THE LANAHAN READINGS

in the

American Polity

FIFTH EDITION

THE LANAHAN READINGS

in the

American Polity

FIFTH EDITION

—

Ann G. Serow
Kingswood Oxford School
Central Connecticut State University

Everett C. Ladd

LANAHAN PUBLISHERS, INC.

Baltimore

The text of this book was composed
in Bembo with display type set in Garamond.
Composition by BYTHEWAY PUBLISHING SERVICES.

ISBN-10 1-930398-16-6
ISBN-13 978-1-930398-16-0

LANAHAN PUBLISHERS, INC.
324 Hawthorne Road
Baltimore, MD 21210-2303
1-866-345-1949 [Toll Free]
LANAHAN@AOL.COM
WWW.LANAHANPUBLISHERS.COM

7 8 9 0

To Our Students

CONTENTS

PART TWO

The Constitution and American Democracy

PART THREE

Separation of Powers

PART FOUR

Federalism

PART FIVE

Congress

PART SIX

The Presidency

PART SEVEN
────────────

The Executive Branch

PART EIGHT
───────────────

The Judiciary

PART NINE

Civil Liberties and Civil Rights

PART TEN

Public Opinion

PART ELEVEN

Interest Groups

PART THIRTEEN

Political Parties

PART FOURTEEN

The Media

PART FIFTEEN

Political Economy and Public Welfare

PART SIXTEEN

America in a Changing World

PREFACE

The first edition of THE LANAHAN READINGS IN THE AMERI-
CAN POLITY began a happy new collaboration of the editors with LANAHAN
PUBLISHERS, INC., and Donald W. Fusting, who founded this new publish-
ing company in 1995. During the previous decade, we had worked close-
ly and confidently with Don on two earlier versions of this book, *The
American Polity Reader*, and we were pleased that the association would
continue—in fact, quite pleased as it turned out: the fourth edition of
THE LANAHAN READINGS was assigned in nearly four hundred schools.

Launching another new edition of an established volume is still a big
step. What matters to students using the volume, however, is what's between the covers. Here, readers of the new fifth edition will find in large
measure both fundamental continuity in basic design and big changes in
specific readings.

There's good reason for continuity. This book is designed to help undergraduates who are taking the basic American government course better understand their country's political system by providing essential readings on American ideas, constitutional system, core political institutions,
public opinion, political competition, and policy debates. All of these
readings have in fact shown exceptional continuity over time because
they reflect the views and values of a society that is strikingly similar now
in this twenty-first century to what it was when the United States was
founded in the late eighteenth century.

At first glance, this proposition might seem surprising. After all, in
some regards the America we now inhabit differs greatly from that of
George Washington, James Madison, and Thomas Jefferson. They traveled
either on foot or, quite literally, by horsepower; we travel faster and more
comfortably in automobiles and jet planes. They could communicate only
face to face or through the written word; we have now gone beyond the
telephone to the Internet. The average life expectancy in their day was
thirty-three years; in ours, seventy-five—and so on is the process of change
across so many of the physical dimensions of life.

But in social and political values, Americans in 1776 and now, in the twenty-first century, are similar people. That's true because America's founding brought the nation to modernity so abruptly and completely. It was a profound break from the aristocratic past that dominated European life—and indeed life in countries all around the world. The great French social commentator, Alexis de Tocqueville, grasped this fact more fully perhaps than anyone else and wrote what is still the most insightful book on American society, *Democracy in America* (Volume I, 1835 and Volume II, 1839). "The emigrants who colonized America at the beginning of the seventeenth century," Tocqueville wrote, "in some way separated the principle of democracy from all those other principles against which they contended when living in the heart of the old European societies, and transplanted that principle only on the shores of the New World." He did not study America, Tocqueville went on, "just to satisfy curiosity, however legitimate; I sought there lessons from which we might profit. . . . I accept that [democratic] revolution as an accomplished fact, or a fact that soon will be accomplished, and I selected of all the peoples experiencing it that nation in which it has come to the fullest and most peaceful completion. . . . I admit that I saw in America more than America; it was the shape of democracy itself which I sought, its inclinations, character, prejudices, and passions."

Now, over 175 years after Tocqueville wrote, America remains a democratic nation and an intensely individualist society—the latter encompassing much of what he understood when he used the term "democracy." This broad continuity in social values and social structure goes far to explain the institutional continuities we find in THE LANAHAN READINGS.

The world of American politics keeps changing, nonetheless. Students need readings on the country's political institutions and its political competition that present the American polity in a fresh, contemporary form. So for the fifth edition of THE LANAHAN READINGS IN THE AMERICAN POLITY, we have replaced over a third of the selections. Among the many new readings:

Cynthia Farrar offers an imaginative model for all of our classrooms on how to sit down for dinner and discover what democracy is all about.

James Davison Hunter examines deeply held, contrasting views about the moral and religious principles underlying American politics.

David Brian Robertson reminds us that politicians, not philosophers, wrote the Constitution, and that national policy can come only from pragmatic coalition building.

Gregory Wawro and Eric Schickler enlighten us about one of the weapons within the Senate chamber: the filibuster.

Senator John McCain's "tweets" on "pork" projects will either amuse or enrage.

Michael Cairo revisits the "imperial presidency" in the post-9/11 climate.

Gil Troy draws a parallel between successful presidents and "leading from the center."

Paul Light offers a performance review of the federal bureaucracy.

Craig Rimmerman delineates the ways by which lesbian and gay movements have sought to attain their goals.

David Bernstein weighs the activists' moral chant of "you can't say that" against the First Amendment's right of free speech in the everyday life of school and work.

David Moore explains how at times separate polls end up with contrasting results on the same topic.

Robert Kaiser narrates the meteoric rise of one lobbying firm.

Joe Garcia sizes up the increasingly influential Latino vote.

David Mark looks at independent groups and their innovative tactics for negative campaigning.

Chuck Todd and Sheldon Gawiser chronicle the 2008 Obama victory.

Ronald Brownstein recounts how far apart the two political parties are from each other.

Kate Zernike offers a glimpse into the Tea Party.

Morley Winograd and Michael Hais focus on "Netroots" political activists and their use of social networking, YouTube, and the Internet in elections.

Cass Sunstein strikes a cautious tone in his examination of the Internet, the blogosphere, and the free exchange of ideas.

Lastly, Michele Wucker highlights the divisive immigration debate; Steven Cohen brings the environmental issue to garbage collecting in New York City; Kevin Phillips narrates the recent financial crisis; and Fareed Zakaria examines America's evolving place in global politics.

To guide readers through these and all other selections, a brief description of each article appears in brackets below its listing in the table of contents. To help orient students, we continue to provide brief introductions to each article. In doing so, we can offer some political, and occasionally, historical and cultural background to the selections. To help students further, we again continue the process of writing footnotes not to dredge up obscure and unnecessary information, but to make clear those words, phrases, and allusions that students need defined or explained in order to understand the particular reading.

As with each new edition, Ann Serow has written the *Instructor's Guide and Quiz Book*. This ancillary gives instructors an ample amount of questions with which to test their students on each of the readings, and also, some further ideas on how the selections can be used. For example, there are a number of readings that can be set up in a point-counterpoint arrangement for instructors who might want to include this approach in their classroom.

Returning to our opening comments, we have been engaged in this project for over twenty years. We believe that the continuity of having the same team, author/editor and publishing editor, has helped keep the goals of the book in focus: This is a book for students of American government and the list of selections was made, and revised, for them. They, too, have contributed heavily to the reader-making process by their in-class comments. The selections can truly be said to have been class-tested. For this, the book is again dedicated to these willing and observant participants, our students.

NOTE OF ACKNOWLEDGMENT   Much appreciation goes to our young political scientist-proofreaders for their many hours of assistance: Mazhar Bokhari (many hours), Chelsea Gelman, Ashley Palma, Theodore Brundage, Myles Alderman, Michael Coulom, Tessa Rose, Erin O'Brien, Max Hoberman, Sarah Giardini, Joel Kruger, Byron Perpetua, and Melody Rosas-Granda. Special thanks go to Alexander Holt and Olivia Brown for their assistance throughout the project and to Margaret Brassil whose knowledge of political science and copyediting improved the manuscript.

AGS

THE LANAHAN READINGS

in the

American Polity

FIFTH EDITION

PART ONE

American Ideology

I

ALEXIS DE TOCQUEVILLE

From *Democracy in America*

In May of 1831, a fancily-dressed, young French aristocrat arrived in the United States to begin his "scientific" study of a new social and political phenomenon, American democracy. After nine months of traveling across the new nation, interviewing numerous Americans from all walks of life, Alexis de Tocqueville returned to France to write Democracy in America, *the single best source with which to begin our exploration of American government and politics. Tocqueville saw the United States as a unique nation. From the start, Americans were all equal. Some were richer and others were poorer, but all who were not indentured or enslaved had an equal opportunity from the start. This clearly was not the case in any other nineteenth-century nation. To the young visitor, this idea of equality was America's identifying mark, a most cherished, if elusive, national virtue.*

AFTER THE BIRTH of a human being his early years are obscurely spent in the toils or pleasures of childhood. As he grows up the world receives him, when his manhood begins, and he enters into contact with his fellows. He is then studied for the first time, and it is imagined that the germ of the vices and the virtues of his maturer years is then formed.

This, if I am not mistaken, is a great error. We must begin higher up; we must watch the infant in his mother's arms; we must see the first images which the external world casts upon the dark mirror of his mind; the first occurrences which he witnesses; we must hear the first words which awaken the sleeping powers of thought, and stand by his earliest efforts, if we would understand the prejudices, the habits, and the passions which will rule his life. The entire man is, so to speak, to be seen in the cradle of the child.

The growth of nations presents something analogous to this: they all bear some marks of their origin; and the circumstances which accompanied their birth and contributed to their rise affect the whole term of their being.

If we were able to go back to the elements of states, and to examine the oldest monuments of their history, I doubt not that we should discover in them the primal cause of the prejudices, the habits, the ruling passions, and, in short, of all that constitutes what is called the national character: we should there find the explanation of certain customs which now seem at variance with the prevailing manners; of such laws as conflict with established principles; and of such incoherent opinions as are here and there to be met with in society, like those fragments of broken chains which we sometimes see hanging from the vault of an edifice, and supporting nothing. This might explain the destinies of certain nations which seem borne on by an unknown force to ends of which they themselves are ignorant. But hitherto facts have been wanting to researches of this kind: the spirit of inquiry has only come upon communities in their latter days; and when they at length contemplated their origin, time had already obscured it, or ignorance and pride adorned it with truth-concealing fables.

America is the only country in which it has been possible to witness the natural and tranquil growth of society, and where the influence exercised on the future condition of states by their origin is clearly distinguishable. . . .

America, consequently, exhibits in the broad light of day the phenomena which the ignorance or rudeness of earlier ages conceals from our researches. Near enough to the time when the states of America were founded, to be accurately acquainted with their elements, and sufficiently removed from that period to judge of some of their results, the men of our own day seem destined to see further than their predecessors into the series of human events. Providence has given us a torch which our forefathers did not possess, and has allowed us to discern fundamental causes in the history of the world which the obscurity of the past concealed from them.

If we carefully examine the social and political state of America, after having studied its history, we shall remain perfectly convinced that not an opinion, not a custom, not a law, I may even say not an event, is upon record which the origin of that people will not explain. The readers of this book will find the germ of all that is to follow in the present chapter, and the key to almost the whole work.

The emigrants who came at different periods to occupy the territory now covered by the American Union, differed from each other in many respects; their aim was not the same, and they governed themselves on different principles.

These men had, however, certain features in common, and they were all placed in an analogous situation. The tie of language is perhaps the strongest and the most durable that can unite mankind. All the emigrants spoke the same tongue; they were all offsets from the same people. Born

in a country which had been agitated for centuries by the struggles of
faction, and in which all parties had been obliged in their turn to place
themselves under the protection of the laws, their political education had
been perfected in this rude school, and they were more conversant with
the notions of right, and the principles of true freedom, than the greater
part of their European contemporaries. At the period of the first emigra-
tions, the parish system, that fruitful germ of free institutions, was deeply
rooted in the habits of the English; and with it the doctrine of the sovereignty of the people. . . .

Another remark, to which we shall hereafter have occasion to recur, is
applicable not only to the English, but to . . . all the Europeans who suc-
cessively established themselves in the New World. All these European
colonies contained the elements, if not the development, of a complete
democracy. Two causes led to this result. It may safely be advanced that on
leaving the mother country the emigrants had in general no notion of
superiority one over another. The happy and the powerful do not go into
exile, and there are no surer guaranties of equality among men than poverty and misfortune. It happened, however, on several occasions, that persons of rank were driven to America by political and religious quarrels.
Laws were made to establish a gradation of ranks; but it was soon found
that the soil of America was opposed to a territorial aristocracy. To bring
that refractory land into cultivation, the constant and interested exertions
of the owner himself were necessary; and when the ground was prepared,
its produce was found to be insufficient to enrich a master and a farmer at
the same time. The land was then naturally broken up into small portions,
which the proprietor cultivated for himself. Land is the basis of an aristocracy, which clings to the soil that supports it; for it is not by privileges
alone, nor by birth, but by landed property handed down from generation
to generation, that an aristocracy is constituted. A nation may present immense fortunes and extreme wretchedness; but unless those fortunes are
territorial there is no true aristocracy, but simply the class of the rich and
that of the poor. . . .

In virtue of the law of partible inheritance, the death of every proprietor brings about a kind of revolution in the property; not only do his
possessions change hands, but their very nature is altered; since they are
parcelled into shares, which become smaller and smaller at each division.
This is the direct and, as it were, the physical effect of the law. It follows,
then, that in countries where equality of inheritance is established by law,
property, and especially landed property, must have a tendency to perpetual diminution. . . .

. . . But the law of equal division exercises its influence not merely upon the property itself, but it affects the minds of the heirs, and brings their passions into play. These indirect consequences tend powerfully to the destruction of large fortunes, and especially of large domains. . . .

Great landed estates which have once been divided never come together again; for the small proprietor draws from his land a better revenue, in proportion, than the large owner does from his; and of course he sells it at a higher rate. The calculations of gain, therefore, which decide the rich man to sell his domain, will still more powerfully influence him against buying small estates to unite them into a large one.

What is called family-pride is often founded upon an illusion of self-love. A man wishes to perpetuate and immortalize himself, as it were, in his great-grandchildren. Where the *esprit de famille* ceases to act, individual selfishness comes into play. When the idea of family becomes vague, indeterminate, and uncertain, a man thinks of his present convenience; he provides for the establishment of his succeeding generation, and no more.

Either a man gives up the idea of perpetuating his family, or at any rate, he seeks to accomplish it by other means than that of a landed estate. . . .

I do not mean that there is any deficiency of wealthy individuals in the United States; I know of no country, indeed, where the love of money has taken stronger hold on the affections of men, and where a profounder contempt is expressed for the theory of the permanent equality of property. But wealth circulates with inconceivable rapidity, and experience shows that it is rare to find two succeeding generations in the full enjoyment of it. . . .

. . . The social condition of the Americans is eminently democratic; this was its character at the foundation of the Colonies, and it is still more strongly marked at the present day. . . .

America, then, exhibits in her social state an extraordinary phenomenon. Men are there seen on a greater equality in point of fortune and intellect, or, in other words, more equal in their strength, than in any other country of the world, or in any age of which history has preserved the remembrance.

The political consequences of such a social condition as this are easily deducible.

It is impossible to believe that equality will not eventually find its way into the political world as it does everywhere else. To conceive of men remaining for ever unequal upon a single point, yet equal on all others, is impossible; they must come in the end to be equal upon all. . . .

2

JAMES BRYCE

From *The American Commonwealth*

The Englishman James Bryce visited the United States in the 1880s, during the so-called Gilded Age. His topic in this excerpt is equality in America. Equality can be measured in several different ways, he says, by money, knowledge, position, and status. The first three measures of equality point up the obvious differences among the American people. But wealthy or poor, educated or not, highly-positioned or lowly, Bryce concludes, Americans regard one another as fundamentally equal as human beings. A fellow citizen may be more famous or more accomplished or more successful, "but it is not a reason for . . . treating him as if he were porcelain and yourself only earthenware." Is Bryce on target over one hundred years later? What has happened to the idea of equality in America in the post-porcelain, post-earthenware age?

THE UNITED STATES are deemed all the world over to be preeminently the land of equality. This was the first feature which struck Europeans when they began, after the peace of 1815 had left them time to look beyond the Atlantic, to feel curious about the phenomena of a new society. This was the great theme of Tocqueville's description, and the starting point of his speculations; this has been the most constant boast of the Americans themselves, who have believed their liberty more complete than that of any other people, because equality has been more fully blended with it. Yet some philosophers say that equality is impossible, and others, who express themselves more precisely, insist that distinctions of rank are so inevitable, that however you try to expunge them, they are sure to reappear. Before we discuss this question, let us see in what senses the word is used.

First there is legal equality, including both what one may call passive or private equality, i.e. the equal possession of civil private rights by all inhabitants, and active or public equality, the equal possession by all of rights to a share in the government, such as the electoral franchise and eligibility to public office. Both kinds of political equality exist in America, in the amplest measure, and may be dismissed from the present discussion.

Next there is the equality of material conditions, that is, of wealth, and all that wealth gives; there is the equality of education and intelligence:

there is the equality of social status or rank: and there is (what comes near to, but is not exactly the same as, this last) the equality of estimation, i.e. of the value which men set upon one another, whatever be the elements that come into this value, whether wealth, or education, or official rank, or social rank, or any other species of excellence. In how many and which of these senses of the word does equality exist in the United States?

Not as regards material conditions. Till about the middle of last century there were no great fortunes in America, few large fortunes, no poverty. Now there is some poverty (though only in a few places can it be called pauperism), many large fortunes, and a greater number of gigantic fortunes than in any other country in the world. . . .

As respects education, the profusion of superior as well as elementary schools tends to raise the mass to a somewhat higher point than in Europe, while the stimulus of life being keener and the habit of reading more general, the number of persons one finds on the same general level of brightness, keenness, and a superficially competent knowledge of common facts, whether in science, history, geography, or literature, is extremely large. This general level tends to rise. But the level of exceptional attainment in that still relatively small though increasing class who have studied at the best native universities or in Europe, and who pursue learning and science either as a profession or as a source of pleasure, rises faster than does the general level of the multitude, so that in this regard also it appears that equality has diminished and will diminish further.

So far we have been on comparatively smooth and easy ground. Equality of wealth is a concrete thing; equality of intellectual possession and resource is a thing which can be perceived and gauged. Of social equality, of distinctions of standing and estimation in private life, it is far more difficult to speak, and in what follows I speak with some hesitation.

One thing, and perhaps one thing only, may be asserted with confidence. There is no rank in America, that is to say, no external and recognized stamp, marking one man as entitled to any social privileges, or to deference and respect from others. No man is entitled to think himself better than his fellows, or to expect any exceptional consideration to be shown by them to him. Except in the national capital, there is no such thing as a recognized order of precedence, either on public occasions or at a private party, save that yielded to a few official persons, such as the governor and chief judges of a State within that State, as well as to the President and Vice-President, the Speaker of the House, the Federal senators, the judges of the Supreme Federal Court, and the members of the President's cabinet everywhere through the Union. In fact, the idea of a regular "rule of precedence" displeases the Americans. . . .

The fault which Americans are most frequently accused of is the worship of wealth. The amazing fuss which is made about very rich men, the descriptions of their doings, the speculation as to their intentions, the gossip about their private life, lend colour to the reproach. He who builds up a huge fortune, especially if he does it suddenly, is no doubt a sort of hero, because an enormous number of men have the same ambition. Having done best what millions are trying to do, he is discussed, admired, and envied in the same way as the captain of a cricket eleven is at an English school, or the stroke of the university boat at Oxford or Cambridge. If he be a great financier, or the owner of a great railroad or a great newspaper, he exercises vast power, and is therefore well worth courting by those who desire his help or would avert his enmity. Admitting all this, it may seem a paradox to observe that a millionaire has a better and easier social career open to him in England than in America. Nevertheless there is a sense in which this is true. In America, if his private character be bad, if he be mean, or openly immoral, or personally vulgar, or dishonest, the best society may keep its doors closed against him. In England great wealth, skilfully employed, will more readily force these doors to open. For in England great wealth can, by using the appropriate methods, practically buy rank from those who bestow it; or by obliging persons whose position enables them to command fashionable society, can induce them to stand sponsors for the upstart, and force him into society, a thing which no person in America has the power of doing. To effect such a stroke in England the rich man must of course have stopped short of positive frauds, that is, of such frauds as could be proved in court. But he may be still distrusted and disliked by the *élite* of the commercial world, he may be vulgar and ill-educated, and indeed have nothing to recommend him except his wealth and his willingness to spend it in providing amusement for fashionable people. All this will not prevent him from becoming a baronet, or possibly a peer, and thereby acquiring a position of assured dignity which he can transmit to his offspring. The existence of a system of artificial rank enables a stamp to be given to base metal in Europe which cannot be given in a thoroughly republican country. The feeling of the American public towards the very rich is, so far as a stranger can judge, one of curiosity and wonder rather than of respect. There is less snobbishness shown towards them than in England. They are admired as a famous runner or jockey is admired, and the talents they have shown, say, in railroad management or in finance, are felt to reflect lustre on the nation. But they do not necessarily receive either flattery or social deference, and sometimes, where it can be alleged that they have won their wealth as the leading spirits in monopolistic combinations, they are made targets for attack, though they may have done nothing more than what other business men have attempted, with less ability and less success.

The persons to whom official rank gives importance are very few indeed, being for the nation at large only about one hundred persons at the top of the Federal Government, and in each State less than a dozen of its highest State functionaries. For these State functionaries, indeed, the respect shown is extremely scanty, and much more official than personal. A high Federal officer, a senator, or justice of the Supreme Court, or cabinet minister, is conspicuous while he holds his place, and is of course a personage in any private society he may enter; but less so than a corresponding official would be in Europe. A simple member of the House of Representatives is nobody. Even men of the highest official rank do not give themselves airs on the score of their position. Long ago, in Washington, I was taken to be presented to the then head of the United States army, a great soldier whose fame all the world knows. We found him standing at a desk in a bare room in the War Department, at work with one clerk. While he was talking to us the door of the room was pushed open, and there appeared the figure of a Western sight-seer belonging to what Europeans would call the lower middle class, followed by his wife and sister, who were "doing" Washington. Perceiving that the room was occupied they began to retreat, but the Commander-in-chief called them back. "Walk-in, ladies," he said. "You can look around. You won't disturb me; make yourselves at home." . . .

Perhaps the best way of explaining how some of the differences above mentioned, in wealth or official position or intellectual eminence, affect social equality is by reverting to what was called, a few pages back, equality of estimation—the idea which men form of other men as compared with themselves. It is in this that the real sense of equality comes out. In America men hold others to be at bottom exactly the same as themselves. If a man is enormously rich, or if he is a great orator, like Daniel Webster or Henry Ward Beecher, or a great soldier like Ulysses S. Grant, or a great writer like R. W. Emerson, or President, so much the better for him. He is an object of interest, perhaps of admiration, possibly even of reverence. But he is deemed to be still of the same flesh and blood as other men. The admiration felt for him may be a reason for going to see him and longing to shake hands with him, a longing frequent in America. But it is not a reason for bowing down to him, or addressing him in deferential terms, or treating him as if he were porcelain and yourself only earthenware.

3

CYNTHIA FARRAR

Dinner with Democracy

Professor Cynthia Farrar invited twenty residents of New Haven, CT, for dinner at Yale University once a week for several months to talk about what democracy means. They were of varied backgrounds and interests, from all walks of life. They found that both individual freedom and the community's well-being were important to true democracy. Also, democracy was not only about politics. Renowned Yale (and University of Chicago) professor Harold Lasswell wrote long ago that politics is "who gets what, when, how." But, Professor Farrar's diners concluded that often, the need to represent group interests and deliver on "who gets what" interfered with real democracy. Exchanging views over dinner in New Haven every week for several months yielded no decisions, no public policy, no budgetary outcomes. It wasn't ancient Athens, just twenty-one people having dinner, sharing their ideas, and that was all; maybe, that was more than enough.

ON A THURSDAY EVENING in January, twenty-one people stood in line in an undergraduate cafeteria, collected their food on trays, and slowly gathered in an adjacent room. A few were affiliated with the university; most were not. Lawyers, political activists, a judge; neighborhood leaders, community organizers, a former mayor; business and religious leaders, a journalist, Yale undergraduates; men and women, of various ages, races, ethnicities, and backgrounds—all stood uncertainly around the room. They had been invited to participate in an extended discussion of democracy. Each week, they would join Yale students and other members of the public at lectures in a special course called Democratic Vistas, taught by fifteen Yale professors from different disciplines. Each week, they would read assigned texts. And each week, they would meet for dinner, with me, and talk.

The first conversation was stilted. I talked too much. Their eyes flicked around the room. They wondered what they had gotten themselves into. To get the discussion going, I asked the group to analyze itself in democratic terms. If this group were to make decisions on behalf of the larger community, how would we assess whether they could legitimately do so? By way of answer, individuals offered guesses as to why they had been invited, why someone (me) had thought they had something to contribute to the discussion: certain kinds of experience or understanding? representing or resembling a particular group in society? commitment to the process itself or to the common good? ability to enlarge the perspectives of others? I posed a further question: if we were to consider ourselves a democratic entity, what would that mean? Would we have to operate in a particular way, such as take turns running the class? What would each person be entitled to expect and be required to contribute? What if some people talked all the time, others not at all? In response, some said that each person brought his or her own agenda. Others questioned the premise that we could act like a democracy: there wasn't enough time; not everyone who needed to be present was there; we weren't trying to produce anything, not even decisions. At the end of the hour and a half, amid the clattering of trays and scraping of chairs, I wondered if anyone would return the following week.

I also wondered what I had gotten them into. I had started from an intuition: that this discussion group would not just talk about democracy, but enrich it. What this might mean became clearer to me over the course of the term. Certainly the initial session was a blind alley. Whatever I may have thought they might accomplish as a group, it would definitely not be defined by adherence to standard democratic procedures and the traditional framework of democratic legitimacy: for example, being chosen by a larger constituency through a fair and open process, making decisions on behalf of that constituency through mechanisms such as majority rule, being accountable for the consequences of those decisions, and the like. Indeed, their contribution might well reside, I thought, in a region not often explored by democratic theorists or reflected in attempts to reform democratic practice. This region was charted by the ancient Athenians and has begun to be mapped more systematically in recent years. Call it participatory democracy, or deliberative democracy. Its defining features are, roughly, these: active participation by a broad range of citizens, a deliberative and at times contentious process of problem solving and decision making, a process that is seen as transforming the individual citizens' civic capacity but preserving their individuality. My own study of the origins of democratic theory in Athens, and my attempts to expand the scope of public participation in local governance, had led me into this territory.

Thirteen weeks after our initial meeting, eighteen people reflected on what we had been through. Their remarks suggest that they too had glimpsed hitherto unfamiliar but appealing democratic terrain:

- "I think it's rare to find oneself in a setting with people who live their lives in a different place in this culture. I don't normally find myself in settings where people have views and experiences that are so totally different from my own. And people who are in the world of business or academia or the judiciary. I think that one of the things that is peculiar, in a way, about this democracy is the extent to which we all do tend to hang out with people who are like ourselves."

- "There's a certain awe and wonder you get when you sit in a large group of people and discuss in an academic context intensely personal ideas and approaches. Because it really forces you to bring more out than you might otherwise."

- "Before the class started, if you had asked me my thoughts about democracy, I probably would have answered in exclusively political terms. And because of the nature of the class, I would hardly exclude the political, but I now think of it as a much more complex mosaic and I can appreciate the fact that democracy has a lot to do with the way that we think and the way that we live, apart from the way that we vote."

- "A lot of my experience with people who disagreed with me politically, or with whom I disagreed politically, was of a nasty contention. And to see that you could do this and if you did it right, you would still be civil to each other and reach some sort of mutual understanding while perhaps not agreeing, but nonetheless, some sort of civility. It was encouraging. And it has made me think very seriously about running for office."

- "I, who am thirteenth generation in the U.S., have always considered myself a persecuted underdog as a woman. And it seems really odd to other people. But I now see people who feel like underdogs in different kinds of ways, and I think that's what I will take forward."

- "The effect of severing these ties that we have with constituencies we normally represent is that we were able to create a little political community in which we were all created equal. While outside of this room, we are really unequal in social status and wealth and ability, age, other variables. So this was sort of an ideal of citizenship, in which people come together and leave aside their constituencies or the social position they represent and are able to interact with each other as equals."

- "I think one of the other things that made this group successful is that it's not only that there's a defined amount of time and structure and an ending point and sort of an abstractness, but also that we all made a commitment to be here. Even when we disagreed, we got to know who the personalities were and how the discussion went and how people interact with each other and how to talk and not talk and listen, and feel part of this group. And knowing that the same faces would be there each time."

The democratic meaning of what we came to think of as Dinner with Democracy rests not primarily in what people said about each week's topic—though what they said was shrewd, thoughtful, and enlightening—but in what they did together and what the experience did to them. This structured, extended, and challenging discourse among a diverse group of individuals offers a glimpse of an aspect of democratic citizenship not comprehended—indeed, sidelined—by most theories, and many practices, of democracy. Some forms of political theory are concerned with abstract questions of legitimacy (and some political theorists of this kind do invoke ideals of collective civic deliberation to make their case). Another kind of political theory considers the actual activity of political communities—which is my concern here—but tends to ignore the as-yet-unrealized potential for different forms of political engagement.

Interpreters of democracy often frame their analysis in terms of contrasting extremes. Discussions of democratic governance offer two alternatives: (1) reliance on the modern structures of the bureaucratic state, overseen to some degree by a system of representative government said to reflect the will of the people; (2) partly in response to the detachment of the administrative model from popular influence, direct involvement by the people in decision making, through a system of initiatives and referendums. Left off the spectrum is the possibility of regular, ongoing, and direct participation of the people in a governance system that requires collective deliberation and a process of mutual political education, not just the casting of individual votes for either a candidate or a proposal.

Discussions of the relationship between individual and society in a democratic context also offer two alternatives: (1) extreme individualism (libertarianism or assimilation of political processes to the workings of the market); (2) partly in response to the perceived excesses of democratic capitalism, an appeal to community solidarity, to the shaping of individual preferences and values through identification with a group. The invocation of community carries the risk of repressing individuality. Left off the spectrum in this second contrast is the possibility of substantive political engagement with others who are not part of a "natural" group, but who are fellow citizens different in other respects from oneself. From this perspective, citizens are neither members of a tribe nor consumers; what they have in common is citizenship, and they engage in constant renegotiation of the inevitable tensions between public goods and private interests, community and individual.

In both cases, what is missing is recognition of the power of structured engagement among political equals, which not only permits them to express and aggregate existing preferences, but also transforms their understanding of and capacity to contribute to civic decision making. The participants in Dinner with Democracy did not in any meaningful sense "choose" what occurred. They agreed to join a process and to be open to the possibility of being transformed by it. The structure of the discussions worked on them. They attended, perhaps, because each in his or her own way had an intuition that however rich their lives, however active their involvement in civic affairs (and they were unusual in their civic commitments, from coaching youth baseball to running a program for ex-cons to serving on every significant nonprofit board in New Haven), some important elements were missing: exposure to people different from themselves, the opportunity to argue and articulate their views under challenge, a chance to reflect on the truths they held to be self-evident. They entered, and sustained, a genuinely "political" space of a kind that modern democracy tends to spurn or, at the very least, to corrode. . . .

Indeed, the conversation continually returned to fundamental questions of power: Is choice freedom? Is equality of opportunity really equality? Or are appeals to "choice" and "equality of opportunity"—at least at times—masks for the exercise of power and freedom by those with resources, and the disempowerment of those without? They wished not to challenge the basic commitment of American democracy to freedom and to equal opportunity, but rather to ask what those commitments yield in practice. The participants recognized that the market simultaneously promotes the general welfare and greater inequality, and that other practices considered essential to our democratic society have a comparable effect. Public education, they acknowledged, both diffuses knowledge among the general population and accelerates the advancement of the talented. What seemed important to many of the diners-with-democracy was the resulting increase in fragmentation and polarization. With respect to both wealth and knowledge, they argued that the greatest risk of investing in freedom of choice at the expense of commonness was isolating those left behind both economically, by technological advances, and physically, in concentrated pockets of rooted poverty and despair created by the choices made by others. . . .

The diners-with-democracy identified two characteristics of their own dinner discussions as the key to dealing with the tensions between liberty and equality inherent in democracy: exposure to difference; and a sense of commonness, initially contrived, and then forged. Their experience offers a distinctively political perspective on citizenship. That is, what the citizen-diners said and what they did suggested that it is essential to create a space within which the claims of the individual and society, of money and power and justice, can be explicitly addressed by those affect-

ed, treated as equal members. They intimated that a threshold level of resources and education is required for this. Yet they were skeptical that the
operation of the existing political system could accomplish any of these
ends. These citizens of New Haven and surrounding towns talked in detail about the ways in which politics, perhaps especially at the local level,
had been corrupted:

- "[If you're running for office], you focus only on those people who are
  for you or leaning for you. Some of those people, after the first phone
  call, never hear again from a political person. And that's the way the
  system works today. And it's become more and more sanitized to the
  point where there isn't really an election anymore. It's who's got the
  most friends to come out to the polls."
- "How do decisions get made and who makes them? . . . It seems to me
  that the aspirations associated with the founding of this country had to
  do with the idea of no taxation without representation. And the idea
  that people should be able to have some degree of power over things
  that they care about, things connected to their own self-realizing activities. How many of us think that we have any power to affect things that
  matter to us?"
- "In my neighborhood, it was a policy of people to state that they had
  no intention of running for office. And they say that in order to develop
  a trust to get things done."
- "Periodically, in my twelve years in New Haven, people have asked me
  about whether or not I would run for mayor. And my response is, 'I am
  queen of my own bedroom, I am captain of my own tub, I am head of
  my own organization.' And the reason why I say that is because it's very,
  very hard not to be corrupted in the current political process. And you
  have to know that the pressure's going to be there and that's going to
  work against the very reason why you decided to run for political office
  or the very reason why you decided to participate in community activities anyway."
- "Last night I had to go in front of the Board of Aldermen to ask the
  mayor to put us in for $35,000 in the Community Development Block
  Grant allocation. . . . One of them says, 'Well, why should we give you
  this money?' By the end of five minutes, it dawned on me, they were
  talking about our money as if it was their money. It's not your money.
  I'm a representative of a community coming to the representatives of
  the people for a piece of the people's money to do people's work. Can
  you stop it? But this is the kind of thing that turns people off."

... Participants in Dinner with Democracy recognized that they were able to engage with each other as equals in part because they left their constituencies and pet projects at the door to the dining hall—and perhaps also precisely *because* they were not being asked to make decisions that would affect others. Members of the group dealt with each other openly and flexibly, as individuals rather than as "representatives" of any particular group or initiative. In a comment quoted earlier, another participant noted that "the effect of severing these ties that we have with constituencies we normally represent is that we were able to create a little political community in which we were all created equal." If they were to make decisions, they would have to take particular groups into account—to act as if they had been selected to represent some group or other, and to be accountable to them for the outcome. This would increase partisanship, inflexibility, a focus on particularist interests, perhaps. As one remarked, "It's a real luxury not to come to any conclusion." But he went on to draw an inference about reforming the way in which existing political structures function: "It's an argument for the point that there ought to be more times when we're not sitting down in a crisis, trying to come out with a conclusion because, then, maybe we'd be more prepared to listen to each other when it was important." ...

... Democracy—alone among political systems—relies on the virtue but also the stubborn individuality of all of its citizens. Disorder is a risk; so is conformity. The challenge is to keep alive both quirkiness and solidarity, both equality and realization of man's individual potential. No system can deliver this result—though some make it easier, while others prevent it entirely. What is required, ... is continual engagement, imagination, persuasion, openness. This can be accomplished only through the process of interaction between self and other, which is often too ragged and contingent, too much influenced by status and power, and too narrowly bounded, to serve democratic purposes. A more varied and rich and demanding fare—dinner with democracy as the table setting, perhaps—may be needed to sustain the democratic experiment.

4

JAMES DAVISON HUNTER

The Enduring Culture War

Professor James Davison Hunter finds deeply held, contrasting views within the United States about the moral and religious principles that underlie our politics. The author compares the "traditionalist or orthodox" view with the "progressivist" view: hold to values that have characterized the nation's past or change culture to be more accepting of new norms. True, only a small number of citizens feel very strongly and are "white-hot" about their position. But many other average citizens feel strongly too, Hunter contends. The author then goes on to explain how the power of language and symbols can affect the views of the citizenry in general by controlling the way "to frame the terms of public discussion." He then provides an interesting example of "framing": the debate that occurred during the 1990s in North Carolina over the issue of outcomes-based education. Influential opposing national interest groups became involved and a "culture war" was underway. Hunter concludes that the middle ground exists, but it is not easily heard.

———

IN THE LAST HALF OF THE TWENTIETH CENTURY, it was widely presumed that distinctions of faith and religious community had been largely settled and were thus no longer politically important. The Catholicism of John F. Kennedy in the 1960 election was the exception that proved the rule, and in this sense, it was the last gasp of a dying fear. In the main, the sense prevailed that every religious faith had been domesticated through its relegation to the private sphere. The diversity that mattered now was a diversity of race, ethnicity, class, gender, and sexual orientation. These have occupied an enormous amount of time and attention over the last forty to fifty years and, . . . to great effect.

But something unexpected is suggested by the idea of a "culture war," especially as it was first articulated. It suggests that the contours of difference have changed yet again in ways that raise a troubling possibility: though configured in ways that are unfamiliar and possibly unprecedented, perhaps religious and moral differences remain politically consequential in late modern America after all. Perhaps, long after it was thought settled, the normative differences rooted in sacred cosmologies (and the communities in which they are embedded) have come to challenge the project of liberal democracy again. . . .

The heart of the culture war argument was that American public culture was undergoing a realignment that, in turn, was generating significant tension and conflict. These antagonisms were playing out not just on the surface of social life (that is, in its cultural politics) but at the deepest and most profound levels, and not just at the level of ideology but in its public symbols, its myths, its discourse, and through the institutional structures that generate and sustain public culture.

Thus underneath the myriad political controversies over so-called cultural issues, there were yet deeper crises over the very meaning and purpose of the core institutions of American civilization. Behind the politics of abortion was a controversy over a momentous debate over the meaning of motherhood, of individual liberty, and of our obligations to one another. Within the politics of government patronage, including the dispute over the National Endowment for the Arts and its funding of controversial art, one could find a more consequential dispute over what constitutes art in the first place and the social ideals it symbolically communicates. Beyond the politics of educational curriculum, the quarrels over textbooks in public schools constituted a more serious disagreement over the national ideals Americans pass on to the next generation. Behind the contentious argument about the legal rights of gays and lesbians was a more serious debate over the fundamental nature of the family and appropriate sexuality. Within the politics of church and state, the various (and seemingly trivial) altercations over Ten Commandment presentations on public property overlaid a more significant debate about the role of religious institutions and religious authority in an increasingly secular society. And so it goes. Cumulatively, these debates concerning the wide range of social institutions amounted to a struggle over the meaning of America.

This, however, was not the end of the matter. Underneath the push and pull of these institutional conflicts were competing moral ideals as to how public life ought to be ordered and maintained. These were not mere political ideologies, reducible to party platforms or political scorecards, but rather moral visions from which the policy discussions and political disputes derived their passion. Embedded within institutions, these ideals were articulated in innumerable ways with every conceivable nuance and shade of variation. *As they were translated into the signs and symbols of public discourse,* however, they lost their complexity and nuance and thus divided into sharply antagonistic tendencies.

One moral vision—the traditionalist or orthodox—is predicated upon the achievements and traditions of the past as the foundation and guide to the challenges of the present. Though this vision is often tinged with nostalgia and is at times resistant to change, it is not simply reactionary, backward looking, or static. Rather, the order of life sustained by this vision is, at its best, one that seeks deliberate continuity with the ordering principles inherited from the past. The social end is the reinvigoration and realization of what are considered to be the very noblest ideals and achievements of civilization.

Against this is a progressivist moral vision that is ambivalent to the legacy of the past, regarding it partly as a useful point of reference and partly as a source of oppression. Instead, the order of life embraced by this vision is one that idealizes experimentation and thus adaptation to and innovation with the changing circumstances of our time. Although sometimes marked by traces of utopian idealism, it is not merely an uncritical embrace of all things new. The aim of the progressivists' vision is the further emancipation of the human spirit and the creation of an inclusive and tolerant world. . . .

Another way to say this is that against the old axis of tension and conflict that was rooted in political economy, a "new" axis of tension and conflict has emerged that is fundamentally cultural in nature. The historical significance of this new axis has been evident in the ways in which it cuts across age-old divisions among Protestants, Catholics, and Jews. The orthodox traditions in these faiths now have much more in common with each other than they do with progressives in their own faith tradition, and vice versa. The polarity of *this* axis seems to better account for the variation in positions on a wide range of popular domestic disputes. In turn, it is the polarities of *these* controversies through which a far-reaching struggle for national identity is carried on. . . .

It is clear that within themselves, traditionalists and permissivists do not have political positions that align perfectly with their moral dispositions. Yet the alignment is fairly close, and for this reason these groups represent a natural and broader constituency receptive to political and social mobilization.

The point is this: no matter how one approaches the question, social dissensus is very much present in public opinion. Forming the grassroots support for competing visions are factions that constitute the white-hot core of difference and dissensus. Disproportionately motivated and active in these issues, they are the most likely to write letters, send checks to the special interest groups and parties that represent them, and volunteer on behalf of their cause. Although these highly partisan citizens may only make up 5 percent of the American population on one side of the cultural divide or the other, in actual numbers they account for 10 to 12 million people on each side. Extending out to less committed constituencies, the numbers who align themselves on one side of the cultural divide or the other can range up to 60 million each.

But this still leaves open the question, are these factions and the larger constituencies of which they are a part politically significant? In his review of [the book titled] *Culture Wars* for *Contemporary Sociology,* Steven Brint posed the question this way: "Can one have a proper war when two-thirds of the army are noncombatants?" The answer brings us back to one of the central contentions of the original argument about the culture war: it has everything to do with the institutions and elites that provide leadership to these factions. . . .

To take the structural and institutional approach in cultural analysis is, in part, to think of culture as objects produced. Culture takes the form of ideas, information, news—indeed, knowledge of all kinds—and these in turn are expressed in pronouncements, speeches, edicts, tracts, essays, books, film, works of art, laws, and the like. At the heart of the production and distribution of cultural output is language. It is, of course, at the root of culture for it provides a medium through which people experience reality. Through both its structure and its meaning, language provides the categories through which people understand themselves, others, and the larger world around them. The power of language resides in its ability to objectify, to make identifiable and "objectively" real the various and ever changing aspects of our experience. When objects are named, when relationships are described, when standards of evaluation are articulated, and when situations are defined, they can acquire a sense of facticity. For this reason formal education, the media of mass communications (including television, radio, newspapers, magazines, and the like), art and music, and religious pronouncements (such as sermons, edicts, policy statements, moral instruction, liturgies and rituals, and the like) all become important conduits for communication and socialization—mechanisms through which a particular vision of reality is defined and maintained. It stands to reason that influence over language, the cultural output through which public language is mediated, and the institutions that produce and manage it all are extraordinarily powerful.

The development and articulation of the more elaborate systems of meaning and the vocabularies that make them coherent are more or less exclusively the realm of elites. They are the ones who provide the concepts, supply the grammar, and explicate the logic of public discussion. They are the ones who define and redefine the meaning of public symbols and provide the legitimating or delegitimating narratives of public figures or events. In all of these ways and for all of these reasons, it is they and the strategically placed institutions they serve that come to frame the terms of public discussion.

In sum, there are elites who are enormously influential for the sway they have over the content and direction of cultural production within specific institutions. These are supported by 5 to 8 percent of the population who are the grassroots activists, the "cultural warriors" who generate and organize resources on behalf of their respective associations and factions. There are yet larger parts of the population whose fundamental orientation leans one way or another but who also tend to be more moderate and less motivated. Yet they can and are mobilized for action in public affairs (even if only by voting) under certain circumstances. . . .

Consider briefly a case concerning school reform in Gaston County, North Carolina, in the early 1990s. The school district there was ranked among the bottom 17 school districts in the state (out of 120) in terms of students' academic performance, high dropout rates, and so on. To rectify this matter, the Board of Education put together the Odyssey Project that incorporated five elements of reform, including a change in pedagogy called "outcomes-based education." The school district won a $2 million grant as the beginning of a $20 million grant in a national competition to implement this reform. Through the work of a local Baptist pastor who drew on the support and materials of Citizens for Excellence in Education (CEE)—a religiously based, special interest organization concerned about secular reforms in the public schools—an opposition was mobilized. The CEE was dead set against outcomes-based education, saying it manipulated and indoctrinated children with secular humanism, New Age thinking, and hostility to Christianity. As its director put it, outcomes-based education marked "the end of academic education in America." It was not long before parents and other citizens "packed school board meetings where they monopolized the use of the microphone, harassed school board members, wrote letters to local newspapers, distributed fliers urging parents to act swiftly in order to save their children from the dire effects of this 'radical' school program, circulated warnings [through e-mail] and gathered signatures on petitions."

Soon enough, another national special interest organization, People for the American Way, became involved in direct ways. People for the American Way claimed that the CEE and other organizations of the religious right posed a dire threat to freedom and tolerance in the United States. Each organization was able to use this local dispute to promote its own larger interests far beyond Gaston County. Neither organization conceded rhetorical space or was willing to consider any compromise. A substantive debate about the merits of the reform proposal never occurred, and in the end, all reform efforts were scuttled, the remaining grant funds were forfeited, the school superintendent was forced to resign, and a community was divided. And still, in the end, it was the children of Gaston County who paid the highest price. . . .

The culture war does not manifest itself at all times in all places in the same way. It is episodic and, very often, local in its expressions. Examples abound: the dispute over the fate of Terri Schiavo in Pinellas Park, Florida; the conflict over teaching "intelligent design" in Kansas City; the controversy over a teacher in the Bronx who was suspended for bringing bibles to P.S. 5; a clash over a Civil War statue in Richmond, Virginia; the tempest over a priest in St. Paul who refused to serve communion to gays at Mass; the fury of parents in Mustang, Oklahoma, after the superintendent excised a nativity scene at the end of the annual Christmas play; the dispute over speech codes at the University of Pennsylvania; the row over release time for religious instruction in the public schools in Staunton, Virginia; and on it goes.

Yet because what is under dispute and what is at stake is culture at its deepest levels, carried by organizations relating to larger movements, these local, often disparate conflicts are played out repeatedly in predictable ways. The nation was not divided by the Odyssey Program, but the community of Gaston County, North Carolina, was for a time and profoundly, with serious consequences. So have been and are communities and regions all over the nation whenever an event fraught with moral meaning and cultural significance occurs that compels communities to take positions and make decisions.

Are local and national elites and the organizations they represent politically significant? They certainly were in this instance, and as it has become clear over the years, they are in virtually every other instance of cultural conflict as well. It is in their interest to frame issues in stark terms, to take uncompromising positions, and to delegitimate their opponents. Clearly, entire populations are not divided at anywhere near the level of intensity of the activists and the rhetoric, but because issues are often framed in such stark terms, public choices are forced. In such circumstances even communities and populations that would prefer other options, and much greater reason and harmony in the process, find themselves divided. . . .

To be sure, elites, activists, the institutions they lead and grassroots support they mobilize, and the larger publics that form their natural constituencies are enormously consequential. Yet their importance is not just measured by the power to frame issues. It is also inversely measured by the lack of influence of the majority of Americans, who are in the middle, to contradict this framing and offer an alternative. If the culture war is a myth and the real story is about the consensus that exists in "the middle," then why is it that the middle cannot put forward, much less elect, a moderate who represents that consensus, with all of its complexity and ambivalence on so many issues? If the center is so vital, then why is it that the extremes are overrepresented in the structures of power—not least, political power? In the case of the dispute over educational reform in Gaston County, where was that contented middle—that consensus that critics suggest is so broad and dynamic? In this dispute and in others like it, the middle was there, but as the outcome showed, it was also, sadly, inconsequential.

5

CORNEL WEST

From *Race Matters*

The opening pages of Professor Cornel West's book tell an unforgettable story of the pervasiveness of racism in the United States. Think about it the next time you wait for a taxi. Think about it when you recall the plight of many of the residents of New Orleans in the aftermath of Hurricane Katrina in 2005. In an America that promises a chance for life, liberty, and the pursuit of happiness to all its citizens, "race matters," West contends. He challenges all Americans to change their thinking about race: the problems of African Americans are not their *problems but* American *problems. West identifies the issues that threaten to disrupt the fabric of the nation—economic, social, political, spiritual—and he suggests a broad outline for solutions.*

THIS PAST SEPTEMBER my wife, Elleni, and I made our biweekly trek to New York City from Princeton. I was in good spirits. My morning lecture on the first half of Plato's *Republic* in my European Cultural Studies course had gone well. And my afternoon lecture on W. E. B. Du Bois's *The Souls of Black Folk* in my Afro-American Cultural Studies course had left me exhausted yet exhilarated. Plato's powerful symbolism of Socrates' descent to the great port of Piraeus—the multicultural center of Greek trade and commerce and the stronghold of Athenian democracy—still rang in my ears. And Du Bois's prescient pronouncement—"The problem of the twentieth century is the problem of the color line"— haunted me. In a mysterious way, this classic twosome posed the most fundamental challenges to my basic aim in life: to speak the truth to power with love so that the quality of everyday life for ordinary people is enhanced and white supremacy is stripped of its authority and legitimacy. Plato's profound—yet unpersuasive—critique of Athenian democracy as inevitably corrupted by the ignorance and passions of the masses posed one challenge, and Du Bois's deep analysis of the intransigence of white supremacy in the American democratic experiment posed another.

As we approached Manhattan, my temperature rose, as it always does when I'm in a hurry near the Lincoln Tunnel. How rare it is that I miss the grinding gridlock—no matter the day or hour. But this time I drove right through and attributed my good luck to Elleni. As we entered the city, we pondered whether we would have enough time to stop at Sweet-water's (our favorite place to relax) after our appointments. I dropped my wife off for an appointment on 60th Street between Lexington and Park avenues. I left my car—a rather elegant one—in a safe parking lot and stood on the corner of 60th Street and Park Avenue to catch a taxi. I felt quite relaxed since I had an hour until my next engagement. At 5:00 P.M. I had to meet a photographer who would take the picture for the cover of this book on the roof of an apartment building in East Harlem on 115th Street and 1st Avenue. I waited and waited and waited. After the ninth taxi refused me, my blood began to boil. The tenth taxi refused me and stopped for a kind, well-dressed, smiling female fellow citizen of European descent. As she stepped in the cab, she said, "This is really ridiculous, is it not?"

Ugly racial memories of the past flashed through my mind. Years ago, while driving from New York to teach at Williams College, I was stopped on fake charges of trafficking cocaine. When I told the police officer I was a professor of religion, he replied "Yeh, and I'm the Flying Nun. Let's go, nigger!" I was stopped three times in my first ten days in Princeton for driving too slowly on a residential street with a speed limit of twenty-five miles per hour. (And my son, Clifton, already has similar memories at the tender age of fifteen.) Needless to say, these incidents are dwarfed by those like Rodney King's beating* or the abuse of black targets of the FBI's COINTELPRO† efforts in the 1960s and 1970s. Yet the memories cut like a merciless knife at my soul as I waited on that godforsaken corner. Finally I decided to take the subway. I walked three long avenues, arrived late, and had to catch my moral breath as I approached the white male photographer and white female cover designer. I chose not to dwell on this everyday experience of black New Yorkers. And we had a good time talking, posing, and taking pictures.

When I picked up Elleni, I told her of my hour spent on the corner, my tardy arrival, and the expertise and enthusiasm of the photographer and designer. We talked about our fantasy of moving to Addis Ababa, Ethiopia—her home and the site of the most pleasant event of my life. I toyed with the idea of attending the last day of the revival led by the Rev.

---

*In 1992, four Los Angeles policemen were charged in criminal court with using unnecessary force in the arrest of Rodney King, a black man whom they had stopped while he was driving.—EDS.

†COINTELPRO was the FBI's "counterintelligence program," conducted over decades but most active in the 1960s. FBI Director J. Edgar Hoover used COINTELPRO to investigate and harass Americans whose activities were considered by the bureau to be subversive: socialist and communist sympathizers; anti-Vietnam War protestors; and especially, black citizens active in the civil rights movement. The press was instrumental in uncovering COINTELPRO's secret machinations in the mid-1970s.—EDS.

Jeremiah Wright of Chicago at Rev. Wyatt T. Walker's Canaan Baptist Church of Christ in Harlem. But we settled for Sweetwater's. And the ugly memories faded in the face of soulful music, soulful food, and soulful folk.

As we rode back to Princeton, above the soothing black music of Van Harper's Quiet Storm on WBLS, 107.5 on the radio dial, we talked about what *race* matters have meant to the American past and of how much race *matters* in the American present. And I vowed to be more vigilant and virtuous in my efforts to meet the formidable challenges posed by Plato and Du Bois. For me, it is an urgent question of power and morality; for others, it is an everyday matter of life and death. . . .

What happened in Los Angeles in April of 1992 was neither a race riot nor a class rebellion.* Rather, this monumental upheaval was a multiracial, trans-class, and largely male display of justified social rage. For all its ugly, xenophobic resentment, its air of adolescent carnival, and its downright barbaric behavior, it signified the sense of powerlessness in American society. Glib attempts to reduce its meaning to the pathologies of the black underclass, the criminal actions of hoodlums, or the political revolt of the oppressed urban masses miss the mark. Of those arrested, only 36 percent were black, more than a third had full-time jobs, and most claimed to shun political affiliation. What we witnessed in Los Angeles was the consequence of a lethal linkage of economic decline, cultural decay, and political lethargy in American life. Race was the visible catalyst, not the underlying cause.

The meaning of the earthshaking events in Los Angeles is difficult to grasp because most of us remain trapped in the narrow framework of the dominant liberal and conservative views of race in America, which with its worn-out vocabulary leaves us intellectually debilitated, morally disempowered, and personally depressed. The astonishing disappearance of the event from public dialogue is testimony to just how painful and distressing a serious engagement with race is. Our truncated public discussions of race suppress the best of who and what we are as a people because they fail to confront the complexity of the issue in a candid and critical manner. The predictable pitting of liberals against conservatives, Great Society Democrats against self-help Republicans, reinforces intellectual parochialism and political paralysis.

The liberal notion that more government programs can solve racial problems is simplistic—precisely because it focuses *solely* on the econom-

*Rioting occurred in Los Angeles after a jury, made up of white citizens, acquitted the policemen who had been accused in the beating of Rodney King.—EDS.

ic dimension. And the conservative idea that what is needed is a change in the moral behavior of poor black urban dwellers (especially poor black men, who, they say, should stay married, support their children, and stop committing so much crime) highlights immoral actions while ignoring public responsibility for the immoral circumstances that haunt our fellow citizens.

The common denominator of these views of race is that each still sees black people as a "problem people," in the words of Dorothy I. Height, president of the National Council of Negro Women, rather than as fellow American citizens with problems. Her words echo the poignant "unasked question" of W. E. B. Du Bois, who, in *The Souls of Black Folk* (1903), wrote:

> They approach me in a half-hesitant sort of way, eye me curiously or compassionately, and then instead of saying directly, How does it feel to be a problem? they say, I know an excellent colored man in my town. . . . Do not these Southern outrages make your blood boil? At these I smile, or am interested, or reduce the boiling to a simmer, as the occasion may require. To the real question, How does it feel to be a problem? I answer seldom a word.

Nearly a century later, we confine discussions about race in America to the "problems" black people pose for whites rather than consider what this way of viewing black people reveals about us as a nation.

This paralyzing framework encourages liberals to relieve their guilty consciences by supporting public funds directed at "the problems"; but at the same time, reluctant to exercise principled criticism of black people, liberals deny them the freedom to err. Similarly, conservatives blame the "problems" on black people themselves—and thereby render black social misery invisible or unworthy of public attention.

Hence, for liberals, black people are to be "included" and "integrated" into "our" society and culture, while for conservatives they are to be "well behaved" and "worthy of acceptance" by "our" way of life. Both fail to see that the presence and predicaments of black people are neither additions to nor defections from American life, but rather *constitutive elements of that life.*

To engage in a serious discussion of race in America, we must begin not with the problems of black people but with the flaws of American society—flaws rooted in historic inequalities and longstanding cultural stereotypes. How we set up the terms for discussing racial issues shapes our perception and response to these issues. As long as black people are viewed as a "them," the burden falls on blacks to do all the "cultural" and "moral" work necessary for healthy race relations. The implication is that only certain Americans can define what it means to be American—and the rest must simply "fit in."

The emergence of strong black-nationalist sentiments among blacks, especially among young people, is a revolt against this sense of having to "fit in." The variety of black-nationalist ideologies, from the moderate views of Supreme Court Justice Clarence Thomas in his youth to those of Louis Farrakhan today, rest upon a fundamental truth: white America has been historically weak-willed in ensuring racial justice and has continued to resist fully accepting the humanity of blacks. As long as double standards and differential treatment abound—as long as the rap performer Ice-T is harshly condemned while former Los Angeles Police Chief Daryl F. Gates's antiblack comments are received in polite silence, as long as Dr. Leonard Jeffries's anti-Semitic statements are met with vitriolic outrage while presidential candidate Patrick J. Buchanan's anti-Semitism receives a genteel response—black nationalisms will thrive.

Afrocentrism, a contemporary species of black nationalism, is a gallant yet misguided attempt to define an African identity in a white society perceived to be hostile. It is gallant because it puts black doings and sufferings, not white anxieties and fears, at the center of discussion. It is misguided because—out of fear of cultural hybridization and through silence on the issue of class, retrograde views on black women, gay men, and lesbians, and a reluctance to link race to the common good—it reinforces the narrow discussions about race.

To establish a new framework, we need to begin with a frank acknowledgment of the basic humanness and Americanness of each of us. And we must acknowledge that as a people—*E Pluribus Unum*—we are on a slippery slope toward economic strife, social turmoil, and cultural chaos. If we go down, we go down together. The Los Angeles upheaval forced us to see not only that we are not connected in ways we would like to be but also, in a more profound sense, that this failure to connect binds us even more tightly together. The paradox of race in America is that our common destiny is more pronounced and imperiled precisely when our divisions are deeper. The Civil War and its legacy speak loudly here. And our divisions are growing deeper. Today, eighty-six percent of white suburban Americans live in neighborhoods that are less than 1 percent black, meaning that the prospects for the country depend largely on how its cities fare in the hands of a suburban electorate. There is no escape from our interracial interdependence, yet enforced racial hierarchy dooms us as a nation to collective paranoia and hysteria—the unmaking of any democratic order.

The verdict in the Rodney King case which sparked the incidents in

Los Angeles was perceived to be wrong by the vast majority of Americans. But whites have often failed to acknowledge the widespread mistreatment of black people, especially black men, by law enforcement agencies, which helped ignite the spark. The verdict was merely the occasion for deep-seated rage to come to the surface. This rage is fed by the "silent" depression ravaging the country—in which real weekly wages of all American workers since 1973 have declined nearly 20 percent, while at the same time wealth has been upwardly distributed.

The exodus of stable industrial jobs from urban centers to cheaper labor markets here and abroad, housing policies that have created "chocolate cities and vanilla suburbs" (to use the popular musical artist George Clinton's memorable phrase), white fear of black crime, and the urban influx of poor Spanish-speaking and Asian immigrants—all have helped erode the tax base of American cities just as the federal government has cut its supports and programs. The result is unemployment, hunger, homelessness, and sickness for millions.

And a pervasive spiritual impoverishment grows. The collapse of meaning in life—the eclipse of hope and absence of love of self and others, the breakdown of family and neighborhood bonds—leads to the social deracination and cultural denudement of urban dwellers, especially children. We have created rootless, dangling people with little link to the supportive networks—family, friends, school—that sustain some sense of purpose in life. We have witnessed the collapse of the spiritual communities that in the past helped Americans face despair, disease, and death and that transmit through the generations dignity and decency, excellence and elegance.

The result is lives of what we might call "random nows," of fortuitous and feeling moments preoccupied with "getting over"—with acquiring pleasure, property, and power by any means necessary. (This is not what Malcolm X meant by this famous phrase.) Post-modern culture is more and more a market culture dominated by gangster mentalities and self-destructive wantonness. This culture engulfs all of us—yet its impact on the disadvantaged is devastating, resulting in extreme violence in everyday life. Sexual violence against women and homicidal assaults by young black men on one another are only the most obvious signs of this empty quest for pleasure, property, and power.

Last, this rage is fueled by a political atmosphere in which images, not ideas, dominate, where politicians spend more time raising money than debating issues. The functions of parties have been displaced by public polls, and politicians behave less as thermostats that determine the climate of opinion than as thermometers registering the public mood. American politics has been rocked by an unleashing of greed among opportunistic public officials—who have followed the lead of their counterparts in the private sphere, where, as of 1989, 1 percent of the population owned 37 percent of the wealth and 10 percent of the population owned 86 percent of the wealth—leading to a profound cynicism and pessimism among the citizenry.

And given the way in which the Republican Party since 1968 has appealed to popular xenophobic images—playing the black, female, and homophobic cards to realign the electorate along race, sex, and sexual-orientation lines—it is no surprise that the notion that we are all part of one garment of destiny is discredited. Appeals to special interests rather than to public interests reinforce this polarization. The Los Angeles upheaval was an expression of utter fragmentation by a powerless citizenry that includes not just the poor but all of us.

What is to be done? How do we capture a new spirit and vision to meet the challenges of the post-industrial city, post-modern culture, and post-party politics?

First, we must admit that the most valuable sources for help, hope, and power consist of ourselves and our common history. As in the ages of Lincoln, Roosevelt, and King, we must look to new frameworks and languages to understand our multilayered crisis and overcome our deep malaise.

Second, we must focus our attention on the public square—the common good that undergirds our national and global destinies. The vitality of any public square ultimately depends on how much we *care* about the quality of our lives together. The neglect of our public infrastructure, for example—our water and sewage systems, bridges, tunnels, highways, subways, and streets—reflects not only our myopic economic policies, which impede productivity, but also the low priority we place on our common life.

The tragic plight of our children clearly reveals our deep disregard for public well-being. About one out of every five children in this country lives in poverty, including one out of every two black children and two out of every five Hispanic children. Most of our children—neglected by overburdened parents and bombarded by the market values of profit-hungry corporations—are ill-equipped to live lives of spiritual and cultural quality. Faced with these facts, how do we expect ever to constitute a vibrant society?

One essential step is some form of large-scale public intervention to ensure access to basic social goods—housing, food, health care, education, child care, and jobs. We must invigorate the common good with a mixture of government, business, and labor that does not follow any existing blueprint. After a period in which the private sphere has been sacralized and the public square gutted, the temptation is to make a fetish of the public square. We need to resist such dogmatic swings.

Last, the major challenge is to meet the need to generate new leadership. The paucity of courageous leaders—so apparent in the response to the events in Los Angeles—requires that we look beyond the same elites and voices that recycle the older frameworks. We need leaders—neither saints nor sparkling television personalities—who can situate themselves within a larger historical narrative of this country and our world, who can grasp the complex dynamics of our peoplehood and imagine a future grounded in the best of our past, yet who are attuned to the frightening obstacles that now perplex us. Our ideals of freedom, democracy, and equality must be invoked to invigorate all of us, especially the landless, propertyless, and luckless. Only a visionary leadership that can motivate "the better angels of our nature," as Lincoln said, and activate possibilities for a freer, more efficient, and stable America—only that leadership deserves cultivation and support.

This new leadership must be grounded in grass-roots organizing that highlights democratic accountability. Whoever *our* leaders will be as we approach the twenty-first century, their challenge will be to help Americans determine whether a genuine multiracial democracy can be created and sustained in an era of global economy and a moment of xenophobic frenzy.

Let us hope and pray that the vast intelligence, imagination, humor, and courage of Americans will not fail us. Either we learn a new language of empathy and compassion, or the fire this time will consume us all.*

---

*In *The Fire Next Time* (1963), African-American writer James Baldwin quotes a black slave's prophecy, found in a song recreated from the Bible, "God gave Noah the rainbow sign, no more water, the fire next time!"—Eds.

6

MICHAEL KAMMEN

From *People of Paradox*

Thinking about the United States, its history, culture, and politics, as a paradox is one of the most useful ways to tie together all the themes and facts in American government. Historian Michael Kammen offers a sometimes-fanciful, sometimes-profound analysis of the many paradoxes that riddle American life. Citizens expect their leaders to be "Everyman and Superman," he perceptively observes. Kammen takes on the difficult issue of the American melting pot; he substitutes the metaphor of a "super-highway" to explain nicely the country and its people. He points out paradoxes in all aspects of American life, ending with a poetic vision of the super-highway, along the side of the road, at Thanksgiving. Many scholars and thinkers are quoted in Kammen's piece, but his top source opens the selection: "We have met the enemy and he is us," cartoon character Pogo recognizes.

We have met the enemy and he is us.

—POGO

. . . OUR INHERITANCE has indeed been bitter-sweet, and our difficulty in assessing it just now arises from the fact that American institutions have had too many uncritical lovers and too many unloving critics. We have managed to graft pride onto guilt—guilt over social injustice and abuses of power—and find that pride and guilt do not neutralize each other, but make many decisions seem questionable, motives suspect, and consciences troubled.

Perhaps so many American shibboleths seem to generate their very opposites because they are often half-truths rather than the wholesome verities we believe them to be. Perhaps we ought to recall Alice in Wonderland playing croquet against herself, "for this curious child was very fond of pretending to be two people. 'But it's no use now,' thought poor Alice, 'to pretend to be two people! Why, there's hardly enough of me left to make one respectable person!'" . . .

This dualistic state of mind may be found also in the domestic political values subscribed to by most Americans. We are comfortable believing in both majority rule and minority rights, in both consensus and freedom, federalism and centralization. It may be perfectly reasonable to support majority rule with reservations, or minority rights with certain other reservations. But this has not been our method. Rather, we have tended to hold contradictory ideas in suspension and ignore the intellectual and behavioral consequences of such "doublethink." . . .

Americans have managed to be both puritanical and hedonistic, idealistic and materialistic, peace-loving and war-mongering, isolationist and interventionist, conformist and individualist, consensus-minded and conflict-prone. "We recognize the American," wrote Gunnar Myrdal in 1944, "wherever we meet him, as a practical idealist." . . .

Americans expect their heroes to be Everyman and Superman simultaneously. I once overheard on an airplane the following fragment of conversation: "He has none of the virtues I respect, and none of the vices I admire." We cherish the humanity of our past leaders: George Washington's false teeth and whimsical orthography, Benjamin Franklin's lechery and cunning. The quintessential American hero wears both a halo *and* horns.

Because our society is so pluralistic, the American politician must be all things to all people. Dwight Eisenhower represented the most advanced industrial nation, but his chief appeal rested in a naive simplicity which recalled our pre-industrial past. Robert Frost once advised President Kennedy to be as much an Irishman as a Harvard man: "You have to have both the pragmatism and the idealism." The ambivalent American is ambitious and ambidextrous; but the appearance of ambidexterity—to some, at least—suggests the danger of double-dealing and deceit. The story is told of a U.S. senator meeting the press one Sunday afternoon. "How do you stand on conservation, Senator?" asked one panelist. The senator squirmed. "Well, I'll tell you," he said. "Some of my constituents are for conservation, and some of my constituents are against conservation, and I stand foresquare behind my constituents." . . .

Raymond Aron, the French sociologist, has remarked that a "dialectic of plurality and conformism lies at the core of American life, making for the originality of the social structure, and raising the most contradictory evaluations." Americans have repeatedly reaffirmed the social philosophy of individualism, even making it the basis of their political thought. Yet they have been a nation of joiners and have developed the largest associations and corporations the world has ever known. Nor has American respect for the abstract "individual" always guaranteed respect for particular persons.

There is a persistent tension between authoritarianism and individualism in American history. The genius of American institutions at their best has been to find a place and a use for both innovators and consolidators, rebellious dreamers and realistic adjudicators. "America has been built on a mixture of discipline and rebellion," writes Christopher Jencks, "but the balance between them has constantly shifted over the years." Our individualism, therefore, has been of a particular sort, a collective individualism. Individuality is not synonymous in the United States with singularity. When Americans develop an oddity they make a fad of it so that they may be comfortable among familiar oddities. Their unity, as Emerson wrote in his essay on the New England Reformers, "is only perfect when all the uniters are isolated."

How then can we adequately summarize the buried historical roots of our paradoxes, tensions, and biformities? The incongruities in American life are not merely fortuitous, and their stimuli appear from the very beginning. "America was always promises," as Archibald MacLeish has put it. "From the first voyage and the first ship there were promises." Many of these have gone unfulfilled—an endless source of ambiguity and equivocation. . . .

Above all other factors, however, the greatest source of dualisms in American life has been unstable pluralism in all its manifold forms: cultural, social, sequential, and political. *E pluribus unum* is a misbegotten motto because we have *not* become one out of many. The myth of the melting pot is precisely that: a myth. Moreover, our constitutional system seems to foster fragmentation of power while our economic-technological system seems to encourage consolidation of power. Thus the imperatives of pluralism under conditions of large-scale technology commonly conflict with principles and practices of constitutional democracy. . . .

It has been the impulse of our egalitarianism to make all men American and alike, but the thrust of our social order and intolerance to accentuate differences among groups. We have achieved expertise at both xenophobia and self-hate! At several stages of our history, population growth has outstripped institutional change. The result in many cases has been violence, vigilante movements, or economic unrest, all with the special coloration of unstable pluralism. Because there are significant variations in state laws regulating economic enterprise, taxation, and welfare payments, people and corporations move to tax-sheltered states and to those with the most generous welfare provisions. In this way mobility becomes a function of pluralism.

I do not argue that pluralism is a peculiarly American phenomenon. But I do believe that unstable pluralism on a scale of unprecedented proportion is especially American. . . .

There is a sense in which the super-highway is the most appropriate

American metaphor. We have vast and anonymous numbers of people rushing individually (but simultaneously) in opposite directions. In between lies a no-man's-land, usually landscaped with a barrier of shrubs and trees, so that we cannot see the road to Elsewhere, but cannot easily turn back either. Indeed, the American experience in some spheres has moved from unity to diversity (e.g., denominationalism), while in other areas it has flowed in the opposite direction, from diversity to unity (e.g., political institutions). Along both roads we have paused from time to time in order to pay substantially for the privilege of traveling these thoroughfares.

There have always been Americans aware of unresolved contradictions between creed and reality, disturbed by the performance of their system and culture. Told how much liberty they enjoy, they feel less free; told how much equality they enjoy, they feel less equal; told how much progress they enjoy, their environment seems even more out of control. Most of all, told that they should be happy, they sense a steady growth in American unhappiness. Conflicts *between* Americans have been visible for a very long time, but most of us are just beginning to perceive the conflicts *within* us individually.

It is a consequence of some concern that our ambiguities often appear to the wider world as malicious hypocrisies. As when we vacillate, for example, between our missionary impulse and our isolationist instinct. From time to time we recognize that the needs of national security and the furtherance of national ideals may both be served by our vigorous but restrained participation in world affairs. At other times these two desiderata tug in opposite directions. However much we desperately want to be understood, we are too often misunderstood. . . .

Because of our ambivalent ambiance, we are frequently indecisive. "I cannot be a crusader," remarked Ralph McGill, "because I have been cursed all my life with the ability to see both sides." Our experience with polarities provides us with the potential for flexibility and diversity; yet too often it chills us into sheer inaction, or into contradictory appraisals of our own designs and historical development. Often we are willing to split the difference and seek consensus. "It is this intolerable paradox," James Reston writes, "of being caught between the unimaginable achievements of men when they cooperate for common goals, and their spectacular failures when they divide on how to achieve the simple decencies of life, that creates the present atmosphere of division and confusion." . . .

We have reached a moment in time when the national condition seems neither lifeless nor deathless. It's like the barren but sensuous serenity of the natural world in late autumn, before Thanksgiving, containing the promise of rebirth and the potential for resurrection. On bare branches whose leaves have fallen, buds bulge visibly in preparation for spring. Along the roadside, goldenrod stands sere and grizzled, and the leafless milkweed with its goosehead pods strews fluff and floss to every breeze, thereby seeding the countryside with frail fertility. The litter of autumn becomes the mulch, and then the humus, for roots and tender seeds. So it was, so it has been, and so it will be with the growth of American Civilization.

7

ROBERT BELLAH/OTHERS

From *Habits of the Heart*

American ideology touches more than just government and politics. It also guides the nation's social, economic, religious, and cultural life. It is fitting, therefore, that an important comment on American ideology comes from the discipline of sociology. Robert Bellah and his colleagues borrow Alexis de Tocqueville's phrase "habits of the heart" to explore the place of individualism in American life. The authors concede that individualism is the single most important ingredient in the nation's values, illustrating it with the symbol of cowboy-heroes Shane and the Lone Ranger. But, they contend, individualism cannot exist without being balanced by a sense of community.

INDIVIDUALISM LIES AT THE VERY CORE of American culture. Every one of the four traditions we have singled out is in a profound sense individualistic. There is a biblical individualism and a civic individualism as well as a utilitarian and an expressive individualism. Whatever the differences among the traditions and the consequent differences in their understandings of individualism, there are some things they all share, things that are basic to American identity. We believe in the dignity, indeed the sacredness, of the individual. Anything that would violate our right to think for ourselves, judge for ourselves, make our own decisions, live our lives as we see fit, is not only morally wrong, it is sacrilegious. Our highest and noblest aspirations, not only for ourselves, but for those we care about, for our society and for the world, are closely linked to our individualism. Yet, as we have been suggesting repeatedly in this book, some of our deepest problems both as individuals and as a society are also closely linked to our individualism. We do not argue that Americans should abandon individualism—that would mean for us to abandon our deepest identity. But individualism has come to mean so many things and to contain such contradictions and paradoxes that even to defend it requires that we analyze it critically, that we consider especially those tendencies that would destroy it from within. . . .

The question is whether an individualism in which the self has become the main form of reality can really be sustained. What is at issue is not simply whether self-contained individuals might withdraw from the public sphere to pursue purely private ends, but whether such individuals are capable of sustaining either a public *or* a private life. If this is the danger, perhaps only the civic and biblical forms of individualism—forms that see the individual in relation to a larger whole, a community and a tradition—are capable of sustaining genuine individuality and nurturing both public and private life. . . .

America is also the inventor of that most mythic individual hero, the cowboy, who again and again saves a society he can never completely fit into. The cowboy has a special talent—he can shoot straighter and faster than other men—and a special sense of justice. But these characteristics make him so unique that he can never fully belong to society. His destiny is to defend society without ever really joining it. He rides off alone into the sunset like Shane,* or like the Lone Ranger moves on accompanied only by his Indian companion. But the cowboy's importance is not that he is isolated or antisocial. Rather, his significance lies in his unique, individual virtue and special skill and it is because of those qualities that society needs and welcomes him. Shane, after all, starts as a real outsider, but ends up with the gratitude of the community and the love of a woman and a boy. And while the Lone Ranger never settles down and marries the local schoolteacher, he always leaves with the affection and gratitude of the people he has helped. It is as if the myth says you can be a truly good person, worthy of admiration and love, only if you resist fully joining the group. But sometimes the tension leads to an irreparable break. Will Kane, the hero of *High Noon*, abandoned by the cowardly townspeople, saves them from an unrestrained killer, but then throws his sheriff's badge in the dust and goes off into the desert with his bride. One is left wondering where they will go, for there is no longer any link with any town. . . .

[T]he cowboy . . . tell[s] us something important about American individualism. The cowboy . . . can be valuable to society only because he is a completely autonomous individual who stands outside it. To serve society, one must be able to stand alone, not needing others, not depending on their judgment, and not submitting to their wishes. Yet this individualism is not selfishness. Indeed, it is a kind of heroic selflessness. One accepts the necessity of remaining alone in order to serve the values of the group. And this obligation to aloneness is an important key to the American moral imagination. Yet it is part of the profound ambiguity of the mythology of American individualism that its moral heroism is always just a step away from despair. . . .

. . . The inner tensions of American individualism add up to a classic case of ambivalence. We strongly assert the value of our self-reliance and

*Shane is the gunfighter-hero of the 1953 western film *Shane*.—EDS.

autonomy. We deeply feel the emptiness of a life without sustaining social commitments. Yet we are hesitant to articulate our sense that we need
one another as much as we need to stand alone, for fear that if we did
we would lose our independence altogether. The tensions of our lives
would be even greater if we did not, in fact, engage in practices that constantly limit the effects of an isolating individualism, even though we cannot articulate those practices nearly as well as we can the quest for autonomy. . . .

   . . . It is now time to consider what a self that is not empty would be
like—one that is constituted rather than unencumbered, one that has, let
us admit it, encumbrances, but whose encumbrances make connection to
others easier and more natural. Just as the empty self makes sense in a
particular institutional context—that of the upward mobility of the
middle-class individual who must leave home and church in order to succeed in an impersonal world of rationality and competition—so a constituted self makes sense in terms of another institutional context, what we
would call, in the full sense of the world, community.

   Communities, in the sense in which we are using the term, have a
history—in an important sense they are constituted by their past—and for
this reason we can speak of a real community as a "community of memory," one that does not forget its past. In order not to forget that past, a
community is involved in retelling its story, its constitutive narrative, and
in so doing, it offers examples of the men and women who have embodied and exemplified the meaning of the community. These stories of collective history and exemplary individuals are an important part of the
tradition that is so central to a community of memory. . . .

   Examples of such genuine communities are not hard to find in the
United States. There are ethnic and racial communities, each with its own
story and its own heroes and heroines. There are religious communities
that recall and reenact their stories in the weekly and annual cycles of
their ritual year, remembering the scriptural stories that tell them who
they are and the saints and martyrs who define their identity. There is the
national community, defined by its history and by the character of its representative leaders from [early colonist] John Winthrop to [civil rights
leader] Martin Luther King, Jr. Americans identify with their national
community partly because there is little else that we all share in common
but also partly because America's history exemplifies aspirations widely
shared throughout the world: the ideal of a free society, respecting all its
citizens, however diverse, and allowing them all to fulfill themselves. Yet
some Americans also remember the history of suffering inflicted and the
gap between promise and realization, which has always been very great. At

some times, neighborhoods, localities, and regions have been communities in America, but that has been hard to sustain in our restless and mobile society. Families can be communities, remembering their past, telling the children the stories of parents' and grandparents' lives, and sustaining hope for the future—though without the context of a larger community that sense of family is hard to maintain. Where history and hope are forgotten and community means only the gathering of the similar, community degenerates into lifestyle enclave. The temptation toward that transformation is endemic in America, though the transition is seldom complete.

People growing up in communities of memory not only hear the stories that tell how the community came to be, what its hopes and fears are, and how its ideals are exemplified in outstanding men and women; they also participate in the practices—ritual, aesthetic, ethical—that define the community as a way of life. We call these "practices of commitment" for they define the patterns of loyalty and obligation that keep the community alive. And if the language of the self-reliant individual is the first language of American moral life, the languages of tradition and commitment in communities of memory are "second languages" that most Americans know as well, and which they use when the language of the radically separate self does not seem adequate.... Sometimes Americans make a rather sharp dichotomy between private and public life. Viewing one's primary task as "finding oneself" in autonomous self-reliance, separating oneself not only from one's parents but also from those larger communities and traditions that constitute one's past, leads to the notion that it is in oneself, perhaps in relation to a few intimate others, that fulfillment is to be found. Individualism of this sort often implies a negative view of public life. The impersonal forces of the economic and political worlds are what the individual needs protection against. In this perspective, even occupation, which has been so central to the identity of Americans in the past, becomes instrumental—not a good in itself, but only a means to the attainment of a rich and satisfying private life. But on the basis of what we have seen in our observation of middle-class American life, it would seem that this quest for purely private fulfillment is illusory: it often ends in emptiness instead. On the other hand, we found many people ... for whom private fulfillment and public involvement are not antithetical. These people evince an individualism that is not empty but is full of content drawn from an active identification with communities and traditions. Perhaps the notion that private life and public life are at odds is incorrect. Perhaps they are so deeply involved with each other that the impoverishment of one entails the impoverishment of the other. Parker Palmer is probably right when he says that "in a healthy society the private and the public are not mutually exclusive, not in competition with each other. They are, instead, two halves of a whole, two poles of a paradox. They work together dialectically, helping to create and nurture one another."

Certainly this dialectical relationship is clear where public life degenerates into violence and fear. One cannot live a rich private life in a state of siege, mistrusting all strangers and turning one's home into an armed camp. A minimum of public decency and civility is a precondition for a fulfilling private life. On the other hand, public involvement is often difficult and demanding. To engage successfully in the public world, one needs personal strength and the support of family and friends. A rewarding private life is one of the preconditions for a healthy public life.

For all their doubts about the public sphere, Americans are more engaged in voluntary associations and civic organizations than the citizens of most other industrial nations. In spite of all the difficulties, many Americans feel they must "get involved." In public life as in private, we can discern the habits of the heart that sustain individualism and commitment, as well as what makes them problematic. . . .

The communities of memory of which we have spoken are concerned in a variety of ways to give a qualitative meaning to the living of life, to time and space, to persons and groups. Religious communities, for example, do not experience time in the way the mass media present it—as a continuous flow of qualitatively meaningless sensations. The day, the week, the season, the year are punctuated by an alternation of the sacred and the profane. Prayer breaks into our daily life at the beginning of a meal, at the end of the day, at common worship, reminding us that our utilitarian pursuits are not the whole of life, that a fulfilled life is one in which God and neighbor are remembered first. Many of our religious traditions recognize the significance of silence as a way of breaking the incessant flow of sensations and opening our hearts to the wholeness of being. And our republican tradition, too, has ways of giving form to time, reminding us on particular dates of the great events of our past or of the heroes who helped to teach us what we are as a free people. Even our private family life takes on a shared rhythm with a Thanksgiving dinner or a Fourth of July picnic.

In short, we have never been, and still are not, a collection of private individuals who, except for a conscious contract to create a minimal government, have nothing in common. Our lives make sense in a thousand ways, most of which we are unaware of, because of traditions that are centuries, if not millennia, old. It is these traditions that help us to know that it does make a difference who we are and how we treat one another.

PART TWO

The Constitution and American Democracy

8

RICHARD HOFSTADTER

From *The American Political Tradition*

Richard Hofstadter, one of the nation's leading historians, explores the real thoughts and motivations behind the men whom all schoolchildren have been taught to revere as Founding Fathers. Hofstadter's classic work points out the ambivalence of those who wrote the Constitution: they viewed human beings as selfish and untrustworthy, yet they strongly believed in the importance of self-government. The founders' ambivalence toward democracy led them to design the political system the United States still lives with today, one in which each interest (or branch or layer of government or economic class or region . . .) would be checked and balanced by competing interests. Hofstadter goes on to interpret what the near-sacred idea of liberty meant to the founders. Liberty was not really related to democracy, he contends, but rather ensured the freedom to attain and enjoy private property. To make this idea clearer, test the author's thesis against current political debates.

———

. . . THE MEN WHO DREW UP the Constitution in Philadelphia during the summer of 1787 had a vivid Calvinistic sense of human evil and damnation and believed with Hobbes that men are selfish and contentious. They were men of affairs, merchants, lawyers, planter-businessmen, speculators, investors. Having seen human nature on display in the marketplace, the courtroom, the legislative chamber, and in every secret path and alleyway where wealth and power are courted, they felt they knew it in all its frailty. To them a human being was an atom of self-interest. They did not believe in man, but they did believe in the power of a good political constitution to control him.

This may be an abstract notion to ascribe to practical men, but it follows the language that the Fathers themselves used. General Knox, for example, wrote in disgust to Washington after the Shays Rebellion that Americans were, after all, "men—actual men possessing all the turbulent passions belonging to that animal." Throughout the secret discussions at the Constitutional Convention it was clear that this distrust of man was first and foremost a distrust of the common man and democratic rule. . . .

And yet there was another side to the picture. The Fathers were intellectual heirs of seventeenth-century English republicanism with its opposition to arbitrary rule and faith in popular sovereignty. If they feared the advance of democracy, they also had misgivings about turning to the extreme right. Having recently experienced a bitter revolutionary struggle with an external power beyond their control, they were in no mood to follow Hobbes to his conclusion that any kind of government must be accepted in order to avert the anarchy and terror of a state of nature. . . .

Unwilling to turn their backs on republicanism, the Fathers also wished to avoid violating the prejudices of the people. "Notwithstanding the oppression and injustice experienced among us from democracy," said George Mason, "the genius of the people is in favor of it, and the genius of the people must be consulted." Mason admitted "that we had been too democratic," but feared that "we should incautiously run into the opposite extreme." James Madison, who has quite rightfully been called the philosopher of the Constitution, told the delegates: "It seems indispensable that the mass of citizens should not be without a voice in making the laws which they are to obey, and in choosing the magistrates who are to administer them." James Wilson, the outstanding jurist of the age, later appointed to the Supreme Court by Washington, said again and again that the ultimate power of government must of necessity reside in the people. This the Fathers commonly accepted, for if government did not proceed from the people, from what other source could it legitimately come? To adopt any other premise not only would be inconsistent with everything they had said against British rule in the past but would open the gates to an extreme concentration of power in the future. . . .

If the masses were turbulent and unregenerate, and yet if government must be founded upon their suffrage and consent, what could a Constitution-maker do? One thing that the Fathers did not propose to do, because they thought it impossible, was to change the nature of man to conform with a more ideal system. They were inordinately confident that they knew what man always had been and what he always would be. The eighteenth-century mind had great faith in universals. . . .

. . . It was too much to expect that vice could be checked by virtue; the Fathers relied instead upon checking vice with vice. Madison once objected during the Convention that Gouverneur Morris was "forever inculcating the utter political depravity of men and the necessity of opposing one vice and interest to another vice and interest." And yet Madison himself in the *Federalist* number 51 later set forth an excellent statement of the same thesis:

Ambition must be made to counteract ambition. . . . It may be a reflection on human nature that such devices should be necessary to control the abuses of government. But what is government itself, but the greatest of all reflections on human nature? If men were angels, no government would be necessary. . . . In framing a government which is to be administered by men over men, the great difficulty lies in this: you must first enable the government to control the governed; and in the next place oblige it to control itself.

. . . If, in a state that lacked constitutional balance, one class or one interest gained control, they believed, it would surely plunder all other interests. The Fathers, of course, were especially fearful that the poor would plunder the rich, but most of them would probably have admitted that the rich, unrestrained, would also plunder the poor. . . .

In practical form, therefore, the quest of the Fathers reduced primarily to a search for constitutional devices that would force various interests to check and control one another. Among those who favored the federal Constitution three such devices were distinguished.

The first of these was the advantage of a federated government in maintaining order against popular uprisings or majority rule. In a single state a faction might arise and take complete control by force; but if the states were bound in a federation, the central government could step in and prevent it. . . .

The second advantage of good constitutional government resided in the mechanism of representation itself. In a small direct democracy the unstable passions of the people would dominate lawmaking; but a representative government, as Madison said, would "refine and enlarge the public views by passing them through the medium of a chosen body of citizens." . . .

The third advantage of the government . . . [was that] each element should be given its own house of the legislature, and over both houses there should be set a capable, strong, and impartial executive armed with the veto power. This split assembly would contain within itself an organic check and would be capable of self-control under the governance of the executive. The whole system was to be capped by an independent judiciary. The inevitable tendency of the rich and the poor to plunder each other would be kept in hand. . . .

It is ironical that the Constitution, which Americans venerate so deeply, is based upon a political theory that at one crucial point stands in direct antithesis to the mainstream of American democratic faith. Modern American folklore assumes that democracy and liberty are all but identical, and when democratic writers take the trouble to make the distinction, they usually assume that democracy is necessary to liberty. But the Founding Fathers thought that the liberty with which they were most concerned was menaced by democracy. In their minds liberty was linked not to democracy but to property.

What did the Fathers mean by liberty? What did Jay mean when he spoke of "the charms of liberty"? Or Madison when he declared that to destroy liberty in order to destroy factions would be a remedy worse than the disease? Certainly the men who met at Philadelphia were not interested in extending liberty to those classes in America, the Negro slaves and the indentured servants, who were most in need of it, for slavery was recognized in the organic structure of the Constitution and indentured servitude was no concern of the Convention. Nor was the regard of the delegates for civil liberties any too tender. It was the opponents of the Constitution who were most active in demanding such vital liberties as freedom of religion, freedom of speech and press, jury trial, due process, and protection from "unreasonable searches and seizures." These guarantees had to be incorporated in the first ten amendments because the Convention neglected to put them in the original document. Turning to economic issues, it was not freedom of trade in the modern sense that the Fathers were striving for. Although they did not believe in impeding trade unnecessarily, they felt that failure to regulate it was one of the central weaknesses of the Articles of Confederation, and they stood closer to the mercantilists than to Adam Smith. Again, liberty to them did not mean free access to the nation's unappropriated wealth. At least fourteen of them were land speculators. They did not believe in the right of the squatter to occupy unused land, but rather in the right of the absentee owner or speculator to preempt it.

The liberties that the constitutionalists hoped to gain were chiefly negative. They wanted freedom from fiscal uncertainty and irregularities in the currency, from trade wars among the states, from economic discrimination by more powerful foreign governments, from attacks on the creditor class or on property, from popular insurrection. They aimed to create a government that would act as an honest broker among a variety of propertied interests, giving them all protection from their common enemies and preventing any one of them from becoming too powerful. The Convention was a fraternity of types of absentee ownership. All property should be permitted to have its proportionate voice in government. Individual property interests might have to be sacrificed at times, but only for the community of propertied interests. Freedom for property would result in liberty for men—perhaps not for all men, but at least for all worthy men. Because men have different faculties and abilities, the Fathers believed, they acquire different amounts of property. To protect property is only to protect men in the exercise of their natural faculties. Among the many liberties, therefore, freedom to hold and dispose [of] property is paramount. Democracy, unchecked rule by the masses, is sure to bring arbitrary redistribution of property, destroying the very essence of liberty. . . .

A cardinal tenet in the faith of the men who made the Constitution was the belief that democracy can never be more than a transitional stage in government, that it always evolves into either a tyranny (the rule of the rich demagogue who has patronized the mob) or an aristocracy (the original leaders of the democratic elements). . . .

What encouraged the Fathers about their own era, however, was the broad dispersion of landed property. The small land-owning farmers had been troublesome in recent years, but there was a general conviction that under a properly made Constitution a *modus vivendi* could be worked out with them. The possession of moderate plots of property presumably gave them a sufficient stake in society to be safe and responsible citizens under the restraints of balanced government. Influence in government would be proportionate to property: merchants and great landholders would be dominant, but small property-owners would have an independent and far from negligible voice. It was "politic as well as just," said Madison, "that the interests and rights of every class should be duly represented and understood in the public councils," and John Adams declared that there could be "no free government without a democratical branch in the constitution." . . .

. . . At the very beginning contemporary opponents of the Constitution foresaw an apocalyptic destruction of local government and popular institutions, while conservative Europeans of the old regime thought the young American Republic was a dangerous leftist experiment. Modern critical scholarship, which reached a high point in Charles A. Beard's *An Economic Interpretation of the Constitution of the United States,* started a new turn in the debate. The antagonism, long latent, between the philosophy of the Constitution and the philosophy of American democracy again came into the open. Professor Beard's work appeared in 1913 at the peak of the Progressive era, when the muckraking fever was still high; some readers tended to conclude from his findings that the Fathers were selfish reactionaries who do not deserve their high place in American esteem. Still more recently, other writers, inverting this logic, have used Beard's facts to praise the Fathers for their opposition to "democracy" and as an argument for returning again to the idea of a "republic."

In fact, the Fathers' image of themselves as moderate republicans standing between political extremes was quite accurate. They were impelled by class motives more than pietistic writers like to admit, but they were also controlled, as Professor Beard himself has recently emphasized, by a statesmanlike sense of moderation and a scrupulously republican philosophy. Any attempt, however, to tear their ideas out of the eighteenth-century context is sure to make them seem starkly reactionary. Consider, for example, the favorite maxim of John Jay: "The people who own the country ought to govern it." To the Fathers this was simply a swift axiomatic statement of the stake-in-society theory of political rights, a moderate conservative position under eighteenth-century conditions of property distribution in America. Under modern property relations this maxim demands a drastic restriction of the base of political power. A large portion of the modern middle class—and it is the strength of this class upon which balanced government depends—is propertyless; and the urban proletariat, which the Fathers so greatly feared, is almost one half the population. Further, the separation of ownership from control that has come with the corporation deprives Jay's maxim of twentieth-century meaning even for many propertied people. The six hundred thousand stockholders of the American Telephone & Telegraph Company not only do not acquire political power by virtue of their stock-ownership, but they do not even acquire economic power: they cannot control their own company.

From a humanistic standpoint there is a serious dilemma in the philosophy of the Fathers, which derives from their conception of man. They thought man was a creature of rapacious self-interest, and yet they wanted him to be free—free, in essence, to contend, to engage in an umpired strife, to use property to get property. They accepted the mercantile image of life as an eternal battleground, and assumed the Hobbesian war of each against all; they did not propose to put an end to this war, but merely to stabilize it and make it less murderous. They had no hope and they offered none for any ultimate organic change in the way men conduct themselves. The result was that while they thought self-interest the most dangerous and unbrookable quality of man, they necessarily underwrote it in trying to control it. . . .

9

ALEXIS DE TOCQUEVILLE

From *Democracy in America*

In 1831, the young French aristocrat observed America's ever-growing equality, an equality that produces reverence for the majority's viewpoint. If all citizens are basically equal, the camp with the most number of people wins fair and square. Tocqueville's assessment? "Dangerous," he believes. The Frenchman explains the way a monarch or a dictator oppresses his people, contrasting that overt kind of oppression with the more covert form that exists in a democracy. His accusation is shocking and unexpected: "I know no country in which there is so little true independence of mind and freedom of discussion as in America." But before you get angry, follow Tocqueville's argument carefully. He explains how a system based on majority rule can be just as—or more—oppressive than a monarchy. Tocqueville discusses the plight of the minority in America and he warns us about the possible consequences of pushing the minority aside. Consider, readers, whether the nation heeded Tocqueville's warning. Consider also whether the nation heeded the warning too well: maybe tyranny of the majority is the least of our problems today.

THE VERY ESSENCE of democratic government consists in the absolute sovereignty of the majority; for there is nothing in democratic states which is capable of resisting it....

...The moral authority of the majority is partly based upon the notion, that there is more intelligence and more wisdom in a great number of men collected together than in a single individual, and that the quantity of legislators is more important than their quality. The theory of equality is in fact applied to the intellect of man; and human pride is thus assailed in its last retreat, by a doctrine which the minority hesitate to admit, and in which they very slowly concur....

The moral power of the majority is founded upon yet another principle, which is, that the interests of the many are to be preferred to those of the few. It will readily be perceived that the respect here professed for the rights of the majority must naturally increase or diminish according to the state of parties. When a nation is divided into several irreconcilable factions, the privilege of the majority is often overlooked, because it is intolerable to comply with its demands.

If there existed in America a class of citizens whom the legislating majority sought to deprive of exclusive privileges, which they had possessed for ages, and to bring down from an elevated station to the level of the ranks of the multitude, it is probable that the minority would be less ready to comply with its laws. But as the United States were colonized by men holding equal rank amongst themselves, there is as yet no natural or permanent source of dissension between the interests of its different inhabitants.

There are certain communities in which the persons who constitute the minority can never hope to draw over the majority to their side, because they must then give up the very point which is at issue between them. Thus, an aristocracy can never become a majority whilst it retains its exclusive privileges, and it cannot cede its privileges without ceasing to be an aristocracy.

In the United States, political questions cannot be taken up in so general and absolute a manner; and all parties are willing to recognize the rights of the majority, because they all hope to turn those rights to their own advantage at some future time. The majority therefore in that country exercises a prodigious actual authority, and a moral influence which is scarcely less preponderant; no obstacles exist which can impede, or so much as retard its progress, or which can induce it to heed the complaints of those whom it crushes upon its path. This state of things is fatal in itself and dangerous for the future. . . .

A majority taken collectively may be regarded as a being whose opinions, and most frequently whose interests, are opposed to those of another being, which is styled a minority. If it be admitted that a man, possessing absolute power, may misuse that power by wronging his adversaries, why should a majority not be liable to the same reproach? . . .

Unlimited power is in itself a bad and dangerous thing; human beings are not competent to exercise it with discretion; and God alone can be omnipotent, because his wisdom and his justice are always equal to his power. But no power upon earth is so worthy of honour for itself, or of reverential obedience to the rights which it represents, that I would consent to admit its uncontrolled and all-predominant authority. When I see that the right and the means of absolute command are conferred on a people or upon a king, upon an aristocracy or a democracy, a monarchy or a republic, I recognize the germ of tyranny, and I journey onwards to a land of more hopeful institutions.

In my opinion the main evil of the present democratic institutions of the United States does not arise, as is often asserted in Europe, from their weakness, but from their overpowering strength; and I am not so much alarmed at the excessive liberty which reigns in that country, as at the very inadequate securities which exist against tyranny.

When an individual or a party is wronged in the United States, to whom can he apply for redress? If to public opinion, public opinion constitutes the majority; if to the legislature, it represents the majority, and implicitly obeys its injunctions; if to the executive power, it is appointed by the majority and remains a passive tool in its hands; the public troops consist of the majority under arms; the jury is the majority invested with the right of hearing judicial cases; and in certain States even the judges are elected by the majority. However iniquitous or absurd the evil of which you complain may be, you must submit to it as well as you can.

If, on the other hand, a legislative power could be so constituted as to represent the majority without necessarily being the slave of its passions; an executive, so as to retain a certain degree of uncontrolled authority; and a judiciary, so as to remain independent of the two other powers; a government would be formed which would still be democratic without incurring any risk of tyrannical abuse.

I do not say that tyrannical abuses frequently occur in America at the present day; but I maintain that no sure barrier is established against them, and that the causes which mitigate the government are to be found in the circumstances and the manners of the country more than in its laws. . . .

It is in the examination of the display of public opinion in the United States, that we clearly perceive how far the power of the majority surpasses all the powers with which we are acquainted in Europe. Intellectual principles exercise an influence which is so invisible and often so inappreciable, that they baffle the toils of oppression. At the present time the most absolute monarchs in Europe are unable to prevent certain notions, which are opposed to their authority, from circulating in secret throughout their dominions, and even in their courts. Such is not the case in America; as long as the majority is still undecided, discussion is carried on; but as soon as its decision is irrevocably pronounced, a submissive silence is observed; and the friends, as well as the opponents, of the measure, unite in assenting to its propriety. The reason of this is perfectly clear: no monarch is so absolute as to combine all the powers of society in his own hands, and to conquer all opposition, with the energy of a majority, which is invested with the right of making and of executing the laws.

The authority of a king is purely physical, and it controls the actions of the subject without subduing his private will; but the majority possesses a power which is physical and moral at the same time; it acts upon the will as well as upon the actions of men, and it represses not only all contest, but all controversy.

I know no country in which there is so little true independence of mind and freedom of discussion as in America. In any constitutional state in Europe every sort of religious and political theory may be advocated and propagated abroad; for there is no country in Europe so subdued by any single authority, as not to contain citizens who are ready to protect the man who raises his voice in the cause of truth, from the consequences of his hardihood. If he is unfortunate enough to live under an absolute government, the people is upon his side; if he inhabits a free country, he may find a shelter behind the authority of the throne, if he require one. The aristocratic part of society supports him in some countries, and the democracy in others. But in a nation where democratic institutions exist, organized like those of the United States, there is but one sole authority, one single element of strength and of success, with nothing beyond it.

In America, the majority raises very formidable barriers to the liberty of opinion: within these barriers an author may write whatever he pleases, but he will repent it if he ever step beyond them. Not that he is exposed to the terrors of an auto-da-fé, but he is tormented by the slights and persecutions of daily obloquy. His political career is closed for ever, since he has offended the only authority which is able to promote his success. Every sort of compensation, even that of celebrity, is refused to him. Before he published his opinions, he imagined that he held them in common with many others; but no sooner has he declared them openly, than he is loudly censured by his overbearing opponents, whilst those who think, without having the courage to speak, like him, abandon him in silence. He yields at length, oppressed by the daily efforts he has been making, and he subsides into silence, as if he was tormented by remorse for having spoken the truth.

Fetters and headsmen were the coarse instruments which tyranny formerly employed; but the civilization of our age has refined the arts of despotism, which seemed however to have been sufficiently perfected before. The excesses of monarchical power had devised a variety of physical means of oppression: the democratic republics of the present day have rendered it as entirely an affair of the mind, as that will which it is intended to coerce. Under the absolute sway of an individual despot, the body was attacked in order to subdue the soul; and the soul escaped the blows which were directed against it, and rose superior to the attempt; but such is not the course adopted by tyranny in democratic republics; there the body is left free, and the soul is enslaved. The sovereign can no longer say, "You shall think as I do on pain of death;" but he says, "You are free to think differently from me, and to retain your life, your property, and all that you possess; but if such be your determination, you are henceforth an alien among your people. You may retain your civil rights, but they will be useless to you, for you will never be chosen by your fellow-citizens if you solicit their suffrages; and they will affect to scorn you, if you solicit their esteem. You will remain among men, but you will be deprived of the rights of mankind. Your fellow-creatures will shun you like an impure being; and those who are most persuaded of your innocence will abandon you too, lest they should be shunned in their turn. Go in peace! I have given you your life, but it is an existence incomparably worse than death."

Monarchical institutions have thrown an odium upon despotism; let us beware lest democratic republics should restore oppression, and should render it less odious and less degrading in the eyes of the many, by making it still more onerous to the few. . . .

The tendencies which I have just alluded to are as yet very slightly perceptible in political society; but they already begin to exercise an unfavourable influence upon the national character of the Americans. I am inclined to attribute the singular paucity of distinguished political characters to the ever-increasing activity of the despotism of the majority in the United States. . . .

In free countries, where every one is more or less called upon to give his opinion in the affairs of state; in democratic republics, where public life is incessantly commingled with domestic affairs, where the sovereign authority is accessible on every side, and where its attention can almost always be attracted by vociferation, more persons are to be met with who speculate upon its foibles, and live at the cost of its passions, than in absolute monarchies. Not because men are naturally worse in these States than elsewhere, but the temptation is stronger, and of easier access at the same time. The result is a far more extensive debasement of the characters of citizens.

Democratic republics extend the practice of currying favour with the many, and they introduce it into a greater number of classes at once: this is one of the most serious reproaches that can be addressed to them. In democratic States organized on the principles of the American republics, this is more especially the case, where the authority of the majority is so absolute and so irresistible, that a man must give up his rights as a citizen, and almost abjure his quality as a human being, if he intends to stray from the track which it lays down. . . .

If ever the free institutions of America are destroyed, that event may be attributed to the unlimited authority of the majority, which may at some future time urge the minorities to desperation, and oblige them to have recourse to physical force. Anarchy will then be the result, but it will have been brought about by despotism. . . .

10

JAMES MADISON

The Federalist 10

This is the most important reading in an American government class. Along with its companion, Federalist 51 *(coming in the next section of the book), James Madison's* Federalist 10 *is the first and last word on U.S. government and politics. In it, he takes up the idea of "faction," by which he means any single group (especially the mob-like majority, but perhaps even a tiny minority) that tries to dominate the political process. Can faction be removed from politics? No, he admits, for a variety of reasons that deeply illuminate his assessment of the American people. But faction can be controlled by a republican (representative) system. Madison favored a large and diverse nation; if there were many groups, no one faction would ever be able to dominate. Signing these papers "Publius," Madison, along with Alexander Hamilton and John Jay, wrote eighty-five essays collectively known as* The Federalist Papers, *which were published in several New York newspapers on behalf of the ratification of the new Constitution in 1787. James Madison's genius is revealed not only in the workable system of government he helped create for America, but also in his vision of the United States in the future, very much as it is today.*

No. 10: Madison

AMONG THE NUMEROUS ADVANTAGES promised by a well-constructed Union, none deserves to be more accurately developed than its tendency to break and control the violence of faction. The friend of popular governments never finds himself so much alarmed for their character and fate as when he contemplates their propensity to this dangerous vice. He will not fail, therefore, to set a due value on any plan which, without violating the principles to which he is attached, provides a proper cure for it. The instability, injustice, and confusion introduced into the public councils have, in truth, been the mortal diseases under which popular governments have everywhere perished, as they continue to be the favorite and fruitful topics from which the adversaries to liberty derive their most specious declamations. The valuable improvements made by the American constitutions on the popular models, both ancient and modern, cannot certainly be too much admired; but it would be an unwarrantable partiality to contend that they have as effectually obviated the danger on this side, as was wished and expected. Complaints are everywhere heard from our most considerate and virtuous citizens, equally the friends of public and private faith and of public and personal liberty, that our governments are too unstable, that the public good is disregarded in the conflicts of rival parties, and that measures are too often decided, not according to the rules of justice and the rights of the minor party, but by the superior force of an interested and overbearing majority. However anxiously we may wish that these complaints had no foundation, the evidence of known facts will not permit us to deny that they are in some degree true. It will be found, indeed, on a candid review of our situation, that some of the distresses under which we labor have been erroneously charged on the operation of our governments; but it will be found, at the same time, that other causes will not alone account for many of our heaviest misfortunes; and, particularly, for that prevailing and increasing distrust of public engagements and alarm for private rights which are echoed from one end of the continent to the other. These must be chiefly, if not wholly, effects of the unsteadiness and injustice with which a factious spirit has tainted our public administration.

By a faction I understand a number of citizens, whether amounting to a majority or minority of the whole, who are united and actuated by some common impulse of passion, or of interest, adverse to the rights of other citizens, or to the permanent and aggregate interests of the community.

There are two methods of curing the mischiefs of faction: the one, by removing its causes; the other, by controlling its effects.

There are again two methods of removing the causes of faction: the one, by destroying the liberty which is essential to its existence; the other, by giving to every citizen the same opinions, the same passions, and the same interests.

It could never be more truly said than of the first remedy that it was worse than the disease. Liberty is to faction what air is to fire, an aliment without which it instantly expires. But it could not be a less folly to abolish liberty, which is essential to political life, because it nourishes faction than it would be to wish the annihilation of air, which is essential to animal life, because it imparts to fire its destructive agency.

The second expedient is as impracticable as the first would be unwise. As long as the reason of man continues fallible, and he is at liberty to exercise it, different opinions will be formed. As long as the connection subsists between his reason and his self-love, his opinions and his passions will have a reciprocal influence on each other; and the former will be objects to which the latter will attach themselves. The diversity in the faculties of men, from which the rights of property originate, is not less an insuperable obstacle to a uniformity of interests. The protection of these faculties is the first object of government. From the protection of different and unequal faculties of acquiring property, the possession of different degrees and kinds of property immediately results; and from the influence of these on the sentiments and views of the respective proprietors ensues a division of the society into different interests and parties.

The latent causes of faction are thus sown in the nature of man; and we see them everywhere brought into different degrees of activity, according to the different circumstances of civil society. A zeal for different opinions concerning religion, concerning government, and many other points, as well of speculation as of practice; an attachment to different leaders ambitiously contending for pre-eminence and power; or to persons of other descriptions whose fortunes have been interesting to the human passions, have, in turn, divided mankind into parties, inflamed them with mutual animosity, and rendered them much more disposed to vex and oppress each other than to co-operate for their common good. So strong is this propensity of mankind to fall into mutual animosities that where no substantial occasion presents itself the most frivolous and fanciful distinctions have been sufficient to kindle their unfriendly passions and excite their most violent conflicts. But the most common and durable source of factions has been the various and unequal distribution of property. Those who hold and those who are without property have ever formed distinct interests in society. Those who are creditors, and those who are debtors, fall under a like discrimination. A landed interest, a manufacturing interest, a mercantile interest, a moneyed interest, with many lesser interests, grow up of necessity in civilized nations, and divide them into different classes, actuated by different sentiments and views. The regulation of these various and interfering interests forms the principal task of modern legislation and involves the spirit of party and faction in the necessary and ordinary operations of government.

No man is allowed to be a judge in his own cause, because his interest would certainly bias his judgment, and, not improbably, corrupt his integrity. With equal, nay with greater reason, a body of men are unfit to be both judges and parties at the same time; yet what are many of the most important acts of legislation but so many judicial determinations, not indeed concerning the rights of single persons, but concerning the rights of large bodies of citizens? And what are the different classes of legislators but advocates and parties to the causes which they determine? Is a law proposed concerning private debts? It is a question to which the creditors are parties on one side and the debtors on the other. Justice ought to hold the balance between them. Yet the parties are, and must be, themselves the judges; and the most numerous party, or in other words, the most powerful faction must be expected to prevail. Shall domestic manufacturers be encouraged, and in what degree, by restrictions on foreign manufacturers? are questions which would be differently decided by the landed and the manufacturing classes, and probably by neither with a sole regard to justice and the public good. The apportionment of taxes on the various descriptions of property is an act which seems to require the most exact impartiality; yet there is, perhaps, no legislative act in which greater opportunity and temptation are given to a predominant party to trample on the rules of justice. Every shilling with which they overburden the inferior number is a shilling saved to their own pockets.

It is in vain to say that enlightened statesmen will be able to adjust these clashing interests and render them all subservient to the public good. Enlightened statesmen will not always be at the helm. Nor, in many cases, can such an adjustment be made at all without taking into view indirect and remote considerations, which will rarely prevail over the immediate interest which one party may find in disregarding the rights of another or the good of the whole.

The inference to which we are brought is that the *causes* of faction cannot be removed and that relief is only to be sought in the means of controlling its *effects*.

If a faction consists of less than a majority, relief is supplied by the republican principle, which enables the majority to defeat its sinister views by regular vote. It may clog the administration, it may convulse the society; but it will be unable to execute and mask its violence under the forms of the Constitution. When a majority is included in a faction, the form of popular government, on the other hand, enables it to sacrifice to its ruling passion or interest both the public good and the rights of other citizens. To secure the public good and private rights against the danger of such a faction, and at the same time to preserve the spirit and the form of popular government, is then the great object to which our inquiries are directed. Let me add that it is the great desideratum by which alone this form of government can be rescued from the opprobrium under which it has so long labored and be recommended to the esteem and adoption of mankind.

By what means is this object attainable? Evidently by one of two only. Either the existence of the same passion or interest in a majority at the same time must be prevented, or the majority, having such coexistent passion or interest, must be rendered, by their number and local situation, unable to concert and carry into effect schemes of oppression. If the impulse and the opportunity be suffered to coincide, we well know that neither moral nor religious motives can be relied on as an adequate control. They are not found to be such on the injustice and violence of individuals, and lose their efficacy in proportion to the number combined together, that is, in proportion as their efficacy becomes needful.

From this view of the subject it may be concluded that a pure democracy, by which I mean a society consisting of a small number of citizens, who assemble and administer the government in person, can admit of no cure for the mischiefs of faction. A common passion or interest will, in almost every case, be felt by a majority of the whole; a communication and concert results from the form of government itself; and there is nothing to check the inducements to sacrifice the weaker party or an obnoxious individual. Hence it is that such democracies have ever been spectacles of turbulence and contention; have ever been found incompatible with personal security or the rights of property; and have in general been as short in their lives as they have been violent in their deaths. Theoretic politicians, who have patronized this species of government, have erroneously supposed that by reducing mankind to a perfect equality in their political rights, they would at the same time be perfectly equalized and assimilated in their possessions, their opinions, and their passions.

A republic, by which I mean a government in which the scheme of representation takes place, opens a different prospect and promises the cure for which we are seeking. Let us examine the points in which it varies from pure democracy, and we shall comprehend both the nature of the cure and the efficacy which it must derive from the Union.

The two great points of difference between a democracy and a republic are: first, the delegation of the government, in the latter, to a small number of citizens elected by the rest; secondly, the greater number of citizens and greater sphere of country over which the latter may be extended.

The effect of the first difference is, on the one hand, to refine and enlarge the public views by passing them through the medium of a chosen body of citizens, whose wisdom may best discern the true interest of their country and whose patriotism and love of justice will be least likely to sacrifice it to temporary or partial considerations. Under such a regulation it may well happen that the public voice, pronounced by the representatives of the people, will be more consonant to the public good than if pronounced by the people themselves, convened for the purpose. On the other hand, the effect may be inverted. Men of factious tempers, of local prejudices, or of sinister designs, may, by intrigue, by corruption, or by other means, first obtain the suffrages, and then betray the interests of the people. The question resulting is, whether small or extensive republics are most favorable to the election of proper guardians of the public weal; and it is clearly decided in favor of the latter by two obvious considerations.

In the first place it is to be remarked that however small the republic may be the representatives must be raised to a certain number in order to guard against the cabals of a few; and that however large it may be they must be limited to a certain number in order to guard against the confusion of a multitude. Hence, the number of representatives in the two cases not being in proportion to that of the constituents, and being proportionally greatest in the small republic, it follows that if the proportion of fit characters be not less in the large than in the small republic, the former will present a greater option, and consequently a greater probability of a fit choice.

In the next place, as each representative will be chosen by a greater number of citizens in the large than in the small republic, it will be more difficult for unworthy candidates to practise with success the vicious arts by which elections are too often carried; and the suffrages of the people being more free, will be more likely to center on men who possess the most attractive merit and the most diffusive and established characters.

It must be confessed that in this, as in most other cases, there is a mean, on both sides of which inconveniencies will be found to lie. By enlarging too much the number of electors, you render the representative too little acquainted with all their local circumstances and lesser interests; as by reducing it too much, you render him unduly attached to these, and too little fit to comprehend and pursue great and national objects. The federal Constitution forms a happy combination in this respect; the great and aggregate interests being referred to the national, the local and particular to the State legislatures.

The other point of difference is the greater number of citizens and extent of territory which may be brought within the compass of republican than of democratic government; and it is this circumstance principally which renders factious combinations less to be dreaded in the former than in the latter. The smaller the society, the fewer probably will be the distinct parties and interests composing it; the fewer the distinct parties and interests, the more frequently will a majority be found of the same party; and the smaller the number of individuals composing a majority, and the smaller the compass within which they are placed, the more easily will they concert and execute their plans of oppression. Extend the sphere and you take in a greater variety of parties and interests;

you make it less probable that a majority of the whole will have a common motive to invade the rights of other citizens; or if such a common motive exists, it will be more difficult for all who feel it to discover their own strength and to act in unison with each other. Besides other impediments, it may be remarked that, where there is a consciousness of unjust or dishonorable purposes, communication is always checked by distrust in proportion to the number whose concurrence is necessary.

Hence, it clearly appears that the same advantage which a republic has over a democracy in controlling the effects of faction is enjoyed by a large over a small republic—is enjoyed by the Union over the States composing it. Does this advantage consist in the substitution of representatives whose enlightened views and virtuous sentiments render them superior to local prejudices and to schemes of injustice? It will not be denied that the representation of the Union will be most likely to possess these requisite endowments. Does it consist in the greater security afforded by a greater variety of parties, against the event of any one party being able to outnumber and oppress the rest? In an equal degree does the increased variety of parties comprised within the Union increase this security? Does it, in fine, consist in the greater obstacles opposed to the concert and accomplishment of the secret wishes of an unjust and interested majority? Here again the extent of the Union gives it the most palpable advantage.

The influence of factious leaders may kindle a flame within their particular States but will be unable to spread a general conflagration through the other States. A religious sect may degenerate into a political faction in a part of the Confederacy; but the variety of sects dispersed over the entire face of it must secure the national councils against any danger from that source. A rage for paper money, for an abolition of debts, for an equal division of property, or for any other improper or wicked project, will be less apt to pervade the whole body of the Union than a particular member of it, in the same proportion as such a malady is more likely to taint a particular county or district than an entire State.

In the extent and proper structure of the Union, therefore, we behold a republican remedy for the diseases most incident to republican government. And according to the degree of pleasure and pride we feel in being republicans ought to be our zeal in cherishing the spirit and supporting the character of federalists.   *Publius*

II

MICHAEL KAMMEN

From *A Machine That Would Go of Itself*

Written at the time of the bicentennial of the United States Constitution, historian Michael Kammen's book is of interest to those seeking greater depth on the evolution of the nation's basic document. Kammen traces the shifts in thought about the Constitution's interpretation, from that of a "machine" that once put in motion would function steadily and unchangingly forever, to a more fluid and malleable plan. Particularly memorable is his analogy of a 1966 "Star Trek" episode, "The Omega Glory," in which we see Captain Kirk and the crew of the Enterprise *grappling with the same questions that we ask today about the Constitution.*

———

THE [METAPHOR], THE NOTION OF a constitution as some sort of machine or engine, had its origins in Newtonian science. Enlightened philosophers, such as David Hume, liked to contemplate the world with all of its components as a great machine. Perhaps it was inevitable, as politics came to be regarded as a science during the 1770s and '80s, that leading revolutionaries in the colonies would utilize the metaphor to suit their purposes. In 1774 Jefferson's *Summary View* mentioned "the great machine of government." . . .

Over the next one hundred years such imagery did not disappear. But neither did it notably increase; and hardly anyone expressed apprehension about the adverse implications of employing mechanistic metaphors. Occasionally an observer or enthusiast might call the Constitution "the best national machine that is now in existence" (1794); or, at the Golden Jubilee in 1839, John Quincy Adams could comment that "fifty years have passed away since the first impulse was given to the wheels of this political machine."

James Fenimore Cooper uttered one of the few expressions of concern couched in this language between 1787 and 1887. "The boldest violations of the Constitution are daily proposed by politicians in this country," he observed in 1848, "but they do not produce the fruits which might be expected, because the nation is so accustomed to work in the harness it has placed on itself, that nothing seems seriously to arrest the movement of the great national car." Although his metaphors are ridiculously muddled, the message is clear enough. Exactly forty years later James Russell Lowell articulated this same apprehension much more cogently in an address to the Reform Club of New York. The pertinent passage marks the apogee of the metaphor, and remains today as profound a warning as it was in 1888.

After our Constitution got fairly into working order it really seemed as if we had invented a machine that would go of itself, and this begot a faith in our luck which even the civil war itself but momentarily disturbed. Circumstances continued favorable, and our prosperity went on increasing. I admire the splendid complacency of my countrymen, and find something exhilarating and inspiring in it. We are a nation which has *struck ile* [sic], but we are also a nation that is sure the well will never run dry. And this confidence in our luck with the absorption in material interests, generated by unparalleled opportunity, has in some respects made us neglectful of our political duties.

That statement epitomizes not merely the main historical theme of this book, but the homily that I hope to convey as well. Machine imagery lingered on for fifty years, casually used by legal scholars, journalists, civics textbooks, even great jurists like Holmes, and by Franklin D. Roosevelt in his first inaugural address. On occasion, during the 1920s and '30s especially, conservatives would declare that the apparatus, being more than adequate, should not be tampered with, whereas reformers insisted that "the machinery of government under which we live is hopelessly antiquated" (a word they loved) and therefore "should be overhauled."

In the quarter century that followed Lowell's 1888 lament, a cultural transition took place that leads us to the last of the major constitutional metaphors. We may exemplify it with brief extracts from three prominent justices: Holmes, who wrote in 1914 that "the provisions of the Constitution are not mathematical formulas . . . they are organic living institutions"; Cardozo, who observed in 1925 that "a Constitution has an organic life"; and Frankfurter, who declared in 1951 that "the Constitution is an organism."

Unlike the other analogies that have been discussed, which were not mutually exclusive, this shift was not merely deliberate but intellectually aggressive at times. The quarter century is punctuated by the declarations of two political scientists deeply involved in public affairs. At the close of the 1880s, A. Lawrence Lowell wrote that "a political system is not a mere machine which can be constructed on any desired plan. . . . It is far more than this. It is an organism . . . whose various parts act and react upon one another." In 1912, when Woodrow Wilson ran for the presidency, a key passage in his campaign statement, *The New Freedom*, elaborated upon Lowell's assertion. "The makers of our Federal Constitution," in Wilson's words, "constructed a government as they would have constructed an orrery,*—to display the laws of nature. Politics in their thought was a variety of mechanics. The Constitution was founded on the law of gravitation. The government was to exist and move by virtue of the efficacy of 'checks and balances.'"

Lowell and Wilson had obviously responded to the same current of cultural change; but they were not attempting to be intellectually trendy by explaining government in terms of evolutionary theory. The word-concept they both used in condemning a Newtonian notion of constitutionalism was "static." Wilson spelled out the implications: "Society is a living organism and must obey the laws of life, not of mechanics; it must develop. All that progressives ask or desire is permission—in an era when 'development,' 'evolution,' is the scientific word—to interpret the Constitution according to the Darwinian principle; all they ask is recognition of the fact that a nation is a living thing and not a machine." . . .

I would describe the basic pattern of American constitutionalism as one of *conflict within consensus*. At first glance, perhaps, we are more likely to notice the consensus. . . .

The volume of evidence is overwhelming that our constitutional conflicts have been consequential, and considerably more revealing than the consensual framework within which they operate. When Americans have been aware of the dynamic of conflict within consensus, most often they have regarded it as a normative pattern for a pluralistic polity. . . .

There is . . . a . . . closely linked aspect of American constitutionalism about which there has been no consensus: namely, whether our frame of government was meant to be fairly unchanging or flexible. Commentators are quick to quote Justice Holmes's "theory of our Constitution. It is an experiment, as all life is an experiment." Although much less familiar, and less eloquent, more Americans have probably shared this sentiment, written in 1936 by an uncommon common man, the chief clerk in the Vermont Department of Highways: "I regard the Constitution as of too much value to be experimented with."

The assumption that our Constitution is lapidary has a lineage that runs, among the justices, from Marshall and Taney to David J. Brewer and George Sutherland. It has been the dominant assumption for most of our history, and provided the basis for Walter Bagehot, Lord Bryce, and others to regard the U.S. Constitution as "rigid" by comparison with the British. The idea that adaptability was desirable emerged gradually during the mid-nineteenth century, appeared in some manuals aimed at a popular audience by the 1880s, and achieved added respectability in 1906 when

*An apparatus for representing the motions . . . of the planets. . . .

Justice Henry Billings Brown spoke at a dinner in his honor. The Constitution, he said, "should be liberally interpreted—interpreted as if it were intended as the foundation of a great nation, and not merely a temporary expedient for the united action of thirteen small States. . . . Like all written Constitutions, there is an underlying danger in its inflexibility." For about a generation that outlook slowly gained adherents, until the two contradictory views were essentially counterpoised in strength by the 1930s.

Meanwhile, a third position appeared during the early decades of the twentieth century—one that might be considered a compromise because it blended facets of the other two. This moderately conservative, evolutionary position was expressed in 1903 by James Ford Rhodes, a nationalistic businessman-turned-historian. The Constitution, in his mind, "is rigid in those matters which should not be submitted to the decision of a legislature or to a popular vote without checks which secure reflection and a chance for the sober second thought, [yet] it has proved flexible in its adaptation to the growth of the country." . . .

Admittedly, our strict constructionists have on occasion stretched the Constitution, as Jefferson did in 1803 to acquire the vast Louisiana Territory. Lincoln, Wilson, and FDR each stood accused of ignoring constitutional restraints; yet each one could honestly respond that, within the framework of a Constitution intended to be flexible in an emergency, his goal had been to preserve the Union, to win a war fought for noble goals, or to overcome the worst and most prolonged economic disaster in American history. In each instance their constitutional critics spoke out clearly, a national debate took place, and clarification of our constitutional values occurred. Sometimes that clarification has come from the Supreme Court; sometimes from a presidential election campaign; sometimes from a combination of the two; and sometimes by means of political compromise. Each mode of resolution is a necessary part of our democratic system. I am led to conclude that Americans have been more likely to read and understand their Constitution when it has been controversial, or when some group contended that it had been misused, than in those calmer moments when it has been widely venerated as an instrument for all time. . . .

During the later 1950s, Robert M. Hutchins and his colleagues at the Center for the Study of Democratic Institutions, located in Santa Barbara, California, began to discuss the desirability of far-reaching constitutional changes. In 1964, following a series of seminars modestly entitled "Drafting a New Constitution for the United States and the World," Hutchins invited Rexford G. Tugwell, once a member of FDR's "Brain Trust," to direct a reassessment of the Constitution. Tugwell accepted and spent two years conferring with hundreds of jurists, politicians, and scholars. . . .

During the 1970s the Center's primary concerns shifted away from constitutionalism; Tugwell's two major volumes (1974 and 1976) received little attention aside from scholarly journals. When Tugwell died in 1979 at the age of eighty-eight, the *New York Times's* appreciative editorial did not even mention the revised constitution on which he labored for more than a decade. The *Times* apparently did not regard it as a fitting culmination for a distinguished career in scholarship and public service.

The negligible impact of this seasoned planner's constitutional vision provides a striking contrast with an extremely tradition-oriented interpolation of the U.S. Constitution in science fiction. One popular episode of the television series "Star Trek," written in 1966, received hundreds of re-runs during the many years when Tugwell labored over his revision. Millions of Americans watched "The Omega Glory" and recognized its affirmation of the good old Constitution that continued to function even though space, time, and ignorance shrouded its meaning.

Reducing the saga to its ideological essence, Captain Kirk and the starship *Enterprise* land on a planet where the inhabitants are guided by a Prime Directive that must not be violated. Those inhabitants are called Yangs (presumably the descendants of colonizers once known as Yanks), and possess "a worn parchment document" that is "the greatest of holies." Kirk and his crew encounter a bizarre political situation that is not so very different from the one criticized by James Russell Lowell in 1888. The Yangs worship "freedom" but do not understand what it means. Through the ages it has become a ritualized "worship word." The Yangs believe that their ancestors must have been very superior people; they swear an oath to abide by all regulations in the Prime Directive; and they can recite the opening lines of the Prime Directive, but "without meaning."

Following a primitive court scene, complete with jury, it becomes clear that institutions of justice are amazingly resilient—capable of enduring even though their rationale has suffered badly from neglect and amnesia. At the culmination Captain Kirk informs the Yangs that they revere a sacred document without understanding what it is all about. Kirk faces Cloud William, chief of the Yangs, and explains the meaning of the Prime Directive's preamble. Enlightenment then occurs and the great question—is the Prime Directive still operative, and does it apply to this planet?—achieves a satisfactory resolution. To use the language of yesteryear, "constitutional morality" would surely be restored.

Unlike Rexford Tugwell's new constitution, which kept "emerging" for so long that after a while no one cared, "Star Trek" had a constitutional homily with a happy ending. Americans like happy endings. Hence many younger Americans can still narrate "The Omega Glory" (Old Glory? Ultimate Glory?) flawlessly. How much of the homily got through, however, is another matter. . . .

Ultimately, however, for better and for worse, it is ideological conflict that most meaningfully calls attention to the Constitution. We are then reminded that all Americans do not agree about the most appropriate division of authority: federalism tilting toward states' rights or federalism leaning toward national authority? We are then reminded that we still have broad and strict constructionists, followers of Hamilton and followers of Madison. And we are then reminded that we have had two complementary but divergent modes of constitutional interpretation: a tradition of conflict within consensus. . . .

It is instructive to recall that the founders did not expect their instrument of government to achieve utopia: "merely" national cohesion, political stability, economic growth, and individual liberty. Despite abundant setbacks and imperfections, much of that agenda has been fulfilled for a great many Americans. During the past generation social justice got explicitly added to the agenda as a high priority, and the American Constitution, interpreted by the Supreme Court, was adapted accordingly. For a society to progress toward social justice within a constitutional framework, even by trial and error, is a considerable undertaking. To do so in good faith, more often than not, is equally commendable. If from time to time we require the assistance of gadflies, what flourishing political culture does not? Senator Lowell P. Weicker of Connecticut, for example, has played that role rather well on occasion. As he thundered in 1981, during debate over a legislative amendment to endorse organized prayer in public schools: "To my amazement, any time the word constitutionalism comes up it's looked upon as a threat. A threat! It shouldn't be; it's what holds us all together."

That has been true more often than not. Perhaps those who feel threatened by constitutionalism do not fully understand it. People frequently feel threatened by the unfamiliar. Perhaps it has not been fully understood because it has not been adequately explained. Perhaps it has perplexed us because aspects of its meaning have changed over time. Back in 1786 Benjamin Rush believed it "possible to convert men into republican machines. This must be done if we expect them to perform their parts properly in the great machine of the government of the state." His contemporaries not only took Rush at his word, but regarded the conversion of men into republican machines as a national imperative. . . .

More than a century later, Woodrow Wilson presented a piece of wisdom that tacked the other way. Call it constitutional revisionism if you like. He declared that if the real government of the United States "had, in fact, been a machine governed by mechanically automatic balances, it would have had no history; but it was not, and its history has been rich with the influences and personalities of the men who have conducted it and made it a living reality." Walter Lippmann chose to quote that sentence in 1913 when he wrote *A Preface to Politics*. But he promptly added that "only by violating the very spirit of the constitution have we been able to preserve the letter of it." What Lippmann had in mind was the role played by that palpable reality the Progressives called "invisible government": political parties, interest groups, trade unions, and so on.

Lippmann's remark was not meant to be as cynical as it might sound. It reflects the Progressive desire to be realistic and tough-minded. It also reflects the fact that Americans have been profoundly ambivalent in their feelings about government. Then, too, it reflects the discovery by three overlapping generations of Americans—represented by James Russell Lowell, Wilson, and Lippmann—that the U.S. Constitution is not, and was not meant to be, a machine that would go of itself.

Above all, Lippmann wanted to build upon his excerpt from Wilson and establish the point that there has been more to the story of constitutionalism in American culture than the history of the Constitution itself. The latter is a cherished charter of institutions and a declaration of protections. The former, constitutionalism, embodies a set of values, a range of options, and a means of resolving conflicts within a framework of consensus. It has supplied stability and continuity to a degree the framers could barely have imagined.

12

C. WRIGHT MILLS

From *The Power Elite*

C. Wright Mills's book The Power Elite *stands as a classic in political science. In it he offers one answer to the question "Who rules America?" A three-part elite rules, he believes, composed of corporate, political, and military leaders. These sectors of American life are connected, creating an "interlocking" power structure with highly centralized decision-making. Mills considers a conspiracy theory to account for the power elite's control, but rejects it for something much more frightening. Average Americans are like "trusting children" who rely on the power elite to run things smoothly and well. Today, a half-century after Mills wrote, his ideas seem a bit ultra-dramatic and overstated. Still, Mills offers a warning about power in America that is timeless, one that many people believe is true.*

———

THE POWERS OF ORDINARY men are circumscribed by the everyday worlds in which they live, yet even in these rounds of job, family, and neighborhood they often seem driven by forces they can neither understand nor govern. "Great changes" are beyond their control, but affect their conduct and outlook none the less. The very framework of modern society confines them to projects not their own, but from every side, such changes now press upon the men and women of the mass society, who accordingly feel that they are without purpose in an epoch in which they are without power.

But not all men are in this sense ordinary. As the means of information and of power are centralized, some men come to occupy positions in American society from which they can look down upon, so to speak, and by their decisions mightily affect, the everyday worlds of ordinary men and women. They are not made by their jobs; they set up and break down jobs for thousands of others; they are not confined by simple family responsibilities; they can escape. They may live in many hotels and houses, but they are bound by no one community. They need not merely "meet the demands of the day and hour"; in some part, they create these demands, and cause others to meet them. Whether or not they profess their power, their technical and political experience of it far transcends that of the underlying population. What Jacob Burckhardt said of "great men," most Americans might well say of their elite: "They are all that we are not."

The power elite is composed of men whose positions enable them to transcend the ordinary environments of ordinary men and women; they are in positions to make decisions having major consequences. Whether they do or do not make such decisions is less important than the fact that they do occupy such pivotal positions: their failure to act, their failure to make decisions, is itself an act that is often of greater consequence than the decisions they do make. For they are in command of the major hierarchies and organizations of modern society. They rule the big corporations. They run the machinery of the state and claim its prerogatives. They direct the military establishment. They occupy the strategic command posts of the social structure, in which are now centered the effective means of the power and the wealth and the celebrity which they enjoy.

The power elite are not solitary rulers. Advisers and consultants, spokesmen and opinion-makers are often the captains of their higher thought and decision. Immediately below the elite are the professional politicians of the middle levels of power, in the Congress and in the pressure groups, as well as among the new and old upper classes of town and city and region. Mingling with them, in curious ways which we shall explore, are those professional celebrities who live by being continually displayed but are never, so long as they remain celebrities, displayed enough. If such celebrities are not at the head of any dominating hierarchy, they do often have the power to distract the attention of the public or afford sensations to the masses, or, more directly, to gain the ear of those who do occupy positions of direct power. More or less unattached, as critics of morality and technicians of power, as spokesmen of God and creators of mass sensibility, such celebrities and consultants are part of the immediate scene in which the drama of the elite is enacted. But that drama itself is centered in the command posts of the major institutional hierarchies.

The truth about the nature and the power of the elite is not some secret which men of affairs know but will not tell. Such men hold quite various theories about their own roles in the sequence of event and decision. Often they are uncertain about their roles, and even more often they allow their fears and their hopes to affect their assessment of their own power. No matter how great their actual power, they tend to be less acutely aware of it than of the resistances of others to its use. Moreover, most American men of affairs have learned well the rhetoric of public relations, in some cases even to the point of using it when they are alone, and thus coming to believe it. The personal awareness of the actors is only one of the several sources one must examine in order to understand the higher circles. Yet many who believe that there is no elite, or at any rate none of any consequence, rest their argument upon what men of affairs believe about themselves, or at least assert in public.

There is, however, another view: those who feel, even if vaguely, that a compact and powerful elite of great importance does now prevail in America often base that feeling upon the historical trend of our time. They have felt, for example, the domination of the military event, and from this they infer that generals and admirals, as well as other men of decision influenced by them, must be enormously powerful. They hear that the Congress has again abdicated to a handful of men decisions clearly related to the issue of war or peace. They know that the bomb was dropped over Japan in the name of the United States of America, although they were at no time consulted about the matter. They feel that they live in a time of big decisions; they know that they are not making any. Accordingly, as they consider the present as history, they infer that at its center, making decisions or failing to make them, there must be an elite of power.

On the one hand, those who share this feeling about big historical events assume that there is an elite and that its power is great. On the other hand, those who listen carefully to the reports of men apparently involved in the great decisions often do not believe that there is an elite whose powers are of decisive consequence.

Both views must be taken into account, but neither is adequate. The way to understand the power of the American elite lies neither solely in recognizing the historic scale of events nor in accepting the personal awareness reported by men of apparent decision. Behind such men and behind the events of history, linking the two, are the major institutions of modern society. These hierarchies of state and corporation and army constitute the means of power; as such they are now of a consequence not before equaled in human history—and at their summits, there are now those command posts of modern society which offer us the sociological key to an understanding of the role of the higher circles in America.

Within American society, major national power now resides in the economic, the political, and the military domains. Other institutions seem off to the side of modern history, and, on occasion, duly subordinated to these. No family is as directly powerful in national affairs as any major corporation; no church is as directly powerful in the external biographies of young men in America today as the military establishment; no college is as powerful in the shaping of momentous events as the National Security Council. Religious, educational, and family institutions are not autonomous centers of national power; on the contrary, these decentralized areas are increasingly shaped by the big three, in which developments of decisive and immediate consequence now occur.

Families and churches and schools adapt to modern life; governments and armies and corporations shape it; and, as they do so, they turn these lesser institutions into means for their ends. Religious institutions provide chaplains to the armed forces where they are used as a means of increasing the effectiveness of its morale to kill. Schools select and train men for their jobs in corporations and their specialized tasks in the armed forces. The extended family has, of course, long been broken up by the industrial revolution, and now the son and the father are removed from the family, by compulsion if need be, whenever the army of the state sends out the call. And the symbols of all these lesser institutions are used to legitimate the power and the decisions of the big three.

The life-fate of the modern individual depends not only upon the family into which he was born or which he enters by marriage, but increasingly upon the corporation in which he spends the most alert hours of his best years; not only upon the school where he is educated as a child and adolescent, but also upon the state which touches him throughout his life; not only upon the church in which on occasion he hears the word of God, but also upon the army in which he is disciplined.

If the centralized state could not rely upon the inculcation of nationalist loyalties in public and private schools, its leaders would promptly seek to modify the decentralized educational system. If the bankruptcy rate among the top five hundred corporations were as high as the general divorce rate among the thirty-seven million married couples, there would be economic catastrophe on an international scale. If members of armies gave to them no more of their lives than do believers to the churches to which they belong, there would be a military crisis.

Within each of the big three, the typical institutional unit has become enlarged, has become administrative, and, in the power of its decisions, has become centralized. Behind these developments there is a fabulous technology, for as institutions, they have incorporated this technology and guide it, even as it shapes and paces their developments.

The economy—once a great scatter of small productive units in autonomous balance—has become dominated by two or three hundred giant corporations, administratively and politically interrelated, which together hold the keys to economic decisions.

The political order, once a decentralized set of several dozen states with a weak spinal cord, has become a centralized, executive establishment which has taken up into itself many powers previously scattered, and now enters into each and every crany of the social structure.

The military order, once a slim establishment in a context of distrust fed by state militia, has become the largest and most expensive feature of government, and, although well versed in smiling public relations, now has all the grim and clumsy efficiency of a sprawling bureaucratic domain.

In each of these institutional areas, the means of power at the disposal of decision makers have increased enormously; their central executive powers have been enhanced; within each of them modern administrative routines have been elaborated and tightened up.

As each of these domains becomes enlarged and centralized, the consequences of its activities become greater, and its traffic with the others increases. The decisions of a handful of corporations bear upon military and political as well as upon economic developments around the world. The decisions of the military establishment rest upon and grievously affect political life as well as the very level of economic activity. The decisions made within the political domain determine economic activities and military programs. There is no longer, on the one hand, an economy, and, on the other hand, a political order containing a military establishment unimportant to politics and to money-making. There is a political economy linked, in a thousand ways, with military institutions and decisions. On each side of the world-split running through central Europe and around the Asiatic rimlands, there is an ever-increasing interlocking of economic, military, and political structures. If there is government intervention in the corporate economy, so is there corporate intervention in the governmental process. In the structural sense, this triangle of power is the source of the interlocking directorate that is most important for the historical structure of the present.

The fact of the interlocking is clearly revealed at each of the points of crisis of modern capitalist society—slump, war, and boom. In each, men of decision are led to an awareness of the interdependence of the major institutional orders. In the nineteenth century, when the scale of all institutions was smaller, their liberal integration was achieved in the automatic economy, by an autonomous play of market forces, and in the automatic political domain, by the bargain and the vote. It was then assumed that out of the imbalance and friction that followed the limited decisions then possible a new equilibrium would in due course emerge. That can no longer be assumed, and it is not assumed by the men at the top of each of the three dominant hierarchies.

For given the scope of their consequences, decisions—and indecisions—in any one of these ramify into the others, and hence top decisions tend either to become co-ordinated or to lead to a commanding indecision. It has not always been like this. When numerous small entrepreneurs made up the economy, for example, many of them could fail and the consequences still remain local; political and military authorities did not intervene. But now, given political expectations and military commitments, can they afford to allow key units of the private corporate economy to break down in slump? Increasingly, they do intervene in economic affairs, and as they do so, the controlling decisions in each order are inspected by agents of the other two, and economic, military, and political structures are interlocked.

At the pinnacle of each of the three enlarged and centralized domains, there have arisen those higher circles which make up the economic, the political, and the military elites. At the top of the economy, among the corporate rich, there are the chief executives; at the top of the political order, the members of the political directorate; at the top of the military establishment, the elite of soldier-statesmen clustered in and around the Joint Chiefs of Staff and the upper echelon. As each of these domains has coincided with the others, as decisions tend to become total in their consequence, the leading men in each of the three domains of power—the warlords, the corporation chieftains, the political directorate—tend to come together, to form the power elite of America. . . .

The conception of the power elite and of its unity rests upon the corresponding developments and the coincidence of interests among economic, political, and military organizations. It also rests upon the similarity of origin and outlook, and the social and personal intermingling of the top circles from each of these dominant hierarchies. This conjunction of institutional and psychological forces, in turn, is revealed by the heavy personnel traffic within and between the big three institutional orders, as well as by the rise of go-betweens as in the high-level lobbying. The conception of the power elite, accordingly, does *not* rest upon the assumption that American history since the origins of World War II must be understood as a secret plot, or as a great and co-ordinated conspiracy of the members of this elite. The conception rests upon quite impersonal grounds.

There is, however, little doubt that the American power elite—which contains, we are told, some of "the greatest organizers in the world"— has also planned and has plotted. The rise of the elite, as we have already made clear, was not and could not have been caused by a plot; and the tenability of the conception does not rest upon the existence of any secret or any publicly known organization. But, once the conjunction of structural trend and of the personal will to utilize it gave rise to the power elite, then plans and programs did occur to its members and indeed it is not possible to interpret many events and official policies of the fifth epoch without reference to the power elite. "There is a great difference," Richard Hofstadter has remarked, "between locating conspiracies *in* history and saying that history *is*, in effect, a conspiracy . . . "

The structural trends of institutions become defined as opportunities by those who occupy their command posts. Once such opportunities are recognized, men may avail themselves of them. Certain types of men from each of the dominant institutional areas, more far-sighted than others, have actively promoted the liaison before it took its truly modern shape. They have often done so for reasons not shared by their partners, although not objected to by them either; and often the outcome of their liaison has had consequences which none of them foresaw, much less shaped, and which only later in the course of development came under explicit control. Only after it was well under way did most of its members find themselves part of it and become gladdened, although sometimes also worried, by this fact. But once the co-ordination is a going concern, new men come readily into it and assume its existence without question.

So far as explicit organization—conspiratorial or not—is concerned, the power elite, by its very nature, is more likely to use existing organizations, working within and between them, than to set up explicit organizations whose membership is strictly limited to its own members. But if there is no machinery in existence to ensure, for example, that military and political factors will be balanced in decisions made, they will invent such machinery and use it, as with the National Security Council. Moreover, in a formally democratic polity, the aims and the powers of the various elements of this elite are further supported by an aspect of the permanent war economy: the assumption that the security of the nation supposedly rests upon great secrecy of plan and intent. Many higher events that would reveal the working of the power elite can be withheld from public knowledge under the guise of secrecy. With the wide secrecy covering their operations and decisions, the power elite can mask their intentions, operations, and further consolidation. Any secrecy that is imposed upon those in positions to observe high decision-makers clearly works for and not against the operations of the power elite.

There is accordingly reason to suspect—but by the nature of the case, no proof—that the power elite is not altogether "surfaced." There is nothing hidden about it, although its activities are not publicized. As an elite, it is not organized, although its members often know one another, seem quite naturally to work together, and share many organizations in common. There is nothing conspiratorial about it, although its decisions are often publicly unknown and its mode of operation manipulative rather than explicit.

It is not that the elite "believe in" a compact elite behind the scenes and a mass down below. It is not put in that language. It is just that the people are of necessity confused and must, like trusting children, place all the new world of foreign policy and strategy and executive action in the hands of experts. It is just that everyone knows somebody has got to run the show, and that somebody usually does. Others do not really care anyway, and besides, they do not know how. So the gap between the two types gets wider.

13

RICHARD ZWEIGENHAFT
G. WILLIAM DOMHOFF

From *Diversity in the Power Elite*

In the previous excerpt, C. Wright Mills presented his interpretation of who holds power in America: a small elite. Mills wrote his classic book decades ago. Richard Zweigenhaft and G. William Domhoff revisit Mills's thesis by examining the composition of today's power elite—assuming, of course, that there is such an elite. The authors offer a fascinating account of Jews, women, blacks, Latinos, Asian Americans, and gay men and lesbians in the elite, including many personal stories of interesting and powerful individuals. The excerpt here looks at corporate women and their discovery that golf is key to · success. Zweigenhaft and Domhoff then explore several prominent African Americans and the relevance of skin color in acceptance into the elite. Among their brief biographies is that of then-senator Barack Obama. Their conclusion? Yes, the elite look different today, but no, they are not really so different than when Mills wrote.

INJUSTICES BASED ON RACE, gender, ethnicity, and sexual orientation have been the most emotionally charged and contested issues in American society since the end of the 1960s, far exceeding concerns about social class and rivaled only by conflicts over abortion. These issues are now subsumed under the umbrella term *diversity*, which has been discussed extensively from the perspectives of both the aggrieved and those at the middle levels of the social ladder who resist any changes.

. . . [W]e look at diversity from a new angle: we examine its impact on the small group at the top of American society that we call the *power elite,* those who own and manage large banks and corporations, finance the political campaigns of conservative Democrats and virtually all Republicans at the state and national levels, and serve in government as appointed officials and military leaders. We ask whether the decades of civil disobedience, protest, and litigation by civil rights groups, feminists, and gay and lesbian rights activists have resulted in a more diverse power elite. If they have, what effects has this new diversity had on the functioning of the power elite and on its relation to the rest of society? . . .

According to many popular commentators, the composition of the higher circles in the United States had indeed changed by the late 1980s and early 1990s. Some went even further, saying that the old power elite had been pushed aside entirely. Enthusiastic articles in mainstream magazines, such as one in the late 1980s in *U.S. News & World Report* entitled "The New American Establishment," have also appeared, celebrating a new diversity at the top and claiming that "new kinds of men and women" have "taken control of institutions that influence important aspects of American life." School and club ties are no longer important, the article announced, highlighting the new role of women with a picture of some of the "wise women" who had joined the "wise men" who dominated the old establishment.

Then, in July 1995, *Newsweek* ran a cover story titled "The Rise of the Overclass," featuring a gallery of one hundred high-tech, media, and Wall Street stars, including women as well as men and previously excluded racial and ethnic groups as well as whites with Western European backgrounds, all of whom supposedly came from all rungs of the social ladder. The term *overclass* was relatively new, but the argument—that the power elite was dead and had been superseded by a diverse meritocratic elite—was not.

More recently, David Brooks, a conservative columnist for the *New York Times*, has made the same kind of claims in two books about the upper-middle class. In the second, *On Paradise Drive: How We Live Now (and Always Have) in the Future Tense*, he refers to a time, presumably in the distant past, "back when the old WASP elite dominated," and contrasts those bad old days with the current era of a "new educated elite." He goes on to reassure the reader, "There is no single elite in America. Hence, there is no definable establishment to be oppressed by and to rebel against."

We are wary about these claims announcing the demise of the old elites and the arrival of new elites because they never have been documented systematically. Moreover, they are suspect because similar claims have been made repeatedly in American history and have been proved wrong each time. In popular books and magazines from the 1830s, 1920s, and 1950s, for example, leading commentators of the day asserted that there used to be a tightly knit and cohesive governing group in the United States, but no longer. A closer look several decades later at each of these supposedly new eras invariably showed that the new power group was primarily the old one after all, with a few additions and alterations here and there. . . .

But is any of the talk about . . . upward mobility true? Can anecdotes, dime novels, and self-serving autobiographical accounts about diversity, meritocracy, and upward social mobility survive a more systematic analysis? Have very many women or members of other previously excluded groups made it to the top? Has class lost its importance in shaping life chances?

... [W]e address these and related questions within the framework provided by the iconoclastic sociologist C. Wright Mills in his classic *The Power Elite*, published half a century ago in 1956 when the media were in the midst of what Mills called the "Great American Celebration," and still accurate today in terms of many of the issues he addressed. In spite of the Great Depression of the 1930s, Americans had pulled together to win World War II, and the country was both prosperous at home and influential abroad. Most of all, according to enthusiasts, the United States had become a relatively classless and pluralistic society, where power belonged to the people through their political parties and public opinion. Some groups certainly had more power than others, but no group or class had too much. The New Deal and World War II had forever transformed the corporate-based power structure of earlier decades.

Mills challenged this celebration of pluralism by studying the social backgrounds and career paths of the people who occupied the highest positions in what he saw as the three major institutional hierarchies in postwar America, the corporations, the executive branch of the federal government, and the military. He found that almost all members of this leadership group, which he called the power elite, were white, Christian males who came from "at most, the upper third of the income and occupational pyramids," despite the many Horatio Algeresque claims to the contrary. A majority came from an even narrower stratum, the 11 percent of U.S. families headed by businesspeople or highly educated professionals like physicians and lawyers. Mills concluded that power in the United States in the 1950s was just about as concentrated as it had been since the rise of the large corporations, although he stressed that the New Deal and World War II had given political appointees and military chieftains more authority than they had exercised previously.

It is our purpose, therefore, to take a detailed look at the social, educational, and occupational backgrounds of the leaders of these three institutional hierarchies to see whether they have become more diverse in terms of gender, race, ethnicity, and sexual orientation, and also in terms of socioeconomic origins. Unlike Mills, however, we think the power elite is more than a set of institutional leaders; it is also the leadership group for the small upper class of owners and managers of large, income-producing properties, the 1 percent of American households that owned 44.1 percent of all privately held stock, 58.0 percent of financial securities, and 57.3

percent of business equity in 2001, the last year for which systematic figures are available. (By way of comparison, the bottom 90 percent, those who work for hourly wages or monthly salaries, have a mere 15.5 percent of the stock, 11.3 percent of financial securities, and 10.4 percent of business equity.) Not surprisingly, we think the primary concern of the power elite is to support the kind of policies, regulations, and political leaders that maintain this structure of privilege for the very rich. . . .

The power elite depicted by C. Wright Mills was, without doubt, an exclusively male preserve. On the opening page of *The Power Elite*, Mills stated clearly that "the power elite is composed of men whose positions enable them to transcend the ordinary environments of ordinary men and women." Although there were some women in the corporate, political, and military worlds, very few were in or near the higher circles that constituted the power elite. Are they there now? If so, how substantial and how visible is their presence? When did they arrive, and how did they get there? What are their future prospects? . . .

In 1990, Elizabeth Dole, then secretary of labor (and, since January 2003, a member of the Senate), initiated a department-level investigation into the question of whether or not there was a "glass ceiling" blocking women and minorities from the highest ranks of U.S. corporations. When the report was issued by the Federal Glass Ceiling Commission in 1995, comments by the white male managers who had been interviewed and surveyed supported the earlier claims that upper management was willing to accept women and minorities only if they were not too different. As one manager explained, "What's important is comfort, chemistry, relationships, and collaborations. That's what makes a shop work. When we find minorities and women who think like we do, we snatch them up."

One *Fortune* 500 labor relations executive used the phrase "comfort zone" to make the same point about "chemistry" and reducing "uncertainty": "You need to build relationships," she said, "and you need to be pretty savvy. And for a woman or a person of color at this company, you have to put in more effort to get into this comfort zone."

Much has been made of the fact that men have traditionally been socialized to play competitive team sports and women have not. In *The Managerial Woman*, Margaret Hennig and Anne Jardim argue that the experience of having participated in competitive team sports provides men with many advantages in the corporate world. Playing on sports teams teaches boys such things as how to develop their individual skills in the context of helping the team to win, how to develop cooperative, goal-oriented relationships with teammates, how to focus on winning, and how to deal with losing. "The experience of most little girls," they wrote in the mid-1970s, "has no parallel." Although the opportunities for young women to participate in competitive sports, including team sports like basketball and soccer, have increased dramatically in recent years, far fewer opportunities were available when many of the women now in higher management in U.S. corporations were young.

Just as football is often identified as the classic competitive and aggressive team sport that prepares men for the rough-and-tumble (and hierarchical) world of the corporation, an individual sport, golf, is the more convivial, but still competitive, game that allows boys to play together, shoot the breeze, and do business. As Marcia Chambers shows in *The Unplayable Lie*, the golf course, and especially the country club, can be as segregated by sex as the football field. Few clubs bar women, but some clubs do not allow women to vote, sit on their governing boards, or play golf on weekend mornings.

Many women managers are convinced that their careers suffer because of discrimination against them by golf clubs. In a study of executives who manage "corporate-government affairs," Denise Benoit Scott found that the women in such positions "share meals with staff members and other government relations officials but never play golf." In contrast, men in such positions "play golf with a broad range of people in business and government, including legislators and top corporate executives." As one of the women she interviewed put it, "I wish I played golf. I think golf is the key. If you want to make it, you have to play golf."

Similarly, when the editors of *Executive Female* magazine surveyed the top fifty women in line-management positions (in sales, marketing, production, and general management with a direct impact on the company's bottom line), they asked them why more women had not made it to the "upper reaches of corporate America." The most frequently identified problem was the "comfort factor"—the men atop their corporations wanted others around them with whom they were comfortable, and that generally meant other men similar to themselves. One of the other most frequently identified problems, not unrelated to the comfort factor, was the exclusion from "the social networks—the clubs, the golf course—where the informal networking that is so important to moving up the ladder often takes place."

Based on the interviews they conducted for *Members of the Club*, Dawn-Marie Driscoll and Carol Goldberg also conclude that there is an important connection between golf and business. Both Driscoll and Goldberg have held directorships on major corporate boards. They establish their insider status at the beginning of their book: "We are both insiders. We always have been and probably always will be." In a section entitled

"The Link That Counts," they explain how they came to realize the importance of golf: "We heard so many stories about golf that we began to pay more attention to the interaction between golf and business. We realized the importance of golf had been right in front of our eyes all the time, but because neither of us played golf, we had missed it as an issue for executive women. But golf is central to many business circles."

A few months before Bill Clinton was elected president, his future secretary of energy had some pertinent comments about the importance of fitting into corporate culture and the relevance of playing golf. "Without losing your own personality," said Hazel O'Leary, then an executive vice president at Northern States Power in Minnesota, "it's important to be part of the prevailing corporate culture. At this company, it's golf. I've resisted learning to play golf all my life, but I finally had to admit I was missing something that way." She took up golf.

There is evidence that the golf anxiety expressed by women executives has its counterpart in the attitudes held by male executives: in its 1995 report, the Federal Glass Ceiling Commission found that many white male executives "fretted" that minorities and women did not know how to play golf.

Whether or not playing golf is necessary to fit in, it is clear that women who make it into the corporate elite must assimilate sufficiently into the predominantly male culture to make it into the comfort zone. As Kathleen Jamieson points out, however, this can place them in a double bind. On the one hand, women in the corporate world are expected to be competitive and tough-minded, but not too competitive or tough-minded, or they risk being called ballbusters. On the other hand, women in the corporate world are expected to be feminine enough to be seen as attractive and caring, but not too feminine, lest their appearance and behavior be seen as inappropriate or as an indication that they are tender-minded. . . .

Throughout the century, scholars have demonstrated that a disproportionate number of black professionals have been light skinned, and that blacks with darker skin are more likely to be discriminated against. Horace Mann Bond found, for example, that many "early Negro scholars" were "light-complexioned" individuals from families that had been part of the antebellum "free colored population" or born to "favored slaves." He explained their success in the following way: "The phenomenon was not due, as many believed, to the 'superiority' of the white blood; it was a social and economic, rather than a natural selection. Concubinage remained an openly sustained relationship between white men and Negro women in the South for fifty years after the Civil War; the children of such unions were more likely to have parents with the money, and the tradition, to send a child to school, than the former field hand slaves who were now sharecroppers and day laborers."

The authors of the Glass Ceiling Commission's report argue that "gradations in skin color" have continued to affect the career chances of men and women of color. They write,

Color-based differences are inescapable but nobody likes to talk about them. These are complicated differences because they are not exclusively racial and not exclusively ethnic. The unstated but ever-present question is, "Do they look like us?"

Though it is mostly covert, our society has developed an extremely sophisticated, and often denied, acceptability index based on gradations in skin color. It is not as simple a system as the black/white/colored classifications that were used in South Africa. It is not legally permissible, but it persists just beneath the surface, and it can be and is used as a basis for decision making, sometimes consciously and sometimes unconsciously. It is applied to African Americans, to American Indians, to Asian and Pacific Islander Americans, and to Hispanic Americans, who are described in a color shorthand of black, brown, yellow, and red. . . .

Colin Powell captured the essence of skin color's role in the broader context of not being too different from, and thus threatening to, whites. In a lengthy New Yorker profile, Henry Louis Gates Jr. asked Powell to explain polls that showed him having greater appeal among whites than among blacks. Powell, described by Gates as "light-skinned and blunt-featured," cut through sociological jargon and the need for statistical analyses:

One, I don't shove it in their face, you know? I don't bring any stereotypes or threatening visage to their presence. Some black people do. Two, I can overcome any stereotypes or reservations they have, because I perform well. Third thing is, I ain't that black. . . . I speak reasonably well, like a white person. I am very comfortable in a white social situation, and I don't go off in a corner. My features are clearly black, and I've never denied what I am. It fits into their general social setting, so they do not find me threatening. I think there's more to it than that, but I don't know what it is." . . .

The three blacks who have served in the U.S. Senate in modern times represent three eras. Indeed, if Edward Brooke, born in 1919, was a product of the old black middle class of the mid-twentieth century, and Carol Moseley-Braun, born in 1947, was a product of the race-conscious 1960s, Barack Obama, born in 1961, is a product of the increasingly biracial and bicultural world of the 1980s and 1990s. . . .

Barack Obama's mother, a white woman born in Kansas, met his father, a Kenyan, in 1959 when they were students at the University of

Hawaii. When Obama was a toddler, his father left Hawaii to do graduate work in economics at Harvard (the scholarship he won was not big enough to enable him to take his wife and son with him), and upon completing his doctoral degree, he returned to Africa.

His parents divorced, and a few years later, Obama's mother met and married an Indonesian. She and six-year-old Barack moved to Jakarta, where Barack lived for four years before returning to Hawaii to live with his maternal grandparents (his grandfather sold insurance and his grandmother worked in a bank).

Despite his family's middle-class background, he was accepted at Punahou Academy, Hawaii's most exclusive prep school. He began college at Occidental before transferring to Columbia, from which he graduated in 1983. After three years working in Chicago as a community organizer, he went to the Harvard Law School, where he became the first black editor of the *Harvard Law Review*. After graduating from law school in 1991, and before returning to Chicago, he spent a year working on the book that was to become *Dreams from My Father*, a memoir that describes his growing up in Hawaii and Indonesia and his search as a young adult to learn more about his father, his family in Kenya, and his own racial identity. He returned to Chicago, practiced civil rights law, and taught at the University of Chicago Law School. When the opportunity arose, he ran for and was elected to the state senate representing a district that included both Hyde Park (home of the university) and some of the most impoverished ghettos on the South Side.

Seven years after his election to the state senate, Obama burst upon the national scene in March 2004 when he beat six others to win the Democratic primary for Senate (he won 53 percent of the vote). The polls indicated that he was well ahead of Jack Ryan, his wealthy, white, Republican opponent, when a sex scandal led Ryan to withdraw from the race. The Illinois Republicans had a hard time finding someone to run against him, and, thus, with no opponent back in Illinois, in July 2004 Obama traveled to Boston to deliver an electrifying keynote address at the Democratic National Convention.

Finally, after various possible candidates turned them down, including former football coach Mike Ditka, the Illinois Republicans came up with Alan Keyes, a hard-core, right-wing, conservative African American who had been an unsuccessful candidate in many previous political races, even though he was a resident of Maryland and a few years earlier had railed against Hillary Clinton for running for the Senate in New York when she was not a resident of that state. When November rolled around, Barack Obama won a landslide victory, with 70 percent of the vote.

Obama is immensely popular with whites, in part, because he is so comfortable among them. As he said about the white voters from rural areas and small towns in Illinois, "I know those people. Those are my grandparents. The food they serve is the food my grandparents served when I was growing up. Their manners, their sensibility, their sense of right and wrong—it's all totally familiar to me."

Whites are also comfortable with him, in part for the same reasons they are comfortable with Colin Powell. His biracial and multicultural background (and his light skin) insulate him from the stereotypes they hold of African Americans, and, as a result, like Powell, he is perceived as nonthreatening. . . .

. . . [The] power elite and Congress are more diverse than they were before the civil rights movement and the social movements that followed in its train brought pressure to bear on corporations, politicians, and government. Although the power elite is still composed primarily of Christian, white men, there are now Jews, women, blacks, Latinos, and Asian Americans on the boards of the country's largest corporations; presidential cabinets are far more diverse than was the case fifty years ago; and the highest ranks of the military are no longer filled solely by white men. In the case of elected officials in Congress, the trend toward diversity is even greater for women and the other previously excluded groups that we have studied. At the same time, we have shown that the incorporation of members of the different groups has been uneven.

. . . [W]e look at the patterns that emerge from our specific findings to see if they help explain the gradual inclusion of some groups and the continuing exclusion of others. We also discuss the impact of diversity on the power elite and the rest of American society. We argue that most of the effects were unexpected and are ironic. The most important of these ironies relates to the ongoing tension between the American dream of individual advancement and fulfillment ("liberal individualism") and the class structure: we conclude that the racial, ethnic, and gender diversity celebrated by the power elite and the media actually reinforces the unchanging nature of the class structure and increases the tendency to ignore class inequalities. . . .

In what may be the greatest and most important irony of them all, the diversity forced upon the power elite may have helped to strengthen it. Diversity has given the power elite buffers, ambassadors, tokens, and legitimacy. This is an unintended consequence that few insurgents or social scientists foresaw. . . .

The black and white liberals and progressives who challenged Christian, white, male homogeneity in the power structure starting in the 1950s and 1960s sought to do more than create civil rights and new job opportunities for men and women who had previously been mistreated and excluded, important though these goals were. They also hoped that new perspectives in the boardrooms and the halls of government would spread greater openness throughout the society. The idea was both to diversify the power elite and to shift some of its power to underrepresented groups and social classes. The social movements of the 1960s were strikingly successful in increasing the individual rights and freedoms available to all Americans, especially African Americans. As we have shown, they also created pressures that led to openings at the top for individuals from groups that had previously been ignored.

But as some individuals made it, and as the concerns of social movements, political leaders, and the courts gradually came to focus more and more on individual rights and individual advancement, the focus on "distributive justice," general racial exclusion, and social class was lost. The age-old American commitment to individualism, reinforced by tokenism and reassurances from members of the power elite, won out over the commitment to greater equality of income and wealth that had been one strand of New Deal liberalism and a major emphasis of left-wing activism in the 1960s.

We therefore conclude that the increased diversity in the power elite has not generated any changes in an underlying class system in which the top 1 percent of households (the upper class) own 33.4 percent of all marketable wealth, and the next 19 percent (the managerial, professional, and small business stratum) have 51 percent, which means that just 20 percent of the people own a remarkable 84 percent of the privately owned wealth in the United States, leaving a mere 16 percent of the wealth for the bottom 80 percent (wage and salary workers). . . .

. . . These intertwined dilemmas of class and race lead to a nation that celebrates individualism, equal opportunity, and diversity but is, in reality, a bastion of class privilege, African American exclusion, and conservatism.

14

ROBERT DAHL

From *Who Governs?* and from
A Preface to Democratic Theory

In any city in the United States—like New Haven, Connecticut—as in the entire nation, political power is no longer in the hands of a few people as it once was early in American history. Nor is power spread evenly among all citizens. Influential political theorist Robert Dahl presents here the classic statement of pluralism: the dispersion of power among many groups of people. Dahl differentiates the "political stratum," made up of interested and involved citizens, from the "apolitical stratum," those who do not take an active part in government. These two segments of society are vastly different in their degree of involvement, yet they are closely tied together in many ways in a pluralist system. At least in theory, anyone can enter the political stratum where numerous interest groups compete and bargain for their goals. Public policy is made by "the steady appeasement of relatively small groups." Because of this "strange hybrid," Dahl contends, pluralism is the best way to describe how power is distributed in America.

IN A POLITICAL SYSTEM where nearly every adult may vote but where knowledge, wealth, social position, access to officials, and other resources are unequally distributed, who actually governs?

The question has been asked, I imagine, wherever popular government has developed and intelligent citizens have reached the stage of critical self-consciousness concerning their society. It must have been put many times in Athens even before it was posed by Plato and Aristotle.

The question is peculiarly relevant to the United States and to Americans. In the first place, Americans espouse democratic beliefs with a fervency and a unanimity that have been a regular source of astonishment to foreign observers . . . [such as] Tocqueville and Bryce. . . .

In the course of the past two centuries, New Haven has gradually changed from oligarchy to pluralism. Accompanying and probably causing this change—one might properly call it a revolution—appears to be a profound alteration in the way political resources are distributed among the citizens of New Haven. This silent socioeconomic revolution has not substituted equality for inequality so much as it has involved a shift from cumulative inequalities in political resources—to use an expression introduced a moment ago—to noncumulative or dispersed inequalities. This point will grow clearer as we proceed. . . .

In the political system of the patrician oligarchy, political resources were marked by a cumulative inequality: when one individual was much better off than another in one resource, such as wealth, he was usually better off in almost every other resource—social standing, legitimacy, control over religious and educational institutions, knowledge, office. In the political system of today, inequalities in political resources remain, but they tend to be *noncumulative*. The political system of New Haven, then, is one of *dispersed inequalities*. . . .

Within a century a political system dominated by one cohesive set of leaders had given way to a system dominated by many different sets of leaders, each having access to a different combination of political resources. It was, in short, a pluralist system. If the pluralist system was very far from being an oligarchy, it was also a long way from achieving the goal of political equality advocated by the philosophers of democracy and incorporated into the creed of democracy and equality practically every American professes to uphold.

An elite no longer rules New Haven. But in the strict democratic sense, the disappearance of elite rule has not led to the emergence of rule by the people. Who, then, rules in a pluralist democracy? . . .

One of the difficulties that confronts anyone who attempts to answer the question, "Who rules in a pluralist democracy?" is the ambiguous relationship of leaders to citizens.

Viewed from one position, leaders are enormously influential—so influential that if they are seen only in this perspective they might well be considered a kind of ruling elite. Viewed from another position, however, many influential leaders seem to be captives of their constituents. Like the blind men with the elephant, different analysts have meticulously examined different aspects of the body politic and arrived at radically different conclusions. To some, a pluralistic democracy with dispersed inequalities is all head and no body; to others it is all body and no head. . . .

Two additional factors help to account for this obscurity. First, among all the persons who influence a decision, some do so more directly than others in the sense that they are closer to the stage where concrete alternatives are initiated or vetoed in an explicit and immediate way. Indirect influence might be very great but comparatively difficult to observe and weigh. Yet to ignore indirect influence in analysis of the distribution of influence would be to exclude what might well prove to be a highly significant process of control in a pluralistic democracy.

Second, the relationship between leaders and citizens in a pluralistic democracy is frequently reciprocal: leaders influence the decisions of constituents, but the decisions of leaders are also determined in part by what they think are, will be, or have been the preferences of their constituents. Ordinarily it is much easier to observe and describe the distribution of influence in a political system where the flow of influence is strongly in one direction (an asymmetrical or unilateral system, as it is sometimes called) than in a system marked by strong reciprocal relations. In a political system with competitive elections, such as New Haven's, it is not unreasonable to expect that relationships between leaders and constituents would normally be reciprocal. . . .

In New Haven, as in other political systems, a small stratum of individuals is much more highly involved in political thought, discussion, and action than the rest of the population. These citizens constitute the political stratum.

Members of this stratum live in a political subculture that is partly but not wholly shared by the great majority of citizens. Just as artists and intellectuals are the principal bearers of the artistic, literary, and scientific skills of a society, so the members of the political stratum are the main bearers of political skills. If intellectuals were to vanish overnight, a society would be reduced to artistic, literary, and scientific poverty. If the political stratum were destroyed, the previous political institutions of the society would temporarily stop functioning. In both cases, the speed with which the loss could be overcome would depend on the extent to which the elementary knowledge and basic attitudes of the elite had been diffused. In an open society with widespread education and training in civic attitudes, many citizens hitherto in the apolitical strata could doubtless step into roles that had been filled by members of the political stratum. However, sharp discontinuities and important changes in the operation of the political system almost certainly would occur.

In New Haven, as in the United States, and indeed perhaps in all pluralistic democracies, differences in the subcultures of the political and the apolitical strata are marked, particularly at the extremes. In the political stratum, politics is highly salient; among the apolitical strata, it is remote. In the political stratum, individuals tend to be rather calculating in their choice of strategies; members of the political stratum are, in a sense, relatively rational political beings. In the apolitical strata, people are notably less calculating; their political choices are more strongly influenced by inertia, habit, unexamined loyalties, personal attachments, emotions, transient impulses. In the political stratum, an individual's political beliefs tend to fall into patterns that have a relatively high degree of coherence and internal consistency; in the apolitical strata, political orientations are disorganized, disconnected, and unideological. In the political stratum, information about politics and the issues of the day is extensive; the apolitical strata are poorly informed. Individuals in the political stratum tend to participate rather actively in politics; in the apolitical strata citizens rarely go beyond voting and many do not even vote. Individuals in the political stratum exert a good deal of steady, direct, and active influence on government policy; in fact some individuals have a quite extraordinary amount of influence. Individuals in the apolitical strata, on the other hand, have much less direct or active influence on policies.

Communication within the political stratum tends to be rapid and extensive. Members of the stratum read many of the same newspapers and magazines; in New Haven, for example, they are likely to read the *New York Times* or the *Herald Tribune*, and *Time* or *Newsweek*. Much information also passes by word of mouth. The political strata of different communities and regions are linked in a national network of communications. Even in small towns, one or two members of the local political stratum usually are in touch with members of a state organization, and certain members of the political stratum of a state or any large city maintain relations with members of organizations in other states and cities, or with national figures. Moreover, many channels of communication not designed specifically for political purposes—trade associations, professional associations, and labor organizations, for example—serve as a part of the network of the political stratum.

In many pluralistic systems, however, the political stratum is far from being a closed or static group. In the United States the political stratum does not constitute a homogeneous class with well-defined class interests. In New Haven, in fact, the political stratum is easily penetrated by anyone whose interests and concerns attract him to the distinctive political culture of the stratum. It is easily penetrated because (among other reasons) elections and competitive parties give politicians a powerful motive for expanding their coalitions and increasing their electoral followings.

In an open pluralistic system, where movement into the political stratum is easy, the stratum embodies many of the most widely shared values and goals in the society. If popular values are strongly pragmatic, then the political stratum is likely to be pragmatic; if popular values prescribe reverence toward the past, then the political stratum probably shares that reverence; if popular values are oriented toward material gain and personal advancement, then the political stratum probably reflects these values; if popular values are particularly favorable to political, social, or economic equality, then the political stratum is likely to emphasize equality. The apolitical strata can be said to "govern" as much through the sharing of common values and goals with members of the political stratum as by other means. However, if it were not for elections and competitive parties, this sharing would—other things remaining the same—rapidly decline. Not only is the political stratum in New Haven not a closed group, but its "members" are far from united in their orientations and strategies. There are many lines of cleavage. . . .

Because of the ease with which the political stratum can be penetrated, whenever dissatisfaction builds up in some segment of the electorate party politicians will probably learn of the discontent and calculate whether it might be converted into a political issue with an electoral payoff. If a party politician sees no payoff, his interest is likely to be small; if he foresees an adverse effect, he will avoid the issue if he can. As a result, there is usually some conflict in the political stratum between intellectuals, experts, and others who formulate issues, and the party politicians themselves, for the first group often demands attention to issues in which the politicians see no profit and possibly even electoral damage.

The independence, penetrability, and heterogeneity of the various segments of the political stratum all but guarantee that any dissatisfied group will find spokesmen in the political stratum, but to have a spokesman does not insure that the group's problems will be solved by political action. Politicians may not see how they can gain by taking a position on an issue; action by government may seem to be wholly inappropriate; policies intended to cope with dissatisfaction may be blocked; solutions may be improperly designed; indeed, politicians may even find it politically profitable to maintain a shaky coalition by keeping tension and discontent alive and deflecting attention to irrelevant "solutions" or alternative issues. . . .

. . . In devising strategies for building coalitions and allocating rewards, one must take into account a large number of different categories of citizens. It would be dangerous to formulate strategies on the assumption that most or all citizens can be divided into two or three categories, for a successful political coalition necessarily rests upon a multiplicity of groups and categories. . . .*

. . . I defined the "normal" American political process as one in which there is a high probability that an active and legitimate group in the population can make itself heard effectively at some crucial stage in the process of decision. To be "heard" covers a wide range of activities, and I do

---

*At this point, the excerpt from *Who Governs?* ends, and the excerpt from *A Preface to Democratic Theory* begins.—EDS.

not intend to define the word rigorously. Clearly, it does not mean that every group has equal control over the outcome.

In American politics, as in all other societies, control over decisions is unevenly distributed; neither individuals nor groups are political equals. When I say that a group is heard "effectively" I mean more than the simple fact that it makes a noise; I mean that one or more officials are not only ready to listen to the noise, but expect to suffer in some significant way if they do not placate the group, its leaders, or its most vociferous members. To satisfy the group may require one or more of a great variety of actions by the responsive leader: pressure for substantive policies, appointments, graft, respect, expression of the appropriate emotions, or the right combination of reciprocal noises.

Thus the making of governmental decisions is not a majestic march of great majorities united upon certain matters of basic policy. It is the steady appeasement of relatively small groups. . . .

To be sure, reformers with a tidy sense of order dislike it. Foreign observers, even sympathetic ones, are often astonished and confounded by it. Many Americans are frequently dismayed by its paradoxes; indeed, few Americans who look upon our political process attentively can fail, at times, to feel deep frustration and angry resentment with a system that on the surface has so little order and so much chaos.

For it is a markedly decentralized system. Decisions are made by endless bargaining; perhaps in no other national political system in the world is bargaining so basic a component of the political process. In an age when the efficiencies of hierarchy have been re-emphasized on every continent, no doubt the normal American political system is something of an anomaly, if not, indeed, at times an anachronism. For as a means to highly integrated, consistent decisions in some important areas—foreign policy, for example—it often appears to operate in a creaking fashion verging on total collapse.

Yet we should not be too quick in our appraisal, for where its vices stand out, its virtues are concealed to the hasty eye. Luckily the normal system has the virtues of its vices. With all its defects, it does nonetheless provide a high probability that any active and legitimate group will make itself heard effectively at some stage in the process of decision. This is no mean thing in a political system.

It is not a static system. The normal American system has evolved, and by evolving it has survived. It has evolved and survived from aristocracy to mass democracy, through slavery, civil war, the tentative uneasy reconciliation of North and South, the repression of Negroes and their halting liberation; through two great wars of worldwide scope, mobilization, far-flung military enterprise, and return to hazardous peace; through numerous periods of economic instability and one prolonged depression with mass unemployment, farm "holidays," veterans' marches, tear gas, and even bullets; through two periods of postwar cynicism, demagogic excesses, invasions of traditional liberties, and the groping, awkward, often savage, attempt to cope with problems of subversion, fear, and civil tension.

Probably this strange hybrid, the normal American political system, is not for export to others. But so long as the social prerequisites of democracy are substantially intact in this country, it appears to be a relatively efficient system for reinforcing agreement, encouraging moderation, and maintaining social peace in a restless and immoderate people operating a gigantic, powerful, diversified, and incredibly complex society.

This is no negligible contribution, then, that Americans have made to the arts of government—and to that branch, which of all the arts of politics is the most difficult, the art of democratic government.

PART THREE

Separation
of Powers

15

JAMES MADISON

The Federalist 51

In Federalist 10, *an earlier selection, one of the Constitution's designers, James Madison, explained his fear of "faction"—any single group that tries to dominate the political process—and why faction cannot be removed from politics. Madison's solution was to accept factions, but control them. Federalist 10 offered a republican (representative) government and a large, diverse nation with many factions as effective controls. In No. 51 he continues, citing the structural features that characterize American government. Power will be separated among different departments, or branches, of government, independent from one another. Power will be divided between the national and state levels, a system called federalism. Madison's philosophy for government is here in this essay too: "Ambition must be made to counteract ambition." Don't miss that paragraph, since it contains warnings that resonate across the centuries.*

No. 51: Madison

To WHAT EXPEDIENT, then, shall we finally resort, for maintaining in practice the necessary partition of power among the several departments as laid down in the Constitution? The only answer that can be given is that as all these exterior provisions are found to be inadequate the defect must be supplied, by so contriving the interior structure of the government as that its several constituent parts may, by their mutual relations, be the means of keeping each other in their proper places. Without presuming to undertake a full development of this important idea I will hazard a few general observations which may perhaps place it in a clearer light, and enable us to form a more correct judgment of the principles and structure of the government planned by the convention.

In order to lay a due foundation for that separate and distinct exercise of the different powers of government, which to a certain extent is admitted on all hands to be essential to the preservation of liberty, it is evident that each department should have a will of its own; and consequently should be so constituted that the members of each should have as little agency as possible in the appointment of the members of the others. Were this principle rigorously adhered to, it would require that all the appointments for the supreme executive, legislative, and judiciary magistracies should be drawn from the same fountain of authority, the people, through channels having no communication whatever with one another. Perhaps such a plan of constructing the several departments would be less difficult in practice than it may in contemplation appear. Some difficulties, however, and some additional expense would attend the execution of it. Some deviations, therefore, from the principle must be admitted. In the constitution of the judiciary department in particular, it might be inexpedient to insist rigorously on the principle: first, because peculiar qualifications being essential in the members, the primary consideration ought to be to select that mode of choice which best secures these qualifications; second, because the permanent tenure by which the appointments are held in that department must soon destroy all sense of dependence on the authority conferring them.

It is equally evident that the members of each department should be as little dependent as possible on those of the others for the emoluments annexed to their offices. Were the executive magistrate, or the judges, not independent of the legislature in this particular, their independence in every other would be merely nominal.

But the great security against a gradual concentration of the several powers in the same department consists in giving to those who administer each department the necessary constitutional means and personal motives to resist encroachments of the others. The provision for defense must in this, as in all other cases, be made commensurate to the danger of attack. Ambition must be made to counteract ambition. The interest of the man must be connected with the constitutional rights of the place. It may be a reflection on human nature that such devices should be necessary to control the abuses of government. But what is government itself but the greatest of all reflections on human nature? If men were angels, no government would be necessary. If angels were to govern men, neither external nor internal controls on government would be necessary. In framing a government which is to be administered by men over men, the great difficulty lies in this: you must first enable the government to control the governed; and in the next place oblige it to control itself. A dependence on the people is, no doubt, the primary control on the government; but experience has taught mankind the necessity of auxiliary precautions.

This policy of supplying, by opposite and rival interests, the defect of better motives, might be traced through the whole system of human affairs, private as well as public. We see it particularly displayed in all the subordinate distributions of power, where the constant aim is to divide and arrange the several offices in such a manner as that each may be a check on the other—that the private interest of every individual may be a sentinel over the public rights. These inventions of prudence cannot be less requisite in the distribution of the supreme powers of the State.

But it is not possible to give to each department an equal power of self-defense. In republican government, the legislative authority necessarily predominates. The remedy for this inconveniency is to divide the legislature into different branches; and to render them, by different modes of election and different principles of action, as little connected with each other as the nature of their common functions and their common dependence on the society will admit. It may even be necessary to guard against dangerous encroachments by still further precautions. As the weight of the legislative authority requires that it should be thus divided, the weakness of the executive may require, on the other hand, that it should be fortified. An absolute negative on the legislature appears, at first view, to be the natural defense with which the executive magistrate should be armed. But perhaps it would be neither altogether safe nor alone sufficient. On ordinary occasions it might not be exerted with the requisite firmness, and on extraordinary occasions it might be perfidiously abused. May not this defect of an absolute negative be supplied by some qualified connection between this weaker department and the weaker branch of the stronger department, by which the latter may be led to support the constitutional rights of the former, without being too much detached from the rights of its own department?

If the principles on which these observations are founded be just, as I persuade myself they are, and they be applied as a criterion to the several State constitutions, and to the federal Constitution, it will be found that if the latter does not perfectly correspond with them, the former are infinitely less able to bear such a test.

There are, moreover, two considerations particularly applicable to the federal system of America, which place that system in a very interesting point of view.

First. In a single republic, all the power surrendered by the people is submitted to the administration of a single government; and the usurpations are guarded against by a division of the government into distinct and separate departments. In the compound republic of America, the power surrendered by the people is first divided between two distinct governments, and then the portion allotted to each subdivided among distinct and separate departments. Hence a double security arises to the rights of the people. The different governments will control each other, at the same time that each will be controlled by itself.

Second. It is of great importance in a republic not only to guard the society against the oppression of its rulers, but to guard one part of the society against the injustice of the other part. Different interests necessarily exist in different classes of citizens. If a majority be united by a common interest, the rights of the minority will be insecure. There are but two methods of providing against this evil: the one by creating a will in the community independent of the majority—that is, of the society itself; the other, by comprehending in the society so many separate descriptions of citizens as will render an unjust combination of a majority of the whole very improbable, if not impracticable. The first method prevails in all governments possessing an hereditary or self-appointed authority. This, at best, is but a precarious security; because a power independent of the society may as well espouse the unjust views of the major as the rightful interests of the minor party, and may possibly be turned against both parties. The second method will be exemplified in the federal republic of the United States. Whilst all authority in it will be derived from and dependent on the society, the society itself will be broken into so many parts, interests and classes of citizens, that the rights of individuals, or of the minority, will be in little danger from interested combinations of the majority. In a free government the security for civil rights must be the same as that for religious rights. It consists in the one case in the multiplicity of interests, and in the other in the multiplicity of sects. The degree of security in both cases will depend on the number of interests and sects; and this may be presumed to depend on the extent of country and number of people comprehended under the same government. This view of the subject must particularly recommend a proper federal system to all the sincere and considerate friends of republican government, since it shows that in exact proportion as the territory of the Union may be formed into more circumscribed Confederacies, or States, oppressive combinations of a majority will be facilitated; the best security, under the republican forms, for the rights of every class of citizen, will be diminished; and consequently the stability and independence of some member of the government, the only other security, must be proportionally increased. Justice is the end of government. It is the end of civil society. It ever has been and ever will be pursued until it be obtained, or until liberty be lost in the pursuit. In a society under the forms of which the stronger faction can readily unite and oppress the weaker, anarchy may as truly be said to reign as in a state of nature, where the weaker individual is not secured against the violence of the stronger; and as, in the latter state, even the stronger individuals are prompted, by the uncertainty of their condition, to submit to a government which may protect the weak as well as themselves; so, in the former state, will the more powerful factions or parties be gradually induced, by a like motive, to wish for a government which will protect all parties, the weaker as well as the more powerful. It can be little doubted that if the State of Rhode Island was separated from the Confederacy and left to itself, the insecurity of rights under the popular form of government within such narrow limits would be displayed by such reiterated oppressions of factious majorities that some power altogether independent of the people would soon be called for by the voice of the very factions whose misrule had proved the necessity of it. In the extended republic of the United States, and among the great variety of interests, parties, and sects which it embraces, a coalition of a majority of the whole society could seldom take place on any other principles than those of justice and the general good; whilst there being thus less danger to a minor from the will of a major party, there must be less pretext, also, to provide for the security of the former, by introducing into the government a will not dependent on the latter, or, in other words, a will independent of the society itself. It is no less certain than it is important, notwithstanding the contrary opinions which have been entertained, that the larger the society, provided it lie within a practicable sphere, the more duly capable it will be of self-government. And happily for the *republican cause*, the practicable sphere may be carried to a very great extent by a judicious modification and mixture of the *federal principle*.   *Publius*

16

DAVID BRIAN ROBERTSON

From *The Constitution and America's Destiny*

*"Politicians, not philosophers, political scientists, or plundering speculators":
that is how Professor David Brian Robertson describes the framers of the
Constitution. They understood how compromises were made. Robertson
takes us into the minds of the framers—or at least into what we think they
were thinking. We learn about James Madison, in particular, and the pragmatic approach he took toward creating a document that all delegates could
accept. In explaining Madison's strategy, Robertson mentions some of the
key features of the Constitution that are basic to an understanding of American government. National and state governmental power, the roles of the
House and the Senate, the power of the executive, the authority of the courts
are all delicately balanced. The result, observes Robertson, is a system that is
"hard to use." That was the plan. Only through the skillful use of the Constitution's many impediments and ambiguities can results be achieved. Many
different groups must be brought together and kept together for any action to
take place. Throughout American history, and today, smart politicians have
known how to do this. That was the plan.*

[T]here can be no doubt but that the result [of the Constitutional Convention]
will in some way or other have a powerful effect on our destiny.

—JAMES MADISON to Thomas Jefferson, June 6, 1787

WHAT PROBLEMS WERE THE U.S. CONSTITUTION'S authors trying
to solve? How did they imagine their Constitution would answer these
problems? We know the framers intended to change America's destiny,
and we know they succeeded. But how did they intend to transform the
way American government uses its power and the way Americans use
their government? What kinds of politics were the delegates to the Constitutional Convention trying to make—and what kinds of politics *did*
their design make? For all that has been written about the Constitution,
we do not have satisfactory answers to these questions.

Practicing politicians wrote the Constitution, and they expected politicians to use it. To understand the enduring effects of the Constitution on
America's destiny, we need to know what its designers thought they were
doing. We need to understand the circumstances that convinced these

politicians that they could and should reconstitute the nation's government. We need to understand precisely how these circumstances shaped their strategies for building a new government. We need to reconstruct how these politicians used such strategies to design their Constitution, provision by provision. Better answers to these questions can help us better understand how Americans have used the government they have inherited. . . .

The delegates who made the Constitution were first and foremost politicians, not philosophers, political scientists, or plundering speculators. These politicians had helped nurture a dozen infant state republics through a devastating war and the turbulence of economic depression. Circumstances forced them to learn the art of sustaining political support while conducting any government's most unpopular activities, such as collecting taxes. These republican politicians had mastered the skills of using policy to balance conflicting demands placed on government. A given set of economic policies could accommodate voters, pacify them, divide them, and selectively mobilize them. At the same time, economic policies could stabilize and grow state economies and secure the support of economic elites. These politicians fully understood that public policy makes politics, and the two are inseparable. Those who seek public office must promise to use government in some beneficial way and deliver on these promises, while those who seek public policy depend on those who win and hold government office.

These politicians set out to change the path of American politics, to alter the nation's destiny. They ultimately succeeded by changing the process for selecting national policy makers, by expanding national government authority, and by building a new process for using that authority. They succeeded, first, because pressing political and economic problems made it an opportune moment to reconstitute the national government. The convention met in a political climate that provided some intense but vague and unfocused support for change. Second, they succeeded because the convention's leaders drew on their own diagnosis of the national situation to propose remedies for these problems. These remedies provided a malleable starting point for deliberating constitutional design. Third, they succeeded because most were willing to come to acceptable political compromises about that design, even though none anticipated the final Constitution or found it fully satisfactory.

At the convention, these delegates behaved like republican legislators because most of them *were* legislators. Even though the convention lacked the features of an established legislature today, the delegates employed familiar legislative scripts to develop the Constitution as they would a major change of law: they agreed to rules for debate and voting, used a Committee of the Whole to facilitate the initial consideration of the agenda, took hundreds of votes on substance and procedure, created special committees to deal with difficult issues, and relied on a Committee of Detail to develop a provisional draft. Although they understood that a constitution had to be different from ordinary legislation, they conducted the *process* for crafting the Constitution much the way they had made public policy in Congress or in state legislatures. The Constitutional Convention, then, can be studied with the analytical tools used to analyze other pathbreaking American policy developments, such as Reconstruction, the Sherman Anti-Trust Act of 1890, the Clayton Act of 1914, the National Industrial Recovery Act of 1933, the Social Security Act of 1935, the Civil Rights Act of 1964, the Clean Air Act of 1970, or other "superstatutes." Like legislators today, some delegates attempted to manipulate the terms of the debates and the scope of conflict, and adjusted provisions to enlarge their political support. Through persuasion, bargaining, threats, and evasion, the delegates built coalitions, undermined others, and produced a series of interdependent, politically satisfactory decisions. The Constitutional Convention, of course, was no ordinary legislative process. The stakes were higher. The Constitution affected a virtually unlimited range of politically significant issues, and the final product necessarily would be more general than a statute law.

The Constitution's design resulted from a series of compromises about substantive issues, policy making procedures, and the control of policy makers. The goals of the Constitution are the collective goals of the thirty-nine individuals willing to sign the final product. The central analytical problem for this book is to describe that zone of acceptable compromise and to explain how the Constitution's provisions together satisfied the framers' goals. . . .

The delegates' strategies matter so much because the framers did not and could not write into the Constitution "directly and unerringly" the interests of the nation's propertied elites. The most influential delegates—particularly James Madison—were rebuilding the American state to make it stable and powerful enough to pursue the nation's long-term interests. Their government had to nurture the nation's prosperity long into the future. These state builders took it for granted that private property, free markets, and commercial expansion were essential for future prosperity, and they appreciated that propertied elites were key agents for expanding markets and driving economic development. But many framers viewed the interests of these elites as too narrow, short-term, uninformed, and conflicted to provide much reliable guidance for redesigning the nation's basic political structure and recasting long-term policy. The framers were trying to balance the government's basic needs (especially for revenue), their own ambitions for the nation's destiny, the clashing claims of different economic interests, and the demands of the more numerous citizens of modest means. Even when they were inclined to implement propertied elites' preferences, policy makers had to balance economic development against the demands of the nation's emerging democracy. Legislators needed a broader constituency to win elections to office. They had to show some responsiveness to the grievances of those with modest means. At the very least, elected policy makers had to make any program of market-driven economic development acceptable and legitimate for a majority of the constituents to whom their political fates were tethered.

In any case, it is impossible to enter the mind of an individual delegate to determine how he balanced principles and interests when he took a position on an issue of constitutional design. Jack Rakove observed that "[w]hat is elusive is the interplay between ideas and interests" in the Constitution's design. A delegate's idealistic argument for strong national powers may have concealed a driving ambition to elevate his state or to seek the personal prestige and power of national office. Another delegate's defense of state prerogatives may have reflected sincere dedication to the principle of constituent representation and a deeply held belief in the superiority of the social, economic, and political order of his state. We can never know for certain. What is certain is that the delegates used ideas as rhetorical weapons to defend positions that closely matched their political interests. Political calculations shaped delegates' views of the stakes in most of the choices about the Constitution's design. Political calculations and negotiations, not just abstract ideas, settled the disputes these choices engendered. By expanding the concept of interest beyond personal pecuniary gain and selfish parochialism to include political interests, it is much easier to see how closely the delegates' ideas and interests aligned with one another in their policy strategies.

James Madison's policy strategy requires an especially careful analysis because Madison's ideas set the convention's agenda and shaped its politics. Madison's Virginia Plan sought to establish a national policy-making system independent of the state governments and armed with most of the authority to govern the national economy. The national government would assume full authority to manage economic development for the interest of the republic as a whole. Even after the defeat of provisions crucial to his agenda, Madison and his allies fought to inject this strategy into national government powers and institutions such as the presidency. Understanding the politics of the Constitution requires a careful understanding of the way Madison defined the nation's problems and the way his plan would mitigate them. . . .

James Madison was in a superb position to shape the convention's initial agenda. Already an experienced politician though barely thirty-six years old, Madison was a knowledgeable and respected authority on American politics and public policy. He had helped write Virginia's Constitution of 1776, served in the state's House of Delegates, and represented Virginia in the Continental Congress. In Congress, he served on many key committees and worked behind the scenes to broker coalitions supportive of extending Congress's powers. He played a major role in initiating the Annapolis Convention of 1786.

Madison, a natural political strategist, had mastered the arts of republican politics and policy making. He was proficient at manipulating agendas, locating points of policy compromise, and building coalitions. He understood how procedural motions could be used tactically to gain leverage in the legislative process. He instinctively appreciated that he could advance his agenda by breaking apart legislative proposals (or by combining them). He creatively coupled problems and solutions to win allies for policy measures he favored. Just three months before the convention, for example, he used national security concerns to justify Confederation aid to Massachusetts for suppressing Shays's Rebellion.* Madison conceded that although "there might be no particular evidence" of British interference, "there was sufficient ground for a general suspicion of readiness in [Great Britain] to take advantage of events in this Country, to warrant precautions ag[ain]st her." He worked behind the scenes to cultivate allies in state legislatures and other political bodies where he had no direct influence. Madison was patient and tenacious in policy combat, displaying a doggedness that may have worn even on his allies. And when his efforts produced results that fell short of his goals, he repeatedly accepted half a loaf rather than none, "much disposed to concur in any expedient not inconsistent with fundamental principles."

Madison was not chiefly a political philosopher but rather a policy strategist, adept at using broad theoretical ideas to advance his goals. It is difficult to read Madison's writings without appreciating his gift for ab-

---

*In the western part of Massachusetts in 1786, Daniel Shays, a Revolutionary War veteran, organized a group of poor farmers whose farms were being foreclosed due to their inability to pay the debts they owed. The mob was angry at judges and bankers who represented the propertied elite. Shays and his followers showed up in Springfield where they tried to attack the armory to seize weapons. Massachusetts was not able to control the mob effectively, causing American political leaders to question the ability of the Articles of Confederation to maintain property rights and leading them to call a convention in 1787 to form a new constitution with a stronger national government.—EDS.

straction and generalization, his tendency to develop theory and then apply its logic to sort through facts, his propensity to use lists of general reasons to justify his claims, and his willingness to use global abstractions to combat adversaries. An opponent at the convention, William Paterson, may well have had Madison's style in mind when he noted that "A little practicable Virtue [is] preferable to Theory." . . .

The Constitutional Convention used no predetermined blueprint to lay out the national policy process. Republican principles demanded only that the powers to legislate, to execute the law, and to judge legal disputes be separated in some way. Practical experience encouraged a bicameral legislature, an executive with veto power, and courts divorced from the play of politics. The delegates assumed that skilled republican politicians would use the process to advantage themselves and their constituents. Beyond these indefinite guidelines, the convention built the policy process piece by piece. Decisions about the policy process were pushed along by an evolving web of agreements about whom each branch would represent, what powers the national government would have, and what role each institution would play in using this process.

As the delegates grew less certain about the consequences of their choices, political logic dictated that they should arm their favored agents with the will and ability to stop policies threatening to their vital interests. They could not agree on the exact boundaries of national authority, but they could agree that by building separate defenses for their favored institutions, they could reduce the danger that the national government would use its authority to take advantage of their constituents. Their choices in turn forced them to adjust the powers and independence of these institutions to one another. The Senate gained extraordinary powers to ratify treaties, confirm presidential appointees, and try impeachments. The House gained nominal authority to initiate revenue measures. The president gained influence over the policy agenda, major appointments, and foreign affairs. Courts gained more autonomy to interpret state and national laws. The convention rejected efforts to build institutional collaboration into national policy making, including proposals to require the joint exercise of veto power by the president and the Supreme Court, the creation of a privy council, and the eligibility of sitting members of Congress to serve in executive offices.

When their work was done, the delegates found that they had created a policy-making process with more complexity and rivalry of purpose than any of them originally anticipated. They had infused each institution with a different perspective on the nation's interests. They had given each institution the power to block the use of government. By doing so, they made it difficult and costly to make effective national public policy, that is, to use the government for any purpose. Public policy would succeed only if it survived a gauntlet of institutions, each deliberately anchored by different constituencies, calendars, and powers.

Members of Congress would be tied to distinct geographical constituencies, and the interests of these constituents would shape their perception of national interests. Most U.S. representatives would concern themselves primarily with the welfare of regions smaller than a state. U.S. senators would act on behalf of the state governments and statewide constituencies. Representatives and senators could pursue reelection. Each Congress would have a two-year frame of reference, because the political dynamics in each house could change after every national election. Veto points would abound: the Senate and House effectively could veto each other, and the president could veto any bill on which they could agree. It would be relatively easy for one institution to exercise its independent power to stop legislation, but it would be relatively difficult to engineer the institutional cooperation required to enact laws. On the other hand, it would be difficult, costly, and time-consuming for representatives of existing regional interests to construct the political majorities necessary for lawmaking. Only an extraordinarily large geographical majority could win concurrent House and Senate approval for any public policy measure. For example, no law could be passed in the first Congress without, at a bare minimum, the consent of representatives of 55 percent of the American population. No treaty or major appointment could be made without the assent of senators representing nine of the thirteen states.

Compared with Congress, the president and his appointees to the national courts would serve much larger constituencies, and their constituencies would greatly broaden their perception of national interests. The president would represent at least a large number of voters in many parts of the nation. Given a four-year term, the president would serve during two Congresses. The possibility of reelection to additional terms further lengthened his time horizon. The president's agenda-setting, administrative, and foreign-policy powers armed the office with the power to change the path of public policy. Presidents could frame policy agendas aimed at directing policy outcomes and building political support well into the future, and so would define the national interest in terms of prospective achievements that cultivate a chosen national constituency. Presidents could be expected to build new national political orders or to articulate existing ones. The president would tend to pursue national interests more proactively than Congress, more coherently, and for longer time horizons. While the Senate embodied [Roger] Sherman's aspiration to protect the interests of the states, the office of the president embodied Madison's ambition to instill in national policy makers the means and motive to pursue national interests, independent of the states.

No institution would view public policy in a longer time horizon than the national judiciary, whose judges would not have to cultivate voters to stay in office. Compared with Congress, and like the president, the national judiciary would have more latitude to define national interests broadly. But judges would lack the policy tools necessary for fine-tuning a future policy agenda. Judges' tools were reactive. They could only respond to disputes about actions already authorized by other institutions. Judges could settle disputes about existing national law and strike down laws inconsistent with the Constitution. Together, these powers would allow judges to defend existing political arrangements rather than to fashion new ones. Judges would have incentives to interpret national interest in the context of the political order in which they had been appointed. The national judiciary would tend to frame national interests more coherently than Congress but more reactively than the president.

The delegates' compromises, in short, produced a policy-making system that would be hard to use. Different institutions with different perspectives on national interest would share responsibility for major steps in the policy process, from setting the policy agenda to implementing law. . . .

The Constitution gave American politicians extraordinary responsibilities, while at the same time made it extraordinarily hard for them to fulfill these responsibilities. It gave the Congress the duty to make laws for the entire nation, but has encouraged its members to view public policy primarily through the lens of the short-term, parochial interests of their local constituents. It gave the president a duty to formulate plans for achieving future national interests, but limited his capacity to pursue these interests. It gave the courts the duty to ensure the supremacy of federal law, but insulated courts so they can only react to individual conflicts about public policy long after the policy's initiation. Founded on the principle of rule by the people, the Constitution tacitly gave unelected judges the duty of rising above politics to protect established national interests. Founded on the principle of majority rule, the Constitution has obstructed and complicated the construction of majorities.

While Americans revere their Constitution, its paradoxes have fostered frustration and cynicism about their government. These frustrations are rooted in the way the framers answered the agonizing questions they confronted: how can a popularly controlled government promote national well-being without also being a threat? James Madison, Roger Sherman, and the other delegates who wrote the Constitution understood this question just as well—and even better—than we do now. These politicians crafted an answer that suited both their ideals and their vital political interests. Politicians designed the United States Constitution. Ingenious politicians use it. Altering the U.S. Constitution therefore can offer no panacea for curing America's political frustrations. Changing the Constitution is hard, and the results are unpredictable. There are no guarantees that any politically feasible change in the Constitution today would do more good than harm. No one who reflects on presidents' struggle for power in the past forty years, for example, can be confident that making it easier for presidents to get their way would unambiguously benefit the nation.

Instead of changing their Constitution, Americans must learn to use it better. To repeat: making this national policy process work requires very broad-based political coalitions and sustained, concerted effort. To use this government, Americans must engage in politics. They must build and sustain the large political coalitions necessary to align the House, the Senate, the presidency, the courts, and a large number of states. Building coalitions requires understanding the interests of many different kinds of people, forging an understanding of the common interests of these people, locating a common set of objectives that can motivate their continuing cooperation, and working constantly to anticipate and remedy the endless, inevitable conflicts that threaten their cooperative effort. American history abounds with ingenious, tough-minded leaders who have constructed politics in this way. These leaders have spotted opportunities in the Constitution's structural constraints, and they have learned to mold the ambiguities of American politics into new possibilities for political cooperation.

17

JAMES STERLING YOUNG

From *The Washington Community: 1800–1828*

Numerous books and articles have been written about the early years of American government, right after the Constitution was ratified. It seems that scholars have left nothing uncovered in their exploration of that crucial era. But historian James Young succeeds in finding a most unusual angle, one that has great significance for students of American government. He relates the physical living arrangements in early Washington to the separation of powers embodied in the Constitution. Young describes the swamp that delineated parts of the town. He recounts stories about the boardinghouses where legislators lived and sometimes argued vehemently. Young's depiction of House and Senate floor activity can certainly match today's C-SPAN for excitement. Early Washington, D.C., established a clear precedent for the future: many interests were represented, but cooperation was minimal. As Young observes, "Some government!"

————

DESOLATE IN SURROUNDING, derogatory in self-image, the governmental community was also distinctive for the extraordinary manner in which the personnel chose to situate themselves in Washington—the social formations into which they deployed on the terrain. The settlement pattern of a community is, in a sense, the signature that its social organization inscribes upon the landscape, defining the groups of major importance in the life of the community and suggesting the relationships among them. In the case of the early Washington community that signature is very clear.

The members did not, in their residential arrangements, disperse uniformly or at random over the wide tract of the intended city. Nor did they draw together at any single place. The governmental community rather inscribed itself upon the terrain as a series of distinct subcommunities, separated by a considerable distance, with stretches of empty land between them. Each was clustered around one of the widely separated public buildings; each was a self-contained social and economic entity. The personnel of the governmental community segregated themselves, in short, into distinct groups, and formed a society of "we's" and "they's." . . .

From data gathered in an 1801 survey, listing the location of houses completed and under construction in the capital, it is possible to recon-

struct the settlement pattern of the early governmental community with
reasonable accuracy. . . .

Members of the different branches of government chose to situate
themselves close by the respective centers of power with which they were
affiliated, seeking their primary associations in extra-official life among
their fellow branch members.

Despite its relative civilization, old Georgetown attracted few members of government as residents, and most of those who stayed there
moved as soon as they could find quarters in Washington, nearer to their
places of work. . . .

At the opposite end of the city, about five miles from Georgetown,
near the Capitol but separated from it by a dense swamp, was the village
of the armed forces. . . .

. . . Commercialization failing, the environs became the site of the
congressional burying ground, a poorhouse, and a penitentiary with an
arsenal "near, much too near" it, thus associating by coresidence the men
and matériel of war with the dead, the indigent, and the incorrigible. The
settlement was generally shunned by civilian members of the government
as a place to live, and high-ranking military and naval officers also forsook
it eventually to take up residence in the executive sector.

The chief centers of activity were the village community of the executives and the village community of the legislators, lying "one mile and
a half and seventeen perches" apart as the crow flies, on the "great heath"
bisected by the River Tiber.

Senators and Representatives lived in the shadow of the Capitol itself,
most of them in knots of dwellings but a moment's walk from their place
of meeting. . . .

The knolltop settlement of legislators was a complete and self-
contained village community from beginning to end of the Jeffersonian
era. Neither work nor diversion, nor consumer needs, nor religious needs
required them to set foot outside it. Eight boardinghouses, a tailor, a shoe-
maker, a washerwoman, a grocery store, and an oyster house served the
congressional settlement in 1801. Within three years a notary, an ironmon-
ger, a saddle maker, several more tailors and bootmakers, a liquor store,
bookstores, stables, bakery, and taverns had been added. In twenty years'
time the settlement had increased to more than two thousand people and
the Capitol was nearly surrounded by brick houses "three stories high,
and decent, without being in the least elegant," where the lawmakers
lodged during the session. An itinerant barber served the community,
shuttling between the scattered villages of the capital on horseback, and a
nearby bathhouse catered to congressional clientele. Legislators with fam-

ilies could send their children to school on the Hill. The members had their own congressional library and their own post office, dispatching and receiving mail—which was distributed on the floor of the Senate and the House daily—without leaving the Hill. Page boys, doorkeepers, sergeants-at-arms, and other ancillary personnel for Congress were supplied from the permanent population of Capitol Hill—mainly the boardinghouse proprietors and their families. . . . The settlement pattern of early Washington clearly reveals a community structure paralleling the constitutional structure of government itself. The "separation of powers" became a separation of persons, and each of the branches of government became a self-contained, segregated social system within the larger governmental establishment. Legislators with legislators, executives with executives, judges with judges, the members gathered together in their extraofficial as well as in their official activities, and in their community associations deepened, rather than bridged, the group cleavages prescribed by the Constitution.

Why did the rulers make this highly contrived, unconventional legal structure into their community structure at Washington? . . . A key factor contributing to social segregation by branch affiliation is suggested by the consistency between such behavior and community attitudes about power and politicians. In the absence of any extrinsic forces compelling the rulers to segregate in community life, patterned avoidance between executives, legislators, and judges indicates that they felt a stronger sense of identification with their constitutional roles than with other more partisan roles they may have had in the community. Social segregation on the basis of branch affiliation suggests, in other words, that the rulers generally considered themselves executives, legislators, or judges first, and politicians or party members second. Such a preference for nonpartisan, constitutionally sanctioned roles fully accords with, and tends to confirm the authenticity of, the members' disparaging image of politicians. Their decided preference for associating with fellow branch members in extraofficial life is also precisely the sort of social behavior that was foreshadowed by the attitudes they held concerning power. Power-holders acculturated to antipower values would, it was predicted, be attracted toward behaviors and associations which were sanctioned by the Constitution. By subdividing into separate societies of executives, legislators, and judges, the rulers could not have more literally translated constitutional principles of organization into social realities nor afforded themselves greater security from reproach in this aspect of their community life at Washington. When one sees, moreover, the remarkable consistency between the organizational precepts of the Constitution of 1787 and the community plan of 1791, on the one hand, and, on the other hand, the actual community structure of the governing politicians from 1800 to 1828, one must presume a consistency also in the attitudes from which these principles of organization originally derived, namely, attitudes of mistrust toward political power. Whatever the underlying causes, here was a community of power-holders who preferred and who sanctioned, in their extraofficial life, a structural configuration that had been designed explicitly to check power. Here was a community of rulers who chose, among all the alternatives of social organization open to them, precisely the one most prejudicial to their capacity to rule. . . . Power made a community of cultural strangers. And power, shared, was hardly a thing to bind strangers together.

To achieve political accord among men of such disparate interests and different acculturation would not have been an easy task even under the most auspicious circumstances. For those gathered to govern on Capitol Hill in the Jeffersonian era, the circumstances were anything but auspicious.

To the political cleavages inherent in any representative assembly were added the deeper social tensions that are generated when men of widely diverging beliefs and behaviors are thrust upon each other in everyday living. Close-quarters living gave rise to personal animus even between "men whose natural interests and stand in society are in many respects similar. . . . The more I know of [two New England Senators] the more I am impressed with the idea how unsuited they are ever to co-operate," commented a fellow lodger; "never were two substances more completely adapted to make each other explode." As social intimacy bared the depth of their behavioral differences, tolerance among men from different regions was strained to the breaking point. Political coexistence with the South and the frontier states was hard enough for New Englanders to accept. Social coexistence was insufferable with slaveholders "accustomed to speak in the tone of masters" and with frontiersmen having "a license of tongue incident to a wild and uncultivated state of society. With men of such states of mind and temperament," a Massachusetts delegate protested, "men educated in . . . New England . . . could have little pleasure in intercourse, less in controversy, and of course no sympathy." Close scrutiny of their New England neighbors in power could convince southerners, in their turn, that there was "not one [who] possesses the slightest tie of common interest or of common feeling with us," planters and gentlemen cast among men "who raised 'beef and pork, and butter and cheese, and potatoes and cabbages'" and carried on "a paltry trade in potash and codfish." Cultural antipathies, crowded barracks, poor rations, and separation from families left at home combined to make tempers wear thin as the winters wore on, leading to sporadic eruptions of violence. In a sudden affray at the table in Miss Shields's boardinghouse, Randolph, "pouring out a glass of wine, dashed it in Alston's face. Alston sent a decanter at his head in return, and these and similar missiles continued to fly to and fro, until there was much destruction of glass ware." The chambers of the Capitol themselves witnessed more than one scuffle, and, though it was not yet the custom for legislators to arm themselves when legislating, pistols at twenty paces cracked more than once in the woods outside the Capitol.

To those who would seek political agreement in an atmosphere of social tensions, the rules of proceeding in Congress offered no aid at all. On the contrary, contentiousness was encouraged by Senate and House rules which gave higher precedence to raising questions than to deciding them and which guaranteed almost total freedom from restraint to the idiosyncratic protagonist. . . . "Political hostilities are waged with great vigour," commented another observer, "yet both in attack and defence there is evidently an entire want both of discipline and organization. There is no concert, no division of duties, no compromise of opinion. . . . Any general system of effective co-operation is impossible."

The result was a scene of confusion daily on the floor of House and Senate that bore no resemblance to the deliberative processes of either the town meeting or the parliamentary assemblies of the Old World. Congress at work was Hyde Park* set down in the lobby of a busy hotel—hortatory outcry in milling throngs, all wearing hats as if just arrived or on the verge of departure, variously attired in the fashions of faraway places. Comings and goings were continual—to the rostrum to see the clerk, to the anterooms to meet friends, to the Speaker's chair in a sudden surge to hear the results of a vote, to the firesides for hasty caucuses and strategy-planning sessions. Some gave audience to the speaker of the moment; some sat at their desks reading or catching up on correspondence; some stood chatting with lady friends, invited on the floor; others dozed, feet propped high. Page boys weaved through the crowd, "little Mercuries" bearing messages, pitchers of water for parched throats, bundles of documents, calling out members' names, distributing mail just arrived on the stagecoach. Quills scratched, bond crackled as knuckles rapped the sand off wet ink, countless newspapers rustled. Desk drawers banged, feet shuffled in a sea of documents strewn on the floor. Bird dogs fresh from the

---

*Hyde Park, in London, has a corner reserved for those in the public who wish to stand up in front of the crowd and offer their views on various issues. At any moment of the day, Hyde Park is filled with raucous, boisterous argument on every subject under the sun.—Eds.

hunt bounded in with their masters, yapping accompaniment to contenders for attention, contenders for power. Some government! . . .

What emerges from a community study of Capitol Hill is, therefore, a social system which gave probably greater sanction and encouragement to constituency-oriented behavior than any institutional norms or organizational features of the modern Congress. . . . Constituency-oriented behavior, in other words, justified the possession of power in a context of personal and national values which seems to have demanded justification for the possession of power. . . .

As a system for the effective representation of citizen interests the social system of Capitol Hill has probably never been surpassed in the history of republican government. But a fragmented social system of small blocs, more anarchic than cohesive, seems hardly to meet the minimal requirements for a viable system of managing social conflict, for performing "the regulation of . . . various and interfering interests" which the author of *The Federalist*, No. 10 acknowledged to be "the principal task of modern legislation." Far from serving as an institution for the management of conflict, the little democracy on the Hill seems more likely to have acted as a source of conflict in the polity. An ironic and provocative judgment is thus suggested by the community record of Capitol Hill: at a time when citizen interest in national government was at its lowest point in history the power-holders on the Potomac fashioned a system of surpassing excellence for representing the people and grossly deficient in the means for governing the people.

PART FOUR

Federalism

18

JAMES MADISON

From *The Federalist 39* and *46*

Ratification of the Constitution in 1787 required delicate and persuasive diplomacy. The Articles of Confederation, flawed as they were in allowing virtually no centralized governmental power, did give each state the near-total independence valued after their experiences as English colonies. The proponents of the new Constitution had to convince the states to adopt a new structure of government that would strengthen national power. In Nos. 39 and 46, Madison first discusses the importance of representative government. Then he turns to the "bold and radical innovation" that both divided and shared power between the national government and the state governments—what we today call federalism. The approval of the Constitution was to be by the people of the states, and once in operation, the government would be both national and federal. But, Madison explained, the American people would be the ultimate repository of power. State governments would always claim the citizenry's top loyalty, unless the people chose otherwise. Publius argued successfully in the great American tradition of compromise; there was something for everyone in the Constitution.

No. 39: Madison

. . . THE FIRST QUESTION that offers itself is whether the general form and aspect of the government be strictly republican. It is evident that no other form would be reconcilable with the genius of the people of America; with the fundamental principles of the Revolution; or with that honorable determination which animates every votary of freedom to rest all our political experiments on the capacity of mankind for self-government. If the plan of the convention, therefore, be found to depart from the republican character, its advocates must abandon it as no longer defensible.

What, then, are the distinctive characters of the republican form? . . .

If we resort for a criterion to the different principles on which different forms of government are established, we may define a republic to be, or at least may bestow that name on, a government which derives all its powers directly or indirectly from the great body of the people, and is administered by persons holding their offices during pleasure for a limited period, or during good behavior. It is *essential* to such a government that it be derived from the great body of the society, not from an inconsiderable proportion or a favored class of it; otherwise a handful of tyrannical nobles, exercising their oppressions by a delegation of their powers, might aspire to the rank of republicans and claim for their government the honorable title of republic. It is *sufficient* for such a government that the persons administering it be appointed, either directly or indirectly, by the people; and that they hold their appointments by either of the tenures just specified; otherwise every government in the United States, as well as every other popular government that has been or can be well organized or well executed, would be degraded from the republican character. According to the constitution of every State in the Union, some or other of the officers of government are appointed indirectly only by the people. According to most of them, the chief magistrate himself is so appointed. And according to one, this mode of appointment is extended to one of the co-ordinate branches of the legislature. According to all the constitutions, also, the tenure of the highest offices is extended to a definite period, and in many instances, both within the legislative and executive departments, to a period of years. According to the provisions of most of the constitutions, again, as well as according to the most respectable and received opinions on the subject, the members of the judiciary department are to retain their offices by the firm tenure of good behavior. . . .

"But it was not sufficient," say the adversaries of the proposed Constitution, "for the convention to adhere to the republican form. They ought with equal care to have preserved the *federal* form, which regards the Union as a *Confederacy* of sovereign states; instead of which they have framed a *national* government, which regards the Union as a *consolidation* of the States." And it is asked by what authority this bold and radical innovation was undertaken? . . .

First.—In order to ascertain the real character of the government, it may be considered in relation to the foundation on which it is to be established; to the sources from which its ordinary powers are to be drawn; to the operation of those powers; to the extent of them; and to the authority by which future changes in the government are to be introduced.

On examining the first relation, it appears, on one hand, that the Constitution is to be founded on the assent and ratification of the people of America, given by deputies elected for the special purpose; but, on the other, that this assent and ratification is to be given by the people, not as individuals composing one entire nation, but as composing the distinct and independent States to which they respectively belong. It is to be the assent and ratification of the several States, derived from the supreme authority in each State—the authority of the people themselves. The act, therefore, establishing the Constitution will not be a *national* but a *federal* act.

That it will be a federal and not a national act, as these terms are understood by the objectors—the act of the people, as forming so many independent States, not as forming one aggregate nation—is obvious from this single consideration: that it is to result neither from the decision of a *majority* of the people of the Union, nor from that of a *majority* of the States. It must result from the *unanimous* assent of the several States that are parties to it, differing not otherwise from their ordinary dissent than in its being expressed, not by the legislative authority, but by that of the people themselves. . . . Each State, in ratifying the Constitution, is considered as a sovereign body independent of all others, and only to be bound by its own voluntary act. In this relation, then, the new Constitution will, if established, be a *federal* and not a *national* constitution.

The next relation is to the sources from which the ordinary powers of government are to be derived. The House of Representatives will derive its powers from the people of America; and the people will be represented in the same proportion and on the same principle as they are in the legislature of a particular State. So far the government is *national*, not *federal.* The Senate, on the other hand, will derive its powers from the States as political and coequal societies; and these will be represented on the principle of equality in the Senate, as they now are in the existing Congress. So far the government is *federal*, not *national.* The executive power will be derived from a very compound source. The immediate election of the President is to be made by the States in their political characters. The votes allotted to them are in a compound ratio, which considers them partly as distinct and coequal societies, partly as unequal members of the same society. . . . From this aspect of the government it appears to be of a mixed character, presenting at least as many *federal* as *national* features. . . . The idea of a national government involves in it not only an authority over the individual citizens, but an indefinite supremacy over all persons and things, so far as they are objects of lawful government. Among a people consolidated into one nation, this supremacy is completely vested in the national legislature. Among communities united for particular purposes, it is vested partly in the general and partly in the municipal legislatures. In the former case, all local authorities are subordinate to the supreme; and may be controlled, directed, or abolished by it at pleasure. In the latter, the local or municipal authorities form distinct and independent portions of the supremacy, no more subject, within their respective spheres, to the general authority than the general authority is subject to them, within its own sphere. In this relation, then, the proposed government cannot be deemed a *national* one; since its jurisdiction extends to certain enumerated objects only, and leaves to the several States a residuary and inviolable sovereignty over all other objects. . . .

If we try the Constitution by its last relation to the authority by which amendments are to be made, we find it neither wholly *national* nor wholly *federal*. Were it wholly national, the supreme and ultimate authority would reside in the *majority* of the people of the Union; and this authority would be competent at all times, like that of a majority of every national society to alter or abolish its established government. Were it wholly federal, on the other hand, the concurrence of each State in the Union would be essential to every alteration that would be binding on all. The mode provided by the plan of the convention is not founded on either of these principles. In requiring more than a majority, and particularly in computing the proportion by *States*, not by *citizens*, it departs from the national and advances towards the *federal* character; in rendering the concurrence of less than the whole number of States sufficient, it loses again the *federal* and partakes of the *national* character.

The proposed Constitution, therefore, even when tested by the rules laid down by its antagonists, is, in strictness, neither a national nor a federal Constitution, but a composition of both. In its foundation it is federal, not national; in the sources from which the ordinary powers of the government are drawn, it is partly federal and partly national; in the operation of these powers, it is national, not federal; in the extent of them, again, it is federal, not national; and, finally in the authoritative mode of introducing amendments, it is neither wholly federal nor wholly national.   *Publius*

No. 46: Madison

. . . I proceed to inquire whether the federal government or the State governments will have the advantage with regard to the predilection and support of the people. Notwithstanding the different modes in which they are appointed, we must consider both of them as substantially dependent on the great body of the citizens of the United States. I assume this position here as it respects the first, reserving the proofs for another place. The federal and State governments are in fact but different agents and trustees of the people, constituted with different powers and designed for different purposes. The adversaries of the Constitution seem to have lost sight of the people altogether in their reasonings on this subject; and to have viewed these different establishments not only as mutual rivals and enemies, but as uncontrolled by any common superior in their efforts to usurp the authorities of each other. These gentlemen must here be reminded of their error. They must be told that the ultimate authority, wherever the derivative may be found, resides in the people alone, and that it will not depend merely on the comparative ambition or address of the different governments whether either, or which of them, will be able to enlarge its sphere of jurisdiction at the expense of the other. Truth, no less than decency, requires that the event in every case should be supposed to depend on the sentiments and sanction of their common constituents. . . .

Many considerations, besides those suggested on a former occasion, seem to place it beyond doubt that the first and most natural attachment of the people will be to the governments of their respective States. . . .

If . . . the people should in future become more partial to the federal than to the State governments, the change can only result from such manifest and irresistible proofs of a better administration as will overcome all their antecedent propensities. And in that case, the people ought not surely to be precluded from giving most of their confidence where they may discover it to be most due; but even in that case the State governments could have little to apprehend, because it is only within a certain sphere that the federal power can, in the nature of things, be advantageously administered.   *Publius*

19

DANIEL ELAZAR

From *American Federalism*

American government has been based on a system of federalism since the Constitution was ratified. Yet, over two centuries, change and flexibility have marked American federalism; the national and state governments have shared power in different ways, to different degrees, with different roles. In the mid-1990s, for example, there was much talk in Washington about moving more governmental programs and policy decisions back to the state level, away from central government edicts. Professor Daniel Elazar offers a classic piece on federalism in which he defends the importance of state governments, even at a time when the national government seemed to dominate. Elazar points to the innovative ideas developed at the state level. He recognizes the states' importance as managers of government programs. Elazar is right on target for today, viewing American federalism as an ever-changing "partnership" between Washington, D.C., and the state capitals.

———

THE SYSTEM of state-federal relations . . . is not the neat system often pictured in the textbooks. If that neat system of separate governments performing separate functions in something akin to isolation is used as the model of what federalism should be to enable the states to maintain their integrity as political systems, then the states are in great difficulty indeed. If, however, the states have found ways to function as integral political systems—civil societies, if you will—within the somewhat chaotic system of intergovernmental sharing that exists, then they are, as the saying goes, in a different ball game. . . . We have tried to show that the states are indeed in a different ball game and as players in that game are not doing badly at all. Viewed from the perspective of that ball game, the strength and vitality of the states—and the strength and vitality of the American system as a whole—must be assessed by different standards from those commonly used.

In the first place, the states exist. This point is no less significant for its simplicity. The fact that the states survive as going concerns (as distinct from sets of historical boundaries used for the administration of centrally directed programs) after thirty-five years of depression, global war, and then cold war, which have all functioned to reduce the domestic freedom necessary to preserve noncentralized government, is in itself testimony to their vitality as political institutions. . . . Every day, in many ways, the states are actively contributing to the achievement of American goals and to the continuing efforts to define those goals.

Consequently, it is a mistake to think that national adoption of goals shared by an overwhelming majority of the states is simply centralization. To believe that is to deny the operation of the dynamics of history within a federal system. Any assessment of the states' position in the federal union must be made against a background of continuous social change. It is no more reasonable to assume that the states have lost power vis-à-vis the federal government since 1789 because they can no longer maintain established churches than it is to believe that white men are no longer as free as they were in that year because they can no longer own slaves. An apparent loss of freedom in one sphere may be more than made up by gains in another. Massachusetts exercises more power over its economy today than its governors ever hoped to exercise over its churches five generations ago. National values change by popular consensus and *all* governments must adapt themselves to those changes. The success of the states is that they have been able to adapt themselves well.

Part of the states' adaptation has been manifested in their efforts to improve their institutional capabilities to handle the new tasks they have assumed. In the twentieth century, there has been an extensive and continuing reorganization of state governments leading to increased executive responsibility, greater central budgetary control, and growing expertise of state personnel (whose numbers are also increasing). . . .

There has also been a great and continuing increase in the states' supervision of the functions carried out in their local subdivisions. The states' role in this respect has grown as fast as or faster than that of the federal government and is often exercised more stringently, a possibility enhanced by the constitutionally unitary character of the states. The states' supervision has been increased through the provision of technical aid to their localities, through financial grants, and through control of the power to raise (or authorize the raising of) revenue for all subdivisions.

In all this, though, there remains one major unsolved problem, whose importance cannot be overemphasized: that of the metropolitan areas. By and large, the states have been unwilling or unable to do enough to meet metropolitan problems, particularly governmental ones. Here, too, some states have better records than others but none have been able to deal with metropolitan problems comprehensively and thoroughly. It is becoming increasingly clear that—whatever their successes in the past—the future role of the states will be determined by their ability to come to grips with those problems.

A fourth factor that adds to the strength and vitality of the states is the manner in which state revenues and expenditures have been expanding since the end of World War II. . . .

Still a fifth factor is the continuing role of the states as primary managers of great programs and as important innovators in the governmental realm. Both management and innovation in education, for example, continue to be primary state responsibilities in which outside aid is used to support locally initiated ideas.

Even in areas of apparent state deficiencies, many states pursue innovative policies. Much publicity has been generated in recent years that reflects upon police procedures in certain states; yet effective actions to eliminate the death penalty have been confined to the state level. The states have also been active in developing means for releasing persons accused of crimes on their own recognizance when they cannot afford to post bail, thus reducing the imprisonment of people not yet convicted of criminal activity.

Because the states are political systems able to direct the utilization of the resources sent their way, federal grants have served as a stimulus to the development of state capabilities and, hence, have helped enhance their strength and vitality. Federal grants have helped the states in a positive way by broadening the programs they can offer their citizens and strengthening state administration of those programs. Conversely, the grants have prevented centralization of those programs and have given the states the ability to maintain their position despite the centralizing tendencies of the times.

For this reason, and because the concerns of American politics are universal ones, there is relatively little basic conflict between the federal government and the states or even between their respective interests. Most of the conflicts connected with federal-state relations are of two kinds: (1) conflicts between interests that use the federal versus state argument as a means to legitimize their demands or (2) low-level conflicts over the best way to handle specific cooperative activities. There are cases, of course, when interests representing real differences are able to align themselves with different levels of government to create serious federal-state conflict. The civil rights question in its southern manifestation is today's example of that kind of situation.

Finally, the noncentralized character of American politics has served to strengthen the states. Noncentralization makes possible intergovernment cooperation without the concomitant weakening of the smaller partners by giving those partners significant ways in which to preserve their integrity. This is because a noncentralized system functions to a great extent through bargaining and negotiation. Since its components are relatively equal in their freedom to act, it can utilize only a few of the hierarchical powers available in centralized systems. In essence, its general government can only use those powers set forth in the fundamental compact between the partners as necessary to the maintenance of the system as a whole. Stated baldly, congressional authorization of new federal programs is frequently no more than a license allowing federal authorities to begin negotiations with the states and localities. . . .

In the last analysis, the states remain viable entities in a federal system that has every tendency toward centralization present in all strong governments. They remain viable because they exist as civil societies with political systems of their own. They maintain that existence because the American political tradition and the Constitution embodying it give the states an important place in the overall fabric of American civil society. The tradition and the Constitution remain viable because neither Capitol Hill nor the fifty state houses have alone been able to serve all the variegated interests on the American scene that compete equally well without working in partnership.

The states remain vital political systems for larger reasons as well as immediate ones, reasons that are often passed over unnoticed in the public's concern with day-to-day problems of government. These larger reasons are not new; though they have changed in certain details, they remain essentially the same as in the early days of the Union.

The states remain important in a continental nation as reflectors of sectional and regional differences that are enhanced by the growing social and economic complexity of every part of the country, even as the older cultural differences may be diminished by modern communications. They remain important as experimenters and innovators over a wider range of fields than ever before, simply because government at every level in the United States has been expanding. The role of the states as recruiters of political participants and trainers of political leaders has in no way been diminished, particularly since the number of political offices of every kind seems to be increasing at least in proportion to population growth.

In at least two ways, traditional roles of the states have been enhanced by recent trends. They have become even more active promoters and administrators of public services than ever before. In part, this is simply because governments are doing more than they had in the past, but it is also because they provide ways to increase governmental activity while maintaining noncentralized government. By handling important programs at a level that can be reached by many people, they contribute to the maintenance of a traditional interest of democratic politics, namely, the maximization of local control over the political and administrative decision-makers whose actions affect the lives of every citizen in ever-increasing ways.

As the population of the nation increases, the states become increasingly able to manage major governmental activities with the competence and expertise demanded by the metropolitan-technological frontier. At the same time, the federal government becomes further removed from popular pressures simply by virtue of the increased size of the population it must serve. The states may well be on their way to becoming the most "manageable" civil societies in the nation. Their size and scale remain comprehensible to people even as they are enabled to do more things better.

In sum, the virtue of the federal system lies in its ability to develop and maintain mechanisms vital to the perpetuation of the unique combination of governmental strength, political flexibility, and individual liberty, which has been the central concern of American politics. The American people are known to appreciate their political tradition and the Constitution. Most important, they seem to appreciate the partnership, too, in some unreasoned way, and have learned to use all its elements to reasonably satisfy their claims on government.

20

ANDREW KARCH

From *Democratic Laboratories*

The title of Andrew Karch's book is taken from Supreme Court Justice Louis Brandeis's use of the phrase in a 1932 dissent. The state governments provide a place to try out new policy ideas that may later be used in other states or in the whole country; the states are "laboratories of democracy." Ideas that come from one state, Karch explains, can become policy in another state through the process of diffusion. The author discusses the importance of state governments, especially since the 1994 Republican congressional victory. "Devolution," as it has been termed, allowed the states a more prominent role in shaping policy and fitting it to the needs of each state. Karch mentions welfare reform as a prime example of devolution. Currently, state experiments with charter schools and with health care reform have provided critical information on the workability of these new programs. The author stresses the significance of the Internet in allowing states to share information efficiently. It's not clear whether the "devolution revolution" that Karch describes will continue in a time of economic problems, increased federal spending, and reliance on the national government for solutions to what ails the nation, but we can be quite sure that ideas developed in Washington, D.C., will have had their start in the states.

HOW DO NEW IDEAS SPREAD? What turns a little-known product or behavior into something with widespread popularity? These straightforward questions have captured the popular imagination. Malcolm Gladwell recently wrote a national best seller devoted to the notion that "ideas and products and messages and behaviors spread just like viruses do." He argued that the best way to understand the emergence of such phenomena as fashion trends and crime waves was to think of them as epidemics. Like an epidemic, modern change tends to occur in one dramatic moment. Rather than building slowly and steadily, change happens in a hurry, with small causes having large effects.

Gladwell's observations resonate with a long-standing scholarly literature on the emergence and diffusion of innovations. In fields ranging from anthropology and rural sociology to marketing and public health, analysts have examined the processes through which new ideas, practices, and objects spread. These innovations need not be new in an objective sense. Instead, they need only be perceived as new by an individual or another unit of adoption. If the idea, practice, or object seems new to a potential adopter, it is an innovation. Diffusion is the process "through which an innovation is communicated through certain channels over time among the members of a social system." Spread is a critical component of this definition. Diffusion is not merely the fact of increasing usage or incidence. It implies movement from the source of an innovation to an adopter. . . .

In a political setting, diffusion implies a process of learning or emulation during which decision makers look to other cities, states, or countries as models to be followed or avoided. Diffusion occurs, in other words, when the likelihood that an innovation will be adopted in jurisdiction A is significantly affected by the existence of that innovation in jurisdiction B. Diffusion does not occur when officials in multiple jurisdictions adopt the same innovation completely independently, nor does it occur when later adopters are unaware of the existence of the innovation elsewhere. In contrast, diffusion implies that extant versions of an innovation affect officials' decisions to create the same political form or to enact the same policy. Diffusion occurs, in sum, when decision makers draw on others' experiences to evaluate the effectiveness of a new political form or idea. . . .

One of the most famous metaphors in American jurisprudential history speaks implicitly to the concept of policy diffusion. In a 1932 dissent, Supreme Court justice Louis Brandeis wrote, "It is one of the happy incidents of the federal system that a state may, if its citizens choose, serve as a laboratory; and try novel social and economic experiments without risk to the rest of the country." Since this landmark dissent, the fifty states have with great regularity been referred to as "laboratories of democracy." Actors from across the political spectrum have invoked this metaphor to describe the states' innovative potential. Liberal and conservative judges have cited Brandeis's metaphor more than three dozen times, and it clearly appeals to a nation of "compulsive tinkerers."

The metaphor of laboratories of democracy implies an almost scientific process, in which the enactment of a policy innovation prompts its evaluation, then other lawmakers use this information to determine whether they, too, will put the program in place. Each new policy is assessed along a set of objective dimensions. If the evaluators agree that the policy achieves its stated goals, other states will enact an identical program once they are made aware of its achievements. For example, if Oklahoma policymakers enact a program to contain health care costs and if this policy innovation succeeds, officials in other states will endorse similar programs. If the innovation is unsuccessful, it will not be adopted elsewhere. Thus, the laboratories metaphor describes a systematic and rational process of trial and error. . . .

Recent developments have catapulted the fifty states to a more prominent place in the American political system. For the past two decades, the states have served as a main locus of policy-making. As a result, now is a timely occasion to examine diffusion in this setting. From abortion and capital punishment to education and the environment, several important policy decisions are being made in state houses across the country, in addition to in the nation's capital. Two main factors contributed to this state resurgence. National political developments, especially the emergence of a Republican congressional majority [from the 1994 elections until the 2006 elections], were one important factor. The second factor was a set of reforms at the state level that strengthened state political institutions.

National developments shifted significant policy-making prerogatives from the national government to the fifty states, with changes in party politics playing a critical role. Republican politicians long considered intergovernmental reform to be a central element of their domestic political agenda. In the early 1970s, President Richard Nixon advanced a proposal called the New Federalism, which emphasized an administrative rationale for devolving policy-making authority to the states. Nixon wanted to restructure the roles and responsibilities of government at all levels in an effort to make the system function more efficiently. Ronald Reagan and Newt Gingrich married these administrative concerns to a larger debate over the legitimate scope and definition of the public sector. For Reagan, Gingrich, and other Republicans, devolution was a way to solve administrative problems and to cut back the reach of government programs.

When the 1994 midterm elections produced a Republican majority in both houses of Congress for the first time in decades, this shift sparked a fundamental rethinking of the relationship between the states and the national government. While many Republican initiatives stalled, others devolved additional policy-making prerogatives to state officials. Perhaps the most prominent example occurred in 1996, when national lawmakers endorsed landmark welfare reform legislation. The Personal Responsibility and Work Opportunity Reconciliation Act placed a time limit on welfare receipt and incorporated stringent work requirements on beneficiaries. It also granted state policymakers unprecedented discretion over the provisions of their welfare programs. Since 1996, state lawmakers have used this discretion to create diverse approaches to welfare policy. Welfare reform is one of many instances in which the states have taken the lead in the making of public policy in response to national legislation.

The partisan shift in Congress was crucial, but other national developments also facilitated the resurgence of the states. Sometimes congressional stalemates, caused by divided government or party polarization, prompted state lawmakers to act in the absence of a national mandate. When national lawmakers could not agree on legislation or did not address specific topics, state officials sometimes developed innovative policy solutions on their own. This dynamic was fairly common in health care policy. During the late 1980s and early 1990s, many states implemented innovative health care programs, such as MinnesotaCare (Minnesota), MassCare (Massachusetts), and the State Health Insurance Program (Hawaii). When legislation for comprehensive national health care reform failed in 1994, state officials attempted to address this vacuum by proposing their own solutions. Over the past two decades, in health care and in other policy arenas, state officials have regularly taken independent action.

In part, state officials' ability to take action grew out of institutional changes that better equipped the states to serve as laboratories of democracy. Reforms of legislatures and executive branches are the second factor that contributed to the resurgence of the states. In institutional terms, the fifty states are stronger than they were a generation ago. In the 1960s, state governments were not professional operations, and many reformers believed that state governments lacked the resources they needed to be effective. Today this is a less pressing concern. James Morone explains: "Once upon a time, good old boys ran the states with winks and backslaps. No more." The institutional capabilities of state governments increased dramatically between the 1960s and the 1980s, thanks to a series of constitutional and institutional reforms. These reforms made state legislatures more professional and enhanced the administrative capacities of the executive branch. As a result, state officials can make a credible claim that they are well equipped to design innovative public policies. . . .

If the fifty states serve as laboratories, they currently are better equipped to take on this task. Institutional changes transformed them from weak backwaters into a strong counterpart to the national government. Around the same time that these state-level changes occurred, developments at the national level granted the states a more prominent place in the American political system. This combination of institutional reforms and national developments contributed to the resurgence of the states and encouraged state officials to design and enact many policy innovations. These laboratories of democracy have been particularly busy in recent years, and the range of recent state activity is quite impressive. In education policy, dozens of states followed suit after the Minnesota state legislature became the first to approve charter school legislation. In health care policy, at least thirty-eight states adopted each of the following policies: small business insurance reforms, high-risk insurance pools, preexisting condition legislation, certificate of need, health care commissions, guaranteed renewal legislation, portability, and guaranteed issue. These and other recent innovations illustrate why the American states are a good setting in which to examine the phenomenon of policy diffusion. . . .

State officials typically have access to libraries and other reference centers whose main job is to collect and distribute information that will be useful during the formulation of public policy. In Virginia, for example, the Legislative Reference Center in Richmond serves the information needs of the Virginia General Assembly. Its collection includes state legislation, legal publications, and topical information to support the research needs of representatives and legislative staff. A shelf near the entrance of the reference center provides introductory materials that describe the information available in the collection. These materials include a bookmark that describes the functions of the center. It states: "We compile state comparative data on a variety of issues. One of our most frequently asked questions is: 'What are other states doing in the area of . . . ?'" The notion of policy diffusion presumes that lawmakers have access to and are sometimes influenced by this type of comparative information. One could reasonably argue that an awareness of and interest in developments elsewhere is the essence of policy diffusion, and this bookmark suggests that such a dynamic is at least a semiregular occurrence. . . .

Public officials currently operate in an information-rich environment. Compared to their predecessors, they generally have more resources at their disposal. These varied resources provide access to a wider range of policy-relevant information. Several recent institutional, technological, and organizational changes facilitate the generation and the collection of policy-relevant information. . . .

In recent decades, institutional changes augmented state officials' ability to gather policy-relevant information. These changes . . . made an especially profound impact on the legislative branch. As late as the mid-1960s, reformers argued that these bodies were ill equipped to process information and to study emerging policy problems. One response to the reformers' complaints was a dramatic increase in the number and the quality of legislative staff. Today, a larger and more qualified staff can gather information for state legislators, although there remain important disparities across states. Legislative staffers are now such an important part of state government, in fact, that a common complaint about the recent imposition of term limits in some states has been that term limits increase the power of unelected legislative staffers. Larger and more professional staffs also serve the executive branch of many state governments. Technological advancements seem to make more information resources available for state officials. The emergence of new information technologies, such as the Internet, increased the ease and speed with which many organizations can provide policy-relevant information. The representative of one professional association explains: "The advances are enormous. Compared with what is going on now, we were asleep fifteen years ago." Technological shifts also increased the ease and speed with which state officials can consult policy-relevant information. State officials can examine model legislation and statutory language online without contacting an organization directly. In addition, they can mark up legislation and send it to a professional association for comment. This electronic exchange is significantly easier than relying on a telephone, a fax machine, or snail mail. In the past, finding information sometimes involved phone calls and waiting for the mail. Today, similar information is often only a click of the mouse away.

Additional technological changes also make it easier for officials to consult their colleagues in other states. Travel is less onerous than it was in the past, facilitating attendance at regional and national meetings of professional organizations that bring together lawmakers and staff from across the country. Alan Rosenthal argues that "legislation tends to spread like wildfire" because of these conferences. Public officials frequently discuss new programs with one another at these meetings, learning about the substantive impact and political feasibility of policy innovations. When state lawmakers and their staff travel to these out-of-state meetings, they often look for bills to introduce when they return to their own states. Attendees also forge long-lasting bonds at these meetings, and they can use these connections to develop legislation once they return to their own states. A legislative staffer in Massachusetts explains the significance of such connections: "If someone called me and asked me to send information on our laws on managed care or HMOs I would know exactly what chapter to go to whereas someone from another state wouldn't. People do the same thing for me when I know exactly what I'm looking for." Communications technologies, such as e-mail and relatively inexpensive long-distance phone calls, facilitate quick correspondence. It is not much of a stretch to imagine that these connections facilitate the dissemination of policy-relevant information. In sum, technological changes suggest that state officials are more closely connected than they were in the past and are therefore better able to exchange ideas and information. . . .

In the foreword to a book on state-level economic policy during the

1980s, Bill Clinton, then governor of Arkansas, used the "laboratories of democracy" metaphor to describe how officials in the states "learn from one another, borrowing, adapting, and improving on each other's best efforts." This quotation alludes to one of the complexities of policy diffusion, because it implies that lawmakers amend the policy templates that they import. Although officials sometimes copy programs that exist elsewhere, it is more common for them to "adapt" and "improve" these examples. In other words, they customize a policy innovation to "fit" their state in the same way that an individual tailors a suit after buying it off the rack. Policy innovations, as a result, take on various forms in the jurisdictions in which they are enacted. Programs that purport to be the same sometimes vary quite significantly across states. . . .

. . . The political forces that affect state lawmaking and the spread of innovative policy ideas are topics of great contemporary significance. The states recently emerged from their worst financial crisis since the Second World War. Constrained by balanced budget requirements that prevented them from running large deficits, state officials responded to this situation in several different ways. Extensive service cuts were one common strategy. Ironically, the scope and magnitude of the cuts testify to the expansive role of state governments. They affected everything from nursing home care and community colleges to homeland security and health care for the poor. It is no exaggeration to claim that state governments reach into almost every corner of American citizens' lives.

In recent years, many officials at the national level have proposed to grant state lawmakers additional policy-making discretion in several areas where the national and state governments currently share responsibility. For example, some of these proposals would provide state governments with lump sum payments to run social programs, such as Head Start and Medicaid. Currently national regulations affect the operation of these programs, but some individuals want state officials to have the power to structure these policies as they see fit. Rather than attaching strings to national grants, they want state policymakers to operate free of any regulations. Proponents of this "devolution revolution" argue that removing these strictures will allow state lawmakers to develop innovative policy ideas and to adapt existing programs to specific conditions within their states. The debate over devolution resonates . . . with the notion that the fifty states can serve as laboratories of democracy. . . .

21

THOMAS BIRKLAND
SARAH WATERMAN

Is Federalism the Reason for Policy Failure in Hurricane Katrina?

Writing in the journal Publius, *a collection of articles that focus on the relationship between the national and state governments, Thomas Birkland and Sarah Waterman ask the question above. The authors review some of the history of American federalism, arriving at a theory of "opportunistic federalism" that may have been responsible for the failures in the federal government's response to Hurricane Katrina. The place of FEMA (Federal Emergency Management Agency) within DHS (Department of Homeland Security) and the effect of the September 11, 2001, terrorist attacks on the World Trade Center and the Pentagon contributed to changes in both state and national disaster planning. From the design of the New Orleans levees to the events in the days after the hurricane, governments at all levels must share blame. Birkland and Waterman believe that the national government needs to re-think how DHS and FEMA integrate state and local governments into planning for another natural disaster. Not federalism, but "the style of federalism" is to blame.*

As THE MOST EXPENSIVE NATURAL DISASTER in American history and one of the deadliest in recent memory, Hurricane Katrina has been seared in the American psyche unlike any other natural disaster. Of particular note is the extent to which the response to Katrina has been cast as a failure of federal initiative and organization, notwithstanding the inherently intergovernmental nature of disaster preparedness, response, recovery, and mitigation in the US. The criticism has been particularly heated given the reforms occasioned by another "focusing event": The September 11 attacks and the concomitant focus on "homeland security," to the detriment of preparedness for and response to natural hazards. Since August 2005, Americans, their elected representatives, and the news media have pointedly asked, "If the federal government cannot prepare for something like Katrina, how can it prepare for a major act of terrorism?" Of course, the mantra of failure, reinforced by media coverage of the supposed overall failure of response to Katrina, failed to consider the things that worked in Katrina. Martha Derthick includes the pre-storm evacuation and the search and rescue function as success stories that involved considerable intergovernmental coordination. But Derthick also notes the failure of flood protection, another intergovernmental function.

The broader failure of disaster mitigation, preparedness, and response was manifest in Katrina. The nature of federalism and intergovernmental relations, particularly post-September 11, has been implicated in these failures. This article explores potential explanations for governmental failure during Hurricane Katrina, including federalism, policy, and administrative failures. The creation of the Department of Homeland Security (DHS) led to substantial changes in the nature of the federal-state-local relationship in emergency management. These changes appear to have validated fears raised by critics before Hurricane Katrina that the reorganization designed to respond to terrorism would undermine the nation's ability to respond to natural disasters. The important question, then, is this: Were the failures in Hurricane Katrina a result of federalism or of a particular style of federalism that characterizes disaster policy in the US? Or did these failures simply reflect the inherent difficulties in preparing for, responding to, and recovering from catastrophes?

Although former eras of federalism were conceptualized as cooperative or competitive, coercive federalism and opportunistic federalism are two terms that might be profitably applied to homeland security and issues raised in Hurricane Katrina. Coercive federalism describes how federal regulations, federal mandates imposed on the states, and federal preemption of state authority seek to compel state and local governments to comply with federal standards in the pursuit of national goals. Many states have claimed that post-September 11 policy is coercive in that it attaches strings to federal preparedness aid. . . .

A potentially more satisfactory model of federalism, which avoids the assumed heavy handedness of coercion and the sometimes naive assumption of shared goals, is called opportunistic federalism, which [Timothy] Conlan defines as

a system that allows—and often encourages—actors in the system to pursue their immediate interests with little regard for the institutional or collective consequences. For example, federal mandates, policy preemptions, and highly prescriptive federal grant programs tend to be driven by opportunistic policy makers who seek to achieve their own policy and political goals regardless of traditional norms of behavior or boundaries of institutional responsibility.

This idea of opportunistic federalism is entirely consistent with the "opportunistic" and episodic nature of nearly all disaster policy, since disaster and crisis policy is almost entirely event-driven, decisions are made rapidly, and policies are often adopted without considering their long-term influence on fundamental constitutional and institutional arrangements. This is an excellent description of federal disaster policy since September 11. In the process of creating the DHS, Congress, with the president's assent, moved FEMA [Federal Emergency Management Agency, created in 1979] into the new agency without regard for its existing organizational and intergovernmental relationships. Furthermore, homeland security "experts" (many of whom had little experience in this new field) made policy in nearly complete ignorance of the vast amounts of knowledge accumulated by social scientists and practitioners on how people and organizations behave in disasters. The creators of the new homeland security establishment were driven by political and policy goals—in particular, the need to act quickly to bolster "homeland security"—rather than by a desire to understand whether the entire disaster preparedness, response, and recovery system really needed to be overhauled at all, or whether small parts needed reform to work better.

The creation of the DHS as it eventually emerged laid the shaky foundation for intergovernmental response that had been partially built before Katrina. This foundation, to be sure, was not undermined solely by opportunistic federalism, but by a patchwork of relationships between and among governments that combined features of coercion and cooperation in ways that were not yet well established after September 11. These relationships reveal challenges of network governance at least as much, if not more, than they reveal problems with the federal nature of disaster policy and practice. . . .

. . . FEMA became known as a poorly performing "turkey farm" because of the Reagan and G. H. W. Bush Administrations' use of FEMA as a source of patronage jobs for third-rate political appointees. FEMA largely ignored natural disasters, even though the National Earthquake Hazards Reduction Act (NEHRA) had indicated that FEMA was the lead disaster response agency in the case of major earthquakes. Indeed, Julius Becton, FEMA director from 1985 to 1989, ranked earthquakes, hurricane, and flood programs at the bottom of FEMA's program priorities. . . .

After the enactment of the Stafford Act [in 1988], FEMA slowly turned its attention to natural disasters; it was forced to turn more quickly in the aftermath of Hurricane Hugo and the Loma Prieta earthquake, both in 1989, and Hurricane Andrew in 1992. The loudest complaints about FEMA came during the two hurricanes. Senator Ernest "Fritz" Hollings famously called FEMA the "sorriest bunch of bureaucratic jackasses" because of FEMA's slow response. The response to Hurricane Andrew was equally deficient, with one local official crying out for help: "Where in the hell is the cavalry on this one? They keep saying we're going to get supplies. For God's sake, where are they?"

President Clinton learned important political lessons from Hurricane Andrew, as reflected in his appointment of FEMA director James Lee Witt, under whom FEMA embarked on a strategy to improve performance and the agency's reputation. The federal government became more generous in its definitions of disasters eligible for federal assistance, a decision that was politically popular but that also lowered federal expectations about the local share of disaster preparedness and management funding and effort. This sort of opportunistic federalism was supported by states and localities, which were able to shift a great deal of the fiscal burden of disaster to the federal government. . . .

The major problem at FEMA post-2001 was not its existence, its location within the bureaucracy, or the nature of its staff. What changed after 2001 was the quality of its leadership and, more to the point, the administration's attitudes toward its mission. It was clear that the Bush administration was unlikely to actively promote the sorts of disaster preparedness and mitigation measures that had been proven at least moderately successful in the 1990s; it cut funding for the various Stafford Act mitigation programs. . . .

Russell Hanson notes that the September 11 attacks caused the national government to "once again [assert] leadership in domestic policy making." As Hanson further notes, the centralization or diffusion of government power to and from the federal government and the states ebbs and flows with events and ideological currents in American life. By defining homeland security as "national security," and by defining emergency management and disaster response as "homeland security events" . . . a strong connection is made between natural disasters and the broader "homeland security" rubric. It seems almost inevitable that there has therefore been a recentralization of the emergency management function—particularly in the leadership of this function—in the federal government. . . .

The creation of the DHS gutted FEMA. Senior personnel left the agency, and many managers either were reassigned within the DHS, left to form consultancies, or departed simply because they were displeased with the new direction. Meanwhile, the federal government was making promises it was unprepared to keep. FEMA continued to operate as if it were a "partner" in emergency management, even as the DHS was inexpertly calling the shots. The FEMA director is now a subcabinet official with no formal access to the president . . . and a reporting line that passes through the DHS secretary. . . .

We can say with confidence that the federal government's attitude toward assisting communities before and after natural disasters has changed considerably since 2001, yet the public pronouncements from FEMA and, particularly, from the DHS suggest that it will continue its pre-2001 mission of rapid response to natural disasters. This message was reinforced by the largely successful FEMA responses to the extremely active 2004 hurricane season, in which four hurricanes in relatively quick succession struck Florida. Both FEMA and the State of Florida responded effectively to these storms, creating the impression that FEMA was prepared to handle disasters of this scale. The comparison is misleading, however: Each 2004 storm was relatively small compared with Katrina, and the State of Florida was much better prepared to handle the storms than Louisiana was in 2005. Furthermore, Katrina was a remarkably large storm that likely would have overwhelmed any jurisdiction it struck, but FEMA's shortcomings seemed particularly painful in light of reassurances that the agency was still focused on its mission. . . .

The normative question raised . . . is this: Why do people blame the federal government more than they do state and local government for the apparent failures in Hurricane Katrina? Potential explanations for the Katrina policy failures reveal a great deal about policy design within and across various levels of government. These explanations are neither definitive nor mutually exclusive. We can define the policy failure as the inability of federal, state, and local governments to take the appropriate steps to mitigate, prepare for, and respond to Hurricane Katrina. The successful application of these aspects of disaster policy leads to disaster-resilient communities that can "bounce back" from disasters. New Orleans, just on population figures alone, cannot be said to have returned to its pre-Katrina state. On these measures, policy failure is clear. What is not yet clear is precisely how and why these policies failed, given the interconnected nature of communities and of cascading failures. . . .

One reason why many people thought that the federal government failed in its perceived duties is because there is evidence that the federal government did fail in fundamental ways. FEMA's response was slow, and then FEMA director Michael Brown was portrayed as being foolish and out of touch.* Later analyses suggested that he was significantly constrained by higher ups in the DHS, and major questions were raised about why the federal government lacked essential supplies and equipment in staging areas much nearer to New Orleans and the Gulf Coast. . . .

Another reason for the fixing of blame on the federal government recognizes that the hurricane's damage was so profound that it quickly overtaxed the ability of Orleans Parish, the neighboring parishes, and the State of Louisiana to effectively respond. One can then make one of two arguments. First, the federal government was inevitably overwhelmed by this catastrophic event, just because the disaster was very big, affecting the Gulf Coast from south-central Louisiana through Mississippi to Mobile, Alabama. The second "causal story" is that the federal government was overwhelmed because, despite assurances to the contrary, it was ill equipped and unable to respond to a disaster of this magnitude. While this has substantially disturbing consequences—if the federal government cannot respond to Hurricane Katrina, how could it handle an act of catastrophic terrorism?—this is less a question of federalism than it is of preparedness organization within the national government. After all, the provision of aid to communities that have been overwhelmed by catastrophic events is at the very heart of the federal role in the emergency management system. . . .

Another candidate explanation for failure is the classic conflict in federal systems: the conflict between federal and state goals. The state and local emergency managers, even after September 11, took the "all hazards" approach much more seriously than the federal government did. The National Strategy for Homeland Security, which still focuses on the "war on terrorism," speaks for itself; meanwhile, the state and local governments have consistently recognized that they are much more likely to have to address a range of natural and technological hazards and disasters as well as terrorism. The federal government's focus on civil defense is therefore neither orthogonal to nor congruent with state and local goals. This stands in rather sharp contrast to the situation during the 1990s, when there was considerably more cooperation between the federal, state, and local governments. One can therefore say that federal policy, on the one hand, and state and local policy, on the other, have been significantly divergent since 2001. . . .

*President George W. Bush's FEMA director, Michael Brown, had previously been an official in the International Arabian Horse Association, but he had resigned from that position after legal problems arose. Eventually, after much criticism due to FEMA's handling of Hurricane Katrina, Brown resigned from the federal agency.—EDS.

While the government at many levels failed in Katrina, it is also possible that citizens' expectations are too great, particularly in relation to their apparent unwillingness to take self-protective measures. One reason for policy failure is "excessive policy demand." That is, some citizens and their leaders call on government to do more than it is able to as a function of resource constraints, limits on governmental authority, or limits on political feasibility. In the first instance, while the federal government has vast resources at its disposal, these resources are not unlimited and often are the object of competition for other needs. Furthermore, at least theoretically, there are limits to what government can do in terms of the usurpation of state and local functions, the role of law enforcement officials, and the like. And some obvious responses to disasters, such as forced evacuations or forced expropriation of land in hazardous areas, are simply incongruent with our political culture and the expectations of most citizens. . . .

Surprisingly, while September 11 triggered wholesale change in federal-state relationships in emergency management, Hurricane Katrina, a truly catastrophic event, has done little to change federal attitudes about the division of responsibilities. Indeed, the public pronouncements from FEMA and the DHS suggest that it will continue its pre-2001 mission of response to natural disasters using a post-2001 model of how the world works. . . .

It is therefore not "federalism" that explains the failure of government initiative but rather the style of federalism evidenced during Hurricane Katrina. The tendencies described in this article suggest a two-fold problem: The centralization of the broader direction of homeland security policy in the federal government and, at the same time, the creation of plans and organizations that are, if history is any guide, doomed to fail during times of "normal" natural disasters, in which the state and local governments still retain considerable responsibility and powers both under the Constitution and under relevant legislation and regulation. Cutting out the state and local governments has deprived the federal government of a considerable body of expertise and has undermined the traditional idea of "defense in depth" for natural disasters, with state and local governments responding first and then seeking federal assistance. If the federal government continues to dominate, state and local capacity could very well be eroded, as it was in Katrina, where capacity to plan for and respond to a Katrina-sized storm was not built in large part because of the federal government's reassignment of resources from natural disaster preparedness to homeland security "needs."

In the end, we cannot have much faith that another catastrophic disaster like Hurricane Katrina will greatly influence federal tendencies to centralize the direction of emergency management policy in Washington. After all, Katrina should have taught the folly of that approach. Rather, it is likely that only change in administration in Washington, akin to the change in 1992 that led to FEMA's reform, is likely to result in change. As long as emergency management is valued by the president and the executive branch primarily as a facet of "homeland security" or "national security," it is unlikely that the federal government will relinquish its domination of this domain, regardless of this stance's actual influence on governmental performance.

PART FIVE

Congress

22

DAVID MAYHEW

From *Congress: The Electoral Connection*

*Congressional scholar David Mayhew admits from the start that his expla-
nation for the motivation of members of Congress is one-dimensional: they
are "single-minded seekers of reelection." While Mayhew's thesis is inten-
tionally narrow and his examples a bit out-of-date (none of the members
cited in the excerpt is still in the House), reelection remains a primary mo-
tivator for congressional behavior. To attain reelection, representatives use
three strategies. They advertise, so that their names are well-known. They
claim credit for goodies that flow to their districts. And they take positions on
political issues. Mayhew's theme, illustrated with amusing examples, may
seem cynical, but it is doubtlessly realistic. Perhaps his analysis should have
been fair warning to members of Congress about the public's growing disillusionment with the national legislature.*

———

. . . I SHALL CONJURE UP a vision of United States congressmen
as single-minded seekers of reelection, see what kinds of activity that goal
implies, and then speculate about how congressmen so motivated are likely to go about building and sustaining legislative institutions and making
policy. . . .

I find an emphasis on the reelection goal attractive for a number of
reasons. First, I think it fits political reality rather well. Second, it puts the
spotlight directly on men rather than on parties and pressure groups,
which in the past have often entered discussions of American politics as
analytic phantoms. Third, I think politics is best studied as a struggle among
men to gain and maintain power and the consequences of that struggle.
Fourth—and perhaps most important—the reelection quest establishes an
accountability relationship with an electorate, and any serious thinking
about democratic theory has to give a central place to the question of accountability. . . .

Whether they are safe or marginal, cautious or audacious, congressmen must constantly engage in activities related to reelection. There will
be differences in emphasis, but all members share the root need to do
things—indeed, to do things day in and day out during their terms. The
next step here is to present a typology, a short list of the *kinds* of activities
congressmen find it electorally useful to engage in. . . .

One activity is *advertising*, defined here as any effort to disseminate one's name among constituents in such a fashion as to create a favorable image but in messages having little or no issue content. A successful congressman builds what amounts to a brand name, which may have a generalized electoral value for other politicians in the same family. The personal qualities to emphasize are experience, knowledge, responsiveness, concern, sincerity, independence, and the like. Just getting one's name across is difficult enough; only about half the electorate, if asked, can supply their House members' names. It helps a congressman to be known. "In the main, recognition carries a positive valence; to be perceived at all is to be perceived favorably." A vital advantage enjoyed by House incumbents is that they are much better known among voters than their November challengers. They are better known because they spend a great deal of time, energy, and money trying to make themselves better known. There are standard routines—frequent visits to the constituency, nonpolitical speeches to home audiences, the sending out of infant care booklets and letters of condolence and congratulation. . . .

Some routines are less standard. Congressman George E. Shipley (D., Ill.) claims to have met personally about half his constituents (i.e. some 200,000 people). For over twenty years Congressman Charles C. Diggs, Jr. (D., Mich.) has run a radio program featuring himself as a "combination disc jockey-commentator and minister." Congressman Daniel J. Flood (D., Pa.) is "famous for appearing unannounced and often uninvited at wedding anniversaries and other events." Anniversaries and other events aside, congressional advertising is done largely at public expense. Use of the franking privilege has mushroomed in recent years; in early 1973 one estimate predicted that House and Senate members would send out about 476 million pieces of mail in the year 1974, at a public cost of $38.1 million—or about 900,000 pieces per member with a subsidy of $70,000 per member. By far the heaviest mailroom traffic comes in Octobers of even-numbered years. There are some differences between House and Senate members in the ways they go about getting their names across. House members are free to blanket their constituencies with mailings for all boxholders; senators are not. But senators find it easier to appear on national television—for example, in short reaction statements on the nightly news shows. Advertising is a staple congressional activity, and there is no end to it. For each member there are always new voters to be apprised of his worthiness and old voters to be reminded of it.

A second activity may be called *credit claiming*, defined here as acting so as to generate a belief in a relevant political actor (or actors) that one is personally responsible for causing the government, or some unit thereof, to do something that the actor (or actors) considers desirable. The political logic of this, from the congressman's point of view, is that an actor who believes that a member can make pleasing things happen will no doubt wish to keep him in office so that he can make pleasing things happen in the future. The emphasis here is on individual accomplishment (rather than, say, party or governmental accomplishment) and on the congressman as doer (rather than as, say, expounder of constituency views). Credit claiming is highly important to congressmen, with the consequence that much of congressional life is a relentless search for opportunities to engage in it.

Where can credit be found? ... For the average congressman the staple way of doing this is to traffic in what may be called "particularized benefits." ...

In sheer volume the bulk of particularized benefits come under the heading of "casework"—the thousands of favors congressional offices perform for supplicants in ways that normally do not require legislative action. High school students ask for essay materials, soldiers for emergency leaves, pensioners for location of missing checks, local governments for grant information, and on and on. Each office has skilled professionals who can play the bureaucracy like an organ—pushing the right pedals to produce the desired effects. But many benefits require new legislation, or at least they require important allocative decisions on matters covered by existent legislation. Here the congressman fills the traditional role of supplier of goods to the home district. It is a believable role; when a member claims credit for a benefit on the order of a dam, he may well receive it. Shiny construction projects seem especially useful. ...

The third activity congressmen engage in may be called *position taking*, defined here as the public enunciation of a judgmental statement on anything likely to be of interest to political actors. The statement may take the form of a roll call vote. The most important classes of judgmental statements are those prescribing American governmental ends (a vote cast against the war; a statement that "the war should be ended immediately") or governmental means (a statement that "the way to end the war is to take it to the United Nations"). ...

The ways in which positions can be registered are numerous and often imaginative. There are floor addresses ranging from weighty orations to mass-produced "nationality day statements." There are speeches before home groups, television appearances, letters, newsletters, press releases, ghostwritten books, *Playboy* articles, even interviews with political scientists. ... Outside the roll call process the congressman is usually able to tailor his positions to suit his audiences. ...

... On a controversial issue a Capitol Hill office normally prepares two form letters to send out to constituent letter writers—one for the pros and one (not directly contradictory) for the antis. Handling discrete audiences in person requires simple agility, a talent well demonstrated in this selection from a Nader profile*:

"You may find this difficult to understand," said Democrat Edward R. Roybal, the Mexican-American representative from California's thirtieth district, "but sometimes I wind up making a patriotic speech one afternoon and later on that same day an anti-war speech. In the patriotic speech I speak of past wars but I also speak of the need to prevent more wars. My positions are not inconsistent; I just approach different people differently." Roybal went on to depict the diversity of crowds he speaks to: one afternoon he is surrounded by balding men wearing Veterans' caps and holding American flags; a few hours later he speaks to a crowd of Chicano youths, angry over American involvement in Vietnam. Such a diverse constituency, Roybal believes, calls for different methods of expressing one's convictions.

Indeed it does.

---

*Ralph Nader is a public-interest activist who has dedicated himself to protecting the American people against both governmental and private industry wrong-doing. One of Nader's best known campaigns came in the 1960s against General Motors, whose Chevrolet Corvair, Nader claimed, was "unsafe at any speed." In the 1996, 2000, 2004, and 2008 presidential elections, he ran as a third-party candidate.—Eds

23

RICHARD FENNO

From *Home Style*

Stated simply, political scientist Richard Fenno had a wonderful idea for a book. Instead of studying members of Congress at work in Washington, D.C., on the House floor, legislating, he researched them in what has always seemed their most obscure, out-of-the-spotlight moments. At home, in their districts, very little was known about legislators until Fenno's work. He opens with the psychological concept of "presentation of self," a technique designed to "win trust" from constituents. Fenno makes mention of the important "delegate" and "trustee" models of representation. Legislators do not explain every detail of their policy positions to the voters, rather, they want voters to trust them enough to allow them "voting leeway" back in Washington.

MOST HOUSE MEMBERS spend a substantial proportion of their working lives "at home." Even those in our low frequency category return to their districts more often than we would have guessed. Over half of that group go home more than once a month. What, then, do representatives do there? Much of what they do is captured by Erving Goffman's idea of *the presentation of self.* That is, they place themselves in "the immediate physical presence" of others and then "make a presentation of themselves to others." Goffman writes about the ordinary encounters between people "in everyday life." But, the dramaturgical analogues he uses fit the political world, too. Politicians, like actors, speak to and act before audiences from whom they must draw both support and legitimacy. Without support and legitimacy, there is no political relationship.

In all his encounters, says Goffman, the performer will seek to control the response of others to him by expressing himself in ways that leave the correct impressions of himself with others. His expressions will be of two sorts—"the expressions that he gives and the expression that he gives off." The first are mostly verbal; the second are mostly nonverbal. Goffman is particularly interested in the second kind of expression—"the more theatrical and contextual kind"—because he believes that the performer is more likely to be judged by others according to the nonverbal than the verbal elements of his presentation of self. Those who must do the judging, Goffman says, will think that the verbal expressions are more controllable and manipulable by the performer. And they will, therefore, read his nonverbal "signs" as a check on the reliability of his verbal "signs." Basic to this reasoning is the idea that, of necessity, every presentation has a largely "promissory character" to it. Those who listen and watch the presentation cannot be sure what the relationship between themselves and the performer really is. So the relationship must be sustained, on the part of those watching, by inference. They "must accept the individual on faith." In this process of acceptance, they will rely heavily on the inferences they draw from his nonverbal expressions—the expressions "given off."

Goffman does not talk about politicians; but politicians know what Goffman is talking about. The response they seek from others is political support. And the impressions they try to foster are those that will engender political support. House member politicians believe that a great deal of their support is won by the kind of individual self they present to others, i.e., to their constituents. More than most other people, they consciously try to manipulate it. Certainly, they believe that what they say, their verbal expression, is an integral part of their "self." But, with Goffman, they place special emphasis on the nonverbal, "contextual" aspects of their presentation. At the least, the nonverbal elements must be consistent with the verbal ones. At the most, the expressions "given off" will become the basis for constituent judgment. Like Goffman, members of Congress are willing to emphasize the latter because, with him, they believe that their constituents will apply a heavier discount to what they say than to how they say it or to how they act in the context in which they say it. In the members' own language, constituents want to judge you "as a person." The comment I have heard most often during my travels is: "he's a good man" or "she's a good woman," unembossed by qualifiers of any sort. Constituents, say House members, want to "size you up" or "get the feel of you" "as a person," or "as a human being." And the largest part of what House members mean when they say "as a person" is what Goffman means by expressions "given off." Largely from expressions given off comes the judgment: "he's a good man," "she's a good woman."

So members of Congress go home to present themselves as a person and to win the accolade: "he's a good man," "she's a good woman." With Goffman, they know there is a "promissory character" to their presentation. And their object is to present themselves as a person in such a way that the inferences drawn by those watching will be supportive. The representatives' word for these supportive inferences is *trust*. It is a word they use a great deal. When a constituent trusts a House member, the constituent is saying something like this: "I am willing to put myself in your hands temporarily; I know you will have opportunities to hurt me, although I may not know when those opportunities occur; I assume—and I will continue to assume until it is proven otherwise—that you will not hurt me; for the time being, then, I'm not going to worry about your behavior." The ultimate response House members seek is political support. But the instrumental response they seek is trust. The presentation of self—that which is given in words and given off as a person—will be calculated to win trust. "If people like you and trust you as individual," members often say, "they will vote for you." So trust becomes central to the representative-constituent relationship. For their part, constituents must rely on trust. They must "accept on faith" that the congressman is what he says he is and will do what he says he will do. House members, for their part, are quite happy to emphasize trust. It helps to allay the uncertainties they feel about their relationship with their supportive constituencies. If members are uncertain as to how to work for support directly, they can always work indirectly to win a degree of personal trust that will increase the likelihood of support or decrease the likelihood of opposition.

Trust is, however, a fragile relationship. It is not an overnight or a one-time thing. It is hard to win; and it must be constantly renewed and re-won. "Trust," said one member, "is a cumulative thing, a totality thing. . . . You do a little here and a little there." So it takes an enormous amount of time to build and to maintain constituent trust. That is what House members believe. And that is why they spend so much of their working time at home. Much of what I have observed in my travels can be explained as a continuous and continuing effort to win (for new members) and to hold (for old members) the trust of supportive constituencies. Most of the communication I have heard and seen is not overtly political at all. It is, rather, part of a ceaseless effort to reenforce the underpinnings of trust in the congressman or the congresswoman as a person. Viewed from this perspective, the archetypical constituent question is not "What have you done for me lately?" but "How have you looked to me lately?" In sum, House members make a strategic calculation that helps us understand why they go home so much. *Presentation of self enhances trust; enhancing trust takes time; therefore, presentation of self takes time. . . .*

Explaining Washington activity, as said at the outset, includes justifying that activity to one's constituents. The pursuit of power, for example, is sometimes justified with the argument that the representative accumulates power not for himself but for his constituents. In justifying their policy decisions, representatives sometimes claim that their policy decisions follow not what they want but what their constituents want. Recall the member who justified his decision not to support his own highway bill with the comment, "I'm not here to vote my own convictions. I'm here to represent my people." Similarly, the member who decided to yield to his constituent's wishes on gun control said, "I rationalize it by saying that I owe it to my constituents if they feel that strongly about it." But this is not a justification all members use. The independent, issue-oriented Judiciary Committee member mentioned earlier commented (privately) with heavy sarcasm,

All some House members are interested in is "the folks." They think "the folks" are the second coming. They would no longer do anything to displease "the folks" than they would fly. They spend all their time trying to find out what "the folks" want. I imagine if they get five letters on one side and five letters on the other side, they die.

An alternative justification, of course, is that the representative's policy decisions are based on what he thinks is good public policy, regardless of what his constituents want. As the Judiciary Committee member told his constituents often, "If I were sitting where you are, I think what I would want is to elect a man to Congress who will exercise his best judgment on the facts when he has them all." At a large community college gathering in the heart of his district, a member who was supporting President Nixon's Vietnam policy was asked, "If a majority of your constituents signed a petition asking you to vote for a date to end the war, would you vote for it?" He answered,

It's hard for me to imagine a majority of my constituents agreeing on anything. But if it did happen, then no, I would not vote for it. I would still have to use my own judgment—especially where the security of the country is involved. You can express opinions. I have to make the decision. If you disagree with my decisions, you have the power every two years to vote me out of office. I listen to you, believe me. But, in the end, I have to use my judgment as to what is in your best interests.

He then proceeded to describe his views on the substantive question.

To political scientists, these two kinds of policy justification are very familiar. One is a "delegate" justification, the other a "trustee" justification. The two persist side by side because the set of constituent attitudes on which each depends also exist side by side. Voters, that is, believe that members of Congress should follow constituents' wishes; and voters also believe that members of Congress should use their own best judgment. They want their representatives, it has been said, to be "common people of uncommon judgment." Most probably, though we do not know, voters want delegate behavior on matters most precious to them and trustee behavior on all others. Nonetheless, both kinds of justification are acceptable as a general proposition. Both are legitimate, and in explaining their

Washington activity members are seeking to legitimate that activity. They use delegate and trustee justifications because both are legitimating concepts.

If, when they are deciding how to vote, House members think in terms of delegates and trustees, it is because they are thinking about the terms in which they will explain (i.e., justify or legitimate) that vote back home if the need to do so arises. If members never had to legitimate any of their policy decisions back home, they would stop altogether talking in delegate or trustee language. . . .

Members elaborate the linkage between presentation and explanation this way: There are at most only a very few policy issues on which representatives are constrained in their voting by the views of their reelection constituencies. They may not *feel* constrained, if they agree with those views. But that is beside the point; they are constrained nevertheless. On the vast majority of votes, however, representatives can do as they wish—provided only that they can, when they need to, explain their votes to the satisfaction of interested constituents. The ability to get explanations accepted at home is, then, the essential underpinning of a member's voting leeway in Washington.

So the question arises: How can representatives increase the likelihood that their explanations will be accepted at home? And the answer House members give is: They can win and hold constituent trust. The more your various constituencies trust you, members reason, the less likely they are to require an explanation of your votes and the more likely they are to accept your explanation when they do ask for it. The winning of trust, we have said earlier, depends largely on the presentation of self. Presentation of self, then, not only helps win votes at election time. It also makes voting in Washington easier. So members of Congress make a strategic calculation: *Presentation of self enhances trust; trust enhances the acceptability of explanations; the acceptability of explanations enhances voting leeway; therefore, presentation of self enhances voting leeway.* . . .

The traditional focus of political scientists on the policy aspects of representation is probably related to the traditional focus on activity in the legislature. So long as concentration is on what happens in Washington, it is natural that policymaking will be thought of as the main activity of the legislature and representation will be evaluated in policy terms. To paraphrase Woodrow Wilson, it has been our view that Congress in Washington is Congress at work, while Congress at home is Congress on exhibition. The extrapolicy aspects of representational relationships have tended to be dismissed as symbolic—as somehow less substantial than the relationship embodied in a roll call vote in Washington—because what goes

on at home has not been observed. For lack of observation, political scientists have tended to downgrade home activity as mere errand running
or fence mending, as activity that takes the representative away from the
important things—that is, making public policy in Washington. As one
small example, the "Tuesday to Thursday Club" of House members who
go home for long weekends—have always been criticized out of hand, on
the assumption, presumably, that going home and doing things there was,
ipso facto, bad. But no serious inquiry was ever undertaken into what
they did there or what consequences—other than their obvious derelic-
tion of duty—their home activity might have had. Home activity has
been overlooked and denigrated and so, therefore, have those extra policy
aspects of representation which can only be studied at home.

Predictably, the home activities described in this book will be regarded by some readers as further evidence that members of Congress spend
too little of their time "on the job"—that is, in Washington, making policy. However, I hope readers will take from the book a different view—a
view that values both Washington and home activity. Further, I hope readers will entertain the view that Washington and home activities may even
be mutually supportive. Time spent at home can be time spent in developing leeway for activity undertaken in Washington. And that leeway in
Washington should be more valued than the sheer number of contact
hours spent there. If that should happen, we might then ask House members not to justify their time spent at home, but rather to justify their use
of the leeway they have gained therefrom—during the legislative process
in Washington. It may well be that a congressman's behavior in Washington is crucially influenced by the pattern of support he has developed at
home, and by the allocational, presentational, and explanatory styles he
displays there. To put the point most strongly, perhaps we can never understand his Washington activity without also understanding his perception of his various constituencies and the home style he uses to cultivate
their support. . . .

24

SARAH BINDER

From *Stalemate*

Writing in 2003, Sarah Binder identifies some reasons for congressional stalemate—gridlock—that became even more pronounced after the 2004 election. First, Binder draws distinctions between lack of legislative action and action based on compromise. She discusses divided government versus control of both houses of Congress and the presidency by the same party. Binder makes the important point that even when the same party controls both branches, stalemate can still happen. As the parties have become more extreme and distant from one another, compromise is less likely. America's bicameral legislature, too, contributes to stalemate. Finally, Binder touches on the Senate filibuster rule that requires a supermajority of 60 votes to end a filibuster as another reason for inaction. Binder's conclusion is that gridlock is a situation not easily remedied and perhaps intrinsic to the "unusual political times" we live in.

GRIDLOCK IS NOT a modern legislative condition. Although the term is said to have entered the American political lexicon after the 1980 elections, Alexander Hamilton complained more than two centuries ago about stalemate, at the time rooted in the design of the Continental Congress. In the very first *Federalist*, Hamilton bemoaned the "unequivocal experience of the inefficacy of the subsisting federal government" under the Articles of Confederation.

More than two hundred years later, innumerable critics of American politics still call for more responsive and effective government. The predominance of divided party government in recent decades disheartens many critics. They charge that divided government brings "conflict, delay, and indecision" and frequently leads to "deadlock, inadequate and ineffective policies, or no policies at all." . . .

In many ways, stalemate, a frequent consequence of separated institutions sharing and competing for power, seems endemic to American politics. Periods of lawmaking prowess are the exception, rather than the norm. When they occur, we give them enduring political labels, like the New Deal and the Great Society. Outside of these episodes of significant policy change, the frequency of gridlock varies considerably, variation that has attracted the attention of political observers and political scientists. In this book, I probe these trends in legislative performance, asking questions about the dynamics of lawmaking. How often does gridlock occur? What explains the historical ups and downs in policy stalemate? What are the consequences of Congress's uneven performance over time? How does legislative performance shape the ambitions of members of Congress, their electoral fortunes, and the reputation of the institution in which they serve? . . .

Why study policy gridlock? Normatively, exploring the causes of stalemate is important, regardless of one's party or ideology. Lawmaking is the process by which governments "legitimize substantive and procedural actions to reshape public problems, perhaps to resolve them." If we care about whether and when our political system is able to respond to problems both new and endemic to our common social, economic, and political lives, then explaining the conditions that underscore policy change and stability is a valuable and worthwhile endeavor.

Some might object that interest in gridlock implies a normative preference for legislative activism and liberal policy change. As Jefferson's maxim implies, "that government is best which governs least." If Jefferson was always right, then gridlock might always be a welcome feature of legislative politics. But views about gridlock tend to vary with one's political circumstance. Former Senate majority leader Bob Dole put it best: "If you're against something, you'd better hope there is a little gridlock." Because legislative activism can move the law in either a conservative or liberal direction, calls to end gridlock are not the exclusive province of liberal interests. In some respects, the confusion lies in the choice of words, as we often use the terms *gridlock, stalemate,* and *deadlock* to describe legislative inaction. In this book, I too refer to stalemate and gridlock, but more precisely I am exploring Congress's relative ability over time and issues to broach and secure policy compromise on issues high on the national agenda. Framed in this way, a study of legislative performance should interest any keen observer, participant, or student of national performance, regardless of her party or ideology. . . .

Unified party control of government cannot guarantee the compromise necessary for breaking deadlock in American politics. As David Mayhew has argued, looking solely at the *structural* component of the American political system—the separation of powers between Congress and the president—tends to obscure important dynamics in American lawmaking. As the analysis suggests, it is the *pluralist* component that deserves our more focused attention. The distributions of policy views within and across the two major political parties have predictable and important effects on the legislative performance of Congress and the president. The timing of party politics also matters. Long-frustrated congressional minorities often capitalize successfully on electoral mandates when their party gains unified control of Congress. Intrabranch politics, it seems, may be as important as the usual culprit of conflict between the branches. . . .

Two . . . other factors shaping Congress's policy performance command attention: the impact of parties and the consequences of bicameralism. First, consider party effects. My findings suggest that it is premature to reject the idea that political parties influence patterns of legislative outcomes. To be sure, the configuration of party control helps explain just a small portion of deadlock in contemporary politics. But . . . elections do more than divide control of the two major branches. Elections also determine the mix of ideologies within each major party. Such ideological divisions within the parties were decried in the 1950s by the "party government" school whose adherents believed that internal party divisions made it nearly impossible for the major parties to assemble and enact party agendas once they took office.

What is striking about the impact of parties in the latter half of the twentieth century is how strongly that impact differs from the expectations of the party government school. As the American Political Science Association's Committee on Political Parties argued in its often-cited 1950 report, cohesive political parties that offered distinctive choices to the electorate were critical for ensuring responsive and accountable government. The consequences of weak parties were steep: "The very heartbeat of democracy," the committee warned, was threatened by the state of the political parties. Democracy was contingent on organizing and responding to majorities, and cohesive parties were deemed the only viable instrument for doing so.

As the two parties have polarized and the political center has stretched thin over the recent past, little evidence indicates that legislative performance has risen in lockstep. Paradoxically, far from ensuring that voters will be given meaningful choices between competing party programs, the polarization of the parties seems to encourage deadlock. Why should polarization have this effect? One prominent scholar of Congress and electoral politics observes that legislators' desire to be responsive to active constituencies affects the incentive to compromise. "I do not think that one must be overcome by nostalgia," notes Morris P. Fiorina, "to imagine that Everett Dirksen, Mike Mansfield, John McCormack, and Gerald Ford [House and Senate party leaders in the 1960s and 1970s] would have found some common ground and acted. Many of today's leaders, however, would rather have issues to use in the upcoming election than accomplishments to point to." There may be a personal element to these temporal differences in leadership styles, but more likely the differences reflect changes in the makeup and activities of contemporary parties, as party organizations are increasingly defined by issue activists, constituency groups, and large-scale financial contributors with pointed policy and ideological agendas. With limited electoral ties to the mass and moderate middle, legislators have only limited and occasional incentive to craft moderate policy compromises to public problems. The statistical evidence ... backs up this impression: the larger the political center and the less polarized the Congress, the greater the prospects for measurable policy compromise and change. Parties do affect Congress's capacity to legislate but not strictly according to whether their control is unified or divided.

Bicameralism is perhaps the most critical structural factor shaping the politics of gridlock. Bicameralism—rather than the separation of power between executive and legislative branches—seems most relevant in explaining stalemate in the postwar period. To be sure, both the separation of powers and bicameralism were central to the framers' late-eighteenth-century beliefs about the proper construction of political institutions. Still, with important recent exceptions, the policy consequences of divided government, not bicameralism, feature prominently in theoretical and empirical treatments of legislative gridlock.

Bicameral differences arise of course because structural differences between House and Senate elections ensure that policy views will not be distributed and aggregated identically in the two chambers. Even when both chambers are controlled by the same party, we cannot assume that the two chambers desire the same policy outcomes. The impact of bicameral differences can be seen clearly in the fate of a patients' bill of rights measure in the 106th Congress (1999-2000). Although both chambers passed a version of the bill with the support of Republican majorities, no final agreement emerged from conference negotiations that took place over several months in mid- to late 2000. As one House Republican observed in trying to explain the bicameral impasse, "Just appreciate the fact that Republicans in the House and Senate sometimes have a gulf as large if not larger than some Republicans and Democrats." The looming presence of a Democratic president ready to veto a bill deemed too responsive to the health insurance industry certainly influenced the Republicans' negotiating strategy, as they probably preferred no bill to the more moderate House bill that the president would have signed. But ideological differences between the two chambers also precluded policy compromise, no matter the views of the president. Given median Senate Republican preferences, Senate Republicans had little incentive to compromise with House Republicans in pursuit of a moderate agreement.

Some speculated that the chief Senate Republican negotiator, Don Nickles of Oklahoma, would move closer to the more moderate House bill if vulnerable Republican senators seeking re-election in 2000 could convince Nickles of the electoral imperative to compromise with the House and pass a bill. Despite some senators' efforts to persuade Nickles, no such compromise toward the House bill occurred. As it turned out, this mattered little to the Democrats, as bicameral negotiations were taking place in the run-up to the tightly contested 2000 presidential election. "For us, it's a win-win," explained Senator Minority Leader Tom Daschle (D-S.D.). "We win if we don't get a bill, politically. We win politically and legislatively if we do get a bill." Not only did bicameral differences limit the feasibility of reaching a conference agreement, the polarization of the parties and the electoral rewards of doing nothing limited the incentive to compromise.

The persistence of bicameral effects across the postwar period also sheds some light on the impact of divided and unified government on legislative performance. Spurred by Mayhew's unconventional finding about the limited impact of divided government, recent studies have re-examined "unified gridlock," stalemate that occurs when a single party controls both chambers of Congress and the White House. Most often fingered as potential causes of unified gridlock are supermajority institutions that limit the policymaking capacity of political parties: procedural rules that require three-fifths majorities to limit debate in the Senate in face of a filibuster and constitutional rules that require a two-thirds majority to override a presidential veto. Because presidential vetoes are rare under unified government, I focus on the impact of the Senate filibuster. A recent and compelling argument is that because a supermajority is needed to pass major policy change in the Senate, the majority party's ability to secure policy outcomes favored by its party median is limited. Thus one cannot predict major policy change based on the policy views of the median legislator of the chamber and the majority party. Instead, the views of the sixtieth senator—the senator whose assent is required to invoke cloture and break a filibuster—are pivotal.

However, the severity of the filibuster threat showed little effect on the frequency of deadlock once bicameral differences and party polarization and control were taken into account. Are interchamber differences a more proximate cause of stalemate than supermajority Senate constraints? . . .

Gridlock under unified government may have more to do with differences between the majority party's House and Senate contingents than with supermajority constraints imposed by Senate rules. . . .

. . . If the frequency of deadlock is largely a function of bicameral differences and polarization of the parties, then Congress's legislative performance is a simple function of electoral outcomes and the evolution of constitutional design. There is little that legislators can do to reduce the barriers to legislative stalemate they typically encounter. Legislators can only wait out electoral change that bolsters the presence of moderates and accept the reality of bicameralism. We cannot engineer electoral outcomes, so we should learn to live with gridlock. In a sense, this perspective commits us to accepting the conventional wisdom about the intentions of the framers: legislative inaction was one of their key goals, and thus they designed a political system of checks and balances that would slow down and often thwart efforts to enact major changes in public law.

I think there is some value to interpreting the causes of stalemate in another way. . . .

It is fair to say that legislators today toil in somewhat unusual political times. The decline of the political center has produced a political environment that more often than not gives legislators every incentive not to reach agreement. There are steady partisan and ideological pressures on members not to compromise on firmly held positions. Legislators also work in a remarkably public environment, are followed by an intensely negative media, and face a revolution in communications technology that grants little time or space for methodical deliberation. Legislators also often face an agenda that requires imposing losses rather than distributing benefits, as the promise of budget surpluses has given way to economic downturns, tax cuts, and politicians' unwillingness to spend from Social Security reserves. . . .

To be sure, the notion of "fixing gridlock" can be troubling. One person's stalemate is another's preferred legislative outcome. In the polarized and polarizing era that legislators inhabit today, it is doubtful that true differences over desirable ends and means can or should always be negotiated away. But neither can we depend on the emergence of cohesive political parties to resolve recurring episodes of gridlock, as we see now that the faith of party government scholars in disciplined parties was misplaced: gridlock only increases as the political center recedes.

25

GREGORY WAWRO
ERIC SCHICKLER

From *Filibuster*

No feature of the U.S. Senate is more important to understanding the inner workings of the chamber than the filibuster. Every senator is allowed to debate a bill or a nomination for an unlimited amount of time, or at least until a supermajority of three-fifths of the Senate votes to end debate. While the filibuster is a custom of the Senate and not a consitutional provision, framer James Madison would approve: an individual or a minority can be heard, protecting them from the majority's power. Gregory Wawro and Eric Schickler explain the origin of the filibuster as well as the cloture rule to end a filibuster. The authors then present a case study of the use of the filibuster in the mid-2000s, when President George W. Bush nominated conservative federal judges whose nominations were filibustered by Democratic senators. Supermajorities, the "nuclear option," the vice president's tie-breaking role, and even cots for an all-night session are all part of Wawro's and Schickler's account; then fourteen senators, both Democrats and Republicans, engineered a compromise. One of the fourteen, Senator John McCain said, "If we don't protect the rights of the minority . . . if you had a liberal president, and a Democrat-controlled Senate, I think that it could do great damage." Enough said. The Senate filibuster offers a possible last refuge for the minority.

———

NO ACTIVITY IN THE UNITED STATES CONGRESS captures the attention of political practitioners, pundits, and the public like filibustering in the Senate. The issue of filibusters has tremendous power to get ink for editorial columns flowing and to rouse even the most somnolent students in lectures on Congress. Perhaps this has something to do with fundamental conflicting concerns about the principles of majority rule and minority rights. Perhaps it is simply that filibusters make good political theater, inducing nostalgia for the days when politics was more of a contact sport. Indeed, it is a supreme irony that some of the loftiest democratic ideals like freedom of speech and minority rights are protected through astonishingly ignoble and bare-knuckle behavior. Whatever the reason, the filibuster is deeply ingrained in the political culture of the United States. Case in point: the word "filibuster" appears on a recently produced list of 100 words that is intended to provide a benchmark by which high school students (and their parents) can measure their command of the English language.... [If] a given person knows anything about the U.S. Congress, they will most likely know that senators can filibuster. Chances are they will know little beyond that, but even well-read students of American politics typically know only the most superficial details about the filibuster and its history....

Yet this lack of attention does not appear to be due to the belief that the filibuster is unimportant or irrelevant to understanding lawmaking.... "The filibuster permeates virtually all senatorial decision making." The principle of unlimited debate and the obstruction that it allows has been a defining feature of the Senate throughout most of its history. Senator Robert Byrd is worth quoting at length on this point:

We must not forget that the right of extended, even unlimited, debate is the main cornerstone of the Senate's uniqueness. It is also a primary reason that the United States Senate is the most powerful upper chamber in the world today....Without the right of unlimited debate, of course, there would be no filibusters, but there would also be no Senate, as we know it.... Filibusters are a necessary evil, which must be tolerated lest the Senate lose its special strength and become a mere appendage of the House of Representatives. If this should happen, which God avert, the American Senate would cease to be "that remarkable body" about which William Ewart Gladstone spoke—"the most remarkable of all the inventions of modern politics."...

The rules of the Senate have been viewed as important not only because of their effect on the internal dynamics of the institution, but also because of their larger ramifications for the operation of the separation of powers system. [One scholar] in arguing that the Senate does "its most notable work" as "a critic of the executive," claimed that "complete freedom of debate and the absence of closure except as a real emergency" are "indispensable" to the Senate's role as a counterpoise to the president. Indeed, in a public relations campaign against senatorial obstruction, Vice President Charles Dawes compared the filibuster with the president's main weapon in inter-branch bargaining, averring that the filibuster "places in the hands of one or of a minority of Senators a greater power than the veto power exercised under the Constitution by the President of the United States, which is limited in its effectiveness by the necessity of an affirmative two-thirds votes."...

Although unlimited debate in the Senate has been roundly praised as an essential component of American democracy, usually by those who have benefited from it the most, the filibuster has also been blamed by many for stalling essential legislation and violating the basic democratic value of majority rule. While in one person's view the filibuster is a protection against majority tyranny, others view it as a device of tyrannical minorities.

If anything, the lack of limits on debate has become more relevant to the uniqueness of the Senate today than it was in the early years of the institution. . . . The Senate's rules that protect unlimited debate and effectively require supermajorities* for the passage of legislation were not part of the Framers' blueprint for the Senate. Nevertheless, these rules are consistent, at least in principle, with their conception of the Senate as a bulwark protecting minorities and as a brake on precipitate action. Perhaps ironically, the rules remain as protections while other institutional safeguards the Framers put into place have become enervated or have disappeared with the passage of time. If anything, Senate rules and practices concerning unlimited debate have become *more* important as the Senate has evolved. . . .

. . . [W]hy does supermajority rule persist in the Senate? One plausible answer is the stickiness of inherited institutions. . . . [It] would require a two-thirds majority to defeat a filibuster of a rules change providing for majority cloture, essentially dooming reform absent an overwhelming majority. As long as at least one-third of senators perceive that eliminating obstruction will lead to policies that they oppose being enacted, supermajority rule will persist.

Inherited institutions are undoubtedly important, but their stickiness itself is not a complete explanation for the refusal of the Senate to move toward majority rule. . . . [A] committed majority could use new precedents to eliminate the tactics available to obstructionists. As we discuss below, such a strategy would entail substantial risks and costs—and the 1917 cloture rule, by codifying a procedure for overcoming filibusters, likely increased those costs. Nonetheless, a simple majority of the Senate with the cooperation of a sympathetic presiding officer could curb obstruction. Thus, the striking feature of Senate history is that such a committed majority has *never* been manifested. Since there have repeatedly been floor majorities that have seen their short-term policy preferences stymied by obstruction, this lack of support for majority cloture cannot be attributed simply to members' immediate policy goals. Instead, bids to eliminate the filibuster in the contemporary Senate run up against indi-

---

*A supermajority refers to a number of votes greater than a majority needed to take an action in Congress. The Constitution contains provisions for certain supermajorities—two-thirds of each house to override a presidential veto, two-thirds of the Senate to ratify a treaty, two-thirds of the Senate to convict an impeached president, for example—but the three-fifths (60) supermajority needed to end a Senate filibuster is a long-standing rule of the Senate, not a constitutional requirement. Sixty votes for cloture means that the majority party needs not just fifty-one but sixty votes to end debate.—EDS.

vidual senators' personal power goals. The right of unlimited debate makes each senator a more prominent player on the national political stage. . . . [S]enators use filibusters to make a name for themselves with donors, interest groups, and constituents. They threaten obstruction to extract concessions of all sorts from the White House and bill proponents. Even as costless filibustering eviscerates the potential informational value of obstruction, it makes the filibuster an even more valuable tool for individualistic senators in an era of candidate-centered elections.

At the same time, the contemporary context of sharp party polarization and narrow majorities in the Senate heightens the potential damage wrought by the filibuster to the majority party's legislative agenda. The prospects of moving toward majority rule will depend ultimately on whether the frustration of the majority party's agenda will become so troublesome that a floor majority will be motivated to bear the risks, uncertainty, and personal power costs of undertaking what has come to be known as the "nuclear option"—that is, eliminating minority rights through that venerable stratagem of rulings from the chair.* Recent battles concerning judicial nominations lead us to expect that demands for majority cloture will only increase as partisan polarization persists. Thus far, enough minority senators have shown the willingness to compromise when confronted with the "nuclear" threat. But it is plausible that the space for compromise will vanish when confronted with a series of high-profile Supreme Court appointments in a political environment of intense interest group mobilization. . . .

In the 109th Congress [2005–2006], the debate over judicial nominees and the Senate's rules consumed Washington to a degree that matches some of the fiercest and most dramatic filibuster fights. Although the Republicans' initial attempt to publicize the obstruction of the judicial nominees through the 108th Congress's all-night session fell more or less flat, the issue took on much greater salience in the following Congress. [President George W.] Bush renominated seven of the filibustered nominees, setting the stage for a showdown. The debate eventually shifted from one about whether the Republicans could invoke the nuclear option to whether they would. Procedurally, there were several different scenarios under which the Republicans could impose majority cloture on judicial nominees. All of these involved violation of past precedents to a degree, but Republicans seemed to be more than willing to undertake them. The real question was whether or not the Republicans had the necessary majority to win key votes on rulings from the chair.

*With the vice president presiding over the Senate, a vote of fifty-one senators could, in theory, remove the 60-vote cloture rule permanently.—EDS.

Senate leaders elevated the issue to the top of the agenda, and the mass media devoted significant column space and air time to the filibuster and the nuclear option. Liberal and conservative groups became involved to a much greater degree, helping to escalate the rhetoric and intensify the controversy. Leaders of conservative groups sent a clear signal that their support of [then Senate majority leader, Dr. Bill] Frist's presidential ambitions (and those of other Republican hopefuls) were tied to the confirmation of the judges.... [A]udience costs for backing down seemed to be central to the dynamics of the conflict.... Democratic and Republican leaders preferred confrontation to compromise because they would be penalized by their allied interest groups should they be seen as caving in.

Although none of the nominations in question were brought to the floor until May 2005, the conflict over them took on a war-of-attrition-like quality. Each side expended resources to convince the other and the public that their position was the right one, hoping that the other side would relent. As the conflict came to a boil, it remained unclear whether Frist had the votes to succeed in his efforts to end the filibuster. He did not appear to have the support of moderates Susan Collins (R–ME), Olympia Snowe (R–ME), Lincoln Chafee (R–RI), and maverick John McCain (R–AZ). A few other Republicans, such as Chuck Hagel (R–NE) and John Warner (R–VA), were non-committal, expressing concern about the long-term impact on the functioning of the Senate. Vice President Dick Cheney stated that he would support Frist's efforts, meaning that Frist needed only 50 votes (if everyone voted) to invoke the nuclear option since Cheney would break the tie in addition to issuing the necessary rulings.... Both sides claimed the other lacked the necessary votes, but it was clear that a vote on the nuclear option would have been extremely close. Much of the posturing seemed to be aimed at convincing wavering Republicans that the votes were there and that it would look bad for them to have broken with their party only to end up on the losing side.

As the Senate prepared for another all-night session on May 23 [2005]—complete with cots set up in the Capitol—the conflict was defused, at least temporarily, by an eleventh-hour compromise agreement entered into by a group of fourteen senators. The "Memorandum of Understanding on Judicial Nominations" explicitly stated that the Democratic signatories would vote to invoke cloture on three nominees—Priscilla Owen, Janice Rogers Brown, and William Pryor. It made no promises about two other contested nominees, William G. Myers III, and Henry Saad, presumably dooming their chances of reaching the bench. In exchange, the Republican signatories would oppose "any amendments to or interpretation of the Rules of the Senate that would force a vote on a judicial nomination by means other than unanimous consent or Rule XXII" in the 109th Congress. The agreement stated that "nominees should only be filibustered under extraordinary circumstances, and each signatory must use his or her own discretion and judgment in determining whether such circumstances exist." The agreement also sent a clear signal to President Bush about the privileged role of senators in the nomination process, encouraging him to consult with senators from both parties prior to submitting nominees to the Senate.

The nuclear threat had succeeded in gaining important concessions from the Democrats. Owen, Brown, and Pryor were regarded by the Democrats—and their interest group allies—as extremists who would provide conservatives with enhanced control of several appeals courts. Yet the deal had prevented the imposition of majority rule. Thus, as it has in every previous instance when the prospect of imposing de jure majority rule through precedents was on the table, the Senate balked. A key question is why a clear majority did not emerge in support of Frist's maneuver. An important strategic consideration for senators concerned the Democrats' response to the execution of the nuclear option and what the impact of such a move would have on individual senators' personal power goals. Democrats threatened to respond with full parliamentary force to an attempt to use rulings from the chair to curtail filibusters of judicial nominations, using every weapon in their arsenal to bring all nonessential work in the chamber to a halt. . . . Indeed the widespread legislative destruction Frist's maneuver would unleash is in part why the approach is referred to as the nuclear option. At a time when the parties are highly polarized and seats in the Senate are almost evenly split between parties, the supermajority requirements in the Senate are the most potent resource the Democrats [then in the minority] possess to stop the Republicans [then in the majority] from rolling them on key agenda items. . . .

With control of the Senate shifting back and forth between the parties in the past decade, senators are highly uncertain about whether they will be in the partisan majority or minority during their careers. In any case, even majority party members have regularly used their extensive prerogatives to affect policy and increase their individual importance in the political system. This suggests a significant role for inherited institutions, but one that is more complex than the suggestion that preexisting rules block the majority from ending obstruction. Instead, a floor majority has the capacity to curtail minority rights, but doing so will involve substantial costs and uncertainties that the floor majority must be willing to bear. The heaviest is the concern that senators will be eliminating a weapon they would want to employ in future legislative or nomination battles. For example, John McCain expressed his concerns by stating, "If we don't protect the rights of the minority . . . if you had a liberal president and a Democrat-controlled Senate, I think that it could do great damage." Fighting back against a minority's efforts to paralyze the institution would most likely require a more extensive clamping down on individual prerogatives, which exacerbates concerns about the long-term effects of the crackdown once today's majority finds itself in the minority. . . .

The increased polarization of the Senate has cast the impact of the filibuster in sharper relief. Polarization and narrow majorities require that more substantial concessions (often painful to core constituencies) need to be made on policy in order to bridge the ideological divide between senators in the two parties. This need to compromise may, in practice, enhance the extent to which Senate outcomes reflect the public's views. Opinion polls show that senators are more polarized than the general public. If the Senate median is more extreme than the median voter in the polity, supermajority requirements can prevent the movement of policies away from the more moderate preferences of ordinary citizens.

Even if one concedes that the filibuster has not paralyzed the Senate and rendered it unable to govern, one must still consider whether supermajority procedures are consistent with the Constitution, especially in light of their exploitation to block judicial nominees. Some have argued that the Constitution implies that only a majority is necessary for those items where a supermajority was not specified as necessary. Therefore, they conclude that the obstruction of judicial nominees, which has translated into a supermajority requirement for confirmation, is unconstitutional. Yet the Constitution also allows the Senate to decide its own rules and does not restrict the Senate from adopting supermajority requirements for any decisions not explicitly specified in the founding document. We have argued that a majority of senators could eliminate supermajority requirements through rulings of the chair, but the bottom line is that a majority of the Senate has never fully committed to going to this extreme. The binding constraint precluding a revolution to date in the 109th Congress is that Republicans have not been able to garner a floor majority for this approach, suggesting that remote majoritarianism still exists concerning Senate rules. True, a majority may not have formed because it would be afraid of what a minority would do in response, but that is a question of preferences regarding policy and not constitutional principles. The majority could fully clamp down on the minority as was done in the House over a century ago, but to do so would likely require a majority of senators to agree to give up the wellspring of their power by curtailing the right of recognition and other prerogatives. At this moment, an insufficient number of senators seem willing to start down the path that would lead to quotidian majority rule. As a result, much like the Senate of the 19th century, today's Senate continues to accord the minority the opportunity to stand in the way of the majority.

Beyond constitutional concerns, one might also question whether supermajority rule is consistent with basic norms of democratic governance. When one considers the severe malapportionment of the Senate with respect to population, however, it is problematic to assume that a move toward majority rule within the institution would help the representation of majority views within the electorate. The diverse, heterogeneous nature of the American electorate adds to the justification for incorporating hurdles that encourage today's majority to consider the views of minority interests. Finally, from a separation of powers standpoint, supermajority rule in the Senate is one of the few remaining barriers to presidential dominance in a context of highly polarized parties and unified control of Congress and the presidency.

26

MICHELE SWERS

From *The Difference Women Make*

The "difference women make" in the House of Representatives and the Senate, scholar Michele Swers finds, is a big difference. Using many examples of female legislators from the past decade, Swers discusses both the way women candidates campaign and the way women in Congress reflect their gender through the views they hold. Female legislators have become important spokespeople for both Democrats and Republicans on a variety of issues. Votes, of course, lie at the core of the parties' goal of attracting women supporters. Swers stresses that beyond just supporters, women legislators bring to congressional issues a distinctive point of view that goes beyond party and politics. In the years after Swers completed her research, the role of women in Congress has continued to grow. Note that Nancy Pelosi (D-CA), cited as a party whip in this selection, became the Democratic leader in the House and in 2007, the Speaker of the House.

━━━━━

ON OCTOBER 20, 1999, a group of largely Democratic women took to the floor of the House of Representatives to support an amendment by Congresswoman Patsy Mink (D-HI) that would restore funding for gender equity programs to a Republican bill reauthorizing parts of the 1965 Elementary and Secondary Schools Education Act. As evidence of the continuing need for gender equity programs, Congresswoman Stephanie Tubbs Jones (D-OH) cited women's underrepresentation in Congress. She proclaimed, "Women need to be encouraged to be right here on the floor ... they need to think about how can we be here on the floor of the U.S. Congress talking about issues that impact the entire country and only fifty-seven of us are women."

Congresswoman Tubbs Jones's comments imply that electing more women to Congress will not just achieve equality but also influence the range of issues considered on the national agenda and the formulation of policy solutions. She is not alone in her belief that electing more women will have a substantive policy impact. Numerous women's Political Action Committees (PACs) raise money to elect liberal or conservative women candidates. For example, the Women in Senate and House (WISH) List raises money for pro-choice Republican women, while the Susan B. Anthony List supports pro-life women. In the 2000 election cycle, Early

Money Is Like Yeast's (EMILY's) List raised $21,201,339 to support pro-choice, Democratic women, thus making it one of the leading fundraisers among all PACs. Some women candidates even point to their gender as one of the reasons voters should elect them. Announcing her candidacy for the Senate in 1998, Blanche Lambert Lincoln (D-AR) proclaimed that she was running because "nearly one of every three senators is a million-aire, but there are only five mothers." Similarly, Patty Murray (D-WA) launched her 1992 Senate campaign as "just a mom in tennis shoes." . . .

How important is it to have a Congress that "looks like America"? Do we need more women as mothers in Congress? Do we need more wom-en as women? . . .

. . . [M]any Democratic and moderate Republican women claim that they do feel a special responsibility to represent women in their commit-tee work, and they do lobby male committee leaders to take into account a policy's potential impact on women. For example, Marge Roukema (R-NJ) explained: "But I have to tell you, when I got to Washington, I found that some of the 'women's issues—the family issues'—weren't be-ing addressed by the men in power. Things like child-support enforce-ment and women's health issues and family safety issues. It wasn't that the men were opposed to these issues—they just didn't get it. They were not sufficiently aware of them. So I realized, in many important areas—if we women in government don't take action, no one else will."

Additionally, in interviews, both Democratic and Republican men and women expressed the belief that women and minorities bring a dif-ferent perspective to the policy process, and it is important to have these groups at the decision-making table. Many of the Republican and Demo-cratic women who have held party leadership posts also feel a sense of responsibility to represent women. For example, in her congressional memoir, Susan Molinari (R-NY) claimed that she used her position as vice-chair of the Republican conference to act as "the party's champion of women's issues." At the height of the budget-cutting battles of the 104th Congress, she convinced the leadership to increase funding for pro-grams to combat violence against women. When other members rolled their eyes at her suggestions for new women's initiatives, Speaker Gin-grich backed her and reminded male members that they could not win the next election without the votes of women. Similarly, in the 103rd Congress, Louise Slaughter (D-NY) used her position on the leadership-controlled Rules Committee to make sure the Freedom of Access to Abortion Clinic Entrances Act was placed on the House calendar before the end of the session and to push a favorable rule through a committee whose members were largely pro-life. Barbara Kennelly (D-CT), who served as a chief deputy whip in the 102nd (1991-92) and 103rd (1993-94) Congresses and conference vice-chair in the 104th (1995-96) Congress, said that "women have a different perspective and you need women to be in the room to make sure it is heard. I worked on women and children's issues over and above committee work, constituent service, and case work."

While both Democratic and Republican women agree that it is important to have women at the table because females bring a different perspective to policy making, Democratic women are more willing to challenge their party leadership explicitly and demand that women be considered for positions because of their gender. According to one Republican staffer, "Republican women do not overtly promote themselves as women" or argue "that we need more women, . . . the Republican Party in general sees a need but it is not overly stated." . . .

On the Democratic side, the more liberal ideological views espoused by the Democratic Party incline members of the caucus to arguments based explicitly on the need for diversity. For example, throughout her campaign to replace David Bonior as whip when he retires in January 2002, Nancy Pelosi maintained that women "deserve a seat at the leadership table." She also argued that her election would allow the party to bring a "fresh face" to the public and would increase the party's advantage with women voters. . . .

Although seniority rules have slowed congresswomen's rise to positions of power in the committees and party leadership, partisan concerns over the potential impact of the gender gap have facilitated women's efforts to raise their profile within their respective party caucuses and to take the lead on gendered issues. Since Republicans seized control of Congress from the Democrats in 1994, they have lost House seats in each succeeding election, and in the 107th Congress their majority control rests on only a six-seat margin. In an era of such tight party competition, party leaders make extra efforts to develop and advertise policy proposals that will attract specific groups of voters and, therefore, both parties are targeting women voters. Although the gender gap is small, women have slightly favored the Democrats since the late 1960s. The gender gap widened in 1996, when 54 percent of women supported Bill Clinton in contrast to only 43 percent of men and when the media focused on the voting behavior of the "soccer mom." Additionally, in 1996, more women voted than men—with 56 percent of women turning out to vote compared to 53 percent of men. The higher turnout among women helped Democrats reclaim House seats in 1996 and 1998. While the Florida recount and the divergence between the popular and Electoral College votes made the 2000 elections a unique historical event, the gender gap continued at the same magnitude, as Al Gore received 12 percent more votes from women than from men. Similarly, across the country, women favored Democratic House candidates, creating a nine-point gender gap, and women helped elect more Democratic women to the Senate.

In response to these trends, Democrats are designing their policy proposals and public appeals with an eye toward maintaining women's support, while Republicans actively work to expand their appeal among women. To achieve these goals, party leaders have increasingly turned to women to act as spokespersons on women's, children's, and family issues and to take a leading role in legislative battles on women's issues. As one Republican congressman complained, "The Democrats will do whatever they can to expand the gender gap." Democratic members and staffers agreed that the party does encourage women to be out in front at press conferences, presidential bill-signing ceremonies, and floor debate on women's issues. As one Democratic staffer explained the dynamic, "The parties are sensitive to the gender gap so they want to appeal to women, children, and family issues. As long as the parties focus on these issues to capture the women's vote, it helps women in office who can be leaders on these issues."

The debates over gun control during the 106th Congress highlight the Democratic strategy. A series of high-profile school shootings brought the issue of gun control back into the public spotlight. Democratic Party polling demonstrated that women care more about gun control legislation than men do and that women are more likely to let their votes be influenced by a candidate's position on gun control. Therefore, Democrats began framing their discussions of gun control in terms of child safety rather than crime, with the presumption that the phrase will resonate especially strongly with women voters. Three Democratic Congresswomen, Carolyn McCarthy (D-NY), Nita Lowey (D-NY), and Assistant Minority Leader Rosa DeLauro (D-CT), took the lead in organizing press conferences, lobbying colleagues, and counting votes to limit Democratic defectors and to attract Republican support for the McCarthy-Roukema Amendment, which would add gun control provisions to a juvenile justice bill. As the congresswomen explained, they "stepped to the foreground of an issue they had long been passionate about and party leaders almost immediately encouraged them to stay there." Indeed, the murder of her husband and injury of her son in a mass shooting on the Long Island Railroad propelled Congresswoman McCarthy to run for office in the first place. After the House defeated the McCarthy-Roukema Amendment in June 1999, the Democratic women organized a floor protest by lining up to make procedural requests to revise and extend their remarks. In the weeks following the amendment's defeat, Democratic congress-women used the unconstrained floor time provided by the period for one-minute speeches at the opening of the legislative day to read the names of children who had been killed as a result of gun violence.

As Democrats turn to congresswomen to expand their support among women voters, Republicans, particularly in the 104th Congress, deploy women in a more defensive manner. Discussing her role as conference vice-chair, Susan Molinari described one of her duties as "putting the friendly face on Republican issues," particularly when Republicans feared that Democrats and President Clinton would portray their policies as un-friendly to women in the battle for public opinion. Another Republican staffer close to the leadership explained that "the Republican leaders will ask women to speak when they know the Democrats will have their women out to demagogue an issue. By having women speak at a press conference or in the floor debate, they get women to put a smiley, soft face on issues and prevent Republicans from looking like mean ogres. This happened most often in the 104th and 105th Congresses on welfare reform and other Contract with America items. In the 106th, they [Re-publicans] have not introduced much extreme legislation. They are not trying to dismantle departments or overhaul social legislation." . . .

Other legislators and staffers explained that, in an effort to narrow the gender gap, Republicans also actively seek out women's issue bills that will improve their standing with women and draw attention away from abortion. As a result, party and committee leaders, often prodded by Re-publican women, have advanced proposals on such issues as breast cancer, child abuse, violence against women, adoption, and foster care. Since the 104th Congress, Republicans have also made efforts to repackage tradi-tional Republican policies on taxes and other fiscal issues in ways that will attract women. In the 105th and 106th Congresses, Republicans courted women by seeking legislation to eliminate the marriage penalty and pro-tect innocent spouses, often divorced women, who are liable for tax debts resulting from the actions of their former spouses. Jennifer Dunn (R-WA), who leads Republican efforts to bridge the gender gap, utilizes press con-ferences and public speeches to explain how tax issues affect women. Her congressional Web site includes a special section for women that lists Re-publican accomplishments on behalf of women and explains how issues like estate taxes disproportionately affect women since, on average, they outlive men. . . .

For the political parties, the crafting of the strategy to sell a policy to the public is as important as the content. Thus, both Democratic and Republican leaders are looking for policies to attract women voters, and they turn to congresswomen to help promote those policies. This concern with the gender gap provides Democratic and Republican women with an opportunity to advance policies related to women's interests, raise their public profiles, and attain power within their party caucuses. Interest groups and individual legislators from both parties seek out women to sponsor or cosponsor gender-related legislation not simply because they have expertise in a particular area but also because they want to connect themselves to the symbolic moral authority these women have as women and/or as mothers.

On the House floor and in press conferences, party leaders rely on women as spokespersons and political symbols in their effort to demonstrate that their party is protecting women's interests. Thus, Democratic leaders turn to their congresswomen to expand the party's traditional advantage with female voters by promoting Democratic initiatives on women's issues and branding Republican policies as antifamily and antiwomen. Similarly, Republicans utilize Republican women to combat Democratic efforts to paint their proposals as hurting women. Republican women also craft messages to explain how traditional Republican issues, such as tax cuts, will benefit women. By speaking out on behalf of their party, female legislators raise their own public profile and collect favors that they can use to advance their positions within the party conference, attain support for favored policy initiatives, or gain leeway to defect from their party's position on another issue. . . .

In the final analysis, understanding how politically significant social identities have an impact on the legislative behavior of representatives is not simply a matter of raw numbers in the legislature. The interplay of presence and power is complex. In the case of gender, the unique policy interests of women provide substantive support to those who call for the inclusion of more women in the cabinet choices of presidents and governors and the leadership ranks of Congress and the state legislatures. Electing women has important consequences for the quality of our representational system, thus making the call for more diversity in Congress more than a mere platitude. Presence, however, is only a first step. Power in Congress also depends on access to influential positions within the institution that allow members to exercise strategic influence over the shape of policy outcomes.

27

RICHARD FENNO

From *Going Home*

Congressman Chaka Fattah is an influential member of the House of Representatives. In this excerpt, renowned scholar Richard Fenno tells readers how he reached his position, beginning with his days growing up in Philadelphia. Fenno's informal interviews with Fattah reveal much about his campaign strategy, his style of representing his Philadelphia district, and his legislative priorities. His emphasis on influencing policy and achieving goals motivates Fattah as a legislator, Fenno finds. Fattah's constituents, both black and white, are firmly behind him, making the district "a comfortable fit" for the congressman. Fattah recounts his desire in the late 1990s to move from the Education Committee where he had become an expert on school equity, to the Appropriations Committee. As an active member of the Congressional Black Caucus and a good money-raiser, Fattah hoped for a seat. It took two attempts, but eventually, Fattah did land a seat on Appropriations, while continuing his commitment to legislation on educational reform. Fenno's visits with the congressman back in his district make it clear why Chaka Fattah has come so far in politics.

———

MY PICTURE OF CHAKA FATTAH is drawn primarily from our six days of shared experiences and conversations in Philadelphia—in June 1996, October 1996, June 1998, June 2000, and April 2001. When we met, he was forty years old and nearing the end of his first term in Congress. His career milestones were these: born, raised, and educated in Philadelphia; attended public schools, Philadelphia Community College, the Wharton School of the University of Pennsylvania, the Fels Institute of State and Local Government of the University of Pennsylvania (earning an M.A.); the Senior Executive Program, Kennedy School, Harvard University; administrative assistant in city government; Pennsylvania state representative, 1982–1988; and Pennsylvania state senator, 1988–1994. . . .

Chaka Fattah is the fourth African American elected from Pennsylvania's Second Congressional District. Robert Nix served from 1959 to 1980, William Gray served from 1981 to 1991, and Lucien Blackwell served from 1991 to 1994. Fattah elaborates his idea of firsts by describing the change in constituency expectations in the quarter-century separating his career from that of Robert Nix: "Congressman Nix was the first black

congressman to be chairman of a House committee—the Post Office and
Civil Service Committee. That was a great accomplishment at the time—
first black chairman. It was his claim to fame. Now, I'm the top Democrat
on the Postal Service Subcommittee and no one ever mentions it." When
he compares himself to his predecessors, Fattah self-consciously places
himself within a contemporary cohort of African American politicians.

He also differentiates between the background experiences of the two
cohorts: "Most of the early generation of African American congressmen
came out of the civil rights movement—or the church," he says. "Most of
the generation now, though they hate to say it, have the orientation of
career or professional politicians. They come out of local government. I'm
doing what I decided to do early in life. I'm doing what I trained myself
to do. . . . There is a different level of preparedness from Nix to Gray to
myself. Bill Gray prepared for the ministry, but I prepared for politics."

Outside observers, too, found a more contemporary pattern. In their
1995 analysis of the Congressional Black Caucus, Richard Champagne
and Leroy Rieselbach single out its "newer, less senior" members as "a
new breed of pragmatists who have become issue activists and coalition
builders eager for influence." Current CBC members, they say, "Often
seek policy influence more as individuals than as a collectivity." And, while
"they still feel an obligation to represent the national black population . . .
[their] strategies seem clearly tipped toward ordinary congressional routines and away from symbolic politics." These distinctions help explain
Chaka Fattah's personal goals and representational strategies. . . .

Chaka Fattah was born into an intensely community-minded and
community-involved family. "My father and mother run the only urban
boys' home [House of Umoja] in the country. [It's] a place to live for
young men who are delinquent or dependent or both. They have several
row houses in west Philadelphia." "So I grew up in a home where there
were always thirty or forty people around," he added. "Maybe that's why I
feel at home in politics."

Earlier in their lives, both parents had multiple community attachments. His mother had once been an editor of the *Philadelphia Tribune,* the
oldest black newspaper in America, and later she became vice president of
the Philadelphia Council of Neighborhood Organizations. His stepfather
had once run the Hartranst Community Center in North Philadelphia,
and later he had become a teacher, pursuing an advanced degree when in
his sixties. His brother still runs a food kitchen for the destitute—Fattah's
Food for Thought—which serves "thousands of people each month."
Chaka Fattah's entire family was deeply involved in the business of helping others less fortunate than they. With considerable understatement, the

congressman says, "I grew up in a home where being involved in community life was a norm."

Helping others through community activism can easily morph into helping others through political activism. And it seems to have done so in Fattah's case. With a story that begins with his own neighborhood organization—the Winnfield Resident's Association—he traces just such a sequence.

My family was very much involved in efforts to deal with youth gang violence. The Winnfield neighborhood was a substantial, integrated, middle-class area that felt exempt from young gang violence. Then one weekend, there were two killings, one in retaliation for the other. My father and I set up meetings between the two groups. There was a picture of me in the *Philadelphia Inquirer.* I was a teenager—sixteen or seventeen. We facilitated a dialogue.

We also fought to close the bars in the area, and I marched in those protests. Ann Jordan was a leader in the Association and she ran against the Speaker of the [Pennsylvania] House. I helped her. She lost. Then we tried to get rid of the ward leader. I got involved in that, and after an eight-year fight, we won. Those committee membership fights were hand-to-hand combat. Then there was a creek that ran under part of the area and there was a settling problem with some of the foundations. When I worked at city hall, I helped work on that problem. I had a history of involvement there by the time I ran for state representative.

He developed a taste for politics and political ambitions early in life. One busy day, when the oil gauge in his car started blinking, he threw up his hands and only half joked, "I don't know anything about cars. I don't know anything except politics. That's all I've cared about since I was a kid." Taste and ambition have combined to propel him steadily up the electoral office ladder. . . .

The fact of his ambition, however, does not tell us about his motivations and his goals—about why he wanted so badly to be in politics. Very early in his life, the sheer allure of politics may have been paramount. "I remember driving to Washington with my mother," he recalls, "to watch her testify at a congressional hearing on gang violence run by John Conyers and Louis Stokes. That experience inspired me to go into politics. And it had nothing to do with policy." As the story of the Winnfield Resident's Association makes clear, however, his actual involvements were, from the outset, policy involvements.

From his earliest days in office, his dominant goal as a legislator has been to participate in making public policy. "I'm dedicated to legislation," he says when discussing his state legislative activity.

I want to be an intricate part of the policy debate. Some people are content to criticize other people's policies. . . . I want to be at the table when policies are being made. I do what you have to do—the grunt work beforehand. As a freshman state representative, I helped get a small group to meet together to do something about the poor economy. We called it "Penn Pride." We worked all summer and produced a package bill, The Employment Opportunity Act, to uplift the state's economy. Some of my colleagues wondered why we would do that—in summer. But I thought that's what a legislator is supposed to do.

As a freshman member of Congress, he articulated the same goal.

I hope that my distinction—not my legacy, I'm too young to speak of that—will be as a legislator. That is my intention—to be able to draft bills, to focus on public policy. I hope my accomplishment, my achievement, will be in legislation, not in how high a position I reached. It wouldn't matter to me what position I had if I got two or three bills passed. Very few people actually drive the policy machine. I want to be one of those people. I don't care about the trappings or the perks, except as they help me to legislate in Congress.

His goals are dominantly policy goals. When he emphasizes his "level of preparedness" and his "training for politics," he means preparedness and training for policy-oriented politics. I will describe his strategy, therefore, as a dominantly *policy-intensive representational strategy.*

This same "policy-intensive" label has been applied usefully to other House members in other constituencies. In Fattah's case, however, an extra measure of intensity should be added. For he is not simply goal oriented, he is goal driven. He is not just policy oriented, he is policy driven. He is not just legislatively oriented, he is legislative-product driven. He is always thinking about establishing and pushing policy goals and legislative goals. He views every situation as a challenge to overcome, and he constantly puts himself to the test. . . .

Chaka Fattah represents a 100 percent urban constituency in a major American city. The district, he says, "is urban, economically and ethnically diverse. It is 60 percent African American. I have—not the poorest section of the city—some of the poorest. I also have some of the most affluent parts of the city, both black and white. And I have more medical colleges in my district than any district in the country." . . .

The district's racial makeup is a faithful predictor of its partisan makeup. The 1972 *Almanac of American Politics* described it as "consistently Philadelphia's most Democratic district in statewide elections." For the eight presidential elections between 1968 and 1996, the district's Democratic vote—with a low of 75 percent and a high of 91 percent—averaged 84 percent. In 1996 Fattah's district gave President Clinton his fifth-highest vote margin. In voting for Congress, only the Democratic primary matters. Since Fattah won there in 1994, he has been unchallenged in the primary and been elected by margins from 86 percent to 100 percent.

"People tell me," he says, "that I have the safest seat in the country." It would be a challenge to find one safer.

Describing his geographical constituency further, he says, "Forty percent is west Philadelphia, 40 percent northwest Philadelphia. And that's the district. The rest is just spicing." He estimates that "the spicing" includes "south Philly, north Philly, center city, and Yeadon [in an adjoining county]," each of which makes up 5 percent of his geographical constituency.

West Philadelphia is Fattah's home area. He describes it as "black, poor working class to middle class." It has been a prototypically declining urban area. Between 1950 and 1990, it lost a third of its population; in 1990 it had over four thousand abandoned structures, and 12 percent of its available housing stock was vacant. During a ride up Market Street, the main artery connecting center city to "west Philly"—with the elevated transit line rumbling overhead—I watched people shopping in small clusters of stores. The clusters were separated by even larger clusters of boarded-up stores and homes, all thickly laced with graffiti. The omnipresence of urban blight bespoke the inequality of resources and the policy needs common to the poorest black communities—jobs, housing, health, schools, and safety. In all these respects, the need for government assistance was observably stark and serious.

The other 40 percent of "the district," northwest Philadelphia, he describes as "black and white, middle class to wealthy." Separated from west Philly by the Schuylkill River, it has a large white population—some of it, as in Chestnut Hill, upper-class Republican. The area has also been a destination of choice for many upwardly mobile, middle-class blacks leaving the west Philly ghetto by "jumping the river" into places like Germantown and Mt. Airy. Congressman Fattah's "strongest support" came from Mt. Airy. "It is thought to be one of the most successful models of racial integration in the country," he says. "It is a very active part of my constituency—filled with civic groups of all sorts. It has the highest income of any place in my district except center city. They vote independently and progressively. And they are very comfortable with a congressman like me."

The Second Congressional District contains, therefore, a measurable element of white, liberal Democrats, with whom a broad-gauged and policy-oriented African American House member can work easily and on equal terms. The presence of this element in Fattah's district brings distinctive characteristics to its politics. Such, at least, is the view of the congressman himself. . . .

When I asked him whether he perceived his congressional district to be homogeneous or heterogeneous, he parried, "I think that there is a harmony of spirit in the district." That "spirit" added an issue-oriented, liberal, white element to his basically black reelection constituency. . . .

The congressman thinks of himself as a particularly good fit for the diverse district he describes. It is not surprising. As a member of the state Senate, he helped draw up the redistricting plan that the courts accepted in 1991. "I drew up the plan for the historically African American Second District," he says. "I had more to do with it than anyone, except the courts. The district I have is the district as I wanted it—hook, line, and sinker. It was even more of what I wanted than I expected to get."

He summarizes his constituency relationship as "comfortable."

It is an easy district to represent—for me. That's because of where I've been and what I've done. I was born in south Philadelphia and moved to west Philadelphia. I went to school here—to community college and to Penn. It is not possible to represent the district without paying a lot of attention to the University of Pennsylvania. It is the outstanding institution of my district and the biggest employer in my district. When I go to speak there, to the young Democrats, the Law School, Wharton [business school], I'm not intimidated. I'm at home. . . .

For me, the district is uniquely easy. I went to the community college. It has branches and it educates more people than any institution in the district. I'm on their Board and I'm tuned in to what they do. I can talk with the environmentalists in the northwest section about their interests. And I can talk to the CEOs in center city. Those are the groups that Lucien [Blackwell, his predecessor in Congress] ignored. It's the comfortability of it. I think that's the best way to put it—it's a *comfortable fit* for me. . . .

Chaka Fattah's constituency relationships resemble the activism of the helping professions. His pattern of involvements was doubtless influenced by the community-regarding activities of his parents. He emphasized the informality of his neighborhood relationships. "I feel so much at home [in the district] that it's like I'm not the congressman. My son and I ride our bikes up and down these streets. . . . I don't make a point about being called 'the congressman.' People call me 'Chaka.' They don't call me 'the congressman.' I'm not interested in the trappings. My interest is in policy." He readily admits that his constituents do not always see him in such an informal light. . . .

The Philadelphia congressman practices representation by immersion. "My politics grows out of the neighborhoods," Fattah generalizes. "And I call my politics 'empowerment politics,' not party politics. When I first went into politics," he says, "I had a big interest in world politics, but the longer I've been in politics, the more I've moved toward issues sorts of groups." When asked, "Who are your strongest supporters?" he moves directly to those "issues sorts of groups." That is, he locates his primary constituency among the policy-oriented groups with whom he works. . . .

My first morning in Philadelphia was spent observing some of those street-level connections at a Community Volunteer Appreciation Fair "hosted" by the congressman. It was a daylong event where representatives of fifty-six different local organizations were scheduled to display materials, hold workshops, and recruit. At their plenary session, Fattah spoke to a dominantly African American gathering of about two hundred people, and he presented awards to one hundred volunteers.

As we entered, he said, "I meet a lot of these same people when I go places. In the beginning, it dawned on me that more or less it's the same group of people. They are the fabric of the community. I didn't start this program, but I could see that, as a public official, I had a unique opportunity to spotlight the contributions of volunteers. So I've been doing it for a number of years. . . . Without them, it would be impossible for the institutions of the community to operate. They deserve recognition, and I want to give it to them. We will stay longer than we will anywhere else today. This meeting is a priority for me."

The mood was upbeat, and so was his short talk. "Volunteers make the everyday things that happen, happen. . . . We did not meet to talk about what's wrong and what did not happen, but to see what's good and what is happening. . . . As a state representative, as a state senator, and now as a congressman, I've worked for affordable housing, and I know that none of it would have been built without volunteers. . . . The great lesson of life is that we grow by helping others." Among the others, he gave awards to individuals from his parents' House of Umoja and from his brother's Fattah's Food for Thought. We spent a couple of hours there while people talked with him and he visited exhibits. Many were, I have since concluded, his strong supporters. Doubtless, many were nonpolitical. But, in general, they fit his self-described mold. On the way out, he noted as a matter of fact that "several [party] committee people were there."

These multiple, overlapping neighborhood involvements give him a depth of constituency immersion that is remarkable and—in my experience—unique. Part of the immersion grows out of the extensiveness of his neighborhood connections and the diversity of his policy connections. Part of the immersion, too, derives from the longevity and the continuity of his efforts.

As he did in his talk at the volunteer fair, he often emphasizes how long he has already been in public life and how crucial that has been to his current constituency connections. "People know me from years of activity with various community groups. Everything I'm doing now I've been doing for years."

All the major players in the district know me personally. That's because I've been around so long—six years in the assembly, six years in the Senate, and now two years in Congress. Bob Haskins, whom you'll meet at the bank—he and I have known each other and worked together in various projects for fifteen years. People know that I've taken the lead on drug-free schools, high-rise housing, putting together $34 million to save the city. Bob knows how much I work in the community.

Indeed, "Because of my involvement, people expect more out of me than they do out of the ordinary run-of-the-mill figure in town." . . .

After six years in Congress, Chaka Fattah had amply met two early challenges posed by his job—winning reelection and influencing legislation. With respect to his personal performance and reputation, he had climbed—and quickly, too—to the top of the political hill in Philadelphia. With respect to a third job challenge—achieving a recognizable power base inside the institution—he still had a lot of climbing to do. The same ambition that had driven him up the electoral and the legislative ladders was also driving him up the chamber's own institutional ladder. . . .

For individual House members, the path to inside power normally runs through positions in the party leadership, or positions on committees, and sometimes through informal member caucuses or coalitions. [Chaka Fattah] had been assigned to two committees: Education, and Work Force and Government Affairs. When we met, well into Fattah's first term, he was already thinking about changing to a more influential committee.

I could stay on the Education Committee and move up. I waged a fight to get on it, even though it was not my first choice, because I wanted a safe harbor. The lion's share of my work has been in education. So I wouldn't be miserable going to work every morning for twelve or fifteen years on the Education Committee, and maybe getting to be chairman. I'd be comfortable there, and I know I would get a lot accomplished. It does important work, even though it has no pizzazz. . . . But I'd like to get on a big, big picture committee—Appropriations, Ways and Means, Rules, Commerce. My preference would be Rules. I've got a lot of interests, and it would give me range.

As for his chances? "Who knows when the train starts and stops. I've done all the things I should do. I've raised money. I've been a key player in the Black Caucus. But there are only a few seats, and seniority is still important. The way things work around here, if you don't get situated where you want to be during your first four years, you stay where you are." I had no idea what, if anything, he was doing to make a change.

Eight months later, in early 1997, circumstances had dictated his path for him. Any plans and prospects he might have developed were altered by the announcement that the congressman from Philadelphia's First District—a sitting member of the Appropriations Committee—would be resigning from Congress soon to take another job. Citing the rationale for a Pennsylvania replacement on that Committee, Fattah seized the opportunity to announce that "I am very interested." And having already talked with "appropriate" people about it, he added that, "No one has dampened my interest." He began to work for membership on the powerful, money-controlling Appropriations Committee. Participation in the decisions of that committee would give him extra leverage in winning funds for his district and an extra measure of influence with his colleagues in the House.

The battle for a top committee position of this sort is not like the battle for legislation. When there is competition, it involves one's own colleagues, not outside interests. Winning a committee assignment is a more exclusively party-oriented and party-dominated process than making a law. Its inside, deal-making processes are more personal, more idiosyncratic, more complicated, less open, and altogether less predictable than lawmaking. In sum, these several factors meant that Chaka Fattah's proven legislative prowess would be of no special help to him in his quest for a seat on the Appropriations Committee.

He had been working toward this new committee goal for over a year when we first talked about it in the summer of 1998. He was confident that his preparatory work had paid off. He had won the support of other aspiring Pennsylvania colleagues, and he had won the support of veteran Pennsylvania Congressman John Murtha who, as a member of the key decision-making body, would argue his case in the party councils. And Murtha apparently thought that he already "had a deal" with the party leader. . . .

In our summertime conversation, Fattah wavered between the view that it was a done deal and the view that it wasn't. "Murtha sees it as a tradition," he said, "that Pennsylvania had two members on Appropriations, one from the west [Murtha himself] and one from the east." As for his party relationships, he added, "I've done all the things I'm supposed to do. I've raised money for the party. I've given speeches for the party. I even went on the Ethics Committee for the party. Unless something goes very wrong, I have crossed another boundary. I have passed my first piece of legislation, and I have gotten on one of the most powerful committees in Congress." A little later, he entertained a small reservation. "It's as close to being done as anything can be in politics."

In December politics intervened and something did go "very wrong." The Capitol Hill newspaper *Roll Call* carried the headline, "Democrats Hand Out Prime Panel Slots: Murtha Storms out of Meeting after Fattah Fails to Get Appropriations Assignment." For one reason or another, seven House members—three of them African Americans—had more support than he. It would be impossible to re-create the inside maneuvering and support patterns. For Fattah, it was an unexpected blow. The press release announcing his appointment had already been written and was ready to go. "Up to now," said a friend afterward, "it's been Appropriations, Appropriations, Appropriations. Now, he's saying 'I could become Chairman of the Education Committee.' But his heart isn't in it. He's in a funk." He made no public comment. . . .

When we next met, Chaka Fattah had achieved his goal. He was a member of the House Committee on Appropriations. But it had not been easy. "After last year," he explained, "everyone expected and agreed that I was in first place next time if another position became available. But several important circumstances intervened." New suitors, with powerful backing, emerged. "I was still in the lead, but I had to worry," he recalled. The Democratic log jam was broken when the Republican majority party leadership reversed its course and agreed to add one more slot to the minority side of the committee. One powerful contender withdrew and two Democrats were chosen. . . .

To close the circle on his accomplishment, I asked, "What if you had not won?" "Education is a major committee and I was moving up. So there was some upside. The only downside was that I would have taken a hit back here. People would say 'Chaka Fattah wanted it, but he couldn't get it.' I would have taken a hit on my reputation back home. I can take that hit. That's not a problem. But if people said 'he wants to pass legislation, but he can't get any passed'—*that* is a hit I could not take. My goal is not to be on Appropriations. My goal is to be a legislator." It was a nice restatement of his personal goal and his policy-centered representational strategy at home. . . .

28

PAUL STAROBIN

Pork: A Time-Honored Tradition Lives On

Journalist Paul Starobin's look at congressional "pork" updates a classic subject. Pork, a project that a representative can secure for her or his district, has been a central part of congressional politics from the start. In times past, pork was easier to notice—edifices like canals, highways, bridges—as well as less controversial. The United States needed these infrastructure improvements, and the money was available for a generous pork barrel. Today, pork carries a different connotation. Starobin lists the new forms that pork takes in the "post-industrial" era. Modern pork projects don't look like those of the past. And the pork barrel, while as popular as always, isn't nearly as deep as it once was. Legislators are under pressure to cut, not spend, and pork—often called "earmarks" today—is a perfect target. But what is pork anyway? Some other district's waste-treatment plant.

———

POLITICAL PORK. Since the first Congress convened two centuries ago, lawmakers have ladled it out to home constituencies in the form of cash for roads, bridges and sundry other civic projects. It is a safe bet that the distribution of such largess will continue for at least as long into the future.*

Pork-barrel politics, in fact, is as much a part of the congressional scene as the two parties or the rules of courtesy for floor debate. . . .

And yet pork-barrel politics always has stirred controversy. Critics dislike seeing raw politics guiding decisions on the distribution of federal money for parochial needs. They say disinterested experts, if possible, should guide that money flow.

And fiscal conservatives wonder how Congress will ever get a handle on the federal budget with so many lawmakers grabbing so forcefully for pork-barrel funds. "Let's change the system so we don't have so much porking," says James C. Miller III, director of the White House Office of Management and Budget (OMB). Miller says he gets complaints on the order of one a day from congressional members taking issue with OMB suggestions that particular "pork" items in the budget are wasteful.

———

*The interesting, little-known, and ignominious origin of the term "pork barrel" comes from early in American history, when a barrel of salt pork was given to slaves as a reward for their work. The slaves had to compete among themselves to get their piece of the handout.—EDS.

But pork has its unabashed defenders. How, these people ask, can lawmakers ignore the legitimate demands of their constituents? When a highway needs to be built or a waterway constructed, the home folks quite naturally look to their congressional representative for help. Failure to respond amounts to political suicide.

"I've really always been a defender of pork-barreling because that's what I think people elect us for," says Rep. Douglas H. Bosco, D-Calif.

Moreover, many accept pork as a staple of the legislative process, lubricating the squeaky wheels of Congress by giving members a personal stake in major bills. . . .

Not only does the flow of pork continue pretty much unabated, it seems to be spreading to areas that traditionally haven't been subject to pork-barrel competition. Pork traditionally was identified with public-works projects such as roads, bridges, dams and harbors. But, as the economy and country have changed, lawmakers have shifted their appetites to what might be called "post-industrial" pork. Some examples:

• *Green Pork.* During the 1960s and 1970s, when dam-builders fought epic struggles with environmentalists, "pork-barrel" projects stereotypically meant bulldozers and concrete. But many of today's projects are more likely to draw praise than blame from environmentalists. The list includes sewer projects, waste-site cleanups, solar energy laboratories, pollution-control research, parks and park improvements and fish hatcheries, to name a few. . . .

• *Academic Pork.* Almost no federal funds for construction of university research facilities are being appropriated these days, except for special projects sponsored by lawmakers for campuses back home. Many of the sponsors sit on the Appropriations committees, from which they are well positioned to channel such funds. . . .

• *Defense Pork.* While the distribution of pork in the form of defense contracts and location of military installations certainly isn't new, there's no question that Reagan's military buildup has expanded opportunities for lawmakers to practice pork-barrel politics. . . .

This spread of the pork-barrel system to new areas raises a question: What exactly is pork? Reaching a definition isn't easy. Many people consider it wasteful spending that flows to a particular state or district and is sought to please the folks back home.

But what is wasteful? One man's boondoggle is another man's civic pride. Perhaps the most sensible definition is that which a member seeks for his own state or district but would not seek for anyone else's constituency.

Thus, pork goes to the heart of the age-old tension between a lawmaker's twin roles as representative of a particular area and member of a national legislative body. In the former capacity, the task is to promote the local interest; in the latter it is to weigh the national interest. . . .

Like other fraternities, the system has a code of behavior and a pecking order. It commands loyalty and serves the purpose of dividing up federal money that presumably has to go somewhere, of helping re-elect incumbents and of keeping the wheels of legislation turning. . . .

When applied with skill, pork can act as a lubricant to smooth passage of complex legislation. At the same time, when local benefits are distributed for merely "strategic" purposes, it can lead to waste. . . .

Just about everyone agrees that the budget crunch has made the competition to get pet projects in spending legislation more intense. Demand for such items has not shrunk nearly as much as the pool of available funds.

29

JOHN ELLWOOD
ERIC PATASHNIK

In Praise of Pork

Pork-barrel spending is high on Americans' list of gripes against Congress. "Asparagus research and mink reproduction" typify the wasteful spending that seems to enrich congressional districts and states while bankrupting the nation. Recently, "earmarks" have been criticized as the newest technique for putting pork into bills. John Ellwood and Eric Patashnik take a different view. Pork is not the real cause of the nation's budget crisis, they believe. In fact, pork projects may be just what members of the House and Senate need to be able to satisfy constituents in order to summon the courage to vote for real, significant, painful budget cuts.

IN A WHITE HOUSE address ... [in] March [1992], President [George H.W.] Bush challenged Congress to cut $5.7 billion of pork barrel projects to help reduce the deficit.* Among the projects Bush proposed eliminating were such congressional favorites as funding for asparagus research, mink reproduction, and local parking garages. The examples he cited would be funny, said the President, "if the effect weren't so serious." ...

Such episodes are a regular occurrence in Washington. Indeed, since the first Congress convened in 1789 and debated whether to build a lighthouse to protect the Chesapeake Bay, legislators of both parties have attempted to deliver federal funds back home for capital improvements and other projects, while presidents have tried to excise pork from the congressional diet. . . .

In recent years, public outrage over government waste has run high. Many observers see pork barrel spending not only as a symbol of an out-of-control Congress but as a leading cause of the nation's worsening bud-

---

*The "pork-barrel" refers to congressional spending on projects that bring money and jobs to particular districts throughout America, thereby aiding legislators in their reelection bids. The interesting, little-known, and ignominious origin of the term "pork barrel" comes from early in American history, when a barrel of salt pork was given to slaves as a reward for their work. The slaves had to compete among themselves to get their piece of the handout.—EDS.

get deficit. To cite one prominent example, *Washington Post* editor Brian Kelly claims in his recent book, *Adventures in Porkland: Why Washington Can't Stop Spending Your Money*, that the 1992 federal budget alone contains $97 billion of pork projects so entirely without merit that they could be "lopped out" without affecting the "welfare of the nation."

Kelly's claims are surely overblown. For example, he includes the lower prices that consumers would pay if certain price supports were withdrawn, even though these savings (while certainly desirable) would for the most part not show up in the government's ledgers. Yet reductions in pork barrel spending have also been advocated by those who acknowledge that pork, properly measured, comprises only a tiny fraction of total federal outlays. For example, Kansas Democrat Jim Slattery, who led the battle in the House in 1991 against using $500,000 in federal funds to turn Lawrence Welk's birthplace into a shrine, told *Common Cause Magazine*, "it's important from the standpoint of restoring public confidence in Congress to show we are prepared to stop wasteful spending," even if the cuts are only symbolic. In a similar vein, a recent *Newsweek* cover story, while conceding that "cutting out the most extreme forms of pork wouldn't eliminate the federal deficit," emphasizes that doing so "would demonstrate that Washington has the political will to reform its profligate ways."

The premise of these statements is that the first thing anyone— whether an individual consumer or the United States government—trying to save money should cut out is the fluff. As *Time* magazine rhetorically asks: "when Congress is struggling without much success to reduce the federal budget deficit, the question naturally arises: is pork *really* necessary?"

Our answer is yes. We believe in pork not because every new dam or overpass deserves to be funded, nor because we consider pork an appropriate instrument of fiscal policy (there are more efficient ways of stimulating a $5 trillion economy). Rather, we think that pork, doled out strategically, can help to sweeten an otherwise unpalatable piece of legislation.

No bill tastes so bitter to the average member of Congress as one that raises taxes or cuts popular programs. Any credible deficit-reduction package will almost certainly have to do both. In exchange for an increase in pork barrel spending, however, members of Congress just might be willing to bite the bullet and make the politically difficult decisions that will be required if the federal deficit is ever to be brought under control.

In a perfect world it would not be necessary to bribe elected officials to perform their jobs well. But, as James Madison pointed out two centuries ago in *Federalist* 51, men are not angels and we do not live in a perfect world. The object of government is therefore not to suppress the imperfections of human nature, which would be futile, but rather to harness the pursuit of self-interest to public ends.

Unfortunately, in the debate over how to reduce the deficit, Madison's advice has all too often gone ignored. Indeed, if there is anything the major budget-reform proposals of the last decade (Gramm-Rudman, the balanced-budget amendment, an entitlement cap*) have in common, it is that in seeking to impose artificial limits on government spending without offering anything in return, they work against the electoral interests of congressmen instead of with them—which is why these reforms have been so vigorously resisted.

No reasonable observer would argue that pork barrel spending has always been employed as a force for good or that there are no pork projects what would have been better left unbuilt. But singling out pork as the culprit for our fiscal troubles directs attention away from the largest sources of budgetary growth and contributes to the illusion that the budget can be balanced simply by eliminating waste and abuse. While proposals to achieve a pork-free budget are not without superficial appeal, they risk depriving leaders trying to enact real deficit-reduction measures of one of the most effective coalition-building tools at their disposal.

In order to appreciate why congressmen are so enamored of pork it is helpful to understand exactly what pork is. But defining pork is not as easy as it sounds. According to *Congressional Quarterly*, pork is usually considered to be "wasteful" spending that flows to a particular state or district in order to please voters back home. Like beauty, however, waste is in the eye of the beholder. As University of Michigan budget expert Edward M. Gramlich puts it, "one guy's pork is another guy's red meat." To a district plagued by double-digit unemployment, a new highway project is a sound investment, regardless of local transportation needs.

Some scholars simply define pork as any program that is economically inefficient—that is, any program whose total costs exceed its total benefits. But this definition tars with the same brush both real pork and programs that, while inefficient, can be justified on grounds of distributional equity or in which geographic legislative influence is small or nonexistent.

---

*Many attempts have been made in past years to lower the deficit. In 1985, the Gramm-Rudman-Hollings law set dollar-limit goals for deficit reduction, to be followed by automatic percentage cuts; however, many programs were exempted. A 1995 balanced-budget amendment passed the House, but failed to get two-thirds of the Senate's approval. Entitlement caps would seek to limit the total amount the federal government could pay out in programs such as Medicare, Medicaid, Social Security, and food stamps.—EDS.

A more promising approach is suggested by political scientist David Mayhew in his 1974 book, *Congress: The Electoral Connection*. According to Mayhew, congressional life consists largely of "a relentless search" for ways of claiming credit for making good things happen back home and thereby increasing the likelihood of remaining in office. Because there are 535 congressmen and not one, each individual congressman must try to "peel off pieces of governmental accomplishment for which he can believably generate a sense of responsibility." For most congressmen, the easiest way of doing this is to supply goods to their home districts.

From this perspective, the ideal pork barrel project has three key properties. First, benefits are conferred on a specific geographical constituency small enough to allow a single congressman to be recognized as the benefactor. Second, benefits are given out in such a fashion as to lead constituents to believe that the congressman had a hand in the allocation. Third, costs resulting from the project are widely diffused or otherwise obscured from taxpayer notice.

Political pork, then, offers a congressman's constituents an array of benefits at little apparent cost. Because pork projects are easily distinguished by voters from the ordinary outputs of government, they provide an incumbent with the opportunity to portray himself as a "prime mover" who deserves to be reelected. When a congressman attends a ribbon-cutting ceremony for a shiny new building in his district, every voter can *see* that he is accomplishing something in Washington. . . .

"It's outrageous that you've got to have such political payoffs to get Congress to do the nation's business," says James Miller, OMB director under Ronald Reagan. Miller's outrage is understandable but ultimately unproductive. Human nature and the electoral imperative being what they are, the pork barrel is here to stay.

But if pork is a permanent part of the political landscape, it is incumbent upon leaders to ensure that taxpayers get something for their money. Our most effective presidents have been those who have linked the distribution of pork to the achievement of critical national objectives. When Franklin Roosevelt discovered he could not develop an atomic bomb without the support of Tennessee Senator Kenneth McKellar, chairman of the Appropriations Committee, he readily agreed to locate the bomb facility in Oak Ridge. By contrast, our least effective presidents—Jimmy Carter comes to mind—have either given away plum projects for nothing or waged hopeless battles against pork, squandering scarce political capital and weakening their ability to govern in the process.

The real value of pork projects ultimately lies in their ability to induce rational legislators into taking electorally risky actions for the sake of the public good. Over the last ten years, as the discretionary part of the budget has shrunk, congressmen have had fewer and fewer opportunities to claim credit for directly aiding their constituents. As Brookings scholar R. Kent Weaver has argued, in an era of scarcity and difficult political choices, many legislators gave up on trying to accomplish anything positive, focusing their energies instead on blame avoidance. The result has been the creation of a political climate in which elected officials now believe the only way they can bring the nation back to fiscal health is to injure their own electoral chances. This cannot be good for the future of the republic.

Politics got us into the deficit mess, however, and only politics can get us out. According to both government and private estimates, annual deficits will soar after the mid-1990s, and could exceed $600 billion in 2002 if the economy performs poorly. Virtually every prominent mainstream economist agrees that reducing the deficit significantly will require Congress to do what it has been strenuously trying to avoid for more than a decade—rein in spending for Social Security, Medicare, and other popular, middle-class entitlement programs. Tax increases may also be necessary. From the vantage point of the average legislator, the risk of electoral retribution seems enormous.

If reductions in popular programs and increases in taxes are required to put our national economic house back in order, the strategic use of pork to obtain the support of key legislators for these measures will be crucial. . . .

. . . [T]he president should ignore the advice of fiscal puritans who would completely exorcise pork from the body politic. Favoring legislators with small gifts for their districts in order to achieve great things for the nation is an act not of sin but of statesmanship. To be sure, determining how much pork is needed and to which members it should be distributed is difficult. Rather than asking elected officials to become selfless angels, however, we would ask of them only that they be smart politicians. We suspect Madison would agree that the latter request has a far better chance of being favorably received.

30

SENATOR JOHN McCAIN

Hey There! SenJohnMcCain Is Using Twitter

Tweeting on Feb. 25, 26, 27 and March 2, 3, 4, 5, 6, 2009, Senator John McCain takes a jab—actually a lot of jabs—at Congress's Omnibus Budget Bill and the amusing earmarks contained in it. In truth, President Barack Obama himself acknowledged that the bill was loaded with pork, much of it decided by Congress before the 2008 election. President Obama stated that he would resist such pork projects in future budget bills. Still, Senator McCain could not resist pointing out such items like Mormon cricket control in Utah ($1 million), genetic improvements to switchgrass ($1.4 million), and pig odor research in Iowa ($1.7 million). Sprinkled among the pork entries are tweets about McCain's daily activities, from voting to speeches to TV appearances. One of his tweets reveals that the senator has had a little help from one of his young aides on how to use Twitter.

February 25–February 27, 2009

1. #6. $1 million for mormon cricket control in Utah—is that the species of cricket or a game played by the brits?   *8:30 AM Feb 27th from web*
2. #7. $300,000 for the Montana World Trade Center—enough said   *8:21 AM Feb 27th from web*
3. #8. $200,000 "tattoo removal violence outreach program to help gang members or others shed visible signs of their past" REALLY?   *7:50 AM Feb 27th from web*
4. going to the floor   *6:40 AM Feb 27th from web*
5. #9. $475,000 to build a parking garage in Provo City, Utah   *6:33 AM Feb 27th from web*
6. #10. $1.7M "for a honey bee factory" in Weslaco, TX   *6:06 AM Feb 27th, from web*
7. top 10 projects on the way . . .   *5:34 AM Feb 27th from web*
8. Tmr I am gonna tweet the TOP TEN PORKIEST PROJECTS in the Omnibus Spending bill the Congress is about to pass   *10:08 AM Feb 26th from web*
9. Mary Hood actually did the interview for CBS on my new found love of twittering.   *8:43 AM Feb 26th from txt*

10. I'm doing an interview with cbs in a few minutes   *8:09 AM Feb 26th from txt*
11. YEs!! I am twittering on my blackberry but not without a little help!   *6:07 AM Feb 26th from txt*
12. house votes 398-24 to freeze auto pay raise! great! who were the 24?   *2:39 PM Feb 25th from web*
13. steve nash hurt? amare too! what now for the suns!   *2:30 PM Feb 25th from web*
14. votes at 5:45   *2:21 PM Feb 25th from web*
15. on my way to an interview with KTVK, channel 3 in PHX . . . tune in tonight   *12:06 PM Feb 25th from web*
16. I appreciate Senator Byrd speaking in favor of my Constitutional point of order   *10:54 AM Feb 25th from web*
17. vote on my Constitutional Point of Order at 2.   *10:45 AM Feb 25th from web*
18. now on my way to AEI to give a speech on Winning the War in Afghanistan   *8:24 AM Feb 25th from web*
19. ICYMI: I filed a constitutional point of order on the DC Representative bill   *8:23 AM Feb 25th from web*
20. on my way to the floor.   *7:11 AM Feb 25th from web*

February 27–March 2, 2009

1. #1. $951,500 for Sustainable Las Vegas   *1:03 PM Mar 2nd from web*
2. and the number 1 porkiest project for today . . .   *1:00 PM Mar 2nd from web*
3. #2. $250,000 to enhance research on Ice Seal populations   *7:58 AM Mar 2nd from web*
4. #3. $150,000 for a rodeo museum in South Dakota   *12:58 PM Mar 2nd from web*
5. #4. $143,000 for Nevada Humanities to develop and expand an online encyclopedia - Anyone heard of Wikipedia?   *12:57 PM Mar 2nd from web*
6. #5. cont: why shouldn't we "float" a Hawaiian voyage for others?   *12:57 PM Mar 2nd from web*
7. #5. $238,000 for the Polynesian Voyaging Society in Hawaii - During these tough economic times with Americans out of work . . .   *12:56 PM Mar 2nd from web*
8. #6. $100,000 for the regional robotics training center in Union, SC - Does R2D2 or CP30 know about this?   *12:48 PM Mar 2nd from web*

9. #7. $1,427,250 for genetic improvements of switchgrass - I thought switchgrass genes were pretty good already, guess I was wrong. *12:38 PM Mar 2nd from web*

10. Hopefully for a Back in the Saddle Again exhibit, Autry's most popular song for those of you too young to remember America's Favorite Cowboy *9:18 AM Mar 2nd from web*

11. #8. $167,000 for the Autry National Center for the American West in Los Angeles, CA *9:14 AM Mar 2nd from web*

12. #9. $143,000 to teach art energy - Art can produce energy? If so, then investing in the arts may lead to energy independence. *8:50 AM Mar 2nd from web*

13. #10. $100,000 for the Central Nebraska World Trade Center *8:36 AM Mar 2nd from web*

14. Back by popular demand, another Top 10 . . . *8:36 AM Mar 2nd from web*

15. #1. $1.7 million for pig odor research in Iowa *2:37 PM Feb 27th from web*

16. and the #1 project is . . . *2:26 PM Feb 27th from web*

17. #2. $2 million "for the promotion of astronomy" in Hawaii - because nothing says new jobs for average Americans like investing in astronomy *1:56 PM Feb 27th from web*

18. #3. $332,000 for the design and construction of a school sidewalk in Franklin, Texas - not enough $ for schools in the stimulus? *12:19 PM Feb 27th from web*

19. #4. $2.1 million for the Center for Grape Genetics in New York - quick peel me a grape. *10:55 AM Feb 27th from web*

20. #5. $650,000 for beaver management in North Carolina and Mississippi *10:52 AM Feb 27th from web*

March 3–March 4, 2009

1. today's top 10 to come shortly *6:50 AM Mar 4th from web*

2. on my way to the wh to meet with the President on contract reform with sen Levin *6:50 AM Mar 4th from web*

3. introduced line item veto with Feingold and congressman ryan *6:45 AM Mar 4th from web*

4. #1. $951,500 for the Oregon Solar Highway *1:48 PM Mar 3rd from web*

5. and the #1 project *1:48 PM Mar 3rd from web*

6. meeting with Henry McMaster - "tell it all. . ." *1:15 PM Mar 3rd from web*

7. #2. $900,000 for fish management – how does one manage a fish
   . . .   *12:57 PM Mar 3rd from web*
8. #3. $380,000 to revitalize downtown Aliceville, AL   *11:32 AM Mar
   3rd from web*
9. 4. $380,000 for lighthouses in Maine   *11:23 AM Mar 3rd from web*
10. meeting with the French Defense Minister, Herve Morin   *11:00
    AM Mar 3rd from web*
11. taking a break for policy lunch   *10:11 AM Mar 3rd from web*
12. #5. $819, 000 for catfish genetics research in Alabama   *9:34 AM
    Mar 3rd from web*
13. #6. $190,000 for the Buffalo Bill Historical Center in Cody, WY
    9:23 AM Mar 3rd from web
14. #7. $400,000 for copper wire theft prevention efforts   *8:50 AM
    Mar 3rd from web*
15. #8. $47,500 to remodel and expand a playground in Ottawa, IL
    8:29 AM Mar 3rd from web
16. #9. $209,000 to improve blueberry production and efficiency in
    GA   *8:20 AM Mar 3rd from web*
17. #10. $285,000 for the Discovery Center of Idaho in Boise, ID
    8:06 AM Mar 3rd from web
18. and coming up, Tuesday's Top 10   *8:04 AM Mar 3rd from web*
19. SASC hearing   *8:04 AM Mar 3rd from web*
20. meeting with PM Tony Blair   *5:24 AM Mar 3rd from web*

March 4–March 5, 2009

1. #4. $95,000 for Hawaii Public Radio   *11:04 AM Mar 5th from
   web*
2. #5. $59,000 for Dismal Swamp and Dismal Swamp Canal in Virgin-
   ia.   *10:52 AM Mar 5th from web*
3. #6. $632,000 for the Hungry Horse Project⁻   *10:47 AM Mar 5th
   from web*
4. off to lunch with Senator Michael Bennett   *10:16 AM Mar 5th from
   web*
5. #7. $95,000 for the state of New Mexico to find a dental school lo-
   cation   *10:15 AM Mar 5th from web*
6. #8. $143,000 for the Historic Jazz Foundation in Kansas City,
   MO   *8:37 AM Mar 5th from web*
7. @ hearing to ensure in the rush to get "out the door" the $787 bil-
   lion in stimulus funds, there isn't waste, fraud and abuse.   *8:02 AM
   Mar 5th from web*

8. on my way to the homeland hearing   *7:46 AM Mar 5th from web*

9. #9. $190,000 for the Guam Public Library in Hagatna, Guam
   7:27 AM Mar 5th from web

10. #10. $3,806,000 for a Sun Grant Initiative in SD   *6:41 AM Mar
    5th from web*

11. Thursday's top 10 porkiest projects coming soon   *5:45 AM Mar
    5th from web*

12. if you wanna know more go to my website: http://mccain.senate
    .gov   *12:10 PM Mar 4th from web*

13. #4. All 13 earmarks for PMA group, which has been raided by the
    FBI for corruption, totaling over $10 million - THE BEST GOV-
    ERNMENT $ CAN BUY   *11:50 AM Mar 4th from web*

14. #5. 150,000 for lobster research - similar to lobster management?
    11:02 AM Mar 4th from web

15. #6. $950,000 for a Convention Center in Myrtle Beach, SC
    9:53AM Mar 4th from web

16. see the sea turtles on your $238,000 Polynesian Voyage   *9:48 AM
    Mar 4th from web*

17. #7. $7,100,000 for the conservation and recovery of endangered Ha-
    waiian sea turtle populations   *9:46 AM Mar 4th from web*

18. #8. $118,750 for a building to house an aircraft display in Rantoul,
    IL   *8:38 AM Mar 4th from web*

19. #9. $380,000 for a recreation and fairground area in Kotzebue,
    AK   *8:37 AM Mar 4th from web*

20. 10. $190,000 to build a Living Science Museum in New Orleans,
    LA   *8:09 AM Mar 4th from web*

March 5–March 6, 2009

1. on with John C. Scott - KVOI-AM (Tucson)   *37 minutes ago from
   web*

2. Just finished fox and now watching Lindsey on MTP   *about 16
   hours ago from txt*

3. #1. $75,000 for the "Totally Teen Zone" in Albany, GA   *11:58
   AM Mar 6th from web*

4. and the number one project of the day . . .   *11:54 AM Mar 6th from
   web*

5. #2. $1,284,525 for Rolls Royce - does that include a car?   *11:51
   AM Mar 6th from web*

6. #3. $122,821 for the Greater Toledo Arts Commission   *11:39 AM
   Mar 6th from web*

7. #4. $190,000 for the Berkshire Theatre in Stockbridge, MA
   11:35 AM Mar 6th from web

8. #5. $2,128,000 for a Ferry Boat, San Juan, PR   *11:22 AM Mar 6th
   from web*

9. #6. $385,000 for the Utah World Trade Center - Utah too?
   10:35 AM Mar 6th from web

10. #7. $228,000 for "streetscaping" in Bridgeville, PA   *10:18 AM Mar
    6th from web*

11. #8. $380,000 for a recreation and fairground area in Kotzebue,
    AK   *9:11 AM Mar 6th from web*

12. #9. $237,500 for a new museum in San Jose, CA   *8:49 AM Mar
    6th from web*

13. on my way to the floor to continue to talk pork   *8:04 AM Mar 6th
    from web*

14. Back by popular demand . . . #10 $190,000 to rebuild a dock in Gold
    Beach, OR   *6:28 AM Mar 6th from txt*

15. Having breakfast with secretary gates @ the pentagon.   *6:11 AM
    Mar 6th from txt*

16. on hannity now!   *1:35 PM Mar 5th from web*

17. #1. $1.9 million for the Pleasure Beach Water Taxi Service Project,
    CT   *1:35 PM Mar 5th from web*

18. #2. $143,000 for the Dayton Society of Natural History in Dayton,
    OH   *12:11 PM Mar 5th from web*

19. attending subcommittee on federal financial management   *11:40
    AM Mar 5th from web*

20. #3. $143,000 for the Historic Jazz Foundation in Kansas City, MO
    11:22 AM Mar 5th from web

31

DAVID PRICE

From *The Congressional Experience*

From a political science classroom at Duke University in Durham, North Carolina, to the U.S. House of Representatives, David Price describes his background, his decision to run for office, and his concerns for the future of the Congress. Price reveals his typical daily schedule as a representative. He discusses his distaste for "Congress-bashing," the favorite pastime of members of the Congress. Price condemns the "hot-button attack politics" campaigning style that has pushed issues aside and created a negative cynical tone in American politics.

In November 1994, Rep. David Price (D-NC) lost his seat in the House of Representatives to his Republican challenger. Then in November, 1996, Price won it back.

———

ON NOVEMBER 4, 1986, I was elected to the U.S. House of Representatives from the Fourth District of North Carolina, a five-county area that includes the cites of Raleigh, Chapel Hill, and Asheboro. Many thoughts crowded in on me on election night, but one of the most vivid was of that spring evening in 1959 when I had first set foot in the part of North Carolina I was now to represent. At the time, I was a student at Mars Hill, a junior college in the North Carolina mountains a few miles from my home in the small town of Erwin, Tennessee. I had taken an eight-hour bus ride from Mars Hill to Chapel Hill to be interviewed for a Morehead Scholarship, a generous award that subsequently made it possible for me to attend the University of North Carolina (UNC). I was awed by the university and nervous about the interview; thinking back on some of the answers I gave the next morning ("Would you say Cecil Rhodes was an imperialist?" "I believe so"), I still marvel that I won the scholarship. But I did, and the next two years were among the most formative and exciting of my life.

I went north in 1961 to divinity school and eventually to graduate school and a faculty appointment in political science at Yale University. But the idea of returning to the Raleigh-Durham-Chapel Hill area of North Carolina exerted a continuing tug on me, particularly as I decided on a teaching career and thought about where I would like to put down personal and academic roots. Fortunately, my wife, Lisa, also found the idea agreeable, despite her budding political career as a member of New Haven's Board of Aldermen. Therefore, when I received an offer to join the political science faculty at Duke University and also to help launch the university's Institute of Policy Sciences and Public Affairs, I jumped at the opportunity. In mid-1973, we moved with our two children—Karen, three, and Michael, one—to Chapel Hill. Though we were delighted with the community and the job and saw the move as a long-term one, I would have been incredulous at the suggestion that within fourteen years I would represent the district in Congress. . . .

Among some voters—and occasionally among congressional colleagues—my academic background has represented a barrier to be overcome. But usually it has not. My district, it is claimed, has the highest number of Ph.D.'s per capita of any comparable area in the country. Certainly, with eleven institutions of higher education and the kind of people who work in the Research Triangle Park, I have some remarkably literate constituents. I sometimes reflect ambivalently on this as I contemplate the piles of well-reasoned letters on every conceivable issue that come into my office. Yet the electoral advantages are considerable. During my first campaign, we polled to test public reactions to my academic affiliation and background, expecting to downplay them in the campaign. Instead, we found highly positive associations and ended up running a television ad that featured me in the classroom! . . .

Becoming a member of the House shakes up not only family life but also the roles and routines associated with one's previous career. I took a special interest, naturally, in [political scientist Richard] Fenno's* interview with a freshman senator who had been a college professor. "Life in the Senate," he said, "is the antithesis of academic life." I would not put it quite that way: Such a view seems both to exaggerate the orderliness and tranquility of modern academic life and to underestimate the extent to which one can impose a modicum of order on life in the Congress. Still, few jobs present as many diverse and competing demands as does service in Congress.

Consider, for example, my schedule for two rather typical days in the spring of 1991, reprinted here without change except for the deletion of some personal names and the addition of a few explanatory notes. By this time, I had moved to the Appropriations Committee from the three com-

---

*Richard Fenno's most well-known book is his 1978 *Home Style*. It represented a whole new way to study Congress. He followed certain representatives as they returned home, to their districts, to meet with constituents. Fenno found that members of Congress try to build "trust" among the voters so that more "leeway" exists for members in their congressional voting. Much of Fenno's work involved interviewing and observing members of Congress as individuals, to gain insight into their behavior as elected officials.—EDS.

mittees on which I sat during my first term, so the hearing schedule was less demanding; nonetheless, the Agriculture Appropriations Subcommittee held hearings on each of these two days. I also testified on a North Carolina environmental matter before a subcommittee of which I was not a member. The Budget Study Group and the Mainstream Forum, two of the informal organizations with which I am affiliated, held meetings, and the Prayer Breakfast, an informal fellowship group, met, as usual, on Thursday morning. I had several scheduled media interviews and probably a number of unscheduled press calls as well. There were a number of party meetings and activities: The Democratic Caucus met to discuss the pending budget resolution; a whip's task force was organized to mobilize Democrats behind the resolution; the caucus held a "party effectiveness" luncheon open to all members to discuss a major pending issue; and I participated in a caucus-organized set of one-minute speeches at the beginning of the House session. The other items are self-explanatory—meetings with North Carolina groups on issues of concern, talks to student groups, and various receptions that substituted for dinner or at least provided enough sustenance to take me through the evening of editing letters and reading in my office. And of course, the schedule does not capture the numerous trips to the House floor for votes, the phone calls, and the staff conferences scattered throughout every day.

These schedules list only events I actually attended; they also reflect the rules of thumb by which my staff and I keep life from getting even more hectic. In general, I talk with groups about pending legislation only when there is a North Carolina connection; most Washington groups are well aware that their delegations need to include at least one representative from the district. I also generally skip receptions at the end of the day unless constituents are to be there or a colleague has asked me to attend.

This sheer busyness in Washington and at home as well surpasses what almost all members have experienced in their previous careers and requires specific survival techniques. Most important, you must set priorities—separate those matters in which you want to invest considerable time and energy from those you wish to handle perfunctorily or not deal with personally at all. Confronted with three simultaneous subcommittee hearings, a member often has a choice: pop in on each of the three for fifteen minutes or choose one and remain long enough to learn and contribute something. It is also essential to delegate a great deal to staff and to develop a good mutual understanding within the office as to when the member's personal direction and attention are required. But there are no management techniques on earth that could make a representative's life totally predictable or controllable or that could convert a congressional

TYPICAL MEMBER'S DAILY SCHEDULE IN WASHINGTON

Wednesday, April 10, 1991

8:00 A.M.	Budget Study Group—Chairman Leon Panetta, Budget Committee, room 340 Cannon Building
8:45 A.M.	Mainstream Forum Meeting, room 2344 Rayburn Building
9:15 A.M.	Meeting with Consulting Engineers Council of N.C. from Raleigh about various issues of concern
9:45 A.M.	Meet with N.C. Soybean Assn. representatives re: agriculture appropriations projects
10:15 A.M.	WCHL radio interview (by phone)
10:30 A.M.	Tape weekly radio show—budget
11:00 A.M.	Meet with former student, now an author, about intellectual property issue
1:00 P.M.	Agriculture Subcommittee Hearing—Budget Overview and General Agriculture Outlook, room 2362 Rayburn Building
2:30 P.M.	Meeting with Chairman Bill Ford and southern Democrats re: HR-5, Striker Replacement Bill, possible amendments
3:15 P.M.	Meet with Close-Up students from district on steps of Capitol for photo and discussions
3:45 P.M.	Meet with Duke professor re: energy research programs
4:30 P.M.	Meet with constituent of Kurdish background re: situation in Iraq
5:30-7:00 P.M.	Reception—Sponsored by National Assn. of Home Builders, honoring new president Mark Tipton from Raleigh, H-328 Capitol
6:00-8:00 P.M.	Reception—Honoring retiring Rep. Bill Gray, Washington Court Hotel
6:00-8:00 P.M.	Reception-Sponsored by Firefighters Assn., room B-339 Rayburn Building
6:00-8:00 P.M.	Reception—American Financial Services Assn., Gold Room

Thursday, April 11, 1991

8:00 A.M.	Prayer Breakfast—Rep. Charles Taylor to speak, room H-130 Capitol
9:00 A.M.	Whip meeting, room H-324 Capitol
10:00 A.M.	Democratic Caucus Meeting, Hall of the House, re: budget
10:25 A.M.	UNISYS reps. in office (staff, DP meets briefly)
10:30 A.M.	Firefighters from Raleigh re: Hatch Act Reform, Manufacturer's Presumptive Liability, etc.
11:00 A.M.	American Business Council of the Gulf Countries re: rebuilding the Gulf, improving competitiveness in Gulf market
11:15 A.M.	Whip Task Force meeting re: Budget Resolution, room H-114 Capitol
12:00 P.M.	Speech—One Minute on House floor re: budget
12:30 P.M.	Party Effectiveness Lunch—re: banking reform, room H-324 Capitol
1:00 P.M.	Agriculture Subcommittee Hearing—Inspector General Overview and the Office of the General Counsel, room 2362 Rayburn Building

TYPICAL MEMBER'S DAILY SCHEDULE IN WASHINGTON (*continued*)

3:00 P.M.	Testify at Oceanography Subcommittee Hearing re: naval vessel waste disposal on N.C. Outer Banks, room 1334 Longworth Building
3:30 P.M.	Speak to Duke public policy students re: operations of Congress, room 188 Russell Building
5:00 P.M.	Interview with Matthew Cross, WUNC stringer re: offshore drilling
6:45 P.M.	Depart National Airport for Raleigh-Durham

office into a tidy bureaucracy. A member (or aide) who requires that kind of control—who cannot tolerate, for example, being diverted to talk to a visiting school class or to hear out a visiting delegation of homebuilders or social workers—is simply in the wrong line of work.

... Former Congressman Bob Eckhardt (D-Texas) suggested that every member of Congress performs three functions: lawmaker, ombudsman, and educator. This last function, as I have shown, may be closely related to the first: Lawmakers who wish to do more than simply defer to the strongest and best-organized interests on a certain matter must give some attention to explaining their actions and educating their constituents, helping them place the issue in broader perspective or perhaps activating alternative bases of support. And the extent to which a member is willing and able to undertake such explanations is ethically as well as politically significant.

Here, I turn to another facet of the legislators' educative role: their portrayal of Congress itself. On traveling with House members around their districts, Richard Fenno noted that the greatest surprise for him was the extent to which each one "polished his or her individual reputation at the expense of the institutional reputation of Congress":

In explaining what he was doing in Washington, every one of the eighteen House members took the opportunity to picture himself as different from, and better than, most of his fellow members in Congress. No one availed himself of the opportunity to educate his constituents about Congress as an institution—not in any way that would "hurt a little." To the contrary, the members' process of differentiating themselves from the Congress as a whole only served, directly or indirectly, to downgrade the Congress.

This was in the mid-1970s, and every indication is that such tactics have become even more prevalent as Congress-bashing by advocacy groups and in the media has intensified. "We have to differentiate me from the rest of those bandits down there in Congress," Fenno heard a member say to a campaign strategy group. "'They are awful, but our guy is wonderful'—that's the message we have to get across."

So much for the traditional norm of institutional patriotism! Opinion polls regularly reveal that public officials in general and Congress in particular rank low in public esteem, an evaluation reinforced by the recent spate of ethics charges in both houses but rooted much more deeply in our country's history and political culture. Every indication is that we members reinforce such an assessment by distancing ourselves from any responsibility for the institution's functioning. And we are phenomenally successful at it, matching a 30 percent approval rate for Congress with a 95+ percent reelection rate for ourselves.

My point is not that a member should defend Congress, right or wrong. I understand very well the disadvantages of being put on the defensive about Congress's ethical problems—pointing out that only a small number of members are involved, for example, or that Ethics Committee proceedings are generally bipartisan and fair—although I believe many of these defenses have merit. Rather, I am speaking of a more general tendency to trash the institution. It is often tempting—but I believe, also deceptive and irresponsible—to pose as the quintessential outsider, carping at accommodations that have been reached on a given issue as though problems could simply be ignored, cost-free solutions devised, or the painful necessities of compromise avoided. Responsible legislators will communicate to their constituencies not only the assembly's failings but also what it is fair and reasonable to expect, what accommodations they would be well advised to accept, and so forth. In the past, institutional patriotism has too often taken an uncritical form, assuming that whatever the process produces must be acceptable. But self-righteous, anti-institutional posturing is no better. The moral quixotism to which reelection-minded legislators are increasingly prone too often serves to rationalize their own nonproductive legislative roles and to perpetuate public misperceptions of the criteria one can reasonably apply to legislative performance.

Therefore, although it may be politically profitable to "run *for* Congress by running *against* Congress," the implications for the institution's effectiveness and legitimacy are ominous. As Fenno concluded, "The strategy is ubiquitous, addictive, cost-free, and foolproof. . . . In the short run, everybody plays and nearly everybody wins. Yet the institution bleeds from 435 separate cuts. In the long run, therefore, somebody may lose. . . . Congress may lack public support at the very time when the public needs Congress the most." . . .

My job keeps me very busy and flying, as they say, "close to the ground"—attending to myriad details in dealing with constituents, tracking appropriations, and all the rest. I sometimes feel that I had a better overview of the current state of American politics and even of certain broad policy questions before I was elected than I do now. I have, however, been in a position to observe some alarming trends in our politics and to develop strong convictions about our need to reverse them. I will therefore conclude with a few thoughts on the ominous gap that has opened up between campaigning and governing. . . . It is in the nature of political campaigns to polarize and to oversimplify, but the negative attacks and distortions have increased markedly. And the link between what candidates say in their campaign advertisements and the decisions they make once in office has become more and more tenuous. . . .

This trend has been reinforced by the new technology of campaign advertising and fund-raising; thirty-second television ads and direct mail financial solicitations, for example, put a premium on hard-hitting, over-simplified appeals and the pushing of symbolic hot buttons. The trend has also been both cause and effect of the modern emergence of cultural and value questions, like abortion, race, patriotism, and alternative life-styles, that lend themselves to symbolic appeals. Republican candidates in particular have found in these issues a promising means of diverting voters' attention from economic and quality-of-life concerns and of driving divisive wedges in the Democratic coalition.

The growing gap between campaigning and governing also bespeaks a certain public alienation and cynicism. Voters complain about the nastiness and irrelevance of campaign advertising, and my campaigns have demonstrated that such tactics can effectively be turned against an opponent. But voters who find little to encourage or inspire them in politics are nonetheless tempted to vote in anger or in protest, inclinations that modern campaign advertising exploits very effectively. As E. J. Dionne suggested, the decline of the "politics of remedy"—that is, politics that attempts "to solve problems and resolve disputes"—seems to have created a vicious cycle:

Campaigns have become negative in large part because of a sharp decline in popular faith in government. To appeal to an increasingly alienated electorate, candidates and their political consultants have adopted a cynical stance which, they believe with good reason, plays into popular cynicism about politics and thus wins them votes. But cynical campaigns do not resolve issues. They do not lead to "remedies." Therefore, problems get worse, the electorate becomes *more* cynical—and so does the advertising.

Responsibility for our descent into attack politics, increasingly divorced from the major problems faced by the American people, is widely shared—by journalists, interest groups, campaign consultants, and the viewing, voting public. Members of Congress are hardly helpless—or blameless—before these trends. For one thing, our defensiveness in the face of tough votes is often exaggerated; members frequently underestimate their ability to deflect attacks or to deal effectively with hostile charges. All of us feel occasionally that "I'd rather vote against this than to have to explain it," but we should worry if we find ourselves taking this way out too often or on matters of genuine consequence. It is our *job* to interpret and explain difficult decisions, and with sufficient effort, we can usually do so successfully.

We also have some choices about the kind of campaigns we run. By making campaign tactics themselves an issue, we can heighten public awareness of and resistance to distorted and manipulative appeals. Above all, we can tighten the link between what we say in our own campaigns and what we have done and intend to do in office. This is not a plea for dull campaigns; on the contrary, it is our duty to arouse people's concern and anger about areas of neglect, to convince them that we can do better, to inspire them to contribute to the solution. Most people believe that politics and politicians ought to have something constructive to offer in the realms of education, housing, health care, economic development, environmental protection, and other areas of tangible concern. Our task is to get to work on these major challenges in both campaigning *and* governing in a credible way that inspires confidence and enthusiasm. As that happens, hot-button attack politics will increasingly be seen as the sham that it is.

PART SIX

The Presidency

32

RICHARD NEUSTADT

From *Presidential Power and the Modern Presidents*

From this often-read book comes the classic concept of presidential power as "the power to persuade." Richard Neustadt observed the essence of presidential power when working in the executive branch during Franklin Roosevelt's term as president. He stayed to serve under President Truman. It is said that President Kennedy brought Presidential Power with him to the White House, and Neustadt worked briefly for JFK. The first half of the excerpt, in which he shows how presidents' well-developed personal characteristics permit successful persuasive abilities, comes from the book's first edition. The excerpt's closing pages reflect Neustadt's later musings on the nation, on world affairs, and on the challenges presidents face.

IN THE EARLY summer of 1952, before the heat of the campaign, President [Harry] Truman used to contemplate the problems of the general-become-President should [Dwight David] Eisenhower win the forthcoming election. "He'll sit here," Truman would remark (tapping his desk for emphasis), "and he'll say, 'Do this! Do that!' *And nothing will happen.* Poor Ike—it won't be a bit like the Army. He'll find it very frustrating."

Eisenhower evidently found it so. "In the face of the continuing dissidence and disunity, the President sometimes simply exploded with exasperation," wrote Robert Donovan in comment on the early months of Eisenhower's first term. "What was the use, he demanded to know, of his trying to lead the Republican Party. . . . " And this reaction was not limited to early months alone, or to his party only. "The President still feels," an Eisenhower aide remarked to me in 1958, "that when he's decided something, that *ought* to be the end of it . . . and when it bounces back undone or done wrong, he tends to react with shocked surprise."

Truman knew whereof he spoke. With "resignation" in the place of "shocked surprise," the aide's description would have fitted Truman. The former senator may have been less shocked than the former general, but he was no less subjected to that painful and repetitive experience: "Do this, do that, and nothing will happen." Long before he came to talk of Eisenhower he had put his own experience in other words: "I sit here all day trying to persuade people to do the things they ought to have sense enough to do without my persuading them. . . . That's all the powers of the President amount to."

In these words of a President, spoken on the job, one finds the essence of the problem now before us: "powers" are no guarantee of power; clerkship is no guarantee of leadership. The President of the United States has an extraordinary range of formal powers, of authority in statute law and in the Constitution. Here is testimony that despite his "powers" he does not obtain results by giving orders—or not, at any rate, merely by giving orders. He also has extraordinary status, ex officio, according to the customs of our government and politics. Here is testimony that despite his status he does not get action without argument. Presidential power is the power to persuade. . . .

The limits on command suggest the structure of our government. The Constitutional Convention of 1787 is supposed to have created a government of "separated powers." It did nothing of the sort. Rather, it created a government of separated institutions *sharing* powers. "I am part of the legislative process," Eisenhower often said in 1959 as a reminder of his veto. Congress, the dispenser of authority and funds, is no less part of the administrative process. Federalism adds another set of separated institutions. The Bill of Rights adds others. Many public purposes can only be achieved by voluntary acts of private institutions; the press, for one, in Douglass Cater's phrase, is a "fourth branch of government." And with the coming of alliances abroad, the separate institutions of a London, or a Bonn, share in the making of American public policy.

What the Constitution separates our political parties do not combine. The parties are themselves composed of separated organizations sharing public authority. The authority consists of nominating powers. Our national parties are confederations of state and local party institutions, with a headquarters that represents the White House, more or less, if the party has a President in office. These confederacies manage presidential nominations. All other public offices depend upon electorates confined within the states. All other nominations are controlled within the states. The President and congressmen who bear one party's label are divided by dependence upon different sets of voters. The differences are sharpest at the stage of nomination. The White House has too small a share in nominating congressmen, and Congress has too little weight in nominating presidents for party to erase their constitutional separation. Party links are stronger than is frequently supposed, but nominating processes assure the separation.

The separateness of institutions and the sharing of authority prescribe the terms on which a President persuades. When one man shares authority with another, but does not gain or lose his job upon the other's whim, his willingness to act upon the urging of the other turns on whether he conceives the action right for him. The essence of a President's persuasive task is to convince such men that what the White House wants of them is what they ought to do for their sake and on their authority. (Sex matters not at all; for *man* read *woman*.)

Persuasive power, thus defined, amounts to more than charm or reasoned argument. These have their uses for a President, but these are not the whole of his resources. For the individuals he would induce to do what he wants done on their own responsibility will need or fear some acts by him on his responsibility. If they share his authority, he has some share in theirs. Presidential "powers" may be inconclusive when a President commands, but always remain relevant as he persuades. The status and authority inherent in his office reinforce his logic and his charm. . . .

A President's authority and status give him great advantages in dealing with the men he would persuade. Each "power" is a vantage point for him in the degree that other men have use for his authority. From the veto to appointments, from publicity to budgeting, and so down a long list, the White House now controls the most encompassing array of vantage points in the American political system. With hardly an exception, those who share in governing this country are aware that at some time, in some degree, the doing of *their* jobs, the furthering of *their* ambitions, may depend upon the President of the United States. Their need for presidential action, or their fear of it, is bound to be recurrent if not actually continuous. Their need or fear is his advantage.

A President's advantages are greater than mere listing of his "powers" might suggest. Those with whom he deals must deal with him until the last day of his term. Because they have continuing relationships with him, his future, while it lasts, supports his present influence. Even though there is no need or fear of him today, what he could do tomorrow may supply today's advantage. Continuing relationships may convert any "power," any aspect of his status, into vantage points in almost any case. When he induces other people to do what he wants done, a President can trade on their dependence now and later.

The President's advantages are checked by the advantages of others. Continuing relationships will pull in both directions. These are relationships of mutual dependence. A President depends upon the persons whom he would persuade; he has to reckon with his need or fear of them. They too will possess status, or authority, or both, else they would be of little use to him. Their vantage points confront his own; their power tempers his. . . .

The power to persuade is the power to bargain. Status and authority yield bargaining advantages. But in a government of "separated institutions sharing powers," they yield them to all sides. With the array of vantage points at his disposal, a President may be far more persuasive than his logic or his charm could make him. But outcomes are not guaranteed by his advantages. There remain the counter pressures those whom he would influence can bring to bear on him from vantage points at their disposal. Command has limited utility; persuasion becomes give-and-take. It is well that the White House holds the vantage points it does. In such a business any President may need them all—and more. . . .

When a President confronts divergent policy advisers, disputing experts, conflicting data, and uncertain outlooks, yet must choose, there plainly *are* some other things he can do for himself besides consulting his own power stakes. But there is a proviso—provided he has done that first and keeps clear in his mind how much his prospects may depend on his authority, how much on reputation, how much on public standing. In the world Reagan inhabited where reputation and prestige are far more intertwined than they had been in Truman's time, or even LBJ's, this proviso is no easy test of presidential expertise. It calls for a good ear and a fine eye. . . .

But when a President turns to others, regardless of the mode, he is dependent on their knowledge, judgment, and good will. If he turns essentially to one, alone, he puts a heavy burden on that other's knowledge. If he chooses not to read or hear details, he puts an even greater burden on the other's judgment. If he consents, besides, to secrecy from everyone whose task in life is to protect his flanks, he courts deep trouble. Good will should not be stretched beyond endurance. In a system characterized by separated institutions sharing powers, where presidential interests will diverge in some degree from those of almost everybody else, that suggests not stretching very far. . . .

Personally, I prefer Presidents . . . more skeptical than trustful, more curious than committed, more nearly Roosevelts than Reagans. I think the former energize our governmental system better and bring out its defects less than do the latter. Reagan's years did not persuade me otherwise, in spite of his appeal on other scores. Every scandal in his wake, for instance, must owe something to the narrow range of his convictions and the breadth of his incuriosity, along with all that trust. A President cannot abolish bad behavior, but he sets a tone, and if he is alert to possibilities he can set traps, and with them limits. Reagan's tone, apparently, was heard by all too many as "enrich yourselves," while those few traps deregulation spared appear to have been sprung and left unbaited for the most part. But this book has not been written to expound my personal preferences. Rather it endeavors to expose the problem for a President of either sort who seeks to buttress prospects for his future influence while making present choices—"looking toward tomorrow from today," as I wrote at the start. For me that remains a crucial enterprise. It is not, of course, the only thing a President should put his mind to, but it is the subject to which I have put my own throughout this book. It remains crucial, in my view, not simply for the purposes of Presidents, but also for the products of the system, whether effective policy, or flawed or none. Thus it becomes crucial for us all.

We now stand on the threshold of a time in which those separated institutions, Congress and the President, share powers fully and uncomfortably across the board of policy, both foreign and domestic. From the 1940s through the 1960s—"midcentury" in this book's terms—Congress, having been embarrassed at Pearl Harbor by the isolationism it displayed beforehand, gave successive Presidents more scope in defense budgeting and in the conduct of diplomacy toward Europe and Japan than was the norm between the two world wars. Once the Cold War had gotten under way, and then been largely militarized after Korea, that scope widened. With the onset of the missile age it deepened. Should nuclear war impend, the President became the system's final arbiter. Thus I characterized JFK against the background of the Cuban missile crisis. But by 1975 the denouement of Watergate and that of Vietnam, eight months apart, had put a period to what remained of congressional reticence left over from Pearl Harbor. And the closing of the Cold War, now in sight though by no means achieved, promises an end to nuclear danger as between the Soviet Union and the United States. Threats of nuclear attack could well remain, from Third World dictators or terrorists, but not destruction of the Northern Hemisphere. So in the realm of military preparations—even, indeed, covert actions—the congressional role waxes as the Cold War wanes, returning toward normality as understood in Franklin Roosevelt's first two terms.

In a multipolar world, crisscrossed by transnational relations, with economic and environmental issues paramount, and issues of security reshaped on regional lines, our Presidents will less and less have reason to seek solace in foreign relations from the piled-up frustrations of home affairs. Their foreign frustrations will be piled high too.

Since FDR in wartime, every President including Bush has found the role of superpower sovereign beguiling: personal responsibility at once direct and high, issues at once gripping and arcane, opposite numbers frequently intriguing and well-mannered, acclaim by foreign audiences echoing well at home, foreign travel relatively glamorous, compared with home, interest groups less clamorous, excepting special cases, authority always stronger, Congress often tamer. But the distinctions lessen—compare Bush's time with Nixon's to say nothing of Eisenhower's—and we should expect that they will lessen further. Telecommunications, trade, aid, banking and stock markets combined with AIDS and birth control and hunger, topped off by toxic waste and global warming—these are not the stuff of which the Congress of Vienna* was made, much less the summits of yore. Moreover, Europeans ten years hence, as well as Japanese, may not resemble much the relatively acquiescent "middle powers" we grew used to in the 1960s and 1970s. Cooperating with them may come to seem to Presidents no easier than cooperating with Congress. Our friends abroad will see it quite the other way around: How are they to cooperate with our peculiar mix of separated institutions sharing powers? Theirs are ordered governments, ours a rat race. Complaints of us by others in these terms are nothing new. They have been rife throughout this century. But by the next, some of the chief complainants may have fewer needs of us, while ours of them grow relatively greater, than at any other time since World War II. In that case foreign policy could cease to be a source of pleasure for a President. By the same token, he or she would have to do abroad as on the Hill and in Peoria: Check carefully the possible effects of present choices on prospective reputation and prestige—thinking of other governments and publics quite as hard as those at home. It is not just our accustomed NATO and Pacific allies who may force the pace here, but the Soviet Union, if it holds together, and potentially great powers—China, India, perhaps Brazil—as well as our neighbors, north and south.

From the multicentered, interdependent world now coming into being, environmentally endangered as it is, Presidents may look back on the Cold War as an era of stability, authority, and glamour. They may yearn for the simplicity they see in retrospect, and also for the solace. Too bad. The job of being President is tougher when incumbents have to struggle for effective influence in foreign and domestic spheres at once, with their

---

*After the 1814 defeat of the French leader Napoleon by Russia, Prussia, Austria, and Britain, these great powers met in Vienna, Austria, to ensure that the future of Europe would be peaceful. At the Congress of Vienna, they created a "balance of power" system so that no single European nation could dominate the continent.—EDS.

command of nuclear forces losing immediate relevance, and the American economy shorn of its former clout. There are, however, compensations, one in particular. If we outlive the Cold War,* the personal responsibility attached to nuclear weapons should become less burdensome for Presidents themselves, while contemplation of their mere humanity becomes less haunting for the rest of us. To me that seems a fair exchange.

---

*The Cold War refers to the hostility that existed between the United States and the Soviet Union from the end of World War II until recent times. The Cold War involved many forms of hostility: democracy versus communism; America's NATO allies versus the Soviet Union's Warsaw Pact military partners; the threat of nuclear war; economic competition; the dividing of Third World nations into pro-U.S. and pro-Soviet camps. With the demise of communism in Eastern Europe and the disintegration of the Soviet Union, the Cold War era has ended.—Eds.

33

ARTHUR SCHLESINGER

From *The Imperial Presidency*

Historian Arthur Schlesinger coined one of the most famous and often-quoted political phrases, used not just in academe but in the real world of government too. The demise of Richard Nixon, because of the Watergate scandal, inspired Schlesinger to look back in U.S. history to locate the roots of the tremendous power that the executive had accumulated. His observations led him to develop the idea of an "imperial Presidency," with all the connotations that phrase carries. The author believes that the imperial presidency initially evolved for a clear and identifiable reason; it then grew due to other secondary factors. Certain presidents—Roosevelt and especially Kennedy—garner praise from Schlesinger for their judicious use of imperial powers. Other presidents he condemns. Schlesinger's discussion of Richard Nixon, the ultimate imperial president, is a frank and unvarnished critique of the man who turned the imperial presidency homeward, against the American people. After Nixon left office, the phrase was little-used, until President George W. Bush responded to the terrorist attacks of September 11, 2001. To some, President Bush's response to 9/11, especially his "War on Terror" and the invasion of Iraq, signified a renewal of the "imperial presidency."

IN THE LAST YEARS presidential primacy, so indispensable to the political order, has turned into presidential supremacy. The constitutional Presidency—as events so apparently disparate as the Indochina War and the Watergate affair showed—has become the imperial Presidency and threatens to be the revolutionary Presidency.

This book ... deals essentially with the shift in the *constitutional* balance—with, that is, the appropriation by the Presidency, and particularly by the contemporary Presidency, of powers reserved by the Constitution and by long historical practice to Congress.

This process of appropriation took place in both foreign and domestic affairs. Especially in the twentieth century, the circumstances of an increasingly perilous world as well as of an increasingly interdependent economy and society seemed to compel a larger concentration of authority in the Presidency. It must be said that historians and political scientists, this writer among them, contributed to the rise of the presidential mystique. But the imperial Presidency received its decisive impetus, I believe, from foreign policy; above all, from the capture by the Presidency of the most vital of national decisions, the decision to go to war.

This book consequently devotes special attention to the history of the war-making power. The assumption of that power by the Presidency was gradual and usually under the demand or pretext of emergency. It was as much a matter of congressional abdication as of presidential usurpation. . . .

The imperial Presidency was essentially the creation of foreign policy. A combination of doctrines and emotions—belief in permanent and universal crisis, fear of communism, faith in the duty and the right of the United States to intervene swiftly in every part of the world—had brought about the unprecedented centralization of decisions over war and peace in the Presidency. With this there came an unprecedented exclusion of the rest of the executive branch, of Congress, of the press and of public opinion in general from these decisions. Prolonged war in Vietnam strengthened the tendencies toward both centralization and exclusion. So the imperial Presidency grew at the expense of the constitutional order. Like the cowbird, it hatched its own eggs and pushed the others out of the nest. And, as it overwhelmed the traditional separation of powers in foreign affairs, it began to aspire toward an equivalent centralization of power in the domestic polity.

. . . We saw in the case of Franklin D. Roosevelt and the New Deal that extraordinary power flowing into the Presidency to meet domestic problems by no means enlarged presidential authority in foreign affairs. But we also saw in the case of FDR and the Second World War and Harry S. Truman and the steel seizure that extraordinary power flowing into the Presidency to meet international problems could easily encourage Presidents to extend their unilateral claims at home. . . . Twenty years later, the spillover effect from Vietnam coincided with indigenous developments that were quite separately carrying new power to the Presidency. For domestic as well as for international reasons, the imperial Presidency was sinking roots deep into the national society itself.

One such development was the decay of the traditional party system. . . . For much of American history the party has been the ultimate vehicle of political expression. Voters inherited their politics as they did their religion. . . . By the 1970s ticket-splitting had become common. Independent voting was spreading everywhere, especially among the young. Never had party loyalties been so weak, party affiliations so fluid, party organizations so irrelevant.

Many factors contributed to the decline of parties. The old political organizations had lost many of their functions. The waning of immigration, for example, had deprived the city machine of its classical clientele. The rise of civil service had cut off the machine's patronage. The New Deal had taken over the machine's social welfare role. Above all, the electronic revolution was drastically modifying the political environment. Two electronic devices had a particularly devastating impact on the traditional structure of politics—television and the computer. . . .

As the parties wasted away, the Presidency stood out in solitary majesty as the central focus of political emotion, the ever more potent symbol of national community. . . .

At the same time, the economic changes of the twentieth century had conferred vast new powers not just on the national government but more particularly on the Presidency. . . .

. . . The managed economy, in short, offered new forms of unilateral power to the President who was bold enough to take action on his own. . . .

. . . The imperial presidency, born in the 1940s and 1950s to save the outer world from perdition, thus began in the 1960s and 1970s to find nurture at home. Foreign policy had given the President the command of peace and war. Now the decay of the parties left him in command of the political scene, and the Keynesian revelation placed him in command of the economy. At this extraordinary historical moment, when foreign and domestic lines of force converged, much depended on whether the occupant of the White House was moved to ride the new tendencies of power or to resist them.

For the American Presidency was a peculiarly personal institution. It remained, of course, an agency of government, subject to unvarying demands and duties no matter who was President. But, more than most agencies of government, it changed shape, intensity and ethos according to the man in charge. . . . The management of the great foreign policy crisis of the Kennedy years—the Soviet attempt to install nuclear missiles in Cuba—came as if in proof of the proposition that the nuclear age left no alternative to unilateral presidential decision. . . .

. . . Time was short, because something had to be done before the bases became operational. Secrecy was imperative. Kennedy took the decision into his own hands, but it is to be noted that he did not make it in imperial solitude. The celebrated Executive Committee became a forum for exceedingly vigorous and intensive debate. Major alternatives received strong, even vehement, expression. Though there was no legislative consultation, there was most effective executive consultation. . . . But, even in retrospect, the missile crisis seems an emergency so acute in its nature and so peculiar in its structure that it did in fact require unilateral executive decision.

Yet this very acuteness and peculiarity disabled Kennedy's action in October 1962 as a precedent for future Presidents in situations less acute and less peculiar. For the missile crisis was unique in the postwar years in that it *really* combined all those pressures of threat, secrecy and time that the foreign policy establishment had claimed as characteristic of decisions in the nuclear age. Where the threat was less grave, the need for secrecy less urgent, the time for debate less restricted—i.e., in all other cases—the argument for independent and unilateral presidential action was notably less compelling.

Alas, Kennedy's action, which should have been celebrated as an exception, was instead enshrined as a rule. This was in great part because it so beautifully fulfilled both the romantic ideal of the strong President and the prophecy of split-second presidential decision in the nuclear age. The very brilliance of Kennedy's performance appeared to vindicate the idea that the President must take unto himself the final judgments of war and peace. The missile crisis, I believe, was superbly handled, and could not have been handled so well in any other way. But one of its legacies was the imperial conception of the Presidency that brought the republic so low in Vietnam. . . .

. . . Johnson talked to, even if he too seldom listened to, an endless stream of members of Congress and the press. He unquestionably denied himself reality for a long time, especially when it came to Vietnam. But in the end reality broke through, forcing him to accept unpleasant truths he did not wish to hear. Johnson's personality was far closer than Truman's to imperial specifications. But the fit was by no means perfect. . . .

Every President reconstructs the Presidency to meet his own psychological needs. Nixon displayed more monarchical yearnings than any of his predecessors. He plainly reveled in the ritual of the office, only regretting that it could not be more elaborate. What previous President, for example, would have dreamed of ceremonial trumpets or of putting the White House security force in costumes to rival the Guards at Buckingham Palace? Public ridicule stopped this. But Nixon saw no problem about using federal money, under the pretext of national security, to adorn his California and Florida estates with redwood fences, golf carts, heaters and wind screens for the swimming pool, beach cabanas, roof tiling, carpets, furniture, trees and shrubbery. . . . Nixon's fatal error was to institute within the White House itself a centralization even more total than that he contemplated for the executive branch. He rarely saw most of his so-called personal assistants. If an aide telephoned the President on a domestic matter, his call was switched to Haldeman's office.* If he sent the President a memorandum, Haldeman decided whether or not the President would see it. "Rather than the President telling someone to do something," Haldeman explained in 1971, "I'll tell the guy. If he wants to find out something from somebody, I'll do it."

Presidents like Roosevelt and Kennedy understood that, if the man at the top confined himself to a single information system, he became the prisoner of that system. Therefore they pitted sources of their own against the information delivered to them through official channels. They understood that contention was an indispensable means of government. But Nixon, instead of exposing himself to the chastening influence of debate, organized the executive branch and the White House in order to shield himself as far as humanly possible from direct question or challenge—i.e., from reality. . . .

As one examined the impressive range of Nixon's initiatives—from his appropriation of the war-making power to his interpretation of the appointing power, from his unilateral determination of social priorities to his unilateral abolition of statutory programs, from his attack on legislative privilege to his enlargement of executive privilege, from his theory of impoundment to his theory of the pocket veto, from his calculated disparagement of the cabinet and his calculated discrediting of the press to his carefully organized concentration of federal management in the White House—from all this a larger design ineluctably emerged. It was hard to know whether Nixon, whose style was banality, understood consciously where he was heading. He was not a man given to political philosophizing. But he was heading toward a new balance of constitutional powers, an audacious and imaginative reconstruction of the American Constitution. He did indeed contemplate, as he said in 1971 State of the Union message, a New American Revolution. But the essence of this revolution was not, as he said at the time, power to the people. The essence was power to the Presidency. . . . His purpose was probably more unconscious than conscious; and his revolution took direction and color not just from the external circumstances pressing new powers on the Presidency but from the needs and drives of his own agitated psyche. This was the fatal flaw in the revolutionary design. For everywhere he looked he saw around him hideous threats to the national security—threats that, even though he would not describe them to Congress or the people, kept his White House

---

*Robert Haldeman headed Richard Nixon's White House staff. He was a stern gatekeeper (the president wished it so) before his resignation in the face of the exploding Watergate scandals during the spring of 1973. He was subsequently convicted of criminal charges and imprisoned for his role in Watergate.—Eds.

in constant uproar and warranted in his own mind a clandestine presidential response of spectacular and historic illegality. If his public actions led toward a scheme of presidential supremacy under a considerably debilitated Constitution, his private obsessions pushed him toward the view that the Presidency could set itself, at will, *above* the Constitution. It was this theory that led straight to Watergate. . . .

Secrecy seemed to promise government three inestimable advantages: the power to withhold, the power to leak and the power to lie. . . .

The power to withhold held out the hope of denying the public the knowledge that would make possible an independent judgment on executive policy. The mystique of inside information—"if you only knew what we know"—was a most effective way to defend the national-security monopoly and prevent democratic control of foreign policy. . . .

The power to leak meant the power to tell the people what it served the government's purpose that they should know. . . .

The power to withhold and the power to leak led on inexorably to the power to lie. The secrecy system instilled in the executive branch the idea that foreign policy was no one's business save its own, and uncontrolled secrecy made it easy for lying to become routine. It was in this spirit that the Eisenhower administration concealed the CIA operations it was mounting against governments around the world. It was in this spirit that the Kennedy administration stealthily sent the Cuban brigade to the Bay of Pigs* and stealthily enlarged American involvement in Vietnam. It was in this spirit that the Johnson administration Americanized the Vietnam War, misrepresenting one episode after another to Congress and the people—Tonkin Gulf, the first American ground force commitment, the bombing of North Vietnam, My Lai and the rest.†

---

*In 1961, President John F. Kennedy accepted responsibility for the disaster at the Bay of Pigs in Cuba. Over a thousand Cuban exiles, trained by the U.S. Central Intelligence Agency (CIA), tried to land in Cuba to overthrow the communist government of Fidel Castro. The invasion was a complete failure, forcing Kennedy to reassess his foreign policy approach, especially toward Latin America.—EDS.

†The Tonkin Gulf incident involved two alleged attacks on American ships in the waters off the coast of Vietnam in 1964. President Lyndon Johnson may have exaggerated the extent of the attacks to gain support for widening the war. In response to the incident, the Senate voted 88 to 2 and the House of Representatives 416 to 0 to allow the president significant latitude in the use of American forces in Vietnam. No formal declaration of war was ever made concerning Vietnam, but the Gulf of Tonkin Resolution became the executive branch's "blank check" to expand the conflict. The 1968 My Lai massacre was a turning point in American public opinion concerning the Vietnam War. U.S. soldiers killed over a hundred Vietnamese villagers. One lieutenant was tried and convicted for the slaughter that had happened because of the inability of American troops to distinguish between enemy soldiers and civilians. Some Americans believed that those higher up in the military, not just Lieutenant William Calley, should have been prosecuted for the massacre.—EDS.

The longer the secrecy system dominated government, the more government assumed the *right* to lie. . . .

God, it has been well said, looks after drunks, children and the United States of America. However, given the number, the brazen presumption and the clownish ineptitude of the conspirators, if it had not been Watergate, it would surely have been something else. For Watergate was a symptom, not a cause. Nixon's supporters complained that his critics were blowing up a petty incident out of all proportion to its importance. No doubt a burglary at Democratic headquarters was trivial next to a mission to Peking. But Watergate's importance was not simply in itself. Its importance was in the way it brought to the surface, symbolized and made politically accessible the great question posed by the Nixon administration in every sector—the question of presidential power. The unwarranted and unprecedented expansion of presidential power, because it ran through the whole Nixon system, was bound, if repressed at one point, to break out at another. This, not Watergate, was the central issue. . . . Watergate did stop the revolutionary Presidency in its tracks. It blew away the mystique of the mandate and reinvigorated the constitutional separation of powers. If the independent judiciary, the free press, Congress and the executive agencies could not really claim too much credit as institutions for work performed within them by brave individuals, nonetheless they all drew new confidence as institutions from the exercise of power they had forgotten they possessed. The result could only be to brace and strengthen the inner balance of American democracy. . . .

If the Nixon White House escaped the legal consequences of its illegal behavior, why would future Presidents and their associates not suppose themselves entitled to do what the Nixon White House had done? Only condign punishment would restore popular faith in the Presidency and deter future Presidents from illegal conduct—so long, at least, as Watergate remained a vivid memory. We have noted that corruption appears to visit the White House in fifty-year cycles. This suggests that exposure and retribution inoculate the Presidency against its latent criminal impulses for about half a century. Around the year 2023 the American people would be well advised to go on the alert and start nailing down everything in sight.

34

MICHAEL CAIRO

The "Imperial Presidency" Triumphant

Foreign policy specialist Michael Cairo begins by citing the important contribution of Arthur Schlesinger, whose phrase "imperial presidency" has been used to explain much in American foreign policy, from Vietnam onward. Both President Bill Clinton and President George W. Bush extended the imperial presidency, Cairo contends, despite expectations that after the fall of the Soviet Union the U.S. Congress would reclaim power. He traces the constitutional basis of the power to conduct war, ultimately moving into the modern era with this blunt assessment: "presidents Clinton and Bush abused their power." Cairo gives readers some often-forgotten background on U.S. hostility toward Iraq and Saddam Hussein. Under both Clinton and Bush, presidential decision making was largely done without Congress's participation. The events of September 11, 2001, accelerated the imperial presidency, Cairo explains, due to President Bush's response to the terrorist attacks. Ultimately, "preemption," striking out against terrorists and nations supportive of terrorism before another attack, represents the imperial presidency "triumphant," Cairo believes. The excerpt provides a good review of the events immediately before and after the terrorist attacks of 2001, and it predicts a future for presidential war power not too different from the past.

━━━━━

THE QUESTION OF WHO has authority to deploy and use U.S. military troops and force abroad is controversial and one that has been present since the Republic's founding. In contemporary U.S. politics, the controversy has been decided in favor of the president. As Arthur Schlesinger Jr. argues, "presidential primacy, so indispensable to the political order, has turned into presidential supremacy," and we have seen an "appropriation by the Presidency . . . of powers reserved by the Constitution and by long historical practice to Congress." According to Schlesinger, this is particularly evident in war powers, where presidents have repeatedly claimed sweeping and unilateral authority, threatening to create an "imperial presidency."

The imperial presidency threatened to emerge during the era of Vietnam and Watergate. Following President Richard Nixon's resignation, however, Congress was resurgent and the foreign policy power of the presidency appeared to be waning. Despite this appearance, President

Ronald Reagan's abuse of powers leading to the Iran-Contra affair* demonstrated that the imperial presidency had not vanished. Contrary to efforts to leash presidential power in foreign affairs, that power has continued to grow, especially with regard to war powers.

In the post–September 11 era, this issue is particularly important. In dealing with terrorism and the threats it presents to the United States, the George W. Bush administration pushes the boundaries on presidential use of force and threatens the constitutional balance between the executive and legislative branches. This trend, however, extends back to the Clinton administration, where a similar abuse of presidential war powers occurred.

Historically, the constitutional ambiguity of war powers has produced tension between the executive and legislative branches, but the Clinton and George W. Bush administrations have advanced the abuse of presidential power in the use of force and exacerbated the already-existing tension. This surprised some because both presidents lacked foreign policy experience when they entered the White House and the cold war† was no longer an emphasis for policymakers. These factors led some to suggest that Congress would be more assertive in foreign policy and recapture its war powers. However, the nature of the new threats that emerged and the ambiguity of the world political environment worked against the rise of a more resolute Congress and served to enhance presidential war power. In addition, and to the chagrin of many, presidents Clinton and Bush used the United Nations (UN) in expanding their presidential power. . . .

. . . [W]ar powers no longer reflect the balance of shared powers the Constitution established. Instead, presidents have claimed and exercised unilateral decision-making authority with regard to war powers. Presidents Clinton and Bush have further contributed to the abuse of war powers not only by subverting Congress and its constitutional authority, but also by using the United Nations as the basis of presidential claims of unilateral war powers. In the area of war powers, the Constitution no

---

*During President Reagan's administration, members of his National Security Council (NSC) were charged with secretly selling arms to Iran in order to fund anti-communist Nicaraguan Contra activities.—EDS.

†The Cold War refers to the hostility that existed between the United States and the Soviet Union from the end of World War II until recent times. The Cold War involved many forms of hostility: democracy versus communism; America's NATO allies versus the Soviet Union's Warsaw Pact military partners; the threat of nuclear war; economic competition; the dividing of Third World nations into pro-U.S. and pro-Soviet camps. With the demise of communism in Eastern Europe and the disintegration of the Soviet Union, the Cold War era has ended. —EDS.

longer reflects the idea of "separated institutions sharing powers," but rather a triumph of the "imperial presidency." . . .

To the casual observer, the president, as commander in chief, appears entitled to unilateral military powers when deploying and using U.S. troops and forces abroad. One of the many arguments in favor of presidential war powers is the [1987] Minority Report of the Congressional Committees Investigating the Iran-Contra Affair. According to the report, no fewer than 118 occasions of force occurred without prior legislative authorization. "The relevance of these repeated examples of the extensive use of armed force," it argues, "is that they indicate how far the President's inherent powers were assumed to have reached when Congress was silent, and even in some cases, where Congress had prohibited an action." . . .

Presidential practice has also relegated Congress to a backseat in decisions on the use of force. Since World War II, Congress has never specifically declared war. In the Korean War, the Truman administration argued, "the President's power to send Armed Forces outside the country is not dependent on Congressional authority." Secretary of Defense Richard Cheney echoed this sentiment prior to the Persian Gulf War. Cheney explained that he did "not believe the president requires any additional authority from Congress" to engage U.S. forces abroad. During his 1992 presidential election campaign, President George H. W. Bush stated that he did not need "some old goat" in Congress to evict Saddam Hussein from Kuwait.

Contrary to these arguments and presidential practice in general, the Founders did not intend to grant presidents exclusive authority in war powers. The belief that Congress should not get in the president's way when national security matters arise is clearly popular, but the Constitution contradicts this. According to the Constitution, Congress and the president are given specific foreign policy powers and each plays a role to ensure that U.S. foreign policy is effective. In fact, the Constitution grants broad power to Congress, not the president. Although the president is given the powers to nominate ambassadors, negotiate treaties, and direct the armed forces as commander in chief, the Congress is granted the powers to regulate commerce, raise and support armies, provide and maintain a navy, and declare war. Thus, the Constitution originally empowered Congress in military matters. . . .

Nothing was more crucial than the successful conduct of foreign policy and the Founders agreed that national safety could best be ensured through trade. The Constitution gave clear priority to commercial relations and vested control over commerce in Congress. Congress was also brought into the treaty-making power. Unlike the monarch, who could approve treaties without Parliament, presidents would have to consult Congress and receive its acceptance of treaties. Congress was also given other weighty powers in foreign policy, including appropriations, and the power to declare war. The Constitution makes clear that the Founders were determined to deny presidents the sole prerogative of making war and peace. The Founders designed a system that, according to James Wilson, would not "hurry us into war; it is calculated to guard against it. It will not be in the power of a single man, or a single body of men, to involve us in such distress." In fact, the Founders chose not to mention the presidency in the war-making power.

This, however, did not deny presidential powers. The Constitution vested the command of the Army and Navy in the presidency. The president's power as commander in chief provided presidents with the ability to respond to national emergencies. The Founders clearly agreed with John Locke that in an emergency responsible rulers could resort to exceptional power. Legislatures were too large and unwieldy to capably cope with a crisis. According to Locke, when the executive perceived an emergency, he could initiate extralegal, or even illegal, measures but the leader would only be vindicated in these actions if the legislature and public sanctioned his actions. . . .

The Founders clearly divided war powers, but the ambiguity of the Constitution left the door open to conflict. Although Congress is given the sole power to initiate offensive war, the Constitution allows presidents to initiate defensive war; this has easily been enlarged. In the nineteenth and twentieth centuries, presidents strengthened their control of information and secured a monopoly on diplomacy and war. . . .

With the collapse of the Soviet Union in 1991 and the subsequent end of the cold war, the United States became the lone superpower. The prospects for international peace seemed considerably better. Many had hopes that the end of the cold war would mean the end of conflict, yet one could argue that conflict has been more prevalent than during the cold war era. Conflict has also not focused on any one issue, but rather multiple issues, including ethnic conflict, civil war, genocide, and terrorism. The uncertainty of the post–cold war environment has increased presidential power because the use of force in U.S. foreign policy remains a key component in this uncertain world.

In dealing with terrorism and Iraq, in particular, presidents Clinton and Bush abused their power. Both of these cases offer good examples for multiple reasons. First, these issues span both presidencies and analysis can uncover patterns. Second, both issues have been central to U.S. national security since the end of the cold war. Finally, both issues demonstrate how each president used the United Nations to justify his use of power.

The Clinton Administration and Saddam Hussein

On August 2, 1990, Saddam Hussein, the leader of Iraq, invaded and annexed Kuwait, seizing Kuwait's vast oil reserves and liquidating billions of dollars of loans provided by Kuwait during the Iran-Iraq War. Within months, the George H. W. Bush administration assembled a coalition of forces, supported by the United Nations, to remove the Iraqi army from Kuwait. On January 17, 1991, Operation Desert Storm, which was authorized by UN Resolution 678 and by a congressional vote endorsing the action, ensued.

The international coalition proved victorious and instituted UN Resolution 687, giving the UN Special Commission (UNSCOM) complete access to Iraqi facilities to search for weapons of mass destruction. In addition, the UN Security Council also passed UN Resolution 688, condemning Iraqi actions against the Kurdish population and authorizing relief organizations to provide humanitarian aid. Pursuant to these resolutions, but without specific UN Security Council authorization, a no-fly zone was established, prohibiting Iraqi flights in northern and southern Iraq.

President-elect Clinton inherited this policy toward Iraq and a hostile Hussein. Almost immediately, Clinton faced mounting tensions between the United States and Iraq. In April 1993 former President Bush visited Kuwait. Prior to his visit, the Central Intelligence Agency (CIA) and Federal Bureau of Investigation (FBI) uncovered an assassination plot against Bush and linked the Iraqi government to that plot. As a response to this plot, Clinton responded with an attack, using precision-guided missiles. Clinton justified the bombings in a statement to Congress, noting "our inherent right to self-defense as recognized in Article 51 of the United Nations Charter and pursuant to [his] constitutional authority with respect to the conduct of foreign relations and as Commander in Chief." In an address to the American public about the strikes, Clinton added, "There should be no mistake about the message we intend these actions to convey to Saddam Hussein. . . . We will combat terrorism. We will deter aggression. . . . While the cold war has ended, the world is not free of danger. And I am determined to take the steps necessary to keep our Nation secure."

In 1996 Clinton used force against Hussein in support of Iraq's Kurdish population. One Kurdish faction, the Patriotic Union of Kurdistan (PUK), accepted arms from Iran and Hussein responded by attacking the

PUK's headquarters in northern Iraq, attempting to crush the opposition. In response, Clinton ordered a missile attack on targets in southern Iraq. In justifying this attack, Clinton relied on humanitarian arguments stressing UN Resolution 688 explaining, "Earlier today I ordered American forces to strike Iraq. Our missiles sent the following message to Saddam Hussein: When you abuse your own people . . . you must pay a price." During his weekly radio address, Clinton added, "America's policy has been to contain Saddam, to reduce the threat he poses to the region, and to do it in a way that makes him pay a price when he acts recklessly."

The next major crisis with Iraq occurred in 1998 when Saddam Hussein refused UNSCOM weapons inspectors access to certain sites, as the provisions of UN Resolution 687 outlined. Hussein argued that U.S. involvement in the inspections was the problem. The Clinton administration suggested that diplomacy was their main instrument in solving the crisis, but reserved the right to use force. Implicit in the administration's argument for the use of force was that the administration had the authority to do so. . . .

In December 1998 Clinton attacked Iraq after a series of diplomatic conflicts over UNSCOM. In an address to the American public, Clinton explained that Iraq had been given numerous opportunities to comply and must face the "consequences of defying the U.N." In a letter to Congress, Clinton justified the attacks citing UN Security Council Resolutions 678 and 687, authorizing "all necessary means" to ensure Iraqi compliance. He also referred to the power granted to the president under Public Law 102–1, which authorized President Bush to use force against Iraq in 1991.

Clinton's actions toward Iraq established a pattern that continued into the George W. Bush administration. First, the Clinton administration took action with little congressional consultation. In fact, Congress remained relatively silent on each occasion. Some of this silence can be attributed to public approval of Clinton's actions. For example, in the 1993 case, 61 percent of the public approved of the action taken. Second, the Clinton administration claimed unilateral powers under the commander in chief clause of the Constitution and UN Security Council authorizations. Justifying the attacks based on UN Security Council authorization broadly defined presidential and U.S. power. . . .

The Bush Administration: Increasing Risks, Increasing Power

In the George W. Bush administration, the war on terrorism and policy toward Iraq are intertwined. This became clear after the September 11,

2001, terrorist attacks on the United States. On that day, terrorists struck the World Trade Center Twin Towers and the Pentagon, killing thousands. Following these attacks, Bush made clear his intentions vowing, "Terrorism against our nation will not stand." He further argued, "War has been waged against us by stealth and deceit and murder," granting the president full authority to defend against the threat. The policy would eventually become the Bush Doctrine, including not only terrorist groups, but rogue states.

On September 12, the UN Security Council adopted a resolution condemning the attacks, declaring that they constituted a "threat to international peace and security." In addition, the resolution recognized the "inherent right of individual or collective self-defense in accordance with the Charter." On September 28, the UN Security Council unanimously adopted a historic resolution directed toward combating terrorism and states that support, harbor, provide safe haven to, supply, finance, help recruit, or aid terrorists. The resolution required cooperation of all member states in a wide range of areas. Resolution 1373 established a comprehensive legal framework for addressing the threat of international terrorism. It also provided a basis for the Bush Doctrine.

On October 7, the U.S. ambassador to the United Nations, John Negroponte, delivered a letter to the president of the UN Security Council stating that the United States, together with other states, had "initiated actions in the exercise of its inherent right of individual and collective self defense." These actions were taken against al Qaeda terrorist camps and military installations in Afghanistan, which had a "central role in the attacks." The letter went on to state that the United States "may find that our self-defense requires further actions with respect to other organizations and other States." This letter was the birth of the Bush Doctrine, which asserted the right of the United States to use military force in "self-defense" against any state that aids, harbors, or supports international terrorism, and it had profound implications. Most significantly, Ambassador Negroponte's letter left open the possibility that a state may intervene in anticipatory self-defense, without UN Security Council authorization, in another state that is alleged to be aiding, harboring, or supporting terrorism. Secretary of Defense Donald Rumsfeld later added:

The only way to deal with the terrorists . . . is to take the battle to them, and find them, and root them out. And that is self-defense. And there is no question but that any nation on Earth has the right of self-defense. And we do. And what we are doing is going after those people, and those organizations, and those capabilities wherever we're going to find them in the world, and stop them from killing Americans. . . . That is in effect self-defense of a preemptive nature.

In his January 2002 State of the Union address, Bush, referring to North Korea, Iran, and Iraq, argued, "States like these, and their terrorist allies, constitute an axis of evil, arming to threaten the peace of the world. . . . America will do what is necessary to ensure our nation's security. . . . I will not wait on events while dangers gather. I will not stand by as peril draws closer and closer. With this statement, the president made clear his intentions to wage war when he felt preventing threats to the United States was necessary. The United States had been attacked, and Bush believed his actions did not require congressional authority or consultation.

Although Bush had a strong argument for unilaterally exercising the decision to use force with regard to the terrorist attacks on September 11, he used that argument to extend his authority and shift U.S. foreign policy. Throughout the spring and summer 2002, the Bush administration devised its strategy for approaching the world. The national security strategy that emerged in September 2002 represents the most sweeping transformation in U.S. foreign policy since the beginning of the cold war. The strategy sets forth three tasks: "We will defend the peace by fighting terrorists and tyrants. We will preserve the peace by building good relations among great powers. We will extend the peace by encouraging free and open societies on every continent."

These tasks have profound implications for the Bush administration's foreign policy. More significantly, the strategy links terrorists with tyrants, the axis of evil and its allies, as sources of danger in the world. Since September 11, it argues, the United States no longer makes a "distinction between terrorists and those who knowingly harbor or provide aid to them." Furthermore, the Bush administration articulates that it does not believe that traditional U.S. strategies such as containment and deterrence will be effective against these new threats. According to the strategy, these terrorists and tyrants are seeking weapons of mass destruction to threaten U.S. security. Faced with this elevated threat to U.S. interests and the American way of life, the strategy argues, "America will act against such emerging threats" and will not "let our enemies strike first."

The national security strategy establishes a doctrine of preemption, relying on the argument that:

nations need not suffer an attack before they can lawfully take action to defend themselves against forces that present an imminent danger of attack. . . . Our priority will be first to disrupt and destroy terrorist organizations. . . . We will disrupt and destroy terrorist organizations by . . . identifying and destroying the threat before it reaches our borders . . . we will not hesitate to act alone, if necessary, to exercise our right of self-defense by acting preemptively against such terrorists, to prevent them from doing harm against our people and our country. . . . [O]ur best defense is a good offense. . . . This strategy will turn adversity into opportunity.

In addition, the strategy links action against rogue states to action against terrorists, expanding preemption:

[N]ew and deadly challenges have emerged from rogue states. . . . These states' pursuit of, and trade in, [weapons of mass destruction have] become a looming threat to all nations. We must be prepared to stop rogue states and their terrorist clients before they . . . threaten or use weapons of mass destruction against the United States. . . . [T]he United States can no longer solely rely on the reactive posture as we have in the past.

The new strategy is proactive, rejecting the reactive strategies of containment and deterrence; its proactive stance is the basis for expanded presidential power. The strategy suggests that due to the nature of the threat a president may act alone to start a war against a perceived aggressor. The strategy presents an incontestable moral claim that in certain situations preemption is preferable to doing nothing and relies on Article 51 of the U.N. Charter for its legitimacy. In fact, the entire strategy is based on the presumption that a president can and must act to prevent future attacks on the United States or U.S. interests. Although such a policy may have its merits, it denies the necessity for congressional action of any kind in the use of force. . . .

The administration consequently negotiated a new UN Security Council resolution. The intent of that resolution was to prepare the way toward military action in Iraq. Resolution 1441 passed the UN Security Council unanimously on November 8, 2002, with a 15–0 vote in support of the resolution, and laid out what Iraq had to do to avoid war. The resolution cited Iraq in "material breach of its obligations under relevant resolutions." Furthermore, it offered Iraq "a final opportunity to comply with its disarmament obligations." In its final phrases, the resolution warned Iraq that it would face "serious consequences" because of continued violations of the UN Security Council resolutions.

Iraq responded to Resolution 1441 by inviting UN weapons inspectors back into the country. Throughout late 2002 and early 2003, the weapons inspectors, headed by Hans Blix and Mohammed el Baredei, pursued their task while the world watched and the United States continued to make its case that Iraqi failure to comply would be met with swift action. . . .

Bush, like Clinton before him, stressed the importance of the United Nations and used UN resolutions as a basis for using force against Iraq. On February 6, 2003, Bush referred to Iraqi noncompliance with UN resolutions as a basis for using force. . . .

Following just over one month of warfare, the Iraqi regime crumbled and U.S. troops occupied Baghdad, Iraq's capital. With rebuilding efforts under way in Iraq, Bush immediately began efforts to focus on another member of the axis of evil—Iran, thus extending the Bush Doctrine of preemption. It is clear that the doctrine is firmly in place and presidential power will remain strong as long as U.S. foreign policy continues to emphasize and expand the war on terrorism. . . .

Presidential abuse of war powers is not a new phenomenon. Since World War II, however, presidential war power has vastly expanded and increased. Despite the constitutional questions that presidential war power raises, it is most likely to remain a problem for a variety of reasons. First, Congress is designed to be the primary check on presidential war powers. Since World War II, however, Congress has been rather ineffective in checking presidential war powers. In some cases, Congress not only fails to combat presidential war power, but also even voluntarily surrenders its legislative functions. In both the Clinton and George W. Bush administrations, Congress never declared war, but actively supported the actions each president took.

Second, contemporary presidents do not believe they need congressional approval and have substituted congressional approval with international legal sanction. Presidents Clinton and George W. Bush both relied on international legal authority in the form of UN Security Council resolutions to pursue military force. This suggests that presidents must no longer garner congressional approval when pursuing war, but must now acquire international support and must meet obligations under international law. This, as the George W. Bush case suggests, opens up the door to an even greater expansion of presidential authority and power in the use of force.

Both presidents relied on Article 51 of the UN Charter, the inherent right of self-defense, to enhance and justify their own and U.S. power. In addition, they both used UN Security Council resolutions as authority for action. This pattern will continue to expand presidential power. As long as the American public and Congress accept the United Nations as providing necessary authority for the use of force, presidents will no longer need congressional authorization.

Third, and perhaps most important, the American public and media have virtually accepted presidents' unilateral use of force. Practice has led most to believe that Congress does not and should not play a significant role in the process. The media age has contributed to this image by increasing the stature of presidents vis-à-vis Congress. As during the Clinton administration, Bush's high popularity ratings, which have until recently consistently been in the 60 percentile, make it unlikely that Congress will challenge him. Ultimately, presidential war power remains strong and will continue to remain strong. Presidents will not willingly give up this power, and Congress is not actively trying to take this power away. Instead of cooperation between the executive and legislative branches of government, the imperial presidency has triumphed. Presidents increasingly take unilateral steps to involve the U.S. military in operations abroad and have substituted the United Nations and international law for congressional sanction of their actions.

35

THOMAS CRONIN
MICHAEL GENOVESE

From *The Paradoxes of the American Presidency*

The United States as a nation of paradoxes is a theme frequently used to explain the contradictions found throughout American life. In an earlier selection, Michael Kammen called Americans "people of paradox." Here, political scientists Thomas Cronin and Michael Genovese use the concept of paradox to explore the many images that citizens hold of their president. Each image they describe is accompanied by a contrary image. For example, Cronin and Genovese note, the president is supposed to be an average person just like us, while simultaneously being outstanding and extraordinary. With such paradoxical expectations of a president, is it any wonder that Americans judge the executive so harshly?

THE MIND SEARCHES FOR answers to the complexities of life. We often gravitate toward simple explanations for the world's mysteries. This is a natural way to try and make sense out of a world that seems to defy understanding. We are uncomfortable with contradictions so we reduce reality to understandable simplifications. And yet, contradictions and clashing expectations are part of life. "No aspect of society, no habit, custom, movement, development, is without cross-currents," says historian Barbara Tuchman. "Starving peasants in hovels live alongside prosperous landlords in featherbeds. Children are neglected and children are loved." In life we are confronted with paradoxes for which we seek meaning. The same is true for the American presidency. We admire presidential power, yet fear it. We yearn for the heroic, yet are also inherently suspicious of it. We demand dynamic leadership, yet grant only limited powers to the president. We want presidents to be dispassionate analysts and listeners, yet they must also be decisive. We are impressed with presidents who have great self-confidence, yet we dislike arrogance and respect those who express reasonable self-doubt.

How then are we to make sense of the presidency? This complex, multidimensional, even contradictory institution is vital to the American system of government. The physical and political laws that seem to constrain one president, liberate another. What proves successful in one, leads to failure in another. Rather than seeking one unifying theory of presidential politics that answers all our questions, we believe that the American presidency might be better understood as a series of paradoxes, clashing expectations and contradictions.

Leaders live with contradictions. Presidents, more than most people, learn to take advantage of contrary or divergent forces. Leadership situations commonly require successive displays of contrasting characteristics. Living with, even embracing, contradictions is a sign of political and personal maturity.

The effective leader understands the presence of opposites. The aware leader, much like a first-rate conductor, knows when to bring in various sections, knows when and how to turn the volume up and down, and learns how to balance opposing sections to achieve desired results. Effective presidents learn how to manage these contradictions and give meaning and purpose to confusing and often clashing expectations. The novelist F. Scott Fitzgerald once suggested that, "The test of a first-rate intelligence is the ability to hold two opposed ideas in the mind at the same time." Casey Stengel, long-time New York Yankee manager and occasional (if accidental) Zen philosopher, captured the essence of the paradox when he noted, "Good pitching will always stop good hitting, and vice versa."

Our expectations of, and demands on, the president are frequently so contradictory as to invite two-faced behavior by our presidents. Presidential powers are often not as great as many of us believe, and the president gets unjustly condemned as ineffective. Or a president will overreach or resort to unfair play while trying to live up to our demands.

The Constitution is of little help. The founders purposely left the presidency imprecisely defined. This was due in part to their fears of both the monarchy and the masses, and in part to their hopes that future presidents would create a more powerful office than the framers were able to do at the time. They knew that at times the president would have to move swiftly and effectively, yet they went to considerable lengths to avoid enumerating specific powers and duties in order to calm the then widespread fear of monarchy. After all, the nation had just fought a war against executive tyranny. Thus the paradox of the invention of the presidency: To get the presidency approved in 1787 and 1788, the framers had to leave several silences and ambiguities for fear of portraying the office as an overly centralized leadership institution. Yet when we need central leadership we turn to the president and read into Article II of the Constitution various prerogatives or inherent powers that allow the president to perform as an effective national leader.

Today the informal and symbolic powers of the presidency account for as much as the formal, stated ones. Presidential powers expand and contract in response to varying situational and technological changes. The powers of the presidency are thus interpreted so differently that they sometimes seem to be those of different offices. In some ways the modern presidency has virtually unlimited authority for almost anything its occupant chooses to do with it. In other ways, a president seems hopelessly ensnarled in a web of checks and balances.

Presidents and presidential candidates must constantly balance conflicting demands, cross pressures, and contradictions. It is characteristic of the American mind to hold contradictory ideas without bothering to resolve the conflicts between them. Perhaps some contradictions are best left unresolved, especially as ours is an imperfect world and our political system is a complicated one, held together by countless compromises. We may not be able to resolve many of these clashing expectations. Some of the inconsistencies in our judgments about presidents doubtless stem from the many ironies and paradoxes of the human condition. While difficult, at the least we should develop a better understanding of what it is we ask of our presidents, thereby increasing our sensitivity to the limits and possibilities of what a president can achieve. This might free presidents to lead and administer more effectively in those critical times when the nation has no choice but to turn to them. Whether we like it or not, the vitality of our democracy depends in large measure upon the sensitive interaction of presidential leadership with an understanding public willing to listen and willing to provide support. Carefully planned innovation is nearly impossible without the kind of leadership a competent and fair-minded president can provide.

The following are some of the paradoxes of the presidency. Some are cases of confused expectations. Some are cases of wanting one kind of presidential behavior at one time, and another kind later. Still others stem from the contradiction inherent in the concept of democratic leadership, which on the surface at least, appears to set up "democratic" and "leadership" as warring concepts. Whatever the source, each has implications for presidential performance and for how Americans judge presidential success and failure. . . .

Paradox #1. Americans demand powerful, popular presidential leadership that solves the nation's problems. Yet we are inherently suspicious of strong centralized leadership and especially the abuse of power and therefore we place significant limits on the president's powers.

We admire power but fear it. We love to unload responsibilities on our leaders, yet we intensely dislike being bossed around. We expect impressive leadership from presidents, and we simultaneously impose constitutional, cultural, and political restrictions on them. These restrictions often prevent presidents from living up to our expectations. . . .

Presidents are supposed to follow the laws and respect the constitutional procedures that were designed to restrict their power, yet still they must be powerful and effective when action is needed. For example, we approve of presidential military initiatives and covert operations when they work out well, but we criticize presidents and insist they work more closely with Congress when the initiatives fail. We recognize the need for secrecy in certain government actions, but we resent being deceived and left in the dark—again, especially when things go wrong, as in Reagan's Iranian arms sale diversions to the Contras.

Although we sometimes do not approve of the way a president acts, we often approve of the end results. Thus Lincoln is often criticized for acting outside the limits of the Constitution, but at the same time he is forgiven due to the obvious necessity for him to violate certain constitutional principles in order to preserve the Union. FDR was often flagrantly deceptive and manipulative not only of his political opponents but also of his staff and allies. FDR even relished pushing people around and toying with them. But leadership effectiveness in the end often comes down to whether a person acts in terms of the highest interests of the nation. Most historians conclude Lincoln and Roosevelt were responsible in the use of presidential power, to preserve the Union, to fight the depression and nazism. Historians also conclude that Nixon was wrong for acting beyond the law in pursuit of personal power. . . .

Paradox #2. We yearn for the democratic "common person" and also for the uncommon, charismatic, heroic, visionary performance.

We want our presidents to be like us, but better than us. We like to think America is the land where the common sense of the common person reigns. Nourished on a diet of Frank Capra's "common-man-as-hero" movies, and the literary celebration of the average citizen by authors such as Emerson, Whitman, and Thoreau, we prize the common touch. The plain-speaking Harry Truman, the up-from-the-log-cabin "man or woman of the people," is enticing. Few of us, however, settle for anything but the best; we want presidents to succeed and we hunger for brilliant, uncommon, and semiregal performances from presidents. . . .

It is said the American people crave to be governed by a president who is greater than anyone else yet not better than themselves. We are inconsistent; we want our president to be one of the folks yet also something special. If presidents get too special, however, they get criticized and roasted. If they try to be too folksy, people get bored. We cherish the myth that anyone can grow up to be president, that there are no barriers and no elite qualifications, but we don't want someone who is too ordinary. Would-be presidents have to prove their special qualifications—their excellence, their stamina, and their capacity for uncommon leadership. Fellow commoner, Truman, rose to the demands of the job and became an apparently gifted decision maker, or so his admirers would have us believe.

In 1976 Governor Jimmy Carter seemed to grasp this conflict and he ran as local, down-home, farm-boy-next-door makes good. The image of the peanut farmer turned gifted governor contributed greatly to Carter's success as a national candidate and he used it with consummate skill. Early in his presidential bid, Carter enjoyed introducing himself as peanut farmer *and* nuclear physicist, once again suggesting he was down to earth but cerebral as well.

Ronald Reagan illustrated another aspect of this paradox. He was a representative all-American—small-town, midwestern, and also a rich celebrity of stage, screen, and television. He boasted of having been a Democrat, yet campaigned as a Republican. A veritable Mr. Smith goes to Washington, he also had uncommon star quality. Bill Clinton liked us to view him as both a Rhodes scholar and an ordinary saxophone-playing member of the high school band from Hope, Arkansas; as a John Kennedy and even an Elvis figure; and also as just another jogger who would stop by for a Big Mac on the way home from a run in the neighborhood....

Paradox #3. We want a decent, just, caring, and compassionate president, yet we admire a cunning, guileful, and, on occasions that warrant it, even a ruthless, manipulative president.

There is always a fine line between boldness and recklessness, between strong self-confidence and what the Greeks called "hubris," between dogged determination and pigheaded stubbornness. Opinion polls indicate people want a just, decent, and intellectually honest individual as our chief executive. Almost as strongly, however, the public also demands the quality of toughness.

We may admire modesty, humility, and a sense of proportion, but most of our great leaders have been vain and crafty. After all, you don't get to the White House by being a wallflower. Most have aggressively sought power and were rarely preoccupied with metaphysical inquiry or ethical considerations.

Franklin Roosevelt's biographers, while emphasizing his compassion for the average American, also agree he was vain, devious, and manipulative and had a passion for secrecy. These, they note, are often the standard weaknesses of great leaders. Significant social and political advances are made by those with drive, ambition, and a certain amount of brash, irrational self-confidence. . . .

Perhaps Dwight Eisenhower reconciled these clashing expectations better than recent presidents. Blessed with a wonderfully seductive, benign smile and a reserved, calming disposition, he was also the disciplined, strong, no-nonsense five-star general with all the medals and victories to go along with it. His ultimate resource as president was this reconciliation of decency and proven toughness, likability alongside demonstrated valor. Some of his biographers suggest his success was at least partly due to his uncanny ability to appear guileless to the public yet act with ample cunning in private. . . .

One of the ironies of the American presidency is that those characteristics we condemn in one president, we look for in another. Thus a supporter of Jimmy Carter's once suggested that Sunday school teacher Carter wasn't "rotten enough," "a wheeler-dealer," "an s.o.b."—precisely the virtues (if they can be called that) that Lyndon Johnson was most criticized for a decade earlier. President Clinton was viewed as both a gifted Southern Baptist-style preacher by some of his followers and a man who was character challenged, by opponents. . . .

Paradox #4. We admire the "above politics" nonpartisan or bipartisan approach, yet the presidency is perhaps the most political office in the American system, a system in which we need a creative entrepreneurial master politician.

The public yearns for a statesman in the White House, for a George Washington or a second "era of good feelings"—anything that might prevent partisanship or politics as usual in the White House. Former French President Charles de Gaulle once said, "I'm neither of the left nor of the right nor of the center, but above." In fact, however, the job of president demands that the officeholder be a gifted political broker, ever attentive to changing political moods and coalitions. . . .

Presidents are often expected to be above politics in some respects while being highly political in others. Presidents are never supposed to act with their eyes on the next election, yet their power position demands they must. They are neither supposed to favor any particular group or party nor wheel and deal and twist too many arms. That's politics and that's bad! Instead, a president is supposed to be "president of all the people," above politics. A president is also asked to lead a party, to help fellow party members get elected or reelected, to deal firmly with party barons, interest group chieftains, and congressional political brokers. His ability to gain legislative victories depends on his skills at party leadership and on the size of his party's congressional membership. Jimmy Carter once lamented that "It's very difficult for someone to serve in this office and meet the difficult issues in a proper and courageous way and still maintain a combination of interest-group approval that will provide a clear majority at election time."

To take the president out of politics is to assume, incorrectly, that a president will be generally right and the public generally wrong, that a president must be protected from the push and shove of political pressures. But what president has always been right? Over the years, public opinion has usually been as sober a guide as anything else on the political waterfront. And, lest we forget, having a president constrained and informed by public opinion is what democracy is all about.

The fallacy of antipolitics presidencies is that only one view of the national interest is tenable, and a president may pursue that view only by ignoring political conflict and pressure. Politics, properly conceived, is the art of accommodating the diversity and variety of public opinion to meet public goals. Politics is the task of building durable coalitions and majorities. It isn't always pretty. "The process isn't immaculate and cannot always be kid-gloved. A president and his men must reward loyalty and punish opposition; it is the only way." . . .

Paradox #5. We want a president who can unify us, yet the job requires taking firm stands, making unpopular or controversial decisions that necessarily upset and divide us.

Closely related to paradox #4, paradox #5 holds that we ask the president to be a national unifier and a *harmonizer* while at the same time the job requires priority setting and *advocacy* leadership. The tasks are near opposites. . . .

Our nation is one of the few in the world that calls on its chief executive to serve as its symbolic, ceremonial head of state *and* as its political head of government. Elsewhere, these tasks are spread around. In some nations there is a monarch and a prime minister; in others there are three visible national leaders—a head of state, a premier, and a powerful party chief.

In the absence of an alternative office or institution, we demand that our president act as a unifying force in our lives. Perhaps it all began with George Washington, who so artfully performed this function. At least for a while he truly was above politics, a unique symbol of our new nation. He was a healer, a unifier, and an extraordinary man for several seasons. Today we ask no less of our presidents than that they should do as Washington did, and more.

We have designed a presidential job description, however, that often forces our contemporary presidents to act as national dividers. Presidents must necessarily divide when they act as the leaders of their political parties, when they set priorities to the advantage of certain goals and groups at the expense of others, when they forge and lead political coalitions, when they move out ahead of public opinion and assume the role of national educators, when they choose one set of advisers over another. A president, as a creative executive leader, cannot help but offend certain interests. When Franklin Roosevelt was running for a second term, some garment workers unfolded a great sign that said, "We love him for the enemies he has made." Such is the fate of a president on an everyday basis; if presidents choose to use power they will lose the goodwill of those who preferred inaction. . . .

Paradox #6. We expect our presidents to provide bold, visionary, innovative, *programmatic* leadership and at the same time to *pragmatically* respond to the will of public opinion majorities; that is to say, we expect presidents to lead and to follow, to exercise "democratic leadership."

We want both pragmatic and programmatic leadership. We want principled leadership and flexible, adaptable leaders. *Lead us,* but also *listen to us.*

Most people can be led only where they want to go. "Authentic leadership," wrote James MacGregor Burns, "is a collective process." It emerges from a sensitivity or appreciation of the motives and goals of both followers and leaders. The test of leadership, according to Burns, "is the realization of intended, real change that meets people's enduring needs." Thus a key function of leadership is "to engage followers, not merely to activate them, to commingle needs and aspirations and goals in a common enterprise, and in the process to make better citizens of both leaders and followers."

We want our presidents to offer leadership, to be architects of the future and to offer visions, plans, and goals. At the same time we want them to stay in close touch with the sentiments of the people. We want a certain amount of innovation, but we resist being led too far in any one direction.

We expect vigorous, innovative leadership when crises occur. Once a crisis is past, however, we frequently treat presidents as if we didn't need or want them around. We do expect presidents to provide us with bold, creative, and forceful initiatives "to move us ahead," but we resist radical new ideas and changes and usually embrace "new" initiatives only after they have achieved some consensus.

Most of our presidents have been conservatives or at best "pragmatic liberals." They have seldom ventured much beyond the crowd. They have followed public opinion rather than shaped it. John F. Kennedy, the author

of the much-acclaimed *Profiles in Courage*, was often criticized for presenting more profile than courage. He avoided political risks where possible.
Kennedy was fond of pointing out that he had barely won election in
1960 and that great innovations should not be forced on the public by a
leader with such a slender mandate. President Kennedy is often credited
with encouraging widespread public participation in politics, but he repeatedly reminded Americans that caution is needed, that the important
issues are complicated, technical, and best left to the administrative and
political experts. Seldom did Kennedy attempt to change the political
context in which he operated. Instead he resisted, "the new form of politics emerging with the civil rights movement: mass action, argument on
social fundamentals, appeals to considerations of justice and morality.
Moving the American political system in such a direction would necessarily have been long range, requiring arduous educational work and
promising substantial political risk."

Kennedy, the pragmatist, shied away from such an unpragmatic undertaking. . . .

Paradox #7. Americans want powerful, self-confident presidential
leadership. Yet we are inherently suspicious of leaders who are arrogant,
infallible, and above criticism.

We unquestionably cherish our three branches of government with
their checks and balances and theories of dispersed and separated powers.
We want our presidents to be successful and to share their power with
their cabinets, Congress, and other "responsible" national leaders. In theory, we oppose the concentration of power, we dislike secrecy, and we resent depending on any one person to provide all of our leadership.

But Americans also yearn for dynamic, aggressive presidents—even if
they do cut some corners. We celebrate the gutsy presidents who make a
practice of manipulating and pushing Congress. We perceive the great
presidents to be those who stretched their legal authority and dominated
the other branches of government. It is still Jefferson, Jackson, Lincoln, and
the Roosevelts who get top billing. Whatever may have been the framers'
intentions for the three branches, most experts now agree that most of the
time, especially in crises, our system works best when the presidency is
strong and when we have a self-confident, assertive president.

There is, of course, a fine line between confidence and arrogance,
between firmness and inflexibility. We want presidents who are not afraid
to exert their will, but at what point does this become antidemocratic,
even authoritarian? . . .

Paradox #8. What it takes to become president may not be what is
needed to govern the nation.

To win a presidential election takes ambition, money, luck, and masterful public relations strategies. It requires the formation of an electoral coalition. To govern a democracy requires much more. It requires the formation of a *governing* coalition, and the ability to compromise and bargain.

"People who win primaries may become good presidents—but 'it ain't necessarily so'" wrote columnist David Broder. "Organizing well is important in governing just as it is in winning primaries. But the Nixon years should teach us that good advance men do not necessarily make trustworthy White House aides. Establishing a government is a little more complicated than having the motorcade run on time."

Ambition (in heavy doses) and stiff-necked determination are essential for a presidential candidate, yet too much of either can be dangerous. A candidate must be bold and energetic, but in excess these characteristics can produce a cold, frenetic candidate. To win the presidency obviously requires a single-mindedness, yet our presidents must also have a sense of proportion, be well-rounded, have a sense of humor, be able to take a joke, and have hobbies and interests outside the realm of politics.

To win the presidency many of our candidates (Lincoln, Kennedy, and Clinton come to mind) had to pose as being more progressive or even populist than they actually felt; to be effective in the job they are compelled to appear more cautious and conservative than they often want to be. One of Carter's political strategists said, "Jimmy campaigned liberal but governed conservative." And as Bill Clinton pointed out toward the end of his first year in office, "We've all become Eisenhower Republicans." ...

We often also want both a "fresh face," an outsider, as a presidential candidate *and* a seasoned, mature, experienced veteran who knows the corridors of power and the back alleyways of Washington. That's why Colin Powell fascinated so many people. Frustration with past presidential performances leads us to turn to a "fresh new face" uncorrupted by Washington's politics and its "buddy system" (Carter, Reagan, Clinton). But inexperience, especially in foreign affairs, has sometimes led to blunders by the outsiders....

Paradox #9. The presidency is sometimes too strong, yet other times too weak.

Presidents are granted wide latitude in dealing with events abroad. At times, presidents can act unilaterally, without the express consent of Congress. While the constitutional grounds for such action may be dubious, the climate of expectations allows presidents to act decisively abroad. This being the case, the public comes to think the president can do the same at home. But this is usually not the case. A clashing expectation is built into the presidency when strength in some areas is matched with weakness in other areas.

It often seems that our presidency is *always too strong* and *always too weak*. Always too powerful given our worst fears of tyranny and our ideals of a "government by the people." Always too strong, as well, because it now possesses the capacity to wage nuclear war (a capacity that doesn't permit much in the way of checks and balances and deliberative, participatory government). But always too weak when we remember nuclear proliferation, the rising national debt, the budget deficit, lingering discrimination, poverty, and the clutch of other fundamental problems yet to be solved.

The presidency is always too strong when we dislike the incumbent. Its limitations are bemoaned, however, when we believe the incumbent is striving valiantly to serve the public interest as we define it. The Johnson presidency vividly captured this paradox: many who believed he was too strong in Vietnam also believed he was too weak to wage his War on Poverty. Others believed just the opposite. . . .

Ultimately, being paradoxical does not make the presidency incomprehensible. Can we rid the presidency of all paradoxes? We couldn't, even if we wanted to do so. And anyway, what is wrong with some ambiguity? It is in embracing the paradoxical nature of the American presidency that we may be able to arrive at understanding. And with understanding may come enlightened or constructive criticism. This is the basis for citizen democracy.

36

CRAIG RIMMERMAN

From *The Rise of the Plebiscitary Presidency*

Scholars who examine American presidents look not only at individuals who have held the position but also at trends that mark different interpretations of the office. Here, Professor Craig Rimmerman builds on Theodore Lowi's concept of the "plebiscitary presidency," in which the president seeks to govern through the direct support of the American people. Likewise, citizens view the plebiscitary presidency as the focal point of government activity. Rimmerman believes this view to be vastly different from the Constitution's intent. He traces changes in the executive's power through several phases, mentioning the contributions of prominent scholars to an understanding of the presidency. From President Roosevelt onward, Rimmerman asks his readers to consider carefully the consequences of such an exalted and unrealistic vision of presidential power.

THE CONSTITUTIONAL framers would undoubtedly be disturbed by the shift to the presidentially centered government that characterizes the modern era. Their fear of monarchy led them to reject the concept of executive popular leadership. Instead, they assumed that the legislative branch would occupy the central policymaking role and would be held more easily accountable through republican government.

Congress has failed, however, to adhere to the framers' intentions and has abdicated its policymaking responsibility. The legislature, with support from the Supreme Court, has been all too willing to promote the illusion of presidential governance by providing the executive with new sources of power, including a highly developed administrative apparatus, and by delegating authority for policy implementation to the executive through vague legislative statutes. . . .

The president-centered government of the modern, plebiscitary era draws much of its power and legitimacy from the popular support of the citizenry, support that is grounded in the development of the rhetorical presidency and the exalted role of the presidency in the American political culture. Theodore Lowi is surely on target when he identifies "the refocusing of mass expectations upon the presidency" as a key problem of presidential governance since Franklin Delano Roosevelt and as a problem associated with the rise of the plebiscitary presidency.

The plebiscitary presidency is characterized by the following: presidential power and legitimacy emanates from citizen support as measured through public opinion polls; in the absence of coherent political parties, presidents forge a direct link to the masses through television; and structural barriers associated with the Madisonian governmental framework make it difficult for presidents to deliver on their policy promises to the citizenry. The framers of the Constitution would hardly have approved of these developments, for they had no intention of establishing a popularly elected monarch. Moreover, the nature of the governmental framework that they created actually prevents occupants of the Oval Office from meeting the heightened citizen expectations associated with the plebiscitary presidency in terms of concrete public policy, especially in the domestic policy arena. This has become particularly clear in the modern era as presidents confront a more fragmented and independent legislature, a decline in the importance of the political party as a governing and coalition-building device, an increase in the power of interest groups and political action committees that foster policy fragmentation, and a bureaucracy that resists centralized coordination. . . .

Throughout much of the nineteenth century, a passive president in domestic policymaking was deemed both acceptable and desirable. Congress took the lead in formulating public policy initiatives and expressed outright hostility toward presidential suggestions that particular legislation should be introduced. In fact, early in the nineteenth century it was commonly believed that the president should not exercise the veto to express policy preferences. The president's primary responsibility was to faithfully execute the laws passed by Congress. For the occupants of the Oval Office in the traditional period, the Constitution imposed "strict limitations on what a President could do." The constitutional separation of powers was taken seriously by all parties, and the prevailing view regarding the proper role of government was "the best government governed least." As opposed to the presidential government of the modern period, the traditional era was characterized by congressional leadership in the policy process.

In the foreign policy arena, however, the president did establish himself through the war-making power. Yet even here the president was restrained when compared to the occupants of the Oval Office in the twentieth century. A prevailing view in the nineteenth century was that the president should avoid involvement with foreign nations, although negotiation with foreign countries was occasionally required. The first president to travel abroad on behalf of the United States was Theodore Roosevelt. Prior to the twentieth century, some members of Congress even argued that the president lacked the necessary legal authority to travel in this manner.

Presidential speechmaking also reflected the largely symbolic chief-of-state roles played by presidents in the traditional era. Jeffrey Tulis's content analysis of presidential speeches reveals that presidents rarely gave the kind of official popular speeches that characterize speech-making in the modern era. When speeches were given, they were considered "unofficial," and they rarely contained policy pronouncements. Tulis concludes that William McKinley's rhetoric was representative of the century as a whole: "Expressions of greeting, inculcations of patriotic sentiment, attempts at building 'harmony' among the regions of the country, and very general, principled statements of policy, usually expressed in terms of the policy's consistency with that president's understanding of republicanism." Virtually all presidents of the time adhered to the same kind of presidential speechmaking. The only exception was Andrew Johnson, who attempted to rally support for his policies in Congress through the use of fiery demagoguery. Johnson's "improper" rhetoric fueled his impeachment charge; yet it is this same kind of rhetoric that today is accepted as "proper" presidential rhetoric.

The reserved role played by the president in the nineteenth century was clearly in keeping with the intention of the constitutional framers....

...Yet as the United States headed into its second full century, this situation was to change, as congressional government began to yield to the presidentially centered form of governance that has characterized the modern period.

Students of the presidency have identified a number of factors that have led to the development of the modern, personal, plebiscitary presidency as we know it today. The personal presidency is "an office of tremendous personal power drawn from the people—directly through Congress and the Supreme Court—and based on the new democratic theory that the presidency with all powers is the necessary condition for governing a large, democratic nation. Its development is rooted in changes in presidential rhetoric, the efforts of the progressive reformers of the early twentieth century, the Great Depression and Franklin Delano Roosevelt's New Deal, the role of Congress in granting the executive considerable discretionary power, and Supreme Court decisions throughout the twentieth century that have legitimated the central role that the president should play in the domestic and foreign policy arenas....

Presidential scholars have contributed to the presidentially centered government and the accompanying citizen expectations of presidential performance that characterize the development of presidential power since Franklin Roosevelt. The "cult of the presidency," "textbook presidency," or "savior model" was developed in response to FDR's leadership during the Great Depression, and it prevailed through the presidency of John F. Kennedy. Underlying this "cult" or model approach is a firm commitment to the presidency as a strong office and to the desirability of this condition for the political system as a whole. Political science texts written during this period concluded approvingly that the presidency was growing larger, while gaining more responsibilities and resources. The use of laudatory labels, such as "the Wilson years," "the Roosevelt revolution," "the Eisenhower period," and "the Kennedy Camelot years" also fostered the cult of the presidency and reinforced the notion that the president is the key figure in the American political system. . . .

Perhaps no other work contributed more to the development of this approach that Richard Neustadt's *Presidential Power*, which was first published in 1960. Representing a sharp break with the legalistic and constitutional approach that had dominated presidential scholarship up until that time, *Presidential Power* reinforced the notion that strong presidential leadership should be linked to good government. Neustadt eschewed strict legalistic interpretations of presidential power and instead conceived of power in the following way: "'Power' I defined as personal influence on governmental action. This I distinguished sharply—a novel distinction then—from formal powers vested in the Presidency." For Neustadt, the Franklin Delano Roosevelt activist presidency was the ideal model for presidential leadership and the exercise of power. Future presidents, according to Neustadt, should be evaluated on the basis of how well they achieved the standards set by Roosevelt. Like presidential scholars of his time and many since, Neustadt rejected the framers' view that the Congress should be the chief policymaking branch and that the president should be constrained by numerous checks and balances. Instead, Neustadt spoke of "separated institutions sharing powers."

As Neustadt and other scholars embraced a presidentially centered form of government, they failed to recognize the consequences of imposing a new interpretation of the political order on a governmental framework rooted in Madisonian principles. One such consequence has been that as presidents attempt to meet the heightened expectations associated with the modern presidency, they are sometimes driven to assert presidential prerogative powers in ways that threaten both constitutional and democratic principles. The Johnson and Nixon presidencies, in particular, provided empirical evidence to support this concern. In response, presidential scholars embraced a new model for evaluating presidential power: "the imperial presidency."

Concerns about excessive presidential power were articulated in light of Lyndon Johnson's legislative victories in the 1960s, Johnson's and Nixon's decisionmaking in the Vietnam War, the Nixon/Kissinger Cambodian debacle, and the Nixon presidency's disgrace in the wake of Watergate.* Presidential scholars began to question whether presidential strength would necessarily lead to the promotion of the general welfare. Scholars spoke of the pathological presidency, reinforcing many of the constitutional framers' fears regarding the consequences of concentrating excessive powers in the executive.

Writing in this vein and responding to presidential excesses in the conduct of the Vietnam War and the Watergate scandal, Arthur Schlesinger, Jr., developed the concept of the "imperial presidency." Schlesinger recognized that the system of checks and balances needed vigorous action by one of the three branches if the stalemate built into the system was to be overcome. Schlesinger believed that the presidency was best equipped to fill this role. Rather than rejecting centralized presidential power per se, he spoke of presidential abuses: "In the last years presidential primacy, so indispensable to the political order, has turned into presidential supremacy. The constitutional Presidency—as events so apparently disparate as the Indochina War and the Watergate affair showed—has become the imperial Presidency and threatens to be the revolutionary Presidency." Schlesinger placed much of the blame for the imperial presidency on presidential excesses in foreign policy. . . . Truman, Kennedy, Johnson, and Nixon interpreted the Constitution to permit the president to commit American combat troops unilaterally, and the prolonged Vietnam War encouraged foreign policy centralization and the use of secrecy. The imperial presidency, or "the presidency as satan model," can also be applied to the Nixon administration's domestic activities, including wiretapping, the use of impoundments, executive branch reorganization for political purposes, and expansive interpretations of executive privilege.

Schlesinger's analysis is an important contribution to the study of presidential power because it recognizes the limitations imposed by the framers and the potentially negative consequences of the plebiscitary presidency. . . .

The plebiscitary presidency has been a key source of presidential power since 1933. For presidents such as Ford and Carter, however, the heightened expectations associated with the personal, plebiscitary presi-

---

*Set in motion by strong presidents, these three episodes—the prolonging of the war in Vietnam, the bombing of Vietnam's neutral neighbor, Cambodia, and a presidential administration's heavy involvement in and coverup of the burglary of the Democratic Party's Watergate Hotel-based election headquarters—all greatly divided the nation.—EDS.

dency have also led to citizen unhappiness and characterizations of presidential failure. The Carter presidency, in particular, reinforced elements of the plebiscitary presidency. As a "trustee" president, Jimmy Carter reinforced the notion that as the elected representative of all the people, "the president must act as the counterforce to special interests" and provide the leadership necessary in setting the policy agenda and introducing "comprehensive policy proposals." Charles Jones makes a persuasive case that Carter's vision of the trustee presidency was anathema to a Congress that had just passed a series of reforms designed to tame the imperial Nixon presidency. When Carter tried to introduce unpopular energy conservation policies and cut back "unnecessary dams and water projects" because they represented the "worst examples of the pork-barrel," he challenged Congress and the American people to reject politics as usual. In this sense, he was displaying a style of presidential leadership unseen in recent years, one that reinforced the plebiscitary presidency while at the same time challenging some of the assumptions on which it is based. Unlike his immediate predecessors and successors, Carter at least tried to heighten the level of dialogue around resource scarcity concerns. He soon learned, however, that his unwillingness to cultivate congressional support for his policies and his call for a shared sacrifice on the part of the American people undermined the plebiscitary foundations of the modern presidency. His 1980 presidential challenger understood Carter's problems quite well and was determined not to repeat them. Ronald Reagan's campaign and governing strategies accepted and extended the plebiscitary presidency. This helps to account for his victories in both 1980 and 1984. . . .

In the American political system, presidents perform two roles that in other countries are often filled by separate individuals. As head of the nation, the president is required to play a unifying role of the kind played by monarchs in Britain, Norway, and the Netherlands or by presidents in France, Germany, and Austria. In addition, presidents serve as political leaders, "a post held in these other nations by a prime minister or chancellor." This dual role virtually guarantees that American presidents will occupy the central political and cultural role as the chief spokesperson for the American way of life. Political scientists, historians, and journalists have all reinforced and popularized the view that the presidency is an office of overwhelming symbolic importance.

Only recently have political scientists begun to challenge this perspective and discuss the negative consequences of such hero worship in a country that purports to adhere to democratic principles. Barbara Hinckley captures these issues well in her recent analysis:

It is the magic of symbolism to create illusion. But illusion has costs that must be considered by journalists, teachers of politics, and future presidents. Is the nation best served by carrying on the symbolism or by challenging it? Should the two contradictory pictures, in a kind of schizophrenic fashion, be carried on together? If so, what line should be drawn and what accommodation made between the two? The questions are compounded by the peculiar openness of the office to changing interpretations. By definition, all institutions are shaped by the expectations of relevant actors. The presidency is particularly susceptible to such influence.

As we have seen in our study of the Reagan and Bush presidencies, presidents attempt to build on their symbolic importance to enhance their public opinion ratings and to extend the plebiscitary presidency. The upshot of this activity over the past sixty years is that the public equates the president with the nation and the values associated with American exceptionalism. A president, such as Jimmy Carter, who attempts to challenge traditional elements of presidential symbolism and demystify the trappings of the White House, is treated with disdain by the public, the press, and to a certain extent by political scientists. . . .

This book suggests that Presidents Reagan and Bush turned to foreign policy when they encountered difficulties in translating their domestic campaign promises into concrete public policy and in meeting the demands of the plebiscitary presidency. Presidents who are caught between citizens' expectations and the constraints of the Madisonian policy-making process* look to the foreign policy arena in an effort to promote the values associated with American exceptionalism.

Any of the examples discussed . . . provide ample opportunity to explore these themes. The Iran-Contra affair,† in particular, raises compelling questions regarding presidential power in the foreign policy arena. In light of the aggrandizement of presidential power that characterized the Vietnam War period and Watergate and the resulting congressional response, it is important to ask students why a president and/or his staff would employ some of the same strategies in dealing with Congress, the media, and the American people. The role of covert activities in a democracy also deserves considerable attention.

If scholars of the presidency are truly concerned with developing a pedagogy and presidential evaluation scheme rooted in critical education

*James Madison's plan for American government limits each branch by checking and balancing the power of one branch against another.—EDS.
†During President Reagan's administration, members of his National Security Council (NSC) were charged with secretly selling arms to Iran in order to fund anti-communist Nicaraguan Contra activities.—EDS.

for citizenship, then their students must be asked to consider why so little questioning generally occurs regarding the role of the president in committing American troops to war. The Persian Gulf war was a case in point.* It begged for serious discussion, reflection, debate, and questioning about the Bush administration's foreign policy decisionmaking. Some argued that those who dissented from the president's foreign policy strategy were un-American and unpatriotic and were trying to undermine the troops who were already in the Middle East. In fact, if citizens fail to question a president's decisionmaking, then they are giving the president virtually unchecked power to do what he wants with their lives. The failure to question a president abdicates all of the principles of a meaningful and effective democracy and embraces the dictates of an authoritarian and totalitarian regime. This is, of course, the logical consequence of the plebiscitary presidency.

Alexis de Tocqueville spoke of a blind and unreflective patriotism that characterized the American citizenry during the nineteenth century. He would surely see evidence of such patriotism in America today. There is little doubt that such patriotism can be connected to the relationship of the citizenry to the state and the office of the presidency. No modern president can expect to succeed without the support of the public. Yet this support must be grounded in a firm rejection of the unrealistic notion of presidential power. Citizens who respond to the presidency in a highly personalized and reverential manner are likely to be disappointed by presidential performance and are also likely to embrace political passivity and acquiescence in the face of presidential power. In the words of Benjamin Barber, "democratic politics thus becomes a matter of what leaders do, something that citizens watch rather than something they do." As this book has pointed out, Ronald Reagan and George Bush heightened these expectations even further by using techniques that emphasize the plebiscitary, personal character of the modern presidency. Ross Perot's 1992 presidential campaign was firmly rooted in plebiscitary principles. His proposals for nation-wide town meetings and an electronic democracy scheme reflected support for government by plebiscite. To Perot, running

*The Persian Gulf War occurred within a two-month period in early 1991. Backed by House and Senate resolutions of support—not an actual declaration of war—President George H. W. Bush sent U.S. troops to the Persian Gulf as part of a multination coalition to force Iraqi President Saddam Hussein's military out of Kuwait. The United States experienced quick and dramatic success, with CNN's coverage bringing the war directly to Americans daily. Years later, questions remained about the long-term effectiveness of the military strikes in weakening the Iraqi threat. In 2003, President George W. Bush ordered an invasion of Iraq, claiming that Saddam Hussein possessed weapons of mass destruction, an allegation later found to be false.—EDS.

as an outsider, anti-establishment candidate, such a plan was desperately needed to challenge the gridlock growing out of the Madisonian policy process and two party system. His proposals also enabled him to emphasize his own leadership abilities and claim that he had the necessary leadership and entrepreneurial abilities to break governmental paralysis. In doing so, Perot reinforced the direct line between the presidency and the American people. Any course on the presidency should examine Perot's government-by-plebiscite proposals and the broader implications of his apparent willingness to bypass the congressional policy process and the two party system. The amount of attention and popularity that Perot's campaign garnered in a short period of time suggests once again that the plebiscitary presidency is an important explanatory construct. It also encourages political scientists to study, with renewed vigor, the relationship between the presidency and the citizenry.

For many students, the presidency is the personification of democratic politics and, as a result, monopolizes "the public space." This view impedes the development of the meaningful and effective participation needed by citizens as they attempt to control decisions that affect the quality and direction of their lives. Presidential scholars have been developing a more realistic understanding of the changing sources of presidential power and how individual presidents have used these powers through the years. We would also do well to consider Murray Edelman's claim that "leadership is an expression of the inadequate power of followers in their everyday lives." This is particularly important as we begin to evaluate the Bush presidency. It is also the first step toward challenging the plebiscitary presidency and achieving a more realistic and successful presidency, one that is grounded in principles of democratic accountability and the development of citizenship.

37

GIL TROY

From *Leading from the Center*

For several decades, American politics has been marked by polarization: Democrats and Republicans, progressives and conservatives, doves and hawks, cultural liberals and traditionalists. Scholar Gil Troy opens this excerpt with a look back at America's early leaders who tried to forge compromises and maintain civility despite deep political differences. Citing George Washington, Abraham Lincoln, Franklin Roosevelt, and John F. Kennedy, Troy characterizes our most successful presidents as "leading from the center." That's where most American citizens are and that's where they want their presidents to be. Presidents Bill Clinton and George W. Bush do not rate highly according to this measure, Troy notes. Moderation does not have to mean weakness or waffling, but it does mean finding common ground and maintaining civility. "Although there is no crystal ball," Troy writes, "history suggests what might work and what will fail." Students of American government can apply Gil Troy's analysis to President Obama, to current politics, and beyond.

———

IT MAY HAVE BEEN THE MOST important dinner party in American history. In June 1790, three titans of the new republic—Secretary of State Thomas Jefferson, Secretary of the Treasury Alexander Hamilton, and Congressman James Madison—broke bread, drank port, and talked late into the night. Dining together, these patriotic statesmen brokered a deal to keep America united. They may be remembered as equally bewigged, staid Founding Fathers, but each was a headstrong individual, and their visions of how America's new Constitution should work clashed. Their political and philosophical disagreements became so intense they would roil George Washington's administration and threaten the states' still fragile, national alliance.

Despite the elegant candlelight at 57 Maiden Lane in New York, the dinner must have been awkward. The host, Thomas Jefferson, an aristocratic polymath but no genius at human relations, was an unlikely mediator who was more partisan than his reputation as the philosopher of freedom would suggest. He had known his fellow Virginian, the shy, cerebral constitutionalist James Madison, for years. Having met the glib, cosmopolitan secretary of the treasury upon returning from France only weeks earlier in March, Jefferson did not yet know Hamilton well enough to loathe him. Within months, the two would become the most famous rivals in early American history, representing opposing camps, ideologies, and sensibilities.

Jefferson had joined Washington's cabinet vowing to avoid petty intrigues; Hamilton and Madison had collaborated on a classic warning against partisanship in writing the *Federalist Papers*. Yet, having fought together to ratify the Constitution, Madison and Hamilton now fought each other over how to implement it. Favoring strong centralized government, Hamilton proposed that the new federal government pay off the states' Revolutionary War debts. More virtuous farmer than sophisticated financier, Madison feared the scheme would penalize responsible states like his native Virginia, which had already settled its debts, and would unfairly reward profligate northern states that had ignored their debts, banking on an eventual federal windfall. Virginia's Revolutionary War hero, Lighthorse Harry Lee, captured the southern sentiment, preferring to dissolve the union rather than succumb to a "fixed insolent northern majority."

"In general I think it necessary to give as well as take in a government like ours," Jefferson magnanimously declared that June. An enlightened rationalist, Jefferson hosted the dinner with Hamilton and Madison because he believed that "men of sound heads and honest views needed nothing more than explanation and mutual understanding to enable them to unite in some measures which might enable us to get along." This repast resulted in the Compromise of 1790.

In this great American accord, the two Virginians, Jefferson and Madison, delivered enough southerners' votes in Congress to pass Hamilton's ambitious, counterintuitive plan to prove America's fiscal responsibility by assuming, then paying off the war debts. In return, Hamilton supported situating the nation's capital farther south along the Potomac River, carving out a city from two slave states, Maryland and Virginia. By August, Jefferson reported that a spirit of compromise had restored the congressional harmony disrupted by the two thorny questions of the debt and the capital's location.

This harmonious tale slights a critical player, President George Washington. Its spirit of moderation testifies to Washington's leadership. George Washington championed the middle course as the best path. As president, he fostered what he called "a spirit of accommodation." Washington embodied Americans' commitment to a "common cause," and he repeatedly urged his squabbling subordinates to find those "mutual concessions which are requisite to the general prosperity," even by sacrificing "individual advantages to the interest of the Community."

Unlike Jefferson, Washington was too discreet to leave a diary entry or write a letter detailing his contribution to what must have been many dinners, exchanges, calculations, and clashes before the legendary meal. Even as the president fought pneumonia during the spring, he warned that discretion remained essential. When Washington went sailing with his secretaries of state and treasury that June, he recorded in his diary the fish caught and the warm sentiments exchanged, not the political give and take that undoubtedly occurred among the men.

As the story of the peacemaking banquet took on legendary proportions, it validated Washington's mission to preserve the union's serenity by finding "sensible men" who could resist democratic politics' tide of vitriol. The two volatile questions, of the debt and the capital city's location, terrified Washington. He realized they could upend the states' still uneasy alliance. After Hamilton and Madison had compromised, the president, invoking one of his favorite phrases, invited all Americans to look forward to "enjoying peace abroad, with tranquility at home."

Washington's way, this often subtle search for the center, has been the secret to American political success. This spirit of compromise is one of America's signature contributions to the noble story of democratic leadership since the 1700s. It is tragic that the capital city named after George Washington, so carefully, sensitively, poised between north and south, would come to represent partisanship, polarization, extremism, and intrigue. By 2007, Connecticut's Senator Joseph Lieberman was complaining, "There is something profoundly wrong when opposition to the war in Iraq seems to inspire greater passion than opposition to Islamist extremism." Defying his party's most passionate partisans, the 2000 Democratic vice presidential nominee denounced this "political climate where, for many people, when George Bush says 'yes,' their reflex reaction is to say 'no.'" In that spirit, New York's legendary Mayor Ed Koch once challenged his constituents, "If you agree with me on nine out of twelve issues, vote for me. If you agree with me on twelve out of twelve issues, see a psychiatrist."

Today's world is too dangerous for Americans to be so deeply, angrily, and unreasonably divided. Enlightened self-interest, wherein the right thing to do is the smart thing to do, calls for reason and unity, not emotion and demagogy. America needs passionate centrists ready to elect presidents leading from the center. And those presidents should be muscular moderates, visionary enough to preserve core values but nationalistic enough and popular enough to root their actions in a broad consensus, which they must often build.

Americans expect their leaders to seek the center. They have long rewarded leaders who built big, broad political tents driven deep into America's rich soil, rather than those who put up partisan lean-tos tilting left or right. Abraham Lincoln's famous Emancipation Proclamation was actually a cautious state document with all the passion of an accountant's ledger. Franklin Roosevelt's New Deal was an incremental zigzag that frustrated communists and plutocrats alike. But rather than representing a failure of leadership, these moments of moderation, like Washington's persistent push for compromise in the 1790s, showcase Americans and their presidents at their best.

In the past, presidents often led from the center boldly. When Abraham Lincoln defined the American nation at Gettysburg, when Franklin Roosevelt restored national confidence during his First Hundred Days, when John F. Kennedy affirmed America's moral commitment to civil rights—they all were leading the country to a new center. But center seeking often required great patience. There were no immediate results when George Washington mediated between warring cabinet secretaries or Abraham Lincoln deliberated and dithered as he wondered how to end slavery without losing the strategic border states. It took tremendous self-control for Theodore Roosevelt to settle 1902's anthracite coal strike by arbitration not fiat and for Franklin D. Roosevelt to inch America step by step toward involvement in World War II. Americans displayed great fortitude as Harry Truman crafted a long-term, bipartisan Cold War containment policy that only truly bore fruit during Ronald Reagan's presidency four decades later. Thinking creatively and cultivating broad alliances, presidents should push voters just enough so they move forward without losing their balance.

George Washington's comportment was contagious. Alexander Hamilton and Thomas Jefferson remained civil toward each other long after they learned to despise one another, as each competed for the great man's blessing. Hamilton in particular became dramatically more vitriolic after he left the cabinet in 1795 and no longer interacted regularly with Washington, his mentor for two decades. Individually and collectively, in his lifetime and after his death, George Washington spread a gospel of civility and centrism that elevated Americans and the presidency. . . .

Alas, America's historic commitment to centrism is menaced by the shrill invective resonating in Washington, in the media, on campus, and on the Internet, particularly the "blogosphere." Our culture and politics are well matched. It is difficult to expect a politics of moderation in an age of excess; temperance cannot flourish in a culture of extravagance.

The middle has long been a very appealing, and very American, place to be—and must remain so. The "great American center" has a long, proud history of offering a muscular moderation, not a mushy middle. . . .

The three two-term presidents since 1980 offer interesting case studies in presidential statesmanship and center seeking. Ronald Reagan was more centrist than his conservative ideology and rhetoric suggested. Reagan repeatedly compromised, showing far more concern for national unity, relative political calm, and his own personal popularity than for conservative purity. Bill Clinton was even more accommodating than Reagan. But whereas Reagan remained anchored in his ideology and frequently demonstrated a muscular moderation, Clinton's need to be loved made for a spineless centrism. Finally, if Bill Clinton was too concerned with public approval, George W. Bush has demonstrated the perils of not being sufficiently sensitive to popular opinion. Bush's characteristic go-it-alone stance sullied the "goodly fabric" George Washington wove so carefully, illustrating the broad dangers to the body politic when a president is imprisoned by his convictions.

The Bill Clinton–George W. Bush obsession with winning at any price resulted in two, two-term presidencies, but at great cost. Both Clinton and Bush maneuvered masterfully to maintain power, but they further divided the American people. Just as Americans are starting to measure their "carbon footprints," assessing how many noxious emissions each individual generates, we need to start measuring our leaders' toxic footprints, measuring the poisonous fallout of particular actions, even if they were successful in the short term. During the Monica Lewinsky scandal,* Bill Clinton kept his office and maintained his popularity, but at what cost to the nation's soul? George W. Bush in 2004 won his reelection campaign, but at what cost to the nation's psyche? Important presidential duties include strengthening democracy, uniting Americans, and reaffirming ideals; a president who leaves office with a nation further divided, demoralized, and doubting its own virtue is a failure, no matter how popular he or she may have been. . . .

The president's job is to preside. And presidents preside most effectively over this diverse country by pursuing centrism rather than riling

---

*The Lewinsky scandal led to President Bill Clinton's 1988–89 impeachment by the House of Representatives and subsequent acquittal in a Senate trial. Clinton was charged with being untruthful, in legal proceedings, about revealing his sexual relationship with Monica Lewinsky, a White House intern.—EDS.

partisans. Using slim majorities to impose radical changes on the country violates the implicit democratic contract between the leader and the people. Great presidents aim for the center, hitting the popular bull's-eye as close as possible, albeit sometimes after repositioning it.

Today, with America threatened by Islamist terrorism and nuclear roguery, presidents must strive to overcome divisive politics and temper extreme positions. America prospers when it has a president who leads by consensus building. "Soldiering is 99% boredom and 1% sheer terror," one Civil War soldier wrote to his wife. Similarly, effective American democratic leadership requires long bouts of compromising, slogging through, and coalition building, punctuated by bursts of boldness and occasional flights of eloquence.

Admittedly, moderation is an odd thing to get passionate about. It is a posture, a tactic, a strategy, that by definition is not intended to make the blood boil. Moreover, it is a relative, ever-changing position. As public opinion fluctuates, conditions change, issues come and go, the elusive center shifts, too. In most Americans' search for heroes, in modern academics' search for radicals, in the media's mania for headlines, moderation often seems to be a synonym for capitulation or indecision.

Mocking moderates is a great American tradition. No politician in the 1970s or 1980s wanted to be called a "wimp." In mid-twentieth-century America, the dismissive term was "Caspar Milquetoast," the name of the reedy, bespectacled, sniveling cartoon character who insisted on wearing a belt *and* suspenders. Prior to that, the pejorative label was "mugwump," early American slang for an Indian chief, which evolved into a nickname for elite political reformers in the late 1800s. By the 1930s, the *Blue Earth Post* in Minnesota was defining mugwump as "a sort of bird that sits on a fence with his mug on one side, and his wump on the other." In 1992 Vice President Dan Quayle dismissed the Democratic centrist Bill Clinton as a "waffler" whose favorite color was "plaid." . . .

Appreciating moderation contradicts pop culture and the latest academic fashions. In Walt Disney's Hall of the Presidents and other popular venues, presidential superheroes save America, often with a rhetorical flourish. On the opposite extreme, academic debunkers ranging from the Afrocentrists to Howard Zinn portray America as a conflict-ridden, rudderless colossus, burdened by impotent leaders or unduly aggressive presidents compensating for individual and national insecurities. Professors honor the antislavery zealotry of John Brown and William Lloyd Garrison over Abraham Lincoln's deliberation. Popularizing the academic trend, History Channel's recent *Ten Days That Unexpectedly Changed America* highlighted Indian massacres, violent clashes between citizens, and radical bombings. These extreme portraits are inaccurate. Balanced analytical history elevates, not just denigrates. We can learn from the coalition builders, not just the partisans; the statesmen, not just the demagogues; and the magnanimous uniters, not just the cranky dividers.

All societies—and especially democracies—need natural mechanisms to resolve conflicts. America's balance seems more difficult to find in a seemingly balkanized world of racial division, ethnic estrangement, religious conflict, geographical tension, and political zeal. Yet American society also functions far more smoothly, effectively, and kindly than the naysayers of the media would ever suggest. . . .

America has a deeper, enduring consensus about the value of liberty, democracy, and equality, as well as the uniqueness of America's mission. If within this solid consensus the two parties quarrel over economic theories, policy details, specific leaders' personalities, or government's exact dimensions, that is natural and healthy. It is the slash and burn, all or nothing, red versus blue, my way or the highway rhetoric from both left and right in the Bush and Clinton years that has been so unnatural and unhealthy. Political parties work when they help individuals come together to solve problems; coalition building works best when people have a variety of affiliations, when people might pray together one morning and go to competing political meetings that night. Political parties become destructive when they demonize and polarize, becoming one of a series of reinforcing elements that pit half the country against the other half. . . .

Although there is no crystal ball, history suggests what might work and what will fail. History teaches us that winning an election or reelection does not guarantee presidential success. Three of the four American presidents since 1980 have been two-term presidents. Bill Clinton and George W. Bush serve as the Scylla and Charybdis* of modern presidential leadership, each offering an alluring but ultimately flawed model that successors should avoid. Clinton's search for the center lacked substance. By preferring policy Band-Aids to serious solutions, he shortchanged his supporters, frittered away his talents, and limited his legacy. Bush stumbled by spurning the center, dissipating much of the goodwill his bold actions had generated in first responding to the 9/11 tragedy. The terrorism issue, which should have been faced in a bipartisan manner, became increasingly controversial and polarizing. Ronald Reagan, for all his flaws, ended his presidency on a high note and is now widely perceived as a success

---

*In Greek mythology, Scylla and Charybdis were sea monsters dwelling on each side of a narrow waterway, waiting to send sailors to their deaths. Each monster, though seemingly seductive, had its own method of destroying sailors, so doom was inevitable regardless of which choice the sailors made. —EDS.

because he never forgot the great American middle or the broader all-American vision. . . .

As George Washington himself emphasized, the spirit of enlightened moderation, a culture of reasonableness, cannot only be generated by the commander in chief. Americans must take more responsibility for what we collectively are doing to our politics, our culture, our country, and ourselves. The escapist combination of partisanship, cynicism, and frivolity embodied in too much of contemporary culture invites flights from responsibility; the privileges of citizenship demand the opposite. We all must begin finding our inner moderate. We must reward those who seek the center. We must repudiate those who through vitriol, demagoguery, or mockery divide, polarize, or distract from important issues at hand to attract our entertainment dollars or score some cheap political points. We need to learn the lessons of George Washington's enlightenment, Abraham Lincoln's flexibility, Theodore Roosevelt's romantic nationalism, Franklin Roosevelt's experimentation, Harry Truman's bipartisanship, Dwight Eisenhower's consensus building, John Kennedy's principled malleability, and Ronald Reagan's muscular moderation.

Citizens in a democracy get the leadership they deserve, for better or worse. If we, collectively, revitalize the center, our presidents will become center seekers. If we demand the best of our leaders, we may just get the best leaders.

38

BRADLEY PATTERSON

From *The White House Staff:* *[Chief of Staff]*

Drawing on many examples, Bradley Patterson paints a detailed picture of one of the least public but most important positions in Washington, D.C. The president's chief of staff is in charge of every aspect of the White House office, from the mundane to the weighty. Patterson is a long-time observer of the inside political scene in the nation's capital, and he brings to his prescription for the chief of staff a vast knowledge both of the individuals who have held the job and of the executive branch. The chief of staff must be all things to the president, Patterson believes, but he must be careful in the process not to become isolated and alienated from the numerous people whose requests he has to reject on behalf of his boss.

———

IT SEEMED AS IF two traditions were in the making: Republican presidents, following the Eisenhower model, emplaced chiefs of staff in their White Houses; Democratic presidents, aghast at the Nixon experience, shunned the idea. The second "tradition" came to a halt with Clinton. As presidential scholar James Pfiffner succinctly put it: "A chief of staff is essential in the modern White House."

... Beyond the chief of staff, there is only the president to try to knit his administration into a coherent set of institutions—and the president has vastly graver, and "undelegatable," responsibilities. The chief of staff is *system manager*: boss of none, but overseer of everything.

Does a new president understand this?

One former aide believes that a new chief executive often has a misconception:

[Presidents] always treat chiefs of staff incorrectly. They . . . think of chiefs of staff as nothing more than foremen, hired hands basically. Whereas chiefs of staff and everybody else think of [them] as exalted kinds of rulers with great power. So I think presidents need to think more about staff functions—how the White House operates, how it's going to operate, and the kind of people they choose to be around them. They don't seem to have that sense of history about them. It's like staff history is below them.

Thirty-eight years of experience—nineteen White House chiefs of staff—have, in this author's view, demonstrated a number of principles for effectiveness in fulfilling that central responsibility.

A chief of staff needs to be familiar with the unique pressures and pitfalls of public life in Washington. This means recognizing—and being comfortable with the existence of—the contravening authorities and forces from the vigorously competing centers of power in the nation and in the nation's capital: the cabinet departments, Congress, the courts, the press, the lobbyists, professional societies, interest groups, and the international community. The more successful chiefs of staff have had some thorough experience in one or more of those institutions. Former chief of staff Leon Panetta emphasized: "You really need to have somebody in that position who has some experience in Washington. It's just absolutely essential. The president can have somebody close to him, but it better be somebody who has some experience with what Washington is about, because that person has to make sure that the president isn't making any obvious mistakes."

The chief of staff needs to have firm, four-way support: not only from the president but from the first lady, the vice president, and the vice president's spouse as well. Nagging doubts or lack of confidence on the part of any of these four will eat away at the chief of staff's stature and authority. The wise chief will stay in especially close communication with the vice president and the two spouses. But communication is one thing; responsibility is another. In the end, the chief of staff has only one boss.

The chief of staff should be someone who is not only close to the president but also very familiar with those who operated the campaign. Most of the campaigners will have their hearts set on positions in Washington, hopefully on the White House staff. The incoming chief of staff must be able to distinguish effectiveness in campaigning from effectiveness in the business of governing—and give preference to those who share the president's political ideology rather than to factional advocates who are not necessarily on the same "policy wavelength" as the president.

The chief of staff has comprehensive control over the activities of the White House staff. Comments Panetta:

I had some military background—which was probably of even greater value than any kind of management background you have when you take a position like that. The role of a chief of staff is more like a battlefield commander: you've got a mission to accomplish, and you have to, sometimes, fight your way through a lot of incoming fire to make sure that the mission is done, but you need to have everybody knowing exactly what he or she has to do, in order to accomplish the mission. . . . It was very important to establish that the chief of staff had control.

But what does "control" mean? One Clinton staff chief allegedly tried to keep most of the policy balls bouncing on his own desk: he acted as the budget director, the legislative liaison head, the economic and domestic policy principal—and was the major White House spokesman. He handled all those functions superbly, it was acknowledged, but how long can such concentration be sustained? Another Clinton chief of staff preferred delegation: each senior presidential staffer was given goals, objectives, and guidelines—and then held firmly accountable for achieving them. "You have to empower people!" he said.

Former president George Bush would advise a president: "Get someone [with whom] you are totally comfortable. He/She must be a strong manager. Must be able to inspire confidence and loyalty in the rest of the staff. Must have had enough experience in some phase of life to walk in the White House door with a certain respect level already in place."

None of the policy centers of the White House—including the National Security Council apparat and the offices of the first lady and the vice president—can be allowed to work independently of the rest of the institution. In the Clinton White House, the national security adviser and the vice president's and the first lady's chiefs of staff all attended the chief of staff's senior staff meetings. The chief of staff attended the NSC principals' (cabinet-level) meetings and the intelligence briefings with the president. If even the most sensitive national security issue is being presented to the president, the national security adviser and the chief of staff jointly go into the Oval Office.

Chief of Staff John Podesta described his relationship with national security adviser Samuel (Sandy) Berger: "The one person I do not view, from a policy perspective, as reporting 'through me' is Sandy. I think it works better that way. I am not only comfortable with that; I think that is the better model. As long as we get along. He runs almost every big decision by me; I don't feel left out by him. He can keep a deeper sense of what is going on in his world; I keep a deeper sense of what is going on in my world—and we are pretty well integrated."

All presentations to the president are subject to the chief of staff's review. Issues—particularly those involving differences of opinion—are first vetted around the chief's table. The chief must ask: Is this an open process? Are the right people here? Have we asked the right questions? Are all the key options included? Has the "underbrush" been cleared out and the issues reduced to their core substance? Can consensus be reached on the lesser, "compromisable" differences?

The chief of staff controls the president's schedule. And the look-ahead period is not days but weeks—often, in fact, months. As for the schedule on a given day, the chief of staff's goal is to keep the focus on *the* principal event, ensuring that activities that would compete with news of that principal happening are downplayed or pushed aside. On policy issues awaiting discussion with the president, the chief of staff determines priorities: Which matters require attention and in what order?

The chief of staff controls the president's doorway. Who is invited to meetings and who is not? There may be some hurt feelings, but temporarily bruised egos are a small price to pay for conserving the president's absolutely invaluable time.

Review, by the chief of staff's office, of all papers that come out of the president's office is as important as scrutiny of those that come in. The president's scribbles and marginal comments are likely to be as important as the check marks in the decision box.

The chief will set up a special system for controlling the White House responses to congressional mail that contains important policy questions. Are budgetary issues being raised that require advice from the Office of Management and Budget? Constitutional ones? Is litigation possible? (The counsel must be consulted.) Who will draft the response? Have all the necessary clearances been obtained? Who will sign the outgoing letter?

The chief of staff may wish to have two or three deputy chiefs of staff. One perhaps will specialize in national security issues, another in management and operations matters, a third in domestic or economic questions. The various White House policy units may be divvied up to report on their work to the appropriate deputy *first*—before the chief of staff and the president get involved. Can such sequencing of reporting procedures be put in place without attenuating the relationships between the chief of staff and the principal White House assistants? The three most recent Clinton chiefs of staff all used this system with apparent success.

The chief of staff cannot avoid dealing with Congress. In fact, he may spend a great deal of time negotiating on the Hill on the president's behalf. The chief will likely have to take calls from governors and meet with the leaders of advocacy groups. As the chief does so, however, he always keeps the appropriate White House colleagues—legislative, intergovernmental, public liaison—closely informed and involved. The effective chief sets a firm practice: other staff members are not to be "disempowered." (Such wide-ranging extramural responsibilities are yet another reason that the contemporary White House chief of staff has deputies: to help create time for the chief to handle such external duties and not shirk his own responsibilities to the president.)

Perhaps the chief of staff's most sensitive judgment call is deciding where to draw the line: when to take an issue to the president and when to settle it before it gets that far. Podesta reflects:

I think I have a regulator that says to me, even if the president is likely to be with the consensus of his advisers, I will still have to take it into the Oval Office. There is a level of importance which, even if there is consensus, requires that the decision be signed off by the president. I think Berger would probably agree with that, from the national security viewpoint. He takes care of a lot of issues over in his office. But there is a certain level of decision which you can't just inform the president about; you really have to have his input. He may say, "I don't have a strong view; you decide." Which he will often do, if everybody is on the same page. "We'll just decide it here."

Podesta's predecessor, Erskine Bowles, expressed similar sentiments:

I made a lot of budget decisions that some people would probably have taken, on balance, right in to the president. But the president made it clear to me that he wanted me to do things like that, and the reason is: everyone has individual strengths and weaknesses. I don't have the vision; I can't dream like Bill Clinton. I can't see the things he can see. . . . But I am a doer; I can get things done. I am a negotiator; I can take tough positions and say no. The president would never say, "Erskine, you go out and make this final decision and just bring me the answer." At the same time, I didn't seek permission every time I did something. We would decide in advance what the ground rules were, what he wanted done and what I thought was practical. We would decide together: "This is what we have to have; it's going to be really tough." My job then was to "go to it." If he didn't like what I had negotiated, I expected him to let me know, which he would, quite clearly. At the same time, whether the results were positive or negative, good or bad, the president had to know it all.

Readers will instantly appreciate what a thin line this is—and will recognize how easily an egotistical chief of staff could be tempted to get into the habit of walling off staff or cabinet pleaders with the dictum "Take it from me: the president has decided!" when in fact the chief, rather than the president, was the decisionmaker.

In the decisionmaking process, the chief of staff is always an honest broker. But only an honest broker? By no means. Presidents expect their chiefs of staff to hold, and to express, their own independent judgments about any issue in the Oval Office neighborhood. They must do so, however, without using their stature and their proximity to give their own arguments an "edge" over competing contentions from other staffers or cabinet disputants.

The chief of staff must be possessed of the exceptional sensitivity to recognize a presidential command that is given in unthinking anger, frustration, or exhaustion—and to lay it aside. Scholar Fred Greenstein quotes Eisenhower: "I told my staff . . . once in a while you people have just got to be my safety-valve. So I'll get you in here and I will let go, but this is for you and your knowledge and your knowledge only. Now I've seen these people going out, and I've gotten a little extreme, a little white, but pretty soon one of them comes in and laughs and says, 'Well, you were in good form this morning, Mr. President.'"

Former presidential assistants Bob Haldeman and Joseph Califano both describe similar experiences. When Nixon issued an intemperate instruction on one occasion, Haldeman remembered: "I said nothing more, then stepped out of the office and placed the order immediately on my mental 'no action ever' shelf." President Johnson had the same habit, and Califano used the same response. Califano commented: "After three years of serving on his White House staff, he would have expected me to have some sense of how to measure his true meaning when he spoke in anger." (It is the author's belief that in May of 1993, when faced with what appeared to be a directive from on high to fire the staff of the White House Travel Office, OMA director David Watkins should have emulated the Haldeman practice.)

The chief of staff or one of the deputy chiefs of staff goes on each presidential journey as principal manager of the overall odyssey, since a presidential trip, particularly one overseas, presents a very special challenge for White House preparers and coordinators.

For nearly half a century it has been the chief of staff's responsibility to convene White House staff meetings. Harry S. Truman was the last president to do so personally. Under President Clinton, Chief of Staff Podesta inaugurated what he called strategic management team meetings, a daily morning gathering of the legislative, domestic, economic policy, and national security heads with the deputy chiefs of staff, the director and deputy director of the OMB, the secretary and deputy secretary of Treasury, and a few other senior staff. One could almost have called the group the "White House Executive Committee."

Because of the chief of staff's stature and proximity to the president, invitations for media appearances—speeches, Sunday television talk shows—pour in. True, the chief is one of those in the White House best positioned to speak for the president—but any chief, even today, remembers Louis Brownlow's long-ago admonition to President Roosevelt: White House staff officers must have a "passion for anonymity." The need to explain or defend a president's actions may be almost overwhelming on some occasions, and a chief may be a spectacularly lucid and persuasive spokesperson. *Each chief of staff and each president will come to their own agreement on how public the chief's persona should be.* The author's personal preference is to give greater weight to Brownlow's advice.

The chief of staff must continually build bridges to the cabinet. While it is the fundamental thesis of this book that policy development and coordination are becoming more and more centralized in the White House staff, there is a risk in this development. Some cabinet secretaries, especially those with narrower and more specialized policy and operational responsibilities—and thus less contact with the White House—may tend to feel isolated, perhaps even alienated. *Locked in the Cabinet*, the memoir of former secretary of labor Robert Reich, evidences this sentiment:

The Secretary of Transportation phones to ask me how I discover what's going on at the White House. I have no clear answer. . . . The decision-making "loop" depends on physical proximity to B—who's whispering into his ear most regularly, whose office is closest to the Oval, who's sitting or standing next to him when a key issue arises. . . . One of the best techniques is to linger in the corridors of the West Wing after a meeting, picking up gossip. Another good place is the executive parking lot between the West Wing and the Old Executive Office Building, where dozens of White House staffers tromp every few minutes. In this administration you're either in the loop or you're out of the loop, but more likely you don't know where the loop is, or you don't even know there *is* a loop.

The chief of staff's antennae must be attuned to pick up such alienation—early.

Concerned that the 1998-99 scandal investigations and impeachment proceedings had led cabinet members to have "gotten kind of distant," Podesta began a series of breakfasts at the White House for small groups of cabinet secretaries. "Seven or eight at a time," he said, "just to kick things around, listen to them, let them tell me what was going on." A former assistant to Chief of Staff Bowles emphasized:

One of the challenges for our office was to act as a nexus, and to remember to keep everyone in the fold, and aware of what was going on in different parts of the White House. It is so big and there are so many different things taking place. There is a certain level of paranoia when you reach certain levels of power in government—in which everybody wants to know what everybody else is doing. The family—the organization—in my mind works better when people understand what's taking place. For the chief of staff to collect information is important, but so is it for the chief of staff to share information.

The chief of staff, finally, runs one more risk: that of becoming insensitive to the perquisites and privileges that necessarily accompany his status. The use of limousines and planes, proximity to the president, the toleration of what may be the chief's personal rudeness, the alacritous attention of subordinates— have gone to the heads of some. Over the years of their incumbency, having had to say no to so many supplicants (including members of Congress) will have added up to a paucity of close friends and a host of enemies. If the chief of staff—a Sherman Adams, a Donald Regan, a John Sununu—makes a stupid, even if unintentional slip, there may be only one friend left: and if he, the president, is embarrassed by the error, there is only the sad and sometimes precipitous exit. Would that the electronics wizards could invent a pocket-size "egometer" that would measure a chief of staff's ego, calculate his insensitivity index—and beep a warning! . . .

PART SEVEN

The Executive Branch

39

HUGH HECLO

From *A Government of Strangers*

To understand Hugh Heclo's intricate analysis of power inside the executive branch, students of American government must first know who the players are. Presidents select a small number (a few thousand) of high-level people to head the executive branch agencies. Among those appointments are cabinet secretaries, undersecretaries, assistant secretaries, and the like. The rest of those who work in the executive branch are civil servants, chosen for government jobs by merit exams, and they remain in government service for many years, even decades. They are the bureaucrats who provide continuity. Appointees come and go—as do presidents—but bureaucrats remain. Heclo identifies the often-unseen tension between a president's appointees and the bureaucrats. Be sure to pay particular attention to his discussion of the "iron triangle," one of the most interesting yet invisible forces in American government.

———

EVERY NEW ADMINISTRATION gives fresh impetus to an age-old struggle between change and continuity, between political leadership and bureaucratic power. Bureaucrats have a legitimate interest in maintaining the integrity of government programs and organizations. Political executives are supposed to have a broader responsibility: to guide rather than merely reflect the sum of special interests at work in the executive branch.

The search for effective political leadership in a bureaucracy of responsible career officials has become extraordinarily difficult in Washington. In every new crop of political appointees, some will have had government experience and a few will have worked together, but when it comes to group commitment to political leadership in the executive branch they constitute a government of strangers. And yet the fact remains that whether the President relies mainly on his White House aides or on his cabinet officials, someone is supposed to be mastering the bureaucracy "out there." For the President, his appointees, and high-ranking bureaucrats, the struggle to control the bureaucracy is usually a leap into the dark.

Despite a host of management and organization studies, Washington exposés and critiques of bureaucracy, very little information is available about the working world and everyday conduct of the top people in government. Even less is known about the operational lessons that could be drawn from their experiences. Congress is widely thought to have lost power to the executive branch, but congressional rather than executive behavior remains a major preoccupation in political research. Observers acknowledge that no president can cope with more than a tiny fraction of the decisionmaking in government, yet we know far more about a president's daily social errands than about the way vital public business is conducted by hundreds of political appointees and several thousand top bureaucrats who take executive actions in the name of the United States government—which is to say, in the name of us all....

If popular impressions are any guide, few job titles are more suspect than "politician" and "bureaucrat." Periodic polls have shown that while most parents might want their offspring to become president, they dislike the notion of their becoming politicians. No pollster has dared to ask Americans what they would think of their children growing up to become Washington bureaucrats.

Yet in many ways the American form of government depends not only on a supply of able politicians and bureaucrats, but even more on a successful interaction between these two unpopular groups....

...The administrative machinery in Washington represents a number of fragmented power centers rather than a set of subordinate units under the President. As many observers have noted, the cracks of fragmentation are not random but run along a number of well-established functional specialties and program interests that link particular government bureaus, congressional committees, and interest groups. People in the White House are aware of these subgovernments but have no obvious control over them. They seem to persist regardless of government reorganizations or, perhaps more to the point, they are able to prevent the reorganizations that displease them. In coping with these Washington subgovernments, the real lines of defense and accommodation are out in the departments, with their mundane operations of personnel actions, program approval, budget requests, regulation writing, and all the rest. These are the unglamorous tools with which political leaders in the agencies either help create a broader approach to the conduct of the public's business or acquiesce to the prevailing interest in business as usual....

...Political executives who try to exercise leadership within government may encounter intense opposition that they can neither avoid nor reconcile. At such times some agency officials may try to undermine the efforts of political executives. Any number of reasons—some deplorable, some commendable—lie behind such bureaucratic opposition. Executive politics involves people, and certain individuals simply dislike each other and resort to personal vendettas. Many, however, sincerely believe in their bureau's purpose and feel they must protect its jurisdiction, programs, and budget at all costs. Others feel they have an obligation to "blow the whistle" as best they can when confronted with evidence of what they regard as improper conduct. In all these cases the result is likely to strike a political executive as bureaucratic subversion. To the officials, it is a question of higher loyalty, whether to one's self-interests, organization, or conscience.

The structure of most bureaucratic sabotage has been characterized as an "iron triangle" uniting a particular government bureau, its relevant interest group, and congressional supporters. The aims may be as narrow as individual profiteering and empire-building. Or they may be as magnanimous as "public interest" lobbies, reformist bureaucrats, and congressional crusaders all claiming somewhat incongruously to represent the unrepresented. There are alliances with fully developed shapes (e.g., the congressional sponsors of a program, the bureaucrats executing it, and its private clients or suppliers) and those made up of only a few diverse lines (e.g., a civil servant looking forward to post-retirement prospects with a particular lobby association or a congressman unconcerned about a bureaucrat's policy aims but aware that his specific favors can help win reelection). Some bureaucratic entrepreneurs initiate their own outside contacts; others have been pushed into becoming involved in outside alliances by former political appointees.

The common features of these subgovernments are enduring mutual interests across the executive and legislative branches and between the public and private sectors. However high-minded the ultimate purpose, the immediate aim of each alliance is to become "self-sustaining in control of power in its own sphere." The longer an agency's tradition of independence, the greater the political controversy surrounding its subject matter, and the more it is allied with outside groups, the more a new appointee can expect sub rosa opposition to develop to any proposed changes. If political leadership in the executive branch is to be more than the accidental sum of these alliances and if political representation is to be less arbitrary than the demands of any group that claims to speak for the unrepresented, then some conflict seems inevitable between higher political leaders and the subgovernments operating within their sphere.

Often sabotage is unrecognizable because of the virtually invisible ways civil servants can act in bad faith toward political executives. In addition to the bureaucracy's power of withholding needed information and services, there are other means. Like a long-married couple, bureaucrats and those in their networks can often communicate with a minimum of words: "If congressional staffs I trust call up and ask me, I might tell them. But I can also tell them I don't agree with the secretary by offering just technical information and not associating myself with the policy."

An official who does not want to risk direct dealings with Congress can encourage a private interest group to go to the agency's important appropriations and legislative committees, as one political executive discovered: "When we tried to downgrade the ... bureau, its head was opposed, and he had a friend in a lobby group. After they got together rumblings started from the appropriations committee. I asked [the committee chairman] if he had a problem with this reorganization, and he said, 'No, you have the problem because if you touch that bureau I'll cut your job out of the budget.'" An experienced bureaucrat may not be able to make the decision, but he can try to arrange things to create the reaction he wants. "A colleague of mine," said a supergrade,* "keeps a file on field offices that can be abolished and their political sensitivity. Depending on who's pressing for cuts, he'll pull out those that are politically the worst for that particular configuration." The everyday relationships between people with specialized interests can shade effortlessly into subversion: "You know what it's like," said a bureau chief. "You've known each other and will have a drink complaining about what's happening and work up some little strategy of your own to do something about it." Or bureaucrats can work to get their way simply by not trying to know what is happening. One assistant secretary reported how his career subordinates agreed there might be mismanagement in the regional offices, "but they also said they didn't know what these offices were doing and so there wasn't enough information to justify doing what I wanted." Ignorance may not be bliss, but it can be security.

Political appointees can sometimes encounter much more vigorous forms of sabotage. These range from minor needling to massive retaliation. Since information is a prime strategic resource in Washington, the passing of unauthorized messages outside channels often approaches an art form. There are routine leaks to build credit and keep channels open for when they might be needed, positive leaks to promote something, negative leaks to discredit a person or policy, and counterleaks. There is even the daring reverse leak, an unauthorized release of information apparently for one reason but actually accomplishing the opposite.†

---

*Though not an official title, a "supergrade" would be a government civil servant in the upper levels of the bureaucracy.—EDS.

†One recent example involved a presidential assistant rather than a bureaucrat. While jockeying with another staff member, the assistant leaked a disclosure of his own impending removal from the West Wing. The opponent, who obviously stood the most to gain from the

There is no lack of examples in every administration. A political executive may discover that an agency subordinate "has gone to Congress and actually written the rider to the legislation that nullified the changes we wanted." A saboteur confided that "no one ever found it was [a division chief] who prepared the list showing which lobbyist was to contact which senator with what kind of argument." Still another official reported he had "seen appointees kept waiting in the outer office while their subordinate bureau officials were in private meetings with the congressional staff members." But waiting lines lack finesse. The telephone can be used with more delicacy, particularly after office hours: "The night before the hearings [a bureaucrat] fed the questions to the committee staff and then the agency witnesses spent the next two days having to reveal the information or duck the questions and catch hell." A young staff civil servant described how his superior operated:

I used to sit in [the bureau chief's] office after 6 P.M. when all the important business got done. He'd call up a senator and say, "Tom, you know this program that you and I got through a while back? Well, there's no crisis, but here are some things I'd like to talk to you about." He'd hang up and get on the phone to [a House committee chairman] and say, "I've been talking with Tom about this issue, and I'd like to bring you in on it." Hell, you'd find [the bureau chief] had bills almost drafted before anybody else in the executive branch had ever heard about them.

Encountering such situations, a public executive becomes acutely aware that experience as a private manager provides scant guidance. As one corporate executive with a six-figure salary said, "The end-runs and preselling were incredible. To find an equivalent you'd have to imagine some of your division managers going to the executive board or a major stockholder behind your back." Learning to deal with sabotage is a function of an executive's political leadership, not his private management expertise.

How do political executives try to deal with bureaucratic sabotage? . . . One approach is simply to ignore bureaucratic sabotage. Since the damage that may be done can easily cripple an executive's aims, diminish his reputation, and threaten his circles of confidence, those adopting this strategy can be presumed to have abdicated any attempt at political leadership in the Washington bureaucracy.

A second approach, especially favored by forceful managers, is to try

---

story, was naturally asked to confirm or deny the report. Since he was not yet strong enough to accomplish such a removal, the opponent had to deny responsibility for the leak and its accuracy, thereby inadvertently strengthening the position of the presidential assistant who first leaked the story.

to root out the leakers and prevent any recurrence. But political executives usually discover that this straightforward approach has considerable disadvantages. For one thing, it is extremely time-consuming and difficult to actually investigate acts of subversion and pin down blame. For another thing, there are few effective sanctions to prevent recurrences. Moreover, a search for the guilty party can easily displace more positive efforts and leadership initiatives an executive needs to make in dealing with the bureaucracy. Even if it were possible, trying to censor bureaucratic contacts would probably restrict the informal help these outside relationships provide, as well as the harm they do. And in the end any serious sabotage will probably be buttressed by some mandate from Congress; punishing the saboteurs can be seen as an assault on legislative prerogatives and thus invite even sterner retribution. It is circumstances such as these that led an experienced undersecretary to conclude:

Of course you can't be a patsy, but by and large you've got to recognize that leaks and end-runs are going to happen. You can spend all your time at trying to find out who's doing it, and if you do, then what? [One of my colleagues] actually tried to stop some of his bureaucrats from accepting phone calls from the press. They did stop accepting the calls, but they sure as hell returned them quickly. In this town there are going to be people running behind your back, and there's not much you can do to stop it.

However, while academics write about the iron triangle as if it were an immutable force, prudent political executives recognize that although they cannot stop bureaucratic sabotage, neither are they helpless against it. They can use personnel sanctions where misconduct can be clearly proven. But far more important, they can work to counteract sabotage with their own efforts—strengthening their outside contacts, extending their own lines of information and competitive analysis, finding new points of countertension. In general, experienced political executives try to use all their means of self-help and working relations so as to reshape the iron triangles into more plastic polygons.

To deal with sabotage, wise political appointees try to render it more obvious:

I make it clear that all the information and papers are supposed to move through me. It increases your work load tremendously, and maybe you don't understand everything you see, but everyone knows I'm supposed to be in on things and that they are accepting risks by acting otherwise.

They try to counteract unwanted messages with their own accounts to the press and others. The more the agency's boat is leaking, "the more you go out and work the pumps. You can't plug all the leaks, but you can make sure to get your side of the story out."

Political executives also make use of timing to deal with sabotage:

I put in a one-year fudge factor for an important change. That's because I know people are going to be doing end-runs to Congress. This year lets congressmen blow off steam, and for another thing it shows me where the sensitive spots are so I can get busy trying to work out some compromises—you know, things that can serve the congressmen's interest as well as mine.

Substantial results can be achieved by bringing new forces into play, dealing not with just one alliance but creating tests of strengths among the triangles:

It's like when officials were getting together with the unions and state administrators to get at some committee chairman. I hustled out to line up governors and show the congressmen that state administrators weren't speaking for all of state government.

Washington offers more opportunities to search for allies than is suggested by any simple image of political executives on one side and bureaucratic opponents on the other. Political appointees may be "backdoored" by other appointees, higher bureaucrats by lower bureaucrats. Fights may be extended to involve some appointees and bureaucrats versus others. As the leader of one faction put it, "Often a guy preselling things on the Hill is hurting people elsewhere, making it tougher for them to get money and approval and straining their relations. I use this fact to get allies."

A political executive who works hard at outside contacts will discover what subversives may learn too late: that many groups are fickle allies of the bureaucracy. This has seemed especially true as Congress has increased its own bureaucracy of uncoordinated staffs. A veteran bureaucrat described the risks run by would-be saboteurs:

Everybody you might talk to weighs the value of the issue to them against the value of keeping you alive for the next time. I've seen [a congressman] ruin many a good civil servant by getting a relationship going with him and then dropping him to score points off the agency brass. Now, too, there are more Hill staffers running around telling appointees, "Hey, these guys from your department said this and that. How about it?" Then the appointee will go back to the agency and raise hell for the bureaucrat.

Thus the political executives' own positive efforts are the necessary—if not always a sufficient—condition for combating sabotage. Since some bureaucratic subversion is an ever-present possibility and since punishment is difficult, the government executives' real choice is to build and use their political relationships or forfeit most other strategic resources for leadership.

40

PAUL LIGHT

From *A Government Ill Executed*

Paul Light is one of the nation's leading authorities on the executive branch. The executive branch is made up of a lot more people than the president and his staff. Millions of civil service workers comprise the ever-growing bureaucracy that administers governmental policies. Light is concerned about the simultaneous growth in the bureaucracy's responsibilities and the decline in the commitment of those who work in the federal service. The fault is not easily assigned. With the impending retirement of many government workers who have been employed for decades, Light sees opportunities for reform. By citing several specific areas for change, the author suggests ways in which the federal workforce can be made more effective. Notable among them is the need to interest capable young citizens in working for the executive branch. Reform is not easy, Light acknowledges, especially when many responsibilities of the federal government are farmed out to a "hidden workforce" of private contractors and state and local employees. Ultimately, it is tough to even figure out what government does and what it costs taxpayers to get the job done.

THIS BOOK IS BASED on Alexander Hamilton's warning about the dangers of a government ill executed. As he argued in *Federalist No. 70*, "A feeble execution is but another phrase for a bad execution; and a government ill executed, whatever it may be in theory must be in practice, a bad government." A government well executed was essential to virtually every challenge that faced the new republic.

More than two hundred years later, however, the federal government seems plagued by bad execution.

The stories are all too familiar: taxpayer abuse by the Internal Revenue Service, security breaches at the nation's nuclear laboratories, missing laptops at the Federal Bureau of Investigation, the Challenger and Columbia space shuttle disasters, breakdowns in policing everything from toys to cattle, the sluggish response to Hurricane Katrina, miscalculations about the war in Iraq, a cascade of wasteful government contracts, continued struggles to unite the nation's intelligence services, agonizing backlogs at the Social Security Administration and the Passport Bureau, near misses on airport runways, staff shortages across the government, porous borders, mistakes on airline passenger screening lines, the subprime mortgage meltdown, destruction of the CIA interrogation tapes, and negligent medical care of veterans. As the stories have accumulated, the federal government's customer service ratings have plummeted, and now rank with those of the airlines and cable TV.

This is not to suggest that the federal government is a wasteland of failure. To the contrary, the federal government accomplishes the impossible every day. Yet, if the federal government is still far from being ill executed, it is not uniformly well executed, either.

Hamilton's warning reflected more than his own experience with a government ill executed during the Revolutionary War. He also recognized that the new government would fail unless it could execute the laws. After all, the Constitution said almost nothing about the administrative state beyond giving the president a role, checked and balanced, in appointing and overseeing the officers of government. Otherwise, it was up to the president to decide how to "take care" that the laws would be faithfully executed. According to Hamilton, that required an energetic executive and a federal service to match. . . .

As the federal government's agenda has expanded over the decades, Hamilton's energetic federal service eventually became the victim of his own vision. Its mission is far broader than its capability; its chains of command are complex and confused; its process for filling the senior offices of government has become a source of embarrassment and delay; its workforce is drawn more by pay, benefits, and security than the chance to make a difference; its future employees would not know how to find a federal job even if they wanted one; its reform agenda has become a destination for fads; and execution of the laws now involves a large and mostly hidden workforce that cannot be held accountable for results. . . .

This erosion of the federal service is no longer a quiet crisis easily dismissed. To the contrary, it is now deafening.

The nation has good reason to worry about the continued erosion. Global warming is working its will on the climate, a new generation of terrorists is flexing its muscle in the Middle East, Medicare is straining under rising health costs, Social Security is bending as the baby boomers prepare for retirement, water wars are rising in the western states, energy independence is decades beyond reach, the nation's infrastructure is rusting, many of its public schools are struggling, and many of its greatest achievements of the past sixty years are in jeopardy as an uncertain future bears down on government.

The question is whether the federal government can rise to the tasks ahead. It has never had a more complex agenda, but has never seemed so confused about its priorities. It has never had a greater need for agility, but has never seemed so thick with bureaucracy. It has never had a bigger budget, but has never been so short on the resources to do its job. It has never had a greater need for decisiveness, but has never seemed so dependent on its hidden workforce to execute decisions. It has never had greater cause for commitment, but has never faced so much reform. Although federal agencies such as the National Institutes of Health and Centers for Disease Control continue to perform at high levels, their laboratories are rusting and their workforces are aging ever closer to retirement.

This [essay] is about reversing the erosion in the capacity to produce a government well executed, whether by creating more flexible careers as the baby boomers leave, building a disciplinary process that actually remedies poor performance, giving federal employees the resources to do their jobs, eliminating layers of needless management, focusing federal agencies and employees on clear priorities, abandoning missions that no longer make sense, or creating an appointments process that makes it easier for America's most talented civic and corporate leaders to say "yes" to a post of honor.

Moreover, with nearly a million baby boomers about to retire from the federal service, the nation has a unique but brief opportunity for radical action to reshape the federal hierarchy, reduce layers of needless management, redistribute resources toward the front lines of government, address the increasing dependency on the hidden workforce of contractors and grantees, and restore student interest in federal careers.

The most powerful advocates for this kind of reform are not outside government, but inside. Federal employees know they do not have enough capacity to do their jobs, and are hungry for change. They also know the time for tinkering is long past. Improving the hiring process will not suffice if new recruits do not have the opportunity to grow; enhancing retention will not help if it produces more layers of management; providing new resources will not matter if they are spread too thin; and setting priorities will not generate clarity if appointees are not in office long enough to make the decisions stick.

There are many reasons to worry about these trends. . . .

At least for now, Americans have little interest in rebuilding the federal service, especially in light of seemingly unending stories of fraud, waste, and abuse. They want the federal government to be involved in great endeavors such as protecting voting rights, reducing disease, and providing health care to low-income Americans, but also think government wastes the vast majority of the money it spends. They think the federal government mostly has the right priorities, but also think federal employees take their jobs for the pay, benefits, and security, not the chance to accomplish something worthwhile, make a difference, or help people. They want the federal government to maintain its programs to deal with important problems, but believe it deserves most of the criticism it receives.

In a very real sense, Americans are getting the government they deserve. They demand more, yet create a climate that encourages their leaders to exploit their distrust. Although the current erosion of the federal service is not just the public's fault, it reflects the tension between what Americans want and what they are willing to pay for. . . .

The weakening of the federal service reflects a series of separate trends that come together to weaken the faithful execution of the laws as a whole. Based on the belief that government can always do more with less, these trends have created a cascade of failures that are harbingers of further, deeper distress.

Both by accident and intent, this belief has been nurtured by repeated campaigns against government, and is reflected in the seven trends embedded in the contemporary erosion. . . . Although each of the trends has contributed to the crisis separately, they have combined to create a desperate moment in bureaucratic time in which the lack of action can only condemn government to greater frustration and failure.

An Ever-Expanding Mission

The threat to the federal service would not be relevant if government did not have such a large list of significant missions. After all, the federal agenda includes many of the most difficult and important problems the nation faces, whether guaranteeing voting rights through decent technology and aggressive enforcement, reducing disease through continued research in modern laboratories, improving the quality of life for older Americans through Social Security and an expanded Medicare program, or protecting the environment through effective implementation of the Clean Air and Water Acts. Americans may not agree on every mission, but the federal government is given little choice but to implement them all. . . .

Still Thickening Government

The federal government's expanding hierarchy reflects its steadily expanding mission, as well as the constant mimicry of new titles. Both by inattention and intent, Congress and the president continue to build a towering monument to their addiction to leadership by layers.

As this book suggests, the federal government has never had more layers of management or more leaders per layer. Despite his promises of businesslike government, George W. Bush's administration now oversees sixty-four discrete titles at the top of the federal government, and almost 2,600 titleholders, up from fifty-one titles and 2,400 titleholders in the final years of the Clinton administration. Although some of the growth reflects the war on terrorism, every department has expanded. Presidents may think the titles create greater leadership, but this book suggests just the opposite—more leaders create more opportunity for delay and obfuscation. . . .

Innocent until Nominated

In theory, tight chains of command should increase executive control at all levels of government. However, the presidential appointments process has become so slow and cumbersome that many layers remain unoccupied for months at the start of a new presidential administration, and continue unoccupied as appointees exit with regularity after eighteen to twenty-four months on the job.

As the scrutiny has increased, the process has slowed. Whereas the Kennedy administration was up and running within three months of inauguration day, the second Bush administration waited more than eight months on average to complete its long list of cabinet and subcabinet appointments. The delays have raised the importance of the de facto subcabinet composed of appointees who serve solely at the pleasure of the president without Senate confirmation.

This . . . does not address the impact of zealous appointees on the erosion of an energetic federal service, though there appears to be an increase in such appointees in Democratic and Republican administrations alike, especially in the rapidly expanding public affairs offices that often seek to politicize unpleasant facts and scientific evidence. However, there is no question that the process itself increasingly discourages appointees, whatever their ideology and intensity, from accepting the call to service. Delays are common, even among highly-qualified appointees, and complaints about the Senate and White House are high. Past appointees report that neither institution acts responsibly, while potential appointees worry that the process will embarrass and confuse them.

Although potential appointees worry more about the process than the past experience of actual appointees suggests is necessary, they also see living in Washington, D.C., as a significant barrier to service, and report significant concerns about the impact of presidential service on their future careers, especially their ability to return to their previous jobs. The result is a dwindling pool of potential appointees, many of whom may be motivated more by the chance to make future contacts and increase their earning power than the chance to serve an admired president.

A Deafening Crisis

Whatever their motivation, presidential appointees oversee a federal workforce that reports serious obstacles to success, especially when compared with business and the nonprofit sector.

On full exertion for the public benefit, many federal employees said they took their jobs for the pay, benefits, and security instead of the chance to accomplish something worthwhile. Compared to nonprofit employees, who emphasize the chance to accomplish something worthwhile and the nature of the work, federal employees have taken Hamilton's model seriously, putting compensation at the top of the list for coming to work each day.

On work that matters, federal employees reported that they do not always receive the kind of work that encourages innovation and high performance. At first glance, the quality of work looks reasonably attractive, especially among employees who said they are surrounded by peers who are committed to the mission, given the chance to do the things they do best, and encouraged to take risks and try new ways of doing things. But when compared with business and nonprofit employment, the quality of federal work suffers.

On the adequate provision of support, federal employees were consistently dissatisfied with access to the tools they need, including training, technology, and enough employees to do the job. Nor did they rate their leadership and coworkers as competent as business and nonprofit employees. At least according to the 2001 and 2002 surveys, most federal employees rated their peers as not particularly competent and not getting better.

On rewards for a job well done and discipline for a job done poorly, most federal employees gave their organization's disciplinary process failing marks and blamed this poor performance in part on their organization's unwillingness to ask enough of all employees. Federal employees also gave their own organizations low ratings on basic tasks such as delivering programs and services, being fair, and spending money wisely.

Finally, on the respect of the public served, ordinary citizens are not the only ones who have come to distrust government. Federal employees themselves showed little trust in their own organizations, in no small part

because the federal government has been so penurious with the basic resources they need to do their jobs well.

Ironically given the urgency of the war on terrorism, many of these
indicators actually decayed following the 9/11 attacks, in part because federal employees may have become less tolerant of bureaucracy and red
tape. The most surprising problems came at the Department of Defense,
where employees simultaneously reported an increased sense of mission,
but more layers of needless management, inadequate staffing levels, and
less access to the technology and training they needed to succeed. Faced
with an urgent mission, they became increasingly angry with the bureaucracy around them, and surprisingly less likely to report high morale among
their colleagues.

The Spirit of Service

All of these trends have contributed to declining interest in federal
service among young Americans, who rightly wonder whether the federal government can deliver on its promises of extensive and arduous enterprise without sacrificing each new generation of talent. In a very real
sense, the federal government's reputation precedes it, whether on college
campuses, in professional schools, or in the halls of government itself.

... [M]any college seniors would not want a federal job even if they
knew how to get one, too many graduates of the nation's top professional
schools see government as a destination for pay, benefits, and security
rather than challenging work.... Having redefined the basic meaning of
public service almost to the point of excluding government work, young
Americans now view nonprofits as the destination of choice for making a
difference and learning new skills. Asked to show them the work, the federal government too often shows young Americans the bureaucracy, including a hiring process that sends the instant message that life will be
difficult at best once on the federal payroll....

The Tides of Reform

The onslaught of reform over the decades has contributed to the federal government's reputation for administrative inertia....

The level of federal reform appears to parallel the frenzy of management improvement fads in business. But as the pace of federal management reform has increased over the past thirty years, so has the mix of
reforms. As Congress has become more involved in making government
work, federal employees have faced one competing reform after another,

leading to confusion, wasted motion, and frustration in setting priorities with fads and fashions that are now out of favor. . . .

The True Size of Government

The rising tides of reform speak to a general frustration with government's ability to perform, but much of that performance is now dependent on a hidden workforce of contractors, grantees, and state and local employees who labor under federal mandates. Although this workforce is essential to implementing the federal mission, there is cause for concern about the costs embedded in continued outsourcing, especially given the lack of an experienced cadre of federal employees to oversee the activity.

There is no question that this hidden workforce is growing. Although the true size of government dropped sharply in the years following the end of the cold war, it began rising in the late 1990s and has been growing ever since. In 1999, for example, the true size of government had reached its lowest level in more than a decade, dropping to just 11 million civil servants, postal workers, military personnel, and contract- and grant-generated employees. Six years later, in 2005, the true size of government had risen to 14.6 million, largely driven by the burgeoning war on terrorism and the Iraq War. Most of the increase did not come from the purchase of goods but from services such as computer programming, management assistance, and temporary labor. . . .

It is impossible to claim that the hidden workforce of contractors and grantees is not doing its job either effectively or at reasonable cost, if only because such a claim would require more information and oversight than overworked federal procurement officers now have. Nevertheless, the increasing use of contractors, grantees, and state and local employees suggests a significant substitution of hidden workers for fulltime federal employees. In turn, this substitution effect creates a series of illusions, including the notion that the federal government can actually track its large and increasing number of megacontracts and the labor they purchase. The hidden workforce may be mostly invisible to the public and press, but it exists nonetheless. . . .

Big problems demand big answers, which is why tinkering will no longer suffice. . . .

41

ROBERT REICH

From *Locked in the Cabinet*

University professor Robert Reich was appointed to President Clinton's cabinet in 1993 to be his Secretary of Labor. Writing with all the candor and humor that is Reich's trademark, he gives readers three important criteria he considered in selecting his assistants and then concludes, "I'm flying blind." His daily schedule is packed, and he is motivated to escape from the "bubble" and actually tour the vast buildings of the Labor Department. Finally, Reich offers an instructive anecdote about an idea developed by an obscure civil servant in the department, an idea that turns out to be a real winner and becomes an important new government policy.

February 1, [1993] Washington

I INTERVIEW TWENTY people today. I have to find a deputy secretary and chief of staff with all the management skills I lack. I also have to find a small platoon of assistant secretaries: one to run the Occupational Safety and Health Administration (detested by corporations, revered by unions); another to be in charge of the myriad of employment and job training programs (billions of dollars), plus unemployment insurance (billions more); another to police the nation's pension funds (four trillion dollars' worth); another to patrol the nation's nine million workplaces to make sure that young children aren't being exploited, that workers receive at least a minimum hourly wage plus time and a half for overtime, that sweatshops are relegated to history.

The Department of Labor is vast, its powers seemingly endless. With a history spanning the better part of the twentieth century—involving every major controversy affecting American workers—it issues thousands of regulations, sends vast sums of money to states and cities, and sues countless employers. I can barely comprehend it all. It was created in 1913 with an ambitious mission: *Foster, promote, and develop the welfare of the wage earners of the United States, improve their working conditions, and advance their opportunities for profitable employment.* That about sums it up.

And yet here I am assembling my team before I've even figured it all out. No time to waste. Bill will have to sign off on my choices, then each of them will be nitpicked for months by the White House staff and the FBI, and if they survive those hurdles each must be confirmed by the Senate.

If I'm fast enough out of the starting gate, my team might be fully installed by June. If I dally now and get caught in the traffic jam of sub-cabinet nominations from every department, I might not see them for a year. And whenever they officially start, add another six months before they have the slightest idea what's going on.

No other democracy does it this way. No private corporation would think of operating like this. Every time a new president is elected, America assembles a new government of 3,000 or so amateurs who only sometimes know the policies they're about to administer, rarely have experience managing large government bureaucracies, and almost never know the particular piece of it they're going to run. These people are appointed quickly by a president-elect who is thoroughly exhausted from a year and a half of campaigning. And they remain in office, on average, under two years—barely enough time to find the nearest bathroom. It's a miracle we don't screw it up worse than we do.

Part of my problem is I don't know exactly what I'm looking for and I certainly don't know how to tell whether I've found it. Some obvious criteria:

1. *They should share the President-elect's values.* But how will I know they do? I can't very well ask, "Do you share the President's values?" and expect an honest answer. Even if they contributed money to the campaign, there's no telling. I've heard of several middle-aged Washington lawyers so desperate to escape the tedium of law practice by becoming an assistant secretary for Anything That Gets Me Out of Here that they've made whopping contributions to both campaigns.

2. *They should be competent and knowledgeable about the policies they'll administer.* Sounds logical, but here again, how can I tell? I don't know enough to know whether someone *else* knows enough. "What do you think about the Employee Retirement Income Security Act?" I might ask, and an ambitious huckster could snow me. "I've thought a lot about this," he might say, "and I've concluded that Section 508(m) should be changed because most retirees have 307 accounts which are treated by the IRS as Subchapter 12 entities." Uttered with enough conviction, bullshit like this could sweep me off my feet.

3. *They should be good managers.* But how to find out? Yesterday I phoned someone about a particular job candidate's management skills, at her suggestion. He told me she worked for him and was a terrific manager. "Ter-

rific?" I repeated. "Wonderful. The best," he said. "You'd recommend her?"
I asked. "Absolutely. Can't go wrong," he assured me. I thanked him, hung
up the phone, and was enthusiastic for about five minutes, until I realized
how little I had learned. How do I know *he* recognizes a good manager?
Maybe he's a lousy manager himself and has a bunch of bozos working for
him. Why should I trust that he's more interested in my having her on *my*
team than in getting her off his?

I'm flying blind. . . .

March 2 Washington

This afternoon, I mount a small revolution at the Labor Department.
The result is chaos.

Background: My cavernous office is becoming one of those hermeti-
cally sealed, germ-free bubbles they place around children born with immune deficiencies. Whatever gets through to me is carefully sanitized.
Telephone calls are prescreened, letters are filtered, memos are reviewed.
Those that don't get through are diverted elsewhere. Only [deputy secre-
tary] Tom [Glynn], chief of staff Kitty [Higgins], and my secretary walk
into the office whenever they want. All others seeking access must first be
scheduled, and have a sufficient reason to take my precious germ-free
time.

I'm scheduled to the teeth. Here, for example, is today's timetable:

6:45 A.M.	Leave apartment
7:10 A.M.	Arrive office
7:15 A.M.	Breakfast with MB from the *Post*
8:00 A.M.	Conference call with Rubin
8:30 A.M.	Daily meeting with senior staff
9:15 A.M.	Depart for Washington Hilton
9:40 A.M.	Speech to National Association of Private Industry Councils
10:15 A.M.	Meet with Joe Dear (OSHA enforcement)
11:15 A.M.	Meet with Darla Letourneau (DOL budget)
12:00	Lunch with JG from National League of Cities
1:00 P.M.	CNN interview (taped)
1:30 P.M.	Congressional leadership panel
2:15 P.M.	Congressman Ford
3:00 P.M.	NEC budget meeting at White House
4:00 P.M.	Welfare meeting at White House
5:00 P.M.	National Public Radio interview (taped)
5:45 P.M.	Conference call with mayors
6:15 P.M.	Telephone time

7:00 P.M.   Meet with Maria Echeveste (Wage and Hour)
8:00 P.M.   Kitty and Tom daily briefing
8:30 P.M.   National Alliance of Business reception
9:00 P.M.   Return to apartment.

I remain in the bubble even when I'm outside the building—ushered from place to place by someone who stays in contact with the front office by cellular phone. I stay in the bubble after business hours. If I dine out, I'm driven to the destination and escorted to the front door. After dinner, I'm escorted back to the car, driven to my apartment, and escorted from the car, into the apartment building, into the elevator, and to my apartment door.

No one gives me a bath, tastes my food, or wipes my bottom—at least not yet. But in all other respects I feel like a goddamn two-year-old. Tom and Kitty insist it has to be this way. Otherwise I'd be deluged with calls, letters, meetings, other demands on my time, coming from all directions. People would force themselves on me, harass me, maybe even threaten me. The bubble protects me.

Tom and Kitty have hired three people to handle my daily schedule (respond to invitations, cull the ones that seem most promising, and squeeze all the current obligations into the time available), one person to ready my briefing book each evening so I can prepare for the next day's schedule, and two people to "advance" me by making sure I get where I'm supposed to be and depart on time. All of them now join Tom and Kitty as guardians of the bubble.

"How do you decide what I do and what gets through to me?" I ask Kitty.

"We have you do and see what you'd choose if you had time to examine all the options yourself—sifting through all the phone calls, letters, memos, and meeting invitations," she says simply.

"But how can you possibly *know* what I'd choose for myself?"

"Don't worry," Kitty says patiently. "We know."

They have no way of knowing. We've worked together only a few weeks. Clare and I have lived together for a quarter century and even she wouldn't know.

I trust Tom and Kitty. They share my values. I hired them because I sensed this, and everything they've done since then has confirmed it. But it's not a matter of trust.

The *real* criterion Tom and Kitty use (whether or not they know it or admit it) is their own experienced view of what a secretary of labor with my values and aspirations *should* choose to see and hear. They transmit to me through the bubble only those letters, phone calls, memoranda, people, meetings, and events which they believe *someone like me* ought to have. But if I see and hear only what "someone like me" should see and hear, no original or out-of-the-ordinary thought will ever permeate the bubble. I'll never be surprised or shocked. I'll never be forced to rethink or reevaluate anything. I'll just lumber along, blissfully ignorant of what I *really* need to see and hear—which are things that don't merely confirm my preconceptions about the world.

I make a list of what I want them to transmit through the bubble henceforth:

1. The angriest, meanest ass-kicking letters we get from the public every week.

2. Complaints from department employees about anything.

3. Bad news about fuck-ups, large and small.

4. Ideas, ideas, ideas: from department employees, from outside academics and researchers, from average citizens. Anything that even resembles a good idea about what we should do better or differently. Don't screen out the wacky ones.

5. Anything from the President or members of Congress.

6. A random sample of calls or letters from real people outside Washington, outside government—people who aren't lawyers, investment bankers, politicians, or business consultants; people who aren't professionals; people without college degrees.

7. "Town meetings" with department employees here at headquarters and in the regions. "Town meetings" in working-class and poor areas of the country. "Town meetings" in community colleges, with adult students.

8. Calls and letters from business executives, including those who hate my guts. Set up meetings with some of them.

9. Lunch meetings with small groups of department employees, randomly chosen from all ranks.

10. Meetings with conservative Republicans in Congress.

I send the memo to Tom and Kitty. Then, still feeling rebellious and with nothing on my schedule for the next hour (the NEC meeting scheduled for 3:00 was canceled) I simply walk out of the bubble. I sneak out of my big office by the back entrance and start down the corridor.

I take the elevator to floors I've never visited. I wander to places in the department I've never been. I have spontaneous conversations with employees I'd never otherwise see. *Free at last.*

Kitty discovers I'm missing. It's as if the warden had discovered an escape from the state pen. The alarm is sounded: Secretary loose! Secretary escapes from bubble! Find the Secretary! Security guards are dispatched.

By now I've wandered to the farthest reaches of the building, to corridors never before walked by anyone ranking higher than GS-12. I visit the mailroom, the printshop, the basement workshop.

The hour is almost up. Time to head back. But which way? I'm at the northernmost outpost of the building, in bureaucratic Siberia. I try to retrace my steps but keep coming back to the same point in the wilderness.

I'm lost.

In the end, of course, a security guard finds me and takes me back to the bubble. Kitty isn't pleased. "You shouldn't do that," she says sternly. "We were worried."

"It was good for me." I'm defiant.

"We need to know where you *are*." She sounds like the mother of a young juvenile delinquent.

"Next time give me a beeper, and I'll call home to see if you need me."

"You *must* have someone with you. It's not safe."

"This is the Labor Department, not Bosnia."

"You might get lost."

"That's *ridiculous*. How in hell could someone get *lost* in this building?"

She knows she has me. "You'd be surprised." She smiles knowingly and heads back to her office. . . .

March 14 Washington

Tom and Kitty suggest I conduct a "town meeting" of Labor Department employees here at headquarters—give them an opportunity to ask me questions and me a chance to express my views. After all, I've been here almost eight weeks and presumably have a few answers and one or two views.

Some of the other senior staff think it unwise. They point to the risk of gathering thousands of employees together in one place with access to microphones. The cumulative frustrations from years of not being listened to by political appointees could explode when exposed to the open air, like a dangerous gas. Gripes, vendettas, personal slights, hurts, malfeasance, nonfeasance, mistreatments, slurs, lies, deceptions, frauds. Who knows what might be in that incendiary mix?

Secretaries of labor have come and gone, usually within two years. Assistant secretaries, even faster. Only a tiny fraction of Labor Department employees are appointed to their jobs because of who's occupying the White House. The vast majority are career employees, here because they got their jobs through the civil service. Most of them will remain here for decades, some for their entire careers. They have come as lawyers, accountants, economists, investigators, clerks, secretaries, and custodians. Government doesn't pay as well as the private sector, but the jobs are more secure. And some have come because they believe that public service is inherently important.

But for years they've been treated like shit. Republican appointees were often contemptuous of or uninterested in most of what went on here. The Reagan and Bush administrations didn't exactly put workplace issues at the top of their agenda. In fact, Reagan slashed the department's budget and reduced the number of employees by about a quarter. His first appointee as secretary of labor was a building contractor.

The career people don't harbor much more trust for Democrats. It's an article of faith among civil servants that political appointees, of whatever party, care only about the immediate future. They won't be here years from now to implement fully their jazzy ideas, or to pick up the pieces if the ideas fall apart. Career civil servants would prefer not to take short-term risks. They don't want headlines. Even if the headlines are positive, headlines draw extra attention, and in Washington attention can be dangerous.

There is a final reason for their cynicism. Career civil servants feel unappreciated by politicians. Every presidential candidate since Carter has run as a Washington "outsider," against the permanent Washington establishment. Almost every congressional and senatorial candidate decries the "faceless bureaucrats" who are assumed to wield unaccountable power. Career civil servants are easy targets. They can't talk back. This scapegoating parallels the public's mounting contempt for Washington. In opinion polls conducted during the Eisenhower administration, about seventy-five percent of the American public thought that their government "could be trusted to act in the public interest most of the time." In a recent poll, only twenty-five percent expressed similar sentiments. But career civil servants aren't to blame. The disintegration has come on the heels of mistakes and improprieties by political leaders—Vietnam, Watergate, the Iran-*contra* imbroglio, the savings-and-loan scandal. And it accelerated as the nation emerged from five decades of Depression, hot war, and cold war—common experiences that forced us to band together and support a strong government—into a global economy without clear borders or evil empires.

Our "town meeting" is set for noon. A small stage is erected on one side of a huge open hall on the first floor of the department. The hall is about the size of football field. On its walls are paintings of former secretaries of labor.

I walk in exactly at noon. Nervous (Wasn't President James Garfield assassinated by a disgruntled civil servant?)

The hall is jammed with thousands of people. Many are sitting on folding chairs, tightly packed around the makeshift stage. Others are standing. Several hundred are standing on risers around the outer perimeter, near the walls. Is it legal for so many employees to be packed so tightly in one place? Tomorrow's Washington *Post*: Labor Secretary Endangers Workers. Subhead: Violates the Occupational Safety and Health Act.

I make my way up to the small stage and face the crowd. I don't want to speak from behind a lectern, because to see over it I'd have to stand on a stool and would look ridiculous. So I hold the microphone. The crowd quiets.

"Hello."

"Hello!" they roar back in unison. Laughter. A good start, anyway. . . .

"Who's first?" I scan the crowd—left, center, right. No hands. I'm back in the classroom, first class of the semester. I've asked the question, but no one wants to break the ice. They have plenty to say, but no one dares. So I'll do what I always do: I'll just stand here silently, smiling, until someone gets up the courage. I can bear the silence.

I wait. Thirty seconds. Forty-five seconds. A minute. Thousands of people here, but no sound. They seem startled. I know they have all sorts of opinions about what should be done. They share them with each other every day. But have they ever shared them directly with the Secretary?

Finally, one timid hand in the air. I point to her. "Yes! You! What's your name?" All eyes on her. The crowd explodes into rumbles, murmurs, and laughs, like a huge lung exhaling. A cordless mike is passed to her.

"Connie," she answers, nervously.

I move to the front of the stage so I can see Connie better. "Which agency do you work in, Connie?"

"Employment Standards."

"What's your idea?"

Connie's voice is unsteady, but she's determined. "Well, I don't see why we need to fill out time cards when we come to work and when we leave. It's silly and demeaning."

Applause. Connie is buoyed by the response, and her voice grows stronger. "I mean, if someone is dishonest they'll just fill in the wrong times anyway. Our supervisors know when we come and go. The work has to get done. Besides, we're professionals. Why treat us like children?"

I look over at Tom. He shrugs his shoulders: Why not?

"Okay, done. Starting tomorrow, no more time cards."

For a moment, silence. The audience seems stunned. Then a loud roar of approval that breaks into wild applause. Many who were seated stand and cheer.

What have I done? I haven't doubled their salaries or sent them on all-expenses-paid vacations to Hawaii. All I did was accept a suggestion that seemed reasonable. But for people who have grown accustomed to being ignored, I think I just delivered an important gift.

The rest of the meeting isn't quite as buoyant. Some suggestions I reject outright (a thirty-five-hour workweek). Others I write down and defer for further consideration. But I learn a great deal. I hear ideas I never would have thought of. One thin and balding man from the Employment and Training Administration has a commonsensical one: When newly unemployed people register for unemployment insurance, why not determine whether their layoff is likely to be permanent or temporary—and if permanent, get them retraining and job-placement services right away instead of waiting until their benefits almost run out? He has evidence this will shorten the average length of unemployment and save billions of dollars. I say I'll look into it. . . .

September 20 Washington

Tom tells me that calls are pouring in from members of Congress demanding that unemployment benefits be extended beyond their normal six months. "We've got to find several billion dollars, quick," says Tom. But I don't know where to find the money other than taking it out of job counseling and training—which would be nuts.

"We *won't* extend unemployment benefits if it means less money for finding new jobs!" I'm defiant.

"I don't think you have a choice," says Tom. "People just don't believe there're new jobs out there. All they know is they had a job. They think it's coming back eventually, and they need money to live on in the meantime."

Kitty rushes in. "I've got it!"

"What?"

"The *answer*. Remember the fellow at the department town meeting who had the idea for fixing the unemployment system?"

"Vaguely." I recall a tall, hollow-eyed career employee who spoke toward the end.

"He suggested that when newly unemployed people apply for unemployment insurance they're screened to determine whether their layoff is temporary or permanent—and if *permanent* they immediately get help finding a new job. *Well* . . . " Kitty pauses to catch her breath. "I spoke with him at some length this morning. His name is Steve Wandner. Seems that a few years ago he ran a pilot project for the department, trying his idea out. Get *this*: Where he tried it, the average length of unemployment dropped two to four weeks! The poor guy has been trying to sell the idea since then, but no one has ever listened."

"I don't get it. How does this help us?"

"Think of it! Do what he did all over the country, and cut the average length of unemployment two to four weeks. This saves the government $400 million a year in unemployment benefits. That's $2 billion over the next five years, if you need help with the math."

"I understand the math. I just don't understand the *point*. So what? That's money saved in the *future*. How does that get us the money we need now?"

Kitty stares at me with her usual what-is-this-man-doing-as-a-cabinet-member expression. "If we can show that we'll save this money over the next five years, we can use it *now* to offset extra unemployment benefits. It's like extra *cash*!" She lunges toward a stack of paper on the corner of my desk and tosses the entire pile into the air. "Manna *from heaven*!"

"I still don't get it. And by the way, you're making a mess."

Kitty is excited, but she talks slowly, as if to a recent graduate of kindergarten. "Try to *understand*. The federal budget law requires that if you want to spend more money, you've got to get the money from somewhere else. Right? One place you can get it is from future savings, but only if the Congressional Budget Office believes you. Follow me?"

"I think so."

"Now comes our brilliant geek from the bowels of the Labor Department with *proof* that we can save around $2 billion during the next five years. And the true *beauty* of it"—Kitty beams—"is that this reform brings us a step closer to what *you've* been talking about. We get a law providing emergency extra unemployment benefits—$2 billion worth—covering the next few months. And *at the same time* we permanently change the whole system so that it's more focused on finding new jobs. It's a twofer! A win-win! Nobody can vote against it! I *love it!*"

I look at Tom. "Is she right?"

"Yup." Tom is impressed.

Kitty begins to dance around the office. She is the only person I have ever met who can fall in love with proposed legislation. . . .

November 24 The White House

B sits at his elaborately carved desk in the Oval Office before the usual gaggle of cameras and spotlights. Clustered tightly around him in order to get into the shot are five smiling senators and ten smiling House members. B utters some sentences about why people who have lost their jobs shouldn't have to worry that their unemployment benefits will run out. He signs the bill into law. The congressmen applaud. He stands and shakes each of their hands. The spotlights go out and the cameras are packed away. The whole thing takes less than five minutes.

Kitty is here, smiling from ear to ear. I congratulate her.

Against a far wall, behind the small crowd, I see Steve Wandner, the hollow-eyed Labor Department employee who first suggested the idea that was just signed into law. I made sure Steve was invited to this signing ceremony. I walk over to where he's standing.

"Good job." I extend my hand.

He hesitates a moment. "I never thought . . . " His voice trails off.

"I want to introduce you to the President."

Steve is reluctant. I pull his elbow and guide him toward where B is chatting energetically with several members of Congress who still encircle him. They're talking football—big men, each over six feet, laughing, telling stories, bonding. It's a veritable huddle. We wait on the periphery.

Several White House aides try to coax the group out of the Oval. It's early in the day, and B is already hopelessly behind schedule. Steve wants to exit, but I motion him to stay put.

The herd begins to move. I see an opening. "Mr. President!" B turns, eyes dancing. He's having fun. It's a good day: signing legislation, talking sports. It's been a good few months: the budget victory, the Middle East peace accord, the NAFTA victory. He's winning, and he can feel it. And when B is happy, the happiness echoes through the White House like a sweet song.

"Come here, pal." B draws me toward him and drapes an arm around my shoulders. I feel like a favorite pet.

"Mr. President, I want you to meet the man who came up with the idea for today's legislation." I motion Steve forward.

With his left arm still around my shoulders, B extends his right hand to Steve, who takes it as if it were an Olympic trophy.

"Good work," is all B says to Steve, but B's tight grip and his fleeting you-are-the-only-person-in-the-world-who-matters gaze into Steve's eyes light the man up, giving him a glow I hadn't thought possible.

It's over in a flash. B turns away to respond to a staffer who has urgently whispered something into his ear. But Steve doesn't move. The hand that had been in the presidential grip falls slowly to his side. He stares in B's direction. The afterglow remains.

I have heard tales of people who are moved by a profound religious experience, whose lives of torment or boredom are suddenly transformed, who actually *look* different because they have found Truth and Meaning. Steve Wandner—the gangly, diffident career bureaucrat who has traipsed to his office at the Labor Department every workday for twenty years, slowly chipping away at the same large rock, answering to the same career executives, coping with silly demands by low-level political appointees to do this or that, seeing the same problems and making the same suggestions and sensing that nothing will ever really change—has now witnessed the impossible. His idea has become the law of the land. . . .

42

JAMES Q. WILSON

From *Bureaucracy*

It's been over twenty years since the "new" ice skating rink was built in New York's Central Park. Many skaters have enjoyed it since 1986. In that time, New York City has experienced much change. New mayors have come and gone. September 11, 2001, happened: The city mourned and then slowly recovered. But some things in New York City have remained the same, even if not exactly. Donald Trump still knows how to get things done. Back in the mid-1980s, before "The Apprentice," real estate developer Trump showed that the efficiency of the private sector could accomplish what no public bureaucracy seemed to be able to do: refurbish the Central Park skating rink, quickly and inexpensively. Today we'd say that the city fired itself and "privatized" the project by hiring Trump. Renowned political scientist James Q. Wilson looks at Trump's success with the skating rink project, but also explains why he had that success. The public sector has many limitations on its actions that the private sector does not have to consider. As privatization becomes increasingly popular on the state and local and even national level of government, it's important to remember Wilson's caveats: efficiency is not the only worthy goal and not all publicly run projects are inefficient.

———

ON THE MORNING OF MAY 22, 1986, Donald Trump, the New York real estate developer, called one of his executives, Anthony Gliedman, into his office. They discussed the inability of the City of New York, despite six years of effort and the expenditure of nearly $13 million, to rebuild the ice-skating rink in Central Park. On May 28 Trump offered to take over the rink reconstruction, promising to do the job in less than six months. A week later Mayor Edward Koch accepted the offer and shortly thereafter the city appropriated $3 million on the understanding that Trump would have to pay for any cost overruns out of his own pocket. On October 28, the renovation was complete, over a month ahead of schedule and about $750,000 under budget. Two weeks later, skaters were using it.

For many readers it is obvious that private enterprise is more efficient than are public bureaucracies, and so they would file this story away as simply another illustration of what everyone already knows. But for other readers it is not so obvious what this story means; to them, business is greedy and unless watched like a hawk will fob off shoddy or overpriced goods on the American public, as when it sells the government $435 hammers and $3,000 coffee-pots. Trump may have done a good job in this instance, but perhaps there is something about skating rinks or New York City government that gave him a comparative advantage; in any event, no larger lessons should be drawn from it.

Some lessons can be drawn, however, if one looks closely at the incentives and constraints facing Trump and the Department of Parks and Recreation. It becomes apparent that there is not one "bureaucracy problem" but several, and the solution to each in some degree is incompatible with the solution to every other. First there is the problem of accountability—getting agencies to serve agreed-upon goals. Second there is the problem of equity—treating all citizens fairly, which usually means treating them alike on the basis of clear rules known in advance. Third there is the problem of responsiveness—reacting reasonably to the special needs and circumstances of particular people. Fourth there is the problem of efficiency—obtaining the greatest output for a given level of resources. Finally there is the problem of fiscal integrity—assuring that public funds are spent prudently for public purposes. Donald Trump and Mayor Koch were situated differently with respect to most of these matters.

Accountability

The Mayor wanted the old skating rink refurbished, but he also wanted to minimize the cost of the fuel needed to operate the rink (the first effort to rebuild it occurred right after the Arab oil embargo and the attendant increase in energy prices). Trying to achieve both goals led city hall to select a new refrigeration system that as it turned out would not work properly. Trump came on the scene when only one goal dominated: get the rink rebuilt. He felt free to select the most reliable refrigeration system without worrying too much about energy costs.

Equity

The Parks and Recreation Department was required by law to give every contractor an equal chance to do the job. This meant it had to put every part of the job out to bid and to accept the lowest without much regard to the reputation or prior performance of the lowest bidder. Moreover, state law forbade city agencies from hiring a general contractor and letting him select the subcontractors; in fact, the law forbade the city from even discussing the project in advance with a general contractor who might later bid on it—that would have been collusion. Trump, by contrast, was free to locate the rink builder with the best reputation and give him the job.

Fiscal Integrity

To reduce the chance of corruption or sweetheart deals the law required Parks and Recreation to furnish complete, detailed plans to every contractor bidding on the job; any changes after that would require renegotiating the contract. No such law constrained Trump; he was free to give incomplete plans to his chosen contractor, hold him accountable for building a satisfactory rink, but allow him to work out the details as he went along.

Efficiency

When the Parks and Recreation Department spent over six years and $13 million and still could not reopen the rink, there was public criticism but no city official lost money. When Trump accepted a contract to do it, any cost overruns or delays would have come out of his pocket and any savings could have gone into his pocket (in this case, Trump agreed not to take a profit on the job).

Gliedman summarized the differences neatly: "The problem with government is that government can't say, 'yes'. . . . . there is nobody in government that can do that. There are fifteen or twenty people who have to agree. Government has to be slower. It has to safeguard the process." . . . .

The government can't say "yes." In other words, the government is constrained. Where do the constraints come from? From us.

Herbert Kaufman has explained red tape as being of our own making: "Every restraint and requirement originates in somebody's demand for it." Applied to the Central Park skating rink Kaufman's insight reminds us that civil-service reformers demanded that no city official benefit personally from building a project; that contractors demanded that all be given an equal chance to bid on every job; and that fiscal watchdogs demanded that all contract specifications be as detailed as possible. For each demand a procedure was established; viewed from the outside, those procedures are called red tape. To enforce each procedure a manager was appointed; those managers are called bureaucrats. No organized group demanded that all skating rinks be rebuilt as quickly as possible, no procedure existed to enforce that demand, and no manager was appointed to enforce it. The political process can more easily enforce compliance with constraints than the attainment of goals.

When we denounce bureaucracy for being inefficient we are saying something that is half true. Efficiency is a ratio of valued resources used to valued outputs produced. The smaller that ratio the more efficient the production. If the valued output is a rebuilt skating rink, then whatever process uses the fewest dollars or the least time to produce a satisfactory rink is the most efficient process. By this test Trump was more efficient than the Parks and Recreation Department.

But that is too narrow a view of the matter. The economic definition of efficiency (efficiency in the small, so to speak) assumes that there is only one valued output, the new rink. But government has many valued outputs, including a reputation for integrity, the confidence of the people, and the support of important interest groups. When we complain about skating rinks not being built on time we speak as if all we cared about were skating rinks. But when we complain that contracts were awarded without competitive bidding or in a way that allowed bureaucrats to line their pockets we acknowledge that we care about many things besides skating rinks; we care about the contextual goals—the constraints—that we want government to observe. A government that is slow to build rinks but is honest and accountable in its actions and properly responsive to worthy constituencies may be a very efficient government, *if* we measure efficiency in the large by taking into account *all* of the valued outputs.

Calling a government agency efficient when it is slow, cumbersome, and costly may seem perverse. But that is only because we lack any objective way for deciding how much money or time should be devoted to maintaining honest behavior, producing a fair allocation of benefits, and generating popular support as well as to achieving the main goal of the project. If we could measure these things, and if we agreed as to their value, then we would be in a position to judge the true efficiency of a government agency and decide when it is taking too much time or spending too much money achieving all that we expect of it. But we cannot measure these things nor do we agree about their relative importance, and so government always will appear to be inefficient compared to organizations that have fewer goals.

Put simply, the only way to decide whether an agency is truly inefficient is to decide which of the constraints affecting its action ought to be ignored or discounted. In fact that is what most debates about agency behavior are all about. In fighting crime are the police handcuffed? In educating children are teachers tied down by rules? In launching a space shuttle are we too concerned with safety? In building a dam do we worry excessively about endangered species? In running the Postal Service is it important to have many post offices close to where people live? In the case of the skating rink, was the requirement of competitive bidding for each contract on the basis of detailed specifications a reasonable one? Probably not. But if it were abandoned, the gain (the swifter completion of the rink) would have to be balanced against the costs (complaints from contractors who might lose business and the chance of collusion and corruption in some future projects).

Even allowing for all of these constraints, government agencies may still be inefficient. Indeed, given the fact that bureaucrats cannot (for the most part) benefit monetarily from their agencies' achievements, it would be surprising if they were not inefficient. Efficiency, in the large or the small, doesn't pay. . . .

Inefficiency is not the only bureaucratic problem nor is it even the most important. A perfectly efficient agency could be a monstrous one, swiftly denying us our liberties, economically inflicting injustices, and competently expropriating our wealth. People complain about bureaucracy as often because it is unfair or unreasonable as because it is slow or cumbersome.

Arbitrary rule refers to officials acting without legal authority, or with that authority in a way that offends our sense of justice. Justice means, first, that we require the government to treat people equally on the basis of clear rules known in advance: If Becky and Bob both are driving sixty miles per hour in a thirty-mile-per-hour zone and the police give a ticket to Bob, we believe they also should give a ticket to Becky. Second, we believe that justice obliges the government to take into account the special needs and circumstances of individuals: If Becky is speeding because she is on her way to the hospital to give birth to a child and Bob is speeding for the fun of it, we may feel that the police should ticket Bob but not Becky. Justice in the first sense means fairness, in the second it means responsiveness. Obviously, fairness and responsiveness often are in conflict.

The checks and balances of the American constitutional system reflect our desire to reduce the arbitrariness of official rule. That desire is based squarely on the premise that inefficiency is a small price to pay for freedom and responsiveness. Congressional oversight, judicial review, interest-group participation, media investigations, and formalized procedures all are intended to check administrative discretion. It is not hyperbole to say that the constitutional order is animated by the desire to make the government "inefficient."

This creates two great tradeoffs. First, adding constraints reduces the efficiency with which the main goal of an agency can be attained but increases the chances that the agency will act in a nonarbitrary manner. Efficient police departments would seek out criminals without reading them their rights, allowing them to call their attorneys, or releasing them in response to a writ of habeas corpus. An efficient building department would issue construction permits on demand without insisting that the applicant first show that the proposed building meets fire, safety, sanitation, geological, and earthquake standards.

The second great tradeoff is between nonarbitrary governance defined as treating people equally and such governance defined as treating each case on its merits. We want the government to be both fair and responsive, but the more rules we impose to insure fairness (that is, to treat all people alike) the harder we make it for the government to be responsive (that is, to take into account the special needs and circumstances of a particular case).

The way our government manages these tradeoffs reflects both our political culture as well as the rivalries of our governing institutions. Both tend toward the same end: We define claims as rights, impose general rules to insure equal treatment, lament (but do nothing about) the resulting inefficiencies, and respond to revelations about unresponsiveness by adopting new rules intended to guarantee that special circumstances will be handled with special care (rarely bothering to reconcile the rules that require responsiveness with those that require equality). And we do all this out of the best of motives: a desire to be both just and benevolent. Justice inclines us to treat people equally, benevolence to treat them differently; both inclinations are expressed in rules, though in fact only justice can be. It is this futile desire to have a rule for every circumstance that led Herbert Kaufman to explain "how compassion spawns red tape."....

In the meantime we live in a country that despite its baffling array of rules and regulations and the insatiable desire of some people to use government to rationalize society still makes it possible to get drinkable water instantly, put through a telephone call in seconds, deliver a letter in a day, and obtain a passport in a week. Our Social Security checks arrive on time. Some state prisons, and most of the federal ones, are reasonably decent and humane institutions. The great majority of Americans, cursing all the while, pay their taxes. One can stand on the deck of an aircraft carrier during night flight operations and watch two thousand nineteen-year-old boys faultlessly operate one of the most complex organizational systems ever created. There are not many places where all this happens. It is astonishing it can be made to happen at all.

PART EIGHT

The Judiciary

43

ALEXANDER HAMILTON

From *The Federalist* 78

The 1787 Federalist Papers *have been quoted extensively in earlier sections of this book. The most famous selections belong to James Madison, writing about separation of powers and federalism. The Federalist actually had three authors: Madison, Alexander Hamilton, and John Jay. In No. 78, Hamilton expounds on the judicial branch. He makes a strong case for an independent judiciary, separate from the legislative and executive branches. He discusses the lifetime appointment of federal judges. Hamilton was a strong proponent of the courts' power, and as such, he believed that the Supreme Court should have the right to declare an act of Congress unconstitutional. This enormous power, termed judicial review, is explained and justified here by Hamilton, although it was not explicitly stated in the Constitution. In 1803, Chief Justice John Marshall established the precedent for the Supreme Court's use of judicial review in the landmark* Marbury v. Madison *case. The year after Marshall's decision, Alexander Hamilton was killed in a duel with Vice-President Aaron Burr.*

No. 78: Hamilton

WE PROCEED now to an examination of the judiciary department of the proposed government. . . .

Whoever attentively considers the different departments of power must perceive that, in a government in which they are separated from each other, the judiciary, from the nature of its functions, will always be the least dangerous to the political rights of the Constitution; because it will be least in a capacity to annoy or injure them. The executive not only dispenses the honors but holds the sword of the community. The legislature not only commands the purse but prescribes the rules by which the duties and rights of every citizen are to be regulated. The judiciary, on the contrary, has no influence over either the sword or the purse; no direction either of the strength or of the wealth of the society, and can take no active resolution whatever. It may truly be said to have neither FORCE nor WILL but merely judgment; and must ultimately depend upon the aid of the executive arm even for the efficacy of its judgments.

This simple view of the matter suggests several important consequences. It proves incontestably that the judiciary is beyond comparison the weakest of the three departments of power;* that it can never attack with success either of the other two; and that all possible care is requisite to enable it to defend itself against their attacks. It equally proves that though individual oppression may now and then proceed from the courts of justice, the general liberty of the people can never be endangered from that quarter; I mean so long as the judiciary remains truly distinct from both the legislature and the executive. For I agree that "there is no liberty if the power of judging be not separated from the legislative and executive powers." And it proves, in the last place, that as liberty can have nothing to fear from the judiciary alone, but would have everything to fear from its union with either of the other departments; that as all the effects of such a union must ensue from a dependence of the former on the latter, notwithstanding a nominal and apparent separation; that as, from the natural feebleness of the judiciary, it is in continual jeopardy of being overpowered, awed, or influenced by its co-ordinate branches; and that as nothing can contribute so much to its firmness and independence as permanency in office, this quality may therefore be justly regarded as an indispensable ingredient in its constitution, and, in a great measure, as the citadel of the public justice and the public security.

The complete independence of the courts of justice is peculiarly essential in a limited Constitution. By a limited Constitution, I understand one which contains certain specified exceptions to the legislative authority; such, for instance, as that it shall pass no bills of attainder, no *ex post facto* laws, and the like. Limitations of this kind can be preserved in practice no other way than through the medium of courts of justice, whose duty it must be to declare all acts contrary to the manifest tenor of the Constitution void. Without this, all the reservations of particular rights or privileges would amount to nothing.

Some perplexity respecting the rights of the courts to pronounce legislative acts void, because contrary to the Constitution, has arisen from an imagination that the doctrine would imply a superiority of the judiciary to the legislative power. It is urged that the authority which can declare the acts of another void must necessarily be superior to the one whose acts may be declared void. As this doctrine is of great importance in all the American constitutions, a brief discussion of the grounds on which it rests cannot be unacceptable.

There is no position which depends on clearer principles than that

---

*The celebrated Montesquieu, speaking of them, says: "Of the three powers above mentioned, the JUDICIARY is next to nothing."—*Spirit of Laws*, Vol. I, page 186.

every act of a delegated authority, contrary to the tenor of the commission under which it is exercised, is void. No legislative act, therefore, contrary to the Constitution, can be valid. To deny this would be to affirm that the deputy is greater than his principal; that the servant is above his master; that the representatives of the people are superior to the people themselves; that men acting by virtue of powers may do not only what their powers do not authorize, but what they forbid.

If it be said that the legislative body are themselves the constitutional judges of their own powers and that the construction they put upon them is conclusive upon the other departments it may be answered that this cannot be the natural presumption where it is not to be collected from any particular provisions in the Constitution. It is not otherwise to be supposed that the Constitution could intend to enable the representatives of the people to substitute their *will* to that of their constituents. It is far more rational to suppose that the courts were designed to be an intermediate body between the people and the legislature in order, among other things, to keep the latter within the limits assigned to their authority. The interpretation of the laws is the proper and peculiar province of the courts. A constitution is, in fact, and must be regarded by the judges as, a fundamental law. It therefore belongs to them to ascertain its meaning as well as the meaning of any particular act proceeding from the legislative body. If there should happen to be an irreconcilable variance between the two, that which has the superior obligation and validity ought, of course, to be preferred; or, in other words, the Constitution ought to be preferred to the statute, the intention of the people to the intention of their agents.

Nor does this conclusion by any means suppose a superiority of the judicial to the legislative power. It only supposes that the power of the people is superior to both, and that where the will of the legislature, declared in its statutes, stands in opposition to that of the people, declared in the Constitution, the judges ought to be governed by the latter rather than the former. They ought to regulate their decisions by the fundamental laws rather than by those which are not fundamental. . . .

If, then, the courts of justice are to be considered as the bulwarks of a limited Constitution against legislative encroachments, this consideration will afford a strong argument for the permanent tenure of judicial offices, since nothing will contribute so much as this to that independent spirit in the judges which must be essential to the faithful performance of so arduous a duty.

This independence of the judges is equally requisite to guard the Constitution and the rights of individuals from the effects of those ill humors which the arts of designing men, or the influence of particular conjunctures, sometimes disseminate among the people themselves, and which, though they speedily give place to better information, and more deliberate reflection, have a tendency, in the meantime, to occasion dangerous innovations in the government, and serious oppressions of the minor party in the community. Though I trust the friends of the proposed Constitution will never concur with its enemies in questioning that fundamental principle of republican government which admits the right of the people to alter or abolish the established Constitution whenever they find it inconsistent with their happiness; yet it is not to be inferred from this principle that the representatives of the people, whenever a momentary inclination happens to lay hold of a majority of their constituents incompatible with the provisions in the existing Constitution would, on that account, be justifiable in a violation of those provisions; or that the courts would be under a greater obligation to connive at infractions in this shape than when they had proceeded wholly from the cabals of the representative body. Until the people have, by some solemn and authoritative act, annulled or changed the established form, it is binding upon themselves collectively, as well as individually; and no presumption, or even knowledge of their sentiments, can warrant their representatives in a departure from it prior to such an act. But it is easy to see that it would require an uncommon portion of fortitude in the judges to do their duty as faithful guardians of the Constitution, where legislative invasions of it had been instigated by the major voice of the community.

But it is not with a view to infractions of the Constitution only that the independence of the judges may be an essential safeguard against the effects of occasional ill humors in the society. These sometimes extend no farther than to the injury of the private rights of particular classes of citizens, by unjust and partial laws. Here also the firmness of the judicial magistracy is of vast importance in mitigating the severity and confining the operation of such laws. It not only serves to moderate the immediate mischiefs of those which may have been passed but it operates as a check upon the legislative body in passing them; who, perceiving that obstacles to the success of an iniquitous intention are to be expected from the scruples of the courts, are in a manner compelled, by the very motives of the injustice they meditate, to qualify their attempts. This is a circumstance calculated to have more influence upon the character of our governments than but few may be aware of. The benefits of the integrity and moderation of the judiciary have already been felt in more States than one; and though they may have displeased those whose sinister expectations they may have disappointed, they must have commanded the esteem and applause of all the virtuous and disinterested. Considerate men of every description ought to prize whatever will tend to beget or fortify that temper in the courts; as no man can be sure that he may not be tomorrow the victim of a spirit of injustice, by which he may be a gainer today. And every man must now feel that the inevitable tendency of such a spirit is to sap the foundations of public and private confidence and to introduce in its stead universal distrust and distress. . . .   *Publius*

44

EUGENE ROSTOW

The Democratic Character of Judicial Review

Written nearly half a century ago, this classic article by legal scholar Eugene Rostow remains the most important analysis written on the theory behind the Supreme Court's power. Judicial review, the ability of the Court to declare an act of Congress or the executive or a state law unconstitutional, may seem on the surface to be "antidemocratic." A handful of lifetime appointees determine the meaning of the Constitution and whether a law passed by Congress and signed by the president is valid. In precise terms and using complex reasoning, Rostow defends the Supreme Court's use of judicial review as being the essence of the American democratic system. In his words, "The political proposition underlying the survival of the power is that there are some phases of American life which should be beyond the reach of any majority, save by constitutional amendment." Rostow's argument is based on what is meant by a democracy. To add a bit to Rostow's explanation, the United States is a "polity" in which the majority rules with protections guaranteed for individuals and minorities. The judiciary ensures that the minority is protected from "tyranny of the majority." Notice the title of this book of readings.

THE IDEA that judicial review is undemocratic is not an academic issue of political philosophy. Like most abstractions, it has far-reaching practical consequences. I suspect that for some judges it is the mainspring of decision, inducing them in many cases to uphold legislative and executive action which would otherwise have been condemned. Particularly in the multiple opinions of recent years, the Supreme Court's self-searching often boils down to a debate within the bosoms of the Justices over the appropriateness of judicial review itself.

The attack on judicial review as undemocratic rests on the premise that the Constitution should be allowed to grow without a judicial check. The proponents of this view would have the Constitution mean what the President, the Congress, and the state legislatures say it means. . . .

It is a grave oversimplification to contend that no society can be democratic unless its legislature has sovereign powers. The social quality of democracy cannot be defined by so rigid a formula. Government and politics are after all the arms, not the end, of social life. The purpose of the Constitution is to assure the people a free and democratic society. The final aim of that society is as much freedom as possible for the individual human being. The Constitution provides society with a mechanism of government fully competent to its task, but by no means universal in its powers. The power to govern is parcelled out between the states and the nation and is further divided among the three main branches of all governmental units. By custom as well as constitutional practice, many vital aspects of community life are beyond the direct reach of government—for example, religion, the press, and, until recently at any rate, many phases of educational and cultural activity. The separation of powers under the Constitution serves the end of democracy in society by limiting the roles of the several branches of government and protecting the citizen, and the various parts of the state itself, against encroachments from any source. The root idea of the Constitution is that man can be free because the state is not.

The power of constitutional review, to be exercised by some part of the government, is implicit in the conception of a written constitution delegating limited powers. A written constitution would promote discord rather than order in society if there were no accepted authority to construe it, at the least in cases of conflicting action by different branches of government or of constitutionally unauthorized governmental action against individuals. The limitation and separation of powers, if they are to survive, require a procedure for independent mediation and construction to reconcile the inevitable disputes over the boundaries of constitutional power which arise in the process of government....

So far as the American Constitution is concerned, there can be little real doubt that the courts were intended from the beginning to have the power they have exercised. The Federalist Papers are unequivocal; the Debates as clear as debates normally are. The power of judicial review was commonly exercised by the courts of the states, and the people were accustomed to judicial construction of the authority derived from colonial charters. Constitutional interpretation by the courts, Hamilton said, does not

by any means suppose a superiority of the judicial to the legislative power. It only supposes that the power of the people is superior to both; and that where the will of the legislature, declared in its statutes, stands in opposition to that of the people, declared in the Constitution, the judges ought to be governed by the latter rather than the former. They ought to regulate their decisions by the fundamental laws, rather than by those which are not fundamental.

Hamilton's statement is sometimes criticized as a verbal legalism. But it has an advantage too. For much of the discussion has complicated the problem without clarifying it. Both judges and their critics have wrapped themselves so successfully in the difficulties of particular cases that they have been able to evade the ultimate issue posed in the Federalist Papers.

Whether another method of enforcing the Constitution could have been devised, the short answer is that no such method has developed. The argument over the constitutionality of judicial review has long since been settled by history. The power and duty of the Supreme Court to declare statutes or executive action unconstitutional in appropriate cases is part of the living Constitution. "The course of constitutional history," Mr. Justice Frankfurter recently remarked, has cast responsibilities upon the Supreme Court which it would be "stultification" for it to evade. The Court's power has been exercised differently at different times: sometimes with reckless and doctrinaire enthusiasm; sometimes with great deference to the status and responsibilities of other branches of the government; sometimes with a degree of weakness and timidity that comes close to the betrayal of trust. But the power exists, as an integral part of the process of American government. The Court has the duty of interpreting the Constitution in many of its most important aspects, and especially in those which concern the relations of the individual and the state. The political proposition underlying the survival of the power is that there are some phases of American life which should be beyond the reach of any majority, save by constitutional amendment. In Mr. Justice Jackson's phrase, "One's right to life, liberty, and property, to free speech, a free press, freedom of worship and assembly, and other fundamental rights may not be submitted to vote; they depend on the outcome of no elections." Whether or not this was the intention of the Founding Fathers, the unwritten Constitution is unmistakable.

If one may use a personal definition of the crucial word, this way of policing the Constitution is not undemocratic. True, it employs appointed officials, to whom large powers are irrevocably delegated. But democracies need not elect all the officers who exercise crucial authority in the name of the voters. Admirals and generals can win or lose wars in the exercise of their discretion. The independence of judges in the administration of justice has been the pride of communities which aspire to be free. Members of the Federal Reserve Board have the lawful power to plunge the country into depression or inflation. The list could readily be extended. Government by referendum or town meeting is not the only possible form of democracy. The task of democracy is not to have the people vote directly on every issue, but to assure their ultimate responsibility for the acts of their representatives, elected or appointed. For judges deciding ordinary litigation, the ultimate responsibility of the electorate has a special meaning. It is a responsibility for the quality of the judges and for the substance of their instructions, never a responsibility for their decisions in particular cases. It is hardly characteristic of law in democratic society to encourage bills of attainder, or to allow appeals from the courts in particular cases to legislatures or to mobs. Where the judges are carrying out the function of constitutional review, the final responsibility of the people is appropriately guaranteed by the provisions for amending the Constitution itself, and by the benign influence of time, which changes the personnel of courts. Given the possibility of constitutional amendment, there is nothing undemocratic in having responsible and independent judges act as important constitutional mediators. Within the narrow limits of their capacity to act, their great task is to help maintain a pluralist equilibrium in society. They can do much to keep it from being dominated by the states or the Federal Government, by Congress or the President, by the purse or the sword.

In the execution of this crucial but delicate function, constitutional review by the judiciary has an advantage thoroughly recognized in both theory and practice. The power of the courts, however final, can only be asserted in the course of litigation. Advisory opinions are forbidden, and reefs of self-limitation have grown up around the doctrine that the courts will determine constitutional questions only in cases of actual controversy, when no lesser ground of decision is available, and when the complaining party would be directly and personally injured by the assertion of the power deemed unconstitutional. Thus the check of judicial review upon the elected branches of government must be a mild one, limited not only by the detachment, integrity, and good sense of the Justices, but by the structural boundaries implicit in the fact that the power is entrusted to the courts. Judicial review is inherently adapted to preserving broad and flexible lines of constitutional growth, not to operating as a continuously active factor in legislative or executive decisions....

Democracy is a slippery term. I shall make no effort at a formal definition here.... But it would be scholastic pedantry to define democracy in such a way as to deny the title of "democrat" to Jefferson, Madison, Lincoln, Brandeis, and others who have found the American constitutional system, including its tradition of judicial review, well adapted to the needs of a free society. As Mr. Justice Brandeis said,

the doctrine of the separation of powers was adopted by the Convention of 1787, not to promote efficiency but to preclude the exercise of arbitrary power. The purpose was, not to avoid friction, but, by means of the inevitable friction incident to the distribution of governmental powers among three departments, to save the people from autocracy.

It is error to insist that no society is democratic unless it has a government of unlimited powers, and that no government is democratic unless its legislature had unlimited powers. Constitutional review by an independent judiciary is a tool of proven use in the American quest for an open society of widely dispersed powers. In a vast country, of mixed population, with widely different regional problems, such an organization of society is the surest base for the hopes of democracy.

45

DAVID O'BRIEN

From *Storm Center*

Professor David O'Brien's fine book on the Supreme Court touches on many landmark cases in constitutional law. Few are more important than Brown v. Board of Education of Topeka, Kansas. Today's students of American government often take Brown for granted, since they've lived with the Court's ruling their whole lives; thus they may forget the dramatic events surrounding the 1954 decision. In this excerpt O'Brien revisits the first Brown case, as well as Brown II, exploring the delicate relationship between the Court and public opinion. He then goes back to President Franklin Roosevelt's infamous 1937 "court-packing" scheme to illustrate another aspect of the impact of public opinion on the judiciary. Unlike the citizenry's direct and immediate reaction to Congress and the president, the communication of views between the public and the judiciary is less easy to measure, O'Brien acknowledges. Yet the Supreme Court lies, as it should, at the heart of the process that resolves the nation's monumental political issues.

———

"WHY DOES the Supreme Court pass the school desegregation case?" asked one of Chief Justice Vinson's law clerks in 1952. *Brown v. Board of Education of Topeka, Kansas* had arrived on the Court's docket in 1951, but it was carried over for oral argument the next term and then consolidated with four other cases and reargued in December 1953. The landmark ruling did not come down until May 17, 1954. "Well," Justice Frankfurter explained, "we're holding it for the election"—1952 was a presidential election year. "You're holding it for the election?" The clerk persisted in disbelief. "I thought the Supreme Court was supposed to decide cases without regard to elections." "When you have a major social political issue of this magnitude," timing and public reactions are important considerations, and, Frankfurter continued, "we do not think this is the time to decide it." Similarly, Tom Clark has recalled that the Court awaited, over Douglas's dissent, additional cases from the District of Columbia and other regions, so as "to get a national coverage, rather than a sectional one." Such political considerations are by no means unique. "We often delay adjudication. It's not a question of evading at all," Clark concluded. "It's just the practicalities of life—common sense."

Denied the power of the sword or the purse, the Court must cultivate its institutional prestige. The power of the Court lies in the pervasiveness of its rulings and ultimately rests with other political institutions and public opinion. As an independent force, the Court has no chance to resolve great issues of public policy. *Dred Scott v. Sandford* (1857) and *Brown v. Board of Education* (1954) illustrate the limitations of Supreme Court policy-making. The "great folly," as Senator Henry Cabot Lodge characterized *Dred Scott*, was not the Court's interpretation of the Constitution or the unpersuasive moral position that blacks were not persons under the Constitution. Rather, "the attempt of the Court to settle the slavery question by judicial decision was simple madness." . . . A hundred years later, political struggles within the country and, notably, presidential and congressional leadership in enforcing the Court's school desegregation ruling saved the moral appeal of *Brown* from becoming another "great folly."

Because the Court's decisions are not self-executing, public reactions inevitably weigh on the minds of the justices. . . .

. . . Opposition to the school desegregation ruling in *Brown* led to bitter, sometimes violent confrontations. In Little Rock, Arkansas, Governor Orval Faubus encouraged disobedience by southern segregationists. The federal National Guard had to be called out to maintain order. The school board in Little Rock unsuccessfully pleaded, in *Cooper v. Aaron* (1958), for the Court's postponement of the implementation of *Brown's* mandate. In the midst of the controversy, Frankfurter worried that Chief Justice Warren's attitude had become "more like that of a fighting politician than that of a judicial statesman." In such confrontations between the Court and the country, "the transcending issue," Frankfurter reminded the brethren, remains that of preserving "the Supreme Court as the authoritative organ of what the Constitution requires." When the justices move too far or too fast in their interpretation of the Constitution, they threaten public acceptance of the Court's legitimacy.

The political struggles of the Court (and among the justices) continue after the writing of opinions and final votes. Announcements of decisions trigger diverse reactions from the media, interest groups, lower courts, Congress, the President, and the general public. Their reactions may enhance or thwart compliance and reinforce or undermine the Court's prestige. Opinion days thus may reveal something of the political struggles that might otherwise remain hidden within the marble temple. They may also mark the beginning of larger political struggles for influence in the country. . . .

When deciding major issues of public law and policy, justices must consider strategies for getting public acceptance of their rulings. When striking down the doctrine of "separate but equal" facilities in 1954 in *Brown v. Board of Education (Brown I)*, for instance, the Warren Court waited a year before issuing, in *Brown II*, its mandate for "all deliberate speed" in ending racial segregation in public education.

Resistance to the social policy announced in *Brown I* was expected. A rigid timetable for desegregation would only intensify opposition. During oral arguments on *Brown II*, devoted to the question of what kind of decree the Court should issue to enforce *Brown*, Warren confronted the hard fact of southern resistance. The attorney for South Carolina, S. Emory Rogers, pressed for an open-ended decree—one that would not specify when and how desegregation should take place. He boldly proclaimed

Mr. Chief Justice, to say we will conform depends on the decree handed down. I am frank to tell you, right now [in] our district I do not think that we will send—[that] the white people of the district will send their children to the Negro schools. It would be unfair to tell the Court that we are going to do that. I do not think it is. But I do think that something can be worked out. We hope so.

"It is not a question of attitude," Warren shot back, "it is a question of conforming to the decree." Their heated exchange continued as follows:

CHIEF JUSTICE WARREN: But you are not willing to say here that there would be an honest attempt to conform to this decree, if we did leave it to the district court [to implement]?

MR. ROGERS: No, I am not. Let us get the word "honest" out of there.

CHIEF JUSTICE WARREN: No, leave it in.

MR. ROGERS: No, because I would have to tell you that right now we would not conform—we would not send our white children to the negro schools. . . .

Agreement emerged that the Court should issue a short opinion-decree. In a memorandum, Warren summarized the main points of agreement. The opinion should simply state that *Brown I* held radically segregated public schools to be unconstitutional. *Brown II* should acknowledge that the ruling creates various administrative problems, but emphasize that "local school authorities have the primary responsibility for assessing and solving these problems; [and] the courts will have to consider these problems in determining whether the efforts of local school authorities" are in good-faith compliance. . . .

Enforcement and implementation required the cooperation and co-ordination of all three branches. Little progress could be made, as Assistant Attorney General Pollack has explained, "where historically there had been slavery and a long tradition of discrimination [until] all three branches of the federal government [could] be lined up in support of a movement forward or a requirement for change." The election of Nixon in 1968 then brought changes both in the policies of the executive branch and in the composition of the Court. The simplicity and flexibility of *Brown*, moreover, invited evasion. It produced a continuing struggle over measures, such as gerrymandering school district lines and busing in the 1970s and 1980s, because the mandate itself had evolved from one of ending segregation to one of securing integration in public schools. . . .

"By itself," the political scientist Robert Dahl observed, "the Court is almost powerless to affect the course of national policy." *Brown* dramatically altered the course of American life, but it also reflected the justices' awareness that their decisions are not self-executing. The rulings [in] *Brown* . . . were unanimous but ambiguous. The ambiguity in the desegregation rulings . . . was the price of achieving unanimity. Unanimity appeared necessary if the Court was to preserve its institutional prestige while pursuing revolutionary change in social policy. Justices sacrificed their own policy preferences for more precise guidelines, while the Court tolerated lengthy delays in recognition of the costs of open defiance and the pressures of public opinion. . . .

Public opinion serves to curb the Court when it threatens to go too far or too fast in its rulings. The Court has usually been in step with major political movements, except during transitional periods or critical elections. It would nevertheless be wrong to conclude, along with Peter Finley Dunne's fictional Mr. Dooley, that "th' supreme court follows th' iliction returns." To be sure, the battle over FDR's "Court-packing" plan and the Court's "switch-in-time-that-saved-nine" in 1937 gives that impression. Public opinion supported the New Deal, but turned against FDR after his landslide reelection in 1936 when he proposed to "pack the Court" by increasing its size from nine to fifteen. In a series of five-to-four and six-to-three decisions in 1935–1936, the Court had struck down virtually every important measure of FDR's New Deal program. But in the spring of 1937, while the Senate Judiciary Committee considered FDR's proposal, the Court abruptly handed down three five-to-four rulings upholding major pieces of New Deal legislation. Shortly afterward, FDR's close personal friend and soon-to-be nominee for the Court, Felix Frankfurter, wrote Justice Stone confessing that he was "not wholly happy in thinking that Mr. Dooley should, in the course of history turn out to have been one of the most distinguished legal philosophers." Frankfurter, of course, knew that justices do not simply follow the election returns. The influence of public opinion is more subtle and complex.

Life in the marble temple is not immune from shifts in public opinion. . . . The justices, however, deny being directly influenced by public opinion. The Court's prestige rests on preserving the public's view that justices base their decisions on interpretations of the law, rather than on their personal policy preferences. Yet, complete indifference to public opinion would be the height of judicial arrogance. . . .

"The powers exercised by this Court are inherently oligarchic," Frankfurter once observed when pointing out that "[t]he Court is not saved from being oligarchic because it professes to act in the service of humane ends." Judicial review is antidemocratic. But the Court's power stems from its duty to give authoritative meaning to the Constitution, and rests with the persuasive forces of reason, institutional prestige, the cooperation of other political institutions, and, ultimately, public opinion. The country, in a sense, saves the justices from being an oligarchy by curbing the Court when it goes too far or too fast with its policy-making. Violent opposition and resistance, however, threaten not merely the Court's prestige but the very idea of a government under law.

Some Court watchers, and occasionally even the justices, warn of "an imperial judiciary" and a "government by the judiciary." For much of the Court's history, though, the work of the justices has not involved major issues of public policy. In most areas of public law and policy, the fact that the Court decides an issue is more important than what it decides. Relatively few of the many issues of domestic and foreign policy that arise in government reach the Court. When the Court does decide major questions of public policy, it does so by bringing political controversies within the language, structure, and spirit of the Constitution. By deciding only immediate cases, the Court infuses constitutional meaning into the resolution of the larger surrounding political controversies. But by itself the Court cannot lay those controversies to rest.

The Court can profoundly influence American life. As a guardian of the Constitution, the Court sometimes invites controversy by challenging majoritarian sentiments to respect the rights of minorities and the principles of a representative democracy. The Court's influence is usually more subtle and indirect, varying over time and from one policy issue to another. In the end, the Court's influence on American life cannot be measured precisely, because its policy-making is inextricably bound up with that of other political institutions. Major confrontations in constitutional politics, like those over school desegregation, school prayer, and abortion, are determined as much by what is possible in a system of free government and in a pluralistic society as by what the Court says about the meaning of the Constitution. At its best, the Court appeals to the country to respect the substantive value choices of human dignity and self-governance embedded in our written Constitution.

46

DAVID YALOF

From *Pursuit of Justices*

In selecting nominees to the Supreme Court, the president faces a daunting task. Legal scholar David Yalof takes readers inside the process, pointing out the many factions in the nation, in the branches of government, and even within the president's own circle that must be considered when making a nomination. The president today has access to large amounts of information about a potential justice, but so does everyone else in the political process. After all, remember that a Supreme Court justice is often the most significant and long lasting legacy that a president leaves behind.

ON JUNE 27, 1992, the Supreme Court inserted itself once again into the national debate over abortion with its surprising decision in *Planned Parenthood v. Casey*. Specifically, five of the nine justices refused to cast aside *Roe v. Wade*, the Court's controversial 1973 opinion establishing a constitutional right to abortion. Included among *Roe's* saviors that day were Sandra Day O'Connor and Anthony Kennedy, both appointees of former President Ronald Reagan. As a candidate for the presidency in 1980 and 1984, Reagan had supported a constitutional amendment to overturn *Roe*, a ruling considered to be among the most vilified of public targets for social conservatives in his party. As president, Reagan had publicly promised to appoint justices to the Supreme Court willing to reverse *Roe v. Wade*. Yet just the opposite occurred in *Casey*: a majority of the Court reaffirmed the core right to privacy first discovered in *Roe*. And in a touch of irony, two of President Reagan's own nominees had played significant roles in safeguarding the decision from the Court's conservatives.

Obviously the selection of Supreme Court nominees is among the president's most significant duties. Yet as the outcome in *Casey* demonstrates, it is a task beset with difficulties and potential frustrations. On one hand, a president ordinarily tries to choose a nominee whose influence will reach beyond the current political environment. As a beneficiary of life tenure, a justice may well extend that president's legacy on judicial matters long into the future. Yet in selecting a nominee the president must also successfully maneuver through that immediate environment, lest he suffer politically or (as in some cases) see his nominee rejected by the Senate outright. In recent years internal strife and factionalism within the executive branch have only further complicated what was already a delicate undertaking. . . .

A central question remains: why were these particular candidates chosen over others possessing similar—and in some cases superior—qualifications? The classic "textbook" portrayal of the Supreme Court nomination process depicts presidents as choosing Supreme Court justices more for their judicial politics than for their judicial talents. By this version of events, presidents, by nominating justices whose political views appear compatible with their own, try to gain increased influence over the Supreme Court. Once on the Court, a justice may then satisfy or disappoint the appointing president by his decisions. Such an oversimplified view of nomination politics usually ignores the more complex political environment in which modern presidents must act, including the various intricacies and nuances of executive branch politics.

. . . I contend that modern presidents are often forced to arbitrate among factions within their own administrations, each pursuing its own interests and agendas in the selection process. At first glance, presidential reliance on numerous high-level officials equipped with a variety of perspectives might seem a logical response to the often hostile and unpredictable political environment that surrounds modern appointments to the Court. Yet conflicts within the administration itself may have a debilitating effect on that president's overall interests. High-level advisors may be sincerely pursuing their own conceptions of what makes up the administration's best interests; but to achieve their own maximum preferred outcomes, they may feel compelled to skew the presentation of critical information, if not leave it out altogether. In recent administrations the final choice of a nominee has usually reflected one advisor's hard-won victory over his rivals, without necessarily accounting for the president's other political interests. . . .

The New Deal marked the beginning of a fundamental transformation in American politics. A national economic crisis demanded national solutions, and the government in Washington grew exponentially to meet these new demands. Beginning in the 1930s, the federal government entered one policy area after another that had previously been the exclusive province of state governments. Emergency conditions required quick institutional responses, and the executive branch in particular was drawn into critical aspects of national policymaking. Just as the character of national politics changed dramatically, the Supreme Court was undergoing a transformation of its own. Fundamental changes in the political landscape

affecting Supreme Court appointments were a by-product of these changes. At least ten critical developments in American politics substantially altered the character of the modern selection process for justices:

1. The *growth and bureaucratization of the Justice Department* facilitated
the investment of considerable manpower and other resources towards the
consideration of prospective Supreme Court candidates. As the size of the
national government grew dramatically during the early twentieth century, the government's overall legal responsibilities quickly expanded.
Congress reacted by increasing the size of the Justice Department and
transferring to it most litigating functions from other federal agencies.
Armed with a full staff of attorneys and more extensive bureaucratic support, attorneys general in modern times have enjoyed more regular input
into the selection of Supreme Court nominees, often consulting with the
president well before a vacancy on the Court even arises. . . .

2. The *growth and bureaucratization of the White House* has also had an
impact on the nomination process. The White House staff, once limited
to a handful of personal assistants, was barely a factor in political decision-
making for most of the nineteenth and early twentieth centuries. Starting
with Franklin Roosevelt's administration, however, the White House staff
experienced prodigious growth, expanding from just thirty-seven employees in the early 1930s to more than nine hundred by the late 1980s. As
the modern presidency has brought more policymaking activities within
the White House, the White House staff has increasingly figured in matters of high presidential priority.

Modern presidents often rely on the White House Counsel's Office to
assist them in screening and selecting prospective Supreme Court nominees. Thus, increasingly, the attorney general's most constant and genuine
competitor for influence has been the White House Counsel. Theodore
Sorenson, John Kennedy's special counsel, asserted that his duties did not
overlap with the attorney general's; rather he was involved "as a policy
advisor to the president with respect to legislation, with respect to his
programs and messages, with respect to executive orders, and with respect
to those few formally legal problems, which come to the White House."
But those supposed lines of demarcation have blurred considerably during the past thirty years. Today, a president has at his disposal two distinct
organizations, each with its own bureaucratic resources; the president may
rely on either or both offices for counsel concerning the selection of Supreme Court nominees.

3. Paralleling the increased role for national political institutions in
American life has been the *growth in size and influence of federal courts.* Congress's willingness in the past to meet increased caseloads with new judge-

ships has steadily multiplied the president's opportunities to place his imprint on lower court policymaking. The total number of district and circuit judgeships rose from under two hundred in 1930 to well over seven hundred by the late 1980s. Thus between thirty and forty vacancies may occur annually on the federal bench. These federal judges must be counted on to interpret, enforce, and in some cases limit the expansion of federal governmental authority. At times federal courts have even fashioned national law and policy, serving as key facilitators of social, economic, and political growth.

Senatorial courtesy, to be sure, remains the dominant factor in lower court selections, but the steady increase in the number of judgeships has provided presidents with more than an occasional opportunity to nominate candidates of their own choosing after the preferences of individual senators have been satisfied. The growing size and prestige of the D.C. Circuit have given presidents additional opportunities to hand out plum assignments: because senatorial courtesy does not apply to those seats, presidents may freely nominate ideologically compatible law professors, former administration officials, and others to positions of considerable prestige in the federal judicial system. Thus more than ever before, the federal courts today provide an especially useful "proving ground" for candidates who might one day be considered for a seat on the high court.

4. *Divided party government* has become a recurring theme in American government since World War II. Between 1896 and 1946, opposing parties controlled the White House and the Senate during just two sessions of Congress. By contrast, split party conditions now seem almost routine. . . .

5. The *confirmation process has become increasingly public.* For much of our nation's history the confirmation process unfolded largely behind closed doors. Though the Senate Judiciary Committee often met and offered recommendations on nominees during the nineteenth century, closed investigative hearings were not conducted until 1873 when President Ulysses Grant unsuccessfully nominated George Williams to be chief justice. Open hearings were held for the first time only in 1916, when the Senate considered Louis Brandeis's candidacy. Nine years later Harlan Fiske Stone became the first nominee in history to appear before the committee personally. Full-fledged public hearings were finally instituted on a regular basis beginning in 1930 with President Hoover's nomination of John J. Parker.

Since 1955, virtually all Supreme Court nominees have formally testified before the Senate Judiciary Committee. Hearings have been televised live since 1981, insuring heightened public access to the process. The increasingly public nature of confirmation-stage politics has placed added strain on senators, many of whom may be reluctant to spend their time and political capital on an arduous process that will only create enemies back home. Meanwhile, the president must now find nominees who, aside from meeting ideological or professional criteria, will fare well in front of television cameras when facing a barrage of senators' questions.

6. The *rise in power of the organized bar* has figured significantly in recent Supreme Court selections. The American Bar Association's Special Committee on the (federal) Judiciary (later renamed the "Standing Committee on Federal Judiciary") was founded in 1947 to "promote the nomination of competent persons and to oppose the nomination of unfit persons" to the federal courts. During the past half-century that committee has played a significant if uneven role in the appointment of lower federal court judges. Not surprisingly, the ABA has taken an especially strong interest in the nomination of Supreme Court justices as well. Beginning with Eisenhower's nomination of Harlan in 1954, the ABA has formally reviewed all Supreme Court nominees for the Senate Judiciary Committee. Thus in selecting nominees, presidents must incorporate into their calculations the possibility that a less-than-exceptional rating from the ABA could serve as a rallying point for opposition during the subsequent confirmation process. Still, the bar's actual influence over the choice of nominees has varied largely depending upon the administration in power. In 1956, the Eisenhower administration began to submit names of potential Supreme Court nominees to the ABA at the same time that the FBI began its background check. During this period the ABA exerted little direct influence during initial deliberations over prospective candidates. By contrast, subsequent administrations have often enlisted the committee's services during much earlier stages of the process. High-ranking officials in the Justice Department have consulted with committee members to gauge potential support for and opposition to a prospective candidate. . . .

7. *Increased participation by interest groups* has also altered the character of the Supreme Court nomination process. This is not an entirely new phenomenon. Organized interests (including the National Grange and the Anti-Monopoly League) figured significantly in defeating Stanley Matthews's nomination to the Court in 1881. Almost fifty years later, an unlikely coalition of labor interests and civil rights groups joined together to defeat the nomination of John Parker. Since World War II, interest groups have extended their influence into the early stages of nominee selection by virtue of their increased numbers and political power. Groups such as the Alliance for Justice, People for the American Way, and the Leadership Conference on Civil Rights have made Supreme Court appointments a

high priority in their respective organizations. Many interest groups now conduct their own research into the backgrounds of prospective nominees and inundate the administration with information and analysis about various individual candidates.

8. *Increased media attention* has further transformed nominee selection politics. Presidents in the nineteenth and early twentieth centuries, working outside the media's glare, could often delay the selection of a nominee for many months while suffering few political repercussions. By contrast, contemporary presidents must contend with daily coverage of their aides' ruminations concerning a Supreme Court vacancy. Reporters assigned to the "Supreme Court beat" often provide their readership with the most recent "shortlists" of candidates under consideration by the president. A long delay in naming a replacement may be viewed by the press as a sign of indecision and uncertainty on the part of the president. Delay may also work to an administration's benefit, especially if media outlets expend their own resources investigating prospective candidates and airing potential political liabilities prior to any formal commitment by the administration.

9. *Advances in legal research technology* have had a pronounced effect on the selection process. All modern participants in the appointment process, including officials within the White House and the Justice Department, enjoy access to sophisticated tools for researching the backgrounds of prospective Supreme Court candidates. Legal software programs such as LEXIS/NEXIS and WESTLAW allow officials to quickly gather all of a prospective candidate's past judicial opinions, scholarship, and other public commentary as part of an increasingly elaborate screening process. Computer searches may be either tailored around narrow subject issues or they may be comprehensive in scope. The prevalence of C-SPAN and other cable and video outlets has made it possible to analyze prospective candidates' speeches and activities that would have otherwise gone unnoticed. Of course, advanced research technology is a double-edged sword: media outlets and interest groups may just as effectively publicize negative information about prospective candidates, undermining the president's carefully laid plans for a particular vacancy.

10. Finally, the *more visible role the Supreme Court has assumed in American political life* has increased the perceived stakes of the nomination process for everyone involved. Several of the critical developments listed above, including increased media attention and interest group influence in the nominee selection process, stem from a larger political development involving the Court itself: during this century the Supreme Court has entrenched itself at the forefront of American politics. Prior to the New

Deal, the Court only occasionally tried to compete with other governmental institutions for national influence. For example, the Taney Court inserted itself into the debate over slavery with its decision in *Dred Scott v. Sanford* (1857). The Court's aggressive protection of property rights in the late nineteenth century pitted it first against state governments, and then later against Congress and the president during the early part of the twentieth century. In each instance the judiciary usually represented a political ideology in decline; after a period of time the Court eventually returned to its role as an essentially reaffirming institution.

Since the early 1940s, however, the Supreme Court has positioned itself at the center of major political controversies on a nearly continuous basis. Driven by a primarily rights-based agenda, the Court has found itself wrestling with matters embedded in the American psyche: desegregation, privacy rights, affirmative action, and law enforcement. With the Court's continuously high visibility in the American political system, each appointment of a new justice now draws the attention of nearly all segments of society. The stakes of Supreme Court appointments may only seem higher than before, but that perception alone has caused a veritable sea change in the way presidents . . . must treat the selection of Supreme Court nominees.

47

RICHARD FALLON

From *The Dynamic Constitution*

The Supreme Court always gets a lot of public attention when vacancies occur and a new president nominates replacements whom the Senate must confirm. Yet behind the media spotlight accorded to Court nominees lie several basic principles necessary to understand the role of the Supreme Court in American government. Constitutional law professor Richard Fallon raises the issue of interpreting "a very old constitution." He discusses the importance of precedent, in terms of the tension between maintaining and overturning past decisions. Giving guidance to lower courts by creating "rules and tests" is another responsibility of the Supreme Court. By selecting the cases it will hear, the Court determines what areas of the law it will influence. Fallon explores several controversial topics in constitutional law today: the Court's relationship to the majority of Americans and to elected officials, the philosophy of "originalism" held by some Supreme Court justices, and the "moral rights" approach to jurisprudence. Cases mentioned in the excerpt such as Brown v. Board of Education *and* Roe v. Wade *are familiar to students of American government. Ultimately, Fallon writes, the resolution of the complicated set of controversies that swirl around the Supreme Court comes from a less lofty, more practical consideration: decisions need to "produce good results overall," results that the American people endorse.*

WRITING IN 1936 IN AN IMPORTANT CASE invalidating the centerpiece of the New Deal's farm program, justice Owen Roberts tried to blunt criticism by saying that the Supreme Court's job was not to exercise any independent judgment about the wisdom or even the possibly urgent necessity of challenged legislation, but simply "to lay the article of the Constitution which is invoked beside the statute which is challenged and to decide whether the latter squares with the former." The Constitution's meaning, he implied, was almost invariably plain. In cases of doubt, others have suggested, research into the "original understanding" will ordinarily resolve any uncertainty.

... Roberts' portrait of the judicial role was more fanciful than realistic. (One wonders whether Roberts himself would not have acknowledged as much in less defensive moments—if not in 1936, then surely a year later, when his so-called "switch in time that saved nine" ended the constitutional crisis that had provoked Franklin Roosevelt's Court-packing plan.) Often the Constitution's plain text will give no simple answer to modern constitutional questions: Which utterances lie within and without "the freedom of speech"? When is a search or seizure "unreasonable" and thus forbidden (rather then reasonable and thus permissible)? Which governmental classifications are consistent and inconsistent with "the equal protection of the laws"?

When the text gives no obvious answer, few would deny that the original understanding of constitutional language is relevant, but it is often hard to apply eighteenth- and nineteenth-century understandings to modern problems. . . .

What is more, many strands of judicial precedent seem inconsistent with the original understandings of constitutional language, and once precedents have been established, nearly everyone acknowledges that they, too, need to be reckoned with in constitutional adjudication. A particularly clear example involves the constitutionality of paper currency. The issuance of paper money very arguably exceeds the original understanding of Congress's power, conferred by Article I, Section 8, Clause 5 of the Constitution, to "coin Money." Had the framers wished to empower Congress to issue "greenbacks," they could easily have said so; the authorization to "coin Money" seems to speak more narrowly. But the Supreme Court held otherwise in 1871, and a reversal on this issue would provoke economic chaos.

Another example involves race-based discrimination by the federal government. Although it seems clear that no provision of the Constitution, even as amended, was originally understood to bar discrimination by Congress (as the Equal Protection Clause, enacted in the aftermath of the civil war, only limits action by the *states*), the Supreme Court has treated race-based discriminations by the federal government as "suspect" for more than sixty years now and has subjected such discriminations to "strict" or "searching" judicial scrutiny. Regardless of whether the earliest cases were rightly reasoned, the matter is now considered by nearly everyone to be settled by precedent and evolving moral understandings. Indeed, even Supreme Court Justices who maintain in other contexts that constitutional adjudication should reflect "the original understanding" of constitutional language have accepted judicial precedents applying equal protection norms to the federal government (and, more controversially, have cited those precedents as authority for condemning federal affirmative action programs).

It is true, of course, that the Supreme Court is not absolutely bound by precedent. Sometimes it chooses to "overrule" itself. But the largely discretionary judgment of when to follow precedent and when to overrule it only adds a further judgmental element to constitutional adjudication in the Supreme Court.

When the various relevant considerations are all put into play, I have suggested repeatedly now—largely following Professor Ronald Dworkin on this point—that Supreme Court Justices typically decide how the Constitution is *best* interpreted in light of history, precedent, and considerations of moral desirability and practical workability. All of these factors are relevant. No clear rule specifies which will be controlling in a particular case. In this context, political scientists repeatedly emphasize that the voting patterns of Supreme Court Justices tend to be relatively (though not perfectly) predictable on the basis of their political ideology. In view of the judgmental character of constitutional adjudication, it would be astonishing if the results were otherwise.

To say this is not to imply that the decisions of Supreme Court Justices are crudely political. The Justices function . . . as a constitutional "practice," which subjects them to a number of role-based constraints. They must reason like lawyers and take account of text and history as well as precedent. They work in the medium of constitutional law, not partisan politics, and the medium of law—with its characteristic techniques of reasoning—limits, shapes, and channels the Justices' search for the best interpretation of the Constitution. Nevertheless, the nature of constitutional interpretation leaves abundant room for the exercise of legal and sometimes moral imagination.

Nor, in assessing the scope of judicial power, is it always helpful or even strictly accurate to think of the Supreme Court as engaged solely in constitutional "interpretation." Among the Court's characteristic modern functions is to formulate rules and tests for application by lower courts in future cases. This process of course begins with an interpretive search for "the meaning of the Constitution." Before reaching a conclusion, however, the Court frequently needs to make a lot of practical judgments, informed by its sense of likely consequences. In my view many of the Court's rules are better viewed as devices to "implement" constitutional values than as "interpretations" of constitutional language. Among the clearest examples of constitutional "implementation" as a function distinct from pure "interpretation" comes from *Miranda v. Arizona* (1966), which introduced the requirement that the police give so-called *Miranda* warnings. Although admittedly an extreme case, the *Miranda* decision exemplifies a broader phenomenon. Many of the doctrinal tests . . . lack clear roots in either the Constitution's language or its history. The Supreme

Court has devised them in order to implement constitutional values, but they do not emerge from the Constitution through a process that would naturally be described as one of interpretation.

One final detail about the role of the Supreme Court deserves mention in a discussion of judicial power. Under the current statutory scheme, the Supreme Court enjoys almost complete discretion about which cases to hear and not to hear. Courts in the United States decide tens of thousands of cases every year. The Supreme Court could not possibly review every decision involving a federal constitutional question. After experimenting with various other schemes, Congress, by statute, has provided that the Supreme Court simply gets to choose which cases decided by lower courts it would like to review. In a typical year, the Court is asked to review more than 7,000 cases, out of which it has recently selected fewer than 100. For the most part, the Court agrees to decide those cases that the Justices think most important. The Supreme Court's power to choose its own cases is an important one, which permits the Court to establish and pursue any agenda that it may wish to adopt—for example, by expanding constitutional rights or powers in some areas or pruning them in others. . . .

The breadth of the power exercised by courts, and especially by the Supreme Court, naturally gives rise to recurrent debates and anxiety. As lawyers and judges worry about whether and when it is legitimate for courts to invalidate legislation based on their interpretation (which others may not share) of a very old constitution, they have at least two concerns in mind. One involves public acceptance of judicial review: Under what circumstances, if any, might the American people simply refuse to put up with having courts invalidate legislation that popular majorities support? What would happen if a popular President defied a very unpopular judicial ruling? Might the people line up behind the President, rather than behind the Court? A second question involves the moral and political justifiability of judicial review, especially in light of the relatively free-wheeling way in which it is sometimes practiced: How, if at all, should courts go about deciding constitutional issues such that the American people *ought* to put up with their doing so?

These are perennial questions in American constitutional law and American politics. But they have arisen with special sharpness at some times in constitutional history—for example, during the *Lochner* era and then when Richard Nixon promised to appoint "strict constructionist" Justices who would halt the excesses (as he saw them) of the Warren Court. In recent years conservative critics of the Supreme Court have found a focal point for criticism in the Court's 1973 decision in *Roe v.*

Wade, which held that absolute prohibitions against abortion violate the Constitution during the period before a fetus becomes viable or capable of surviving outside the womb. Although restrictions on abortion undoubtedly curtail "liberty," no one believes that the Due Process Clause—the provision on which the Court based its decision—was originally understood or intended to protect abortion rights. The Court based its ruling partly on precedent, partly on a contestable judgment that it is unreasonable to make women bear an unwanted fetus.

In objecting to decisions such as *Roe*, critics often maintain not just that the Court reached the wrong decision, but that it is not fair or "legitimate" for the unelected Justices of the Supreme Court to exercise a power to thwart the judgments of political majorities—at least when legislation is not in flat contravention of the Constitution's originally understood meaning. This challenge, to which Alexander Bickel gave the label of "the counter-majoritarian difficulty," deserves to be taken seriously. But it bears emphasis that charges of "countermajoritarianism" can be leveled at conservative as well as liberal judicial decisions.... [I]n recent years, the five Justices of the Supreme Court who are generally labeled most "conservative" have invalidated numerous pieces of federal regulatory legislation, including the so-called Violence Against Women Act, on the ground that Congress lacks authority to enact it. Conservative Justices have also voted to subject federal affirmative action programs to strict judicial scrutiny, even though no provision of the Constitution was originally understood to bar affirmative action (or other forms of race-based discrimination) by the federal government. Conservative Justices have also voted to strike down popularly enacted restrictions on commercial advertising, even though it seems highly doubtful, at best, that the First Amendment was originally understood to protect commercial advertising.

Against the background of the countermajoritarian difficulty and related anxieties, judges and Justices openly debate questions of judicial role and interpretive methodology, often in the course of opinions deciding actual cases. Nor are debates about constitutional methodology confined to the courts. When Presidential candidates talk about the kind of judges and Justices that they would like to appoint, issues of proper interpretive methodology enter a broader public arena. Similar debates occur when the Senate considers whether to approve the nominations of candidates put forward by the President to become federal judges.

In recent years, at least two (highly conservative) Justices of the Supreme Court, Antonin Scalia and Clarence Thomas, have occasionally maintained that judges and Justices should renounce interpretive methodologies that require them to decide how the Constitution would "best" or most fairly be applied to modern conditions and should decide cases based solely on the original understanding of constitutional language— what it was understood to mean by those who ratified it. Because virtually no one denies that the original understanding is *relevant* to constitutional adjudication, it is often hard to gauge the precise scope of the difference between so-called originalists and their opponents. But originalists often claim that their methodology is sharply distinctive.

Insofar as originalism is sharply distinctive, however, critics urge two forceful objections. First, the "original understanding" of some constitutional provisions may be far out of touch with current realities. For example, . . . the principal basis for claims of federal authority to regulate the economy is a constitutional provision empowering Congress to regulate "Commerce . . . among the several States." It is highly questionable whether Congress's regulatory authority in this vital area should depend entirely on the understanding that prevailed in what President Franklin Roosevelt, in championing the need for federal power to defeat the Great Depression, referred to as "horse and buggy" days.

A second problem, to which I have called attention already, is that a great deal of modern constitutional doctrine that is now too entrenched to be given up seems impossible to justify by reference to the original understanding. Originalists do not maintain otherwise. They generally concede that their theory must make an *exception* for issues settled by past, entrenched judicial decisions—or at least some of them. It is issues of consistency that give originalists trouble, for they do not contend that all erroneous precedents should be immune from correction. To take perhaps the best known example, prominent originalists insist tirelessly that *Roe v. Wade*'s recognition of constitutional abortion rights ought to be overruled. But what distinguishes *Roe* from the precedents that originalists would leave unaltered? In essence, originalists reserve the right to pick which precedents to reject and which to accept, largely on the basis of their own judgments concerning which are important, desirable, and undesirable. Once it is recognized that Justices must make judgments of this kind, originalism fails in its own aspiration to exclude the Justices' moral and political views from constitutional adjudication. It is a philosophy available to be trotted out in some cases and ignored in others.

Confronted with objections such as these, originalists commonly insist that it takes a theory to beat a theory. Many originalists believe the best defense of their method is that it is the least bad of an imperfect lot. Others believe that alternative approaches to constitutional adjudication are better.

Another prominent theory of constitutional adjudication rests on the premise that the Constitution embodies "moral" rights. According to this view, the Constitution's framers and ratifiers did not invent such rights as those to freedom of speech and religion and to the equal protection of the laws. Rather, they recognized that such rights already existed as moral rights, and they incorporated those moral rights into the Constitution. Those holding this view would say, for example, that the Equal Protection Clause extends as far as the moral right to treatment as an equal and thus justifies the result in *Brown v. Board of Education,* even if the framers and ratifiers of the Fourteenth Amendment would have thought otherwise. At its foundation, a "moral rights" approach to constitutional adjudication must posit that the courts are better at identifying moral truths than are members of Congress and the state legislatures, perhaps because the latter are subject to political pressures to which the former—who have more opportunity to be long-sighted and deliberative—are not. Critics of course maintain that this approach invites judges simply to impose their personal moral views. Judges, they insist, have no monopoly on, and indeed no special insight into, moral truth.

In view of the objections to both originalism and a "moral rights" approach, some observers call for greater "judicial restraint" in invalidating legislation. When members of Congress and state legislators enact statutes, they have presumably considered whether the legislation violates the Constitution and determined that it does not. In light of this presumption, advocates of judicial restraint have long contended—since the *Lochner* era and even before—that the Supreme Court should accord "deference" to the constitutional judgments of other branches of government. According to one famous formulation of this position, the Court should invalidate statutes only when Congress or a state legislature has made a "clear mistake" about what the Constitution permits. This is by no means a wholly implausible position, but it would call for a dramatically reduced judicial role. It would also cast retrospective doubt on many of the Supreme Court's most celebrated decisions, including some that have protected the rights of racial minorities, safeguarded political speech, and enforced voting rights.

Believing that the Court should retain a robustly protective role in these areas, the late constitutional scholar John Hart Ely argued for deference to majorities *except* in cases involving claims of minority rights or rights to participate in the political process. He justified this approach by arguing that the Constitution's predominant commitment is to political democracy, and that courts should therefore intervene to make sure that the processes of political democracy function fairly. Among its implications, Ely's theory would stop courts from invalidating affirmative action programs (which disadvantage the white majority, not a racial minority) and recently enacted statutes that discriminate against women (who are a numerical majority, not a minority, of the population). Ely did not claim that the Supreme Court actually follows his theory, only that it should.

Other participants in constitutional practice defend a more flexible approach to constitutional adjudication, such as they believe the Court has characteristically practiced, partly based on an analogy to the way that judges decided cases under the so-called common law. Well into the nineteenth century, Congress and the state legislatures still had enacted comparatively few statutes, and the most basic law—called the common law—was developed by judges on the basis of custom and reason. In deciding cases at common law, judges begin with the rules as formulated in prior judicial decisions, but they also enjoy some flexibility to adapt those rules as circumstances change or as custom and reason require. Under the approach advocated by common-law constitutionalists, Supreme Court Justices should employ a comparably flexible approach in deciding constitutional issues. They should always begin with the text of the written Constitution, with which any interpretation must at least be reconciled. And they should treat the original understanding as always relevant and often decisive. But, it is argued, judges and especially Justices should also give weight to previous judicial decisions, including those that depart from original constitutional understandings, and they should take express account of what is fair, reasonable, workable, and desirable under modern circumstances, because we will get better constitutional law if they do so than if they do not. Critics, notably including originalists, argue that the common-law approach gives too large a role to judges, who are invited to thwart the wishes of democratic majorities based on their personal notions of justice and workability.

As the seemingly endless debate perhaps suggests, it may well be that questions of appropriate interpretive methodology admit no *general* answer—and that there can be no categorically persuasive rejoinder to the countermajoritarian difficulty either. The justification of the Supreme Court's role and interpretive methodology, if any, may well depend on the substantive fairness and popular acceptability of the particular decisions that it makes across the sweep of time. For now, at least, the people of the United States appear to have accepted a judicial role in adapting the Constitution to changing perceptions of need and fairness. But their acceptance of a flexible judicial role should surely be regarded as contingent, based on an assumption—grounded in our traditions—that judicial review as historically practiced has tended to produce good results overall: It is a useful device for promoting substantive justice and for reaching results that are broadly acceptable to the American public in ways that are at least tolerably consistent with the constitutional ideal of "a government of laws, and not of men."

Alexander Bickel may have had a thought such as this in mind when he wrote, somewhat enigmatically, that the Court "labors under the obligation to succeed." If the Court must somehow succeed in order to justify the role that it plays, and if success depends on reconciling the contestable demands of substantive justice with sometimes competing imperatives of adhering to settled rules of law and of rendering decisions that the public deems acceptable, it is easy to understand why the practice of judicial review should provoke ongoing anxieties and debate....

PART NINE

Civil Liberties and Civil Rights

48

ANTHONY LEWIS

From *Gideon's Trumpet*

Written in 1964, Gideon's Trumpet *is one of the most-assigned books in American government courses. The excerpt presented here touches on all the major points in the legal and personal story of Clarence Earl Gideon, the Florida prisoner whose case,* Gideon v. Wainwright *(1963), transformed American justice. As Gideon's story unfolds, notice the following elements in journalist Anthony Lewis's account of the landmark case that ensured all defendants legal counsel in state criminal cases:* in forma pauperis; *writ of certiorari;* Betts v. Brady; *stare decisis; Attorney Abe Fortas; Fourteenth Amendment; selective incorporation of the Bill of Rights; "a great marble temple"; "Oyez, oyez, oyez"; Justice Black; 9-0; court-appointed attorney Fred Turner; public defenders; not guilty; the Bay Harbor Poolroom.*

IN THE MORNING MAIL of January 8, 1962, the Supreme Court of the United States received a large envelope from Clarence Earl Gideon, prisoner No. 003826, Florida State Prison, P.O. Box 221, Raiford, Florida. Like all correspondence addressed to the Court generally rather than to any particular justice or Court employee, it went to a room at the top of the great marble steps so familiar to Washington tourists. There a secretary opened the envelope. As the return address had indicated, it was another petition by a prisoner without funds asking the Supreme Court to get him out of jail—another, in the secretary's eyes, because pleas from prisoners were so familiar a part of her work. . . .

. . . A federal statute permits persons to proceed in any federal court *in forma pauperis,* in the manner of a pauper, without following the usual forms or paying the regular costs. The only requirement in the statute is that the litigant "make affidavit that he is unable to pay such costs or give security therefor."

The Supreme Court's own rules show special concern for *in forma pauperis* cases. Rule 53 allows an impoverished person to file just one copy of a petition, instead of the forty ordinarily required, and states that the Court will make "due allowance" for technical errors so long as there is substantial compliance. In practice, the men in the Clerk's Office—a half dozen career employees, who effectively handle the Court's relations with the outside world—stretch even the rule of substantial compliance.

Rule 53 also waives the general requirement that documents submitted to the Supreme Court be printed. It says that *in forma pauperis* applications should be typewritten "whenever possible," but in fact handwritten papers are accepted.

Gideon's were written in pencil. They were done in carefully formed printing, like a schoolboy's, on lined sheets evidently provided by the Florida prison. Printed at the top of each sheet, under the heading Correspondence Regulations, was a set of rules ("Only 2 letters each week . . . written on one side only . . . letters must be written in English . . .") and the warning: MAIL WILL NOT BE DELIVERED WHICH DOES NOT CONFORM TO THESE RULES. Gideon's punctuation and spelling were full of surprises, but there was also a good deal of practiced, if archaic, legal jargon, such as "Comes now the petitioner . . .".

Gideon was a fifty-one-year-old white man who had been in and out of prisons much of his life. He had served time for four previous felonies, and he bore the physical marks of a destitute life: a wrinkled, prematurely aged face, a voice and hands that trembled, a frail body, white hair. He had never been a professional criminal or a man of violence; he just could not seem to settle down to work, and so he had made his way by gambling and occasional thefts. Those who had known him, even the men who had arrested him and those who were now his jailers, considered Gideon a perfectly harmless human being, rather likeable, but one tossed aside by life. Anyone meeting him for the first time would be likely to regard him as the most wretched of men.

And yet a flame still burned in Clarence Earl Gideon. He had not given up caring about life or freedom; he had not lost his sense of injustice. Right now he had a passionate—some thought almost irrational—feeling of having been wronged by the State of Florida, and he had the determination to try to do something about it. Although the Clerk's Office could not be expected to remember him, this was in fact his second petition to the Supreme Court. The first had been returned for failure to include a pauper's affidavit, and the Clerk's Office had enclosed a copy of the rules and a sample affidavit to help him do better next time. Gideon persevered. . . .

Gideon's main submission was a five-page document entitled "Petition for a Writ of Certiorari Directed to the Supreme Court State of Florida." A writ of certiorari is a formal device to bring a case up to the Supreme Court from a lower court. In plain terms Gideon was asking the Supreme Court to hear his case.

What was his case? Gideon said he was serving a five-year term for "the crime of breaking and entering with the intent to commit a misdemeanor, to wit, petty larceny." He had been convicted of breaking into the Bay Harbor Poolroom in Panama City, Florida. Gideon said his conviction violated the due-process clause of the Fourteenth Amendment to the Constitution, which provides that "No state shall . . . deprive any person of life, liberty, or property, without due process of law." In what way had Gideon's trial or conviction assertedly lacked "due process of law"? For two of the petition's five pages it was impossible to tell. Then came this pregnant statement:

"When at the time of the petitioners trial he ask the lower court for the aid of counsel, the court refused this aid. Petitioner told the court that this Court made decision to the effect that all citizens tried for a felony crime should have aid of counsel. The lower court ignored this plea."

Five more times in the succeeding pages of his penciled petition Gideon spoke of the right to counsel. To try a poor man for a felony without giving him a lawyer, he said, was to deprive him of due process of law. There was only one trouble with the argument, and it was a problem Gideon did not mention. Just twenty years before, in the case of *Betts v. Brady*, the Supreme Court had rejected the contention that the due-process clause of the Fourteenth Amendment provided a flat guarantee of counsel in state criminal trials.

Betts v. Brady was a decision that surprised many persons when made and that had been a subject of dispute ever since. For a majority of six to three, Justice Owen J. Roberts said the Fourteenth Amendment provided no universal assurance of a lawyer's help in a state criminal trial. A lawyer was constitutionally required only if to be tried without one amounted to "a denial of fundamental fairness." . . .

Later cases had refined the rule of *Betts v. Brady*. To prove that he was denied "fundamental fairness" because he had no counsel, the poor man had to show that he was the victim of what the Court called "special circumstances." Those might be his own illiteracy, ignorance, youth, or mental illness, the complexity of the charge against him or the conduct of the prosecutor or judge at the trial. . . .

But Gideon did not claim any "special circumstances." His petition made not the slightest attempt to come within the sophisticated rule of *Betts v. Brady*. Indeed, there was nothing to indicate he had ever heard of the case or its principle. From the day he was tried Gideon had had one idea: That under the Constitution of the United States he, a poor man, was flatly entitled to have a lawyer provided to help in his defense. . . .

Gideon was wrong, of course. The United States Supreme Court had not said he was entitled to counsel; in *Betts v. Brady* and succeeding cases it had said quite the opposite. But that did not necessarily make Gideon's petition futile, for the Supreme Court never speaks with absolute finality when it interprets the Constitution. From time to time—with due solemnity, and after much searching of conscience—the Court has overruled its own decisions. Although he did not know it, Clarence Earl Gideon was calling for one of those great occasions in legal history. He was asking the Supreme Court to change its mind. . . .

Clarence Earl Gideon's petition for certiorari inevitably involved, for all the members of the Court, the most delicate factors of timing and strategy. The issue he presented—the right to counsel—was undeniably of first-rank importance, and it was an issue with which all of the justices were thoroughly familiar. . . .

. . . Professional comment on the Betts case, in the law reviews, had always been critical and was growing stronger, and within the Supreme Court several justices had urged its overruling. On the other hand, a majority might well draw back from so large a step. . . . At the conference of June 1, 1962, the Court had before it two jurisdictional statements asking the Court to hear appeals, twenty-six petitions for certiorari on the Appellate Docket, ten paupers' applications on the Miscellaneous Docket and three petitions for rehearing. . . .

The results of the deliberations at this conference were made known to the world shortly after ten A.M. the following Monday, June 4th, when a clerk posted on a bulletin board the mimeographed list of the Supreme Court's orders for that day. One order read:

Gideon v. Cochran 890 Misc.

The motion for leave to proceed *in forma pauperis* and the petition for writ of certiorari are granted. The case is transferred to the appellate docket. In addition to other questions presented by this case, counsel are requested to discuss the following in their briefs and oral argument:

"Should this Court's holding in *Betts v. Brady*, 316 U.S. 455, be reconsidered?" . . .

In the Circuit Court of Bay County, Florida, Clarence Earl Gideon had been unable to obtain counsel, but there was no doubt that he could have a lawyer in the Supreme Court of the United States now that it had agreed to hear his case. It is the unvarying practice of the Court to appoint a lawyer for any impoverished prisoner whose petition for review has been granted and who requests counsel.

Appointment by the Supreme Court to represent a poor man is a great honor. For the eminent practitioner who would never, otherwise, dip his fingers into the criminal law it can be an enriching experience, making him think again of the human dimensions of liberty. It may provide the first, sometimes the only, opportunity for a lawyer in some distant corner of the country to appear before the Supreme Court. It may also require great personal sacrifice. There is no monetary compensation of any kind—only the satisfaction of service. The Court pays the cost of the lawyer's transportation to Washington and home, and it prints the briefs, but there is no other provision for expenses, not even secretarial help or a hotel room. The lawyer donates that most valuable commodity, his own time. . . .

The next Monday the Court entered this order in the case of *Gideon v. Cochran:*

"The motion for appointment of counsel is granted and it is ordered that Abe Fortas, Esquire, of Washington, D.C., a member of the Bar of this Court be, and he is hereby, appointed to serve as counsel for petitioner in this case.

Abe Fortas is a high-powered example of that high-powered species, the Washington lawyer. He is the driving force in the firm of Arnold, Fortas and Porter. . . . A lawyer who has worked with him says: "Of all the men I have met he most knows why he is doing what he does. I don't like the s.o.b., but if I were in trouble I'd want him on my side. He's the most resourceful, the boldest, the most thorough lawyer I know." . . .

. . . "The real question," Fortas said, "was whether I should urge upon the Court the special-circumstances doctrine. As the record then stood, there was nothing to show that he had suffered from any special circumstances. . . .

When that transcript was read at Arnold, Fortas and Porter, there was no longer any question about the appropriateness of this case as the vehicle to challenge *Betts v. Brady*. Plainly Gideon was not mentally defective. The charge against him, and the proof, were not particularly complicated. The judge had tried to be fair; at least there was no overt bias in the courtroom. In short, Gideon had not suffered from any of the special circumstances that would have entitled him to a lawyer under the limited rule of *Betts v. Brady*. And yet it was altogether clear that a lawyer would have helped. The trial had been a rudimentary one, with a prosecution case that was fragmentary at best. Gideon had not made a single objection or pressed any of the favorable lines of defense. An Arnold, Fortas and Porter associate said later: "We knew as soon as we read that transcript that here was a perfect case to challenge the assumption of *Betts* that a man could have a fair trial without a lawyer. He did very well for a layman, he acted like a lawyer. But it was a pitiful effort really. He may have committed this crime, but it was never proved by the prosecution. A lawyer—not a great lawyer, just an ordinary, competent lawyer—could have made ashes of the case." . . .

As Abe Fortas began to think about the case in the summer of 1962, before Justice Frankfurter's retirement, it was clear to him that overruling *Betts v. Brady* would not come easily to Justice Frankfurter or others of his view. This was true not only because of their judicial philosophy in general, but because of the way they had applied it on specific matters. One of these was the question of precedent.

"In most matters it is more important that the applicable rule of law be settled than that it be settled right." Justice Brandeis thus succinctly stated the basic reason for *stare decisis*, the judicial doctrine of following precedents. . . .

Another issue . . . cut even deeper than *stare decisis*, and closer to Gideon's case. This was their attitude toward federalism—the independence of the states in our federal system of government. . . .

The Bill of Rights is the name collectively given to the first ten amendments to the Constitution, all proposed by the First Congress of the United States in 1789 and ratified in 1791. The first eight contain the guarantees of individual liberty with which we are so familiar: freedom of speech, press, religion and assembly; protection for the privacy of the home; assurance against double jeopardy and compulsory self-incrimination; the right to counsel and to trial by jury; freedom from cruel and unusual punishments. At the time of their adoption it was universally agreed that these eight amendments limited only the Federal Government and its processes. . . .

There matters stood until the Fourteenth Amendment became part of the Constitution in 1868. A product of the Civil War, it was specifically designed to prevent abuse of individuals by state governments. Section 1 provided: "No State shall make or enforce any law which shall abridge the privileges or immunities of citizens of the United States; nor shall any State deprive any person of life, liberty, or property, without due process of law; nor deny to any person within its jurisdiction the equal protection of the laws." Soon the claim was advanced that this section had been designed by its framers to *incorporate*, and apply to the states, all the provisions of the first eight amendments.

This theory of wholesale incorporation of the Bill of Rights has been adopted by one or more Supreme Court justices from time to time, but never a majority. . . .

But if wholesale incorporation has been rejected, the Supreme Court has used the Fourteenth Amendment to apply provisions of the Bill of Rights to the states *selectively*. The vehicle has been the clause assuring individuals due process of law. The Court has said that state denial of any right deemed "fundamental" by society amounts to a denial of due process and hence violates the Fourteenth Amendment. . . .

The difficult question has been which provisions of the first eight amendments to absorb. . . .

Grandiose is the word for the physical setting. The W.P.A. Guide to Washington* called the Supreme Court building a "great marble temple" which "by its august scale and mighty splendor seems to bear little relation to the functional purposes of government." Shortly before the justices moved into the building in 1935 from their old chamber across the street in the Capitol, Justice Stone wrote his sons "The place is almost bombastically pretentious, and thus it seems to me wholly inappropriate for a quiet group of old boys such as the Supreme Court." He told his friends that the justices would be "nine black beetles in the Temple of Karnak."

The visitor who climbs the marble steps and passes through the marble columns of the huge pseudo-classical facade finds himself in a cold, lofty hall, again all marble. Great bronze gates exclude him from the area of the building where the justices work in private—their offices, library and conference room. In the courtroom, which is always open to the public, the atmosphere of austere pomp is continued: there are more columns, an enormously high ceiling, red velvet hangings, friezes carved high on the walls. The ritual opening of each day's session adds to the feeling of awe. The Court Crier to the right of the bench smashes his gavel down sharply on a wooden block, everyone rises and the justices file in through the red draperies behind the bench and stand at their places as the Crier intones the traditional opening: "The honorable, the Chief Justice and the Associate Justices of the Supreme Court of the United States. Oyez, oyez, oyez. All persons having business before the honorable, the Supreme Court of the United States, are admonished to draw near and give their attention, for the Court is now sitting. God save the United States and this honorable Court."

But then, when an argument begins, all the trappings and ceremony seem to fade, and the scene takes on an extraordinary intimacy. In the most informal way, altogether without pomp, Court and counsel converse. It is conversation—as direct, unpretentious and focused discussion as can be found anywhere in Washington. . . .

*The WPA, the Works Progress Administration, was started by President Franklin Roosevelt as part of the New Deal in 1935. WPA projects, designed to put people back to work during the Depression, included school and park building, theater and music performances, and map and guidebook writing.—EDS.

Chief Justice Warren, as is the custom, called the next case by reading aloud its full title: Number 155, Clarence Earl Gideon, petitioner, versus H. G. Cochran, Jr., director, Division of Corrections, State of Florida....

The lawyer arguing a case stands at a small rostrum between the two counsel tables, facing the Chief Justice. The party that lost in the lower court goes first, and so the argument in *Gideon v. Cochran* was begun by Abe Fortas. As he stood, the Chief Justice gave him the customary greeting, "Mr. Fortas," and he made the customary opening: "Mr. Chief Justice, may it please the Court...."

This case presents "a narrow question," Fortas said—the right to counsel—unencumbered by extraneous issues....

"This record does not indicate that Clarence Earl Gideon was a person of low intelligence," Fortas said, "or that the judge was unfair to him. But to me this case shows the basic difficulty with Betts versus Brady. It shows that no man, however intelligent, can conduct his own defense adequately."...

"I believe we can confidently say that overruling Betts versus Brady at this time would be in accord with the opinion of those entitled to an opinion. That is not always true of great constitutional questions.... We may be comforted in this constitutional moment by the fact that what we are doing is a deliberate change after twenty years of experience—a change that has the overwhelming support of the bench, the bar and even of the states."...

It was only a few days later, as it happened, that *Gideon v. Wainwright* was decided. There was no prior notice; there never is. The Court gives out no advance press releases and tells no one what cases will be decided on a particular Monday, much less how they will be decided. Opinion days have a special quality. The Supreme Court is one of the last American appellate courts where decisions are announced orally. The justices, who divide on so many issues, disagree about this practice, too. Some regard it as a waste of time; others value it as an occasion for descending from the ivory tower, however briefly, and communicating with the live audience in the courtroom....

Then, in the ascending order of seniority, it was Justice Black's turn. He looked at his wife, who was sitting in the box reserved for the justices' friends and families, and said: "I have for announcement the opinion and judgment of the Court in Number One fifty-five, Gideon against Wainwright."

Justice Black leaned forward and gave his words the emphasis and the drama of a great occasion. Speaking very directly to the audience in the courtroom, in an almost folksy way, he told about Clarence Earl Gideon's case and how it had reached the Supreme Court of the United States.

"It raised a fundamental question," Justice Black said, "the rightness of a case we decided twenty-one years ago, Betts against Brady. When we granted certiorari in this case, we asked the lawyers on both sides to argue to us whether we should reconsider that case. We do reconsider Betts and Brady, and we reach an opposite conclusion."

By now the page boys were passing out the opinions. There were four—by Justices Douglas, Clark and Harlan, in addition to the opinion of the Court. But none of the other three was a dissent. A quick look at the end of each showed that it concurred in the overruling of *Betts v. Brady*. On that central result, then, the Court was unanimous. . . .

That was the end of Clarence Earl Gideon's case in the Supreme Court of the United States. The opinions delivered that Monday were quickly circulated around the country by special legal services, then issued in pamphlets by the Government Printing Office. Eventually they appeared in the bound volumes of Supreme Court decisions, the United States Reports, to be cited as *Gideon v. Wainwright*, 372 U.S. 335—meaning that the case could be found beginning on page 335 of the 372nd volume of the reports.

Justice Black, talking to a friend a few weeks after the decision, said quietly: "When *Betts v. Brady* was decided, I never thought I'd live to see it overruled." . . .

The reaction of the states to *Gideon v. Wainwright* was swift and constructive. The most dramatic response came from Florida, whose rural-dominated legislature had so long refused to relieve the problem of the unrepresented indigent such as Gideon. Shortly after the decision Governor Farris Bryant called on the legislature to enact a public-defender law. . . .

Resolution of the great constitutional question in *Gideon v. Wainwright* did not decide the fate of Clarence Earl Gideon. He was now entitled to a new trial, with a lawyer. Was he guilty of breaking into the Bay Harbor Poolroom? The verdict would not set any legal precedents, but there is significance in the human beings who make constitutional-law cases as well as in the law. And in this case there was the interesting question whether the legal assistance for which Gideon had fought so hard would make any difference to him. . . .

. . . After ascertaining that Gideon had no money to hire a lawyer of his own choice, Judge McCrary asked whether there was a local lawyer whom Gideon would like to represent him. There was: W. Fred Turner.

"For the record," Judge McCrary said quickly, "I am going to appoint Mr. Fred Turner to represent this defendant, Clarence Earl Gideon." . . .

The jury went out at four-twenty P.M., after a colorless charge by the judge including the instruction—requested by Turner—that the jury must believe Gideon guilty "beyond a reasonable doubt" in order to convict him. When a half-hour had passed with no verdict, the prosecutors were less confident. At five twenty-five there was a knock on the door between the courtroom and the jury room. The jurors filed in, and the court clerk read their verdict, written on a form. It was *Not Guilty*.

"So say you all?" asked Judge McCrary, without a flicker of emotion. The jurors nodded. . . .

After nearly two years in the state penitentiary Gideon was a free man. . . . That night he would pay a last, triumphant visit to the Bay Harbor Poolroom. Could someone let him have a few dollars? Someone did.

"Do you feel like you accomplished something?" a newspaper reporter asked.

"Well I did."

49

Miranda v. Arizona

Chief Justice Earl Warren, the great liberal judge whose Court had already handed down a number of landmark rulings—among them, Brown v. Board of Education (1954) on desegregation in public schools, Mapp v. Ohio (1961) on search and seizure by police, and Gideon v. Wainwright (1963) on the right to counsel in criminal trials in state courts—wrote the opinion in another major case, Miranda v. Arizona (1966). The case involved Ernesto Miranda, who had been arrested for kidnap and rape, and who had been identified by the victim in a police lineup. Police officers then interrogated Miranda, who subsequently signed a confession at the top of which read that he had done so "with full knowledge of my legal rights, understanding that any statement I make may be used against me." During the trial, Miranda's confession was entered as evidence, and despite the officer's testimony that Miranda had not been told of his right to have an attorney present during interrogation, Miranda was found guilty. The Supreme Court of Arizona upheld the conviction on the grounds that Miranda had not specifically requested an attorney. The case went to the U.S. Supreme Court whose ruling resulted in what we now know as the "Miranda rights," a statement read to any suspect by law enforcement officers during an arrest.

Miranda v. Arizona
384 U.S. 436, 86 S.Ct. 1602 (1966)

CHIEF JUSTICE WARREN DELIVERED the opinion of the Court.

The cases before us raise questions which go to the roots of our concepts of American criminal jurisprudence: the restraints society must observe consistent with the Federal Constitution in prosecuting individuals for crime. More specifically, we deal with the admissibility of statements obtained from an individual who is subjected to custodial police interrogation and the necessity for procedures which assure that the individual is accorded his privilege under the Fifth Amendment to the Constitution not to be compelled to incriminate himself.

We dealt with certain phases of this problem recently in *Escobedo v. Illinois*, 378 U.S. 478 (1964). There, as in the four cases before us, law enforcement officials took the defendant into custody and interrogated him in a police station for the purpose of obtaining a confession. The police did not effectively advise him of his right to remain silent or of his right to consult with his attorney. Rather, they confronted him with an alleged accomplice who accused him of having perpetrated a murder. When the defendant denied the accusation and said "I didn't shoot Manuel, you did it," they handcuffed him and took him to an interrogation room. There, while handcuffed and standing, he was questioned for four hours until he confessed. During this interrogation, the police denied his request to speak to his attorney, and they prevented his retained attorney, who had come to the police station, from consulting with him. At his trial, the State, over his objection, introduced the confession against him. We held that the statements thus made were constitutionally inadmissible. . . . We adhere to the principles of *Escobedo* today.

Our holding will be spelled out with some specificity in the pages which follow but briefly stated it is this: the prosecution may not use statements, whether exculpatory or inculpatory, stemming from custodial interrogation of the defendant unless it demonstrates the use of procedural safeguards effective to secure the privilege against self-incrimination. By custodial interrogation, we mean questioning initiated by law enforcement officers after a person has been taken into custody or otherwise deprived of his freedom of action in any significant way. As for the procedural safeguards to be employed, unless other fully effective means are devised to inform accused persons of their right of silence and to assure a continuous opportunity to exercise it, the following measures are required. Prior to any questioning, the person must be warned that he has a right to remain silent, that any statement he does make may be used as evidence against him, and that he has a right to the presence of an attorney, either retained or appointed. The defendant may waive effectuation of these rights, provided the waiver is made voluntarily, knowingly and intelligently. If, however, he indicates in any manner and at any stage of the process that he wishes to consult with an attorney before speaking there can be no questioning. Likewise, if the individual is alone and indicates in any manner that he does not wish to be interrogated, the police may not question him. The mere fact that he may have answered some questions or volunteered some statements on his own does not deprive him of the right to refrain from answering any further inquiries until he has consulted with an attorney and thereafter consents to be questioned. . . .

The constitutional issue we decide in each of these cases [being decided today] is the admissibility of statements obtained from a defendant questioned while in custody or otherwise deprived of his freedom of action in any significant way. In each, the defendant was questioned by police officers, detectives, or a prosecuting attorney in a room in which he was cut off from the outside world. In none of these cases was the defendant given a full and effective warning of his rights at the outset of the interrogation process. In all the cases, the questioning elicited oral admissions, and in three of them, signed statements as well which were admitted at their trials. They all thus share salient features—incommunicado interrogation of individuals in a police-dominated atmosphere, resulting in self-incriminating statements without full warnings of constitutional rights. . . . We stress that the modern practice of in-custody interrogation is psychologically rather than physically oriented. . . . Interrogation still takes place in privacy. Privacy results in secrecy and this in turn results in a gap in our knowledge as to what in fact goes on in the interrogation rooms. A valuable source of information about present police practices, however, may be found in various police manuals and texts which document procedures employed with success in the past, and which recommend various other effective tactics. . . .

The officers are told by the manuals that the "principal psychological factor contributing to a successful interrogation is *privacy*—being alone with the person under interrogation." The efficacy of this tactic has been explained as follows:

"If at all practicable, the interrogation should take place in the investigator's office or at least in a room of his own choice. The subject should be deprived of every psychological advantage." . . .

After this psychological conditioning, however, the officer is told to point out the incriminating significance of the suspect's refusal to talk:

"Joe, you have a right to remain silent. That's your privilege and I'm the last person in the world who'll try to take it away from you. If that's the way you want to leave this, O.K. But let me ask you this. Suppose you were in my shoes and I were in yours and you called me in to ask me about this and I told you, 'I don't want to answer any of your questions.' You'd think I had something to hide, and you'd probably be right in thinking that. That's exactly what I'll have to think about you, and so will everybody else. So let's sit here and talk this whole thing over."

Few will persist in their initial refusal to talk, it is said, if this monologue is employed correctly.

In the event that the subject wishes to speak to a relative or an attorney, the following advice is tendered:

"[T]he interrogator should respond by suggesting that the subject first tell the truth to the interrogator himself rather than get anyone else involved in the matter. If the request is for an attorney, the interrogator may suggest that the subject save himself or his family the expense of any such professional service, particularly if he is innocent of the offense under investigation. The interrogator may also add,

'Joe, I'm only looking for the truth, and if you're telling the truth, that's it. You can handle this by yourself.'" . . .

Even without employing brutality, the "third degree" or the specific stratagems described above, the very fact of custodial interrogation exacts a heavy toll on individual liberty and trades on the weakness of individuals. . . .

. . . In each of the cases [heard by the court], the defendant was thrust into an unfamiliar atmosphere and run through menacing police interrogation procedures. The potentiality for compulsion is forcefully apparent, for example, in *Miranda*, where the indigent Mexican defendant was a seriously disturbed individual with pronounced sexual fantasies, and in *Stewart*, in which the defendant was an indigent Los Angeles Negro who had dropped out of school in the sixth grade. To be sure, the records do not evince overt physical coercion or patent psychological ploys. The fact remains that in none of these cases did the officers undertake to afford appropriate safeguards at the outset of the interrogation to insure that the statements were truly the product of free choice.

It is obvious that such an interrogation environment is created for no purpose other than to subjugate the individual to the will of his examiner. This atmosphere carries its own badge of intimidation. To be sure, this is not physical intimidation, but it is equally destructive of human dignity. The current practice of incommunicado interrogation is at odds with one of our Nation's most cherished principles—that the individual may not be compelled to incriminate himself. Unless adequate protective devices are employed to dispel the compulsion inherent in custodial surroundings, no statement obtained from the defendant can truly be the product of his free choice. . . .

To summarize, we hold that when an individual is taken into custody or otherwise deprived of his freedom by the authorities in any significant way and is subjected to questioning, the privilege against self-incrimination is jeopardized. Procedural safeguards must be employed to protect the privilege, and unless other fully effective means are adopted to notify the person of his right of silence and to assure that the exercise of the right will be scrupulously honored, the following measures are required. He must be warned prior to any questioning that he has the right to remain silent, that anything he says can be used against him in a court of law, that he has the right to the presence of an attorney, and that if he cannot afford an attorney one will be appointed for him prior to any questioning if he so desires. Opportunity to exercise these rights must be afforded to him throughout the interrogation. After such warnings have been given, and such opportunity afforded him, the individual may knowingly and intelligently waive these rights and agree to answer questions or make a statement. But unless and until such warnings and waiver are demonstrated by the prosecution at trial, no evidence obtained as a result of interrogation can be used against him....We turn now to these facts to consider the application to these cases of the constitutional principles discussed above....

On March 13, 1963, petitioner, Ernesto Miranda, was arrested at his home and taken in custody to a Phoenix police station. He was there identified by the complaining witness. The police then took him to "Interrogation Room No. 2" of the detective bureau. There he was questioned by two police officers. The officers admitted at trial that Miranda was not advised that he had a right to have an attorney present. Two hours later, the officers emerged from the interrogation room with a written confession signed by Miranda. At the top of the statement was a typed paragraph stating that the confession was made voluntarily, without threats or promises of immunity and "with full knowledge of my legal rights, understanding any statement I make may be used against me."

At his trial before a jury, the written confession was admitted into evidence over the objection of defense counsel, and the officers testified to the prior oral confession made by Miranda during the interrogation. Miranda was found guilty of kidnapping and rape. He was sentenced to 20 to 30 years' imprisonment on each count, the sentences to run concurrently. On appeal, the Supreme Court of Arizona held that Miranda's constitutional rights were not violated in obtaining the confession and affirmed the conviction. 98 Ariz. 18, 401 P. 2d 721. In reaching its decision, the court emphasized heavily the fact that Miranda did not specifically request counsel.

We reverse. From the testimony of the officers and by the admission of respondent, it is clear that Miranda was not in any way apprised of his right to consult with an attorney and to have one present during the interrogation, nor was his right not to be compelled to incriminate himself effectively protected in any other manner. Without these warnings the statements were inadmissible.

50

DONALD KETTL

From *System under Stress*

The USA PATRIOT Act was one of the American government's first responses to the September 11, 2001, terrorist attacks. It is also one of the most controversial responses. Professor Donald Kettl first recounts some of the bureaucratic failures that led up to the attacks. He then discusses the legislation proposed immediately after September 11. The debate over the USA PATRIOT Act exposed the tension between officials who favored a broad expansion of government's power to ensure security and those who feared a drastic loss of civil liberties. The Act, itself, is long and complicated; learn here a little about the key provisions. Finally, Kettl takes up the question of whether the PATRIOT Act was passed too quickly, without sufficient consideration of the civil liberties that Americans were sacrificing. This excerpt raises important questions about the balance between protecting the nation and guarding people's freedoms. The real question is: Can we find the right balance?

———

OF ALL THE SURPRISES IN THE AFTERMATH of the September 11 terrorist attacks, one of the biggest was the discovery that the four teams of hijackers had been living undetected in the United States for many months. Two had settled in San Diego in January 2000. Several had spent time in the United States in the early 1990s, taking language instruction and, later, flight lessons. The "muscle" hijackers, whose job it was to overcome the pilots and control the passengers, began arriving in April 2001. The four pilot hijackers flew dry runs across the country early in the year and, for reasons investigators could never determine, spent layovers in Las Vegas.

All of the hijackers had entered the country with what appeared to be valid passports. By the day of the attacks, the visas of two of them had expired, and a third hijacker had failed to register for classes and thus violated the terms of his student visa. But federal authorities did not discover any of this until after the attacks. Just as importantly, sixteen of the hijackers were in the country legally. All managed to live comfortable lives, blending into the fabric of American society.

Americans have always treasured their ability to go where they want when they want. They have long valued the freedom to choose their jobs and chart their careers, to live their lives without government scrutiny, and to associate with people of their own choosing. So important are these values, in fact, that many states refused to ratify the U.S. Constitution until, in 1789, Congress proposed a bill of rights. But at the same time, Americans have always expected their government to protect them from threats. That the country was attacked by people who had so easily integrated themselves into the nation's daily life raised a dilemma: How much should government intrude into the lives of citizens in its quest to provide protection?

That question raised a second point. Americans have always accepted any expansion of government power grudgingly. When government has expanded, people have tended to trust state and local governments, to which they are closer, more than the federal government. But to the degree that homeland security strengthens government power, it tends to strengthen the power of the federal government. Therefore, it not only shifts the balance from individual freedom to government control, but it also shifts the balance from state and local authority to federal power. In the long run, the most lasting and important effects of the September 11 attacks could prove to be these changes in individual liberty and governance.

The discovery that the attackers had so easily entered the country and managed to plot the attacks without detection (except by a handful of suspicious FBI agents, whose memos had not gained attention at headquarters) stunned federal officials. A congressional investigation, completed in 2002 but whose report was not released until six months later in early 2003, offered a scathing assessment. "At home, the counterterrorism effort suffered from the lack of an effective domestic intelligence capability. The FBI was unable to identify and monitor effectively the extent of activity by al Qaeda and other international terrorist groups operating in the United States." Coupled with the CIA's problems in tracking foreign threats, "these problems greatly exacerbated the nation's vulnerability to an increasingly dangerous and immediate international terrorist threat inside the United States." Sixteen of the nineteen hijackers had come from Saudi Arabia, and an American who had worked for the Saudi foreign ministry said, "The visa operation is a joke over there." Nationals from other countries handled the initial processing of the applications, and that made it easy for even questionable individuals to slip through the process. "The State Department does not do a quality control check," the former employee charged. As a result, *Boston Globe* reporters concluded, "With its borders so porous and its recordkeeping so unreliable, the United States has little ability to keep all criminals—or terrorists—out of the country and has no system to track them once they're in."

According to the *Washington Post*, the whole star-crossed system was "a portrait of terrorists who took advantage of America's open society as they planned their murderous assault on the Pentagon and the World Trade Center." The story was dismaying: a student visa process that one terrorist had exploited; easy issuance of new passports to foreign travelers; a lack of careful screening at American immigration facilities; failure to create effective watch lists and match them to those trying to enter the country; and weak information systems to track foreign travelers once they entered the country. Americans and their officials wondered if the nation's tradition of openness and minimal intrusion of government had allowed the hijackers an advantage that they had exploited to horrendous result.

Americans were rocked not only by the enormity of the attacks but also by the fact that the terrorists had walked among them for months or years. Even worse, intelligence analysts warned that more al Qaeda operatives might be waiting in "sleeper cells" to stage more attacks. Investigators found evidence that some of the September 11 hijackers had studied crop dusters. Was al Qaeda planning to distribute anthrax or some other bio-toxin from the air? Was another round of airline hijackings in the offing? How could the nation protect itself without turning into a police state? The *Boston Globe* said that the terrorists "exploited one of the most enduring tenets of American freedom: its open society." A week after the attacks, columnist Martin Wolf sharply summarized the budding dilemma in London's *Financial Times*. "The biggest long-term challenge to any open society vulnerable to assaults on so vast a scale is striking the balance between safety and freedom. The attack of September 11 took advantage of the ease of movement and low security levels of air transport inside the U.S." He concluded, "We must balance the needs of security with the demands of freedom."

Even the staunchest advocates of civil liberties knew that the horror of the September 11 attacks and the fact that the terrorists had exploited American freedom in an effort to weaken the nation would inevitably mean some sacrifice of civil rights and civil liberties to provide greater security. Intelligence analysts discovered that the terrorists were using satellite phones and coded e-mail. By contrast, American officials charged with guarding the borders and ferreting out terrorist cells had to sift through reams of paper and deal with databases that did not connect and computer systems that could not network. Sen. Edward M. Kennedy of Massachusetts, long an advocate of an open immigration policy, nonetheless recognized that things had to change. "We're dealing with horse-and-buggy technology," he said. "We're dealing with handwritten notes. It's a shocking indictment." U.S. intelligence had to enter the twenty-first century. . . .

Attorney General John Ashcroft, along with other senior administration officials, was at a secure location, a carefully guarded and undisclosed site away from Washington, for the first days after the attacks. But Ashcroft sent word to his staff that he wanted tough, new authority to help the FBI and the Justice Department find and break up terrorist cells. One of his aides later remembered that Ashcroft's charge was clear: "all that is necessary for law enforcement, within the bounds of the Constitution, to discharge the obligation to fight this war against terror." Not only did department officials feel the need to act, but the heat of press scrutiny created an inescapable need to be *seen* to be acting as well.

That imperative created a flurry of proposals on the floor of Congress. Some members proposed an aggressive new authority that would allow the federal government to intercept e-mail and telephone calls. Proposals surfaced to allow the government to increase monitoring of foreign agents and to infiltrate religious services even if there was no prior evidence of criminal activity. Investigators, in fact, had complained that the law made it easier to infiltrate the Mafia than al Qaeda cells and this had to be corrected. For their part, civil libertarians worried that Congress would rush to enact sweeping new legislation without stopping to consider what impact it might have on civil rights and civil liberties. Security experts struggled to find a way to balance concerns for liberty with the need for stronger homeland defense.

A plan began to take shape. Members of Congress agreed on new legislation to make it easier to track the origin and destination of telephone calls and to increase the authority of government to track e-mail. They agreed on broader wiretap authority and new measures to track the flow of money to terrorist groups. The Bush administration, however, wanted to go much further. Ashcroft, for example, wanted the authority to indefinitely detain noncitizens who the Justice Department believed might be planning acts of terrorism. He wanted greater flexibility in sharing grand jury and eavesdropping data throughout the federal government and in tapping into e-mail chats. And he wanted the new authority to be made permanent, so that the federal government could create new and aggressive long-term strategies to go after potential terrorists. Just a week after the attacks, Ashcroft announced at a press conference that he expected the administration's proposal to be ready very shortly—and that he wanted Congress to act on it within a few days. "We need these tools to fight the terrorism threat which exists in the United States," Ashcroft said.

Most members of Congress agreed that the nation needed tougher penalties for terrorists and that the federal government needed broader investigative powers. But Sen. Patrick J. Leahy, D-Vt., chair of the Judiciary Committee, warned that "the biggest mistake we could make" was to conclude that the terrorist threat was so great "that we don't need the Constitution." He added, "The first thing we have to realize is this is not either/or—this is not the Constitution versus capturing the terrorists. We can have both." The American Civil Liberties Union echoed Leahy's concern in a set of ten principles endorsed by scores of civil rights and civil liberties groups. "We need to consider proposals calmly and deliberately with a determination not to erode the liberties and freedoms that are at the core of the American way of life," the ACLU said on September 20.

Fundamental issues were at stake. Citizens expect a right of privacy in their homes and workplaces, but government intelligence analysts believed that they needed broader powers to wiretap phones and track e-mail. They sought new powers to search the homes and belongings of individuals suspected to have terrorist links, without informing the individuals in advance. The rationale behind all of this was that the government suspected that terrorists worked in secret cells. Conducting a search of one cell member's home might alert the others that the government was on to them and frustrate the government's ability to arrest all of the cell's members.

Civil libertarians worried that in its zeal to capture and interrogate potential terrorists, the government might violate the long-standing principle of habeas corpus. Literally translated as "you have the body," the principle traces its lineage back to the Magna Carta. A writ of habeas corpus, issued by a court, requires the government to bring a prisoner to court to show that it has reasonable cause for holding the person or the prisoner must be released. Federal officials said they believed that some potential terrorists should be held as "enemy combatants," which would allow them to be imprisoned indefinitely, without trial, to permit prolonged investigation and questioning. That, civil libertarians worried, would open the door to broad abuse of government power.

Congress did not come close to meeting Ashcroft's deadline, but it did complete its work in near-record time. The legislation's authors formally labeled it the "Uniting and Strengthening America by Providing Appropriate Tools Required to Intercept and Obstruct Terrorism Act"—or the "USA Patriot Act," surely one of the most clever and symbolically powerful Washington acronyms of all time. It not only found the right words to spell out the title for the act, but it wrapped the legislation in the cloak of patriotism, which the drafters hoped no one could resist in the frightening days after September 11. The bill won House approval on October 24. The Senate agreed the next day by a vote of 98–1, with Sen. Russ Feingold, D-Wis., casting the only "nay" vote. President Bush signed the bill promptly on October 26, just six weeks after the attacks. "Today, we take an essential step in defeating terrorism, while protecting the constitutional rights of all Americans," Bush said that morning. "With my signature, this law will give intelligence and law enforcement officials important new tools to fight a present danger."

The USA Patriot Act gives the federal government broad new powers to investigate and detain potential terrorists:

• It facilitates the tracking and gathering of information with new technologies. The law allows federal officials greater authority to use a kind of "secret caller ID," which can identify the source and destination of calls made to and from a particular telephone. Existing laws allowed such "trap and trace" orders for phone calls. The new law permits them for other electronic communications, including e-mail.

• The law permits "roving surveillance," which means that surveillance can occur without being limited to a particular place or instrument. In the past, court orders allowed surveillance only on telephones or places identified in advance. Since terrorists often change locations and sometimes discard cellular telephones after a single use, court orders could not keep up with their activities. The new law permits investigators to obtain authority to track targets as they move or switch phones and e-mails. It also allows investigators to obtain a court order to examine any "tangible item," rather than just business records. For example, investigators can probe voice mails and library records showing who borrowed which books.

• It increases federal authority to investigate money laundering. The new law requires financial institutions to keep more complete records of the financial activities of suspicious individuals and to allow federal investigators broader access to them. In the aftermath of September 11, federal officials had discovered that hundreds of thousands of dollars had flowed through the financial system to terrorist cells undetected, and they wanted stronger authority to trace this flow of money.

• The law strengthens the authority of border agents to prevent possible terrorists from entering the United States. It gives authorities greater power to detain and deport suspicious individuals and those suspected of supporting them. To signal that these provisions were not aimed at punishing foreigners, the law also provides humanitarian assistance for foreign victims of the September 11 attacks.

• The law defines a broad array of activities—terrorist attacks on mass transportation facilities, biological attacks, harboring of terrorists, money laundering to support terrorism, and fraudulent solicitation of money to support terrorism—as federal crimes. Federal officials were concerned that the ingenuity of terrorists had grown faster than criminal law, and they were intent on capturing the full range of terrorist activities as crimes.

• It allows so-called sneak-and-peek searches in which investigators can enter homes and facilities and conduct searches without informing those searched until sometime later. Under previous law, those searched had to be informed before the search began. Federal officials said that giving even a few minutes' notice might disrupt their investigations and tip off members of a terrorist cell. Sneak-and-peek searches, they said, permit more effective investigations.

• It expands the government's authority to prosecute computer hackers. Government officials increasingly worried that terrorists, or even ordinary hackers, would exploit vulnerabilities in the Internet to flood the system with e-mail or to damage computer records. With the growing dependence of the world economy on electronic commerce and communication, officials wanted to increase the system's protection against cyber-terror attacks and to provide stronger remedies to those hurt by hackers. Such attacks had not occurred on a broad scale at that point, but security analysts warned that the system was vulnerable and that they could occur in the future. Over the next few years, hackers proved them right.

Administration officials maintained that the USA Patriot Act gave the government valuable new powers that only terrorists needed to fear. The line, often repeated, was that the government needed the same power to investigate potential terrorists that it had long used to stop organized crime. Civil rights experts acknowledged the need for new government powers but worried that there were few checks on the new powers and that the government would push them too far. The government could conduct searches without informing those searched. It could hold prisoners without informing them of the charges or bringing them to trial. And the issue not only was *what* the government could do. It was also the uncertainty about how the new powers would be used and what protections citizens would have to ensure that government officials did not abuse those powers.

For the new wiretap and surveillance powers, the law created a "sunset" (an automatic expiration of the authority) at the end of 2005, unless

Congress extended them. Within an hour of Bush's signing the act, Ashcroft put ninety-four federal attorneys and fifty-six FBI field offices to work implementing its provisions. In September 2003, he hailed the Patriot Act as one of the Justice Department's best tools to "connect the dots" in fighting terrorist activity. Congress passed the law with overwhelming, bipartisan support. But almost immediately, critics began worrying about just how the government would use the act's new powers. . . .

In the months after the passage of the USA Patriot Act, worries about the ramifications of post-September 11 policies on civil rights and civil liberties steadily grew. Constant criticism from international human rights organizations of U.S. treatment of Taliban and al Qaeda prisoners failed to attract much attention within the United States. At least initially, many Americans were simply in no mood to worry about the possible mistreatment of those allied with the September 11 terrorists. For the USA Patriot Act, however, domestic criticism was broad based and sharp. The legislatures of Alaska and Hawaii passed resolutions condemning it. So did the councils of more than 160 local governments, including Baltimore, Denver, Detroit, Minneapolis, Oakland, San Francisco, and Seattle. Alaska Rep. Don Young, a Republican, said, "I think the Patriot Act was not really thought out." He added, "I'm very concerned that, in our desire for security and our enthusiasm for pursuing supposed terrorists, sometimes we might be on the verge of giving up the freedoms which we're trying to protect." Attorney General Ashcroft decided to meet the critics head-on by going on an eighteen-city speaking tour in August 2003 to sell the act and its accomplishments. It was an unusual tactic by such a senior official for a program that had been in place so long.

Critics on both the right and the left complained that Congress had rushed to judgment. They charged that, under heavy pressure to act, Congress had given too little attention to the measure's effects on civil rights and civil liberties. At the conservative Cato Institute, Robert A. Levy said that "Congress's rush job" had produced a bill that was "unconstitutionally vague" and dangerous. In fact, he charged, the bill gutted "much of the Fourth Amendment [the protection against unreasonable searches and seizures] in far less time than Congress typically expends on routine bills that raise no constitutional concerns." The Patriot Act, Levy said, did not provide sufficient judicial oversight to prevent possible abuses. He contended that the law was too broad and that it aggressively threatened the rights of individual citizens under the guise of protecting against terrorism. He worried that the sunset was too narrow and too long—that the law did not provide a sufficient opportunity to revisit the broad questions to see how well it was working. "Any attempt by government to chip away at constitutionally guaranteed rights must be subjected to the most painstaking scrutiny to determine whether less invasive means could accomplish the same ends. The USA-Patriot anti-terrorism bill does not survive that demanding test. In a free society, we deserve better," he concluded.

From the left came equally harsh criticism. "In its rush to pass the Patriot Act just six weeks after the September 11 attacks, Congress overlooked one of our most fundamental rights—the right to express our political beliefs, especially those that are controversial," said senior attorney Nancy Chang of the Center for Constitutional Rights, which filed suit to block the act. Chang added, "Now it is up to the judiciary to correct Congress's excesses." The ACLU filed its own suit against the Patriot Act, claiming that the provision allowing broader searches of "tangible things" was unconstitutional. Even librarians found themselves in the battle. They feared that the extensive powers the act gave the government to probe "tangible things" would enable federal investigators to examine the reading habits of their patrons without their knowledge or consent. These actions, the American Library Association (ALA) warned in a 2003 resolution, could "threaten civil rights and liberties guaranteed under the United States Constitution and Bill of Rights." That drew a retaliatory charge from Ashcroft, in the midst of his multicity campaign, that the ALA was fueling a "baseless hysteria."

The charges and countercharges finally led the Justice Department to release a count of how many times the "tangible thing" provision had been used in the act's first two years: zero. Department officials argued that this was evidence that the critics did not need to worry. The critics countered that if the provision had not been used at all, it could not have been important in the antiterror war. Rep. John Conyers Jr., D-Mich., said that "if this authority was not needed to investigate September 11," he wondered if "it should stay on the books any longer." . . .

Nevertheless, the USA Patriot Act was a highly unusual piece of federal legislation. Rarely had any public policy issue united critics from both conservative and liberal ends of the political spectrum. On the right, condemnation came from those who had long worried that a strong government might hinder the exercise of individual freedom. On the left, opponents were concerned that innocent individuals would be swept up in the administration's zeal to fight terrorists. Critics from both sides quietly suggested that the administration was using the war against terrorism to promote new governmental powers that Congress had rejected in years past. No one argued for being soft on terrorists, and no one wanted to risk another big attack, but many involved felt that some kind of line had to be drawn in the shifting sand of homeland security legislation. . . .

While the debate raged, there was widespread disagreement on just where to draw this line between the stronger powers the government said it needed and the protections of civil rights and civil liberties that had, for many decades, been fundamental to American democracy. Having stood atop the pile of debris that once had been the World Trade Center, inhaling the pungent smoke and surrounded by determined rescue workers, President Bush had developed an unshakable commitment to making the country as safe as possible. Civil libertarians, conservatives and liberals alike, worried that the post-September 11 changes could transform American society. The USA Patriot Act and the president's proposals for a second, stronger version, they feared, could have as lasting an impact on the country as the American Revolution. This time, however, the legacy would be one of enduring restrictions on liberty, the opposite of the legacy of freedom established by the nation's founders. Both sides knew that the struggle was titanic. Rarely does a nation face such fundamental choices about its future.

The debate gained steam as the issue developed. Unlike most public policy controversies, in which debate peaks during the congressional battle over proposed legislation and then wanes with time, concern about the Patriot Act only grew following its passage. The number of state and local governments passing resolutions against it swelled. The confidence of critics—and the concern of Bush administration officials—increased, in part because of what now appeared to be legitimate worry that in the weeks after September 11 high emotions had led Congress to pass the measure too quickly, without careful examination. As the act's details became clearer, they stirred up more worry. Moreover, as the immediate effects of September 11 faded slightly, so did concern about another imminent attack, and concerns about the threat to traditional liberties grew. Reports such as the one about the imprisonment of children at Guantanamo and the complaints of the librarians motivated critics to ask what the administration truly had in mind. The second wave of Bush administration proposals led both members of Congress and civil liberties activists to dig in for what they expected would be a protracted battle. . . .

"When dangers increase, liberties shrink. That has been our history, especially in wartime," explains Stuart Taylor Jr. Unquestionably, the nation must recalibrate the balance between liberty and security, but in determining how best to do so, Taylor argues, "We are also stuck in habits of mind that have not yet fully processed how dangerous our world has become or how ill-prepared our legal regime is to meet the new dangers."

This predicament proved especially devilish because the only way to know how low to set the security bar was to take a chance on an attack and risk the devastating consequences that could occur from miscalculation. After September 11, administration officials did not want to be in a position of having to defend themselves against charges that they failed to protect the nation ever again. They realized that there were risks to civil liberties in their approach, but they believed that they had to take those risks to secure the nation.

How could officials know whether they had gone too far? The absence of a terrorist attack might mean that the administration had calibrated its strategy just right, or simply that terrorists had changed their strategies and were planning something different. On the other hand, an attack could occur in the future because it is fundamentally impossible to protect everyone against everything all of the time. Even seemingly absurd and paranoid government restrictions on civil rights and civil liberties might not necessarily defend against all terrorist threats. It is impossible ever to know where best to set the balance—safety is no guarantee that the government did not go too far, and attack is not necessarily a sign that the government did not go far enough. As cases challenging the USA Patriot Act and the Bush administration's strategy of detaining prisoners in Guantanamo began wending their way through the federal courts, even some early proponents began worrying that the policies had gone too far.

Thus, homeland security is about setting a balance. Where that balance is set must ultimately be a political judgment, made by political officials through the rough-and-tumble debates of the political process. The tough and sometimes nasty battles over the USA Patriot Act in many ways represent the process at its best. With the nation tiptoeing into new problems it had never faced before, it needed to devise untested policies to solve uncertain issues. To make the problem even more devilish, it was one in which citizens, quite rightly, expected their public officials to provide them protection and safety in their homes and workplaces—as well as freedom and liberty in their daily lives.

51

RICHARD KLUGER

From *Simple Justice*

No Supreme Court case has so changed the United States as did Brown v. Board of Education of Topeka, Kansas (1954). Volumes have been written on Brown and the aftermath of Brown, but the best place to start is with Richard Kluger's classic work. The selection here focuses on Earl Warren, the chief justice who wrote the landmark decision. The case that would reverse Plessy v. Ferguson (1896) and the "separate but equal" doctrine that the Court had upheld for half a century, was waiting to be heard when the death of Chief Justice Fred Vinson put Warren on the Court. Kluger quotes Justice Frankfurter as saying on hearing of Vinson's death, "This is the first indication I have ever had that there is a God." Kluger explores the intricate process Warren faced in forging a majority, and eventually unanimity, for overturning "separate but equal." While those Americans who were born after Brown cannot remember a time when it was not the law of the land, Kluger takes us back to that thrilling moment of change.

———

IN THE TWO AND A HALF YEARS since they had last sat down to decide a major racial case, the Justices of the Supreme Court had not grown closer. Indeed, the philosophical and personal fissures in their ranks had widened since they had agreed—unanimously—to side with the Negro appellants in *Sweatt, McLaurin,* and *Henderson* in the spring of 1950. That had been a rare show of unanimity. By the 1952 Term, the Court was failing to reach a unanimous decision 81 percent of the time, nearly twice as high a percentage of disagreement as it had recorded a decade earlier. . . .

It was perhaps the most severely fractured Court in history—testament, on the face of it, to Vinson's failure as Chief Justice. Selected to lead the Court because of his skills as a conciliator, the low-key, mournful-visaged Kentuckian found that the issues before him were far different from, and far less readily negotiable than, the hard-edged problems he had faced as Franklin Roosevelt's ace economic troubleshooter and Harry Truman's Secretary of the Treasury and back-room confederate.

Fred Vinson's lot as Chief Justice . . . had not proven a happy one. . . .

What, then, could be expected of the deeply divided Vinson Court as it convened on the morning of December 13, 1952, to deliberate on the

transcendent case of *Brown v. Board of Education*? The earlier racial cases—
Sweatt and *McLaurin*—they had managed to cope with by chipping away
at the edges of Jim Crow but avoiding the real question of *Plessy's* continued validity.* The Court could no longer dodge that question, though it
might continue to stall in resolving it. Hovering over the Justices were all
the repressive bugaboos of the Cold War era. The civil rights of Negroes
and the civil liberties of political dissenters and criminal defendants were
prone to be scrambled together in the public mind, and every malcontent
was a sitting target for the red tar of anti-Americanism. No sector of the
nation was less hospitable to both civil-liberties and civil-rights claimants
than the segregating states of the South, and it was the South with which
the Justices had primarily to deal in confronting *Brown*....

And so they were divided. But given the gravity of the issue, they
were willing to take their time to try to reconcile their differences. They
clamped a precautionary lid on all their discussions of *Brown* as the year
turned and Fred Vinson swore in Dwight David Eisenhower as the thirty-
fourth President of the United States. The Justices seemed to make little
headway toward resolving the problem, but they all knew that a close vote
would likely be a disaster for Court and country alike. The problem of
welding the disparate views into a single one was obviously complicated
by the ambivalence afflicting the Court's presiding Justice. As spring came
and the end of the Court's 1952 Term neared, Fred Vinson seemed to be
in increasingly disagreeable and edgy spirits. Says one of the people at the
Court closest to him then: "I got the distinct impression that he was dis-
tressed over the Court's inability to find a strong, unified position on such
an important case."

What evidence there is suggests that those on or close to the Court
thought it was about as severely divided as it could be at this stage of its
deliberations....

During the last week of the term in June, the law clerks of all the
Justices met in an informal luncheon session and took a two-part poll.
Each clerk was asked how he would vote in the school-segregation cases
and how he thought his Justice would vote. According to one of their
number, a man who later became a professor of law: "The clerks were al-

---

*The Supreme Court in *Plessy v. Ferguson* (1896) interpreted the equal protection clause of
the Fourteenth Amendment to mean that the states could require separation of the races in
public institutions if these institutions were equal (the "separate but equal doctrine"). From
1937 until 1954 the Court subjected "separate but equal" to increasingly rigorous scrutiny. In
Sweatt v. Painter (1950) and *McLaurin v. Oklahoma State Regents* (1950), for example, the Court
invalidated specific state racial segregationist practices in higher education on grounds that
they did not permit truly equal access to black students. Yet, the Court had not overturned
Plessy.—EDS.

most unanimous for overruling *Plessy* and ordering desegregation, but, according to their impressions, the Court would have been closely divided if it had announced its decision at that time. Many of the clerks were only guessing at the positions of their respective Justices, but it appeared that a majority of the Justices would not have overruled *Plessy* but would have given some relief in some of the cases on the ground that the separate facilities were not in fact equal." ...

All such bets on the alignment of the Court ended abruptly a few days later when the single most fateful judicial event of that long summer occurred. In his Washington hotel apartment, Fred M. Vinson died of a heart attack at 3:15 in the morning of September 8 [1953]. He was sixty-three.

All the members of the Court attended Vinson's burial in Louisa, Kentucky, his ancestral home. But not all the members of the Court grieved equally at his passing. And one at least did not grieve at all. Felix Frankfurter had not much admired Fred Vinson as judge or man. And he was certain that the Chief Justice had been the chief obstacle to the Court's prospects of reaching a humanitarian and judicially defensible settlement of the monumental segregation cases. In view of Vinson's passing just before the *Brown* reargument, Frankfurter remarked to a former clerk, "This is the first indication I have ever had that there is a God." ... Fred Vinson was not yet cold in his grave when speculation rose well above a whisper as to whom President Eisenhower would pick to heal and lead the Supreme Court as it faced one of its most momentous decisions in the segregation cases....

Dwight Eisenhower's principal contribution to the civil rights of Americans would prove to be his selection of Earl Warren as Chief Justice—a decision Eisenhower would later say had been a mistake. The President was on hand, at any rate, on Monday, October 5, when just after noon the clerk of the Supreme Court read aloud the commission of the President that began, "Know ye: That reposing special trust and confidence in the wisdom, uprightness and learning of Earl Warren of California, I do appoint him Chief Justice of the United States.... " Warren stood up at the clerk's desk to the side of the bench and read aloud his oath of office. At the end, Clerk Harold Willey said to him, "So help you God." Warren said, "So help me God." Then he stepped quickly behind the velour curtains and re-emerged a moment later through the opening in the center to take the presiding seat. His entire worthy career to that moment would be dwarfed by what followed.... At the reargument, Earl Warren had said very little. The Chief Justice had put no substantive questions to any of the attorneys. Nor is it likely that he had given any indication of his views to the other Justices before they convened at the Saturday-morning conference on December 12. But then, speaking first, he made his views unmistakable.

Nearly twenty years later, he would recall, "I don't remember having any great doubts about which way it should go. It seemed to me a comparatively simple case. Just look at the various decisions that had been eroding *Plessy* for so many years. They kept chipping away at it rather than ever really facing it head-on. If you looked back—to *Gaines*, to *Sweatt*, to some of the interstate-commerce cases—you saw that the doctrine of separate-but-equal had been so eroded that only the *fact* of segregation itself remained unconsidered. On the merits, the natural, the logical, and practically the only way the case could be decided was clear. The question was *how* the decision was to be reached."

At least two sets of notes survive from the Justices' 1953 conference discussion of the segregation cases—extensive ones by Justice Burton and exceedingly scratchy and cryptic ones by Justice Frankfurter. They agree on the Chief Justice's remarks. The cases had been well argued, in his judgment, Earl Warren told the conference, and the government had been very frank in both its written and its oral presentations. He said he had of course been giving much thought to the entire question since coming to the Court, and after studying the briefs and relevant history and hearing the arguments, he could not escape the feeling that the Court had "finally arrived" at the moment when it now had to determine whether segregation was allowable in the public schools. Without saying it in so many words, the new Chief Justice was declaring that the Court's policy of delay, favored by his predecessor, could no longer be permitted.

The more he had pondered the question, Warren said, the more he had come to the conclusion that the doctrine of separate-but-equal rested upon the concept of the inferiority of the colored race. He did not see how *Plessy* and its progeny could be sustained on any other theory—and if the Court were to choose to sustain them, "we must do it on that basis," he was recorded by Burton as saying. He was concerned, to be sure, about the necessity of overruling earlier decisions and lines of reasoning, but he had concluded that segregation of Negro schoolchildren had to be ended. The law, he said in words noted by Frankfurter, "cannot in 'this day and age' set them apart." The law could not say, Burton recorded the Chief as asserting, that Negroes were "not entitled to *exactly same* treatment of all others." To do so would go against the intentions of the three Civil War amendments.

Unless any of the other four Justices who had indicated a year earlier their readiness to overturn segregation—Black, Douglas, Burton, and

Minton—had since changed his mind, Warren's opening remarks meant that a majority of the Court now stood ready to strike down the practice.

But to gain a narrow majority was no cause for exultation. A sharply divided Court, no matter which way it leaned, was an indecisive one, and for Warren to force a split decision out of it would have amounted to hardly more constructive leadership on this transcendent question than Fred Vinson had managed. The new Chief Justice wanted to unite the Court in *Brown*. . . .

He recognized that a number of Court precedents of long standing would be shattered in the process of overturning *Plessy*, and he regretted that necessity. It was the sort of reassuring medicine most welcomed by Burton and Minton, the least judicially and intellectually adventurous members of the Court.

He recognized that the Court's decision would have wide repercussions, varying in intensity from state to state, and that they would all therefore have to approach the matter in as tolerant and understanding a way as possible. Implicit in this was a call for flexibility in how the Court might frame its decree.

But overarching all these cushioning comments and a tribute to both his compassion as a man and his persuasive skills as a politician was the moral stance Earl Warren took at the outset of his remarks. Segregation, he had told his new colleagues, could be justified only by belief in the inferiority of the Negro; any of them who wished to perpetuate the practice, he implied, ought in candor to be willing to acknowledge as much. These were plain words, and they did not have to be hollered. They cut across all the legal theories that had been so endlessly aired and went straight to the human tissue at the core of the controversy. . . .

The Warren opinion was "finally approved" at the May 15 conference, Burton noted in his diary. The man from California had won the support of every member of the Court.

. . . Not long before the Court's decision in *Brown* was announced, Warren told *Ebony* magazine twenty years later, he had decided to spend a few days visiting Civil War monuments in Virginia. He went by automobile with a black chauffeur.

At the end of the first day, the Chief Justice's car pulled up at a hotel, where he had made arrangements to spend the night. Warren simply assumed that his chauffeur would stay somewhere else, presumably at a less expensive place. When the Chief Justice came out of his hotel the next morning to resume his tour, he soon figured out that the chauffeur had spent the night in the car. He asked the black man why.

"Well, Mr. Chief Justice," the chauffeur began, "I just couldn't find a place—couldn't find a place to ... "

Warren was stricken by his own thoughtlessness in bringing an employee of his to a town where lodgings were not available to the man solely because of his color. "I was embarrassed, I was ashamed," Warren recalled. "We turned back immediately. ... "

... In the press room on the ground floor, reporters filing in at the tail end of the morning were advised that May 17, 1954, looked like a quiet day at the Supreme Court of the United States.

All of the opinions of the Court were announced on Mondays in that era. The ritual was simple and unvarying. The Justices convened at noon. Lawyers seeking admission to the Supreme Court bar were presented to the Court by their sponsors, greeted briefly by the Chief Justice, and sworn in by the clerk of the Court. Then, in ascending order of seniority, the Justices with opinions to deliver read them aloud, every word usually, without much effort at dramaturgy. Concurrences and dissents were read after the majority opinion. And then the next case, and then the next. There was no applause; there were no catcalls. There were no television or newsreel cameras. There were no questions from the newsmen in the audience. There was no briefing session in the press room or the Justices' chambers after Court adjourned. There were no weekly press conferences. There were no appearances on *Meet the Press* the following Sunday. There were no press releases elaborating on what the Court had said or meant or done. The opinions themselves were all there was. ...

Down in the press room, as the first three routine opinions were distributed, it looked, as predicted, like a very quiet day at the Court. But then, as Douglas finished up, Clerk of the Court Harold Willey dispatched a pneumatic message to Banning E. Whittington, the Court's dour press officer. Whittington slipped on his suit jacket, advised the press-room contingent, "Reading of the segregation decisions is about to begin in the courtroom," added as he headed out the door that the text of the opinion would be distributed in the press room afterward, and then led the scrambling reporters in a dash up the marble stairs.

"I have for announcement," said Earl Warren, "the judgment and opinion of the Court in No. 1—*Oliver Brown et al. v. Board of Education of Topeka.*" It was 12:52 P.M. In the press room, the Associated Press wire carried the first word to the country: "Chief Justice Warren today began reading the Supreme Court's decision in the public school segregation cases. The court's ruling could not be determined immediately." The bells went off in every news room in America. The nation was listening.

It was Warren's first major opinion as Chief Justice. He read it, by all accounts, in a firm, clear, unemotional voice. If he had delivered no other opinion but this one, he would have won his place in American history. Considering its magnitude, it was a short opinion. During its first part, no one hearing it could tell where it would come out. . . .

Without in any way becoming technical and rhetorical, Warren then proceeded to demonstrate the dynamic nature and adaptive genius of American constitutional law. . . . Having declared its essential value to the nation's civic health and vitality, he then argued for the central importance of education in the private life and aspirations of every individual. . . . That led finally to the critical question: "Does segregation of children in public schools solely on the basis of race . . . deprive the children of the minority group of equal educational opportunities?"

To this point, nearly two-thirds through the opinion, Warren had not tipped his hand. Now, in the next sentence, he showed it by answering that critical question: "We believe that it does." . . .

This finding flew directly in the face of *Plessy*. And here, finally, Warren collided with the 1896 decision. . . .

The balance of the Chief Justice's opinion consisted of just two paragraphs. The first began: "We conclude"—and here Warren departed from the printed text before him to insert the word "unanimously," which sent a sound of muffled astonishment eddying around the courtroom—"that in the field of public education the doctrine of 'separate but equal' has no place. Separate educational facilities are inherently unequal." The plaintiffs and others similarly situated—technically meaning Negro children within the segregated school districts under challenge—were therefore being deprived of the equal protection of the laws guaranteed by the Fourteenth Amendment.

The concluding paragraph of the opinion revealed Earl Warren's political adroitness both at compromise and at the ready use of the power of his office for ends he thought worthy. "Because these are class actions, because of the wide applicability of this decision, and because of the great variety of local conditions," he declared, "these cases present problems of considerable complexity. . . . In order that we may have the full assistance of the parties in formulating decrees," the Court was scheduling further argument for the term beginning the following fall. The attorneys general of the United States and all the states requiring or permitting segregation in public education were invited to participate. In a few strokes, Warren thus managed to (1) proclaim "the wide applicability" of the decision and make it plain that the Court had no intention of limiting its benefits to a handful of plaintiffs in a few outlying districts; (2) reassure

the South that the Court understood the emotional wrench desegregation would cause and was therefore granting the region some time to get
accustomed to the idea; and (3) invite the South to participate in the en-
tombing of Jim Crow by joining the Court's efforts to fashion a temper-
ate implementation decree—or to forfeit that chance by petulantly ab-
staining from the Court's further deliberations and thereby run the risk of
having a harsh decree imposed upon it. It was such dexterous use of the
power available to him and of the circumstances in which to exploit it
that had established John Marshall as a judicial statesman and political
tactician of the most formidable sort. The Court had not seen his like
since. Earl Warren, in his first major opinion, moved now with that same
sure purposefulness. . . .

It was 1:20 P.M. The wire services proclaimed the news to the nation.
Within the hour, the Voice of America would begin beaming word to
the world in thirty-four languages: In the United States, schoolchildren
could no longer be segregated by race. The law of the land no longer
recognized a separate equality. No Americans were more equal than any
other Americans.

52

CHARLES OGLETREE

From *All Deliberate Speed*

The impact of the Supreme Court case, Brown v. Board of Education, *certainly did not end in 1954 when the decision was handed down. Legal scholar Charles Ogletree picks up the story of* Brown *with the events after the landmark decision. Ogletree looks at* Brown II, *the subsequent decision that required school desegregation "with all deliberate speed." Contrary to common belief, the real meaning of this phrase, Ogletree asserts, is that change could come slowly, not right away. Ogletree then takes readers decades ahead to three classic civil rights cases based on affirmative action. He explores the 1978* Bakke *decision and the more recent 2003* Gratz *and* Grutter *cases from the University of Michigan: the issues in all three involve the value of diversity and the means to achieve it. To close the excerpt, Ogletree looks ahead to the way in which all these cases may affect education in the United States in the coming decades. The meaning of "all deliberate speed" has proven crucial to the lives of millions of American young people.*

———

ON MAY 17, 1954, AN OTHERWISE UNEVENTFUL Monday afternoon, fifteen months into Dwight D. Eisenhower's presidency, Chief Justice Earl Warren, speaking on behalf of a unanimous Supreme Court, issued a historic ruling that he and his colleagues hoped would irrevocably change the social fabric of the United States. "We conclude that in the field of public education the doctrine of 'separate-but-equal' has no place. Separate educational facilities are inherently unequal." Thurgood Marshall, who had passionately argued the case before the Court, joined a jubilant throng of other civil rights leaders in hailing this decision as the Court's most significant opinion of the twentieth century. The *New York Times* extolled the *Brown* decision as having "reaffirmed its faith and the underlying American faith in the equality of all men and all children before the law." . . .

At the time, no one doubted the far-reaching implications of the Court's ruling. The *Brown* lawyers had apparently accomplished what politicians, scholars, and others could not—an unparalleled victory that would create a nation of equal justice under the law. The Court's decision seemed to call for a new era in which black children and white children would have equal opportunities to achieve the proverbial American Dream. It did not come too soon for the families whose children were victims of segregation. . . .

Having broadly proclaimed its support of desegregating public schools, the Supreme Court shortly thereafter issued [a second] opinion [*Brown II*]—the opinion that legitimized much of the social upheaval that forms the central theme of this book. Fearful that southern segregationists, as well as the executive and legislative branches of state and federal governments, would both resist and impede this courageous decision, the Court offered a palliative to those opposed to *Brown's* directive. Speaking again with one voice, the Court concluded that, to achieve the goal of desegregation, the lower federal courts were to "enter such orders and decrees consistent with this opinion as are necessary and proper to admit to public schools on a racially nondiscriminatory basis *with all deliberate speed* the parties to these cases."

As Thurgood Marshall and other civil rights lawyers pondered the second decision, they tried to ascertain what the Court meant in adding the crucial phrase "all deliberate speed" to its opinion. It is reported that, after the lawyers read the decision, a staff member consulted a dictionary to confirm their worst fears—that the "all deliberate speed" language meant "slow" and that the apparent victory was compromised because resisters were allowed to end segregation on their own timetable. These three critical words would indeed turn out to be of great consequence, in that they ignore the urgency on which the *Brown* lawyers insisted. When asked to explain his view of "all deliberate speed," Thurgood Marshall frequently told anyone who would listen that the term meant S-L-O-W. . . .

Nearly twenty-five years after the landmark *Brown* decision, a major challenge to its underlying principles of equality in education was emerging. The timing was significant for me in that I was among the large wave of first-generation African-Americans going to college and graduate school. Even though *Brown* paved the way by removing the barrier of segregated educational systems, it remained to be seen who would now have the opportunity to attend the prestigious institutions that had been substantially, if not completely, closed to African-Americans. While the battle for integration continued in the courtrooms around America, the shocking assassination of Martin Luther King, Jr., in April 1968, triggered a chain reaction of nationwide black protest; it also forced many institutions to open their doors much faster than they had contemplated. Harvard Law School was no different. A private institution, it claimed that its doors had always been open to people regardless of color (although women were not admitted until 1953), and it could point out that George Lewis Ruffin, an African-American, had graduated from the law school in 1869 (which, coincidentally, was the year that Howard Law School was founded), but there was still no real effort to seek out and admit African-Americans. . . .

When I arrived in the fall of 1975, Harvard Law School was admitting fifty to sixty African-American students each year, nearly 10 percent of its entering class. Harvard was, in fact, admitting more African-American students than any of its peer institutions and, with the exception of Howard Law School, was at the top of all law schools in the number of minority students enrolled. Some twenty-five years after *Brown*, diversity appeared to be a permanent part of Harvard's educational mission. Our sense of comfort was nearly shattered, however, when Allan Bakke, a white student who had applied to the University of California at Davis Medical School and been rejected, filed a suit challenging an admissions program that affirmatively recruited and admitted African-American and Chicano applicants. The lawsuit called the *Brown* case into question, and squarely raised the issue of what public institutions could do, or not do, to increase the deplorably low representation of minorities in their universities and graduate schools. . . .

In *Bakke*, Justice Powell asserted that Title VI of the Civil Rights Act of 1964 proscribed only racial classifications that would be unconstitutional if used by a state. He applied strict scrutiny and concluded that, although achieving a diverse student body constituted a compelling state interest, the California program was not narrowly tailored to meet that end. He upheld the aspect of the UC Davis plan as that allowed the consideration of diversity, as articulated in the Harvard plan, as one factor, in selecting a class of students to pursue higher education. . . .

What differentiates *Brown* from *Bakke* is the forced abandonment of a legal and intellectual justification of integration based on remedying past discrimination. *Bakke* placed the legitimacy of affirmative action in universities squarely on educational diversity rather than on remedial aims. . . .

I routinely discuss legal, personal, and social issues with my friend John Payton, and in 1997, John called with some exciting news. His law firm had been approached by the University of Michigan to represent it in a lawsuit filed by some white applicants who had unsuccessfully applied to Michigan's law school and undergraduate program. The white applicants were represented by the Center for Individual Rights (CIR), a conservative Washington, D.C.-based organization. . . .

The Michigan lawsuits demanded, among other things, the end to any program that considered an applicant's race, the immediate admission of those whites who were allegedly qualified and denied admission, and money damages. . . .

The civil rights community and those private and public universities committed to maintaining a diverse pool of applicants for their institutions learned some painful lessons from the *Bakke* case, and they decided to develop a more focused effort this time around. More than 150 groups filed briefs in support of the Michigan diversity plan; they included law schools, universities, members of Congress, and corporations. Retired members of the armed forces, reporting that the military could not have credibility without an affirmative action plan that recruited minority officers into its ranks, filed a highly influential brief. Their brief caused a stir, in that it went against the public position of President George W. Bush, who filed a brief opposing the Michigan plan and labeled it a quota. There were further splits within the Republican ranks, as the highest-ranked and best-known African-Americans in the Bush administration, Colin Powell and Condoleezza Rice, also supported diversity and, in Powell's case, supported Michigan explicitly. Despite all of this external agitation, only nine votes counted, and I was carefully counting to see whether we could muster five votes. . . .

In *Gratz v. Bollinger* and *Grutter v. Bollinger*, the Supreme Court answered the central question, debated since *Bakke*, of the propriety of university or college affirmative action programs. The results were, at best, a moderate success for affirmative action. They remain, in the context of the Court's jurisprudence on race- and economic-based educational programs, an important setback to the mission established in *Brown*. By a vote of 5 to 4, the Court upheld the Michigan Law School's affirmative action plan. By a vote of 6 to 3, it held that the undergraduate program was tantamount to a quota system, and unconstitutional. It was a day to celebrate, largely because a contrary decision in the law school case would have been unfathomable.

In *Grutter*, O'Connor presented a robust endorsement of the principle of diversity as a factor in university admissions. Justice O'Connor not only endorsed Justice Powell's broad mandate in *Bakke* but went even further in embracing the significance of diversity in the *Grutter* decision:

> Justice Powell emphasized that *nothing less* than the "nation's future depends upon leaders trained through wide exposure to the ideas and mores of students as diverse as this Nation of many peoples."

So long as the admissions program does not constitute the type of quota system of "racial balancing" outlawed by *Bakke*, it may admit a "critical mass" of minority students in an effort to obtain a racially diverse student body. Educational institutions are permitted to use race as a factor (in the words of *Bakke*, quoted in *Grutter*, as a "plus") in minority admissions, so long as the decision to admit the student is "flexible enough to ensure that each applicant is evaluated as an individual and not in a way that makes an applicant's race or ethnicity the defining feature of his or her application."

In the *Gratz* opinion, Chief Justice Rehnquist, writing for a 6-to-3 majority, found the undergraduate admissions program unconstitutional. He was joined by the conservative justices Scalia, Kennedy, O'Connor, and Thomas. The centrist justice Breyer concurred in the judgment of the Court while not joining the chief justice's opinion. The chief justice found that awarding a blanket score—in this case, 20 points, or just over 13 percent of the maximum 150 points used to rank applicants—ensured that the university would admit all qualified minority applicants. He held that the scoring system, "by setting up automatic, predetermined point allocations for the soft variables [including race], ensures that the diversity contributions of applicants cannot be individually assessed." The university's failure to consider individualized features of the diversity of each applicant rendered its affirmative action plan unconstitutional and required the Court to strike it down.

Grutter held that attainment of the educational benefits flowing from diversity (such as promoting cross-racial understanding that breaks down racial stereotypes) constitutes a compelling interest, and deferred to the university's determination that diversity is essential to its educational mission. The law school's position was further bolstered by numerous expert studies and reports, as well as the experience of major American businesses, retired military officers, and civilian military officials. Finally, universities and, more especially, law schools are training grounds for future leaders, and "the path to leadership must be visibly open to talented and qualified individuals of every race and ethnicity."

Moreover, the individualized consideration, the absence of quotas, and the recognition of diversity stemming from sources other than race (all of which resemble the Harvard approach that Justice Powell praised in *Bakke*) render the plan narrowly tailored. However, affirmative action must be limited in time, and the Court expects it will no longer be necessary twenty-five years from now. . . .

Collectively, *Grutter* and *Gratz* preserved the institution of affirmative action in American higher education and, to that extent, are important. Nonetheless, both cases—*Grutter* by what it did *not* say and *Gratz* by what it *did* say—are troubling in that they will likely fail to be the catalysts for dispensing with the "all deliberate speed" mentality adopted in *Brown*. With the decisions, the Court did not erect a further barrier in the path of the struggle to true integration and equality; it also did little to promote that struggle. . . .

. . . My fear that *Brown's* vision is being accomplished only with "all deliberate speed" is now supplanted by my greater fear that resegregation of public education is occurring at a faster pace. While we celebrate the Michigan decision as a vindication of the principles articulated in *Brown*, we must also be vigilant to make sure that the progress of fifty years is not compromised any further. . . .

Racial segregation today is the result of a complicated mix of social, political, legal, and economic factors, rather than the result of direct state commands ordering racial separation. Yet, whatever the causes, it remains overwhelmingly true that black and Latino children in central cities are educated in virtually all-minority schools with decidedly inferior facilities and educational opportunities. Even when students in suburban and rural schools are included, a majority of black and Latino students around the country still attend predominantly minority schools.

The effective compromise reached in the United States at the close of the twentieth century is that schools may be segregated by race as long as it is not due to direct government fiat. Furthermore, although *Brown I* emphasized that equal educational opportunity was a crucial component of citizenship, there is no federal constitutional requirement that pupils in predominantly minority school districts receive the same quality of education as students in wealthier, largely all-white suburban districts. Although these suburban districts appear as healthy as ever, the public school system in many urban areas is on the brink of collapse. Increasing numbers of parents who live in these urban areas are pushing for charter schools, home schooling, or vouchers for private schools in order to avoid traditional public school education. At the start of the twenty-first century, the principle of *Brown* seems as hallowed as ever, but its practical effect seems increasingly irrelevant to contemporary public schooling.

Indeed, the United States has been in a period of resegregation for some time now. Resegregation is strongly correlated with class and with poverty. Today, white children attend schools where 80 percent of the student body is also white, resulting in the highest level of segregation of any group. Only 15 percent of segregated white schools are in areas of concentrated poverty; over 85 percent of segregated black and Latino schools are. Schools in high-poverty areas routinely show lower levels of educational performance; even well-prepared students with stable family backgrounds are hurt academically by attending such schools.

U.S. public schools as a whole are becoming more nonwhite as minority enrollment approaches 40 percent of all students, nearly twice the percentage in the 1960s. In the western and southern regions of the country, almost half of all students are minorities. In today's schools, blacks make up only 8.6 percent of the average white student's school, and just over 10 percent of white students attend schools that have a predominantly minority population. Even more striking is the fact that over 37 percent of black and Latino students attend 90-100 percent minority schools.

This trend has led to the emergence of a substantial number of public schools where the student body is almost entirely nonwhite. The 2000 United States Department of Calculation data showed that there has been a very rapid increase in the number of multiracial schools where three different racial groups comprise at least one-tenth of the total enrollment. However, these schools are attended by only 14 percent of white children. Most of the shrinking white enrollment occurs in the nation's largest city school systems.

Minority segregated schools have much higher concentrations of poverty and much lower average test scores, lower levels of student and teacher qualifications, and fewer advanced courses. They are often plagued by limited resources and social and health problems. High-poverty schools have been shown to increase educational inequality for the students who attend them because of such problems as a lack of resources, shortage of qualified teachers, lower parent involvement, and higher teacher turnover. Almost half of the students in schools attended by the average black or Latino student are poor or nearly poor. By contrast, less than one student in five in schools attended by the average white student is classified as poor. As Gary Orfield, co-director of the Civil Rights Project (CRP) at Harvard University, and Susan E. Eaton, researcher at CRP, note, "Nine times in ten, an extremely segregated black and Latino school will also be a high-poverty school. And studies have shown that high-poverty schools are overburdened, have high rates of turnover, less qualified and experienced teachers, and operate a world away from mainstream society." . . .

Certainly, there must be some form of social change on the education front. Whether this occurs through separation or in an integrated environment is a matter of great consequence for American society. Our experiment with integration started with a pronouncement, half a century ago in *Brown*, that integration was an important value with positive social consequences that should be embraced by all Americans. Twenty years later, real action to integrate our schools had only just started. We are but one generation into an integrated society, and the signs are that the majority of the population is tired with the process. Those at the top want to stay there, and those in the middle would rather hold on to what they have than give a little to get a lot. We have to decide whether this is a country that is comfortable with discrimination. Are we satisfied with the fact that many whites find minorities so repellent that they will move and change their children's schooling to avoid us? For, make no mistake, that is what underpins the supposedly "rational" decisions based on racial stereotyping: an inability on the part of the majority of Americans to acknowledge that minority citizens are "just like us."

There is little surprise in acknowledging that there was substantial resistance by the white community to integration and later to affirmative action. But the theory of interest convergence suggests that most Americans cannot be bothered to engage that problem unless it directly affects them. They would rather turn away, uninterested, and perpetuate racial disadvantage than acknowledge it, let alone confront it. We have witnessed the *Brown* decision, followed by *Bakke* and, more recently, *Grutter v. Bollinger*. We have witnessed Dr. King's historic "I Have a Dream" speech and his subsequent assassination. We have heard the powerful words of President Johnson in his commitment to affirmative action, and President Bush's criticism of the Michigan plan as a program promoting racial preferences. We have seen diversity plans approved by the Supreme Court and, in the same year, some HBCUs [historically black colleges and universities] lose their accreditation and close. We continue to make progress, and suffer setbacks, in grappling with the persistent problem of race in America. But we must remain vigilant in our commitment to confront racial inequalities, even when we face persistent, even increasing resistance. . . .

The decision in *Brown I*, ending segregation in our public schools—and by implication de jure segregation everywhere—is justly celebrated as one of the great events in our legal and political history. Precedent did not compel the result, nor was the composition of the Court indicative of a favorable outcome. There is no doubt that the circumstances of many African-Americans are better now than they were before the *Brown* decision. But the speed with which we have embraced the society made possible by *Brown I* has indeed been all too deliberate. It has been deliberate meaning "slow," "cautious," "wary," as if Americans remained to be convinced of the integration ideal. It has been deliberate in the sense of "ponderous" or "awkward," as if each step had been taken painfully and at great cost. Yet the speed with which we have embraced integration has not been deliberate in the sense of "thoughtful" or "reflective"—on the contrary, our response has been emotional and instinctive, perhaps on both sides of the debate. These reactions, anticipated and epitomized in *Brown II*, I suggest, are the real legacy of *Brown I*.

It would be foolhardy to deny that progress has been made, or to dismiss the reality that *Brown I* is a momentous decision both for what it says and for what it has achieved. But there is more yet to do. *Brown I* should be celebrated for ending de jure segregation in this country—a blight that lasted almost four hundred years and harmed millions of Americans of all races. Far too many African-Americans, however, have been left behind, while only a relative few have truly prospered. For some, the promise of integration has proved ephemeral. For others, short-term gains have been replaced by setbacks engendered by new forms of racism. School districts, briefly integrated, have become resegregated. Some distinctively African-American institutions have been permanently destroyed and others crippled. As we stand near the end or the transformation of affirmative action, things look set to get worse, not better.

For all their clear vision of the need to end segregation, *Brown I* and *II* stand as decisions that see integration as a solution that is embraced only grudgingly. Subsequent courts do not even seem to recognize integration as an imperative. And that, perhaps, is the worst indictment of the *Brown* decisions: their faith in progress and their failure to see how quickly people of a different mind could not only resist but, once the tide had turned, even reverse the halting progress toward a fully integrated society. . . .

53

CRAIG RIMMERMAN

From *The Lesbian and Gay Movements*

The past decade has brought much attention to issues involving the gay and lesbian community. Noted political science professor Craig Rimmerman mentions the "tangible accomplishments" that have occurred, both in changing public attitudes and in changing laws. His pessimism about the possibility of gay marriage, expressed in this book published in 2008, may well be replaced by a degree of optimism as gay marriage has now become legal in several states. Rimmerman considers two different approaches to achieving lesbian and gay rights: the "assimilationist" and the "liberationist." Proponents of slow, evolutionary legal change—assimilationists—advocate a different strategy than the more confrontational liberationists. Rimmerman proposes that both strategies be used, and just a few short years after he wrote, changes are happening, although not without some push-back from traditionalists.

THIS IS A PARTICULARLY AUSPICIOUS TIME to engage in . . . critical examination, . . . given the cultural visibility that lesbians, gays, bisexuals, and those who are transgendered have faced in recent years. This cultural visibility has been increasingly reflected in an array of popular television shows, including *The L Word, Queer as Folk, Six Feet Under, Will and Grace, The Sopranos, Rescue Me, Nip/Tuck, Buffy the Vampire Slayer, OZ, NYPD Blue,* and *The Shield,* to name a few. And when a moving, mainstream Hollywood film, *Brokeback Mountain,* receives considerable critical praise from reviewers and enthusiastic attention by the moviegoing public, one recognizes the sea change that has taken place since even the mid-1990s. But what does this visibility really mean in terms of people's daily lives? In recent years we have seen increased public tolerance and support for people coming out of the closet. The students I teach now are more likely to be supportive of their "out" peers than others were even ten years ago. And courses related to the lesbian and gay movements across academic disciplines are often among the most popular offerings on college campuses. This undoubtedly reflects the political organizing and education of earlier eras and the salience of these complicated and challenging issues for young people's lives.

At the same time, the lesbian and gay movements have achieved tangible accomplishments in the political arena at all levels of government, but especially in communities throughout the United States. For example, there are open communities of lesbians and gay men in urban areas throughout the United States. In addition, openly gay men and lesbians have been successful in the electoral arena, as they have been elected to city councils, state legislatures, and the U.S. Congress. Community organizations and businesses target the interests of the lesbian and gay movements. And some progress has been made through the legal system, most notably in the Supreme Court's 2003 *Lawrence v. Texas* decision that essentially ruled state sodomy laws unconstitutional.

But for all of the so-called progress, lesbians and gay men remain second-class citizens in vital ways. Fewer than one-tenth of 1 percent of all elected officials in the United States are openly lesbian, gay, or bisexual; very few transgendered people have been elected to public office. Lesbians and gay men are forbidden to marry, to teach in many public schools, to adopt children, to provide foster care, and to serve in the armed forces, National Guard, reserves, and the ROTC. If evicted from their homes, expelled from their schools, fired from their jobs, or refused public lodging, they usually are not able to seek legal redress. The topic of homosexuality is often deemed inappropriate for discussion in public schools, including in sex education courses. Many public school libraries refuse to own some of the many books that address the issue in important ways. Lesbians and gays are often reviled by the church and barred from membership in the clergy. They are the victims of hate crimes and targets of verbal abuse, and the possibility still exists that they will be beaten, threatened, attacked, or killed for simply loving another human being. And there is still no national hate-crimes legislation.* Their parents reject them, and many gay youth have either attempted or contemplated suicide. Indeed, one political scientist concludes that "no other group of persons in American society today, having been convicted of no crime, is subject to the number and severity of legally imposed disabilities as are persons of same-sex orientation."

What does all of this mean for how the contemporary lesbian and gay movements conceive of their political organizing strategies, especially

---

*In 2009, after four previous attempts, Congress passed and President Barack Obama signed a national anti-hate crimes bill into law. Officially called the Matthew Shepard and James Byrd, Jr. Hate Crimes Prevention Act, after the two men who died horrific deaths because of sexual orientation (Shepard) and race (Byrd), the bill expanded the 1969 federal hate-crimes law to include crimes motivated by a victim's actual or perceived gender, sexual orientation, gender identity or disability. The act gave federal authorities greater ability to prosecute hate crimes and provided $5 million a year in funding to help state and local agencies pay for investigating and prosecuting hate crimes. —EDS.

given the determination by the Christian Right to use lesbian and gay issues, such as same-sex marriage, as wedge issues in elections at all levels of government? Should policy and cultural change reflect a top-down model, or should it be inspired by grassroots organizing in local communities throughout the United States? And should the goal be a more assimilationist, rights-based approach to political and social change, or should movement activists embrace a more liberationist, revolutionary model, one that might embrace a full range of progressive causes? This last question is the central dilemma of this book, given how the assimilationist and liberationist approaches have been integral to the lesbian and gay movements' organizing over the past sixty years.

Throughout their relatively short history, the lesbian and gay movements in the United States have endured searing conflicts over whether to embrace the assimilationist or liberationist strategy. . . . The assimilationist approach typically embraces a rights-based perspective, works within the broader framework of pluralist democracy—one situated within classical liberalism—and fights for a seat at the table. In doing so, the assimilationists celebrate the "work within the system" insider approach to political and social change. Typically, they espouse a "let us in" approach to political activism, rather than the "let us show you a new way of conceiving the world" strategy associated with lesbian and gay liberation. Assimilationists are more likely to accept that change will have to be incremental and to understand that slow, gradual progress is built into the very structure of the U.S. framework of government. In this way, they typically embrace an insider approach to political change.

A second approach, the liberationist perspective, favors more radical cultural change, change that is transformational in nature and often arises outside the formal structures of the U.S. political system. Liberationists argue that there is a considerable gap between access and power and that it is simply not enough to have a seat at the table. For many liberationists, what is required is a shift in emphasis from a purely political strategy to one that embraces both structural political and cultural change, often through "outsider" political strategies. The notion of sexual citizenship embraced by liberationist activists and theorists is much more broadly conceived, as sociologist Steven Seidman describes: "Buoyed by their gains, and pressured by liberationists, the gay movement is slowly, if unevenly, expanding its political scope to fighting for full social equality—in the state, in schools, health-care systems, businesses, churches, and families." Political theorist Shane Phelan claims that liberationists often "attempt to subvert the hierarchies of the hegemonic order, pointing out the gaps and contradictions in that order, thus removing the privilege of innocence from the dominant group." As I will demonstrate, the assimilationist and liberationist strategies are not mutually exclusive....

In Laramie, Wyoming, on the night of October 6, 1998, a twenty-one-year-old gay University of Wyoming senior stopped in downtown Laramie for a drink at the Fireside Bar. One day later, that same student was found by a mountain biker "lashed to a fence on the outskirts of town, beaten, pistol-whipped, unconscious, and barely breathing." The young man never regained consciousness and died five days later, on October 12. His name was Matthew Shepard. His murder, funeral, and the subsequent trials of his killers—Russell Henderson and Aaron McKinney—received international attention. His killers, also from Laramie, were in their early twenties, like the young man whom they had brutally murdered.

Why did his murder happen? One explanation offered in the aftermath of the murder is that Matthew made a pass at his killers in a space that had become known as a "hospitable" place for lesbians and gays to gather, to share a drink, and to find the kind of community and solace that bars have often provided in the face of a hostile world. But another more important explanation is it occurred because we live in a country where we do not provide the young with appropriate education at all levels regarding the importance of respecting and understanding racial, gender, and sexual-orientation differences. As one of my colleagues said to me in the wake of the murder, "This underscores the crucial importance of education." Had Russell Henderson and Aaron McKinney been given the opportunity to confront their anxieties regarding their own sexualities and their views of those who fall outside the "heterosexual norm" in an educational setting many years before, perhaps the murder would not have happened. And had we had national hate-crimes legislation on the books that applied to bias crimes related to the victim's sexual orientation, perhaps the crime might not have occurred, and even if it had, we would have had a clear policy regarding how to punish the perpetrators. But . . . we also live in a country where people who are lesbian, gay, bisexual, and transgender are reviled and targeted by many. For example, soon after Matthew Shepard's death, Fred Phelps, a defrocked minister from Kansas and creator of the Internet site GODHatesFags.com, "faxed reporters images of the signs he and his followers intended to carry at the funeral: 'Fag Matt in Hell,' 'God Hates Fags,' 'No Tears for Queers.'" The media's coverage of Phelps's attacks publicized his hatred and vitriol, thus giving them more attention than they deserved. Not to be outdone, in the wake of the September 11 attacks, the late Rev. Jerry Falwell, founder of the Moral Majority, said on the Rev. Pat Robertson's *700 Club* television show, "I really believe that the pagans and the abortionists, and the feminists, and the gays and the lesbians who are actually trying to make that an alternative lifestyle, the ACLU, People for the American Way, all of them who have tried to secularize America, I point the finger in their face and say 'you helped this happen.'" His remarks were publicized and denounced by many, though once again the media saw fit to highlight them at a particularly difficult time for the country and the world. The revulsion expressed by Phelps and Falwell is reflected in the public debates that we have had about sex education, HIV/AIDS, military integration, and same-sex marriage (to name just a few of the most contentious issues) and in our laws. We are a country that forbids openly lesbian and gay people to get married, to serve in the military, to teach in our schools in many places, and, in most states, to adopt children as well. It is no surprise, then, that the laws that we have crafted as a nation reflect a country that is and has been retrograde in its ability to have open, honest, mature, and dignified discussions of many of the issues underlying this book....

... [M]uch of the work of the contemporary national lesbian and gay organizations has relied on an insider assimilationist strategy, one that strives for access to those in power and is rooted in an interest-group and legislative-lobbying approach to change. The strategy is largely based on civil rights, legal reform, legitimation, political access, and visibility. It is an approach that works within the political and economic framework that is associated with our classical liberal ideology. And it highlights the importance of allowing lesbians, gays, and bisexuals (but rarely those who are transgender) to have access to power and to have a seat at the table. This strategy often emphasizes national-level policymaking as opposed to organizing at the grassroots level, though in recent years the mainstream lesbian and gay movements have increasingly recognized the importance of organizing and educating at the local level.

The assimilationist approach recognizes that the American political system and the policy process growing out of that system are characterized by slow, gradual, incremental change. One way of thinking of political, policy, and cultural change is to think of it in terms of cycles of change. Incremental change means "creeping along" the path to reform, whereas more radical change means "leaping" toward more radical goals. The period of "creeping" is often associated with "strategic incoherence" on the part of social movements. Assimilationists are typically more patient with creeping toward long-term movement goals, whereas liberationists are more likely to try to force more radical and ambitious structural challenges to the system at large. The lesbian and gay movements have witnessed cycles of creeping change and cycles of leaping change throughout their history. There have been three key moments of "leaping change" throughout the development of the lesbian and gay movements. The first leap forward occurred in the 1950s with the founding of the Mattachine Society and the Daughters of Bilitis, organizations that engaged in acts of courage and resistance, especially given the context of the times. By the time of the 1969 Stonewall Riot* another great leaping moment, the rights-based strategy called for by the Mattachine Society and the Daughters of Bilitis seemed too assimilationist in the face of greater liberationist calls for change. The third major leap forward was framed "by the 1987 March on Washington and the debate over the military exclusion policy in 1993. Like gay liberation of the Stonewall era, activists in these years frequently used militant direct action tactics. But unlike the two earlier periods of leaping ahead, this one witnessed movement and community organizations sinking secure roots in every region of the country." We are now clearly in a period of creeping political, social, and policy change....

... Same-sex marriage is the issue that has dwarfed nearly all others on the lesbian and gay movements' policy agenda in recent years. For a positive interpretation of the progress made in the fight for same-sex marriage and how that progress connects to larger movements' accomplishments, political scientist David Rayside claims:

The United States is an unusual case, in part because of the extraordinary range of legal and political outcomes across states and localities. It is also unusual in several characteristics that impede the march to equity. But it is not as exceptional as is widely believed. A great majority of Americans now believe in extending recognition to lesbian and gay couples, if only a minority favor marriage. Most large corporations extend their family benefits coverage to the same-sex partners of employees. A steadily growing number of U.S. states and municipalities extend some form of recognition to such partners of their own employees. Openly lesbian and gay characters make regular appearances on American television dramas, even if their portrayals have limitations. In everyday life, sexual diversity is as visible in American society as in any. And across a wide range of regions and localities in the United States, countless lesbians, gays, bisexuals, and the transgendered are asserting their right to be visible....

But if the rights-based assimilationist strategy has provided us with the "virtual equality" that ... liberationists deride, then why might the movements want to embrace a more fully developed liberationist strategy

---

*The events at New York City's Stonewall Inn in 1969 mark the beginning of the modern gay rights movement. Police arrived at the bar to hassle gay patrons, and a violent confrontation ensued which continued for several days. After the Stonewall raid, gay and lesbian residents began to organize to prevent further harassment.—EDs.

and policy agenda? And what would such a strategy and agenda look like in practice? One scholar-activist offers an insightful overview of the challenges facing those who embrace a liberationist approach:

> Queer radicals today face a dilemma. Should we try to steer the mainstream GLBT [gay, lesbian, bisexual, transgender] movement in a more progressive direction or work with other progressive activists in groups that are not queer-focused? Can—and should—a movement focused on gay and lesbian identity expand to encompass a full range of progressive causes? And how can a movement organized around sexual identity embrace the intersecting identities of gay men and lesbians (and bisexuals? and transgendered people?) who are also women, people of color, disabled, youth, or working class?

These theoretical and practical considerations challenge the larger lesbian and gay movements in compelling ways, and as we have seen in this book, they have been the source of considerable disagreement and tension among the movements over time. These are questions that the Gay Liberation Front was forced to confront coming out of Stonewall in the early 1970s. Activist-scholar Michael Bronski provides an excellent rationale for the importance of embracing a broader coalition-based, progressive organizing strategy:

> We need to reassess what kind of a movement we want it to be. Will it be a movement that continues arguing, with diminishing success, for the rights of its own people—and even at that, only for those who want to formalize a relationship? Or will we argue for a broader vision of justice and fairness that includes all Americans? If the movement does not choose the latter course, we risk becoming not just irrelevant, but a political stumbling block to progressive social change in general.

Bronski's vision will require the movements to develop a broad coalition-building strategy, which is no easy task, especially given the disagreements among lesbians, gays, bisexuals, and transgender individuals over what the movements' central issues should be and how they should be addressed. . . .

And what does all of this mean for the central dilemma . . . the tensions between the assimilationist and liberationist approaches to political and social change—that has characterized the lesbian and gay movements over the years? One clear answer is it means that the movements should pursue a dual organizing strategy, one that builds on the best of the assimilationist perspective, but one that also always considers the possibilities for more radical, liberationist, structural, social, and policy change. . . .

. . . The answer is we need to build on the best of what the assimilationist and liberationist strategies have to offer. The assimilationist strategy, in and of itself, is far too limiting. And in the words of the late civil rights activist Bayard Rustin, those who embrace radical, outsider, unconventional, liberationist politics must eventually recognize the importance of moving "from protest to politics." All social movements recognize over time the importance of building coalitions with others across issues of common interest that will help bridge sexual-orientation, gender, race, and class divides. We have discussed the barriers to doing so throughout this book, but these barriers are not insurmountable. Indeed, much of the hope for the future resides in the attitudes and values of young people today, many of whom have indicated to pollsters and in classrooms across the country that those who are lesbian, gay, bisexual, and transgender deserve to live in a world free from prejudice, discrimination, and harassment, and deserve, at a bare minimum, the rights afforded to those in the heterosexual majority. What we must ultimately do is reconceptualize what it is to be an American, challenge what Audre Lorde has called the American norm: someone who is "white, thin, male, young, heterosexual, christian, and financially secure." It is important to do so because "this mythical American norm" is socially constructed and is the locus of considerable power and privilege in American society. No single political strategy can begin to accomplish this goal; multiple strategies for political, social, cultural, and economic transformation are at the core of this radical democratic conception of politics. . . .

54

ELLEN ALDERMAN
CAROLINE KENNEDY

From *In Our Defense*

Two noted attorneys have chosen to examine the Bill of Rights not from the perspective of landmark Supreme Court cases, but from a grassroots perspective. Ellen Alderman and Caroline Kennedy present the story behind an obscure federal case involving the First Amendment and freedom of religion. The U.S. Forest Service had decided to build a logging road through public lands in northern California. The land is sacred to the Yurok tribe, and the tribe hoped that the Constitution's First Amendment would protect them in their free exercise of religion. However, in 1987 the Supreme Court, in a close vote, decided otherwise. Alderman and Kennedy note, however, that Congress intervened, and the land was named protected wilderness in 1990. For now, the Yurok's sacred land is undisturbed, but without the Supreme Court's help.

"Congress shall make no law respecting an establishment of religion, or prohibiting the free exercise thereof . . . "

WHEN THE DOGWOOD TREE blossomed twice and a whale swam into the mouth of the Klamath River, the Yurok medicine man knew it was time for the tribe to perform the White Deer Skin Dance. He knew that these natural signs were messengers sent by the Great Spirit to tell the people things were out of balance in the world. The White Deer Skin Dance and Jump Dance are part of the World Renewal Ceremonies of the Yurok, Karok, Tolowa, and Hoopa Indian tribes of northern California. The World Renewal Ceremonies are performed to protect the earth from catastrophe and humanity from disease and to bring the physical and spiritual world back in balance. Preparations for the ceremonies begin far up in the mountains, in the wilderness known to the Indians as the sacred "high country."

According to Indian mythology, the World Renewal Ceremonies were initiated by the *woge*, spirits that inhabited the earth before the coming of man. The *woge* gave culture and all living things to humanity, and the ceremonies are held at sites along the river where these gifts were given. The *woge* then became afraid of human contamination and retreated to the mountains before ascending into a hole in the sky. Because the mountains were the *woge*'s last refuge on earth, they are the source of great spiritual power.

In recent years, there has been a quiet resurgence of traditional Indian religion in the high country. Young Indians who left to find jobs on the "other side of the mountain" are returning to their ancestral grounds. Lawrence "Tiger" O'Rourke, a thirty-two-year-old member of the Yurok tribe, worked for eight years around the state as a building contractor before returning to raise fish in the traditional Indian way.

"In the white man's world . . . you just spend all of your lifetime making money and gathering up things around you and it doesn't really have any value," Tiger says. "Here, the Spirit is still in everything—the trees, the rocks, the river . . . the different kinds of people. It's got a life spirit, so we're all connected. . . . The concrete world, it's kind of dead. It feels like something's missing and the people are afraid. . . . So this place is just right for me, I guess."

There are about five thousand others who, like Tiger, are happy to live in isolation from the "white man's world"; indeed the spiritual life of the high country depends on it. But when the U.S. Forest Service announced plans to build a logging road through the heart of the high country, many of the Yurok tribe decided they could not remain quiet any longer.

They went to court, claiming that the logging road would violate their First Amendment right to freely exercise their religion. They said it was like building a "highway through the Vatican." What the Indians wanted the courts to understand was that the salmon-filled creeks, singing pines, and mountain trails of the high country were their Vatican.

To prepare for the World Renewal Ceremony, the medicine man first notifies the dance givers that it is time. According to Indian law, only certain families are allowed to give dances and to own dance regalia. The privilege and the responsibility are passed down from generation to generation.

"In the beginning," says Tiger, a member of such a family, "the Spirit came up the river and he stayed at different people's houses. He only knocked and went in where he knew the people would take care of him. They would have a responsibility to the people, and the world, and the universe to make the ceremony, and they would always do it. It's a lot of work. You have to live a good life, you have to live with truth. Not everybody could do it."

The dance giver is also responsible for paying up all debts before the dance. Indian law puts a price on everything, and by paying the price the social balance is restored. If you insult someone, you owe that person a certain amount; if you kill a person, you must pay that person's family. Payment prevents hatred and anger from spreading to infect the community and brings the world back into harmony. . . .

The most sacred area of the high country is known as Medicine Mountain, a ridge dominated by the peaks of Doctor Rock, Peak 8, and Chimney Rock. Chimney Rock, a majestic outcropping of pinkish basalt, rises sixty-seven hundred feet above sea level. From its summit, views of receding blue waves of mountain ridges fade into the horizon in all directions. On a clear day, the shimmer of the Pacific Ocean gleams at the end of the winding silver ribbon of the Smith River below. . . .

Although only a few medicine men and Indian doctors actively use the sacred sites of the high country, the spiritual well-being of the entire tribe depends on performance of the ancient rituals. Despite more than a half century during which the government removed Indians from their villages and prohibited them from speaking their own language or practicing their religion, a few elderly Indians never left or gave up the old ways. Some young Indians, like Tiger, are returning to their homeland. And others, like Walter "Black Snake" Lara, are trying to balance the old world with the new.

Black Snake works felling trees. He says it is an honorable job in many parts of the lush California forests, but not in the high country. Of the sacred grounds he says, "The Creator fixed it that way for us. We're responsible for it."

Tiger, Black Snake, and others are struggling to maintain their fragile way of life. They are succeeding in part because the steep mountains, dense forests, and nonnavigable streams have protected their cemeteries, villages, and high country from encroachment by the "concrete" world. To them, the proposed highway was more than just a symbol of that concrete world. By the Forest Service's own estimates, each day it would bring about seventy-two diesel logging trucks and ninety other vehicles within a half mile of Chimney Rock.

Actually, the Forest Service started constructing a logging road through the Six Rivers National Forest in the 1930s. It began at either end, in the lumber-mill towns of Gasquet to the north and Orleans to the south, thus becoming known as the G-O Road. Under the Forest Service's management plan, once the road was completed, the towns would be connected and timber could be hauled to mills at either end of the forest. In the meantime, as construction inched toward Chimney Rock, new areas of timber were opened up to logging. "They snuck that road in from both sides," says Black Snake.

By the 1970s, the two segments of the seventy-five-mile road dead-ended in the forest. Black pavement simply gave way to gravel and dirt, and then the side of a mountain. The final six-mile section needed to complete the road was known as the Chimney Rock section of the G-O Road.

The Indians feared that if the road was built it would destroy the sanctity of the high country forever. As Sam Jones, a full-blooded Yurok dance giver put it. "When the medicine lady goes out there to pray, she stands on these rocks and meditates. The forest is there looking out. [She] talks to the trees and rocks, whatever is out there. After they get through praying, their answer comes from the mountain. Our people talk in their language to them and if it's all logged off and all bald there, they can't meditate at all. They have nothing to talk to."

An influx of tree fellers, logging trucks, tourists, and campers would also destroy the ability to make medicine in the high country. The consequences were grave; if the medicine man could not bring back the power for the World Renewal Ceremonies, the people's religious existence would be threatened. And because the land itself is considered holy by the Indians, they could not move their "church" to another location. "People don't understand about our place," Black Snake says, "because they can build a church and worship wherever they want."

The Indians filed a lawsuit in federal district court in San Francisco: *Northwest Indian Cemetery Protective Association v. Peterson.* (R. Max Peterson was named as defendant in his capacity as chief of the U.S. Forest Service.) They claimed that construction of the G-O Road would destroy the solitude, privacy, and undisturbed natural setting necessary to Indian religious practices, thereby violating their First Amendment right to freely exercise their religion.

By invoking the First Amendment, the Indians joined those before them who had sought religious freedom in America. After all, many colonists came to the New World to escape religious persecution in the Old, establishing colonies that reflected the varied beliefs of their inhabitants. The Puritans of Massachusetts sought to build their "City on a Hill," Lord Baltimore founded Maryland as a colony where Catholics and Protestants would live together and prosper, William Penn led the Quakers to Philadelphia, and the Virginia planters were strong supporters of the Church of England. . . .

[Thomas] Jefferson's [1785 Virginia] statute served as one of [James] Madison's models for the First Amendment, which, as adopted and ratified, has two components: the establishment clause and the free exercise clause. In general terms, according to the Supreme Court, the "establishment of religion clause of the First Amendment means at least this: Neither a state nor the Federal Government can set up a church. Neither can pass laws which aid one religion, aid all religions, or prefer one religion over another. . . . In the words of Jefferson, the clause against establishment of religion by law was intended to erect 'a wall of separation between church and State.'" Courts have relied on the establishment clause to strike down state support for parochial schools, statutes mandating school prayer, and the erection of religious displays (for example, nativity scenes or menorahs) on public property.

In contrast, the free exercise clause forbids the government from outlawing religious belief. It also forbids the government from unduly burdening the exercise of a religious belief. However, some regulation of conduct expressing belief is permitted. If a person claims that a government action violates his right to freely exercise his religion, courts must first determine if the asserted religious belief is "sincerely held." If so, then the burden on individual worship must be balanced against the state's interest in proceeding with the challenged action. Only if the state's interest is "compelling" will it outweigh the individual's right to the free exercise of religion.

In the two hundred years since the First Amendment was ratified, the free exercise clause has protected many whose religious beliefs have differed from those of the majority. For example, the Supreme Court has held that unemployment benefits could not be denied to a Seventh-Day Adventist fired for refusing to work on Saturday, her sabbath; nor to a Jehovah's Witness who quit his job in a weapons production factory for religious reasons. Forcing these individuals to choose between receiving benefits and following their respective religious practices violated their right to the free exercise of religion.

In 1983, the Federal District Court for the Northern District of California held that completion of the G–O Road would violate the Northwest Indians' right to freely exercise their religion. The court concluded that the G–O Road would unconstitutionally burden their exercise of sincerely held religious beliefs, and the government's interest in building the road was not compelling enough to override the Indians' interest. Therefore, the court enjoined, or blocked, the Forest Service from completing the road. When the decision was announced, the group of fifty to a hundred Indians who had traveled south to attend the trial were convinced that their medicine had been successful.

The government appealed the decision to the Ninth Circuit Court of Appeals. While the case was pending, Congress passed the California Wilderness Act, which designated much of the sacred high country as a wilderness area. Thus all commercial activity, including mining or timber harvesting, was forever banned. But as part of a compromise worked out to secure passage of the act, Congress exempted a twelve-hundred-foot-wide corridor from the wilderness, just enough to complete the G-O Road. So although the surrounding area could not be destroyed, the road could still be built. That decision was left to the Forest Service. The medicine was still working, however; in July 1986, the Ninth Circuit affirmed the district court's decision and barred completion of the road.

The government then appealed the case to the U.S. Supreme Court. It filed a "petition for certiorari," a request that the Court hear the case. The Supreme Court receives thousands of these "cert" petitions each year, but accepts only about 150 for argument and decision. In order to take the case, four justices must vote to grant "cert." If they do not, the lower-court ruling stands. Because freedom of religion is so important in the constitutional scheme, and because the case involved principles affecting the management of vast tracts of federal land, *Northwest Indian Cemetery Protective Association* was one of the 150 cases accepted.

The Indians based their Supreme Court arguments on their victories in the lower courts and on a landmark 1972 Supreme Court case, *Wisconsin v. Yoder*. In *Yoder*, three Amish parents claimed that sending their children to public high school, as required by law, violated their right to free exercise of religion. They explained that the Old Order Amish religion was devoted to a simple life in harmony with nature and the soil, untainted by influence from the contemporary world. The Amish said that public schools emphasized intellectual accomplishment, individual distinction, competition, and social life. In contrast, "Amish society emphasize[d] informal learning-through-doing; a life of 'goodness,' rather than a life of intellect; wisdom, rather than technical knowledge; community welfare, rather than competition; and separation from, rather than integration with, contemporary worldly society." The Amish said that forcing their children out of the Amish community into a world undeniably at odds with their fundamental beliefs threatened their eternal salvation. Therefore, they claimed, state compulsory education laws violated their right to freely exercise their religion. The Supreme Court agreed.

If the Supreme Court could find that freedom of religion outweighed the state's interest in compulsory education, the Indians believed that the Constitution would make room for them too. After all, Chief Justice Warren Burger had written in *Yoder*, "A way of life that is odd or even erratic but interferes with no rights or interests of others is not to be condemned because it is different." The Indians argued that, like the Amish, they wanted only to be left alone to worship, as they had for thousands of years.

But the Forest Service argued that the Indians were seeking something fundamentally different from what the Amish had won. Whereas the exemption from a government program in *Yoder* affected only the Amish, and "interfere[d] with no rights or interests of others," the Indians were trying to stop the government from managing its own resources. From the government's point of view, if the courts allowed these Indians to block the G-O Road, it would open the door for other religious groups to interfere with government action on government lands everywhere. (It did not matter to the government that the Indians considered the high country to be *their* land.) The Forest Service produced a map marked to indicate sacred religious sites in California; the red markers nearly covered the state. Giving the Indians veto power over federal land management decisions was not, in the government's view, what the free exercise clause was intended to protect. As Justice William O. Douglas once wrote, "The Free Exercise Clause is written in terms of what the government cannot do to the individual, not in terms of what the individual can exact from the government."

The singing pines, soaring eagles, and endless mountain vistas of northern California are about as far from the white marble Supreme Court on Capitol Hill as it is possible to get in the United States. Yet like thousands of Americans before them, a small group of Indians came in November 1987 to watch their case argued before the highest court in the land. Though the Indians had never put much faith in any branch of the government, they had come to believe that if the justices could see the case through "brown eyes," they would finally make room in the Bill of Rights for the "first Americans."

Some did not realize that by the time a case reaches the Supreme Court, it no longer involves only those individuals whose struggle initiated it, but has enduring repercussions throughout the country. Unlike a legal code or statute that is written with specificity, "a constitution," wrote Chief Justice John Marshall, "is framed for ages to come, and is designed to approach immortality, as nearly as human institutions can approach it." When the Supreme Court decides a case based on the Bill of Rights, it enunciates principles that become the Supreme Law of the Land, and are used by lower courts across the United States to guide their decisions.

The Indians lost by one vote. "The Constitution simply does not provide a principle that could justify upholding [the Indians'] legal claims," Justice Sandra Day O'Connor wrote for the majority. "However much we wish that it were otherwise, government simply could not operate if it were required to satisfy every citizen's religious needs and desires."

The Court accepted that the G-O Road could have "devastating effects on traditional Indian religious practices." Nonetheless, it held that the G-O Road case differed from *Yoder* because here, the government was not *coercing* the Indians to act contrary to their religious beliefs. In what may prove to be an important development in the law, the Court concluded that unless the government *coerces* individuals to act in a manner that violates their religious beliefs, the free exercise clause is not implicated, and the government does not have to provide a compelling reason for its actions.

The Court also noted the broad ramifications of upholding the Indians' free exercise claim. While the Indians did not "at present" object to others using the high country, their claim was based on a need for privacy in the area. According to the Court, under the Indians' reasoning there was nothing to prevent them, or others like them, from seeking to exclude all human activity but their own from land they held sacred. "No disrespect for the [Indian] practices is implied when one notes that such beliefs could easily require *de facto* beneficial ownership of some rather spacious tracts of public property," the Court wrote.

Justice William Brennan's emotional dissent rejected the Court's reasoning and result. The religious freedom remaining to the Indians after the Supreme Court's decision, according to Justice Brennan, "amounts to nothing more than the right to believe that their religion will be destroyed . . . the safeguarding of such a hollow freedom . . . fails utterly to accord with the dictates of the First Amendment." Justice Brennan and the two justices who joined him, Thurgood Marshall and Harry Blackmun, rejected the Court's new "coercion test."

"The Court . . . concludes that even where the government uses federal land in a manner that threatens the very existence of a Native American religion, the Government is simply not 'doing' anything to the practitioners of that faith," Justice Brennan wrote. "Ultimately the Court's coercion test turns on a distinction between government actions that compel affirmative conduct inconsistent with religious belief, and those governmental actions that prevent conduct consistent with religious belief. In my view, such a distinction is without constitutional significance." The dissenters believed instead that the Indians' religion would be severely burdened, indeed made "impossible," by the government's actions, and that the government had not shown a compelling interest in completing the road.

"They might as well rewrite the Constitution. They teach us we have freedom of religion and freedom of speech, but it's not true," says Tiger O'Rourke. "This was our place first time, our home. It's still our home, but we don't have the same rights as other Americans."

Currently, the G-O Road is stalled. The Indians are challenging the

Forest Service on environmental grounds and attempting to get Congress to add the G–O Road corridor to the existing, protected wilderness area.

Like many Americans, Tiger and Black Snake say they never thought much about the Constitution until it touched their lives directly. Among the tribes of northern California, defeat has fired a new fight for their way of life, spurred intertribal outreach and educational efforts, and brought a new awareness of the legal system. "We *have* to understand the Constitution now," says Tiger O'Rourke. "We still need our line of warriors, but now they've got to be legal warriors. That's the war now, and it's the only way we're going to survive."

N.B. On October 28, 1990, the last day of its session, the 101st Congress passed legislation adding the G–O Road corridor to the Siskiyou Wilderness. This legislation ensures that the logging road will not be completed; its two spurs will remain dead-ended in the forest beneath Chimney Rock. Because the area was protected to preserve the environment rather than the Indians' religion, the Indians found their victory bittersweet. "It's all right for us. We'll use the area as we always have," says Black Snake. "But we didn't accomplish what we set out to accomplish for other tribes. [We] can't win one on beliefs." But, he adds, "maybe it's the Creator's way of seeing just how sincere we are."

55

MARY ANN GLENDON

From *Rights Talk*

Individual rights lie at the heart of America's political system. Unfortunately, in the view of legal scholar Mary Ann Glendon, today's "rights talk" makes a mockery of the real meaning of rights. Legitimate, deeply-rooted rights have given way to what are nothing more than demands. Little thought is given to whether a right is basic or merely a convenience; to the effect of one person's claim of a right on others; to the weighing of rights versus responsibilities. Glendon, as a strong supporter of individual rights, asks people to return to a more common-sense, less artificial, definition of rights. Daily, in their private lives, Americans embrace a genuine and true concept of rights, not the "rights talk" of the public arena.

———

IN THE SPRING of 1990, men and women in East Germany and Hungary participated in the first fully free elections that had taken place in any of the East European countries since they came under Soviet control in 1945. Excitement ran high. The last people to have voted in that part of the world were now in their seventies. Some young parents, casting a ballot for the first time, brought their children with them to see the sight. Many, no doubt, will long remember the day as one marked with both festivity and solemnity. Meanwhile, in the United States, public interest in politics appears to be at an all-time low. Two months before the 1988 presidential election, polls revealed that half the voting-age public did not know the identity of the Democratic vice-presidential candidate and could not say which party had a majority in Congress. In that election, only half the eligible voters cast ballots, thirteen percent less than in 1960. Americans not only vote less than citizens of other liberal democracies, they display a remarkable degree of apathy concerning public affairs. Over a period of twenty years, daily newspaper readership has fallen from seventy-three percent of adults to a mere fifty-one percent. Nor have the readers simply become viewers, for ratings of network evening news programs have dropped by about twenty-five percent in the past ten years, and the slack has not been taken up by cable television news. Cynicism, indifference, and ignorance concerning government appear to be pervasive. By all outward indicators, the right and obligation to vote—a subject of wonder to East Europeans, and the central concern of many of us who worked in the civil rights movement in the 1960s—is now held here in rather low esteem.

Poor voter turnouts in the United States are, of course, mere symptoms of deeper problems, not least of which are the decline of broadly representative political parties, and the effect of the "sound-bite" on serious and sustained political discussion. On this deeper level lies the phenomenon with which this book is concerned: the impoverishment of our political discourse. Across the political spectrum there is a growing realization that it has become increasingly difficult even to define critical questions, let alone debate and resolve them.

Though sound-bites do not permit much airing of issues, they seem tailor-made for our strident language of rights. Rights talk itself is relatively impervious to the other more complex languages we still speak in less public contexts, but it seeps into them, carrying the rights mentality into spheres of American society where a sense of personal responsibility and of civic obligation traditionally have been nourished. An intemperate rhetoric of personal liberty in this way corrodes the social foundations on which individual freedom and security ultimately rest. While the nations of Eastern Europe are taking their first risk-laden and faltering steps toward democracy, the historic American experiment in ordered liberty is thus undergoing a less dramatic, but equally fateful, crisis of its own. It is a crisis at the very heart of the American experiment in self-government, for it concerns the state of public deliberation about the right ordering of our lives together. In the home of free speech, genuine exchange of ideas about matters of high public importance has come to a virtual standstill.

This book argues that the prominence of a certain kind of rights talk in our political discussions is both a symptom of, and a contributing factor to, this disorder in the body politic. Discourse about rights has become the principal language that we use in public settings to discuss weighty questions of right and wrong, but time and again it proves inadequate, or leads to a standoff of one right against another. The problem is not, however, as some contend, with the very notion of rights, or with our strong rights tradition. It is with a new version of rights discourse that has achieved dominance over the past thirty years.

Our current American rights talk is but one dialect in a universal language that has developed during the extraordinary era of attention to civil and human rights in the wake of World War II. It is set apart from rights discourse in other liberal democracies by its starkness and simplicity, its prodigality in bestowing the rights label, its legalistic character, its exaggerated absoluteness, its hyper-individualism, its insularity, and its silence with respect to personal, civic, and collective responsibilities.

This unique brand of rights talk often operates at cross-purposes with our venerable rights tradition. It fits perfectly within the ten-second formats currently preferred by the news media, but severely constricts opportunities for the sort of ongoing dialogue upon which a regime of ordered liberty ultimately depends. A rapidly expanding catalog of rights—extending to trees, animals, smokers, nonsmokers, consumers, and so on—not only multiplies the occasions for collisions, but it risks trivializing core democratic values. A tendency to frame nearly every social controversy in terms of a clash of rights (a woman's right to her own body vs. a fetus's right to life) impedes compromise, mutual understanding, and the discovery of common ground. A penchant for absolute formulations ("I have the right to do whatever I want with my property") promotes unrealistic expectations and ignores both social costs and the rights of others. A near-aphasia concerning responsibilities makes it seem legitimate to accept the benefits of living in a democratic social welfare republic without assuming the corresponding personal and civic obligations.

As various new rights are proclaimed or proposed, the catalog of individual liberties expands without much consideration of the ends to which they are oriented, their relationship to one another, to corresponding responsibilities, or to the general welfare. Converging with the language of psychotherapy, rights talk encourages our all-too-human tendency to place the self at the center of our moral universe. In tandem with consumerism and a normal dislike of inconvenience, it regularly promotes the short-run over the long-term, crisis intervention over preventive measures, and particular interests over the common good. Saturated with rights, political language can no longer perform the important function of facilitating public discussion of the right ordering of our lives together. Just as rights exist for us only through being articulated, other goods are not even available to be considered if they can be brought to expression only with great difficulty, or not at all.

My principal aim . . . has been to trace the evolution of our distinctive current rights dialect, and to show how it frequently works against the conditions required for the pursuit of dignified living by free women and men. With stories and examples drawn from disputes over flag-burning, Indian lands, plant closings, criminal penalties for homosexual acts, eminent domain, social welfare, child support, and other areas, I have endeavored to demonstrate how our simplistic rights talk simultaneously reflects and distorts American culture. It captures our devotion to individualism and liberty, but omits our traditions of hospitality and care for the community. In the images of America and Americans that it projects, as well as in the ideals to which it implicitly pays homage, our current rights talk is a verbal caricature of our culture—recognizably ours, but with certain traits wildly out of proportion and with some of our best features omitted.

Our rights-laden political discourse does provide a solution of sorts to the communications problems that beset a heterogeneous nation whose citizens decreasingly share a common history, literature, religion, or customs. But the "solution" has become part of the problem. The legal components of political discourse, like sorcerers' apprentices, have taken on new and mischief-making connotations when liberated from their contexts in the speech community of lawyers. (A person has no duty to come to the aid of a "stranger.") With its nonlegal tributaries rapidly dwindling, political rhetoric has grown increasingly out of touch with the more complex ways of speaking that Americans employ around the kitchen table, in their schools, workplaces, and in their various communities of memory and mutual aid.

Under these circumstances, what is needed is not the abandonment, but the renewal, of our strong rights tradition. But it is not easy to see how we might develop a public language that would be better suited in complexity and moral seriousness to the bewildering array of difficulties that presently face us as a mature democracy in an increasingly interdependent world. Nor is it readily apparent how the public forum, dominated as it is by images rather than ideas, could be reclaimed for genuine political discourse.

We cannot, nor would most of us wish to, import some other country's language of rights. Nor can we invent a new rhetoric of rights out of whole cloth. A political Esperanto* without roots in a living cultural tradition would die on the vine. . . . In many settings, employing a grammar of cooperative living, American women and men sound better and smarter than our current political discourse makes them out to be. The best resource for renewing our political discourse, therefore, may be the very heterogeneity that drives us to seek a simple, abstract, common language. The ongoing dialogue between freedom and responsibility, individualism and community, present needs and future plans, that takes place daily in a wide variety of American speech communities could help to revitalize our rights tradition as well as our political life.

---

*Esperanto was a language created in the late 1880s using simplified grammar and vocabulary borrowed from many languages in an attempt to create a common, universal method of communication. Esperanto was not accepted by people, however, and never achieved wide popularity.—EDS.

56

DAVID BERNSTEIN

From *You Can't Say That!*

Not all attacks on civil liberties, such as free speech, come from groups on the right side of the political spectrum, claims law professor David Bernstein. The author cites several memorable examples of the application of laws that prohibit discrimination against groups of people to situations that seem extreme. The results are sometimes bizarre, Bernstein believes, and civil liberties are sacrificed. Of particular interest is the author's examination of speech codes on college campuses. There are two sides to every issue, and especially to this issue, so you, the readers, will have to find your own position. "Idle chatter of a sexual nature," the "South of the Border party" T-shirt, and the "friend, lover, or partner" terminology are up for debate. How should the First Amendment's right to free speech fit into everyday life in school or at work?

INTOLERANT ACTIVISTS ARE DETERMINED to impose their moralistic views on all Americans, regardless of the consequences for civil liberties. These zealots are politically well organized and are a dominant force in one of the two major political parties. They have already achieved many legislative victories, especially at the local level, where they often wield disproportionate power. Courts have often acquiesced to their agenda, even when it conflicts directly with constitutional provisions protecting civil liberties. Until the power of these militants is checked, the First Amendment's protection of freedom of speech and freedom of religion will be in constant danger.

To many civil libertarians, the preceding paragraph reads like a description of the Christian right. But it also describes left-wing egalitarian activists, many of whom are associated with the "civil rights" establishment. Their agenda of elevating antidiscrimination concerns above all others poses an acute threat to civil liberties. The First Amendment prohibits the government from interfering with freedom of expression, which includes free exercise of religion, freedom of speech, freedom of the press, and the right to petition the government for a redress of grievances. All of these civil libertarian restrictions on government power are at risk from antidiscrimination laws. For example:

• In Berkeley, the federal Department of Housing and Urban Development threatened to sanction three neighborhood activists for organizing community opposition to a plan to turn a rundown hotel into a homeless center. HUD alleged that the activists had violated the Fair Housing Act by interfering with a project that would serve a group of people who would be disproportionately mentally ill or recovering substance abusers, protected groups under the Act. HUD spokesperson John Phillips, trying to parry free speech concerns raised by the media, instead stoked them. "To ask questions is one thing," Phillips told reporters. "To write brochures and articles and go out and actively organize people to say, 'We don't want those people in those structures,' is another."

• In San Francisco, Krissy Keefer is using an antidiscrimination law to challenge the artistic autonomy of the San Francisco Ballet. She is suing the ballet for height and weight discrimination for refusing to accept her daughter Fredrika into its preprofessional program. Fredrika is of average height and weight, while modern ballet's aesthetic standards require that dancers be tall and lithe.

• In Denver, the city government refused to issue a Columbus Day parade permit unless the organizers signed an agreement stating that "there will be no references, depictions, or acknowledgment of Christopher Columbus during the parade; and no speeches or wreath laying for Christopher Columbus will be conducted." The city was responding to pressure from American Indian activists, who alleged that a parade celebrating Columbus would create an illegal "hostile public environment."

• In New York City, Michelle Ganzy sued the Allen Christian School for firing her after she became pregnant out of wedlock. Ganzy, like all of the school's teachers, had agreed to serve as a role model for her students, in part by behaving in accordance with the school's conservative moral beliefs. Nevertheless, Ganzy sued for sex discrimination. A federal court, seemingly oblivious to the threat this lawsuit posed to the autonomy of religious institutions, ruled in her favor, holding that "[r]estrictions on pregnancy are not permitted because they are gender discriminatory by definition."

• In Minneapolis, a group of librarians complained of sexual harassment because patrons using the library computers viewed images the librarians saw and found offensive. The Equal Employment Opportunity Commission found that the librarians had "probable cause" to pursue their claim. Because of this and similar cases, public and private libraries throughout the United States are under pressure to install filtering software on their computers, lest a librarian inadvertently view offensive material and file a sexual harassment lawsuit. Defining the issue precisely backwards, a representative of the National Organization for Women told the *New York Times* that she wondered "how far First Amendment rights may go before they infringe on sexual harassment laws."

• In Eugene, Oregon, the state Newspaper Publishers Association published a list of 80 words and phrases that its members should ban from real estate advertisements to avoid liability under federal, state, or local fair housing laws. The forbidden words and phrases include language that signifies an obvious intent to violate fair housing laws (e.g., "no Mexicans"), but also language that is merely descriptive, such as "near church" or "walking distance to synagogue." Fair housing officials overzealously interpret such phrases as expressing an illicit preference for Christians and Jews, respectively. The list also includes phrases that some fair housing officials believe are used as codes to discourage minorities ("exclusive neighborhood," "board approval required") or families with children ("quiet tenants," "bachelor pad"). There are a number of other phrases that did not make the Oregon list, but that some realtors avoid nonetheless for fear of liability, including the following: master bedroom (either sexist or purportedly evocative of slavery and therefore insulting to African Americans), great view (allegedly expresses preference for the nonblind), and walk-up (supposedly discourages the disabled).

• Religious conservatives have also jumped on the antidiscrimination bandwagon. In Wellsville, Ohio, Dolores Stanley celebrated her new job as manager of the local Dairy Mart by removing *Playboy* and *Penthouse* from the store's shelves. "It goes against everything I believe in as a Christian," Stanley said. "There's no way I could participate in that." Stanley's superiors at corporate headquarters, attempting to exercise Dairy Mart's First Amendment right to sell legal magazines, told Stanley to replace the periodicals. She refused and was fired. The American Family Association, a conservative antipornography organization, represented Stanley in a lawsuit against Dairy Mart for sex and religious discrimination and for subjecting her to a "hostile workplace environment." The case settled before trial for a sum "well into the six figures."

These anecdotes are just a few examples of the growing threat antidiscrimination laws pose to civil liberties. Some civil libertarians have attempted to finesse the issue by redefining civil liberties to include protection from the discriminatory behavior of private parties. Under this view, conflicts between freedom of expression and antdiscrimination laws could be construed as clashes between competing civil liberties. For purposes of this book, however, civil liberties retains its traditional definition, referring to constitutional rights protected by the First Amendment and related constitutional provisions.

The clash of civil liberties and antidiscrimination laws has emerged due to the gradual expansion of such laws to the point at which they regulate just about all aspects of American life. This expansion of antidiscrimination laws, in turn, reflects a shift in the primary justification for such laws from the practical, relatively limited goal of redressing harms visited upon previously oppressed groups, especially African Americans, to a moralistic agenda aimed at eliminating all forms of invidious discrimination. Such an extraordinarily ambitious goal cannot possibly be achieved—or even vigorously pursued—without grave consequences for civil liberties. . . .

By the mid-1980s, antidiscrimination laws had emerged as a serious threat to civil liberties. Courts found that these laws punished everything from refusing to cast a pregnant woman as a bimbo in a soap opera, to giving speeches extolling the virtues of stay-at-home mothers, to expressing politically incorrect opinions at work, to refusing to share one's house with a gay roommate, to refusing to fund heretical student organizations at a Catholic university. Defendants protested that their First Amendment rights were being trampled on, but to no avail. Through the early 1990s, courts consistently refused to enforce First Amendment rights and other constitutionally protected civil liberties when their enforcement would have limited the reach of antidiscrimination laws. The trend of recent court decisions seems more friendly to civil liberties, largely because the courts have been populated with conservatives less committed to the antidiscrimination agenda. However, the final outcome of the conflict between civil liberties and antidiscrimination laws remains unresolved. Meanwhile, the fear of litigation—fear not only of actually losing a lawsuit, but also fear of being vindicated only after a protracted, expensive legal battle—is having a profound chilling effect on the exercise of civil liberties in workplaces, universities, membership organizations, and churches throughout the United States. . . .

Given the moral authority of antidiscrimination law in a society still recovering from a viciously racist past, writing a book critical of many of antidiscrimination law's applications is necessarily perilous, the law professor's equivalent of a politician disparaging mom and apple pie. The laudable goal of the ever-broadening antidiscrimination edifice is to achieve a fairer, more just society. Yet even—or perhaps especially—well-meaning attempts to achieve a praiseworthy goal must be criticized when the means used to achieve that goal become a threat to civil liberties.

The student who callously utters a racial epithet, the business executive who excludes Jews from his club, the coworker who tells obnoxious sexist jokes, the neighbor who lobbies against housing for the mentally ill—the actions of these individuals can be infuriating, especially to those who, like the author of this book, have been personally victimized by bigots. But the alternative to protecting the constitutional rights of such scoundrels is much worse: the gradual evisceration of the pluralism, autonomy, and check on government power that civil liberties provide. . . .

Public universities, like all government entities, must comply with the First Amendment. Nevertheless, many public universities have established speech codes to censor expression potentially offensive to women, African Americans, or other groups protected by civil rights laws. Universities commonly justify these rules as being necessary to prevent the creation of an illegal "hostile environment" on campus. University officials have not, however, been able to reconcile suppression of potentially offensive expression with the First Amendment.

The first wave of public university speech codes appeared in the late 1980s, with the rise of censorious political correctness. The University of Michigan's code, for example, banned speech "that stigmatizes or victimizes an individual on the basis of race" or that "has the purpose or reasonably foreseeable effect of interfering with an individual's academic efforts." Another part of the code prohibited speech relating to sex or sexual orientation that "creates an intimidating, hostile or demeaning environment for educational pursuits."

In furtherance of its code, the university distributed a handbook with examples of illicit speech. For example, a student organization, the book stated, would violate the speech code if it "sponsors entertainment that includes a comedian who slurs Hispanics." The handbook also noted that expression of certain politically incorrect opinions, such as remarks by male students that "women just aren't as good in this field as men," were prohibited. Beyond these two examples, students could only guess at what speech was forbidden. A federal court concluded "that the University had no idea what the limits of the [p]olicy were and it was essentially making up the rules as it went along." . . .

In any case, many public universities retain speech codes despite the lurking First Amendment issues. Some codes are so broad that, when taken literally, they are absurd. The University of Maryland's sexual harassment policy, for example, bans "idle chatter of a sexual nature, sexual innuendoes, comments about a person's clothing, body, and/or sexual activities, comments of a sexual nature about weight, body shape, size, or figure, and comments or questions about the sensuality of a person." So, at the University of Maryland, saying "I like your shirt, Brenda" is a punishable instance of sexual harassment. Further, because under Maryland's code the prohibited speech need not be specifically directed at an individual to constitute harassment, even saying "I really like men who wear bow ties" is out of bounds, at least if a man who wears bow ties hears about it.

Public university censorship to prevent a hostile environment extends well beyond the sex discrimination issues raised in the Santa Rosa case. Federal law also bans discrimination in education on the basis of race, religion, veteran status, and other criteria, and universities argue that they must censor speech to prevent a hostile environment for groups protected by those laws, as well. As a measure of just how far the law extends, consider the actions of the Office of Federal Contract Compliance Programs. That office charged illegal harassment based on Vietnam-era veteran status when an exhibit at Ohio State University displayed pictures and postings criticizing the actions of American military personnel during the Vietnam War. So much for academic freedom and the spirit of open debate in higher education.

A more typical case arose when a member of Phi Kappa Sigma at the University of California, Riverside, designed a T-shirt advertising a "South of the Border" party. The shirt featured a figure wearing a serape and sombrero sitting on a beach looking at the setting sun and holding a bottle of tequila, along with a picture of a set of steel drums and a wooden tiki head, in which was carved the word "Jamaica." The bottom of the shirt depicted a smiling Rastafarian carrying a six-pack of beer while standing in a Mexican cantina frequented by Riverside students, humming a lyric from an antiracist song by Bob Marley: "It doesn't matter where you come from long as you know where you are going." Although not exactly a brilliant artistic gem, the shirt was nonetheless a little more creative and diverse than the average frat party ad.

Campus Latino activists, however, were not favorably impressed. They charged that the shirt "dehumanizes and promotes racist views of Mexican people" and they formally accused the fraternity of violating university rules by circulating "offensive racial stereotypes." The fraternity president, Rich Carrez, apologized to the activists and pointed out that he was part Native American, the vice president of the fraternity was Latino, the T-shirt creator was Latino, and the fraternity was the most racially diverse on campus, with 25 white and 22 nonwhite members. The activists were unmoved and stubbornly clung to their view that the innocuous T-shirt promoted offensive stereotypes.

Ultimately, the university required fraternity members to destroy all of the T-shirts, apologize in writing, engage in community service, and attend two seminars on multiculturalism—an ironic punishment given that almost half the fraternity members were themselves minorities. The university also stripped the fraternity of its charter and expelled it from campus for three years. The university eventually lifted all of the sanctions, but only after legal intervention by the Individual Rights Foundation, a national network of lawyers that responds to threats to the First Amendment by college administrators and government officials.

Lawsuits, or even the threat of lawsuits, certainly seem to get campus officials' attention. At some public universities, civil libertarians have used the threat of legal action to persuade school officials to abandon their speech codes. For example, in 1997, the Office of Social Justice at West Virginia University published a brochure defining illicit discriminatory behavior as, among other things, expression of politically incorrect sentiments. An example of such forbidden discrimination was provided: claiming that "women never do well" in a particular science class regardless, apparently, of whether the statement is true. With such strict limits on what thoughts and feelings could be publicly shared, WVU students might well have had trouble finding anything neutral and sensitive enough to say to each other. But not to worry, the brochure provided helpful "advice" for encouraging a welcome environment, such as substituting "friend, lover, or partner" for the word boyfriend or girlfriend. The brochure further cheerfully suggested that failure to comply with its advice would be punishable.

Concerned faculty members wrote to the president of the university, David Hardesty Jr., seeking assurance that the brochure was not a speech and behavior code for students and faculty. Hardesty instead confirmed his correspondents' fears by writing that "[t]he right to free speech and the concept of academic freedom do not exist in isolation," and that freedom of speech does not include the right "to create a hostile environment on campus." The university ultimately withdrew the brochure, but, as is no doubt becoming a familiar theme in these tales, only after the West Virginia Civil Liberties Union threatened to sue. . . .

Regardless of whether their universities have formal speech codes, public university officials frequently restrict "offensive" student speech on an ad hoc basis. For example, UCLA suspended an editor of the student newspaper for running an editorial cartoon ridiculing affirmative action preferences. In the cartoon, a student asks a rooster on campus how it got into UCLA. The rooster responds, "affirmative action." After the editor was sanctioned by UCLA, student editor James Taranto reproduced the cartoon in the California State University, Northridge, student newspaper and criticized UCLA officials for suspending the paper's editor for engaging in constitutionally protected expression. Northridge officials suspended Taranto from his editorial position for two weeks for publishing controversial material "without permission." However, when Taranto threatened a lawsuit, the school removed the suspension from his transcript. Taranto continued to pursue a career in journalism and currently edits Opinionjournal.com.

In another incident, administrators at the University of Minnesota, Twin Cities, prohibited the College Republicans from distributing at the school's orientation fliers critical of then-president Bill Clinton. Several fliers contained R-rated humor, and one of them vulgarly satirized the president's views on gay rights. University officials argued that the fliers violated the university's nondiscrimination policy, violated orientation guidelines that require orientation to provide students with an "appreciation of diversity," and were not "consistent with the goals of the university."

After severe criticism from the American Civil Liberties Union and the local media—especially the *Minneapolis Star Tribune*—the university relented and permitted the distribution of the fliers. However, university president Nils Hasselmo stubbornly insisted that the flyer incident had only had the "appearance of" suppressing speech. He maintained that the orientation regulations that the fliers had violated were constitutional and had only been suspended, not repealed. Subsequently, an outraged Minnesota law student sued the university for violating its students' constitutional rights. The university capitulated, agreeing not only to stop censoring student materials but also, in a welcome twist on the usual forced sensitivity training ritual, to have its administration attend a lecture on the protection of freedom of speech afforded by the First Amendment. . . .

PART TEN

Public Opinion

57

V. O. KEY

From *Public Opinion and American Democracy*

Professor V. O. Key was a pioneer in the study of many facets of modern American politics, including elections, political parties, and public opinion. His detailed study of public opinion attempted to explain the relationship between the people's opinions and the political leadership's opinions. Key's analysis is complicated but clear in its recognition of both elite and mass influence. A particularly useful concept is Key's "opinion dike." He believed that the public's opinion keeps leaders from straying too far outside the parameters acceptable to the people in the making of policy. Most important, Key lifted the blame for "indecision, decay, and disaster" from the shoulders of the public onto the leadership stratum where, he alleged, it really belongs.

THE EXPLORATION of public attitudes is a pursuit of endless fascination—and frustration. Depiction of the distribution of opinions within the public, identification of the qualities of opinion, isolation of the odd and of the obvious correlates of opinion, and ascertainment of the modes of opinion formation are pursuits that excite human curiosity. Yet these endeavors are bootless unless the findings about the preferences, aspirations, and prejudices of the public can be connected with the workings of the governmental system. The nature of that connection has been suggested by the examination of the channels by which governments become aware of public sentiment and the institutions through which opinion finds more or less formal expression.

When all these linkages are treated, the place of public opinion in government has still not been adequately portrayed. The problem of opinion and government needs to be viewed in an even broader context. Consideration of the role of public opinion drives the observer to the more fundamental question of how it is that democratic governments manage to operate at all. Despite endless speculation on that problem, perplexities still exist about what critical circumstances, beliefs, outlooks, faiths, and conditions are conducive to the maintenance of regimes under which public opinion is controlling, at least in principle, and is, in fact, highly influential. . . . Though the preceding analyses did not uncover the secret of the conditions precedent to the practice of democratic politics, they pointed to a major piece of the puzzle that was missing as we sought to assemble the elements that go into the construction of a democratic regime. The significance of that missing piece may be made apparent in an indirect manner. In an earlier day public opinion seemed to be pictured as a mysterious vapor that emanated from the undifferentiated citizenry and in some way or another enveloped the apparatus of government to bring it into conformity with the public will. These weird conceptions, some of which were mentioned in our introductory chapter, passed out of style as the technique of the sample survey permitted the determination, with some accuracy, of the distribution of opinions within the population. Vast areas of ignorance remain in our information about people's opinions and aspirations; nevertheless, a far more revealing map of the gross topography of public opinion can now be drawn than could have been a quarter of a century ago.

Despite their power as instruments for the observation of mass opinion, sampling procedures do not bring within their range elements of the political system basic for the understanding of the role of mass opinion within the system. Repeatedly, as we have sought to explain particular distributions, movements, and qualities of mass opinion, we have had to go beyond the survey data and make assumptions and estimates about the role and behavior of that thin stratum of persons referred to variously as the political elite, the political activists, the leadership echelons, or the influentials. In the normal operation of surveys designed to obtain tests of mass sentiment, so few persons from this activist stratum fall into the sample that they cannot well be differentiated, even in a static description, from those persons less involved politically. The data tell us almost nothing about the dynamic relations between the upper layer of activists and mass opinion. The missing piece of our puzzle is this elite element of the opinion system. . . .

While the ruling classes of a democratic order are in a way invisible because of the vagueness of the lines defining the influentials and the relative ease of entry to their ranks, it is plain that the modal norms and standards of a democratic elite have their peculiarities. Not all persons in leadership echelons have precisely the same basic beliefs; some may even regard the people as a beast. Yet a fairly high concentration prevails around the modal beliefs, even though the definition of those beliefs must be imprecise. Fundamental is a regard for public opinion, a belief that in some way or another it should prevail. Even those who cynically humbug the people make a great show of deference to the populace. The basic doctrine goes further to include a sense of trusteeship for the people generally and an adherence to the basic doctrine that collective efforts should be dedicated to the promotion of mass gains rather than of narrow class advantage; elite elements tethered to narrow group interest have no slack for maneuver to accommodate themselves to mass aspirations. Ultimate expression of these faiths comes in the willingness to abide by the outcome of popular elections. The growth of leadership structures with beliefs including these broad articles of faith is probably accomplished only over a considerable period of time, and then only under auspicious circumstances.

If an elite is not to monopolize power and thereby to bring an end to democratic practices, its rules of the game must include restraints in the exploitation of public opinion. Dimly perceptible are rules of etiquette that limit the kinds of appeals to public opinion that may be properly made. If it is assumed that the public is manipulable at the hands of unscrupulous leadership (as it is under some conditions), the maintenance of a democratic order requires the inculcation in leadership elements of a taboo against appeals that would endanger the existence of democratic practices. Inflammation of the sentiments of a sector of the public disposed to exert the tyranny of an intolerant majority (or minority) would be a means of destruction of a democratic order. Or by the exploitation of latent differences and conflicts within the citizenry it may at times be possible to paralyze a regime as intense hatreds among classes of people come to dominate public affairs. Or by encouraging unrealistic expectations among the people a clique of politicians may rise to power, a position to be kept by repression as disillusionment sets in. In an experienced democracy such tactics may be "unfair" competition among members of the politically active class. In short, certain restraints on political competition help keep competition within tolerable limits. The observation of a few American political campaigns might lead one to the conclusion that there are no restraints on politicians as they attempt to humbug the people. Even so, admonitions ever recur against arousing class against class, against stirring the animosities of religious groups, and against demagoguery in its more extreme forms. American politicians manifest considerable restraint in this regard when they are tested against the standards of behavior of politicians of most of those regimes that have failed in the attempt to establish or maintain democratic practices. . . .

. . . Certain broad structural or organizational characteristics may need to be maintained among the activists of a democratic order if they are to perform their functions in the system. Fundamental is the absence of sufficient cohesion among the activists to unite them into a single group dedicated to the management of public affairs and public opinion. Solidification of the elite by definition forecloses opportunity for public choice among alternative governing groups and also destroys the mechanism for the unfettered expression of public opinion or of the opinions of the many subpublics. . . .

. . . Competitive segments of the leadership echelons normally have their roots in interests or opinion blocs within society. A degree of social diversity thus may be, if not a prerequisite, at least helpful in the construction of a leadership appropriate for a democratic regime. A series of independent social bases provide the foundations for a political elite difficult to bring to the state of unification that either prevents the rise of democratic processes or converts them into sham rituals. . . .

Another characteristic may be mentioned as one that, if not a prerequisite to government by public opinion, may profoundly affect the nature of a democratic order. This is the distribution through the social structure of those persons highly active in politics. By various analyses, none founded on completely satisfactory data, we have shown that in the United States the political activists—if we define the term broadly—are scattered through the socio-economic hierarchy. The upper-income and occupational groups, to be sure, contribute disproportionately; nevertheless, individuals of high political participation are sprinkled throughout the lesser occupational strata. Contrast the circumstances when the highly active political stratum coincides with the high socioeconomic stratum. Conceivably the winning of consent and the creation of a sense of political participation and of sharing in public affairs may be far simpler when political activists of some degree are spread through all social strata. . . .

Allied with these questions is the matter of access to the wider circles of political leadership and of the recruitment and indoctrination of these political activists. Relative ease of access to the arena of active politics may be a preventive of the rise of intransigent blocs of opinion managed by those denied participation in the regularized processes of politics. In a sense, ease of access is a necessary consequence of the existence of a somewhat fragmented stratum of political activists. . . .

This discussion in terms of leadership echelons, political activists, or elites falls painfully on the ears of democratic romantics. The mystique of democracy has in it no place for ruling classes. As perhaps with all powerful systems of faith, it is vague on the operating details. Yet by their nature governing systems, be they democratic or not, involve a division of social labor. Once that axiom is accepted, the comprehension of democratic practices requires a search for the peculiar characteristics of the political influentials in such an order, for the special conditions under which they work, and for the means by which the people keep them in check. The vagueness of the mystique of democracy is matched by the intricacy of its operating practices. If it is true that those who rule tend sooner or later to prove themselves enemies of the rights of man—and there is something to be said for the validity of this proposition—then any system that restrains that tendency however slightly can excite only awe. . . .

Analytically it is useful to conceive of the structure of a democratic order as consisting of the political activists and the mass of people. Yet this differentiation becomes deceptive unless it is kept in mind that the democratic activists consist of people arranged along a spectrum of political participation and involvement, ranging from those in the highest posts of official leadership to the amateurs who become sufficiently interested to try to round up a few votes for their favorite in the presidential campaign. . . . It is in the dynamics of the system, the interactions between these strata, that the import of public opinion in democratic orders becomes manifest. Between the activists and the mass there exists a system of communication and interplay so complex as to defy simple description; yet identification of a few major features of that system may aid in our construction of a general conception of democratic processes.

Opinion Dikes

In the interactions between democratic leadership echelons and the mass of people some insight comes from the conception of public opinion as a system of dikes which channel public action or which fix a range of discretion within which government may act or within which debate at official levels may proceed. This conception avoids the error of personifying "public opinion" as an entity that exercises initiative and in some way functions as an operating organism to translate its purposes into governmental action.

In one of their aspects the dikes of opinion have a substantive nature in that they define areas within which day-to-day debate about the course of specific action may occur. Some types of legislative proposals, given the content of general opinion, can scarcely expect to attract serious attention. They depart too far from the general understandings of what is proper. A scheme for public ownership of the automobile industry, for example, would probably be regarded as so far outside the area of legitimate public action that not even the industry would become greatly concerned. On the other hand, other types of questions arise within areas of what we have called permissive consensus. A widespread, if not a unanimous, sentiment prevails that supports action toward some general objective, such as the care of the ill or the mitigation of the economic hazards of the individual. Probably quite commonly mass opinion of a permissive character tends to develop in advance of governmental action in many areas of domestic policy. That opinion grows out of public discussion against the background of the modal aspirations and values of people generally. As it takes shape, the time becomes ripe for action that will be generally acceptable or may even arouse popular acclaim for its authors. . . .

The idea of public opinion as forming a system of dikes which channel action yields a different conception of the place of public opinion than does the notion of a government by public opinion as one in which by some mysterious means a referendum occurs on very major issue. In the former conception the articulation between government and opinion is relatively loose. Parallelism between action and opinion tends not to be precise in matters of detail; it prevails rather with respect to broad purpose. And in the correlation of purpose and action time lags may occur between the crystallization of a sense of mass purpose and its fulfillment in public action. Yet in the long run majority purpose and public action tend to be brought into harmony. . . .

The argument amounts essentially to the position that the masses do not corrupt themselves; if they are corrupt, they have been corrupted. If this hypothesis has a substantial strain of validity, the critical element for the health of a democratic order consists in the beliefs, standards, and competence of those who constitute the influentials, the opinion-leaders, the political activists in the order. That group, as has been made plain, refuses to define itself with great clarity in the American system; yet analysis after analysis points to its existence. If a democracy tends toward indecision, decay, and disaster, the responsibility rests here, not in the mass of the people.

58

THOMAS CRONIN

From *Direct Democracy*

Although the United States is a representative—republican—system of government, elements of direct democracy have been introduced on the state and local levels over time, especially in the early twentieth century during the Progressive era. Initiative, referendum, and recall give citizens an immediate and direct voice in their government, beyond just electing officials. Professor Thomas Cronin explains these instruments of direct democracy and cites California's 1978 tax-cutting Proposition 13 as a leading example of an important statewide ballot question. Controversy swirls over the wisdom of such exercises in direct democracy. Cronin weighs the advantages against the potential problems of allowing voters to have a direct say in policy-making. His conclusion is that initiative, referendum, and recall will neither destroy American government nor save it. Yet in the twenty-first century, with voters' openly-expressed distrust of public officials, direct democracy will surely become more and more a part of the state and local political scene.

FOR ABOUT A hundred years Americans have been saying that voting occasionally for public officials is not enough. Political reformers contend that more democracy is needed and that the American people are mature enough and deserve the right to vote on critical issues facing their states and the nation. During the twentieth century, American voters in many parts of the country have indeed won the right to write new laws and repeal old ones through the initiative and referendum. They have also thrown hundreds of state and local officials out of office in recall elections.

Although the framers of the Constitution deliberately designed a republic, or indirect democracy, the practice of direct democracy and the debate over its desirability are as old as English settlements in America. Public debate and popular voting on issues go back to early seventeenth-century town assemblies and persist today in New England town meetings.

Populist democracy in America has produced conspicuous assets and conspicuous liabilities. It has won the support and admiration of many enthusiasts, yet it is also fraught with disturbing implications. Its most important contributions came early in this century in the form of the initiative, referendum, and recall, as a reaction to corrupt and unresponsive state legislatures throughout the country. Most of us would not recognize what then passed for representative government. "Bills that the machine and its backers do not desire are smothered in committee; measures which they do desire are brought out and hurried through their passage," said Governor Woodrow Wilson at the time. "It happens again and again that great groups of such bills are rushed through in the hurried hours that mark the close of the legislative sessions, when everyone is withheld from vigilance by fatigue and when it is possible to do secret things." The threat, if not the reality, of the initiative, referendum, and recall helped to encourage a more responsible, civic-minded breed of state legislator. These measures were not intended to subvert or alter the basic character of American government. "Their intention," as Wilson saw it, was "to restore, not to destroy, representative government."

The *initiative* allows voters to propose a legislative measure (statutory initiative) or a constitutional amendment (constitutional initiative) by filing a petition bearing a required number of valid citizen signatures.

The *referendum* refers a proposed or existing law or statute to voters for their approval or rejection. Some state constitutions require referenda; in other states, the legislature may decide to refer a measure to the voters. Measures referred by legislatures (statutes, constitutional amendments, bonds, or advisory questions) are the most common ballot propositions. A *popular* or *petition referendum* (a less frequently used device) refers an already enacted measure to the voters before it can go into effect. States allowing the petition referendum require a minimum number of valid citizen signatures within a specified time. There is confusion about the difference between the initiative and referendum because *referendum* is frequently used in a casual or generic way to describe all ballot measures.

The *recall* allows voters to remove or discharge a public official from office by filing a petition bearing a specified number of valid signatures demanding a vote on the official's continued tenure in office. Recall procedures typically require that the petition be signed by 25 percent of those who voted in the last election, after which a special election is almost always required. The recall differs from impeachment in that the people, not the legislature, initiate the election and determine the outcome with their votes. It is a purely political and not even a semijudicial process.

American voters today admire and respect the virtues of representative government, yet most of them also yearn for an even greater voice in how their laws are made. They understand the defects of both representative and direct democracy and prefer, on balance, to have a mixture of the two. Sensible or sound democracy is their aspiration.

Although Americans cannot cast votes on critical national issues, voters in twenty-six states, the District of Columbia, and hundreds of localities do have the right to put measures on their ballots. Legislatures can also refer measures to the public for a general vote. And constitutional changes in every state except Delaware must be approved by voters before becoming law. Voters in fifteen states and the District of Columbia can also recall elected state officials, and thirty-six states permit the recall of various local officials.

When Americans think of their right to vote, they think primarily of their right to nominate and elect legislators, members of school boards and of city councils, and the American president. Yet California's famous Proposition 13 in June 1978 focused nationwide attention on the public's right to participate in controversial tax decision making, as Californians voted to cut their property taxes by at least half. More voters participated in this issue contest than in the same day's gubernatorial primaries.

California's Proposition 13 had two additional effects. It triggered similar tax-slashing measures (both as bills and as direct legislation by the people) in numerous other states, and it encouraged conservative interest groups to use the initiative and referendum processes to achieve some of their goals. In the past decade conservative interests have placed on state and local ballots scores of measures favoring the death penalty, victims' rights, English-only regulations, and prayer in schools, and opposing taxation or spending, pornography, abortion, and homosexuality. Several states have regularly conducted referenda on issues ranging from a nuclear freeze to seat-belt laws. Citizens are now voting on hundreds of initiatives and referenda at state and local levels. . . .

Skeptics, however, worry about tyranny by the majority and fear voters are seldom well enough informed to cast votes on complicated, technical national laws. People also worry, and justifiably, about the way well-financed special interest groups might use these procedures. Corruption at the state level is much less common today than it was early in the century, but special interests are surely just as involved as ever. The power of campaign contributions is clear. The advantages to those who can afford campaign and political consultants, direct mail firms, and widespread television and media appeals are very real. Although in theory Americans are politically equal, in practice there remain enormous disparities in individuals' and groups' capacities to influence the direction of government. And although the direct democracy devices of the initiative, referendum, and recall type are widely available, the evidence suggests it is generally the organized interests that can afford to put them to use. The idealistic notion that populist democracy devices can make every citizen a citizen-legislator and move us closer to political and egalitarian democracy is plainly an unrealized aspiration.

The initiative, referendum, and recall were born in an era of real griev-ances. They made for a different kind of democracy in those areas that permitted them. At the very least, they signaled the unacceptability of some of the most corrupt and irresponsible political practices of that ear-lier era. It is fashionable among political analysts today to say that although they have rarely lived up to their promises, neither have they resulted in the dire outcomes feared by critics. Yet they have had both good and questionable consequences. . . .

By examining direct democracy practices we can learn about the strengths and weaknesses of a neglected aspect of American politics, as well as the workings of representative democracy. We seek to understand it so we can improve it, and to improve it so it can better supplement rather than replace our institutions of representative government. . . .

A populist impulse, incorporating notions of "power to the people" and skepticism about the system has always existed in America. Ameri-cans seldom abide quietly the failings and deficiencies of capitalism, the welfare state, or the political decision rules by which we live. We are, as historian Richard Hofstadter wrote, "forever restlessly pitting ourselves against them, demanding changes, improvements, remedies." Demand for more democracy occurs when there is growing distrust of legislative bodies and when there is a growing suspicion that privileged interests exert far greater influences on the typical politician than does the com-mon voter.

Direct democracy, especially as embodied in the referendum, initia-tive, and recall, is sometimes viewed as a typically American political re-sponse to perceived abuses of the public trust. Voters periodically become frustrated with taxes, regulations, inefficiency in government programs, the inequalities or injustices of the system, the arms race, environmental hazards, and countless other irritations. This frustration arises in part be-cause more public policy decisions are now made in distant capitals, by remote agencies or private yet unaccountable entities—such as regulatory bodies, the Federal Reserve Board, foreign governments, multinational alliances, or foreign trading combines—instead of at the local or county level as once was the case, or as perhaps we like to remember.

Champions of populist democracy claim many benefits will accrue from their reforms. Here are some:

• Citizen initiatives will promote government responsiveness and accountability. If officials ignore the voice of the people, the people will have an available means to make needed law.

• Initiatives are freer from special interest domination than the legislative branches of most states, and so provide a desirable safeguard that can be called into use when legislators are corrupt, irresponsible, or dominated by privileged special interests.

• The initiative and referendum will produce open, educational debate on critical issues that otherwise might be inadequately discussed.

• Referendum, initiative, and recall are nonviolent means of political participation that fulfill a citizen's right to petition the government for redress of grievances.

• Direct democracy increases voter interest and election-day turnout. Perhaps, too, giving the citizen more of a role in governmental processes might lessen alienation and apathy.

• Finally (although this hardly exhausts the claims), citizen initiatives are needed because legislators often evade the tough issues. Fearing to be ahead of their time, they frequently adopt a zero-risk mentality. Concern with staying in office often makes them timid and perhaps too wedded to the status quo. One result is that controversial social issues frequently have to be resolved in the judicial branch. But who elected the judges?

For every claim put forward on behalf of direct democracy, however, there is an almost equally compelling criticism. Many opponents believe the ordinary citizen usually is not well enough informed about complicated matters to arrive at sound public policy judgments. They also fear the influence of slick television advertisements or bumper sticker messages.

Some critics of direct democracy contend the best way to restore faith in representative institutions is to find better people to run for office. They prefer the deliberations and the collective judgment of elected representatives who have the time to study complicated public policy matters, matters that should be decided within the give-and-take process of politics. That process, they say, takes better account of civil liberties.

Critics also contend that in normal times initiative and referendum voter turnout is often a small proportion of the general population and so the results are unduly influenced by special interests: big money will win eight out of ten times.

A paradox runs throughout this debate. As the United States has aged, we have extended the suffrage in an impressive way. The older the country, the more we have preached the gospel of civic participation. Yet we also have experienced centralization of power in the national government and the development of the professional politician. The citizen-politician has become an endangered species.

Representative government is always in the process of development and decay. Its fortunes rise and fall depending upon various factors, not least the quality of people involved and the resources devoted to making it work effectively. When the slumps come, proposals that would reform and change the character of representative government soon follow. Direct democracy notions have never been entirely foreign to our country—countless proponents from Benjamin Franklin to Jesse Jackson, Jack Kemp, and Richard Gephardt have urged us to listen more to the common citizen. . . .

The American experience with direct democracy has fulfilled neither the dreams and expectations of its proponents nor the fears of its opponents.

The initiative and referendum have not undermined or weakened representative government. The initiative, referendum, and recall have been no more of a threat to the representative principle than has judicial review or the executive veto. Tools of neither the "lunatic fringe" nor the rich, direct democracy devices have become a permanent feature of American politics, especially in the West.

The initiative, referendum, and recall have not been used as often as their advocates would have wished, in part because state legislatures have steadily improved. Better-educated members, more-professional staff, better media coverage of legislative proceedings, and longer sessions have transformed the legislative process at the state level, mostly for the better. Interest groups once denied access to secret sessions now regularly attend, testify, and participate in a variety of ways in the legislative process. Although individuals and some groups remain frustrated, the level and intensity of that frustration appear to be lower than the discontent that prompted the popular democracy movements around the turn of the century.

Still, hundreds of measures have found their way onto ballots in states across the country, and 35 to 40 percent of the more than 1,500 citizen-initiated ballot measures considered since 1904 have won voter approval. About half of these have been on our ballots since World War II. A few thousand legislatively referred measures have also been placed on the ballot, and at least 60 percent of these regularly win voter approval. Popular, or petition, referenda, placed on the ballot by citizens seeking a voter veto of laws already passed by state legislatures, have been used infrequently. . . .

Recall, used mainly at the local and county level, is seldom used against state officials. The marvel is that all these devices of popular democracy, so vulnerable to apathy, ignorance, and prejudice, not only have worked but also have generally been used in a reasonable and constructive manner. Voters have been cautious and have almost always rejected extreme proposals. Most studies suggest that voters, despite the complexity of measures and the deceptions of some campaigns, exercise shrewd judgment, and most students of direct democracy believe most American voters take this responsibility seriously. Just as in candidate campaigns, when they give the benefit of the doubt to the incumbent and the burden of proof is on the challenger to give reasons why he or she should be voted into office, so in issue elections the voter needs to be persuaded that change is needed. In the absence of a convincing case that change is better, the electorate traditionally sticks with the status quo.

Few radical measures pass. Few measures that are discriminatory or would have diminished the rights of minorities win voter approval, and most of the exceptions are ruled unconstitutional by the courts. On balance, the voters at large are no more prone to be small-minded, racist, or sexist than are legislators or courts.

A case can be made that elected officials are more tolerant, more educated, and more sophisticated than the average voter. "Learning the arguments for freedom and tolerance formulated by notables such as Jefferson, Madison, Mill, or the more libertarian justices of the Supreme Court is no simple task," one study concludes. "Many of those arguments are subtle, esoteric, and difficult to grasp. Intelligence, awareness, and education are required to appreciate them fully." Yet on the occasional issues affecting civil liberties and civil rights that have come to the ballot, voters have generally acted in an enlightened way. This is in part the case because enlightened elites help shape public opinion on such occasions through endorsements, news editorials, talk-show discussions, public debates, and legislative and executive commentary. Further, those voting on state and local ballot measures are usually among the top 30 or 40 percent in educational and information levels.

The civic and educational value of direct democracy upon the electorate has been significant, but this aspect of the promise of direct democracy was plainly overstated from the start. Most voters make up their minds on ballot issues or recall elections in the last few days, or even hours, before they vote. The technical and ambiguous language of many of these measures is still an invitation to confusion, and about a quarter of those voting in these elections tell pollsters they could have used more information in making their decisions on these types of election choices.

Like any other democratic institution, the initiative, referendum, and recall have their shortcomings. Voters are sometimes confused. On occasion an ill-considered or undesirable measure wins approval. Large, organized groups and those who can raise vast sums of money are in a better position either to win, or especially to block, approval of ballot measures. Sometimes a recall campaign is mounted for unfair reasons, and recall campaigns can stir up unnecessary and undesirable conflict in a community. Most of these criticisms can also be leveled at our more traditional institutions. Courts sometimes err, as in the *Dred Scott* decision and in *Plessy v. Ferguson* or *Korematsu*. Presidents surely make mistakes (FDR's attempt to pack the Supreme Court, 1937; Kennedy's Bay of Pigs fiasco, 1961; Nixon's involvement in the Watergate break-in and subsequent coverup, 1972–1974; Reagan's involvement in the Iran-contra arms deal, 1986). And legislatures not only make mistakes about policy from time to time but wind up spending nearly a third of their time amending, changing, and correcting past legislation that proved inadequate or wrong. In short, we pay a price for believing in and practicing democracy—whatever the form.

Whatever the shortcomings of direct democracy, and there are several, they do not justify the elimination of the populist devices from those state constitutions permitting them. Moreover, any suggestion to repeal the initiative, referendum, and recall would be defeated by the voters. Public opinion strongly supports retaining these devices where they are allowed. . . .

In sum, direct democracy devices have not been a cure-all for most political, social, or economic ills, yet they have been an occasional remedy, and generally a moderate remedy, for legislative lethargy and the misuse and nonuse of legislative power. It was long feared that these devices would dull legislators' sense of responsibility without in fact quickening the people to the exercise of any real control in public affairs. Little evidence exists for those fears today. When popular demands for reasonable change are repeatedly ignored by elected officials and when legislators or other officials ignore valid interests and criticism, the initiative, referendum, and recall can be a means by which the people may protect themselves in the grand tradition of self-government.

59

LAWRENCE JACOBS
ROBERT SHAPIRO

From *Politicians Don't Pander*

Lawrence Jacobs and Robert Shapiro challenge the premise popular in the 1990s that politicians cater to what the public wants: a finger in the wind of public opinion makes policy. No, they find, politicians don't pander. In fact, the authors suggest that the opposite is true. More often, politicians ignore what the mainstream of the public wants, attempting instead to create a version of public opinion that accords with the politicians' views. Media coverage aids in this upside-down relationship between the people and their representatives. The end result is that the American people do not believe that the government reflects their views; they do not trust their leaders. To Jacobs and Shapiro, the question of how much public opinion truly shapes policy lies at the heart of American democracy.

———

THE WAY CONGRESS HANDLED the impeachment of President Bill Clinton revealed a lot about American politics. Commentators and the American public were visibly struck by the unyielding drive of congressional Republicans to remove Clinton from office in the face of clear public opposition. The Republicans' disregard for the preferences of the great majority of Americans contradicted perhaps the most widely accepted presumption about politics—that politicians slavishly follow public opinion.

There was little ambiguity about where Americans stood on Clinton's personal behavior and impeachment. The avalanche of opinion polls during 1998 and early 1999 showed that super-majorities of nearly two-thirds of Americans condemned the president's personal misdeeds, but about the same number approved his job performance, opposed his impeachment and removal from office, and favored a legislative censure as an appropriate alternative punishment.

Despite Americans' strong and unchanging opinions, congressional Republicans defied the public at almost every turn. Beginning in the fall of 1998, the Republican-led House of Representatives initiated impeachment proceedings; its Judiciary Committee reported impeachment articles; and it passed two articles of impeachment on the House floor. Neither the House nor the Senate allowed a vote on the option supported by the public—censure. For all the civility in the Senate trial of the president on the House-passed articles of impeachment, the Republicans' pursuit of Clinton was checked not by a sudden attentiveness to public opinion but rather by the constitutional requirement of a two-thirds vote and the bipartisan support that this demanded.

The impeachment spectacle reveals one of the most important developments in contemporary American politics—the widening gulf between politicians' policy decisions and the preferences of the American people toward specific issues. The impeachment of Clinton can be added to the long list of policies that failed to mirror public opinion: campaign finance reform, tobacco legislation, Clinton's proposals in his first budget for an energy levy and a high tax on Social Security benefits (despite his campaign promises to cut middle-class taxes), the North American Free Trade Agreement (at its outset), U.S. intervention in Bosnia, as well as House Republican proposals after the 1994 elections for a "revolution" in policies toward the environment, education, Medicare, and other issues.

Recent research . . . provides evidence that this list is not a quirk of recent political developments but part of a trend of declining responsiveness to the public's policy preferences. The conventional wisdom that politicians habitually respond to public opinion when making major policy decisions is wrong. . . .

The Republicans' handling of impeachment fits into a larger pattern in contemporary American politics. . . .

. . . First, Republicans disregarded public opinion on impeachment because their political goals of attracting a majority of voters was offset by their policy goals of enacting legislation that politicians and their supporters favored. The ideological polarization of congressional Republicans and Democrats since the mid-1970s, the greater institutional independence of individual lawmakers, and other factors have raised the political benefits of pursuing policy goals that they and their party's activists desire. Responding to public opinion at the expense of policy goals entailed compromising their own philosophical convictions and risked alienating ideologically extreme party activists and other supporters who volunteer and contribute money to their primary and general election campaigns. Only the heat of an imminent presidential election and the elevated attention that average voters devote to it motivate contemporary politicians to respond to public opinion and absorb the costs of compromising their policy goals.

Indeed, the Republicans' relentless pursuit of impeachment was largely driven by the priority that the domineering conservative wing of the party attached to their policy goal (removing Clinton) over their political goals (appealing to a majority of Americans). Moderate Republicans could not ignore the risk of opposing impeachment—it could lead to a challenge in the next primary election and diminished campaign contributions.

Our second point is that politicians pursue a strategy of *crafted talk* to change public opinion in order to offset the potential political costs of not following the preferences of average voters. Politicians track public opinion not to make policy but rather to determine how to craft their public presentations and win public support for the policies they and their supporters favor. Politicians want the best of both worlds: to enact their preferred policies and to be reelected.

While politicians devote their resources to changing public opinion, their actual influence is a more complex story. Politicians themselves attempt to change public opinion not by directly persuading the public on the merits of their policy choices but by "priming" public opinion: they "stay on message" to highlight standards or considerations for the public to use in evaluating policy proposals. Republicans, for example, emphasized "big government" to prompt the public to think about its uneasiness about government. Politicians' efforts to sway the public are most likely to influence the perceptions, understandings, and evaluations of specific policy proposals such as Republican proposals in 1995 to significantly reduce spending on Medicare to fund a tax cut. But even here, politicians' messages promoting their policy proposals often provoke new or competing messages from their political opponents and the press that complicate or stymie their efforts to move public opinion. In addition, efforts to influence the public's evaluations of specific proposals are unlikely to affect people's values and fundamental preferences (such as those underlying support for Medicare, Social Security, and other well-established programs). We distinguish, then, between political leaders' attempts to alter the public's perceptions, evaluations, and choices concerning very specific proposals (which are susceptible but not certain to change) and Americans' values and long-term preferences (which tend to be stable and particularly resistant to short-term manipulation). In short, politicians' confidence in their ability to move public opinion by crafting their statements and actions boosts their willingness to discount majority opinion; but the reality is that efforts to change public opinion are difficult and are often most successful when deployed against major new policy proposals by the opposition, which has the more modest task of increasing the public's uncertainty and anxiety to avoid risk.

Politicians respond to public opinion, then, but in two quite different ways. In one, politicians assemble information on public opinion to design government policy. This is usually equated with "pandering," and this is most evident during the relatively short period when presidential elections are imminent. The use of public opinion research here, however, raises a troubling question: why has the derogatory term "pander" been pinned on politicians who respond to public opinion? The answer is revealing: the term is deliberately deployed by politicians, pundits, and other elites to belittle government responsiveness to public opinion and reflects a long-standing fear, uneasiness, and hostility among elites toward popular consent and influence over the affairs of government. It is surely odd in a democracy to consider responsiveness to public opinion as disreputable. We challenge the stigmatizing use of the term "pandering" and adopt the neutral concept of "political responsiveness." We suggest that the public's preferences offer both broad directions to policymakers (e.g., establish universal health insurance) and some specific instructions (e.g., rely on an employer mandate for financing reform). In general, policymakers should follow these preferences.

Politicians respond to public opinion in a second manner—they use research on public opinion to pinpoint the most alluring words, symbols, and arguments in an attempt to move public opinion to support their desired policies. Public opinion research is used by politicians to manipulate public opinion, that is, to move Americans to "hold opinions that they would not hold if aware of the best available information and analysis. . . ." Their objective is to *simulate responsiveness*. Their words and presentations are crafted to change public opinion and create the *appearance* of responsiveness as they pursue their desired policy goals. Intent on lowering the potential electoral costs of subordinating voters' preferences to their policy goals, politicians use polls and focus groups not to move their positions closer to the public's but just the opposite: to find the most effective means *to move public opinion closer to their own desired policies*.

Political consultants as diverse as Republican pollster Frank Luntz and Clinton pollster Dick Morris readily confess that legislators and the White House "don't use a poll to reshape a program, but to reshape your argumentation for the program so that the public supports it." Indeed, Republicans' dogged pursuit of impeachment was premised on the assumption that poll-honed presentations would ultimately win public support for their actions. We suggest that this kind of overconfidence in the power of crafted talk to move public opinion explains the political overreaching and failure that was vividly displayed by Clinton's health reform effort during the 1993–94 period and the Republicans' campaign for their policy objectives beginning with their "Contract with America" during 1995–96. Crafted talk has been more effective in opposing rather than promoting policy initiatives partly because the news media represent and magnify disagreement but also because politicians' overconfidence in crafted talk has prompted them to promote policy goals that do not enjoy the support of most Americans or moderate legislators.

Our argument flips the widespread image of politicians as "pandering" to public opinion on its head. Public opinion is not propelling policy decisions as it did in the past. Instead, politicians' own policy goals are increasingly driving major policy decisions and public opinion research, which is used to identify the language, symbols, and arguments to "win" public support for their policy objectives. Responsiveness to public opinion and manipulation of public opinion are not mutually exclusive: politicians manipulate public opinion by tracking public thinking to select the actions and words that resonate with the public.

Our third point is that politicians' muted responsiveness to public opinion and crafting of their words and actions has a profound impact on the mass media and on public opinion itself. In contrast to others who emphasize the nearly unlimited independence and power of the mass media, we argue that press coverage of national politics has been driven by the polarization of politicians and their reliance on crafting their words and deeds. The press focuses on political conflict and strategy because these are visible and genuine features of contemporary American politics. The combination of politicians' staged displays and the media's scrutiny of the motives behind them produced public distrust and fear of major government reform efforts. We do not treat policymaking, media coverage, and public opinion as parts that can be studied one at a time; rather, we study their dynamic configurations and processes of interdependence. Democratic governance and the process of public communications are inseparably linked. . . .

We argue that politicians' pursuits of policy goals have created a reinforcing spiral or cycle that encompasses media coverage and public opinion. It is characterized by three features. First, the polarization of Washington political elites and their strategies to manipulate the media and gain public support have prompted the press to increasingly emphasize or frame its coverage in terms of political conflict and strategy at the expense of the substance of policy issues and problems. Although news reports largely represent the genuine contours of American politics, the media's organizational, financial, and professional incentives prompt them to exaggerate the degree of conflict in order to produce simple, captivating stories for their audiences.

Second, the increased political polarization and politicians' strategy of crafting what they say and do (as conveyed through press coverage) raise the probability of both changes in public understandings and evaluations of specific policy proposals, and public perceptions that proposals for policy change make uncertain or threaten the personal well-being of individual Americans. The presence of a vocal political opposition, combined with the media's attentiveness to the ensuing conflict and the public's skittishness about change, often prevents reformers from changing public opinion as they intended.

Third, the cycle closes as the media's coverage and the public's reaction that was initially sparked by politicians' actions feed back into the political arena. How politicians appraise the media's coverage of their initial actions affects their future strategy and behavior. Politicians latch on to any evidence of changes in public opinion that are favorable to their positions in order to justify their policies and to increase the electoral risk of their rivals for opposing them. . . .

The public's perception that government officials do not listen to or care much about their views accelerated in the 1970s and peaked in the 1990s. Paralleling this trend, polls by Gallup, the Pew Center, and the Center on Policy Attitudes during the second half of the 1990s consistently found that large majorities doubted the founding premise of American government—popular sovereignty and consent of the governed. Over 60 percent of the public (according to responses to a diverse set of survey questions) believed that elected officials in Washington and members of Congress "lose touch" or are "out of touch with average Americans" and do not understand what "most Americans" or "people like you" think. . . .

Increasing political responsiveness to centrist opinion would not produce neutral changes in government policy but ones that can have profound political implications. Politicians who respond to public opinion would enact policies that defied today's calcified political categories of liberal and conservative. The public, on balance, is more conservative on social issues than Democrats; it is less liberal, for instance, toward homosexuality and criminal behavior. On the other hand, the public is supportive of proposals for political reforms and progressive economic, health, and environmental programs, which Republicans reject. More responsive government might well pursue more conservative social policies and more progressive economic and political ones.

The most important implication of raising responsiveness is to reaffirm the spirit and content of democracy in America. The continued slippage in government responsiveness threatens the foundation of our democratic order and the meaning of rule by and for the people. Whether *democratic* government survives is not foreordained or guaranteed; it is the challenge of each generation to be vigilant and reassert its importance. Insisting that politicians follow the popular will and allow citizens to engage in unfettered public debate is central to that struggle.

60

DAVID MOORE

From *The Opinion Makers*

Using an example from 2004 and 2005 polling on Americans' attitudes toward oil drilling in the Artic National Wildlife Refuge, public opinion expert David Moore reveals the reason behind the sometimes contrasting results that different polls find on the same topic. Many people who respond don't know much about the topic being explored; many don't feel strongly one way or the other. Therefore, the poll results are "soft" and easily manipulated. Moore exposes several pitfalls in polling that can produce inaccurate data. The author then moves to a famous 2008 incident that brought a lot of attention to the issue of polling accuracy: the pollsters' prediction that candidate Hillary Clinton would lose the New Hampshire primary to Senator Barack Obama. Surprise! Clinton beat Obama by a couple of percentage points. Moore assesses where the polls went wrong, providing some important warnings for future polling efforts. He then takes on the polling-in-the-era-of-cell-phones controversy. Moore's concluding words address the need to acknowledge that many people do not feel strongly about an issue and that their opinions are easily swayed—even by the order in which questions are asked.

———

THE GREAT PROMISE of public opinion polls was not that they would be able to predict election winners, but that they would give voice to the people between elections. That at least was the hope of George Gallup when he launched "America Speaks" in the early 1930s, and it remains the universal vision of media pollsters today. The question from the beginning of modern polling, however, has always been the same: How well do the polls measure what people are thinking? Election predictions can be checked for accuracy against the electoral results, but there is nothing comparable against which to measure the accuracy of the typical public policy poll. Pollsters try to establish their overall credibility by demonstrating how well they can predict elections, the assumption being that if they are successful there, they must have good samples that represent the American public on more general policy issues. That's not necessarily a good assumption, of course, since even in election campaigns the polls are not especially reliable in describing the public mind.

Beyond the credibility of the pollster, there is another, though still imperfect, way to assess the potential accuracy of a public policy poll—whether or not it agrees with other polls asking roughly the same question at roughly the same time. If they all agree, it doesn't mean they are all right. They could all be wrong in the same way. But if the polls disagree with one another, we definitely know that at least one is inaccurate. Comparisons over the past several years suggest some real problems with public policy polls, which are increasingly more likely to confuse than they are to enlighten us about what Americans are thinking.

One of the major problems is that opinions on public policy are more complex than those expressing a vote choice. A single question will rarely suffice, because there are so many facets of any given policy. Moreover, the policy may be so arcane, or the public so unengaged in the issue, that large numbers of Americans have no opinion about it at all—a fact that media pollsters generally do everything in their power to conceal. Rather than allow respondents to freely acknowledge they don't have an opinion, pollsters pressure them to choose one of the available options. Respondents in turn try to come up with some plausible reason for choosing one answer over another. If they don't have much information about the issue, they pick up cues from the way the question is framed or from other questions in the survey. The net result is that many respondents are influenced by the questionnaire itself.

An extreme example of how drastically polls can manipulate public opinion occurred shortly after President Bush's re-election, when he announced that he would try once again to have Congress pass legislation to permit oil drilling in Alaska's Arctic National Wildlife Refuge (ANWR). A national poll released by Republican Frank Luntz in January 2005, on behalf of the Arctic Power interest group, found a public that supported oil drilling in ANWR by a margin of 17 percentage points (51 percent to 34 percent). Yet in direct contradiction, a similar poll conducted December 13 through 15, 2004, by John Zogby for the Wilderness Society found the public opposed to oil drilling in ANWR, by the exact same margin (55 percent opposed to 38 percent in favor).

It seemed more than coincidental that the poll results happened to conform with the desires of the sponsoring organizations. And a look at the questionnaires shows how easy it was to shape the findings into mirror opposites. Luntz preceded his question on oil drilling with 13 questions that dealt with the cost of oil and with energy dependence on foreign countries. By the time the interviewer got to the question of exploring and developing oil reserves in ANWR, many respondents were primed to solve the country's energy needs by opening up that area to the oil industry. Zogby, on the other hand, framed the issue in a less biased way, asking only one question related to the oil industry before the drilling question. But that one question helped present the issue as an environmental matter, and in that context a solid majority of the respondents opposed oil drilling.

A key to understanding how easy it was to manipulate respondents into giving the desired answers is recognizing that most people had little knowledge about ANWR going into the survey. Eighty-seven percent of Luntz's respondents, for example, could not say where the Arctic National Wildlife Refuge is located—the same percentage could not accurately identify even one word of the acronym ANWR. In addition, only 8 percent said they knew either a lot or a good deal about the area. Despite this lack of knowledge, only 7 percent of Zogby's sample and 15 percent of Luntz's sample declined to offer an opinion. Clearly, information presented over the course of the interview helped many respondents form an instantaneous opinion.

Although the contradictory results make it difficult to specify what the "true" state of public opinion was, there are some useful indicators. Even a biased poll in favor of oil drilling found 34 percent opposed, and a biased poll opposed to oil drilling found 37 percent in favor—suggesting a mostly divided public, with a substantial proportion not having a deeply held opinion. But there were no intensity questions, so we don't know how engaged the public was—how many people had a deeply held view compared with how many expressed top-of-mind opinions.

A Gallup poll in March 2005, just a couple of months after the Zogby and Luntz polls, tried to get at that intensity dimension when it first asked a neutral question: "Do you think the Arctic National Wildlife Refuge in Alaska should or should not be opened up for oil exploration?" People were opposed 53 percent to 42 percent, with just 5 percent unsure. The follow-up question asked respondents if they would be upset if what occurred was the opposite of what they had just said they preferred. The result was that 19 percent of respondents wanted oil drilling and would be upset if it didn't happen, 45 percent were opposed and would be upset if it did happen, and 36 percent essentially didn't care. Among those who cared, opposition to the proposal was greater than 2 to 1, but there's a catch. The question was asked after numerous questions on global warming and on the ability of various government agencies to protect the nation's environment. In that context, the intense opposition measured by Gallup among its respondents might well be greater than among the public as a whole.

Unlike the other two polls, the Gallup poll on oil drilling in ANWR was not sponsored by a group with a vested interest in the results. Having worked on that specific Gallup poll myself, I can personally attest to the fact that we did not intend to bias the results. The poll itself was part of Gallup's monthly Social Series surveys, which measure public opinion about various matters regularly. In January of each year, for example, Gallup devotes a poll to measuring the mood of the country, in February to public opinion on world affairs, in March to the environment, in April to the economy, and so on. Because there are so many questions related to the environment in the March poll, it would be impossible not to ask some questions after respondents had already heard several about the environment. Inevitably, the early questions will influence how some respondents answer the later ones. Generally, the more questions on the environment, the more likely respondents are to give environmentally positive responses as the interview continues.

The Luntz and Zogby examples illustrate how pollsters are often treated as guns-for-hire. In each case, the policy question itself was neutral, but the questionnaire context of each poll was manipulated to produce the desired results. Find the right pollster, get the right answer. This is not to say that on every topic, polls can produce whatever a sponsoring organization might want. But on topics about which most people know very little, enormous swings in results can easily be obtained by careful questionnaire designs.

The Gallup example illustrates what's wrong with most media polls that purport to measure an objective public opinion. Though it did measure the intensity of the expressed opinions, it failed in several other areas. There was no attempt to measure how much people knew about the issue, and the question was posed in a forced-choice format. Whether avoidable or not, the ANWR question was asked after several other questions about the environment, which clearly biased the answers of respondents who had been unengaged on the issue before the survey. And no attempt was made to discover why people supported or opposed the oil drilling. George Gallup wanted his polls to provide a guide for political leaders, but the results of the Gallup poll in this case were hardly useful for that purpose. . . .

On January 8, 2008, the date of the New Hampshire primary, media pollsters suffered their biggest failure in election prediction since the 1948 presidential contest, when the three major scientific polls of the day all confidently predicted Republican Thomas Dewey to beat incumbent Democratic president Harry S. Truman. At the time, expectation of a Republican victory was so pervasive, news stories analyzing what a Dewey administration would look like were being written days before the actual election.

A similar national consensus emerged in the days just before the New Hampshire primary, when pundits of all stripes across the country were predicting the demise of Hillary Clinton's candidacy in light of eleven different polls forecasting her almost certain defeat on primary day. On average, these polls showed Barack Obama winning with 38 percent to Clinton's 30 percent. Obama's lead varied from 3 percentage points, reported by Franklin Pierce College, to 13 points, reported by both Gallup and Zogby. The stunning final vote count: Clinton won with 39 percent to Obama's 37 percent.

The magnitude of the pollsters' failure was highlighted by ABC's Gary Langer, who referred to it as "New Hampshire's Polling Fiasco," saying that it was "essential" to have a "serious critical look" at those results. "It is simply unprecedented for so many polls to have been so wrong," he wrote. "We need to know why." Langer's ABC News poll and its partner the *Washington Post* poll conducted a single survey in New Hampshire in early December but wisely avoided polling toward primary day, which meant that their poll results were too far removed to be compared with the vote count. Later Langer joked online, "What I like best about the final New Hampshire pre-election polls is that I didn't do any of them."

Langer's call for a serious critical look at other news media's polls was shared by key members of the American Association for Public Opinion Research. Five days after the election, the association's president, Nancy Mathiowetz, announced the formation of an ad hoc committee "to evaluate pre-election primary methodology and the sponsorship of a public forum on the issue." After reassuring the public that polls have long been "remarkably accurate," Mathiowetz wrote that, "Sixty years ago the public opinion profession faced a crisis related to the poll predictions of the Truman-Dewey race. The way survey researchers reacted then—with a quick, public effort to identify the causes—played a key role in restoring public confidence and improving research methodology."

Many pollsters and pundits attributed the New Hampshire meltdown to the long-standing problem of "nonresponse"—the increasing difficulty in reaching respondents who are willing to be interviewed. These days, more and more people screen their calls with answering machines and caller ID. Even if pollsters can get through, Americans are increasingly unwilling to participate. The question posed by "New Hampshire's Polling Fiasco" was whether pollsters simply hadn't been able to reach enough Clinton supporters—and whether this portended a terrible polling performance for the presidential election campaign. . . .

In my estimation, the main reason the polls were wrong is that they stopped too early. A last-minute television news blitz on Sunday and

Monday, too late to be picked up by the polls, showed an emotional Clinton coming close to tears and looking both vulnerable and strong as she explained why she was campaigning so hard for president. Another video clip shown repeatedly in the last forty-eight hours before the election was former president Bill Clinton's passionate speech that Obama's claim to wiser judgment on the Iraq war was a "fairy tale," an argument that could have relieved doubts among antiwar voters concerned about Hillary Clinton's vote in favor of war. The frequent broadcasts of these two videos during the final hours leading up to the primary almost certainly influenced New Hampshire voters. And polling shows just who among those voters were most heavily influenced. Two days before the primary, the last Granite State poll showed only 34 percent of Democratic women intending to vote for Clinton. Postprimary exit polls, however, revealed that 46 percent of women wound up voting for her.

Though nonresponse was almost certainly not a major factor in the New Hampshire Democratic primary miscalls, it represents an ever-present threat to the validity of all polls. And there's not much pollsters can do about it. . . .

Related to the nonresponse issue is the steep increase in the number of Americans, especially young people, who rely on cell phones, which have typically been excluded from the samples used in most media polls. The cell phone issue burst into politics as a major issue for pollsters during the 2004 presidential election, when advocates for John Kerry claimed his support was underestimated by polls that had not been able to reach youthful voters. After the election, however, Pew's Scott Keeter analyzed the exit polls and concluded that while 7 percent of all voters were reachable by cell phone only, including a much higher percentage among young voters, that did not mean that the regular telephone preelection polls underestimated Kerry's vote. Polls that weighted their results to account for the underrepresentation of young voters generally were able to compensate for the lack of young voters with cell phones. Apparently, there were few differences in attitudes between young voters who could be reached only by cell phones and those who could be reached by landline. At least for the time being, telephone polls could continue without fear of a youth bias. . . .

In a special issue of *Public Opinion Quarterly* published at the end of 2007, various researchers arrived at very different conclusions about the need for pollsters to include cell phones in their samples. Pew researchers reported on four separate surveys conducted in 2006 to compare the views of cell-phone-only respondents with those of landline-phone respondents, and found that excluding cell phones did not bias poll results for *the population as a whole*. However, the authors cautioned that some results as they applied exclusively to young adults were biased because of the cell-phone exclusion. Young people with landlines are more likely to attend church and less likely to drink alcohol or approve of smoking marijuana, for example, than are young people with cell phones only. Still, the authors of the study concluded that overall, the utility of including cellphone samples with the regular landline samples "appears marginal, at least at present."

Two other teams of researchers reached quite a different conclusion, and both argued that overall results applying to the general population would be biased if cell phones are excluded. . . .

On January 14, 2008, Frank Newport of the Gallup Poll announced that as of the beginning of the year, Gallup had added "cell phone interviewing as part of the sample for general population studies." He admitted that it was a "complex and costly modification in methodology," and that Gallup was making the change despite the fact that "study after study has shown that in general, the effect of excluding from the interview process those who only have cell phones has not seemed to affect the overall marginal results of political studies." So, why did Gallup make such a bold change? Newport didn't say. Mark Blumenthal, founder of pollster.com, however, suggested that the real significance of the change was "symbolic." And because Gallup is the "granddaddy" of the polling industry, Blumenthal expected the change to have a "big ripple effect on the polling industry." . . . .

The power of polls today far exceeds the visions of the early pollsters, who simply hoped that their scientific measurements of the public will would enhance the democratic process. But as I've made clear, that power is not always positive. The problem is that media polls today are designed to conceal the truth about the American public, a truth that everybody knows but that journalists and pollsters are reluctant to acknowledge.

Virtually everyone who studies or measures public opinion today recognizes that there is a distinction between what Daniel Katz called "a superficially held view which may be discarded the next moment" and "a cherished conviction which will change only under unusual pressure." The current academic debate focuses mostly on how to differentiate between the two extremes. Some researchers suggest there is a spectrum, from non-attitudes to quasi-attitudes to real attitudes. Quasi-attitudes are in the middle of the spectrum, because they signify lightly held views that tend to correlate with other opinions and demographic characteristics but also tend to be quite "labile." The issue is where along this spectrum it makes sense to draw the line between opinion and non-opinion. . . .

To tell the truth about Americans' opinions on policy matters, pollsters should routinely measure the extent of public ignorance. It will never be zero, and in most cases it will represent a substantial proportion of the citizenry. Measuring it costs nothing; all it requires is offering an option that allows respondents to admit that they don't have an opinion. Because it's an important element in understanding the public, suppressing it for commercial or other purposes is simply unacceptable.

In addition, pollsters should include at least one additional question to measure the intensity of respondents' opinions. I would prefer . . . asking respondents if they would be "upset" if their opinion were not followed. There are other approaches, such as asking whether the issue is important to the respondents, or whether it would affect their vote for a political candidate. Whatever the approach, it's important to distinguish between the lightly held, top-of-mind response, which can change in an instant, and the more deeply held opinions that respondents want to see prevail. . . .

Any description of the general public's orientation toward specific policy proposals needs to mention explicitly how large is the size of the disengaged public—the proportion of people who admit up front that they have no opinion, plus those who initially express a view but immediately say that they don't care if it is ignored by elected leaders. Anytime a poll reports less than 20 percent of the public disengaged, it's almost certain the results have been manipulated and should be viewed with deep suspicion. . . .

Pollsters have known for a long time that election and public policy polls alike produce, at best, rough estimates of what the public is thinking. From the beginning of modern polling, experiments have shown that even small differences in question wording, or the order in which questions are read, can have a profound effect on results. The gender and race of interviewers, as well as whether surveys are conducted by telephone or online, through the mail, or in person can also affect responses. George Gallup was the first to conduct experiments that revealed the fuzziness of opinion, but he maintained a belief that the right questions, objectively worded, could accurately measure the will of the people. His vision was that polls would be able to continuously monitor "the pulse of democracy." It turns out that on most issues the public's pulse is either a bit weak or harder to discern than Gallup had hoped. . . .

The real problem with telling the truth about the public and the electorate is not that the elected leaders or the public can't handle it, but that the news media might find it dull. Journalists like sharply divided groups and extreme reactions because that makes their stories more exciting.

They like the fake stories about voter preferences years ahead of the election, and the exciting horse race of a fully decided electorate that nevertheless keeps changing its mind. They have become addicted to the fictitious national primary electorate, and entranced by their own illusion of a completely rational, all-knowing, and fully engaged public. Should they be forced to report on the real public, a more prosaic public of which large segments are minimally informed or disengaged or have opinions that are ambiguous or tentative, journalists might lose their obsessive fascination with polls. That could happen to some extent, though I doubt even polls that told the unvarnished truth about the public would lose their journalistic appeal completely. But even if pollsters believed that a reformed polling system would cause the news media to rely less often on poll reports, that's no argument for pollsters to continue pumping up false numbers to satisfy the press's unrealistic expectations.

I'm hopeful, if not wildly optimistic, that we are witnessing a historical phase that will soon pass, and that a more responsible approach to measuring public opinion lies in the not-too-distant future. Widespread dissatisfaction with polls can only increase as their dismal performances continue. Eventually, the many conflicting and nonsensical results should shame pollsters and the news media into reform. Only if that happens will polls achieve their ideal role in the democratic process—telling the truth about the public, warts and all.

PART ELEVEN

Interest Groups

61

ALEXIS DE TOCQUEVILLE

From *Democracy in America*

Interest-group politics remains a big part of U.S. government today—for good and bad. But it is not as new a part as it may seem. Young French aristocrat Alexis de Tocqueville, visiting in 1831, observed how naturally Americans formed "associations." Just like today, groups were formed "to promote the public safety, commerce, industry, morality, and religion." In a country that emphasized individuality, Tocqueville thought, group allegiances gave people the power to work together to reach shared goals. American interest groups were out in the open, meeting freely to advance their viewpoints. Tocqueville, whose earlier selection from Democracy in America *opened this book, placed great faith in interest groups as a way that minorities could protect themselves from "tyranny of the majority." Today, one wonders how he would suggest that the nation protect itself from the tyranny of interest groups.*

IN NO COUNTRY IN the world has the principle of association been more successfully used, or more unsparingly applied to a multitude of different objects, than in America. Besides the permanent associations, which are established by law under the names of townships, cities, and counties, a vast number of others are formed and maintained by the agency of private individuals.

The citizen of the United States is taught from his earliest infancy to rely upon his own exertions, in order to resist the evils and the difficulties of life; he looks upon the social authority with an eye of mistrust and anxiety, and he only claims its assistance when he is quite unable to shift without it. This habit may even be traced in the schools of the rising generation, where the children in their games are wont to submit to rules which they have themselves established, and to punish misdemeanors which they have themselves defined. The same spirit pervades every act of social life. If a stoppage occurs in a thoroughfare, and the circulation of the public is hindered, the neighbors immediately constitute a deliberative body; and this extemporaneous assembly gives rise to an executive power, which remedies the inconvenience, before anybody has thought of recurring to an authority superior to that of the persons immediately concerned. If the public pleasures are concerned, an association is formed to provide for the splendor and the regularity of the entertainment. Societies are formed to resist enemies which are exclusively of a moral nature, and to diminish the vice of intemperance: in the United States associations are established to promote public order, commerce, industry, morality, and religion, for there is no end which the human will seconded by the collective exertions of individuals, despairs of attaining. . . .

An association consists simply in the public assent which a number of individuals give to certain doctrines; and in the engagement which they contract to promote the spread of those doctrines by their exertions. The right of associating with such views is very analogous to the liberty of unlicensed writing; but societies thus formed possess more authority than the press. When an opinion is represented by a society, it necessarily assumes a more exact and explicit form. It numbers its partisans, and compromises their welfare in its cause: they, on the other hand, become acquainted with each other, and their zeal is increased by their number. An association unites the efforts of minds which have a tendency to diverge in one single channel, and urges them vigorously towards the one single end which it points out.

The second degree in the right of association is the power of meeting. When an association is allowed to establish centres of action at certain important points in the country, its activity is increased, and its influence extended. Men have the opportunity of seeing each other; means of execution are more readily combined; and opinions are maintained with a warmth and energy which written language cannot approach.

Lastly, in the exercise of the right of political association, there is a third degree: the partisans of an opinion may unite in electoral bodies, and choose delegates to represent them in a central assembly. This is, properly speaking, the application of the representative system to a party.

Thus, in the first instance, a society is formed between individuals professing the same opinion, and the tie which keeps it together is of a purely intellectual nature: in the second case, small assemblies are formed which only represent a faction of the party. Lastly, in the third case, they constitute a separate nation in the midst of the nation, a government within the Government. . . .

It cannot be denied that the unrestrained liberty of association for political purposes is the privilege which a people is longest in learning how to exercise. If it does not throw the nation into anarchy, it perpetually augments the chances of that calamity. On one point, however, this perilous liberty offers a security against dangers of another kind; in countries where associations are free, secret societies are unknown. In America, there are numerous factions, but no conspiracies. . . .

The most natural privilege of man, next to the right of acting for himself, is that of combining his exertions with those of his fellow-creatures, and of acting in common with them. I am therefore led to conclude that the right of association is almost as inalienable as the right of personal liberty. . . .

62

E. E. SCHATTSCHNEIDER

From *The Semisovereign People*

The late 1950s and early 1960s was a time when political scientists placed their focus on the interest group theory of American politics. Although hardly a new idea, interest group politics was studied intensely, sometimes to be idealized as the perfect model of government and other times critiqued as the downfall of democracy. Scholar E. E. Schattschneider's much-cited book explored the "pressure system" in American politics, dominated by "organized" (as opposed to informal), "special-interest" (not public-interest) groups. Schattschneider's conclusion was that "the pressure system has an upper-class bias." Decades later, political scientists might not use the exact same language as Schattschneider, who relied on the concept of class in his analysis. Today, vastly different degrees of organization, financial resources, and intensity separate interest group claimants in the competition for getting their issues heard by the government.

———

MORE THAN any other system American politics provides the raw materials for testing the organizational assumptions of two contrasting kinds of politics, *pressure politics* and *party politics.* The concepts that underlie these forms of politics constitute the raw stuff of a general theory of political action. The basic issue between the two patterns of organization is one of size and scope of conflict; pressure groups are small-scale organizations while political parties are very large-scale organizations. One need not be surprised, therefore, that the partisans of large-scale and small-scale organizations differ passionately, because the outcome of the political game depends on the scale on which it is played.

To understand the controversy about the scale of political organization it is necessary first to take a look at some theories about interest-group politics. Pressure groups have played a remarkable role in American politics, but they have played an even more remarkable role in American political theory. Considering the political condition of the country in the first third of the twentieth century, it was probably inevitable that the discussion of special interest pressure groups should lead to development of "group" theories of politics in which an attempt is made to explain everything in terms of group activity, i.e., an attempt to formulate a universal group theory. Since one of the best ways to test an idea is to ride it into the ground, political theory has unquestionably been improved by the heroic attempt to create a political universe revolving about the group. Now that we have a number of drastic statements of the group theory of politics pushed to a great extreme, we ought to be able to see what the limitations of the idea are. . . .

One difficulty running through the literature of the subject results from the attempt to explain *everything* in terms of the group theory. On general grounds it would be remarkable indeed if a single hypothesis explained everything about so complex a subject as American politics. Other difficulties have grown out of the fact that group concepts have been stated in terms so universal that the subject seems to have no shape or form.

The question is: Are pressure groups the universal basic ingredient of all political situations, and do they explain everything? To answer this question it is necessary to review a bit of rudimentary political theory.

Two modest reservations might be made merely to test the group dogma. We might clarify our ideas if (1) we explore more fully the possibility of making a distinction between public interest groups and special-interest groups and (2) if we distinguished between organized and unorganized groups. . . .

As a matter of fact, the distinction between *public* and *private* interests is a thoroughly respectable one; it is one of the oldest known to political theory. In the literature of the subject the public interest refers to general or common interests shared by all or by substantially all members of the community. Presumably no community exists unless there is some kind of community of interests, just as there is no nation without some notion of national interests. If it is really impossible to distinguish between private and public interests the group theorists have produced a revolution in political thought so great that it is impossible to foresee its consequences. For this reason the distinction ought to be explored with great care.

At a time when nationalism is described as one of the most dynamic forces in the world, it should not be difficult to understand that national interests actually do exist. It is necessary only to consider the proportion of the American budget devoted to national defense to realize that the common interest in national survival is a great one. Measured in dollars this interest is one of the biggest things in the world. Moreover, it is difficult to describe this interest as special. The diet on which the American leviathan feeds is something more than a jungle of disparate special interests. In the literature of democratic theory the body of common agreement found in the community is known as the "consensus" without which it is believed that no democratic system can survive.

The reality of the common interest is suggested by demonstrated capacity of the community to survive. There must be something that holds people together.

In contrast with the common interests are the special interests. The implication of this term is that these are interests shared by only a few people or a fraction of the community; they *exclude* others and may be *adverse* to them. A special interest is exclusive in about the same way as private property is exclusive. In a complex society it is not surprising that there are some interests that are shared by all or substantially all members of the community and some interests that are not shared so widely. The distinction is useful precisely because conflicting claims are made by people about the nature of their interests in controversial matters. . . .

Is it possible to distinguish between the "interests" of the members of the National Association of Manufacturers and the members of the American League to Abolish Capital Punishment? The facts in the two cases are not identical. First, *the members of the A.L.A.C.P. obviously do not expect to be hanged.* The membership of the A.L.A.C.P. is not restricted to persons under indictment for murder or in jeopardy of the extreme penalty. *Anybody* can join A.L.A.C.P. Its members oppose capital punishment although they are not personally likely to benefit by the policy they advocate. The inference is therefore that the interest of the A.L.A.C.P. is not adverse, exclusive or special. It is not like the interest of the Petroleum Institute in depletion allowances. . . .

We can now examine the second distinction, the distinction between organized and unorganized groups. The question here is not whether the distinction can be made but whether or not it is worth making. Organization has been described as "merely a stage or degree of interaction" in the development of a group.

The proposition is a good one, but what conclusions do we draw from it? We do not dispose of the matter by calling the distinction between organized and unorganized groups a "mere" difference of degree because some of the greatest differences in the world are differences of degree. As far as special-interest politics is concerned the implication to be avoided is that a few workmen who habitually stop at a corner saloon for a glass of beer are essentially the same as the United States Army because the difference between them is merely one of degree. At this point we have a distinction that makes a difference. . . .

If we are able, therefore, to distinguish between public and private interests and between organized and unorganized groups we have marked out the major boundaries of the subject; *we have given the subject shape and scope.* We are now in a position to attempt to define the area we want to explore. Having cut the pie into four pieces, we can now appropriate the piece we want and leave the rest to someone else. For a multitude of reasons *the most likely field of study is that of the organized, special-interest groups*. The advantage of concentrating on organized groups is that they are known, identifiable and recognizable. The advantage of concentrating on special-interest groups is that they have one important characteristic in common: they are all exclusive. This piece of the pie (the organized special-interest groups) we shall call the *pressure system*. The pressure system has boundaries we can define; we can fix its scope and make an attempt to estimate its bias. . . .

The organized groups listed in the various directories (such as *National Associations of the United States*, published at intervals by the United States Department of Commerce) and specialty yearbooks, registers, etc., and the *Lobby Index*, published by the United States House of Representatives, probably include the bulk of the organizations in the pressure system. All compilations are incomplete, but these are extensive enough to provide us with some basis for estimating the scope of the system. . . .

When lists of these organizations are examined, the fact that strikes the student most forcibly is that *the system is very small*. The range of organized, identifiable, known groups is amazingly narrow; there is nothing remotely universal about it. There is a tendency on the part of the publishers of directories of associations to place an undue emphasis on business organizations, an emphasis that is almost inevitable because the business community is by a wide margin the most highly organized segment of society. Publishers doubtless tend also to reflect public demand for information. Nevertheless, the dominance of business groups in the pressure system is so marked that it probably cannot be explained away as an accident of the publishing industry. . . .

The business or upper-class bias of the pressure system shows up everywhere. Businessmen are four or five times as likely to write to their congressmen as manual laborers are. College graduates are far more apt to write to their congressmen than people in the lowest educational category are. . . .

Broadly, the pressure system has an upper-class bias. There is overwhelming evidence that participation in voluntary organizations is related to upper social and economic status; the rate of participation is much higher in the upper strata than it is elsewhere. . . .

The bias of the system is shown by the fact that *even nonbusiness organizations reflect an upper-class tendency*. . . .

The class bias of associational activity gives meaning to the limited scope of the pressure system, because *scope and bias are aspects of the same tendency.* The data raise a serious question about the validity of the proposition that special-interest groups are a universal form of political organization reflecting *all* interests. As a matter of fact, to suppose that everyone participates in pressure-group activity and that all interests get themselves organized in the pressure system is to destroy the meaning of this form of politics. The pressure system makes sense only as the political instrument of a segment of the community. It gets results by being selective and biased; *if everybody got into the act the unique advantages of this form of organization would be destroyed, for it is possible that if all interests could be mobilized the result would be a stalemate.*

Special-interest organizations are most easily formed when they deal with small numbers of individuals who are acutely aware of their exclusive interests. To describe the conditions of pressure-group organization in this way is, however, to say that it is primarily a business phenomenon. Aside from a few very large organizations (the churches, organized labor, farm organizations, and veterans' organizations) the residue is a small segment of the population. *Pressure politics is essentially the politics of small groups.*

The vice of the groupist theory is that it conceals the most significant aspects of the system. The flaw in the pluralist heaven is that the heavenly chorus sings with a strong upper-class accent. Probably about 90 percent of the people cannot get into the pressure system.

The notion that the pressure system is automatically representative of the whole community is a myth fostered by the universalizing tendency of modern group theories. *Pressure politics is a selective process* ill designed to serve diffuse interests. The system is skewed, loaded and unbalanced in favor of a fraction of a minority. . . .

The competing claims of pressure groups and political parties for the loyalty of the American public revolve about the difference between the results likely to be achieved by small-scale and large-scale political organization. Inevitably, the outcome of pressure politics and party politics will be vastly different.

63

RICHARD SKINNER

From *More Than Money*

Interest groups play an important role in American politics. Critics may condemn the tactics of interest groups, while defenders cite their role in voicing citizens' views to their government. Author Richard Skinner gives some solid background for understanding the world of interest groups. He discusses groups' knowledge about their specific issues, their ability to locate voters who believe a particular issue to be important, and their skill in helping to run campaigns. Skinner's examples are many and varied: the Sierra Club, the National Rifle Association, the National Abortion and Reproductive Rights Action League, the National Association for the Advancement of Colored People, the American Federation of Labor–Congress of Industrial Organizations, the Association of Trial Lawyers of America, the National Federation of Independent Business, EMILY's List. The excerpt concludes by mentioning the complex relationship between interest groups and political parties. In this era, Skinner believes, interest groups have become critical parts of "party networks," further underscoring the link between groups and parties.

———

[ANOTHER] RESOURCE AVAILABLE to groups is expertise. In this context, expertise consists of special abilities and knowledge that groups can bring to bear in order to win elections. While expertise is necessary to use the other resources effectively, and money and membership are needed to build expertise, expertise is still a separate and distinct resource. Longtime staffers may have skills, acquired from years of activity, that are not easy to duplicate—although political professionals do frequently change jobs, moving from group to group, working for this or that campaign. An organization may have established credibility with members or other voters that can be difficult to replicate. A group may have been closely identified with an issue through decades of activism, such as the Sierra Club and the environment or Planned Parenthood and sexual health. This can build a reputation among voters that can pay off at election time. Or a group may have built a close relationship with its members by advocating for their interests, as organized labor has. Expertise is not simply money transmuted into another form.

There are several types of expertise that an organization can employ in order to win elections. One is *issue credibility,* the ability to speak on a particular issue in a way than affects voters' decisions. Closely aligned with issue credibility is *targeting voters,* the ability to reach specific voters outside the organization, usually ones who care about a priority issue. Another form of expertise is *targeting races,* that is, selecting which races will receive priority involvement. Finally, some groups provide *campaign services,* such as polls, demographic research, candidate training, or fund-raising. . . .

Perhaps the most important form of expertise is issue credibility, the ability to speak out on particular issues in a way that sways a significant number of voters. Issue credibility comes from years of activity, from public visibility, from ties to other organizations, and from spending money. Groups may aim their efforts at a particular segment of voters, often compiled in a computerized list, or at a much broader audience. Groups can use issue credibility not just to win elections, but to raise the salience and visibility of their issue. If politicians believe that a given issue sways voters, they will treat it as important.

Issue credibility has been the Sierra Club's stock-in-trade. . . . In 1998, the club targeted twenty-four races; its favored candidates won in twenty-two of them. . . . But its most visible weapon has been issue ads, which allow the club to use its treasury funds without dipping into its PAC money. Generally speaking, the club has preferred to run issue ads early during campaigns, so it can make the environment a priority issue for candidates and to avoid being drowned out by ads by candidates or by richer interest groups. *National Journal* estimated the club's overall spending in the 2000 elections as between $9 million and $9.5 million.

Perhaps the most visible aspect of its 2000 efforts was the Environmental Voter Education Campaign, an $8 million issue advocacy campaign. EVEC targeted mostly Republicans. . . . The club also thanked eleven members for their environmental records; most of these members were Democrats. . . . In 2000, EVEC included mailings, broadcast ads, "video voter guides," and a website. The club targeted women ages twenty-five to forty-five who have children; the club's staff believed that they are more likely to care about environmental issues such as clean air and water. For the first time, the club also produced Spanish-language ads; one former club official argued that Hispanic families have the same concerns as their Anglo counterparts, especially recreation. . . .

Since the environment is an issue with broad public appeal, the Sierra Club has mostly pursued highly visible methods of getting out its message, as opposed to the "under-the-radar" techniques used by other groups. But, with their fund-raising down and the environment off the public agenda after 9/11, the Sierra Club mostly shifted to "ground war" techniques in 2002, particularly in Senate races in Colorado, Minnesota, New Hampshire, and Missouri. The Sierra Club continued this approach in 2004.

The Sierra Club's staff believe that they have greatest credibility when they speak about local issues and when they attack an incumbent for a poor voting record, rather than praising a good one. Local issues mean more to voters than abstract concerns about the Amazon rain forest or global warming. In addition, local issues allow the club to speak to voters in areas not usually seen as sympathetic to environmentalists; for example, pollution from hog farms has become an important issue in the rural Midwest and South. Going negative works better than going positive because voters expect officials to protect the environment, and are shocked when they do not.

Deanna White, deputy political director of the Sierra Club, said that her group's greatest success in 2000 was

the increased visibility of the environment as an issue. And ultimately that's the goal of our program—to get people to talk about the environment. Because the more visibility it gets, the more aware decision makers are that people care about the environment and the more they will be held accountable for what they do.

Other groups capitalize on issue credibility in order to move voters. But many of these groups target their efforts far more than the Sierra Club does. Activists who are interested in "hot-button" issues such as abortion and gun control know that their issues are not salient to many or even most voters. (For example, in four meetings with NRA staff, at no time did they mention contacting voters who do not own guns.) They also know that their opponents care passionately about these issues, and could be activated by a broadcast campaign. So groups concerned with these issues usually target their efforts narrowly at identified supporters.

The National Rifle Association (NRA) mostly eschews broadcast advertising; its main television campaign in 2000 was a series of infomercials aimed at encouraging gun owners to join the organization. Instead of "broadcasting" its message, the NRA "narrow-casts" to a selected audience of gun owners. The National Right to Life Committee (NRLC) also avoids broadcast advertising; instead, it and its state affiliates focus on those voters who share their antiabortion commitment. (The exceptions to these rules are telling. The NRA has broadcast some advertisements on cable outlets such as the Outdoor Life Network and in rural TV markets. In both cases, few unsympathetic voters are likely to see the spots. Similarly, Right to Life occasionally runs advertisements on Christian radio.) NARAL [The National Abortion and Reproductive Rights Action League; Pro-Choice America] has sponsored broadcast advertising before, especially in 1992, a year of unusually high activism by abortion rights advocates. But in 2000, it switched to communicating with identified pro-choice voters by phone, mail, and e-mail. An official with Planned Parenthood suggested that NARAL made its switch because it had exhausted its credibility with "swing" voters because it appeared too partisan and too focused on the single issue of abortion. By contrast, Planned Parenthood, which had built up credibility and a nonpartisan "public service" image over many decades, was able to capitalize on these assets in 2000. It conducted a $7 million television campaign decrying George W. Bush's views on abortion and sex education that was targeted at such key states as Florida and Pennsylvania.

These groups may target their pitches to sympathetic audiences because they do not want to risk mistakenly activating the opposition: a pro-choice Republican who sees a Right to Life advertisement backing an antiabortion GOP candidate may decide to vote Democratic this year. It may also allow the groups to use tougher, more persuasive pitches than they could if their messages were going to the general public. Finally, it may simply be more efficient to spend their money on phone banks or mass mailings rather than TV time for ads that will reach many voters who are apathetic or antagonistic on the groups' issues. . . .

[A] group that relied heavily on a voter list was the NAACP [National Association for the Advancement of Colored People] National Voter Fund, created in 2000 to increase political participation by African Americans. It used a voter file of 3.8 million black voters; the fund staff decided to concentrate on infrequent voters because most groups preferred to contact those likely to vote. According to Heather Booth, director of the fund, only about one-fifth of the people included in the list voted frequently. Almost half rarely voted. The fund assembled the file in cooperation with other groups and with a vendor. The vendor acted as a broker, helping the fund buy the best lists in targeted states. The list could be broken down by state, congressional district, age, gender, or marital status. By contacting these voters, the NAACP could translate the issue credibility built through decades of advocating for African Americans into results at the ballot box.

Lists can also be compiled from publicly available sources. While the National Rifle Association boasts more than 4 million members, that is only a small percentage of the estimated 80 million Americans who own a gun. (Polls have shown that about two out of five American adults own a firearm; for example, a 1999 Louis Harris survey found that 39 percent of respondents reported having a gun in their home or garage. . . .) Since there is no national registry of gun owners—thanks in part to the NRA's efforts—the organization has to put together its own list for voter contact. The NRA buys some lists that are likely to contain many gun owners, for example, subscribers to outdoor-sports magazines such as *Field and Stream, Guns and Ammo,* and *Outdoor Life.* But the NRA also uses many publicly available lists: those of licensed hunters and holders of concealed weapon permits, for example. NRA volunteers attend gun shows and visit gun stores, where they obtain lists of customers. The NRA can then add these names to its lists of gun owners targeted for voter turnout. . . .

Once groups have targeted voters, they have to reach them. The most common means of contacting voters are phone, mail, and e-mail. Usually, reaching voters by phone simply means using phone banks, whether staffed by volunteers or paid workers, whether in-house or outside. But telemarketers have worn out Americans' patience for being called at home. So groups have had to get more creative. One of the most distinctive means of reaching voters by phone is "robo-calling." This is the use of a taped message sent out by computer to thousands of potential voters, usually on the eve of an election, with the purpose of reminding them to vote. Often the message is intended more for being recorded on an answering machine rather than being heard directly by the recipient. The message is frequently recorded by a celebrity or by a politician. NARAL used messages recorded by Sarah Jessica Parker, star of HBO's *Sex and the City,* while Planned Parenthood used Barbra Streisand. The NAACP National Voter Fund used Bill Clinton. (Interestingly, the fund found that the infrequent voters it targeted welcomed phone calls at home; unlike more politically active people, they were not used to people asking for their votes.) By contrast, and perhaps illustrating the importance of grassroots organization, the National Education Association used the leaders of the local affiliates. While robo-calls seem cutting edge, the evidence of their effectiveness is mixed at best. Certainly they are no substitute for more personal means of contacting voters.

The other classic means of reaching targeted voters is by mail. The NRA has long sent distinctive orange postcards reminding gun owners of its endorsements. It also mails bumper stickers that serve as visible evidence of the NRA's support for a candidate. The Sierra Club sends voter guides to its members and others. While its mailings are not as focused as some other group's, they are primarily sent to its primary target audience of women ages twenty-five to forty-five who are registered to vote. The lists have been purchased from vendors.

With the growth of the Internet, most politically active groups have developed an online presence. All of the groups included in this study have sophisticated websites where visitors can get lists of endorsements and statements on public issues and sign up for e-mail lists. On the AFL-CIO's [American Federation of Labor–Congress of Industrial Organizations] site, workers could download flyers that could then be printed and distributed. The Sierra Club experimented with banner ads on popular Internet sites, but did not find them particularly helpful. The National Rifle Association is collecting e-mail addresses from its members to supplement "snail mail" addresses and telephone numbers. In May 2001, NRA federal affairs director Chuck Cunningham estimated that his organization had collected about 200,000 e-mail addresses, but hoped to have 2 million within a year. NARAL collects e-mail address through mail and its website. Planned Parenthood also uses e-mail to contact its activists, and the e-mails may even include links to streaming video. But one top official expressed skepticism about e-mail, since it is not organized geographically. The National Education Association also e-mails its members, and it has the added difficulty that it is not allowed to send e-mail to teachers' work addresses. . . .

Interest groups possess expertise that is not easily transferred and that is not simply an outgrowth of spending. While unions can contribute millions of dollars to Democratic candidates and committees, they cannot so easily transfer their expertise at turning out their members to vote. The NRA has invested years of work and treasure in building its credibility with gun owners; a start-up organization could not expect to duplicate the NRA's clout, even if it could match its spending. The Sierra Club, the NAACP, and Planned Parenthood all have "brand names" that may be as relevant to voters as Coca-Cola, Kellogg, and Budweiser are to consumers.

For many organizations, their political expertise helps justify their very existence. Group leaders can boast of their effectiveness to potential members, to journalists, to other political activists. Belonging to a group that has shown political prowess can itself be an incentive for members to join.

Groups' areas of expertise allow them to fulfill different roles in the party networks. The NRA can mobilize gun owners, while Right to Life organizations can turn out antiabortion voters, both usually in support of Republican candidates. Arguably, both can speak to their constituencies more effectively than the party committees can. Similarly, unions can turn out their members, the Sierra Club can talk to "soccer moms" about the environment, and ATLA [Association of Trial Lawyers of America] can encourage trial lawyers to contribute to Democratic candidates. While these webs of relationships are not precisely the same as formal party organizations, they are still essential parts of party politics today—"extended parties" or "party networks." . . . .

. . . [P]olitical scientists have tended to view groups and parties as competing forms of political organization. Parties aggregate voters; groups disaggregate them. Parties serve to counteract the inegalitarian biases of the American system; groups exacerbate them. During the 1960s, 1970s, and 1980s, commentators decried the simultaneous decline of political parties and the proliferation of interest groups. On the fate of political parties, however, a new conventional wisdom is beginning to emerge: that parties have actually experienced a revival over the past two decades.

With this strengthening and polarization of political parties, we may be seeing an evolution by some interest groups toward closer ties to the parties. With the current atmosphere of polarization, it may no longer be as easy for groups to work with members of both parties. Narrow margins of control make every seat count. Close group-party alliances, such as those between the Democrats and organized labor and between the Republicans and the Christian Right, have been flourishing. These ties may be growing strong enough that we can treat some groups as actual parts of a party network. As part of this party network, groups can perform valuable tasks that are beyond the capabilities of the party committees. . . .

. . . [S]ome interest groups clearly have developed closer relationships with the political parties. They are often part of the same partisan and ideological networks of individuals and organizations. These party networks not only include party committees and friendly interest groups, they include individual politicians and the leadership PACs under their control, think tanks, lobbyists, and perhaps even media figures. The Republican National Committee, the NFIB [National Federation of Independent Business], Tom DeLay and his [now defunct] leadership PAC (Americans for a Republican Majority), the Heritage Foundation, Vin Weber (a onetime House Republican, now a well-connected lobbyist), and Rush Limbaugh are part of a Republican network. This network shares information and coordinates activity.

The professionalization of politics has allowed more individuals to both live "off" politics and live "for" politics. Rather than being rewarded with deputy postmasterships or sinecures in the city Parks Department, today's political professionals can instead seek jobs as chiefs of staff or communications directors, perhaps with an eye to an eventual corner office on K Street.* As they move from position to position, professionals remain enmeshed in webs of relationships within their own partisan universes. Even when working as lobbyists or consultants, they remain active in support of their party and its candidates. . . .

We need to expand our notion of what a political party is. It is not simply a series of committees. It is instead a matrix of relationships between politicians, whether they work in party organizations, in interest groups, in the media, in political action committees, in consulting firms, or in government itself. The activists at the Sierra Club, EMILY's List [Early Money is Like Yeast—it makes the dough rise], or the AFL-CIO may not get their checks from the Democratic National Committee, but they are part of the same Democratic Party network. The people working for the NRA, the NFIB, or other Republican-leaning organizations are essential parts of the Republican Party network. Rather than tearing down the party system, they are among its most important pillars. . . .

---

*K Street, in Washington, D.C., is filled with many prosperous firms that engage in lobbying for businesses, foreign nations, and, well, basically any organization that will pay for their services. The lobbying firms can be called law firms, public relations firms, or consultants, but the bottom line is that K Street is synonymous with lobbying.—EDS.

64

ROBERT KAISER

From *So Damn Much Money*

The inside story of lobbying firms in Washington, DC, is told through the story of the rise and fall of Gerald Cassidy, co-founder of Schlossberg-Cassidy & Associates, once the preeminent K Street lobbying organization. Robert Kaiser tells us about the young consultants' (Cassidy and his partner, Kenneth Schlossberg) start in the 1970s when their efforts on behalf of Tufts University yielded an early "earmark"—a word later to become one of every American government student's key terms. Kaiser points out the "deep conflict of American values" that lobbying provokes. Of course, influence over the decisions that government makes is central to the U.S. political system. But lobbying became a big industry—a big-money industry. Kaiser follows the firm, which became Cassidy & Associates, into the 1980s and 1990s, as the nation's economy prospered and wealth grew. Lobbyists got their share. In the new millennium, with the cost of political campaigns soaring, lobbyists became deeply involved in fundraising on behalf of members of Congress. While alas, the fate of Cassidy & Associates is not an entirely happy one, Kaiser reveals, the interrelationships of members of Congress, PACs, lobbyists and money continue on. The more important government becomes in the lives of Americans, the higher the stakes for interested groups and the lobbyists who carry their messages.

FRIENDS WHO KNEW BOTH MEN at the time agree that the firm was [Kenneth] Schlossberg's idea, and that he was the moving force in its creation. The firm's original name suggests as much: Schlossberg-Cassidy & Associates. Schlossberg was the president, [Gerald] Cassidy the secretary-treasurer. The only "associate" was Loretta Cassidy, who did some secretarial work. . . .

The official address of Schlossberg-Cassidy & Associates was 623 South Carolina Avenue, Schlossberg's Capitol Hill townhouse. The office was in the basement. The firm's original articles of incorporation, filed in May 1975, described its "purposes" in terms that reflected Schlossberg's original idea: "To provide a broad range of services to industry and government including but not limited to research, counseling, evaluation, planning, policy making and analysis of agricultural, food, nutrition and health programs, policies and products." No lobbying there.

Nor, it soon became clear, was there much business. The two sent hundreds of letters to everyone they could think of, announcing the creation of their new firm and offering to help solve problems in Washington. No one responded. . . .

Cassidy wanted to be a big-time lobbyist like Claude Desautels, who once worked on John F. Kennedy's White House staff as a liaison to Congress, then lobbied Congress for Kennedy's longtime political advisor Lawrence O'Brien Jr. when O'Brien became postmaster general, then became an almost invisible but effective and successful Washington lobbyist.

Desautels was one of the people Cassidy consulted when he was just starting out, and his advice made a deep impression: always work on a retainer basis—a fixed monthly fee—and always insist on payment in advance. "He had a lot of very large clients," Cassidy remembered—just what Cassidy wanted himself.

Asked to summarize his ambition for the new firm, Cassidy replied: "I wanted to be successful and financially secure." This would be the theme of his life and career.

Alan Stone, of the nutrition committee, probably had it right when he said their relationship was doomed.

After six months in operation, Schlossberg-Cassidy was a going concern. Pillsbury, Nabisco, and General Mills had joined its roster of clients. Schlossberg and Cassidy had real income, several thousand dollars a month each. "In about December," Cassidy said, "I thought we had enough money to get an office."

This was the sort of matter that he handled. He and Loretta found an office in L'Enfant Plaza, a hulking office complex designed by I. M. Pei then several years old. Part of an urban renewal project, it was wedged between Independence Avenue and the Southeast Freeway, about half a mile from the Capitol. "It was a single office. You could have a little reception area if you put in bookcases to block it off. That was our first office. We moved in there like March or so. We rented furniture," Cassidy remembered.

On its first birthday, Schlossberg-Cassidy & Associates was pretty much what Schlossberg had envisioned: a modest consulting firm specializing in food and nutrition issues. Lobbying Congress was not yet an important part of its repertoire. Its one-room office accurately signified its insignificance on the Washington scene. "We couldn't afford parking," Cassidy remembered, "so we would find parking spaces down on Maine Avenue," near the Anacostia River. Then in the summer and fall of 1976, their world changed.

The agent of this change was a charismatic Frenchman named Jean

Mayer, a biologist and physician who earned doctorates from the Sorbonne and Yale, and became famous as a nutritionist on the faculty of the Harvard School of Public Health. His fame grew in the late 1960s when Americans began looking seriously at hunger and malnutrition in their own country. When the Nixon White House called a White House Conference on Food, Nutrition and Health, Mayer was invited to be its chairman, giving him a highly visible national platform.

As an immigrant Mayer was an outsider in American academic life, but this did not diminish his ambition. When a search began for a new president of Harvard in 1971, Mayer threw his hat into the ring. Harvard's trustees picked Derek Bok, a law professor, instead, but the experience whetted Mayer's appetite. Five years later he accepted an offer from Tufts University to become its president.

Tufts, a venerable institution founded in 1852, was located in Medford, Massachusetts, just a few miles from Harvard. But in the academic world the distance between the two was far greater. Tufts had a middling reputation and modest ambitions when Mayer took over in 1976. But he was determined to change its status. "He had a vision of rebuilding Tufts, turning it from a commuter school into an elite school," Cassidy recalled, "and he thought the key to it was federal funding." Even before he was inaugurated as Tufts' tenth president in September 1976, Mayer approached the young partners of Schlossberg-Cassidy to seek their help.

How he approached them is, typically, disputed by Cassidy and Schlossberg. Mayer died in 1993, so he cannot resolve the dispute. Cassidy's version: "In June [of 1976] I got a call from Jean Mayer and [he asked] where the hell were we located? He came by, it was the first real business meeting I had in that office. It was me, Jean. . . . He wanted to get [federal] funds appropriated. . . . He wanted to build a national nutrition center."

Schlossberg's version: Yes, Mayer called the office in Washington and reached Gerry, but he asked for Schlossberg, who was then at his family's beach house in Massachusetts. He and Mayer had been working together for years. They became friends at the 1969 White House conference on nutrition that Mayer chaired. Mayer had invited Schlossberg to speak to his class at Harvard, then helped him organize a National Nutrition Policy Conference in the Senate. Schlossberg remembered that "Gerry called me and told me that Jean was looking for me to call him from my beach house at his office at Tufts." So, Schlossberg said, he placed the call.

"Jean said he was going to become the president of Tufts, and invited me to come see him for a chat. . . . I went from my beach house to Jean's office. . . . He said Tufts is a sort of second or third sister to Harvard, it doesn't have wealthy alumni, but I want to do some serious things here. I want to establish a human nutrition research center, and a school of veterinary medicine. Could you help me with this? How?

"I don't know what I can do," Schlossberg remembered saying, "but for $10,000 I'll take a hard look." Mayer agreed to his terms.

The fulfillment of Mayer's dream ultimately changed the way Congress spends much of the money that America's taxpayers provide to their government.

Cassidy and Schlossberg agree about what happened next: Cassidy, the lawyer and detail man, began looking for legislation on the books that they might exploit to help Mayer fulfill his ambitions.

The rules and procedures of the House and Senate can be maddeningly opaque and confusing. One of the most basic is also one of the least understood: the relationship between authorizing and appropriating. Traditionally, to spend the taxpayers' money, both houses must pass two pieces of legislation: the first to authorize the project on which money is to be spent, the second to allocate dollars from the Treasury to that project. This is why, for example, the Senate and House both have armed services committees and appropriations subcommittees on defense. The armed services committees are supposed to write legislation authorizing military programs; the defense appropriations subcommittees work on bills to fund what has been authorized. Eventually, the full House and Senate must approve versions of both kinds of legislation, and the president must sign the bills in order for the money to be spent.

Cassidy found a law on the books "that you could say authorized a national nutrition center," as he put it. It had been sponsored by Senator Quentin Burdick of North Dakota, and money had been appropriated for a project in North Dakota under the authorization. As Cassidy realized, its wording seemed to allow room to fund the facility Mayer hoped to create at Tufts.

Still, there were few precedents for what Mayer was seeking: a specific appropriation of federal funds to a single university for a particular facility, the nutrition research center. In years to come this kind of legislative provision would become so common that it acquired a widely used nickname—an earmark, short for an earmarked, or specifically directed, appropriation. But in 1976 this was an unusual idea.

Mayer was inaugurated president of Tufts on July 1, 1976. A reception was held for the new president, and the local congressman attended. Fortuitously, this was Tip O'Neill, who grew up a stone's throw from Tufts and was then the majority leader of the House of Representatives. Months later he would be its speaker.

Mayer shared some exciting news with Schlossberg and Cassidy after that reception. O'Neill, he reported, had told him he had a soft spot for Tufts. As boys, he and his brother used to sneak onto a football field there to play ball. If there is anything I can do for you while you are president of Tufts, he told Mayer, just let me know.

"Well, you can imagine having something like that fall into your lap," Schlossberg said years later. "It's like being at the casino and pulling the arm on the one-dollar machine with a million-dollar payoff and seeing the thing go *Gzing! Gzing! Gzing!* It didn't take me more than two seconds to start to have my own wheel in my own mind go *Gzing! Gzing! Gzing!* I'm sure it did the same thing with Gerry."

Soon afterward Cassidy and Schlossberg went to O'Neill's office in the Capitol to talk about the possibility of appropriating money for a human nutrition research center at Tufts. Schlossberg recounted a meeting with O'Neill, who "brought in his staff guy and said, 'These two guys work for President Mayer at Tufts. We're going to try to help them out. I want you to work with these guys.' Manna from heaven. We now have what would turn out to be—you know, like a prospector finding the first nugget with gold in it. This was what Tufts University was going to turn into." . . .

And there was nothing new about members of Congress bringing home the bacon. Extracting money and other benefits from the federal government for one's state or district has been part of the job for as long as there has been a Congress. When O'Neill, [Rep. Silvio] Conte, and [Sen. Edward] Kennedy shared credit for the creation of what became the Jean Mayer USDA Human Nutrition Research Center on Aging, they performed an ancient ritual by which members have long advertised their effectiveness to voters. The fact that Americans understand the phrase "bringing home the bacon" as a description of one aspect of politics is telling. The *Oxford English Dictionary* says that the origin of this usage involved farmers, not politicians. Not in America.

But Schlossberg-Cassidy & Associates had brought something new to an old game by stationing themselves at a key intersection between a supplicant for government assistance, Tufts, and the people who could respond—members of Congress and the executive branch. Their success for Tufts would create a new kind of Washington business and a new political art form, the earmark.

Schlossberg's evocation of a slot machine's *Gzing!* says it all. He, Cassidy, and Mayer all realized that they had stumbled on to something with big potential. Tufts was paying Schlossberg-Cassidy $10,000 a month. The federal government was providing the money Mayer needed. The Massachusetts politicians were delighted. This was a winning formula. . . .

The early earmarks for Tufts (another soon followed to help build a medical library) marked an unspoken victory for Gerry Cassidy over his partner. With them, the debate over Schlossberg-Cassidy's corporate identity ended. This was now a lobbying firm—*Gzing!* could have been the company motto. Schlossberg, making more money than he had ever seen in his life, did not complain, though he had misgivings.

The firm soon acquired a string of university clients, all looking for their own earmarks, each paying a handsome retainer. Cassidy had also brought in a substantial corporate client, a source of tension in the partnership but also of money in the bank. This was the Ocean Spray cranberry cooperative, a marketing organization owned by cranberry farmers that promoted and developed cranberry-based products.... Ocean Spray was having trouble getting cranberry juice approved by the Department of Agriculture for the federal school lunch program because its sugar content was high. ("Did you ever try to drink raw cranberry juice?" Cassidy likes to ask, even today. The sugar compensated for the cranberry's natural bitterness.) At Cassidy's suggestion, Ocean Spray set up one of the early political action committees, to funnel campaign contributions from cranberry farmers to politicians who could affect their business. Cassidy would run the PAC and help decide who got its money.

Schlossberg recalled this with discomfort. He remembered Cassidy "explaining to me what was going on in town with the DNC [Democratic National Committee] and corporate PACs [whose money both parties wanted], and what the law was, how this could make us a bigger player and help get things done."

Cassidy asked him to come to an Ocean Spray convention in San Diego, where Schlossberg played golf with members of the board. One of them, he recalled, "delivered a diatribe against FDR and his works—you'd have thought it was 1932." He found the Ocean Spray people distasteful, Schlossberg said. He was taken aback by Cassidy's enthusiasm for the Ocean Spray relationship, which had fulfilled his desire for a corporate client who would agree to set up a PAC. "He never got excited about anything the way he did about that," Schlossberg said.

Soon the two of them were making contributions to members themselves. In the beginning the amounts were small, but the role of money in politics was changing palpably.

So was the role of money in the Schlossberg-Cassidy partnership. They were paying themselves handsome salaries. They moved offices at L'Enfant Plaza, trading in their one room for a more spacious suite. Both bought bigger houses and fancier cars....

Both men had new Washington identities. They had met and made friends as warriors for the hungry and poor—underpaid aides to a Senate committee. Quite suddenly, they looked a lot like fat-cat Washington lobbyists. . . .

When Schlossberg-Cassidy & Associates moved unabashedly into the ranks of Washington's lobbyists, they joined an ancient profession. Lobbyists were present at the first session of the first Congress when it convened in New York City in March 1789, in the persons of wealthy New York merchants eager to delay congressional action on a tariff bill they thought would cost them money. They exploited what quickly became the most typical transaction between moneyed favor-seeker and elected legislator—a good dinner, well lubricated with wine and spirits, allowing the supplicant to make his case to the legislator in congenial circumstances. These merchants offered "treats, dinners, attentions," Senator William Maclay of Pennsylvania wrote in his diary. There would be many more such treats and attentions in the decades and centuries that followed. . . .

Despite the rich history of venality associated with influence peddling in Washington, there has always been more to lobbying than corruption. Americans can wax indignant at perceived abuses or at a system they consider crooked, but they also believe, often fervently, in the right to "petition the government for a redress of grievances," a right forcefully guaranteed in the First Amendment to the Constitution* and in the English common law from which the Constitution grew. To petition for the redress of grievances—to make a formal complaint about a perceived injustice committed by king or governors, and demand action to correct it—is often to do something that can fairly be described as lobbying. Of course lobbying can be corrupt, nefarious, even disgusting—Jack Abramoff demonstrated all of that. But lobbying can also express one of Americans' fundamental rights.

The lobbying profession elicits conflicting responses because it symbolizes a deep conflict of American values. Lobbying is corrupt and deplorable . . . until one's own ox is gored or threatened, at which point, let the lobbying begin! . . .

There is no evading this very American moral conundrum—a classic dilemma for a society and culture that loves to romanticize its history and avoid facing up to the gulf that so often separates its mythology from the

---

*"Congress shall make no law respecting an establishment of religion, or prohibiting the free exercise thereof; or abridging the freedom of speech, or of the press; or the right of the people peaceably to assemble, and to petition the government for a redress of grievances."

truth. In the matter of lobbying, Americans seem doomed to accept what often feel like contradictory propositions. So, for example, Americans tend to believe that people should not be getting rich by influencing government decisions after contributing money to the people who make them. But many of America's noblest institutions, among them the Red Cross, the United Way, the Kiwanis clubs, and the March of Dimes, pay handsome fees to Washington lobbyists to help them influence government decisions. If Americans enjoy an inalienable right to petition their government, are they not also entitled to some help from an expert who might actually know how the government works, and how its decisions might be influenced?

As a matter of historical fact, Americans have "lobbied" their governments for more than four hundred years, from the earliest days of the Virginia colony. Historians interpret this as evidence that a strong democratic impulse was operating in America long before independence or the founding of the modern republic. Seeking benefits, protection, or just a fair shake from the authorities of the day is an American reflex long taken for granted. . . .

Ethical ambiguity is the inevitable accompaniment to organized lobbying. The lobbyist is paid, often handsomely, to make something happen that might not have happened without his efforts. The worst of these transactions can be utterly venal, but how should we evaluate the best of them? Was the country well served by the creation, at taxpayers' expense, of a top-flight nutrition research center at Tufts? By the construction of new buildings for two of its best training academies for diplomats?

Cassidy and Schlossberg cast themselves on the side of the angels, helping deserving colleges and universities with the creative use of politics and government money. Happily for them, the work paid well.

. . . [By the early 1980s] Schlossberg-Cassidy's tactics were also examples of the new Washington mores—for example, promoting those earmarks for Columbia and Catholic University by helping the speaker's son sell insurance and by raising and contributing money to [Florida] Congressman [Don] Fuqua's re-election campaign. Not that using money and favors to achieve legislative objectives was a new idea—it is as old as the republic. But for the young and evolving lobbying firm of Schlossberg-Cassidy, this was new terrain.

Schlossberg said these maneuvers made him uncomfortable. "I didn't much care for how the whole thing developed and finally went down," he said of those efforts to cultivate O'Neill and Fuqua. "It reeked of quid pro quo and buying influence." He said he feared he could get into serious trouble, even go to jail. "Was what was going on legal? . . . I actually got a copy of the ethics rules governing House members and I discovered that there was no legal prohibition on doing business with children of members. So, I sucked it up."

Electoral politics, Washington lobbying, political fund-raising, and the nature of Congress were all changing in the years when Schlossberg-Cassidy's lobbying business was taking off. Members of Congress were discovering the benefits they could gain by helping the growing new class of lobbyists, which included many others besides Cassidy and Schlossberg. The lobbying business was growing because of the benefits lobbyists could win for clients from members who were realizing that they needed ever-increasing amounts of money to run the campaigns that could keep them in office.

In the early 1980s a new relationship began to develop between lobbyists and their clients "downtown," where a growing number of lobbying firms, trade associations, labor unions, and corporations maintained Washington offices, and "the Hill," Capitol Hill, home of the House and Senate. It was a relationship of mutual dependency. It was just beginning then and has strengthened significantly since, altering the public life of the country. . . .

The fate of Cassidy & Associates during 1989 was revealing. On one hand this was a year of public embarrassments: *The Washington Post* exposed the firm's modus operandi, the ways it exploited its relationships with members of Congress and greased them with campaign contributions and honoraria. The chairman of the Senate Appropriations Committee and former majority leader, Robert Byrd, had described Cassidy & Associates lobbyists (not by name, but unmistakably) as "influence peddlers" who "sell themselves as hired guns to the highest bidder." And yet, business boomed. Between January and September 1989, the firm signed up thirty new clients. Cassidy expected more than $21 million in revenue for that year. No lobbying firm in the history of Washington had taken in so much money.

This apparent contradiction disconcerted Cassidy, who never enjoyed criticism. He particularly disliked the opening that the *Post*'s articles and Byrd's statements gave to a growing group of competitors, lobbyists who finally caught on to how well Cassidy had done in the earmark business and were entering it themselves. "This is a very competitive city, and for a long time, people who we might be competing with would hand out an article about the Byrd Amendment [to prospective clients]. It went on for several years," Cassidy recalled.

Nevertheless, wasn't this a boom time for the firm?

"It was," Cassidy said. "But it was also a very difficult time. It was a boom time because we didn't stop. There's an old Irish expression, 'It's a great life if you don't weaken'—and we didn't weaken. We just pushed as hard as we could. Personally it was a very difficult time, and very stressful. . . .

What had been a rather small, narrowly focused lobbying firm turned into a big business, with a big payroll, big debts, a big list of clients, and a big "revenue number," to use the favored term of the lobbying industry. This transformation reflected Cassidy's ambitions, and also the spirit of the times." . . .

By the beginning of the new millennium, Washington was famous for cash of a different sort—campaign contributions. In the 2000 elections, the campaigns of all the candidates for president, the House, and the Senate cost $2.8 *billion*—three times what was spent in the 1976 elections, even after adjusting for inflation. In 2004, the total was $4.2 billion. This steady increase appears now to be a permanent fixture of our politics.

The escalation of the cost of politics has had many repercussions, altering the public life of the country and the political culture in Washington. Higher campaign costs contributed, for example, to a steadily rising number of wealthy men and women sitting in the House and Senate, as "self-funded" candidates exploited their natural advantages in electoral politics. John Corzine, a retired investment banker and a Democrat, spent $62 million of his own money in 2000 to win a Senate seat from New Jersey—the most ever spent on a Senate campaign. (What would the founding fathers, so suspicious of inherited wealth and power, have made of *that*?) As spending on campaigns grew, campaign consultants and pollsters—recipients of a lion's share of the money—became more important in Washington, and a lot more rich. A new kind of political technician entered the game, the fund-raising consultant. By the late 1990s most candidates for the House and Senate employed professionals who helped them raise money, for a fee or a percentage of the money raised. Another new elite in the capital consisted of PAC directors—the people who ran the political action committees that gave steadily increasing amounts to campaigns. Most PACs were connected to corporations, trade associations, and labor unions. Their contributions to congressional campaigns grew from $55 million for the election of 1980 to $363 million in the 2006 election cycle. PAC contributions rose by more than 600 percent in a quarter century.

The most significant repercussion has been on Congress itself. Today's members of the House and Senate lead lives that their predecessors of a generation or two ago would not recognize, because so much of their time is devoted to the search for money. "Most members hate fund-raising," Gerald Cassidy observed. "It's the most frequent complaint you hear from members. . . . Lobbyists complain about it, the members complain about it. It just goes back to this trap they're in, that campaign funding has created. . . . No one will disarm. No one will stop fund-raising because it could end their career. They raise money out of fear."

The more important money became to the politicians, the more important its donors became to them. This was a boon to Cassidy and all his colleagues and competitors. "The lobbyists are in the driver's seat," observed Leon Panetta. "They basically know that the members have nowhere else to turn" for money. This was not literally true, because the PACs were so big and so numerous, but lobbyists often told the PACs where to give their money (as Cassidy had with the Ocean Spray cranberry cooperative's PAC for many years). Panetta's remark precisely captured a fundamental truth about modern Washington, however: lobbyists had become indispensable to politicians. They served as advisors, fundraisers, even finance chairmen of their campaigns. . . .

"Money is the great equalizer for lobbyists," observed Jonathan Orloff, a former Cassidy employee. "Even if you are not very smart or charming, money makes up for a lot." . . .

Cassidy observed that in the twenty-first century, senators typically "spend ten, twenty million dollars on their campaigns. I don't believe our small contributions would sway them in any direction."

But if the money won't sway them, why give so much of it, and why give to so many different recipients? Because, as Cassidy said, the goal of these donations is usually not to achieve any particular objective, but rather to reinforce established connections: "A lot of money is given because of long-term relationships and friendships." Much of the money donated to politicians is Washington's version of frankincense and myrrh—symbolic tribute, meant to signal fealty and respect. . . .

Cassidy lived by those rules also. For him, as we've seen, nothing was more important than loyalty. In Cassidy's world, giving money is a meaningful expression of loyalty.

An honest lobbyist will acknowledge how their contributions help them function. "Why do lobbyists give so much money to politicians?" Dan Tate Sr., the former Cassidy lobbyist, once asked, rhetorically. "What's the purpose? Well, it isn't good government. It's to thank friends, and to make new friends. It opens up channels of communication."

Without access to members and their staffs, lobbyists have no hope of achieving their goals or impressing their clients. Everyone on Capitol Hill knows giving money leads to access. From time to time a member of Congress blurts out the truth. Congressman Romano Mazzoli, a Democrat from Kentucky from 1971 to 1995, did so soon after he retired from the House: "People who contribute get the ear of the member," he said. "They have the access, and access is it. Access is power. Access is clout. That's how this thing works." . . .

Cassidy & Associates began to slip down the list of top lobbying firms. From second place in 2003, when [new chief operating officer Gregg] Hartley came to the firm, it fell to fourth in the 2007 rankings. More ominously, its revenue declined by nearly 15 percent in those five years, from $28 million to $24.3 million. In 2003 it was just $1.4 million behind Patton Boggs, the leader; in 2007 it was $17.6 million behind. The other top firms were growing; Cassidy was not. Early in 2008, the firm lost one of its marquee names. Jack Quinn, the former congressman from Buffalo, decided to give up lobbying and to accept the presidency of Erie Community College in his hometown.

Many of the new, big-name clients fell off the list of Cassidy accounts, among them the Business Roundtable, Deutsche Telekom, Fidelity Investments, General Electric, Lucent Technologies, News Corporation, Swift, Wal-Mart, and Walt Disney. Five years into the Hartley era, 123 of the 203 clients added since his arrival had already left the firm.

"Cassidy & Associates has gone into eclipse," said an old friend of Cassidy's who had worked in the firm for many years. . . .

. . . Once the firm had been unique; for years it enjoyed huge competitive advantages. All that was gone, as the numbers made clear.

Nevertheless, the changes in Washington and its politics that Gerry Cassidy had witnessed, and often contributed to, endured. The nation's capital was now a big-money town, its politics utterly dependent on money. Tens of thousands of lobbyists worked the corridors of power—it was impossible to count them accurately. According to the filings that lobbyists and their clients had to make under the law, customers spent nearly $3 billion to lobby the government in 2007, but that was a fraction of the real amount spent to try to influence decisions in Congress and the executive branch. Lobbying was Washington's biggest business, and business was still booming. . . .

The sad political realities of the early twenty-first century were not the product of any decision to undermine American politics and government—there is no mastermind or villain in this story. Gerry Cassidy did not hope for this outcome—indeed, he deplored it. . . .

The mess was created by ordinary people responding logically to powerful incentives. In the memorable phrase of George Washington Plunkitt of New York City, holder of numerous public offices in the late nineteenth and early twentieth centuries, these men and women "seen [their] opportunities and [they] took 'em." . . .

Robert Strauss, a great Washington fixer, gets the last word. Cassidy worked for Strauss in 1973, soon after the Texan came to town, when he was the chairman of the Democratic National Committee. Strauss built his law firm into a powerhouse. Its $31.4 million in lobbying revenue in 2007 put the Strauss firm second in the official standings, just behind Patton Boggs, two slots and $7 million ahead of Cassidy & Associates.

Why, Strauss was asked, did the lobbying business prosper so in the years when he and Gerry Cassidy were part of it? Strauss paused for a long moment. "There's just so damn much money in it," he finally replied. "There's so many people with issues in Washington, and people are more and more turning to the government because it is involved in their lives. It's a company town, and the business is lobbying."

65

JOE GARCÍA

La Gran Oportunidad/Up for Grabs/
The Hispanic Opportunity

In 2008, Joe García ran for—and lost—a seat in the House of Representatives from Florida. However, his influence as a spokesman for the Latino community in America remains strong. García begins by recalling the massive protests that occurred across the United States in 2006 on behalf of rights for Hispanics. The author reminds us of the demographics that spurred on the protests. Latinos are the nation's fastest growing ethnic group (or groups, since there are many diverse ethnicities that are encompassed by the label "Hispanic" or "Latino") and they are a very young population group. García discusses the desire of Hispanics to maintain their own culture, rejecting the traditional American one as "lacking in warmth and human relations and the joys of life." Keep in mind as you read about his strategy for future elections that García is a Democratic party activist; it remains to be seen if his scenario for the future is entirely accurate. One thing that cannot be denied in American politics, though, is "the Latino wave."

ON MAY 1, 2006, thousands upon thousands of protesters flooded the streets, parks, and public plazas of cities throughout the United States, calling for the right to live and work here. Many marchers carried banners and posters that read, "Today, we march. Tomorrow, we vote." The vast majority of those marching were of Latin American origin, most without the papers necessary to live and work permanently or even temporarily in this country. Those without papers—the undocumented—were joined in their marches by other Latinos, many of whom were U.S.-born, naturalized citizens or permanent residents.

Demonstrations were by and large peaceful, and they were not limited to cities with traditionally large Latino populations. To the surprise of many in mainstream media, some of the largest demonstrations took place in Chicago and Milwaukee, cities far from the U.S.-Mexican border.

Those demonstrations should have been a wake-up call to politicians, policymakers, the media, and corporate America, for if you were to scan the crowds, it would have been difficult to tell just by looking who was born in this country and who wasn't, who had papers and who didn't, who could vote and who couldn't.

The Mayday protests were a watershed in the history of U.S. Latino political power. Latinos as a group finally began to see the power in their numbers and in their ability to organize themselves and to express themselves politically without benefit of a traditional leadership or party structure. The marches were a pure expression of people power, and how this group defines itself, is defined, is understood, and what its aspirations are is at the heart of getting their vote for this and for future generations.

Although the Latino vote has been a fairly reliable one for the Democratic Party, it has never completely been in the Democratic camp to the extent that the African American vote is. Latinos have demanded that politicians earn their vote, and as was demonstrated by the immigration protests, the community learned quickly how to flex its political muscle. Words to the wise: The Latino vote may be up for grabs, but it has to be earned.

The Democratic Party or, for that matter, anyone else who wants the Latino vote for the long run, has to understand what's at stake. They also have to understand that that vote needs to be courted but not with empty promises. The Latino community clearly demonstrated in its reactions to the protracted immigration debate in 2006 and 2007 that it is far more sophisticated, far more diverse, and much more American than many observers had realized before.

Those marches—the largest the country had seen since the civil rights marches of the 1960s—provided tangible evidence of the dramatic demographic change this country has been undergoing for several decades. By 2008, Hispanics made up 14 percent of the population of the United States, having surpassed the largest minority group, African Americans, only four short years previously. Numbering over forty million, Hispanics are a young population—with a median age of 25 years old compared to the general population's thirty-six years—and the country's fastest-growing minority. Their growth is spurred both by a high birth rate and a continuous flow of immigrants from Latin America.

There are significant Hispanic communities in all fifty states, whose members hail from more than twenty different countries. Each state has a different make-up of countries of origin, immigrant and native-born, citizen and noncitizen, making every state and local Hispanic population unique. The oldest communities, predating the Pilgrims, are in the southwest, and are predominantly Mexican in origin.

But there are also relatively newer communities with strong ties to their places of origin as well as deep roots in their new homes, such as the Puerto Ricans who migrated from the island in the 1950s and the more recent Dominican arrivals in New York. There are large pre-Castro Cuban communities in the northeast, notably in New Jersey, and, for the past half century, Miami has seen successive waves of Cubans fleeing communism. Working-class Colombians seeking economic opportunities migrated to New York, specifically Queens, decades ago, and in this last decade entrepreneurial Colombians have left the almost endemic violence of their homeland and settled in suburban Miami, neighbors once more to Venezuelans escaping an increasingly undemocratic regime. Civil wars, violence, poverty, or a combination of all three have long driven Central Americans from their homelands. They have settled throughout the United States, creating vibrant and close-knit communities in Los Angeles, Washington, D.C. and along the Gulf Coast.

The Latino wave, as it has been called, is the single most important element of the recent demographic and sociological change in the United States, a country that is becoming increasingly suburban and exurban, southern and western, Hispanic and Asian, immigrant and Spanish-speaking, aging boomer and millennial, and more digital and information age in its orientation toward life and work than during the industrial age. . . .

Of the 29 million Hispanic adults, 13 million or so were registered to vote in 2008. Close to half of these 13 million registered were foreign born U.S. citizens. (And it's a young voting population. According to Pew Hispanic Center figures from September 2007, there were 5 million Hispanic voters between the ages of 18 and 29. That number just keeps growing—an estimated 400,000 U.S.-born Hispanics turn 18 every year.)

With each election in recent history, the number of Latinos registering to vote, and voting, has increased. In 1980, Hispanics represented 2.5 percent of total registered voters; by 1996, they were 4.9 percent, and in 2004, 9.3 percent. Not only do they register, Hispanics exercise their right to vote in percentages higher than the national average. Clearly the potential and the future potential of the Hispanic vote are enormous.

So, the demographic transformation of the United States represents not a challenge but an opportunity for politicians of both parties to be truly inclusive. Or, to put it more bluntly, given their size and the trend of rapidly increasing numbers, it will be hard for an ideological movement or political party to be dominant without Hispanics. To quote that great philosopher Karl Rove, "You cannot ignore the aspirations of the fastest-growing minority in America."

The immigration debate is but a smokescreen for the larger debate about identity, the Anglo-American identity versus the Hispanic identity. Unlike previous waves of immigration, Hispanics have held strong to their roots and their culture. To some, the power and endurance of this identity is a threat to their own culture. Unlike previous waves, Hispanics don't want to "melt" into a culture that they see as lacking in warmth and human relations and the joys in life. They want to hold fast to their culture and values, and they see no conflict in being good Americans and good Hispanics at the same time.

Prior to the debate and the tabling of serious legislation, immigration ranked 7th or 8th as an issue of importance among Latino voters. U.S.-born Latinos by and large did not take the issue personally for they did not see what it had to do with them as good, law-abiding U.S. citizens. When the hate mongers got involved, when the tone turned venomous and xenophobic, the dynamic changed. The debate became about whether Hispanics belong in America, whether Hispanic culture is a good thing or a bad thing for America.

Hispanics, documented and undocumented, decided that their culture and their contributions were good for this country. They rose and took to the streets to let their politicians and their countrymen know how they felt. The issue touched their souls. Terms like "anchor babies," "welfare cheats," and "law-breakers" were unfair, they felt, to describe people who had come to this country to work hard and to contribute. Some of the name-calling was directed toward their own family members for, remember, the definition of family as the "nuclear family" is virtually unknown in the Hispanic community. The broader description of family means that many U.S.-born Latinos might well have an undocumented cousin or two at their dinner table.

In much the same way as the Catholic Church's opposition to abortion benefited Republicans, the church's support of immigrants' rights benefited Democrats. The Church, which still yields great influence among many Latinos, vigorously defended immigrants, helping to turn the issue into a wedge issue like abortion and gay marriage. And immigration reform became a family-values issue for the toll the broken immigration system had taken on many families. Suddenly, it wasn't just a parish priest talking about abortion and driving the faithful into the Republican camp; there were bishops speaking to crowds of thousands, talking about immigration reform as a social justice issue, a more typical part of the Democratic agenda.

Since taking to the streets didn't work, Hispanics went to the polls in record numbers in November 2006. They went to punish the party that told them that their culture and their contributions were unwelcome in this society. And punish they did. Their vote was key, in some cases, decisive, to Democrats' victories in the House and Senate. . . .

If the Democrats could earn the Hispanic vote, the resulting power shift would likely also last for generations to come. What do the Democrats have to do to gain power via the Hispanic vote?

The 2008 primary race for the White House represented much of what is best about the Democratic Party and what is most attractive to potential Hispanic voters. The race was historic not only because it was the first open field race since 1928 (i.e., no incumbent or vice president was in the running), it was also truly the first race with serious and viable candidates representative of America: a woman, an African American, a Hispanic, all of them qualified, all of them Democrats. Two Democratic candidates, New Mexico Governor Bill Richardson and Senator Chris Dodd of Connecticut are fluently bilingual, and both actively campaigned in Spanish among the Hispanic community. Two candidates, Senators Hillary Clinton and Joe Biden, had Hispanics leading the charge as their campaign managers.

The Democratic contenders also very quickly accepted an invitation to a debate sponsored by Univision, the leading Spanish-language network. The debate, held at the University of Miami on September 9, broke records for the network, with over 2 million viewers. (Republican candidates initially declined to participate in a forum originally scheduled to be held at the same venue a week later on September 16. No doubt due to the success of the debate among Hispanic viewers, all but one candidate reconsidered, and a Univision-sponsored Republican candidates' debate was held December 9 at the University of Miami.)

This reflected part of an overall strategy by the candidates to approach Hispanics earlier in the game. The unprecedented media blitz in 2008 outstripped earlier primary campaigns—previously, attempts to reach Hispanics didn't start until the general election and usually only in the waning moments of the campaign.

Another important step forward was the rise of a serious southwest strategy. With the country's demographic shift to the south and the west, politicians need to spend time and money where their potential voters are. In 2004, the Democrats couldn't find the southwest on a map; for their 2008 nominating convention they chose a major western city, Denver, as their venue and they selected as convention chair Senator Ken Salazar, a compelling figure and rising star in the party. (It was the second straight convention chaired by a Hispanic—Bill Richardson chaired the 2004 Democratic Convention in Boston.)

The Democrats also moved up their Nevada caucus, holding it very early in the primary cycle, on January 19, just after the Iowa caucus and the New Hampshire primary. Nevada, as a western state, was especially significant. One of the fastest growing states in the nation, Nevada's growth is largely attributed to the Hispanic population, who currently make up about 25 percent of the state's residents.

California and Texas also held early votes. Delegate-rich California, which historically has held its primaries as late as June, moved up the contest to February 5. It was one of twenty-four states to vote in a quasi-national referendum that day. Texas moved up its primary and caucus vote to March 4.

The Latino vote was decisive in those three western states. Although [Barack] Obama had received the endorsement of the powerful culinary workers' union in Nevada, Hillary Clinton beat him there, winning the Latino vote 2 to 1, as she did in California and Texas. In those contests, Latinos turned out in higher numbers than most voters. In Texas, Latinos made up approximately 20 percent of registered voters, but accounted for 32 percent of voter turnout (up from 24 percent in 2004). In California, where one in four residents is Hispanic, 29 percent of those casting ballots were Hispanic. (In 2004, Latinos accounted for 16 percent of voters in the primary.)

Florida, one of the nation's most populous swing states, is where the Democrats stand to make some serious long-term gains. The country's most racially complex state seems to be in a constant demographic flux. Immigration from the south and migration from the north both drive growth in the state. As fast as Nevada is growing, Florida is changing. Huge new waves of Hispanic immigration in Florida—largely Puerto Rican and Central and South American—have left the long-dominant Cuban Americans a minority of the statewide Hispanic vote. The exit polls report that in 2006 Cubans were 5 percent of the total statewide vote; other Hispanics were at 6 percent.

With an increase of participation of two groups much more Democratic than the original exiles—second-generation Cuban Americans and those who came after 1980—the Cuban vote itself is becoming less Republican. In 2006, the Democratic candidates for governor and Senate received 29 percent and 37 percent, respectively, of the Cuban vote, twice the total historically achieved by a Democrat.

Newly arrived Puerto Ricans from New York and the island tend to be Democrat, as do Dominicans who have resettled in Florida from New York. Nicaraguans, who are politically active but make up a small portion of the Latino electorate in Florida, tend to be more conservative, their experiences colored by the Cold War. Their arrival in large numbers to Florida coincided with the rise of the conservative movement in the 1980s.

Taken together, what all this means is that Florida Hispanics are no longer majority Republican, and may in fact now be majority Democratic. . . .

Latino leadership remains a challenge for the Democrats. At least 45 percent of the nationwide Hispanic electorate is foreign born while most Latino Democratic leaders come from families who have been in this country for generations, if not centuries. Part of the problem the modern Democratic movement has with these foreign born voters is that it is mired in the civil rights successes of the past. The foreign born voters don't see the tangible fruits of those victories, nor were they part of the struggle. The foreign born electorate relates more readily to its own struggles with the demagogic Hugo Chávez than it does to the struggles of the iconic César Chávez.*

As Hispanic power increases across the country, the Democrats are going to have to compete with other interest groups, so they need to take a hard look at Latino numbers nationwide and to try to appreciate the complexity of the Latino community or communities. Latinos are black, Caucasian, Asian; a majority are at least nominally Roman Catholic but Latino evangelicals make up a growing portion of the Hispanic electorate (and they are twice as likely to identify with the GOP, according to 2007 Pew Hispanic Center figures). . . .

Hispanics are now in every region, in every state, and in every walk of life. And although their presence is leaving a broad effect on America, they have embraced American culture and have contributed to it. But in the end, American culture changes immigrants more than immigrants change American culture.

The biggest change of all for those from other countries is often their belief in the power of the political process. Even those who do not have a vote believe strongly in the power free expression has to change a society. Imagine the faith in the political process of those who have fought long and hard to attain citizenship.

Today, they march; tomorrow, they vote. And vote they will.

---

*Hugo Chávez is the controversial president of Venezuela who pushed for an end to presidential term limits so that he could stay in power; his stance toward the United States has been extremely hostile. César Chávez was a Mexican-American activist who led many civil rights protests on behalf of migrant farm workers during the 1970s and 1980s as head of the United Farm Workers.—EDS.

PART TWELVE

Voting and Elections

66

DANTE SCALA

From *Stormy Weather*

It's the fall of 2011. You're in school. Congress and the president are at work in Washington, D.C. A presidential election is a year away, far into the future. But for the candidates, the future is now and the place is New Hampshire. How can a tiny northern non-demographically representative locale be the critical focus of American politics? The New Hampshire primary, held early in the winter of a presidential election year, can become the source of "momentum," explains Dante Scala: that precious and unmeasurable quality that can make or break a campaign. Scala points to the realities of momentum and the media attention it garners; with media attention come donations. Scala takes readers through the Exhibition Season, a bizarre combination of grassroots politics based on winning over local activists and simultaneously catering to the national press corps. Then comes the Media Fishbowl, the New Hampshire primary that occurs right after the Iowa caucuses. New Hampshire has had its moment in the spotlight. It has given and taken away candidates' momentum. All too soon, the fall of 2015 will be here.

THE FACT THAT CANDIDATES for the highest office in the land must pass muster with the residents of New Hampshire, a small New England state, is one of the greatest eccentricities of the American electoral calendar. This eccentricity is embraced by those who consider New Hampshire the last bastion of grassroots politics in the presidential selection process, a place where a politician seeking the highest office in the land must look a voter in the eye, shake hands, and answer questions on a one-to-one basis. Critics dismiss the New Hampshire primary as an annoying appendix to the presidential nomination process, a model of grassroots democracy now much more myth than reality. They charge that the primary gives vastly disproportionate influence to a relatively small group of voters who are unrepresentative of the national electorate, pointing to the Granite State's peculiarly libertarian brand of conservatism, its aversion to taxes, and its homogeneous, white population.

That such a small state came to play such a large role in choosing major-party nominees for president—and thus a significant role in choosing the next occupant of the White House—is a uniquely American story of the idiosyncrasies of local politics mixing with national trends to produce an unforeseen development. When the state's political elites scheduled the presidential primary to coincide with Town Meeting Day in March, they did so in order to save the money and trouble of holding two separate events. Not in their wildest dreams did the frugal Yankees realize that they were gaining squatter's rights to the most valuable real estate in presidential nomination politics. . . .

The fuel New Hampshire has provided, in a word, is "momentum." Momentum sometimes takes on a mystical, ill-defined quality for observers and participants in a campaign, something akin to "team chemistry" in sports. A losing team is often said to suffer from bad chemistry among its members, but that chemistry magically transforms when the same team has a winning streak. Candidates often claim to have momentum until results at the polls prove otherwise. . . .

. . . In the presidential primaries, a candidate's momentum is judged on a weekly, even daily, basis by the answer to a single question: What is the likelihood that the candidate will go on to win the support of a majority of the delegates to the party's national convention and the nomination? A candidate is said to have momentum if that likelihood is on the rise. In the course of the campaign, that likelihood will rise and fall as political handicappers compare a candidate's progress in relation to his competitors and consider what opportunities are left for the candidate to pick up more delegates. . . .

. . . Media attention along with financial contributions and standings in the polls are the three main measurements of momentum. Often these measures all affect one another in a cyclical manner. A flurry of stories on a candidate boosts name recognition; increased name recognition leads to better standings in the polls; and better showings in the polls prompt more contributors to send funds to the campaign. . . . At a certain point, the momentum may be seen as ineluctable as the candidate takes on, or is given, an "aura of success."

A candidate gains that aura by exceeding expectations or a series of markers that observers such as the national media lay down as criteria for successful results. The media's expectations are often criticized as arbitrary, especially by those candidates who fail to meet them or feel that the media have been too lenient on their opponents. Expectations, however, do have their roots in a comparison of assumptions about how a candidate will do—based on evidence such as historical precedents, poll standings, results from neighboring states, and the efforts of campaigns—with how a candidate actually does. Expectations and momentum are a zero-sum game: a *better than expected performance* fuels momentum, increasing the candidate's likelihood of winning the nomination while reducing that of the opponent; *performing no better than expectations but no worse* means the candidate remains moving at the same pace toward the nomination, with little advantage for either the candidate or the opponent; *performing worse than expectations* puts the brakes on a candidate's momentum, harming his chances of winning the nomination and advancing those of the opponent.

Momentum can thus be fleeting, an important consideration given that the presidential nomination "process" is really more a series of loosely connected electoral contests held at irregular intervals over a prolonged period of time. Each state has its own peculiarities, its own set of factions and differing proportions of factions, so that momentum created in one primary can be dashed as the successful message employed there backfires in subsequent states.

Momentum can be a valuable addition to the other types of resources that a candidate carries with him into the presidential nomination process. Some of these, such as a candidate's ideological reputation or his inherent abilities as a campaigner, are established prior to the beginning of the campaign. A candidate's liberalism, for example, will aid him in a liberal state but harm him in a conservative one. The availability of vital resources—money, attention from the media, and overall popularity—may depend on the success of the candidate's campaign, such as a strong performance in a competitive primary that attracts media coverage. With all other factors equal, candidates with more resources will do better than candidates with fewer resources, and early success can generate increased resources, such as the backing of donors who prefer to send their donations to perceived winners. . . .

First Stage: The Exhibition Season

Also referred to as the invisible primary, this is the period that extends from the morning after a general presidential election, until the first contests in Iowa and New Hampshire more than three years later. "The exhibition season is a building and testing period," Cook wrote, "in which candidates are free to fashion campaign themes and to discover which constituencies are receptive to their appeals." Key tasks include fundraising; the early stages of organization building in various primary states; and seeking the support of key interest groups such as labor unions. Although no votes are cast in the exhibition season, the games played at this time clearly count on the candidate's record.

The ability to raise money is one of the chief benchmarks for a successful campaign during the exhibition season. Conventional political wisdom places the prerequisite amount for a viable primary campaign at roughly $20 million. Candidates with lots of cash on hand have obvious advantages in a nomination campaign, including the capability to pay for staffers, to put advertising on the airwaves, and to garner valuable data from polling. Money alone may not necessarily decide a nomination, but money does make it possible for a candidate to employ certain means that help to secure a victory, such as advance polling.

The task of raising campaign funds, however, has been greatly complicated by the campaign finance reforms of the 1970s. Prior to these reforms, a presidential candidate was able to rely on a small group of wealthy donors to provide invaluable seed money for the initial stages of a campaign. After the reforms, which placed a ceiling of $1,000 on individual donations (now raised to $2,000 for the 2004 election cycle, after the passage of the McCain-Feingold campaign finance reform legislation), reliance on a few fat-cat donors was no longer possible. In order to run a viable campaign, presidential candidates instead have to collect thousands upon thousands of donations, in addition to obtaining matching public funding. Campaigns employ a variety of strategies to accomplish this daunting task. While insurgent ideological candidates can patch together a viable campaign by using direct mail or even 1-800 numbers, candidates who can raise money in thousand-dollar increments, as opposed to hundred-dollar increments, undoubtedly are able to raise large amounts of money more efficiently while still being eligible for matching public financing as well. The ability to raise funds is, in many ways, the first real contest of the nomination season. . . .

Much media speculation inevitably focuses on how candidates are doing in the first-in-the-nation primary in New Hampshire. Thus, in addition to fundraising trips to money centers such as New York and California, New Hampshire's Manchester International Airport is a frequent stop for candidates playing in the exhibition season. One weekend in fall 2002, for instance, Senator John Edwards of North Carolina did no fewer than a dozen events in a three-day tour of the state, beginning with a speech at the state Democratic Party's annual Jefferson-Jackson dinner Friday night in Manchester. The events ranged widely in size and were held all over the state, from the smallest, a coffee with four or five people, to house parties with dozens of people, including one at the home of Peter Burling, leader of the Democratic delegation in the New Hampshire House of Representatives. At one point during Edwards's whirlwind weekend, the van taking the candidate from Claremont to Cornish in western New Hampshire got lost. Edwards's political consultant, Nick Baldick, himself a New

Hampshire primary veteran, chalked this up as par for the course: "This is New Hampshire," he said. "There are no signs. People are going to get lost."

For many aspiring presidential candidates, a trip to New Hampshire is indeed similar to an educated business traveler's first voyage to a far-off land. The traveler needs to accomplish a number of things on his first visit. He needs to make acquaintances and discover friends. He needs a base of operations that will run and expand while he is away on business elsewhere. Most of all, though, the traveler needs a guide from among the natives. But how should he choose? Dayton Duncan, veteran New Hampshire activist and author of *Grass Roots*, a book on activists in the 1988 presidential campaign, described the dilemma of finding good advice this way:

You're a wealthy Englishman going big-game hunting in a foreign country.... [You] might be very good at firing your big gun. But you're in a foreign country, and [depending on] which guides you hire when you arrive, they might lead you to where you get a good shot off, or they might lead you to where all you get is malaria. And part of it is, before you made your choice of guides, had you done some previous work on that, of trying to determine who the guides ought to be? Or, do you also just have innate, common sense or innate political ability to figure it out?

Answering these questions, Duncan said, is key to this first stage of the New Hampshire primary: the competition among the candidates to lure activists and build an organization. This contest ends by the close of September or early October, months before the primary; by this time, the courtship of activists is mostly complete, and organizations are well along in their setup. Courting activists is more an art than a science, in part because there are as many motivations that draw activists to candidates as there are activists, said Manchester Democratic party chair Ray Buckley:

Some people just like personal attention. If you're running for president, and you call this person once a week for six months, you've got him. Other people, they want you to be the ... craziest liberal. Another person, it's because you're on a particular committee in the Senate, and so you did something on an issue, they're attracted on the issue.... They happened to have been at an event, and you gave an amazing speech, and you showed charisma, so the person was excited by that. You get this one person in, because they know forty other activists, you happen to get that whole clique.

Unlike the early days of the New Hampshire primary, candidates must now undertake this competition in the media spotlight, knowing that their every move is scrutinized by the political cognoscenti. When the

New Hampshire Democratic Party held a fund-raising dinner in February 2003, for instance, the list of presidential candidate attendees made not just the *Manchester Union Leader* but also ABCNews.com's "The Note," a daily must-read for the national political elite. American politics today, including media coverage of politics, "lends itself to endless speculation, and gum-chewing, and thumb-sucking about what's going to happen, versus real reporting on what actually is happening," Duncan said. In that type of environment, grassroots campaigning in New Hampshire is important in part because of the image such action conveys to the watching media. "Having that as your backdrop to how you're campaigning is a good backdrop to have. It also saves you from getting a rap going, particularly early on, that you're doing it wrong." . . .

Second Stage: The Media Fishbowl

The seemingly interminable exhibition season finally ends in January of the year of the presidential election, when Iowa holds its caucuses and, soon after, New Hampshire its primary.

The Iowa caucuses are both inconclusive and definitive for candidates' fortunes. On one hand, the January caucuses held in precincts across the state do not actually award convention delegates to candidates; this occurs months later at state party conventions. On the other hand, and more important, the Iowa caucuses are "the gateway to a long and complex nomination process, and all players and all observers very much want whatever information they can glean" from the results, however transitory they may be. The media turn their attention from speculation on a candidate's prospects to analysis of the verdict from actual voters: "Iowa results, plus media spin" set the story line for New Hampshire and establish the roles of front runner, lead challenger (or challengers), and the remaining bit players who have the unenviable parts of long shots or also-rans.

For the week between the Iowa caucuses and New Hampshire's first-in-the-nation primary, the attention of the national political media descends on New Hampshire in a deluge. "That week is full of electricity," said Pat Griffin, executive vice president for the advertising firm O'Neil Griffin Bodi and a veteran of several political campaigns. In jest, he compared the last week before the primary to being on the set of *Doctor Zhivago*:

All these Washington types buy their mukluks . . . to come up once every four years. . . . They come up and say, "My God, where can I get my hair done? Where can I find arugula salad?" . . . Go to [Manchester restaurant] Richard's Bistro at night, they're all at the same places, [saying] "My goodness, can you believe this tundra where these people live?"

The national political media venture into the tundra—at least as far as Manchester and its environs, if not the seacoast or the Connecticut River valley or the North Country—because the people who live there possess something they want dearly: information on how actual voters feel about the presidential candidates. The Iowa caucuses, in which participants have to devote hours of time on a single evening, are usually low-turnout events attended by party faithful, in which strong organizations are often vital to a good showing. The New Hampshire primary, in contrast, turns out a much higher percentage of voters, and candidates must therefore be able to appeal to a variety of constituencies. Iowa and New Hampshire together, plus the media's interpretations of those two contests, winnow the field to a front runner and one or, at most, two or three challengers. . . .

Perhaps one of the reasons New Hampshire has been and remains an indicator is that it is an early testing ground of candidates' organizational skills, charisma, and appeal to the broad range of the relevant electorate. For, notwithstanding its idiosyncrasies—and what state is not idiosyncratic?—New Hampshire's populace is composed of various factions that have their analogues in the rest of the nation. How a candidate crafts a message to appeal to those factions or constituencies in New Hampshire does affect how he or she will be perceived thereafter. New Hampshire's ability to determine the nomination may be in question; that it is an early indicator of how a candidate plans on running a campaign and the likely chances of the success of that message, however, is not.

67

DENNIS JOHNSON

From *No Place for Amateurs*

Behind the scenes of every political campaign today is a political consultant. Political consulting is a thriving business whose skills are employed not just by candidates for national office, but those running for state and local positions, too. No race is too small or too obscure to be aided by consulting firms, whether big-time ones led by the famous (James Carville, Dick Morris) or the anonymous one- or two-person basement operation. Dennis Johnson reveals the multitude of tasks that consultants perform for a campaign. He also gives some good tips on movies to rent on the topic: The War Room *and* Wag the Dog *are particularly good choices for those who enjoy the blend of fact and fiction.*

I don't want to read about you in the press.
I'm sick and tired of consultants getting famous at my expense.
Any story that comes out during the campaign undermines my candidacy.

—BILL CLINTON to his new 1996 reelection consultants
Dick Morris and Doug Schoen

JUST DAYS BEFORE THE 1996 Democratic National Convention, a smiling, confident Bill Clinton was featured on the cover of *Time* magazine. Pasted on Clinton's right shoulder was a cut-out photo of political consultant Dick Morris, "the most influential private citizen in America," according to *Time*. On the eve of Clinton's renomination, *Time* was sending its readers a backhanded pictorial message: here is the most powerful man in the world, who fought his way back from political oblivion, and perched on his shoulder is the reason why. Suddenly the once-secretive, behind-the-scenes consultant was a household name. In the early months of the reelection campaign, Morris worked hard at being the unseen political mastermind and strategist. "Being a man of mystery helps me work better," he confided to George Stephanopoulos. While Bill Clinton's 1992 consultants were talk-show regulars, wrote best-sellers, and traveled the big-dollars lecture circuit, Morris was the backroom schemer. Many media outlets had trouble even finding a file photo of the elusive Dick Morris, adding to the mystery and illusion of power.

Morris had been Clinton's earliest political adviser back in Arkansas during the first run for governor. They had a rocky relationship over the years, but following the Republican takeover of Congress in November 1994, Bill Clinton began meeting secretly with Morris. Working out of the Jefferson Hotel in Washington, using the code name "Charlie," Morris plotted the president's comeback. He was the anonymous, behind-the-scenes consultant who would retool Clinton's image, reposition his policies, and help revive his faltering presidency.

Throughout his career, Bill Clinton had a reputation for discarding political consultants. Those who helped him capture the White House in 1992—Mandy Grunwald, Stanley Greenberg, Paul Begala, and James Carville—were nowhere to be seen following the 1994 election upheaval. By the spring of 1995, Morris had assembled his own team, including veteran media consultants Bob Squier, Bill Knapp, and Hank Sheinkopf, and pollsters Mark Penn and Doug Schoen. They met regularly with several White House insiders to plan the remarkable political comeback of Bill Clinton.

Morris's anonymity was shattered when he was caught with his long-time prostitute companion by the supermarket tabloid the *Star*. The tabloid deliberately timed its bombshell story for maximum effect on the Democratic convention, with the scandal erupting on the day that Bill Clinton accepted his party's renomination for the presidency. Morris and his wife immediately left the Chicago convention and the Clinton campaign, retreating to their Connecticut home, besieged by reporters and photographers. Morris, the political consultant turned nefarious celebrity, had become a late-night dirty joke, damaged goods, and certainly a political liability. There were rumors that he was sharing sensitive White House information with his prostitute girlfriend, and Morris shocked many by announcing that months earlier he had signed a secret book deal to write the inside story of Clinton's reelection comeback. Morris now had plenty of free time to write his version of the 1996 campaign, work the talk-show circuit, join a twelve-step sex addiction program, retool his tarnished image, and pocket his $2.5 million book advance. Though the Morris scandal scarcely damaged the Clinton campaign, it ended up being everything President Clinton objected to: Dick Morris was getting famous—and rich—at his expense. For the moment, Morris joined a short list of celebrity political consultants who became as famous and often far more handsomely paid than their clients.

For years Americans had been unwittingly exposed to campaign posturing and manipulation engineered by political consultants. In the 1990s they grew curious about the manipulators. Suddenly, political consultants

DENNIS JOHNSON

were hot properties. Movies, documentaries, and books gave us a glimpse of consultants at work. A film documentary, *The War Room*, made media stars of James Carville and George Stephanopoulos in Bill Clinton's 1992 presidential campaign headquarters. Reporter Joe Klein's best-selling roman à clef, *Primary Colors*, detailed with unnerving accuracy the seamy side of the presidential quest by an ambitious young Southern governor and his avaricious campaign team. Later John Travolta starred as the silver-haired young presidential candidate in the inevitable movie version. *Vote for Me*, a PBS documentary, showed hard-charging New York media consultant Hank Sheinkopf patiently coaching his candidate, an Alabama Supreme Court judge, on the fine points of camera angles and voice projection. Another film documentary, *The Perfect Candidate*, chronicled the highly charged campaign of conservative lightning rod Oliver North and his consultant Mark Goodin as they battled and lost to the uninspiring, wooden Charles Robb in the 1994 Virginia Senate race.

In the movie *Wag the Dog*, the president's spin doctor (Robert De Niro) and a high-powered Hollywood myth-maker (Dustin Hoffman) conjure up a wartime incident in Albania to cover up the president's sexual indiscretions with a twelve-year-old girl. Michael J. Fox portrayed the energetic, earnest young White House aide, a George Stephanopoulos clone, in the film *An American President* (1995), and later reprised the role in a television series, *Spin City*, with Fox serving as an aide to an unprincipled, vacuous mayor of New York City.

The bookshelf was suddenly filling up with insider accounts by political consultants. Well-traveled, controversial Republican consultant Ed Rollins skewered many of his campaign rivals and former clients in a book entitled *Bare Knuckles and Back Rooms*. On the dust jacket was the middle-aged, balding Rollins, poised with his boxing gloves, ready to take on the rough and tumble of politics. Carville and his Republican-operative wife, Mary Matalin, teamed up on the lecture circuit, hawked credit cards and aspirin in television commercials, and wrote a best-selling memoir, *All's Fair: Love, War, and Running for President*.

Carville, Stephanopoulos, and Paul Begala reappeared during the Lewinsky scandal* and the impeachment hearings. Begala returned as the loyal defender inside the White House bunker, while Carville attacked special prosecutor Kenneth Starr on television talk shows and through an angry book. . . . *And the Horse He Rode in On: The People v. Kenneth Starr*.

---

*The Lewinsky scandal led to President Bill Clinton's 1998-99 impeachment by the House of Representatives and subsequent acquittal in a Senate trial. Clinton was charged with being untruthful, in legal proceedings, about revealing his sexual relationship with Monica Lewinsky, a White House intern.—EDS.

Stephanopoulos, meanwhile, singed by the president's betrayal, distanced himself from the White House and publicly criticized Clinton's behavior in his 1999 book, *All Too Human*. Morris, too, resurfaced on talk shows, wrote political columns, advised Clinton on how to deflect criticism during the Lewinsky scandal, and penned another book, immodestly titled *The New Prince: Machiavelli Updated for the Twenty-first Century*.

Despite the notoriety and self-promotion of Morris, Carville, and others, the celebrity consultant is the exception, not the rule. Most political consultants toil in the background, content to ply their craft in anonymity. Even at the presidential campaign level, consultants generally labor in obscurity. Few Americans had ever heard of Don Sipple or Bill McInturff, consultants in Bob Dole's dysfunctional 1996 presidential race, or Bill Clinton's 1996 consultants Bill Knapp, Doug Schoen, and Marius Penczner. Very few have ever heard of George W. Bush's chief strategist Karl Rove, Al Gore's media consultant Carter Eskew, or John McCain's consultant Mike Murphy.

Political consultants, both controversial and anonymous, have become essential players in the increasingly technological, fast-paced, often brutal world of modern elections. Through it all, they have changed the face of modern American politics.

Political Consultants at Work

In earlier decades, campaigns were financed and run by local or state political parties. They were fueled by local party activists and volunteers, by family, friends, and close political supporters. By the early 1960s presidential campaigns and statewide campaigns for governor and senator began seeking out media and polling firms to help deliver their messages to voters. During the next two decades, there emerged both a new industry, political management, and a new professional, the campaign consultant. By the 1980s every serious presidential candidate, nearly every statewide candidate, and a large number of congressional candidates were using the services of professional political consultants.

The 1990s witnessed yet another transformation. Candidates for office below the statewide level were beginning to seek the advice of professional political consultants. For many candidates, the dividing line was the $50,000 campaign: those who could not raise that kind of money had to rely solely on volunteer services, and those above this threshold usually sought professional assistance. In some local political jurisdictions, record amounts of campaign funds were being raised to pay for campaign services, and races for medium-city mayor, county sheriff, or local judge took on the techniques and tactics once seen only in statewide, professionally managed contests. Professional consulting services, such as phone banks, telemarketing, and direct mail, were supplanting the efforts once provided by volunteers and party loyalists. This multibillion-dollar industry is now directed by professional consultants who make the key decisions, determine strategy, develop campaign communications, and carry out campaign tactics for their clients.

The influence of political consultants goes well beyond getting candidates elected to office. They play an increased role in ballot measures by helping clients determine ballot strategy, framing issues, and even providing the campaign foot soldiers who gather signatures for ballot petitions. Consultants use marketing and mobilization skills to orchestrate pressure on legislators. Political telemarketers link angered constituents directly with the telephones of members of Congress. Overnight, they can guarantee five thousand constituent telephone calls patched directly to a legislator's office. Political consultants are also finding lucrative markets internationally, serving presidential and other candidates throughout the world.

In the commercial world, a business that generates less than $50 million is considered a small enterprise. By that measure, every political consulting firm, except for some of the vendors, is a small business. Most of the estimated three thousand firms that specialize in campaigns and elections have ten or fewer staffers and generate just several hundred thousand dollars in revenue annually. Only a few firms, such as media consultant Squier, Knapp, and Dunn, generate millions of dollars in revenue; most of this money, however, passes through the consultants' hands to pay television advertising costs.

Leading polling firms, such as the Tarrance Group or Public Opinion Strategies, may have forty to eighty employees; most are support staff working the telephones and part of the back office operations. Quite a few firms are cottage enterprises—one- or two-person boutiques, often in speciality markets such as event planning, opposition research, fundraising, or media buying. Many political consulting firms operate out of the basement of the principal's home with no more than telephone lines, computers, fax machines, and online access. For example, even after he became famous as Clinton's principal political adviser, James Carville and his assistants worked out of the "bat cave," a basement studio apartment on Capitol Hill that served as Carville's home and nerve center for his far-flung political operations.

Firms that rely solely on campaign cycles are exposed to the roller-coaster of cash flow: many lean months, with very little money coming in from clients, countered by a few fat months, when the bulk of the revenue pours in. In addition to the on-off flow of cash, the firms must deal with the logistical difficulties of juggling many candidates during the crucial last weeks of the campaign cycle and the enormous time pressures of a busy campaign season. Some consulting firms have around-the-clock operations during critical weeks of the campaign. These political emergency rooms are geared to handle any last-minute crisis. During long stretches when there are few campaign opportunities, professionals and support staff may have to be let go until the cycle picks up again.

One of the most difficult but necessary tasks is to even out the steep curves in the election cycle so that money and resources flow more regularly. Consultants have developed several strategies for this: convincing candidates to hire consultants earlier in the cycle, stretching out the amount of time they stay with campaigns, and seeking out off-year races, especially down the electoral ladder, such as mayoral races, general assembly, and other local contests, many of which in past years would not have sought professional assistance. Consultants are becoming more involved in the growing business of initiatives, referenda, and issues management. Many of these campaigns are tied to the same election cycle as candidate campaigns, but others are tied to local, state, or congressional issue cycles. Political consulting firms also pursue clients from the corporate and trade association world and international clients. By spreading out business, consulting firms are able to stay competitive, smooth out the peaks and valleys of the election cycle, and keep their heads above water.

In the 1980s firms began to shift away from heavy reliance on candidate campaigns. For example, the late Matt Reese, one of the founders of the political consulting business, who had worked for more than four hundred Democratic candidates, changed direction after the 1982 elections to concentrate on corporate and trade association clients. Republican consultant Eddie Mahe shifted his business from 100 percent candidate-based in 1980 to about fifteen percent candidate-based in the early 1990s, picking up corporate and other clients. In the mid-1970s Wally Clinton's pioneering political telemarketing firm, the Clinton Group, gained 90 percent of its work from candidates, but has since moved away from reliance on candidates to issues and corporate work. Many successful consulting firms have followed this pattern and now have much of their business coming from noncandidate campaigns.

As corporations have discovered the value of grassroots lobbying and issues management, consultants who specialize in direct mail and political telemarketing have shifted focus to legislative and issues work. Corporate and trade association organizations took special notice of the successful political consultant-orchestrated grassroots campaign run against President

Clinton's 1993–94 health care proposal. For political consultants, such work is often far more lucrative, more reliable, and less stress-inducing than working for candidates in competitive election cycles. Some of the most successful political consulting firms have less than half of their revenue coming from candidate campaigns. . . .

What Consultants Bring to Campaigns

Candidates, not consultants, win or lose elections. In 1996 voters chose Bill Clinton, not media consultant Bob Squier; they rejected Bob Dole, not pollster Bill McInturff. Candidates alone face the voters and ultimately bear the responsibility for the tone and expression of their campaign. Sometimes reputations are diminished and images tarnished by the campaign itself. For example, George Bush will be remembered for permitting a down-and-dirty campaign that included the infamous "Revolving Door" and Willie Horton* commercials in his 1988 presidential campaign. In that same year, Michael Dukakis will be remembered for his ride in a military vehicle, hunkered down in an oversized battle helmet, looking goofy. Alphonse D'Amato and Charles Schumer will be remembered for the abusive, in-your-face campaigns they waged in the 1998 New York Senate race.

While candidates are ultimately responsible for their campaigns, there is no way they can compete, let alone win, without professional help. Professional consultants bring direction and discipline to the campaign. Few enterprises are as unpredictable, vulnerable, and chaotic as a modern campaign. So much can go wrong: the candidate might go "off message," in which case the campaign loses focus; internal party feuds might threaten the success of the entire campaign; fund-raising might fall short of expectations, choking the life out of the entire enterprise. All the while, the opponent's campaign is raising more money, attacking with a sharp, clear message, redefining the race in its own terms, grabbing media attention, and efficiently mobilizing its resources. Campaign professionals are needed to bring order out of chaos, maintain message and strategy discipline, and keep the campaign focused.

The best consultants are able to define the race on their own terms—

---

*The Willie Horton ad is a famous—or infamous—negative ad from the 1988 Bush-Dukakis presidential campaign. An independent PAC created the initial ad that accused Democratic candidate, Gov. Michael Dukakis of Massachusetts, of allowing convicted murderer William Horton out of prison on a weekend furlough; Horton committed several violent crimes while on furlough. Because Horton was black and his victims were white, the ad stirred up racial tensions that lurked not too far beneath the surface of the 1988 Bush-Dukakis campaign.—EDS.

not the terms set by the opposition, the media, or outside third parties. In the end, the campaign boils down to letting voters know the answers to some very simple questions: who the candidate is, what the issues are, and why this race is important. Following are some examples of defining issues and messages.

From the 1996 Clinton-Gore reelection campaign:

DEFINING ISSUE: Who is better prepared to lead this country into the next century?
MESSAGE: "Building a bridge to the twenty-first century."

From the 1980 Reagan-Bush campaign:

DEFINING ISSUE: The shortcomings of the Carter administration's policies.
MESSAGE: "Are you better off today than you were four years ago?"

Republican consultant Lee Atwater was fond of saying that he knew that the message of his campaign was hitting home when he would go to a local Kmart and ask shoppers what they thought of the contest, and they'd simply parrot the message he had developed.

Professionals also take campaign burdens off the candidate. Campaigns are exhausting, placing extraordinary physical and emotional demands upon the candidate. The campaign staff, and especially the campaign manager, absorb as much of the stress of the campaign as possible. A campaign manager may serve as official campaign optimist, psychologist, and handholder for the candidate or, often, the candidate's spouse. The manager will make the tough personnel and tactical choices when the campaign starts going bad, and be the unofficial heavy (or whipping boy) when needed.

Consultants, particularly those in niche or vendor industries, provide legal, tax, and accounting services for the increasingly complex financial disclosure reporting requirements. They provide expertise in buying television time and placing radio and television commercials. Consulting firms capture and analyze television commercials aired by opponents and other races, and offer both quantitative and qualitative analysis from survey research, focus-group, and dial-group findings. Increasingly campaigns depend on specialists who also can provide a technological edge. Consultants provide online retrieval systems and websites, computer-assisted telephone technology, voter and demographic databases, and geo-mapping and sophisticated targeting techniques so that a campaign can know, block by block and house by house, who is likely to vote and for whom they would cast a ballot. Strategists are able to use predictive technologies, traditional statistical techniques such as regression analysis, and new artificial intelligence technologies such as neural nets and genetic algorithms to target potential voters.

Above all, consultants bring experience from other campaigns. Every campaign has its unique circumstances, events, and dynamics. But campaigns are also great recycling bins. When a consultant has worked for fifteen or twenty-five races, campaigns begin to fall into predictable patterns: messages and themes, issues, and tactics reappear, taking on slight variations—new twists to old challenges. Veteran consultants can save a candidate from making mistakes, spot opportunities quickly, and take advantage of changing circumstances. As veteran consultant Joseph R. Cerrell put it, tongue in cheek, we need consultants—"to have someone handy who has forgotten more about media, mail, fund-raising and strategy than most candidates will ever know."

Growing reliance on professional consultants is costly: the price of admission to elections has risen substantially. The campaign, for many candidates, becomes a perverse full-time game of chasing dollars. Consultants have seen business grow because of the superheated fund-raising activities of the national Democratic and Republican parties, the explosion of soft money, and issues advocacy.

The best consultants aren't afraid of a fight. They know that in many cases an election can be won only if they drop the pretense of reasoned, civilized campaigning and take the gloves off. Campaigns engage in rough tactics because they work. Opposition researchers dig deep into personal lives, seeking out misdeeds and character flaws. Pollsters test-market negative material before focus and electronic dial meter groups. Then the media team cuts slash-and-burn thirty-second clips, using all the tricks of the trade: unflattering black-and-white photos of the opponent, ominous music and sound effects, and distorted features, salted with authentic-sounding textual material, often taken out of context. The direct mail pieces may get even uglier. The goal is to drive up the opponent's negatives, to paint the opponent in such unflattering ways that enough voters have only a negative view of that candidate.

Certainly not all campaigns use negative tactics. Candidates are often very reluctant to engage in mudslinging or demagoguery. Voters are turned off by negative campaigns and feel alienated from the democratic process. But campaign consultants see negative campaigning as a tool, not so much a question of political ethics or morality. If the only way to win is to go negative, then negative it is.

Professional consultants bring many weapons to a campaign. The campaign's theme and message are communicated through television and radio commercials, through direct mail pieces, and increasingly through campaign websites. Those communications are developed and honed through the use of sophisticated research analyses, especially survey research, focus groups, and dial meter sessions. Even more fundamental is the campaign's deadliest weapon, candidate and opposition research. . . .

Professional campaigns and the political consulting industry will flourish in the decades to come. Candidates for public office—both incumbents and challengers—will not hesitate to raise increasingly larger sums of campaign funds to pay for professional consultants and their services. Despite the occasional outburst from elected officials or the public, candidates need, want, and for the most part appreciate the assistance they receive from professional consultants. We may see profound changes in campaign financing, communications, and technology. Through it all, professional consulting will endure, adapt, and prosper. Professionals have become indispensable players in modern campaigns.

68

DAVID MARK

From *Going Dirty*

Don't assume that negative campaigning is new, or that it is worse now than ever, or that only today's YouTube technology encourages it. Negative campaigning has a long history, much of it even before David Mark starts his story in 1964. When you finish reading the excerpt, go to YouTube for a trip down negative advertising's memory lane: look at the 1964 Lyndon Johnson "Daisy Girl" ad against Barry Goldwater; the 1988 "Willie Horton" ad that George H.W. Bush used against Michael Dukakis (a classic negative ad mentioned briefly in the excerpt); and the 2004 Swift Boat Vets' ad against John Kerry. We learn about 527 groups and about the campaign finance reform of 2002 (McCain-Feingold). The 527s are not confined to any one political party's loyalists or to any one ideological position. Democrat, Republican, liberal, conservative: with strong views, lots of money, and a good ad writer, the 527s are on the scene.

FIRST, I WANT TO DISTINGUISH negative campaigning—charges and accusations that, while often distorted, contain at least a kernel of truth—from dirty tricks or cheating. Examples abound of campaign dirty tricks, most famously the tactics of Richard M. Nixon's 1972 Committee to Reelect the President (CREEP), which were exposed in the Watergate proceedings of 1973 to 1974. Perhaps the most notorious dirty trick was a letter planted in a New Hampshire newspaper alleging that a leading Democratic presidential candidate, Senator Edmund Muskie of Maine, had approved a slur that referred to Americans of French-Canadian descent as "Canucks." On a snowy New Hampshire day, standing outside the offices of the newspaper, Muskie gave a rambling denial in which tears seemed to drip from his eyes (some contend they were actually melting snowflakes). His emotional conduct, replayed on television, caused him to drop in the New Hampshire polls shortly before the presidential primary. Senator George McGovern of South Dakota, considered a weaker candidate by Nixon political strategists, eventually won the 1972 Democratic nomination and lost the general election to the Republican president in a landslide. . . .

Yet even beyond dirty tricks, many people still recoil at legitimate negative political ads on television, radio, the Internet, and in other forms.

Negative campaigning has become a catchall phrase that implies there is something inherently wrong with criticizing an opponent. Negative campaigning is one of the most bemoaned aspects of the American political system, particularly by academics and journalists who say it diminishes the level of political discourse and intensifies the divisions among voters.

These complaints emerge each election cycle, partly because political spots are so different in content, style, and form than ads for commercial products. Anyone peddling breakfast cereal needs to be careful about criticizing competitors too overtly or else run the risk of turning off consumers so much that they'll start their day with another form of breakfast food. Rarely do product advertisements include hard-hitting direct comparisons to competitors. (And when they do, the contrasts are usually mild and fleeting.)

The goal of political marketing is entirely different, whether in a Republican versus Democrat match or a tough party primary. Unlike product campaigns, political campaigns do not mind at all turning off some "consumers," the voters. In fact, political operatives often *prefer* to keep voter participation down among those inclined to vote for the opposition. They are perfectly happy to drive down turnout, as long as those who do show up vote for them. And then there's the timing. The stakes of elections are higher than everyday consumer purchases. Consumers do not have to live with the same cereal or beer for the next few years, but they do have to live with the same president, governor, or member of Congress. . . .

For better or worse, aggressive campaign tactics have been a vital part of the American political system from the very start. . . . [The] tenor of modern political campaigns is actually considerably milder than that of old. And, . . . negative campaign tactics have been constantly reinvented, to adapt to the latest technologies and to fit the prevailing mood of the electorate during different eras of American history. . . .

Few candidates have needed to employ negative campaigning less than President Lyndon Baines Johnson in 1964. The assassination of President John F. Kennedy in November 1963 ensured that the Republicans would face an up-hill battle no matter whom they pitted against the Texas Democrat. After all, the new president had ridden a wave of goodwill after the tragic events of Dallas, toward swift passage of much of his predecessor's idling legislative agenda. Most notably, LBJ, the former Senate majority leader, muscled through a recalcitrant Congress the landmark Civil Rights Act of 1964, which guaranteed blacks access to all public facilities and accommodations and banned discrimination because of race, religion, national origin, or sex. The Vietnam War, later to be Johnson's downfall, was escalating. But on Election Day' of 1964, it had yet to become a real liability.

The ambitious Johnson did not just want to win his own term as president; he craved a resounding victory that would establish a new White House power base. Then he could push forward his own legislative agenda, which included creation of Medicare and Medicaid, aid to education, regional redevelopment and urban renewal, and scores of other proposals to establish a "Great Society." . . .

So as he looked toward a victory of historic proportions as president in 1964, Johnson approved his campaign's launch of the first media campaign centered on the rapidly growing medium of television, much of it an assault on the Republican presidential nominee, Senator Barry Goldwater of Arizona. Johnson adviser Bill Moyers said the president "was determined to roll up the biggest damned plurality ever and he felt that anything that could help—and he believed advertising could help—was worth the price."

Goldwater himself became the focus of the election, not foreign policy, taxation, or other issues. According to Johnson's ads, Goldwater would destroy Social Security, end government programs to aid the poor, and potentially launch a nuclear war that could endanger all humanity. While LBJ's victory was never really in doubt, his campaign set the precedent for the television attack ads Americans now take for granted. Many of the spots seem tame and downright quaint compared to the commercials that followed forty years later, but at the time the massive television onslaught of political commercials stunned the Republican opposition.

The 1964 presidential race also offers a vivid illustration of how effectively negative campaigning has worked when it has played into voters' preconceived notions about candidates. The Johnson ads did a masterful job of using Goldwater's words against him, which typecast the Republican. The vaunted "Daisy Girl" ad that suggested Goldwater would start a nuclear war (it never mentioned his name) was consistent with many voters' views of the Republican candidate. "The commercial evoked a deep feeling in many people that Goldwater might actually use nuclear weapons," wrote Tony Schwartz, creator of the famous ad. "This distrust was not in the Daisy spot. It was in the people who viewed the commercial." . . .

A couple of ads by the Johnson campaign aired only one time each. The "Daisy Girl" spot, perhaps the most famous campaign ad of all time, ran during NBC's *Monday Night at the Movies* on September 7; it turned Goldwater's outspokenness on military action and nuclear weapons into a story of nuclear apocalypse (he had once joked about tossing a nuclear weapon into the men's room of the Kremlin.) The 30-second ad showed a little girl in a field picking petals from a daisy. As she counted, the camera moved closer, finally freezing on a close-up of her eye. At the same, time, an announcer started to intone a countdown. Suddenly, the screen erupted in a nuclear mushroom. The voiceover of Lyndon Johnson then admonished: "These are the stakes; to make a world in which all God's children can live, or to go into the darkness. Either we must love each other or we must die." Then words appeared on the screen: "On November 3rd, vote for President Johnson."

The ad served to remind American voters of Goldwater's propensity for warlike statements, even though the spot never mentioned the Republican or made reference to him. More than forty years after the ad ran, its creator, Tony Schwartz, said it was fair game based on Goldwater's record. "He had made two speeches" on the use of nuclear weapons, Schwartz recalled. "It was a very effective commercial." The Goldwater campaign actually filed a complaint with the Fair Campaign Practices Committee to stop the ad, which didn't go through when the Johnson team made it clear the commercial would only be run once. (Even Senator Hubert Humphrey, the Democratic vice-presidential candidate, publicly disapproved of the spot.) Still, for many Republicans, the Daisy Girl ad eviscerated whatever goodwill existed toward LBJ after he assumed office in place of Kennedy, the martyred president. "That's negative campaigning carried to an unbelievable excess," said Bill Brock, who in 1964 was a freshman Republican House member from Tennessee and later won election to the U.S. Senate.

Though the ad ran only once on commercial television, it earned tremendous airtime through repetition and discussion on news shows. In a sense, the ad served as a precursor of the "free media" effect the Swift Boat Vets would have forty years later, when the group's spots, purchased on an initially small budget, attacked the military record of Senator John F. Kerry, the 2004 Democratic presidential nominee. In 1964 most of the Daisy Girl ad's repetitious playing came from three television networks' nightly news shows. Forty years later, the ability to post such controversial ads on the Internet and send them by e-mail had increased their visibility exponentially. . . .

During the heated 2004 campaign season, television viewers in Ohio, Florida, and other presidential battleground states learned that Senator John Kerry had once accused American servicemen in Vietnam of committing war crimes. Viewers were also told, in another commercial, that a former officer in the Alabama Air National Guard and his friends never saw George W. Bush at their unit in 1972, when he was temporarily assigned there.

Such accusations, hurled against Kerry by the Swift Vets and POWs for Truth (originally known as the Swift Boat Veterans for Truth) and toward Bush by Texans for Truth, made liberal use of facts on the public record. But the ads didn't tell the whole truth. In testimony before a Senate committee in 1971, Kerry did not accuse specific people of war crimes; he said he was describing atrocities alleged by other veterans. And Bush pointed to his honorable discharge from the Air National Guard as evidence that he had fulfilled his service.

Such nuances and finer points were lost on many television viewers. That was exactly the point. The ads played on viewers' emotions and aimed to drive true believers to the polls on Election Day. The spots were among a slew of hard-edged television attacks aired during the 2004 presidential election cycle, the first to operate under the rules of the 2002 Bipartisan Campaign Finance Reform Act (BCRA), also known as McCain-Feingold, for its sponsors, Senators John McCain (R-Ariz.) and Russ Feingold (D-Wis.).

Notably, neither Bush nor Kerry sponsored the ads. Instead, they came from independent groups bankrolled by wealthy individuals who wanted to affect the election outcome. Ironically, their donations were the very things BCRA sought to block, or at least reduce. Unlimited fat-cat donations simply shifted from national party organizations—the Republican National Committee and Democratic National Committee—to private groups that aimed not just to support their favored candidate but to tear down the opposition with the bluntest possible words and images as well.

The biggest recipients of the campaign cash were 527 groups,* named for the federal tax code provision that governed their operations. These organizations eagerly threw out charges and criticized the opposition more virulently than the candidates themselves did. Bush's campaign did not criticize Kerry for his decorated service while in Vietnam because

---

*So-called 527 groups first appeared in the 2004 election, in response to changes in campaign finance law. The Bipartisan Campaign Finance Reform Act of 2002 (McCain-Feingold) closed a loophole that had allowed political parties to use wealthy donors' money to create campaign ads and spend for other campaign activities above and beyond what the candidates themselves could raise and spend. In the place of party spending, private 527s appeared. Named for their designation in the tax code, 527s were independent of the campaigns and therefore could spend whatever "soft money" amount they wanted, on whatever they wanted: negative ads were their contribution of choice. Prominent 527s include groups of all political viewpoints, from ultra-liberal to ultra-conservative.—EDS.

that could have easily brought a backlash, considering the president had stayed stateside during the war. The Swift Vets, Kerry's key critics among the 527 groups, felt no such restraints. "The Bush campaign would never have said the things the Swift Boat Vets said noted Chris LaCivita, the group's chief strategist. "If people want to complain about 527s, thank McCain-Feingold."

The new, complex campaign finance rules—upheld virtually in their entirety by the U.S. Supreme Court'—helped spawn a dramatic increase of negative campaigning over the airwaves, on the Internet, and through direct mail. The 527s ratcheted up the shrillness, nastiness, and outright distortions in political ads, all the while injecting massive sums of money into the political process. According to a postelection study by the nonpartisan Campaign Finance Institute, 527 committees raised $405 million in 2004, up dramatically from the $151 million they collected in 2002. GOP Senator Trent Lott of Mississippi—who had voted against BCRA—called contributions to 527s "sewer money" after the election. . . .

The stakes in the 2004 election were huge: Executing the global war on terror in the post–9/11 world; a costly, divisive war in Iraq; and an economy in recovery that still lost hundreds of thousands of jobs. Adding to the intensity was the near even split between registered Republicans and Democrats, lingering bitterness over the disputed 2000 election, and the deep, personal dislike many Democrats had for the president, along with the disdain Republicans held for the Democratic challenger.

So it was no surprise that big money would find a way into the system, especially to opponents of the legislation who predicted just such an outcome. Recent campaign history showed outside organizations would seek to fill in the gaps where candidates were limited in collecting donations. The 527s that proliferated during the 2004 election cycle were only the latest type of independent-expenditure group to be active in national politics. During the 1980 election cycle, the National Conservative Political Action Committee (NCPAC) spent more than $1 million on independent-expenditure ads in an effort to defeat several Democratic U.S. senators. After sending out millions of direct mail pieces and running scores of television commercials knocking the Democratic incumbents, NCPAC succeeded wildly; the Republicans won control of the Senate for the first time in 26 years. NCPAC also ran several independent ads in favor of Republican presidential candidate Ronald Reagan that criticized President Jimmy Carter's handling of the Iranian hostage crisis and other matters. And the most memorable ad of the 1988 presidential election—one that linked Democratic nominee and Massachusetts Governor Michael

Dukakis with furloughed criminal Willie Horton—came from an independent group called the National Security Political Action Committee. (The independent ad showed a picture of Horton, who was black, while a spot by the campaign of Vice President George H. W. Bush focused solely on the Massachusetts prison-furlough program and did not feature the criminal's image or name.)

Even two of the Supreme Court justices whose decision upheld the constitutionality of BCRA acknowledged that large amounts of money would still find a way into the political system, which Congress would eventually have to regulate again: "[We are] under no illusion that this will be the last congressional statement on the matter. Money, like water, will always find an outlet. What problems will arise, and how Congress will respond, are concerns for another day," wrote John Paul Stevens and Sandra Day O'Connor....

In tone, the outside groups were much more likely to connect the dots in a conspiratorial fashion and draw the worst possible conclusions about the opposition. "You had both sides feeling essentially the world was going to turn into a black hole if the other side won," said Brooks Jackson, director of FactCheck.org, an authoritative website that monitors the veracity of campaign ads....

Arguably no ads were more memorable—or controversial—than those run by the Swift Vets. The group consisted of Vietnam veterans who patrolled the Mekong Delta in Swift boats similar to those that Kerry piloted. Kerry had tried to inoculate himself on national security issues by making his heroism in Vietnam the centerpiece of his nominating convention and a reason he was fit to be commander in chief. To critics, that strategy opened Kerry up to the torrent of criticism about his military service that followed.

The Swift Vets wanted to destroy Kerry's heroic image and raise questions about his ability to lead the nation during a time of war. Their ads started with an initially small media buy, $500,000, in Wisconsin, Ohio, and West Virginia. But cable shows played the ads repeatedly, and pundits chewed them over on air for weeks. Senator Kerry's critics furiously e-mailed the spots to anyone they could. Even criticisms of the Swift Vets' charges helped increase their exposure. "We wanted to generate controversy," said Chris LaCivita, the Swift Vets' chief strategist. That strategy succeeded wildly. The ads had the effect of confronting Kerry on one of his perceived strong issues, said LaCivita, a combat Marine veteran from the Gulf War, who said he was drawn to the group by their disgust with Kerry for criticizing active-duty troops after he returned from Vietnam.

The commercials were a milestone in the history of negative campaigning in presidential politics. Candidates had long been chastised for avoiding combat service, whether it was Grover Cleveland for hiring a substitute during the Civil War or Bill Clinton for pulling strings to avoid going to Vietnam. But the Swift Vets' ads in 2004 marked the first time a candidate's active-duty military service had been used *against* him during a campaign, rather than in his own favor. . . .

The issues and themes of negative campaigning will vary by decade and era, but the use of those tactics by ambitious politicians is not going away. Nor should it. Voters should be given as many facts about potential officeholders as possible, so they can make up their own minds about what is and is not important and relevant. Positive ads can be more misleading because candidates omit key pieces of information about themselves. What a candidate chooses *not* to discuss is usually as important as what he or she prefers to emphasize. If a candidate has a deep character flaw, voters should know that before casting their votes.

Further, despite claims that negative campaigning turns voters off, it's the most partisan races that often bring more people to the polls. The 2004 presidential campaign, one of the most heated in recent memory, produced a voter turnout of roughly 60 percent, the highest in 36 years. Senator John Kerry's vote total was up 16 percent from Vice President Al Gore's; President George W. Bush's vote total was up 23 percent from what it had been four years before. That fits a historical pattern, as turnout rose during the years following the Civil War, when campaigns were very biting; Republicans were accused of "waving the bloody shirt" and Democrats labeled "disloyal." "Enthusiasm in politics usually contains a large element of hatred," noted political commentator Michael Barone, coauthor of the biannual *The Almanac of American Politics.*

Finally, the way candidates respond to negative campaign tactics can be indicative of how they would perform in office. In a democratic society, public officials must be willing to accept a tremendous amount of criticism about their public actions and personal lives—much of it unfair. If they wilt under attacks or fail to respond to negative charges, it may be a sign they would not perform particularly well in the rough and tumble of elected office. "Part of what people look for is how he answers it. Does he stand up to it? Does he hide from it?" said Carter Wrenn, the veteran North Carolina Republican political consultant and former captain of Senator Jesse Helms's old political machine, the Congressional Club.

Ultimately, much of the responsibility for the tone of American political campaigns rests with voters themselves. In the Internet age, with news sources legion, voters have no excuse for not finding sufficient information to make decisions on whether to support or oppose political candidates. Yes, votes in a legislative body can be twisted to make it seem something they are not. But there's plenty of information available to overcome such distortions, if voters only make minimal efforts to educate themselves.

69

DAVID CAMPBELL

From *Why We Vote*

A young voter in a local Boston election inspired scholar David Campbell to examine why she voted, despite her newness to the area and her uncertainty about the candidates running. Campbell considers two reasons, citing Constitution framer James Madison and French observer Alexis de Tocqueville. Voters can be motivated by self interest or by a sense of duty. Campbell then traces the young voter's background to see why she felt she ought to vote. Little River, Kansas, is the reason. Often, voting is a habit, he finds, and one that is instilled in younger years. It depends on the expectations of the community in which a youngster is raised. Campbell's conclusions are especially important in the aftermath of the 2008 primaries and general election which drew in large numbers of new young voters. Are these voters here to stay?

ON SEPTEMBER 26, 1989, Traci Hodgson cast her ballot in Boston's City Council election. It was the only vote cast in her precinct. For a number of reasons, the political science literature predicts that Traci should have been like the other 275 registrants in her precinct and not turned out to vote. She was only twenty-one, she had lived in Boston for less than two months, and she admitted that she was "not very familiar with the candidates running." So why did she vote? When asked she replied, "I just think it's important to vote. If you have the right, you ought to exercise it—whether you are going to make a difference or not."

This book is about why Traci voted, and why she voted alone.

Madison and Tocqueville: A Tale of Two Motivations

Our starting point in answering this question is not what *did* motivate Traci, but rather what did *not*. Clearly she did not vote to protect or advance her interests, as she admitted that she did not know enough about the candidates to select them on the basis of who best represented her. To someone with only a cursory familiarity with the study of American politics this may seem difficult to explain, as politics is typically described as a forum for the "clash of interests." Equating politics with conflict underpins much of the political science literature and is an assumption shared by scholars working within many theoretical frameworks. I recall an introductory political science course in which a professor defined politics as the "scarcity of consensus." In 1960, E. E. Schattschneider wrote simply, "At the root of all politics is the universal language of conflict." Forty years later, Morris Fiorina and Paul Peterson note matter-of-factly in their introductory textbook on American politics that "politics is fundamentally about conflict." For all the ink spilled by contemporary political scientists, however, no one has ever expressed this way of understanding politics better than James Madison in *Federalist 10*. Madison writes compellingly of how "the latent causes of faction are thus sown in the nature of man," and that "the most frivolous and fanciful distinctions have been sufficient to kindle their unfriendly passions and excite their most violent conflicts."

It does not seem, however, that Traci had her passions kindled as Madison describes. Instead, by her own account she was motivated by the glowing embers of obligation. She felt that she ought to vote, that it was her duty.

In invoking a sense of duty as a motivation to vote, Traci highlights a second, if more subtle, theme in both contemporary and classic writings on political engagement. If, in *Federalist 10,* Madison has written the quintessential statement on political participation as "protecting one's interests," then perhaps Tocqueville has written an equally quintessential description of political participation as driven by "fulfilling one's duty." In *Democracy in America,* Tocqueville observes that American political institutions lead citizens to see that "it is the duty as well as the interest of men to be useful to their fellows. . . . What had been calculation becomes instinct. By dint of working for the good of his fellow citizens, he in the end acquires a habit and taste for serving them."

These two opposing views of politics are not merely the abstract statements of theoreticians, the political science rendition of how many angels can dance on the head of a pin. They also inform the writings and doings of political practitioners, with some of America's founders as notable examples. Of course, Madison was one of the founders and, as noted, in his words we find a cogent description of how politics is inevitably defined by conflict. However, George Washington's vision was of a republic free from strife among its citizens, in which citizens were involved in public affairs out of duty. Ironically, given their disagreements on so many other matters, Thomas Jefferson's vision for the new republic mirrored Washington's. Jefferson idealized a nation of small Tocquevillian communities, mentioning his ideal in almost every speech he gave.

The ongoing debate between civic republican and liberal political philosophers over the nature of political life at the time of America's founding underscores the two competing visions of democracy's nature. In summarizing this extensive literature, James Morone writes,

> [T]he dominant interpretation of liberal America focuses on the pursuit of self-interest. . . . In the republican view, the colonial and Revolutionary ideal lay, not in the pursuit of private matters, but in the shared public life of civic duty, in the subordination of individual interests to the *res publica*. Citizens were defined and fulfilled by participation in political community.

The distinction between engagement driven by interests versus duty need not be seen as either/or. The very fact that evidence can be mustered to support both interpretations of the founders' ideals suggests that neither one dominated to the exclusion of the other. Nor should we assume that the essential difference between engagement spurred by a threat to one's interests and engagement motivated by a sense of civic obligation has faded over time. Indeed, the distinction between interest-driven and duty-driven engagement is at the core of this book, which is about contemporary patterns of public engagement in the United States.

Traci and Tocqueville

While articulating that engagement in the public square is driven by Tocquevillian as well as Madisonian impulses underscores that there are two fundamentally different motivations for political activity, this observation alone does not provide much theoretical traction for empirical analysis. On its own, "fulfilling one's duty" remains at best a tautological explanation for political participation. It is far more interesting to ask *why* Traci felt that voting was her duty.

A potential answer to that question was intuitively included in the newspaper article that told of Traci's lonely ballot. Traci, the reader learns, had just moved to Boston from Kansas. She was born and raised in the town of Little River, population 693—a community that advertises itself as a "town with a lot of civic pride." Significantly, in 1992 voter turnout in Little River was 67 percent, 12 percentage points higher than turnout nationwide, and *27 points higher* than in Boston. Armed with this information about Traci's hometown it seems plausible, even probable, that Traci voted because she hails from a community where voting is common. One might say that you can take the girl out of Kansas, but you can't take the Kansas out of the girl. . . .

. . . I suggest that people vote out of both Madisonian and Tocquevillian motivations. In some communities more voters come to the polls in order to protect their interests, whereas in other places more of them cast a ballot because they feel it is their duty to do so. In these latter communities, civic norms are strong. Those norms are strong, in turn, because of consensus over values—what political scientists are more likely to call interests, and what economists call preferences. Where many people share the same values social norms are more easily enforced, specifically a norm encouraging civic participation. Diverse interests breed conflict, while uniformity fosters consensus; voter turnout can spring from both, but for different reasons. Furthermore, some forms of engagement in the community are more common in consensual communities, other forms in places better characterized as conflictual.

Assuming that I convince the reader that communities vary in the degree to which they can be characterized by their consensus over values, and thus in the extent to which their residents act in accordance with civic norms, Traci's vote will nonetheless remain unexplained. Remember that when she cast her ballot, Traci was not actually living in homogeneous Little River, Kansas, but heterogeneous Boston, Massachusetts. Why would Traci vote out of a sense of duty once she had moved away from a place with strong civic norms? Tocqueville hints at the answer when in the quotation above he refers to people acting out of duty because it had become their "instinct," having acquired a "habit and taste" for it. Traci had internalized the norm that voting is a duty and continued her duty-driven behavior even when she moved to a place where those norms would not be enforced. Critically, she spent her adolescence enmeshed in a community where civic norms were strong. During this particularly formative period of our lives, we are prone to developing habits that stay with us throughout our lives. In short, one can be socialized into acting out of a sense of duty, and an important (probably the most important) period of our lives for that socialization to occur is adolescence. . . .

Why did Traci vote? Because she was raised in a community where she internalized the norm that voting is her civic duty. The simplicity of this statement, however, belies the complexity of the theoretical foundation upon which it rests. Implicit within it are a number of claims, none of which is necessarily conventional wisdom within political science. To make the case that the communities in which we spend our adolescence affect whether we vote in adulthood first requires establishing that

a. communities shape the civic and political engagement of the people who live within them, or *what you do now depends on where you are now*

b. the engagement of adolescents in particular is shaped by where they live, or *what you did then depends on where you were then*

c. adolescents' engagement links to their engagement as adults, or *what you do now depends on what you did then*

Together these claims lay the foundation for the . . . central argument: the civic norms within one's adolescent social environment have an effect on civic participation well beyond adolescence: *what you do now depends on where you were then*. . . .

In places characterized by conflict, politically motivated public engagement is more common. Conversely, communities where there is relative consensus are more likely to host civic engagement, because these communities have strong civic norms encouraging engagement in publicly spirited activities. This, in a nutshell, is what I have labeled the *dual motivations theory* of public engagement. . . .

Political participation refers to those activities by private citizens that are more or less directly aimed at influencing the selection of governmental personnel and/or the actions they take.

The key to the definition is the *end* to which the activity is directed—actions taken or policies enacted by public officials.

What other authors have characterized as activity driven by expressive, Tocquevillian, or duty-driven motivations, I will refer to as *civic participation*. It, too, is defined by its end.

Civic participation refers to public-spirited collective action that is not motivated by the desire to affect public policy.

These definitions necessitate that I make three things clear.

First, the motivations described in these definitions are at the end points of a continuum, as many activities are driven by a mixture of both impulses. Dahl's distinction between *homo politicus* and *homo civicus* is instructive, as he has clearly constructed two ideal types. Just as some—probably most—people have a mix of these characteristics, so are various activities driven by more than one motivation. But just as some people more closely resemble *homo politicus* than *civicus* (and vice versa), there are clearly activities that tilt more to the political than civic side (and vice versa). For example, we would expect writing a letter to one's member of Congress to have a predominantly political motivation, while volunteering to tutor a child is likely to be civically motivated. . . .

Second, these two motivations are not exhaustive. I recognize that the activities I discuss, like all human behavior, really have multiple motivations. The key for the discussion at hand, however, is that civic and political motivations are both systematically related to the nature of the social environments in which we live. And it is people's social environments that will occupy our attention.

Third, I do not mean to attach any normative weight to one motivation or another. This is the point on which I might most fairly be accused of asking to both eat and have my cake, since I have consciously adopted language from normative theory. Furthermore, I readily acknowledge that in common discourse, the terms "political" and "civic" have a normative flavor. "Political," of course, is generally a pejorative term. To accuse someone of being political is to label him as self-serving and manipulative. To be civic, or civic-minded, though, connotes selflessness and virtue. I question, however, whether these terms deserve their common connotations, at least as I have defined them. Essentially, I have defined political as the desire to influence public policy. By this definition, being political does not seem so deserving of opprobrium. Is it really so bad that people vote or otherwise participate in public affairs because they have an interest in a policy outcome? In the United States generally, and within the discipline of political science particularly, there is a common lament that voters are woefully uninformed. Why else should voters be informed but to determine where they stand on the issues? To flip the question around, is it really such a good thing for individuals to participate in politics without an interest in the outcome? The example of Traci Hodgson drives this point home. Recall that Traci voted because she felt that it was her duty, not because she knew anything about the candidates. Having voters drawn to the polls out of obligation, only to cast totally uninformed ballots, seems far from the democratic ideal. . . .

Community Heterogeneity

It is probably not immediately obvious how the findings of the literature on community heterogeneity and civic engagement lead to the hypothesis that noncompetitive elections produce high turnout. The claim rests on two propositions, both of which will be elaborated upon. First, community homogeneity *in general* lifts rates of civically oriented participation *in general*. Second, by the logic of the existing literature on community heterogeneity, we should expect that political homogeneity—another way of saying "noncompetitive elections"—should produce high voter turnout.

In an article reviewing the literature on heterogeneity and participation, economists Dora L. Costa and Matthew E. Kahn note that "at least fifteen different empirical economic papers have studied the consequences of community heterogeneity, and all of these studies have the same punch line: heterogeneity reduces civic engagement." This conclusion holds across different measures of heterogeneity, whether ethnic, racial, or economic, and different measures of civic engagement: group membership, response rates to the 2000 census, and interpersonal trust. If voter turnout has civic underpinnings, we should therefore expect it to fall as ethnic, racial, and economic heterogeneity rise.

Figures 1, 2, and 3 constitute simple tests of the relationship between three different types of heterogeneity and voter turnout in the 2000 presidential election. Both heterogeneity and turnout have been measured at the level of the county, an approximation of an individual's "mid-range" social context—smaller than the state or metropolitan area but larger than the neighborhood. The measures of heterogeneity have been taken directly from the existing literature. The first is *ethnic heterogeneity* (or what some authors call "birthplace fragmentation"). Always a tricky concept to measure, for this purpose ethnicity is operationalized using seven broad ethnic categories: Anglo-American, Western European, Scandinavian, Latino/Hispanic, Mediterranean, Eastern European/ Balkan, and West Indian, which mirror the categories used by other researchers. I have created an index of ethnic heterogeneity, in which a higher number represents a greater degree of heterogeneity. *Racial heterogeneity* is measured in a manner comparable to *ethnic heterogeneity,* only with racial categories in the place of the ethnic groups. *Income heterogeneity* is operationalized with the Gini coefficient, a standard measure of the income distribution within a community. The greater a county's Gini coefficient, the greater its degree of income inequality, or income heterogeneity. To simplify the graphical presentation, for all three figures the counties have been divided into deciles based on their level of heterogeneity (thus, the value for each decile represents the mean level of heterogeneity for roughly 300 counties).

The figures clearly show that as each type of heterogeneity increases, voter turnout decreases. If one has the perspective that voting is a form of civic participation, this negative relationship should not be surprising. The explanation for why heterogeneity dampens civic activity—whether voting, volunteering, or some other form of publicly spirited collective action—rests on two premises. The first is that a primary reason people engage in civically oriented collective action is in adherence to a social

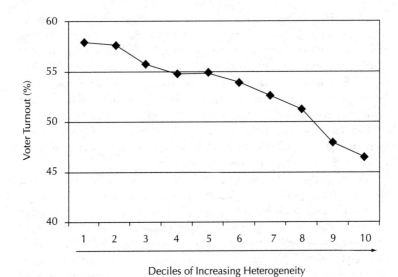

Figure 1 • ETHNIC HETEROGENEITY AND VOTER TURNOUT IN THE 2000
PRESIDENTIAL ELECTION, COUNTIES

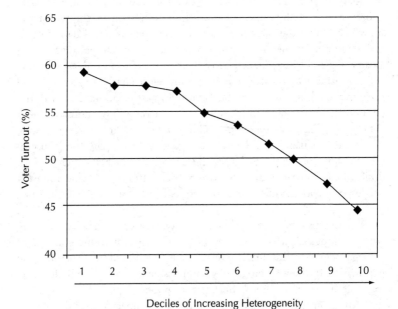

Figure 2 • RACIAL HETEROGENEITY AND VOTER TURNOUT IN THE 2000
PRESIDENTIAL ELECTION, COUNTIES

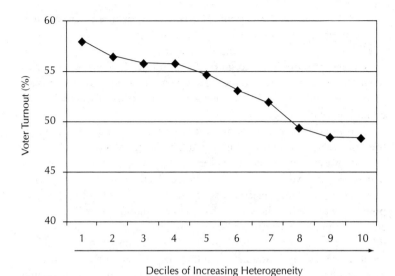

Figure 3 • Income Heterogeneity and Voter Turnout in the 2000
Presidential Election, Counties

norm encouraging it, which is another way of saying that people vote out
of a sense of civic duty. The second is that norms are more easily enforced
in homogeneous communities.

What do I mean by a social norm? Like any term employed in social
science, the definition is contested. For some, a norm is simply a behavioral regularity, something people generally do. The definition I employ,
however, specifies that a norm is rooted in a sense of obligation. . . .

[My] objective is to demonstrate that whether you vote depends on
where you are. We have seen empirical results that are, I argue, a synthesis
of two literatures that, taken alone, would each lead us to opposite conclusions about the relationship between the political composition of a
community and its level of voter turnout. A longstanding body of research concludes that voter turnout is high in places characterized by
political heterogeneity, where elections are most competitive. The social
capital literature, however, suggests voter turnout should be high where
political preferences are homogeneous. We have seen that both expectations are met. There is a curvilinear relationship between heterogeneity
and turnout—it is high in the most homogeneous counties, dropping off
toward the mean and then increasing as counties become more heterogeneous. This relationship holds across multiple years, in both aggregate-
and individual-level data, and upon controlling for a host of rival causes.

The explanation for the curvilinear relationship between heterogeneity and turnout rests on understanding the dual motivations for voter turnout. In homogeneous communities, turnout is *civically motivated*. On average, voters are more likely to go to the polls out of adherence to a civic norm. In places that are heterogeneous, however, people are more likely to vote because they feel their interests are threatened. Turnout in these communities is *politically motivated*. . . .

It is important to underscore just what we have learned thus far. In toto, this array of empirical findings provides support for the theory of dual motivations, and thus can explain the otherwise puzzling observation that presidential voter turnout rises where elections are not competitive. Turnout in presidential elections aside, however, a more fundamental purpose . . . is to explore how it is that the communities in which we live affect our public engagement. Simply put, living in different places has different consequences for participation. With this insight, it is possible to reconcile a seeming contradiction in the current literature on community heterogeneity. On the one hand, one line of research (conducted mainly by economists) has found that "heterogeneity reduces civic engagement." On the other hand, another line of research (primarily done by political scientists) has found that heterogeneity fosters engagement. Who is right? The answer is both. While at first glance these conclusions appear empirically incompatible, they are actually theoretically consistent with one another, once we recognize that they are looking at different forms of participation. Participation motivated by the advancement or defense of political interests is sparked within heterogeneous communities—places where people have divergent interests or preferences. Places where interests or preferences are held in common facilitate publicly spirited collective action that is outside the arena of political combat. As the United States becomes increasingly heterogeneous (or in the vernacular outside of social science, diverse), increasing attention will be paid to heterogeneity's consequences. The lesson of the foregoing analysis is that, at least when it comes to public engagement, those consequences do not lend themselves to simplistic assertions. One should be wary of claims to the contrary. . . .

. . . Remember Traci Hodgson? She was the young woman . . . who cast the only ballot at her precinct in a Boston city election. Our objective has been to explain why she was the lonely voter. The explanation is deceivingly simple: she voted in Boston because she had come to see voting as her duty. And she came to see voting as a civic obligation because she had internalized voting as a civic norm. Furthermore, she internalized that norm because she spent her formative years in a community characterized by strong civic norms. . . . [We] have examined the plausibility of this explanation for her vote, building a theoretical structure to explain Traci's vote as driven by a civic motivation, implanted during her adolescent years.

First, we saw evidence that *what you do depends on where you are*. Heterogeneous communities like Boston have a very different civic character than homogeneous places like Traci Hodgson's hometown of Little River, Kansas. In politically heterogeneous communities, voter turnout is more likely to be ignited by political conflict. People vote because they see their interests threatened. In homogeneous communities, however, voter turnout is more likely to be motivated by a sense of civic obligation. Similarly, politically heterogeneous communities are more likely to be the site of political combat, as their residents are more likely to work on political campaigns and march in demonstrations, while communities characterized by relative political homogeneity are more likely to host civically motivated activities like volunteering in the community.

Traci grew up in a community where public engagement likely had a stronger civic than political flavor, from which we can infer that her adolescence was shaped by civic norms. . . . [We] saw that adolescents' public engagement is shaped by the communities in which they live. Or, in other words, I examined whether *what you did then depends on where you were then*. The pattern paralleled what we observed for adults. In communities with greater political heterogeneity, adolescents have a greater degree of political efficacy—the sense that engagement in politics is worth the effort because it brings substantive results. On the other hand, with political homogeneity comes a higher level of civically motivated activity, specifically engagement in community service.

The next step was to see whether civic behavior in adolescence links to adulthood. It is one thing to say that while living in some communities over others, teens are more likely to engage in civically motivated activity. It is quite another to say that once they leave those communities, they continue to be civically involved. Remember that Traci cast her solitary vote in Boston, where she was a newcomer, and not in Little River, where she spent her adolescence. And so, the analysis next turned to the question of whether *what you do now depends on what you did then*. We found strong links between young people's participation in civically oriented activity and their civic involvement later on in life. . . .

Recent years have seen the embrace of diversity become a defining characteristic of contemporary American society. In the American public creed, it is now placed firmly beside other bedrock values like liberty and equality. While diversity perhaps does not have the longevity of these other ideals—the word did not roll off the lips of the Framers—it has quickly made up for lost time. Legal scholar Peter Schuck begins his book *Diversity in America* by noting, "In the pantheon of unquestioned goods, diversity is right up there with progress, motherhood, and apple pie."

The rising attention to diversity has led to research on its consequences, including the question of whether public engagement rises or falls as a community's level of diversity rises. The answer is "yes." Or, it depends. Community heterogeneity and public engagement share a nuanced connection, as it is not as simple as asking whether engagement rises or falls as heterogeneity rises. The answer depends on the type of engagement in question. Civically motivated participation is more common in politically homogeneous communities, while people are more likely to engage in politically motivated activity in politically heterogeneous communities. Political diversity pulls civic involvement down while pushing political involvement up. . . .

. . . For the foreseeable future there will continue to be much discussion of diversity, much of it from a Panglossian perspective. Americans' abiding interest in—and celebration of—diversity is noble, deeply rooted in our history as a pluralist nation. But we should never forget that there is no free lunch. Increased diversity, particularly in a political context, appears to mean a trade-off between one type of public engagement and another, with normatively ambiguous consequences. To put our thumb on the purely civic side of the scale is to withdraw from the public decision making that is integral to a pluralist democracy, thus impoverishing our politics. Too much politics and too little civic involvement, however, runs the risk that contention will supplant community. I suspect that most of us would not want to live in a place constantly riven with political discord. . . .

CHUCK TODD
SHELDON GAWISER

From *How Barack Obama Won*

The historic 2008 presidential election occurred after a wild series of politi-cal events in the past decades. NBC's Chuck Todd and Sheldon Gawiser characterize 2008 as the "exclamation point on the country's post–Cold War search for its political center." Todd and Gawiser trace the landmarks leading up to 2008, beginning with then-Senator Hillary Clinton's path to the Democratic nomination, a path that initially seemed unobstructed. Barack Obama's candidacy was different than Clinton's (or Republican McCain's) from the start, since Obama established early on the reason he was seeking the office: that reason was "change from Bush." The authors then turn to the Clinton-Obama primary contest, and the vice presidential choices. Todd and Gawiser mention a few other memorable 2008 campaign moments including Joe the Plumber. Was the result of the November 2008 vote the start of a realignment? Honestly, write Todd and Gawiser, "we don't know yet."

SO HOW DOES ONE sum up the 2008 presidential campaign in just 12,000 words? Who is arrogant enough to think he or she can capture precisely the historical nature of this campaign and election, at a time when the nation seems vulnerable on so many fronts?

It's possible a historian 50 years from now might be able truly to un-derstand what happened and why the country was ready to break through the color barrier, particularly if said historian looks at the 2008 election through the prism of post–Cold War America.

Since 1992, the country has witnessed nearly two decades of political tumult of a kind it has experienced only once or twice a century. Right now, the country is so enamored with the fact that we've broken the po-litical color barrier of the American presidency that we haven't stepped back and appreciated just what a wild political ride our country has been on.

Since the Cold War ended and America lost its most significant ene-my, the Soviet Union, the country has been looking for its political center. Consider the upheaval we've experienced as a nation since 1992. First, we had a three-way presidential election in which the third-party candidate was the front-runner for a good part of the campaign. Then, in 1994, we saw the House of Representatives switch control for the first time in 40 years. Next, in 1996, the winning presidential candidate failed to secure 50% of the vote for the second straight election, something that hadn't happened before in two straight presidential elections in 80 years. Then, in 1998, the nation watched as a tabloid presidential soap opera became a Constitutional crisis, and Congress impeached a president for only the second time in this nation's history. In 2000, the nation's civics lesson on the Constitution continued, thanks to the first presidential election in over 100 years in which the winner of the Electoral College failed to win the popular vote, followed by the Supreme Court ruling, which eventually ended the protracted vote count controversy in Florida. In 2001, this nation was the victim of the worst terrorist attack in our history. Then, in 2004, a president won reelection by the smallest margin of any successfully reelected president in modern times. Finally, in 2006, control of Congress flipped after what, historically, was a fairly short stint for the Republicans. All of which brings us to 2008 and what for many Americans is the campaign commonly referred to as "the election of our lifetimes."

Is this the election that ends a 20-year period of political chaos? The serious problems this country is facing may be the reason that 2008 puts the exclamation point on the country's post–Cold War search for its political center. . . .

. . . The [2008] campaign began in 1999, when word first leaked that then first lady Hillary Clinton was seriously contemplating a run for U.S. senator from New York. Her election in 2000 set off the anticipation for what would be a historic first: the potential election of this country's first woman president.

There was some scuttlebutt that Clinton would run for president in 2004, but ultimately she decided to keep her eye on the 2008 ball. That was when she'd be into her second term as senator and when the field would be cleared of an incumbent president. This country rarely fires presidents after one term. It's happened just three times in the last 100 years.

The long march of the Hillary Clinton candidacy shaped much of the presidential fields for both parties. The Republicans who announced in 2008 all made their cases within the framework of challenging Hillary. In fact, it was Hillary's presence on the Democratic side that gave Rudy Giuliani the opportunity to be taken seriously by Republicans as a 2008 presidential candidate. As for the Democrats, consider that many an analyst and media critic like to talk about how wrong so-called conventional wisdom was during the 2008 campaign. But much of it was right. One early piece of such wisdom was that the Democratic primary campaign would be a primary within the primary between all the Democrats not named Clinton to establish an alternative to Hillary.

This sub-Democratic primary, which started in earnest after the 2004 presidential election, looked as if it was going to be a campaign between a lot of white guys and Washington insiders looking for their last chance at the brass ring. Familiar faces like Joe Biden, Chris Dodd, John Edwards, and Bill Richardson must have thought to themselves, *If I could only get into a one-on-one with Hillary, I could beat her.* Some new names were also seriously considering a run, like Virginia Governor Mark Warner and Iowa Governor Tom Vilsack. None of these potential candidates scared the Clinton camp, because they all were just conventional enough that Hillary's ability to put together a base of women and African-Americans would be sufficient to achieve the Democratic nomination.

But there was one potential candidate whose name was being talked about by activists and the blogosphere who did have the Clinton crowd nervous: the freshman senator from Illinois, Barack Obama. The factor that kept the Clintons confident about their 2008 chances was the notion that there was just no way, despite his popularity with the Democratic activist base, that a guy who, until 2004, was in the Illinois state senate would somehow have the audacity to run for president so soon. The Clintons were very familiar with the strategy of figuring out the timing of when best to run. They knew 1988 was too soon for Bill, and they took the advice of many and waited until 1992, and they knew that 2004 was too soon for Hillary, and she took the advice of many and waited. Surely, the Clintons must have thought, Obama would follow the same advice. . . .

While the Republican nomination [of Arizona Senator John McCain] was fascinating, it didn't hold a candle to what was going on inside the Democratic party. The decision by Obama to run transformed the Democratic primary instantly from a subprimary campaign to determine the anti-Hillary alternative to a two-person clash of the titans. From the moment Obama formalized his candidacy, Clinton's campaign was transformed into a rapid response operation focused solely on Obama.

When word leaked that Obama was going to form an exploratory committee and would do so on YouTube, Clinton quickly crafted her "I'm in it to win it" announcement, which was also done via the Web.

Interestingly, though, while Obama used new media to announce the formation of his exploratory committee, he went the old school route when formally announcing his actual candidacy—he gave a "Why I'm running for president" announcement speech in front of thousands of supporters in his home state. Clinton never gave a formal "Why I'm running" speech akin to what Obama delivered on February 10, 2007, in front of the Old State Capitol in Springfield, Illinois. This fundamental fact sums up the primary contest about as well as any primary result or delegate count. . . .

Obama outlined the organizing principle for that candidacy via his announcement speech. In fact, the basic themes Obama introduced in that first speech in Springfield would be repeated on the stump throughout the campaign—all the way until his victory speech on Election Night in November 2008.

That initial announcement speech included plenty of phrases which would become familiar to his supporters, such as: "What's stopped us is the failure of our leadership, the smallness of our politics—the ease with which we're distracted by the petty and trivial, our chronic avoidance of tough decisions, our preference for scoring cheap political points instead of rolling up our sleeves and building a working consensus to tackle big problems." In that first speech, Obama also constantly used the refrain, "Let's be the generation," as a way to talk directly to new voters; he hinted that his speeches would be a big part of his campaign strategy when he uttered the phrase, "There is power in words."

While much of Obama's campaign rationale was evident in his announcement speech, the same cannot be said for either Clinton or McCain. Stunningly, neither gave a "Why I'm running for president" speech. Neither made a formal announcement in his or her home state or any other. Neither outlined in the traditional way a philosophy or program as Obama had done. Clinton made her Web video speech and that was it, nothing else other than "I'm in it to win it." McCain announced on *The Tonight Show with Jay Leno.* Just on the basis of announcement strategies, is it any wonder why Obama appeared to be the candidate who constantly was able to stay on message while his two opponents, Clinton in the primary and McCain in the general, were grasping for anything that would stick?

There are several reasons why Obama ultimately won the presidency, but one of the central factors was he always made the case for why he was the candidate of change, the candidate who was change from Bush. Clinton and McCain, when running against Obama, were always caught up in trying to contrast themselves with Obama and highlight his inexperience. Neither offered consistent "change from Bush" arguments. And in a time when President Bush had approval ratings ranging from 25% to 30%, change mattered the most to voters over any other issue. . . .

As close followers of the Democratic nominating fight will remember, the Democratic Party awards delegates to any candidate earning at least 15% of the vote in any congressional district of any state. So even if Clinton won California by some 20 points, Obama was still picking up sizable chunks of delegates. But Clinton was getting trounced in the caucus states, so badly that she came close to getting shut out in a few states. The most glaring example of this Clinton miscalculation was the delegates earned by Obama in Idaho versus the number earned by Clinton in New Jersey. Obama won Idaho and netted 15 more delegates than Clinton. She won New Jersey, not by an insignificant margin, but netted fewer delegates than Obama's gain in Idaho. It was miscalculations like this one that cost the Clinton campaign dearly.

The Obama delegate operation ran circles around the Clinton campaign and by the time all of the delegates were counted after Super Tuesday, it was Obama, not Clinton, who won more delegates that day. (He also won more states and was about even in total votes so there really wasn't a barometer for the Clintons to prove they were ahead.) Clinton may have won the bigger states, but Obama was garnering the votes that mattered. When Super Tuesday came and went, the Clinton campaign was broke and behind. The Obama campaign was just getting started. A week later, Obama would sweep the Potomac primaries, Maryland, Virginia, and D.C., and go on to win 11 straight contests, forcing Clinton to make a final stand on Junior Tuesday, the March 4 primaries in Ohio and Texas.

But while the news media was soaking up the Clinton theatrics about the Ohio-Texas do-or-die, a very important event had already occurred: Obama had built a delegate lead that was close to insurmountable, thanks to the proportional system of delegates. His 100-plus delegate lead from his February sweep through post-Super Tuesday states may have looked close in the raw total, but it wasn't.

While Clinton did well on Junior Tuesday by winning Ohio and Texas, she netted less than a dozen delegates for her efforts. The die was cast and all Obama had to do was run out the clock. But all was not smooth going: there was the Reverend Wright episode* in the run-up to the

---

*Reverend Jeremiah Wright was the former pastor of the church in Chicago that Barack Obama had long attended. Over several decades, Wright had preached sermons that contained views seen as inflammatory to many Americans. For example, Wright made the statement "God damn America." He said that the United States bore some blame for the 2001 World Trade Center attack. Wright made many comments that could be interpreted as anti-

Pennsylvania primary. And Obama's loss in the Pennsylvania primary raised concerns among some Democrats that he couldn't win the working-class white vote in the general election and gave Clinton even more life, or so it seemed. Then Obama won North Carolina by double digits and nearly upset Clinton in white working-class-heavy Indiana on May 6, leading smart observers to publicly acknowledge that the race was over. In fact, on that famous May night, the late Tim Russert said first what every smart politico knew, "We now know who the Democratic nominee is going to be." And that nominee was Barack Obama.

It was a primary campaign for the ages; one that probably lasted longer than it should have because of the media's fascination with the Clintons. But it was still something else. Every Tuesday night, more and more folks kept tuning in to see what would happen next in America's favorite reality show. Could Obama win working-class white voters? Would college-educated white women start breaking more for Clinton? Would Hillary finally drop out? What would Bill Clinton say next?

To think that we're writing a book on how Obama won and mostly talking about the general election is to dismiss a very important, if not more important, part of Obama's rise and maturation as a presidential candidate. The long, drawn-out primary campaign with Clinton did more to help Obama than hurt him. He became a better debater, not a great debater, but a better one. He became a candidate who could speak a bit more from the heart than the head on economic issues. And of course, without Clinton, he never would have had to run campaigns in all 50 states (and Guam and the Virgin Islands and Puerto Rico . . .). If Obama never had to run a 50 state campaign in the primaries, would he have been able to put Indiana in play in the general election? What about North Carolina? And would Virginia have turned blue so easily without Obama's early primary efforts?

Many an Obama operative seethed at the selfishness of the Clinton campaign during those draining primary moments in March, April, and May, because they knew she couldn't win and she had to know that as well. But Clinton staying in this race as long as she did only helped Obama. And Obama, the candidate-turned-president, knows it. It's why the highest-ranking cabinet slot went to her. . . .

The most interested spectator for the greatest reality show on earth in the spring of 2008 was John McCain. While Obama had to trudge through 48 states (not including Florida and Michigan) and Puerto Rico to fend

---

Jewish. Initially, Obama tried to explain Wright's comments in the context of his experiences, but eventually Obama left the church and cut his ties with Wright.—EDS.

off Clinton, McCain was able to wrap up his nomination by campaigning in all of four states. Being the nominee on the sidelines should have been an enormous advantage. This should have been the time for McCain to ratchet up his national organization, hone his general election message, begin the VP vetting process, and raise the boatload of money he would need to keep up with the financial juggernaut that was and still is Barack Obama.

As it turns out, McCain apparently did very little of those things. Many a McCain apologist argues that his candidacy was doomed by outside events, like the economic meltdown in the fall of 2008 or the fact that President George W. Bush had the lowest ratings of any two-term president since the archiving of polling numbers began. But while Bush and the economy were enormously heavy anchors on McCain, it does not excuse the wasted three month head start he had on Obama. . . .

The general election really didn't take off until Obama set out on his weeklong international tour of world hotspots and European capitals. The culmination of the trip was a speech in Berlin in front of some 200,000 spectators, a scene that seemed to leave much of this country awestruck by Obama's worldwide popularity

With their backs against the wall, the McCain campaign was desperate to bring Obama back down to earth. They launched perhaps the most famous TV ad of the 2008 campaign, calling Obama the "biggest celebrity in the world" and comparing him to Paris Hilton and Britney Spears. Needless to say, this ad served as cable news catnip and got tons of attention. The McCain strategy was clear; they intended to make Obama's popularity a liability. The McCain campaign was attempting to win the experience argument against Obama by invoking celebrity lightweights like Paris Hilton.

The tactic worked. Obama didn't get the big bump from his very well orchestrated international trip. If anything, Obama's narrow three to six point lead throughout the summer started to shrink a bit, as the race fell within the margin of error in the polls. The more important aspect about this moment in the campaign is that it really did signal the start of the general election. And everything from this point on in the race was a blur.

The McCain folks were proud of their ability to deflate the bounce they expected Obama to receive from his overseas adventure. But the campaign leadership may have learned the wrong lesson from this moment: that tactics were the secret to keeping McCain viable. The campaign would never have as effective a hit on Obama after the Paris Hilton ad but would spend a lot of energy trying. Whether it was the pick of

Sarah Palin as running mate, the decision to suspend the campaign, or the introduction of "Joe the Plumber,"* the McCain campaign used a series of tactics with no overall strategy.

... [It] is telling that McCain never gave a formal announcement speech for president. If he had no organizing principle from the beginning, how was he expected to find it as the campaign wore on? Our NBC colleague, Tom Brokaw, liked to compare the McCain campaign team to guerilla war fighters. They could do quick strikes and shock their foes for a day or two, but like many unsuccessful guerilla armies, the McCain campaign could never advance on the general election battlefield. They never took new ground, never forced the Obama campaign into retreat. The best the McCain campaign could ever do was slow the Obama campaign from advancing; they never stopped them. . . .

Obama's vice presidential selection process was fairly predictable. This is another case in which the campaign and the conventional wisdom crowd were in sync. Despite all of the cable chatter by uninformed hype-analysts about putting Hillary Clinton on the ticket, the campaign believed Obama needed someone safe, and safe meant an older white guy with impeccable foreign policy credentials. Obama, himself, wanted to be a bit more daring. He was personally impressed with two of his early primary supporters, Kansas Governor Kathleen Sebelius and Virginia Governor Tim Kaine. But the political reality was that he couldn't pick a woman running mate not named Clinton, and he couldn't pick a running mate who had been in his current position for less time than Obama's own tenure as senator. So the campaign quickly zeroed in on Delaware Senator Joe Biden, one of Obama's primary opponents.

The Biden pick checked all of the conventional wisdom boxes, including experience, working-class roots (the Scranton, Pennsylvania–raised Democrat was one of the poorest members of the Senate, one of just a handful who were not millionaires), and he'd been publicly vetted [in] a more than 30 year Senate career. . . .

McCain's search for a running mate was much less chronicled in the media because the campaign seemed to do a pretty good job keeping their short list close to the vest. One thing they were counting on though, was Obama not picking Biden. It was the one pick the leadership of the

---

*"Joe the Plumber" was a guy from Ohio who attended one of candidate Barack Obama's impromptu question sessions in October 2008. Joe Wurzelbacher asked Obama about tax policy, challenging the candidate's approach to taxation. Joe become a symbol used by the McCain campaign to express middle America's views on some of Obama's policies. Despite a few tax and plumbing-license problems of his own, Joe became a campaign celebrity, appearing in several McCain ads and sitting for television news interviews.—EDS.

McCain campaign thought would be the safest and smartest choice for Obama, the pick that would create the least amount of drama. As one McCain senior adviser put it, "Obama doesn't have the guts to pick Biden." What did he mean by that? Biden's too logical of a choice and too qualified for the job; Obama doesn't believe he needs that, so pontificated this senior McCain strategist.

But that's just the thing: the McCain folks constantly misjudged Obama. They believed the stereotype they were trying to create, that he was this out-of-control, egomaniacal, power-hungry politician. It's one thing to attempt to create that image; it's another to believe it when you are in charge of setting the campaign's strategy.

. . . So he went back to the drawing board and asked about a candidate whom two of McCain's close aides, Steve Schmidt and Rick Davis, had been pushing for for some time: Alaska Governor Sarah Palin. After a fairly brief meeting, McCain gave the nod.

The Palin pick was announced approximately 12 hours after Obama finished giving what the Democratic campaign believed was a historically significant acceptance speech, in front of 80,000 Democrats. The speech was so effective that 13 hours later, barely a word was being replayed. Why? The entire political world was focused on one person, Sarah Palin.

That she took the country by storm is an understatement. The irony, of course, is that she instantly became a celebrity of the level the McCain campaign hadn't seen since, well, Obama in Europe. There were so many things to learn about her: her husband was half-Eskimo; she had five children, one of whom was less than a year old; her oldest daughter was pregnant; she was a dead-ringer for *Saturday Night Live* veteran Tina Fey; and she was a self-described "hockey mom."

Notice what wasn't on that list: she was a successful governor who had done X, Y, and Z. Or, she was an expert in subject matter X. The pop culture story of Sarah Palin and the image of a working mother was a great narrative. But after that, a perception quickly developed that there wasn't a lot of "there" there. Of course, she became fodder for the media, was even ridiculed, and that only got the Republican base fired up. To the GOP base, she was a breath of fresh air; the *Republican* the Republican Party had been waiting to rally around for two years. While the base had never been enamored with McCain, they were taken with Palin. Here was a woman who was practicing what many in the social conservative movement were preaching, whether it was choosing to have a Down syndrome child or pushing her unmarried daughter to keep her baby and get married.

But it would be Palin's lack of experience that would eventually prove her undoing. Was she the reason McCain lost? No. Did she, in fact, help McCain in certain states like North Carolina and Georgia? Absolutely. But the campaign did her no favors when she was rolled out more as a pop icon and less as someone ready to be president, particularly when voters consistently told pollsters that McCain's age was a bigger factor than Obama's race. One of the issues McCain said she was an expert on was energy. But did the campaign ever allow Palin to hold an event in front of an oil rig or a nuclear power plant or a wind farm? The campaign did nothing to reinforce the energy issue in Palin's background other than to insinuate that any elected official from Alaska is by definition an energy expert because of energy's importance to the state's economy.

Palin proved to be an excellent political performer in controlled settings but stumbled in some TV interviews, most famously with Katie Couric of CBS. The experience seemed to scar Palin a bit as she became harder to deal with for the rest of the campaign. This was always going to be a tougher political marriage than the McCain campaign team understood. Palin's political experiences were limited. Sure, she had run for quite a few offices and mostly won, but her staff was limited and her chief strategist was her husband. When she parachuted onto the national stage, she suddenly found herself with political handlers. And when those handlers, in her mind, failed her during the early rollout, she rebelled and refused to take any advice from anyone, relying instead on her gut instincts and her husband. . . .

As for the verdict of voters, it's clear, according to the 2008 National Exit Poll, Palin was polarizing. Four out of ten voters said Palin's selection was an important factor in their vote, but those voters split their votes about evenly between the Republican and Democratic tickets. Fully two-thirds of voters believed Joe Biden was ready to serve as president if required, but 60% of voters nationwide held the opposite view of Palin, saying she was not qualified.

	Total	Obama	McCain
Importance of Palin Selection			
Important	41	48	51
Not Important	53	53	45
Palin Qualified to Be President			
Yes	38	8	91
No	60	82	16
Biden Qualified to Be President			
Yes	66	71	28
No	32	17	80

Palin energized social conservatives behind McCain. There was greater consensus on the qualifications of the two vice presidential candidates. For example, 74% of Republicans, 66% of conservatives, and 62% of white Evangelicals thought Palin was qualified to be president. She may have helped shore up the Republican base, but she made it far more difficult for McCain to broaden his appeal. Outside of core Republican groups, Palin's standing was weak. Sixty-four percent of Independents believed her to be unqualified, as did college graduates. Even voters who say they favored Hillary Clinton over Obama as the Democratic nominee, a group some Republicans expected to defect to McCain because of his inclusion of a woman on the ticket, were not enthusiastic about Palin's qualifications. Only 12% of Clinton supporters thought Palin had the necessary background to become president. . . .

The Palin pick did prove to be a short-term spark in early September 2008, as McCain took the lead in many of the national polls for the first time all year. But that lead wouldn't last for long, as the Palin bounce was nothing more than a bubble just waiting to be popped. And it was. On September 15, Lehman Brothers, one of the financial world's biggest institutions, failed, leading to a panicky feeling in the country that the worst was yet to come for the economy. It was just after the Lehman announcement that McCain voiced a phrase on the campaign trail, which he will regret for the rest of his life. As the country was watching its economy collapse, McCain claimed that the "fundamentals of our economy are strong." Within an hour of uttering the phrase at a rally in Florida, a claim McCain had made nearly two dozen times before this dark day, Obama was on the trail mocking McCain's statement and implying the Republican, like Bush, was deeply out of touch on the economy.

McCain, to his credit, tried to fix the error, but the seeds were sewn; he had lost the economic issue and with it, any remote chance he may have had at the presidency. From this point on, Obama's numbers would only go up, slowly building a five to ten point lead in the national polls and substantial leads in states like Pennsylvania and Michigan, two blue states McCain was hoping to pick off. In addition, the economic turn for the worse hit four red states particularly hard and created an electoral map that was unnavigable for McCain. Florida, North Carolina, Indiana, and Ohio were all red states that were especially hit hard by the economic downturn.

McCain would try various gambits to attempt to get back in control of his fortunes, from suspending his campaign to work out the deal to get a financial bailout package passed in Congress to introducing the country to a working-class hero named "Joe the Plumber." None worked, and if anything the public saw through the efforts as nothing but political stunts. . . .

There are plenty of ways to slice this election and proclaim that X is what won Obama the election. X could equal Bush or the economy or African-Americans or new voters or money or the suburbs or, well, you get the picture.

But let's start with the simple question on the minds of many political observers; was the 2008 election the start of a political realignment in favor of the Democrats?

The answer is: we don't yet know. Political realignments aren't known until a few years after they happen. Frankly, it wasn't crystal clear that 1980 was a political realignment until as early as 1988 and maybe as late as 1994.

But here's what we do know: there is an opportunity for Democrats to make 2008 a realignment election; they simply have to govern smartly and popularly. If they do that, they could see themselves in power with a 52% to 55% coalition of supporters for a decade or more. . . .

The building blocks for a political realignment are clearly in place. The Democratic Party's advantages in fast-growing states and fast-growing demographics indicate the possibility the party could go on a run that mirrors the Republican success story from 1980 to 2004.

The rest of this book takes a detailed look at each state, how it voted, and where it's headed on the political spectrum. It's a scary book to some Republican strategists because the numbers in 2008 were so dire. It's possible Obama was a unique candidate, running in a unique year that will never be mirrored again. After all, maybe a soft-spoken Midwestern African-American Democratic politician is a more powerful political weapon to defeat Republicans than moderate Southern Democrats, the previous recipe for Democrats. Obama's dominance in the region of Illinois (Iowa, Wisconsin, and Indiana), combined with his ability to mobilize minority and new voters in New South states like Virginia, North Carolina, and Florida, allowed him to put together an unparalleled electoral coalition, which even Bill Clinton couldn't do and Clinton had the help of Ross Perot peeling away Republican voters. . . .

It's unclear where the GOP will head next. More than likely, there will be an ideological debate about whether the party was conservative enough. The argument will be that Bush campaigned as a conservative but didn't govern as one and McCain never governed as a conservative and only masked himself as one during the campaign. But if conservatives win this debate, will that help them win back the northern Virginia suburbs? Will that help the party compete more effectively in Pennsylvania? What about New Hampshire, Colorado, and Arizona?

And then there is the GOP's Hispanic problem. After two straight elections making gains among Hispanics, the party's support levels slipped badly to numbers the party hadn't seen since 1996. The GOP already loses African-Americans by large margins. Can the party afford to see a faster growing minority group voting in larger and larger majorities for the Democrats?

Finally, there's the GOP's education deficit. For yet another cycle, college-educated white voters have moved toward the Democrats. Some in the GOP are warning that all of this anti-intellectual rhetoric is chasing away onetime suburban Republicans.

Republicans can always hope the Democrats overreach with their political power; it's something all political parties eventually do when they achieve the status that the Democrats now have, which is control of both houses of Congress and the presidency. But Obama's campaign team turned governing team doesn't look like a gang that will shoot itself in the foot often. And for the GOP, rebuilding its party can't start with hoping the other guys self-destruct; it starts with getting its act together state by state, county by county, demographic group by demographic group.

PART THIRTEEN

Political Parties

71

WALTER DEAN BURNHAM

From *Critical Elections and the Mainsprings of American Politics*

Political science can offer few clear-cut theories of how politics works. Because of the variable of human nature as well as the impossibility of measuring and predicting political events with exactness, political science is often less a "science" and more an "art." A few attempts at developing major theories to explain and predict politics have been made, however. One is the theory of "critical realignments." Professor Walter Dean Burnham was one of the first to try to explain why certain presidential elections throughout American history mark significant long-term changes in the social and economic direction of the nation. Citing 1800, 1828, 1860, 1896, and 1932, Burnham describes the characteristics of a critical or realigning election, the most dramatic being its supposed "uniform periodicity." They occur at roughly equal intervals apart in time.

———

FOR MANY DECADES it has been generally recognized that American electoral politics is not quite "all of a piece" despite its apparent diverse uniformity. Some elections have more important long-range consequences for the political system as a whole than others, and seem to "decide" substantive issues in a more clear-cut way. There has long been agreement among historians that the elections of those of 1800, 1828, 1860, 1896, and 1932, for example, were fundamental turning points in the course of American electoral politics.

Since the appearance in 1955 of V. O. Key's seminal article, "A Theory of Critical Elections," political scientists have moved to give this concept quantitative depth and meaning. . . .

It now seems time to attempt at least an interim assessment of the structure, function, and implications of critical realignments for the American political process. Such an effort is motivated in particular by the author's view that critical realignments are of fundamental importance not only to the system of political action called "the American political process" but also to the clarifications of some aspects of its operation. It seems particularly important in a period of obvious political upheaval not only to identify these phenomena and place them in time, but to integrate them into a larger (if still very modest) theory of movement in American politics.

Such a theory must inevitably emphasize the elements of stress and abrupt transformation in our political life at the expense of the consensual, gradualist perspectives which have until recently dominated the scholar's vision of American political processes and behavior. For the realignment phenomenon focuses our attention on "the dark side of the moon." It reminds us that politics as usual in the United States is not politics as always; that there are discrete types of voting behavior and quite different levels of voter response to political stimuli, depending on what those stimuli are and at what point in time they occur; and that American political institutions and leadership, once defined (or redefined) in a "normal phase" of our politics, seem to become part of the very conditions that threaten to overthrow them. . . .

In its "ideal-typical" form, the critical realignment differs from stable alignments eras, secular [gradual] realignments, and deviating elections in the following basic ways.

1. The critical realignment is characteristically associated with short-lived but very intense disruptions of traditional patterns of voting behavior. Majority parties become minorities; politics which was once competitive becomes noncompetitive or, alternatively, hitherto one-party areas now become arenas of intense partisan competition; and large blocks of the active electorate—minorities, to be sure, but perhaps involving as much as a fifth to a third of the voters—shift their partisan allegiance.

2. Critical elections are characterized by abnormally high intensity as well.

a. This intensity typically spills over into the party nominating and platform-writing machinery during the upheaval and results in major shifts in convention behavior from the integrative "norm" as well as in transformations in the internal loci of power in the major party most heavily affected by the pressures of realignment. Ordinarily accepted "rules of the game" are flouted; the party's processes, instead of performing their usual integrative functions, themselves contribute to polarization.

b. The rise in intensity is associated with a considerable increase in ideological polarizations, at first within one or more of the major parties and then between them. Issue distances between the parties are markedly increased, and elections tend to involve highly salient issue-clusters, often with strongly emotional and symbolic overtones, far more than is customary in American electoral politics. One curious property of established leadership as it drifts into the stress of realignment seems to be a tendency to become more rigid and dogmatic, which itself contributes greatly to the explosive "bursting stress" of realignment. . . .

c. The rise in intensity is also normally to be found in abnormally heavy voter participation for the time. . . .

3. Historically speaking, at least, national critical realignments have not occurred at random. Instead, there has been a remarkably uniform periodicity in their appearance. . . .

4. It has been argued, with much truth, that American political parties are essentially constituent parties. That is to say, the political-party subsystem is sited in a socioeconomic system of very great heterogeneity and diversity. . . .

Critical realignments emerge directly from the dynamics of this constituent-function supremacy in American politics. . . . In other words, realignments are themselves constituent acts: they arise from emergent tensions in society which, not adequately controlled by the organization or outputs of party politics as usual, escalate to a flash point; they are issue-oriented phenomena, centrally associated with these tensions and more or less leading to resolution adjustments; they result in significant transformations in the general shape of policy; and they have relatively profound aftereffects on the roles played by institutional elites. They are involved with redefinitions of the universe of voters, political parties, and the broad boundaries of the politically possible.

To recapitulate, then, eras of critical realignment are marked by short, sharp reorganizations of the mass coalitional bases of the major parties which occur at periodic intervals on the national level; are often preceded by major third-party revolts which reveal the incapacity of "politics as usual" to integrate, much less aggregate, emergent political demand; are closely associated with abnormal stress in the socioeconomic system; are marked by ideological polarizations and issue-distances between the major parties which are exceptionally large by normal standards; and have durable consequences as constituent acts which determine the outer boundaries of policy in general, though not necessarily of policies in detail. . . . There is much evidence . . . that realignments do recur with rather remarkable regularity approximately once a generation, or every thirty to thirty-eight years.

The precise timing of the conditions which conduce to realignment is conditioned heavily by circumstance, of course: the intrusion of major crises in society and economy with which "politics as usual" in the United States cannot adequately cope, and the precise quality and bias of leadership decisions in a period of high political tension, cannot be predicted in specific time with any accuracy. Yet a broadly repetitive pattern of oscillation between the normal inertia of mass electoral politics and the ruptures of the normal which realignments bring about is clearly evident from the data. So evident is this pattern that one is led to suspect that the truly "normal" structure of American electoral politics at the mass base is precisely this dynamic, even dialectic polarization between long-term inertia and concentrated bursts of change in this open system of action. It may well be that American political institutions, including the major political parties, are so organized that they have a chronic, cumulative tendency toward underproduction of other than currently "normal" policy outputs. They may tend persistently to ignore, and hence not to aggregate, emergent political demand of a mass character until a boiling point of some kind is reached.

In this context, the rise of third-party protests as what might be called protorealignment phenomena would be associated with the repeated emergence of a rising gap between perceived expectations of the political process and its perceived realities over time, diffused among a constantly increasing portion of the active electorate and perhaps mobilizing many hitherto inactive voters. . . .

The periodic rhythm of American electoral politics, the cycle of oscillation between the normal and the disruptive, corresponds precisely to the existence of largely unfettered developmental change in the socioeconomic system and its absence in the country's political institutions. Indeed, it is a prime quantitative measure of the interaction between the two. The socioeconomic system develops but the institutions of electoral politics and policy formation remain essentially unchanged. Moreover, they do not have much capacity to adjust incrementally to demand arising from socioeconomic dislocations. Dysfunctions centrally related to this process become more and more visible, until finally entire classes, regions, or other major sectors of the population are directly injured or come to see themselves as threatened by imminent danger. Then the triggering event occurs, critical realignments follow, and the universe of policy and of electoral coalitions is broadly redefined. It is at such moments that the constitution-making role of the American voter becomes most visible, and his behavior, one suspects, least resembles the normal pattern. . . .

In this context, then, critical realignment emerges as decisively important in the study of the dynamics of American politics. It is as symptomatic of political nonevolution in this country as are the archaic and increasingly rudimentary structures of the political parties themselves. But even more importantly, critical realignment may well be defined as the chief tension-management device available to so peculiar a political system. Historically it has been the chief means through which an underdeveloped political system can be recurrently brought once again into some balanced relationship with the changing socioeconomic system, permitting a restabilization of our politics. . . . Granted the relative inability of our political institutions to make gradual adjustments along vectors of *emergent* political demand, critical realignments have been as inevitable as they have been necessary to the normal workings of American politics. Thus once again there is a paradox: the conditions which decree that coalitional negotiation, bargaining, and incremental, unplanned, and gradual policy change become the dominant characteristic of American politics in its normal state also decree that it give way to abrupt, disruptive change with considerable potential for violence. . . .

Such a dynamically oriented frame of reference presupposes a holistic view of American politics which is radically different from that which until very recently has tended to dominate the professional literature. The models of American political life and political processes with which we are most familiar emphasize the well-known attributes of pluralist democracy. There are not stable policy majorities. Intense and focused minorities with well-defined interests exert influence on legislation and administrative rule making out of all proportion to their size. The process involves gradual, incremental change secured after bargaining has been completed among a wide array of interested groups who are prepared to accept the conditions of bargaining. It is true that such descriptions apply to a "politics as usual" which is an important fragment of political reality in the United States, but to describe this fragment as the whole of that reality is to assume an essentially ideological posture whose credibility can be maintained only by ignoring the complementary dynamics of American politics as a whole. . . .

The reality of this process taken as a whole seems quite different from the pluralist vision. It is one shot through with escalating tensions, periodic electoral upheavals, and repeated redefinitions of the rules and outcomes-in-general of the political game, as well as redefinitions—by no means always broadening ones—of those who are in fact permitted to play it. One very basic characteristic of American party politics which emerges from a contemplation of critical realignments is a profound incapacity of established political leadership to adapt itself sequentially—or even incrementally?—to emergent political demand generated by the losers in our stormy socioeconomic transformations. American political parties are not action instrumentalities of definable and broad social collectivities; as organizations they are, consequently, interested in control of offices but not of government in the broader sense of which we have been speaking. It follows from this that once successful routines are established or reestablished for winning office, there is no motivation among party leaders to disturb the routines of the game. These routines are disturbed not by adaptive change within the party-policy system, but by the application of overwhelming external force.

72

MORLEY WINOGRAD
MICHAEL HAIS

From *Millennial Makeover*

You, kind readers, are the Millennial Generation. In terms of politics, Morley Winograd and Michael Hais believe the Millennials have major differences with those voters who came before them. Many of the differences center around new technologies, but they also reflect new values and ideas about government. In the excerpt, the authors note the large size of the Millennial Generation and their diversity. Where they are not diverse, however, is in their hope of finding solutions to America's social and economic problems, often with government as the major agent of change. Winograd and Hais describe the use of MySpace, YouTube, and Facebook in creating a new means of political communication. Writing right before the 2008 election, the authors identify the Democrats as well-positioned to benefit from the new campaign technologies; they identify then-candidate Obama as particularly adept at using social networking sites. The selection concludes with a revealing analysis of Hillary Clinton's and Barack Obama's presentations in Selma, Alabama, in 2007, to mark an anniversary of a tragic event in American civil rights history. Knowing what we know now about the 2008 election and especially about young voters, Obama was establishing himself as a voice of the Millennials.

SINCE THE ESTABLISHMENT of the current two-party system in the United States, American electoral politics have been characterized by a persistent pattern of relatively long periods of great stability in electoral outcomes, lasting about forty years, interspersed with shorter periods of sharp and decisive change. Usually, but not invariably, this realignment makes what had been the minority political party the new majority party. America is now primed for its next political realignment or makeover.

Each of the five major political realignments in U.S. history has been triggered by a crucial event, such as the Civil War or the Great Depression that then became the subject of extensive examination. But the real driving forces behind this constant and predictable shift in the fortunes of America's political parties and in its political institutions and public policy are underlying changes in generational size and attitudes and contemporaneous advances in communication technologies. Technology serves to enable these changes by creating powerful ways to reach new voters with messages that relate directly to their concerns. But without new generations, with their new attitudes and beliefs and a passion for communicating in new ways, advancements in technology would have little impact on political outcomes.

Today, our political institutions face another test from these same twin forces of change. A new generation, Millennials, born between 1982 and 2003, is coming of age in unprecedented numbers. The Millennials bring with them a facility and comfort with cutting-edge communication and computing technologies that is creating the same kind of bewilderment and bemusement that parents of television-addicted Baby Boomers felt in the 1950s and 1960s. Every generation defines itself first by making it clear how and why it is unlike the generation that preceded it. Then, as it moves into positions of power and influence in society, the new generation demands that the nation's institutions change to accommodate its beliefs and its values. The Millennials are about to make those demands on America.

The Millennial Generation is larger than any that has come before it. It is the most ethnically diverse generation in American history. Because of the way in which they have been reared, Millennials are more positive than older generations, both about the present and future state of their own lives and about the future of their country. Recent survey research on the political attitudes of this generation shows a high tolerance for lifestyle and ethnic differences and support for an activist approach by government to societal and economic issues. Unlike the generally conservative Gen-Xers, who immediately preceded them, or the harshly divided Baby Boom Generation, Millennials are united across gender and race in their desire to find "win-win" solutions to America's problems.

Millennials are also particularly adept in the use of the new peer-to-peer communication technologies that will increasingly be used to inform and shape American public opinion. Their embrace of this technology began with the original Napster web site that allowed them to share music with all their friends, without regard to copyright laws—and without any cost. Then they made social networking sites like MySpace, an enormously popular way to share personal opinions even in the most intimate detail, online and with their friends. Now they have added video to that extended conversation, making YouTube, a company in existence since only 2005, one of the five most visited sites on the Net. As Millennials become the target demographic for all types of media, this approach to creating as well as absorbing content and information without filtering by experts will soon become the way America prefers to get all of its information.

The presidential campaign of 2008 is the first real test of the willingness of candidates to embrace social networking technologies, and the generation that uses them, as Millennials become a significant portion of the electorate. The initial launches of exploratory committees and official presidential candidate web sites demonstrated a wide range of comfort with "Netroots" campaigning. Most of the major Republican candidates' early web sites failed to go beyond the brochure stage—with appeals for money and volunteers the only interactive aspect, leaving them Internet years behind their Democratic competitors. Within the Democratic field, some, such as Hillary Rodham Clinton, went further than that but still hesitated to venture into the land of peer-to-peer technology, preferring to control interactions through online chats or "American Idol"–like voting for her campaign's theme song. Other Democrats, such as John Edwards and Barack Obama, have actively embraced social networking. Edwards racked up 10,000 "friends" on MySpace within a month of his announcement, and Obama used his web site, built on Facebook's platform, to help secure more money for his campaign from more individual donors than any Democrat in history.

In 2007, survey research data, as well as the approach and tone of the announced 2008 presidential candidates, provided some clues as to who might be best positioned among the candidates to capture the hearts and minds of a new generation. Senator Obama, the youngest major party candidate, a late Baby Boomer born on the cusp of Generation X, distanced himself from the rest of the candidates in a crucial way that demonstrated his awareness of generational differences and his sensitivity to the concerns and political style of the Millennial Generation. In a You-Tube video prior to his announcement, Obama said the country needed "to change our politics first" and "come together around common interests and concerns as Americans," clearly signaling his awareness of the debilitating effect that the Baby Boom Generation's continuation of the culture wars of the 1960s was having on American politics. He and Senator Clinton were the only two candidates from either party who registered significant support from 18- to 29-year-olds in a *New York Times/* CBS poll in June 2007. But as much fun as it is to speculate which candidate will take advantage of the technological and generational trends impacting the country's mood in order to win the ultimate prize in American politics in 2008, the complexity of current events, candidate missteps, and campaign tactics makes any such speculation a fool's errand.

What does seem clear is that the Democrats' approach to political and societal issues appears more compatible with Millennial attitudes. This is clearly reflected in that generation's perceptions of the two parties and voting results from the 2004 and 2006 elections. The Democratic Party also seems to have taken the early lead in its willingness and ability to use the new communication technology to create a sophisticated, "Netroots" approach to political campaigning. But all of this is just the tip of the iceberg, both in terms of the use of peer-to-peer technology in political campaigns and in the impact that the Millennial Generation will have on American politics.

One way to think about Millennials, in comparison to the two generations that preceded them, is to picture a generational cohort made up solely of Harry Potter and his friends and then to compare those bright-eyed, overachieving wizards with the adults at Hogwarts, who try to mold their upbringing for good or ill. J. K. Rowling, the author of the series that revolutionized the book industry and sparked a desire to read among an entire generation, shows Harry and his team working hard to do their best within the rules set for them to follow and, of course, using their own special ingenuity to save the world whenever necessary. In this reading, Baby Boomers are the teachers and directors at Hogwarts—every one of them individualistic, judgmental egotists who talk more than they act. A few characters such as Hagrid, not in power but always around to try to help, despite less-than-perfect pasts, represent Generation X, the unlucky group sandwiched between two dynamic and dominating generations. As much as *The Wizard of Oz* was an allegory for the politics of the Populist era of the 1890s, the *Harry Potter* series, in spite of its British origin and setting, provides just the right metaphor for understanding contemporary American politics. And while Rowling understands and captures this dynamic perfectly, many other media moguls, authors, and even politicians make the fundamental error of thinking that today's young people think and act just like they did when they were young. Nothing could be further from the truth. . . .

By 2012 the first half of the entire Millennial Generation, approximately 42 million young Americans, will be eligible to vote. The history of political realignments suggests that the realignment shaped in 2008 by this generation's oldest members will be confirmed and solidified when whoever is elected that year runs for reelection. Just as FDR's landslide victory in 1936 made the Democrats the dominant power in American politics for another thirty years, so too will the party that captures the White House in 2008 have a historic opportunity to become the majority party for at least four more decades.

But the stakes for the country in the outcome of the 2008 election are even higher than for either political party. Regardless of which party successfully recombines the four M's of political campaigns—money, media, message, and messenger—to become the dominant party in the coming realignment, the end result will be major changes in the style, tone, and structure of America's government, politics, and society. If past history is any guide, over the next twenty or thirty years, America will positively and forcefully resolve many of the issues and problems that have concerned it for the past four decades. Which path the country takes in resolving these issues will be determined by the choices Millennials and their technologies help America make in 2008. . . .

On Sunday, March 4, 2007, leaders of the African American community gathered in two churches in Selma, Alabama, to commemorate the forty-second anniversary of the attempted march to Montgomery across the Edmund Pettis Bridge by a group of civil rights activists led by the Reverend Martin Luther King Jr. That nonviolent march was met with police dogs, batons, and fire hoses, and its violent ending so horrified the nation that the Voting Rights Act of 1965 was passed within five months of what came to be known as "Bloody Sunday." Since those historic events of March 1965, two generations of Americans had been born into a country profoundly reshaped by the courage and cause that the congregations had come to celebrate and honor.

Gathering in the same churches that were used on that infamous Sunday, Brown Chapel AME and First Baptist Church of Selma, were living heroes of the nation's civil rights movement, including Congressman John Lewis, who was at the front of the Selma marchers on the bridge in 1965, and those who benefited from their leadership, such as Congressman Artur Davis from Alabama's Seventh Congressional District that encompasses Selma. The congregations each had the privilege of hearing from one of the two leading contenders for the 2008 Democratic presidential nomination—Senators Hillary Clinton and Barack Obama.

Senator Clinton is a member of the Baby Boom Generation, most of whose members were in their teens and twenties at the time of the Selma march. This dynamic and idealistic generation forced the country to confront many of its fundamental beliefs about equality, freedom, and opportunity throughout the 1960s and 1970s. Senator Clinton used her remarks to trace the lineage of Selma's "spirit and logic" to the opportunity for her, as a woman, to seek the presidency of the United States—as well as for New Mexico governor Bill Richardson, a Hispanic, and Senator Barack Obama, an African American, to do the same. She even pointed to a childhood memory of her pastor giving her "a chance to see this phenomenon," the Reverend Martin Luther King Jr., in Chicago, in January 1963. King's speech, she recalled, was on the importance of "Remaining Awake through a Great Revolution," and she took his message on the importance of involvement to heart.

What she didn't talk about was her own political ideology at that time. After seeing Dr. King, she was still motivated to campaign for Republican Barry Goldwater's presidential candidacy in 1964. She did so in spite of the fact that Goldwater based his campaign on his opposition to the Civil Rights Act, enacted that year, which guaranteed blacks legal access to public facilities throughout the country.

But Senator Clinton was not being duplicitous or insincere in the remarks she delivered in Selma. Her clarion call to continue the march "for freedom, justice, opportunity and everything America can be" was very much in line with her generation's commitment to using ideals as the driving force to provide meaning in their lives. The impulse was the same whether it was being exercised by a young woman caught up in the Republican politics of her parents, or the questioning college student who as she matured became just as ardent on behalf of liberal causes, such as civil rights, women's rights, and the anti–Vietnam War movement. For an idealistic Baby Boomer of that era, it was not really a stretch to move from being a conservative Republican to a liberal Democrat in less than five years.

Senator Obama took a different approach to tracing his lineage to the events at the Edmund Pettis Bridge in 1965. He told his audience, in cadences that fit comfortably in that Sunday's church setting, that President John F Kennedy, as part of the ideological war with Communism, had instituted an exchange program for young Africans to visit the United States so they could see that America was not the nation of hate and discrimination that Bloody Sunday seemed to portray. One of the people selected by the State Department was the son of a houseboy in British colonial Kenya. While in this country he met a woman from Kansas, and their son grew up to become a U.S. senator.

Barack Obama told his Selma audience that his mother's family could trace its American lineage back to "a great, great, great, great grand-father who had owned slaves." This heritage allowed him to make it clear to the audience that he owed his very political existence to that historic day forty-two years ago in Selma. "Don't tell me I'm not coming home when I come to Selma," he shouted to a crowd enraptured with this personal testament to what its sacrifices had made possible.

But the main theme of Obama's remarks on that Sunday was even more poignant and biblical. He compared the efforts of those who led the civil rights movement to leaders of the "Moses generation" who had led the Hebrew people out of slavery in Egypt. "We are in the presence today of a lot of Moseses, giants whose shoulders we stand on, who battled for America's soul." But, he pointed out, the Bible makes it clear that God did not let Moses cross the River Jordan to see the Promised Land before he died. Instead, all of Moses' generation, and its children as well, had to wander in the desert until a new generation, which Obama called the "Joshua generation," was born. Once that generation was ready to lead the Israelites into battle, they were given permission to enter the land of milk and honey and to engage in the great civic endeavor that created the kingdom of Israel. Obama pointed out that those who followed the heroes of the civil rights movement were very much like that "Joshua generation." The newer generation owed a debt to their own "Moses generation" and to its ideals of "liberty, equality, opportunity and hope" that could never be fully repaid. Nevertheless, it was only the members of a "Joshua generation," who had the new skills and focus needed to close the "gaps" in "educational achievement, health care, empathy, and hope" that still permeated American life.

Obama's remarks were not only politically effective, but insightful in ways that many in his Selma audience and TV viewers across the country may not have appreciated. After first paying homage to the Baby Boomers of the "Moses generation," whose idealism was the spur for the civil rights movement, Obama pointed to the work of another, older generation, the GI Generation, whose values of sacrifice and discipline he constantly praised. His identification of gaps that the "Joshua generation" needed to close between the promise of the civil rights vision and the reality of today's America echoed John F. Kennedy's campaign assertion of a "missile gap" with Russia. Senator Obama's call to "ask not just what our government can do for us, but what we can do for ourselves" had an even more direct connection to the inaugural address of the first GI Generation president of the United States.

Whether Senator Obama was aware of it or not, his remarks in Selma referred to an explanation of American political history based on the concept of generational cycles. According to this explanation, every eighty years or so a civic-oriented generation, like the one he called the "Joshua generation," reappears in America. This civic generation sets about the task of rebuilding or repairing a society that seems to have lost its way, after a period of upheaval caused by the idealistic fervor of a "Moses generation" (such as the Baby Boomers in America's current generational cycle). Although Obama didn't mention it by name, there was another generation in addition to those of Moses and Joshua. This cohort, like all the Israelites, was made to wander in the desert for forty years because the Lord was punishing them for their sins. It, too, has a parallel in America's current generational cycle, Generation X—a generation whose members often felt as if they had to endure a nomadic existence without guidance or support from their parents or from society as a whole.

But, as Senator Obama realized, the generational cycle of American politics is about to turn again. The newest version of a "Joshua generation" is starting to emerge and make its mark. The two people who literally wrote the book on America's generations, William Strauss and Neil Howe, call this most recent incarnation of a rebuilding civic generation the Millennial Generation. The Millennials, whose members were born in the period from 1982 to 2003, possess all the characteristics of the previous "Joshua generations" in American history. By identifying with the rising Millennial Generation, Senator Obama was not only deferentially and personally assuming the mantle of the civil rights movement, he was also speaking to a new generation ready to leave its own distinctive mark on American politics. . . .

73

JOHN JUDIS

America the Liberal: The Democratic Majority: It Emerged!

*President Obama and the Democrats in Congress should move ahead rap-
idly and forcefully with their plans for the nation, writes John Judis, because
they are the vanguard of a Democratic realignment that will shape American
politics for decades ahead. Judis reviews the theory of realigning elections,
pointing out major demographic changes that have contributed to this new
era in politics. Professional workers, ethnic and racial minorities, and women
are the heart of the new Democratic majority, bolstered by other voters who
voted Democratic based on economic factors. Judis explores the changing attitudes on social and economic issues; his data supports his view of increasingly progressive, liberal views among the American people. Realignments
can be "hard" or "soft," the author notes. He urges President Obama and the
Democrats to lock in the former kind, a Democratic realignment that will
last for decades into the future. Strong, daring policy changes will ensure it.*

———

THESE GUYS—AND THE OTHERS who are counseling Barack
Obama and the Democrats to "go slow"—couldn't be more wrong. They
are looking at Obama's election through the prism of Jimmy Carter's win
in 1976 and Bill Clinton's victory in 1992. Both Carter and Clinton did
misjudge the mood of the electorate. They tried unsuccessfully to govern
a country from the center-left that was moving to the right (in Carter's
case) or that was only just beginning to move leftward (in Clinton's case)
and they were rebuked by voters as a result.

Obama is taking office under dramatically different circumstances. His
election is the culmination of a Democratic realignment that began in the
1990s, was delayed by September 11, and resumed with the 2006 election.
This realignment is predicated on a change in political demography and
geography. Groups that had been disproportionately Republican have become disproportionately Democratic, and red states like Virginia have
turned blue. Underlying these changes has been a shift in the nation's
"fundamentals"—in the structure of society and industry, and in the way
Americans think of their families, jobs, and government. The country is
no longer "America the conservative." And, if Obama acts shrewdly to
consolidate this new majority, we may soon be "America the liberal."

Realignments—which political scientist Walter Dean Burnham called "America's surrogate for revolution"—are not scientifically predictable events like lunar eclipses. But they have occurred with some regularity over the last 200 years—in 1828, 1860, 1896, 1932, and 1980. The two most recent realignments were essentially belated political acknowledgments of tectonic changes that had been occurring in the country's economic base. In the case of the New Deal, it was the rise of an urban industrial order in the North; in the case of Reagan conservatism, it was the shift of industry and population from the North to the lower-wage, non-unionized, suburban Sunbelt stretching from Virginia down to Florida and across to Texas and southern California.

The new Democratic realignment reflects the shift that began decades ago toward a post-industrial economy centered in large urban-suburban metropolitan areas devoted primarily to the production of ideas and services rather than material goods. . . . Clustered in the regions that have undergone this economic transition are the three main groups that constitute the backbone of the new Democratic majority: professionals (college-educated workers who produce ideas and services); minorities (African Americans, Latinos, and Asian Americans); and women (particularly working, single, and college-educated women). . . .

The rise of these voting groups within the post-industrial economy has brought in its wake a new political worldview. Call it "progressive" or "liberal" or even "Naderite" (for Ralph Nader the consumer advocate, not the misbegotten presidential candidate). If unionized industrial workers were the vanguard of the New Deal majority, professionals are the vanguard of the new progressive majority. Their sensibility is reflected in the Democratic platform and increasingly in the country as a whole. It has sometimes been described as socially liberal and fiscally conservative, but that doesn't really get it right. Professionals are generally liberal on civil rights and women's rights; committed to science and to the separation of church and state; internationalist on trade and immigration; skeptical of, but not necessarily opposed to, large government programs; and gung-ho about government regulation of business, especially K Street lobbyists. . . .

There have been two kinds of realignments in American history—hard and soft. The realignments of 1896 and 1932 were hard: They laid the basis for 30 years of party dominance, periods when the same party would win the bulk of national, state, and local elections. (During the New Deal realignment, from 1932 to 1968, Republicans controlled the presidency for only eight of 36 years and Congress for only four years.) The conservative Republican realignment of 1980, by contrast, was soft: It began in 1968, was interrupted by Watergate, resumed during Carter's presidency, and climaxed in Reagan's landslide. Yet, even then, Democrats retained control of the House and got back the Senate in 1986. Republicans did win Congress in 1994, but a Democrat was president and was reelected easily in 1996. Burnham characterized the '90s as a period of "unstable equilibrium" between the parties.

Will the Democratic realignment of 2008 be hard or soft? Initially, it seemed it would be soft. Initially, it seemed it would be soft. Like the Reagan realignment, it began in fits and starts—Clinton's victory in 1992 was comparable to Richard Nixon's victory in 1968, with Ross Perot playing the schismatic role that George Wallace had played in 1968. The Democratic trend was slowed by the Clinton scandals and interrupted by September 11. By this measure, 2008 seemed to be more analogous to 1980 than to 1932 or 1896.

But the onset of the financial crisis may have changed this. . . .

If Obama and congressional Democrats act boldly, they can not only arrest the downturn but also lay the basis for an enduring majority. As was the case with Franklin Roosevelt's New Deal, many of the measures necessary to combat today's recession will also help ensure long-term Democratic electoral success. Many Southerners remained Democrats for generations in part because of Roosevelt's rural electrification program; a similar program for bringing broadband to the hinterland could lure these voters back to the Democratic Party. And national health insurance could play the same role in Democrats' future prospects that Social Security played in the perpetuation of the New Deal majority.

Americans, to be sure, are always reluctant to undertake ambitious government initiatives. This is a country, historian Louis Hartz once pointed out, founded on Lockean liberalism. But, as Roosevelt discovered when he was elected, a national crisis creates popular willingness to entertain dramatic initiatives. Moreover, Obama will not face the same formidable adversaries that Jimmy Carter and Bill Clinton had to confront. The Republican Party will be divided and demoralized after this defeat. And, just as the Great Depression took Prohibition and the other great social issues of the 1920s off the popular agenda, this downturn has pushed aside the culture war of the last decades. It simply wasn't a factor in the presidential election.

If, however, Obama and the Democrats take the advice of official Washington and go slow—adopting incremental reforms, appeasing adversaries that have lost their clout—they could end up prolonging the downturn and discrediting themselves. What might have been a hard realignment could become not merely a soft realignment, but perhaps even an abortive one. That's not the kind of change America needs—or wants.

74

STUART ROTHENBERG

Is 2008 a Realigning Election?
Numbers Offer Some Clues

On the surface, Stuart Rothenberg acknowledges that the 2008 election (and the 2006 congressional election) seem to portend a bright future for the Democratic party—a realignment that could last for decades, maybe. But wait, writes the author, the 2008 victory was caused by several factors beyond a new Democratic allegiance: President Obama as a candidate, the economic crisis, a shift by certain demographic groups that may not be permanent. Rothenberg mentions several alternative reasons that voters may have decided as they did in 2008. Yet he admits that "Obama will have a chance to change the nation's political landscape." The elections of 2010 and 2012, and the many new policy initiatives undertaken by President Obama's administration, will test the validity of Rothenberg's thesis.

THE BIG QUESTION that everyone is asking is whether [the November 2008] general election marked the beginning of a political realignment that will create a new dominant party. Have Americans shifted their loyalties and fundamental assumptions about the parties and about the government, or did we just witness a short-term reaction to years of bad news?

Let's be clear: The election results in 2006 and 2008 constitute the kind of one-two punch that is rare in modern American political history. It would be silly to portray this year's election as a minor hiccup. The nation elected a liberal African-American Democrat from the North as president, and it gave him a majority of all votes cast.

Moreover, in the past two elections, Democrats gained at least a dozen Senate seats and at least 50 House seats, taking total control of Congress. At the state level, they now have 4,090 state legislators to the GOP's 3,221.

Polls show that the Republican advantages on foreign policy and pocketbook issues have either shrunk or disappeared. While there remains a stark contrast on cultural matters between the parties, Democrats have sought to mute that difference on both guns and values, and those issues clearly were not what the 2008 elections were about.

If demographics are indeed destiny, then the 2008 national exit poll at the very least raises questions about where the GOP goes from here.

For the first time ever, whites constituted less than 75 percent of the electorate, a considerable problem for the Republican Party given its historical problems attracting minorities. Sen. John Kerry (D–Mass.) drew just 55 percent of the Hispanic vote in 2004, but Sen. Barack Obama (D–Ill.) drew 67 percent of it four years later—a remarkable showing considering that many of those voters preferred Sen. Hillary Rodham Clinton (N.Y.) in the Democratic contest and supposedly were resistant to voting for a black candidate.

While the highly anticipated surge in younger voters never materialized, those voters younger than 30 who did participate went overwhelmingly for Obama, 66 percent to 32 percent. That 34-point margin was almost four times the 9-point margin that Kerry had with voters younger than 30.

As many analysts have pointed out, if these younger voters carry that Democratic preference with them through their lives, they could constitute a strongly Democratic cohort for the next 40 or 50 years.

Just as bad for Republicans is the fact that over the past dozen years, there has been a noticeable shift in voters' attitudes toward government, according to an exit poll question that has also been asked for years in the NBC News/*Wall Street Journal* survey.

In December 1995, only a third of respondents said that "government should do more to solve our country's problems," while 62 percent said that government "is trying to do too many things that should be left to individuals and businesses." But in this year's exit poll, a slim majority, 51 percent, said government should do more, while only 43 percent said it was doing too many things better left to businesses and individuals.

That's a potentially significant change in attitudes that suggests voters may be more willing to accept a more activist government that regulates business and seeks to affect outcomes, rather than merely ensures a neutral playing field.

Democrats and liberals would prefer the story to end here, but it doesn't. Other data paint a different picture.

First, in an election with a highly unpopular Republican president and a severely damaged Republican brand, the Democratic share of the presidential vote increased from 48 percent of the vote in 2000 and 2004 to 53 percent of the vote in 2008, hardly a landslide figure or evidence of a new dominant political coalition.

Obama's victory was built largely on a number of factors: higher black turnout, a bigger Hispanic vote, big numbers among younger voters and first-time voters, and more support from independents. It's far from clear that any of those numbers will be replicated in 2010 or 2012, because these groups could well have been motivated by Obama's personal appeal, not ideological or partisan dogma.

Second, one of Sen. John McCain's (R–Ariz.) biggest problems among core groups was a 5-point drop among white men. President Bush carried 62 percent of white men in 2004, while McCain won only 57 percent of them.

The drop easily could have been caused by growing concerns about the economy, as well as the lesser salience of national security concerns between 2004 and 2008, rather than a fundamental shift in partisan loyalties.

Third, the lack of any statistically significant shift in self-described ideology of voters also argues against a fundamental realignment. In 2004, 21 percent of voters called themselves liberals, while 34 percent said they were conservatives. This year, 22 percent said they were liberals and the same 34 percent identified as conservative.

Finally, the 2008 exit poll found far more Democrats turned out than Republicans. In the exit poll four years ago, self-identified Democrats and Republicans each constituted 37 percent of the sample, but this year 39 percent of voters were Democrats compared with 32 percent of Republicans. Fewer Republican voters meant fewer votes for Republican candidates.

While this change could reflect a fundamental shift in self-identified partisanship, it could merely be a dip in GOP turnout caused by any number of factors (possibly dissatisfaction with McCain's candidacy, the selection of Alaska Gov. Sarah Palin as his running mate or the issue agenda of 2008) or a one-time shift in partisanship. Party ID, after all, reflects the popularity of the party at any moment, and the damage to the Republican brand certainly could have caused a short-term dip in GOP identification.

At this point, it is far too premature to claim that 2008 was anything more than a dramatic reaction to an unpopular president and to a party hurt by its own ineptness. Obama will have a chance to change the nation's political landscape. But his election, by itself, isn't necessarily a sign of a new partisan alignment.

75

RONALD BROWNSTEIN

From *The Second Civil War*

Writing before President Barack Obama's 2008 election, journalist Ronald Brownstein described a political party system that is locked in nearly mortal combat, with no middle path possible. In his campaign, Obama suggested a post-partisan approach in which he would go beyond the two parties' clashing positions to find common ground. But Brownstein's view may prove to be the more valid one. He describes the loyalty that politicians owe to their "base," adding to the influence of the most extreme partisans in both parties. While clear-cut differences between the parties have been a mark of American politics at certain times in our history, the willingness to forge compromise solutions has been just as important. Those compromises are missing from Washington, D.C., today, Brownstein believes. Quoting several high-profile Democratic and Republican political figures, Brownstein makes the case that American government was not always so polarized. "Hyperpartisanship," as Brownstein terms it, does have positive byproducts, such as much more citizen participation. But at what price? Despite the fact that issues are no more divisive now than in the past, the cost of so much partisanship is paid by the American people. Perhaps the nation will find a post-partisan solution. Or perhaps there'll be a "second civil war."

———

AMERICA IS THE RICHEST and most powerful country in the world. It may be the richest and most powerful country in the history of the world.

But it cannot agree on a plan to reduce its dependence on foreign oil.

Nor can it balance its federal budget.

It can't provide health insurance for the nearly one in six Americans without it, either.

It can't agree on a plan to improve security at its borders and provide a humane way to deal with the estimated twelve million illegal immigrants working in its fields and factories and restaurants.

It can't align the promises it has made to seniors through Social Security and Medicare with the tax burdens that future generations realistically can bear.

It can't agree on the steps to rebuild economic security for middle-class Americans in the age of global economic competition. It can't formulate a strategy for reducing the emissions of the gases that contribute to global warming and potentially disruptive changes in the climate.

It cannot agree on an approach to fight the threat of Islamic terrorism, at home and abroad, in a way that unites the country with shared purpose.

None of these problems are new. All have been discussed for years in the media. All are the subject of constant debate in Washington. In most cases the options for dealing with them are limited and familiar.

Why, then, has America failed to make more progress against these challenges?

The answer, above all, is that the day-to-day functioning of American politics now inhibits the constructive compromises between the parties required to confront these problems. The political system has evolved to a point where the vast majority of elected officials in each party feel comfortable only advancing ideas acceptable to their core supporters—their "base," in the jargon of modern campaigns. But progress against these problems, and almost all other challenges facing America, requires comprehensive solutions that marry ideas favored by one party and opposed by the other. It's implausible, for instance, to imagine that we can address the long-term challenge of Social Security and Medicare without both reducing benefits and increasing taxes. Or that we can regain control of our borders without significantly toughening enforcement and creating a legal framework for the millions of illegal immigrants already in the United States. Or that we can reduce our dependence on foreign oil without reducing consumption and increasing domestic production. Yet in each of those cases, and all the others listed above, most elected officials in one of the two major parties will not accept half of that solution. The result is to prevent us from using all of the tools available to attack our problems. One side proposes to control the deficit solely through spending cuts; the other side almost entirely through tax increases. One party proposes to produce more energy, the other to conserve more energy. In fact, to make meaningful progress against any of these problems, the answer is almost always that we will need to do both. Yet because each party seeks to impose its will on the other—and recoils from actions that might challenge its core supporters—it cannot propose comprehensive solutions. We are left with either-or alternatives—increase production or reduce consumption, cut benefits or raise taxes—when the challenges demand that we apply solutions built on the principle of both-and.

This book examines how we have reached this dangerous impasse. It rests on an unambiguous conclusion: The central obstacle to more effective action against our most pressing problems is an unrelenting polarization of American politics that has divided Washington and the country into hostile, even irreconcilable camps. Competition and even contention between rival parties has been part of American political life since its founding. That partisan rivalry most often has been a source of energy, innovation, and inspiration. But today the parties are losing the capacity to recognize their shared interest in placing boundaries on their competition—and in transcending it when the national interest demands. On some occasions—notably efforts to balance the federal budget and reform the welfare system under Bill Clinton, and an initiative to rethink federal education policy in George W. Bush's first year—they have collaborated on reasonable compromises. But for most of the past two decades the two sides have collided with such persistent and unwavering disagreement on everything from taxes to Social Security to social and foreign policy that it sometimes seems they are organizing not only against each other, but against the idea of compromise itself.

Against this backdrop of perpetual conflict, America is living through a transformation of its political life. For most of our history American political parties have functioned as loose coalitions that lightly tether diverse ideological views. Because the parties were so diverse, they have usually operated as a force that synthesized the diverse interests in American society. As the great political historian Richard Hofstadter once wrote, "In our politics, each major party has become a compound, a hodge-podge, of various and conflicting interests; and the imperatives of party struggle, the quest for victory and for offices, have forced the parties to undertake the business of conciliation and compromise among such interests."

That definition is obsolete. From Congress and the White House through the grassroots, the parties today are becoming less diverse, more ideologically homogeneous, and less inclined to pursue reasonable agreements. American government . . . usually has worked best when it is open to a broad array of views and perspectives, and seeks to harmonize a diverse range of interests. Today the dynamics of the political competition are narrowing the perspectives of each party in a manner that pushes them toward operating as the champion of one group of Americans against another—with dangerous results for all Americans. Reconfigured by the large forces we will explore, . . . our politics today encourages confrontation over compromise. The political system now rewards ideology over pragmatism. It is designed to sharpen disagreements rather than construct consensus. It is built on exposing and inflaming the differences that separate Americans rather than the shared priorities and values that unite them. It produces too much animosity and too few solutions.

Political leaders on both sides now feel a relentless pressure for party discipline and intellectual conformity more common in parliamentary systems than through most of American history. Any politician who attempts to build alliances across party lines is more likely to provoke suspicion and criticism than praise. "People want you to choose sides so badly in modern politics, there is no ability to cross [party lines]," said Senator Lindsey Graham, a conservative but iconoclastic Republican from South Carolina. "You are one team versus the other and never shall the twain meet. If it's a Democratic idea, I have to be against it because it came from a Democrat. And vice versa."

Richard A. Gephardt of Missouri, the former Democratic leader in the House of Representatives, used almost the exact same terms to describe the changes he experienced during the twenty-eight years he served in the House before retiring after 2004. "There is no dialogue [between the parties]," he said. "You are either in the blue team or the red team, and you never wander off. It's like the British Parliament. And I never thought about it that much when I came, but it was very different then. It wasn't a parliamentary system, and people wandered off their side and voted in committee or on the floor with the other side. There was this understanding that we were there to solve problems."

The wars between the two parties that take place every day in Washington may seem to most Americans a form of distant posturing, like border clashes between two countries they could not find on the map. But this polarization of political life imposes a tangible cost on every American family—a failure to confront all of the problems listed above with sensible solutions that could improve life for average Americans. Less tangibly but as importantly, extreme partisanship has produced a toxic environment that empowers the most adversarial and shrill voices in each party and disenfranchises the millions of Americans more attracted to pragmatic compromise than to ideological crusades. The reflexive, even ritualized, combat of modern politics leaves fewer and fewer attractive choices for all Americans who don't want to be conscripted into a battle between feuding ideologues or forced to link arms with Michael Moore or Ann Coulter.* . . .

. . . [T]he trends in election results over the past several decades add to the portrait of a political system increasingly divided between stable, di-

---

*Michael Moore and Ann Coulter—on the left and right, respectively—represent the more extreme sides of the political spectrum. Moore is a television and movie producer, famous for films such as *Bowling for Columbine* and *Capitalism: A Love Story*. Coulter, a prolific author, is known for her books including *Godless: The Church of Liberalism* and *Guilty: Liberal "Victims" and Their Assault on America.*—EDS.

vergent, and antagonistic camps. Ideologically, culturally, and geographically, the electoral coalitions of the two major parties have dispersed to the point where they now represent almost mirror images of each other. As this resorting has proceeded, each party has established powerful regional strongholds in which it dominates the presidential vote as well as House and Senate races. Each party, in other words, is consolidating its control over a formidable sphere of influence that provides it a stable foundation of support. The flip side is that each party is losing the ability to speak for the entire nation as it loses the capacity to effectively compete in large sections of the country. . . .

The polarization of American politics is an enormously complex, interactive phenomenon. Its roots trace into factors far beyond the workings of the political system itself, into changes in social life, cultural attitudes, and America's place in the world. The tendency toward polarization has been fueled, on the one hand, by the rise of feminism and the gay rights movement, and on the other by the increasing popularity of fundamentalist and evangelical churches. It draws strength from the questions about America's international role opened by the end of the cold war. And it has been influenced by changes in residential patterns that appear to have increased the tendency of Americans to settle among neighbors who share their political views.

This book, though, will focus on the changes within the political system that have carried America into the age of hyperpartisanship: the changing nature of the party coalitions; the role of organized constituency groups in shaping the political debate; the shifts in the way the media interacts with political life; the changes in the rules and practices of Congress; and the strategies pursued by presidents and other political leaders. All of these changes are diminishing our capacity to resolve conflicts. Indeed, . . . almost every major force in American political life now operates as an integrated machine to push the parties apart and to sharpen the disagreements in American life.

The consequences of hyperpartisanship are not all negative. The new alignment offers voters clear, stark choices. As recently as 1980 less than half of Americans told pollsters they saw important differences between the Republican and Democratic parties. Today, three fourths of Americans say they see important differences. With the choices so vividly clarified, more Americans are participating in the political system. Over 122 million people voted in 2004 [and over 130 million in 2008], nearly 17 million more than just four years earlier. The number of people who volunteered and contributed money to campaigns has soared too. One study found that the number of small donors to the presidential campaign increased at least threefold, and perhaps even fourfold, from 2000 to 2004. Many of those small donors made their contributions through the Internet, which has demonstrated an extraordinary ability to connect ordinary citizens to politics. . . .

American politics isn't breaking down because the country's disagreements are inherently more difficult to bridge today. . . . It is breaking down because too few political leaders resist the rising pressures inside the parties for ideological and partisan conformity that make it more difficult to bridge our disagreements. Ideological voices are louder than perhaps ever before in all aspects of American politics, from Congress to the media, but that isn't because deeply ideological voters now dominate the American electorate. At its core, the problem isn't too many ideologues but too few conciliators willing to challenge the ideologues, and partisan warriors on each side demanding a polarized politics. The first step toward lowering the temperature in American politics is a political leadership that would rather douse fires than start them.

Today, though, the impulse to harmonize divergent interests has almost vanished from the capital. Rather than promoting consensus, Washington manufactures disagreement. In both parties, many politicians see it in their interests to widen, not narrow, the underlying divisions in society. Americans today are sincerely divided over the role of government in the economy, foreign policy (especially the Iraq War), and perhaps most intractably, cultural and social issues. But no one would say Americans are divided as violently and passionately as they were over civil rights and the Vietnam War in the 1960s, or the rise of the corporate economy in the 1890s, much less slavery in the 1850s. In each of those periods, the differences between Americans were so profound that they were expressed not just with words, but with fists, and clubs, and ultimately guns. (Think Kent State, the Homestead Steel strike, and John Brown, not to mention the Civil War.) Clearly the *country* has been more polarized than it is today. What's unusual now is that the *political system* is more polarized than the country. Rather than reducing the level of conflict, Washington increases it. That tendency, not the breadth of the underlying divisions itself, is the defining characteristic of our era and the principal cause of our impasse on so many problems.

The road to this point has been paved by the long list of factors. . . . It has been manifest in hundreds, even thousands, of discrete decisions, yet the overall direction has been unwavering. The center in American politics is eroding. Confrontation is rising. The parties are separating. And the conflict between them is widening.

With so many centrifugal forces at work, this era of hyperpartisanship won't unwind easily or quickly. No one any time soon will confuse American politics with the era of good feeling that virtually eradicated partisan competition early in the nineteenth century. The forces encouraging polarization are now deeply entrenched, and they are unlikely to be entirely neutralized: Many of the most antagonistic features of American politics over the past fifteen years are likely to endure indefinitely. But that doesn't mean the country has to be as sharply and relentlessly divided as it is today. The parties have cooperated before to reach commonsense solutions that advance the national interest and could do so again. . . .

76

KATE ZERNIKE

From *Boiling Mad*

"I have a message, a message from the Tea Party. . . . We have come to take our government back. . . . " Quoting a much-cited phrase from 2010 Kentucky Senate candidate Rand Paul the night he won the Republican nomination, author Kate Zernike explains the motivations that created the controversial Tea Party movement. She introduces readers to several activists from the movement, and lets them define the Tea Party's central goals: "limited government, fiscal responsibility, and free markets." Yet critics have pointed to another side of the movement, charging some Tea Partiers with racism and right-wing extremism. To capture the intensity surrounding the organization, Zernike gives a brief look into Rand Paul's Tea Party challenge to establishment Republicans. The young eye surgeon, son of Texas Representative (and, briefly, presidential candidate) Ron Paul, won the Republican nomination convincingly despite the fact that he had held no political office previously—or maybe because he had held no political office previously. Zernike's account ends that night, but the Tea Party story continues. With the nation deep in debt and many Americans concerned about the long recession and a decade of big spending in Washington, D.C., Rand Paul was elected to the U.S. Senate in November 2010, along with several other Tea Party-backed candidates—a momentary tantrum from outside the mainstream or the first round in the American voters' fight to regain control of their government?

———

AT ITS HEART, the Tea Party movement was deeply divided. The people who held virulent signs at rallies were a very different group from those who sat through meetings about organizing local precincts, who in turn were different from those who stayed home but sympathized with the cause. Younger Tea Partiers extolling the wisdom of Friedrich Hayek and Ludwig von Mises had different priorities from the older Tea Partiers who wanted change but also wanted their Medicare left alone. Even the movement's harshest critics acknowledged a kind of "good Tea Party" / "bad Tea Party" divide. The liberal group Media Matters for America had devoted a great deal of time and effort to tracking the Fox News Channel's promotion of the Tea Parties and debunking the movement's received wisdom, but when it sent a researcher undercover to the Tea Party Convention in Nashville, she reported back how "affable and welcoming" her fellow conventioneers were. "A nice surprise was the lack of violent language," wrote the researcher, Melinda Warner, who described herself as an evangelical conservative-turned-progressive. "The members who make those horrible signs and make violent and hateful comments either were not in attendance or kept their mouths shut and left their signs at home." They were, of course, all part of the whole. As it entered its second year, the Tea Party movement had become a mirror as well as a magnet: it reflected back whatever its individual members wanted to project onto it. To some Tea Partiers it was a vessel for grievance, inchoate or specific. To others it was a means to electoral victory against the Democrats. Libertarians hoped it would force the Republican Party to fight more for fiscal discipline, while constitutional purists hoped it would cleanse the country of its New Deal–Great Society sins. The Tea Party was like the proverbial blind men and the elephant; it had a different shape and texture depending on what was in front of you.

Even people within the movement were not always clear about its goals. Tea Party Patriots, which, as an umbrella of more than two thousand local Tea Party groups, best reflected the grassroots origins of the movement, declared as its motto, "Limited government, fiscal responsibility, and free markets." This was in line with the priorities advocated by Freedom-Works and by those who promoted libertarian philosophy. Most local groups embraced some version of this motto, saying they wanted to focus on fiscal problems and not divisive social issues like abortion or gay marriage or immigration. "Every social issue you bring in, you're adding planks to your mission," said Frank Anderson, a founder of the Independence Caucus, which worked with Tea Party groups to evaluate candidates' positions on issues. "And planks become splinters." Yet as Tea Party Patriots invited people to submit ideas for the Contract from America, which was the closest thing to a manifesto of what the Tea Party movement wanted Congress to do, among the more popular suggestions were "an official language of the United States" and "amend the Endangered Species Act." (Another proposal: "Legalize hemp.") Any armchair originalist could tell you that these were not among the powers enumerated in the Constitution.

And if some goals championed by Tea Partiers weren't envisioned by the more purist strains of the movement, others directly contradicted it. Wendy Day, a leader of the Michigan Tea Party, told an interviewer that one good use of government would be to "force credit card companies to lower interest rates for everyone." Jeff McQueen, the creator of the Tea Party flag, had been laid off from his job in international sales for an auto parts company, and he argued that the government had pushed him into unemployment because it had failed to promote American car companies. McQueen pointed out that in Japan and Korea, government policy forced everyone to drive cars manufactured there.

Most Tea Partiers did not see themselves as racists, and you could go to their meetings and not get a whiff of racist attitudes. But with its talk of states' rights and protecting what was rightfully yours, the movement was inherently attractive to people who believed that the government had coddled minorities and the disadvantaged. Along a rural stretch of road near Akron, Ohio, the resident of a ranch house that was well maintained and decorated with more than a dozen American flags displayed a Tea Party manifesto in six precisely placed lawn signs:

YOU ARE ENTERING THE ZONE OF A VAST
RIGHT-WING CONSPIRACY

WE ARE FOR THE TEA PARTY, GUNS, GOD AND LIFE

IMPEACH OBAMA

THE USA NEEDS A FRESH, LIGHT PAINT JOB

TRICKLE UP SOCIALISM AT WORK

YOU ARE NOW LEAVING THE ZONE OF A VAST
RIGHT-WING CONSPIRACY

The rallies themselves best captured the scrum of interests competing for attention. They were a mix of the committed, the curious, and the cantankerous (and sometimes, the crazy). But just as important were the people who had never been to a rally but supported the movement from afar. "For every one of us, there's two or three hundred at home," said Bob Glover, a chemist for the U.S. Customs Service who had come from Savannah, Georgia, to a rally in Washington, D.C. Even if Glover's guess overstated the numbers, there was fertile ground among ordinary Americans for the Tea Party's arguments. You couldn't ignore the rallies. But you had to listen to the folks at home, too, because they represented the growth potential for the Tea Party. It was striking how many people came out for their first demonstrations in the spring of 2010, even as those activists who had started the movement had begun to tire of the public spectacles. Both groups would be voting for Tea Party candidates. And both groups revealed different things about the free-floating discontent in the land. . . .

. . . But 2010 was not any other year. It was the year of the Tea Party. . . .

No campaign better captured the trends that had converged in the Tea Party than the race for the Republican nomination for the U.S. Senate in Kentucky; no contest would be a better test of the new movement's electoral power. Yes, it had won with Scott Brown in Massachusetts, but that was about saying no to health care reform. It had won in Utah, but that was about getting rid of an incumbent who had dared to reach across the aisle. Charlie Crist had been driven from the primary in Florida, but Marco Rubio pointedly identified himself as a conservative, not a Tea Party candidate.

If Trey Grayson was Establishment, Rand Paul was Tea Party, having attended some of the earliest rallies in Kentucky. "If they had cards," he said, "I'd be a card-carrying member." And through his father, he laid claim to a long embrace of libertarian philosophy. (Though many people assumed he had been named for the libertarian novelist and philosopher Ayn Rand, the truth was that his full name was Randal.) He brought together the idealistic wing that had started the movement and the angry wing that had swelled its ranks; the young and tech-savvy Tea Partiers and the older ones concerned about taxes and the national debt. As an eye surgeon, with no previous political experience, he had an anti-Washington appeal that resonated with the people who had been cheering the Tea Party from the sidelines and rooting to throw the bums out. In the videos on his campaign website outlining his policy positions, he appeared wearing scrubs, suggesting he had more important things to do.

Paul had the backing of Sarah Palin and Dick Armey. He also had his father's [Ron Paul, R-Texas] national fundraising network, so he would not lack for cash. (This one would be hard work *and* Daddy's money.)

Paul's supporters spoke about his campaign in terms of a mission, and so did he, declaring that a "reckoning" was at hand. It was a reckoning for big government, but also for the Republican Party. The Republican establishment knew it had a problem; they had known it from the uproar over Charlie Crist in Florida, and when Dede Scozzafava was driven from the race in upstate New York. Those contests might have suggested that the only adjustment needed was to follow the script from the past: move further to the right, especially on social issues. After all, the challengers, Marco Rubio and Doug Hoffman, were more reliably prolife and anti-gay marriage. But Paul's campaign made clear to Republicans in Washington that this wasn't just a center-versus-right debate. This was antigovernment; this was anti-Them. As much as Trey Grayson was going to have to contend with Rand Paul, the Republicans were going to have to contend with the Tea Party. They had hoped they could harness its energy toward victory in the midterm elections. Rand Paul made clear that the Tea Party might actually make things more difficult.

The Tea Party was going to be tested, too, on the strength of its unlikely coalition. The libertarians who saw Paul as their standard-bearer recognized that the Tea Party had been a boon for their numbers and that he was their best chance for a big electoral victory. But they worried that the new grassroots recruits did not truly understand the implications of small government, that popular programs like Social Security were inconsistent with constitutional fidelity, as they saw it.

"There's a larger group that doesn't get it," said Tim Quinn, an environmental consultant in Louisville who had campaigned for Ron Paul in 2008 before jumping on the son's bandwagon. "People want change," he said, "but they need to look deeper."

The Tea Party had always been better about defining what it was against than what it was for. As Rand Paul toured Kentucky, he talked about what he supported, his interpretations of Austrian economics, and the Constitution. Voters talked about a range of grievances and, mostly, economic anxiety. It wasn't always clear that they were really listening to what he was saying. Until the end. . . .

Paul's campaign staff, a combination of former Ron Paulites and local Tea Party leaders, relentlessly mocked Grayson as a country club Republican, referring to him by his full name, including the Roman numeral, instead of "Trey." Paul, by contrast, came off as authentic.

In early April 2010, six weeks before the Republican primary, Paul was touring the state in a luxury bus owned by Ryan Renshaw's sister, who had dropped out of theater school in New York City and become a NASCAR driver. David Adams was rallying the crowd of about a hundred people gathered for a Tea Party in the parking lot outside Ol' Harvey's Eats when the bus pulled in. Paul ambled toward the front of the crowd, wearing a short-sleeved denim shirt and brown rubber-soled shoes, his hair tousled. As he listened to the warm-up speakers, his head down, brow furrowed, he gave the sense of a man with a lot on his mind. It was an appealing pose to Tea Partiers who believed that the founders intended us to have citizen legislators rather than governing elites, men who served their country and then went back to what they really wanted to do, which was to tend their farms. As Adams introduced him, Paul demurred: "I thought we were going to have some music first." His three young sons took the makeshift stage with guitars, singing "This Land is Your Land," and "America the Beautiful." Then the crowd joined in to sing "Happy Birthday" to Robert, the youngest.

Paul stayed long at every stop to answer questions, and he gave expansive, sometimes rambling answers. His message was more apocalyptic than the usual uplift of a politician's speech. "The end is coming, the times are growing short to fix the situation," he said ominously. He often quoted Thomas Paine—"These are the times that try men's souls"—or the Canadian band Rush, known for their libertarian views: "Glittering prizes and endless compromises / shatter the illusion of integrity." The glittering prizes, Paul told the audience outside Ol' Harvey's, were the pork-barrel projects that politicians bring home even though there is no money to pay for them. It was like the last days of Rome, he told the audience, where leaders used bread and circuses to placate the mob.

"When they promise you things, they're promising something they don't have to give," he said. "They have picked the pig clean."

But if his speeches were downers, his crowds loved them. To them, the language felt honest.

"It's really freeing to see people coming out for the Tea Party who would never have said anything," said Cliff Pike, an Episcopalian minister who had retired to Kentucky after his last parish in West Chester, Pennsylvania. Wearing a pressed gingham dress shirt and khakis, he was leaving the rally in Lawrenceburg with a RAND PAUL U.S. SENATE 2010 lawn sign. "They don't usually talk politics or religion. As a minister, I couldn't even put up a sign on my lawn."

"It's hard for us to come out here and, you know, clap clap," agreed his wife, Nancy. "We don't usually show our emotions that way."

The Pikes had been to their first Tea Party in Louisville a year earlier, concerned about the bailouts of the banks and auto companies, the proposed cap-and-trade legislation, and the prospect of health care reform. "All of a sudden you've had it up to here and you want to do something," Cliff Pike said. "It's like the frog in the kettle—only I'm a human being and we're smart enough to know we're in hot water as a country."

They were also angry about how Tea Party supporters had been portrayed in the media. "These were stockbrokers, university professors, normal people," Cliff said. "You don't see racists or bigots. You see your next door neighbors."

Rand Paul told it like it was, Cliff said. "Grayson's a career politician. It's about time we broke the mold."

While Rand Paul brought a message of strict constitutional interpretation and smaller government, his audiences, like the Tea Party itself, greeted him with sprawling concerns. They wanted him to be the answer to all of them.

Mostly they asked about jobs, and how to bring them back. A woman at Bruce's Country Store in Mason complained that food safety laws were hurting small farmers; Paul agreed, criticizing laws that banned the sale of raw milk and then those that regulated homeschooling. At the rally in Lawrenceburg, a woman asked his position on cyberbullying. Paul said that he thought schools had rules on that, and that parents had to take some responsibility for knowing what their children were writing and seeing online. "You have to balance freedom of expression," he said.

"They're taking advantage of freedom of speech to use slander and violence," the woman insisted.

Paul urged her, again, to work with school officials. The woman persisted. Kelley Paul, standing in the audience, smiled hard and said in a sweet Kentucky singsong, "I think he's answered the question." . . .

The conservatives on Twitter began jumping as polls closed in Kentucky on Tuesday, May 18, just as they had after Rick Santelli's rant fifteen months earlier. "Randslide!" someone declared it, and others picked up the phrase; #randslide soon became its own hashtag, to identify tweets about Paul's victory.

Rand Paul had won by twenty-four percentage points.

More than a hundred supporters had gathered for the victory party at the Bowling Green Country Club, with its lush greens, popping azaleas, and limpid turquoise pool. Around the fireplace on the outdoor patio, they clinked beer bottles and tumblers of scotch. Andrew Demers, the campaign's twenty-eight-year-old political director and a veteran of the Ron Paul New Hampshire campaign, had invited Rand's father to join the celebration, and Ron stood by proudly as his son stuffed a pipe. Jim Johnson, a seventy-year-old car dealer and a neighbor of Rand Paul's, said he still thought of himself as a conservative, but he was getting to be more of a libertarian. "I'm not 100 percent libertarian, I'm about 78 percent," he said, "but I'm getting there."

Sarah Palin called Paul as soon as the results were in, followed by Mitt Romney. Finally, Paul came out to the booming sounds of the Rush lyric and the cheers of the crowd. He paid tribute to his wife, his sons, his siblings, his parents, his staff, and mostly, the movement that had propelled him.

"I have a message, a message from the Tea Party," he proclaimed. "We have come to take our government back. . . . We are encountering a day of reckoning and this movement, this Tea Party movement is a message to Washington that we're unhappy and that we want things done differently.

The Tea Party movement is huge. The mandate of our victory tonight is huge. What you have done and what we are doing can transform America."

As Rand Paul departed the stage, supporters and reporters mobbed Ron Paul. Supporters asked for autographs, and congratulated him as the one truly responsible for the victory that night. "What you did for Rand is what Barry Goldwater did for Ronald Reagan," one gushed.

The success of his son's campaign, the elder Paul told reporters, showed that Americans were finally catching on to Austrian economics. He had noticed it in 2007, that college students started nodding their heads when he mentioned von Mises and Hayek—ideas he had been talking about for forty years. Now, he said, the word was spreading, and politicians would have to pay attention. "And get rid of the power people," he said, "the people who run the show, the people who think they're above everybody else. That's what the people are sick and tired of, that's the message."

The primary had been open to Republicans only, which meant that it reflected the state's most conservative voters. To win in November, Rand Paul would have to win among Democrats, who dominated Kentucky voter rolls. He vowed to resist calls to moderate his message, to abandon the Tea Party. . . .

The men and women of the Tea Party, this coalition of young and old, were the new young idealists in town. As the 2010 midterms approached, they would be faced with reality: Would they keep pushing for ideals that had been beating against the march of the nation's history for decades? Or would they support people who made compromises that would still get them closer to their goals on spending?

Washington was also a city of endless compromises, as Rand Paul's favorite Rush lyric had it. But if that would turn the Tea Partiers into old cynics, it was no cause for concern. Young idealists were more than just part of the fabric of Washington; they were part of the fabric of American politics, and had been for more than two hundred years. The Tea Partiers of today might one day become cynical, they might one day be co-opted. But even if that happened, history argued that a new generation of young idealists would be back soon.

PART FOURTEEN

The Media

77

LARRY SABATO

From *Feeding Frenzy*

When political scientist Larry Sabato published his 1991 book on the media's role in campaigning, he gave a term to a phenomenon others had already seen: a feeding frenzy. The press en masse attacks a wounded politician whose record—or more accurately, his or her character—has been questioned. Every network and cable station participates, often without any real evidence to back up the rumor. Sabato's list of thirty-six examples ends in 1990; knowledgeable readers will be able to update the list. Paradoxically, the spectacular success of the Washington Post's *Bob Woodward and Carl Bernstein in investigating Watergate set the stage for recent feeding frenzies. Today, just the fear of being a media target may deter many qualified people from entering public service, Sabato notes.*

IT HAS BECOME a spectacle without equal in modern American politics: the news media, print and broadcast, go after a wounded politician like sharks in a feeding frenzy. The wounds may have been self-inflicted, and the politician may richly deserve his or her fate, but the journalists now take center stage in the process, creating the news as much as reporting it, changing both the shape of election-year politics and the contours of government. Having replaced the political parties as the screening committee for candidates and officeholders, the media propel some politicians toward power and unceremoniously eliminate others. Unavoidably, this enormously influential role—and the news practices employed in exercising it—has provided rich fodder for a multitude of press critics.

These critics' charges against the press cascade down with the fury of rain in a summer squall. Public officials and many other observers see journalists as rude, arrogant, and cynical, given to exaggeration, harassment, sensationalism, and gross insensitivity. . . .

Press invasion of privacy is leading to the gradual erasure of the line protecting a public person's purely private life. This makes the price of public life enormously higher, serving as an even greater deterrent for those not absolutely obsessed with holding power—the kind of people we ought least to want in office. Rather than recognizing this unfortunate consequence, many in journalism prefer to relish their newly assumed role of "gatekeeper," which, as mentioned earlier, enables them to substitute for party leaders in deciding which characters are virtuous enough to merit consideration for high office. As ABC News correspondent Brit Hume self-critically suggests:

> We don't see ourselves institutionally, collectively anymore as a bunch of journalists out there faithfully reporting what's happening day by day. . . . We have a much grander view of ourselves: we are the Horatio at the national bridge. We are the people who want to prevent the bad characters from crossing over into public office.

Hume's veteran ABC colleague Sander Vanocur agrees, detecting "among some young reporters a quality of the avenging angel: they are going to sanitize American politics." More and more, the news media seem determined to show that would-be emperors have no clothes, and if necessary to prove the point, they personally will strip the candidates naked on the campaign trail. The sheer number of journalists participating in these public denudings guarantees riotous behavior, and the "full-court press" almost always presents itself as a snarling, unruly mob more bent on killing kings than making them. Not surprisingly potential candidates deeply fear the power of an inquisitorial press, and in deciding whether to seek office, they often consult journalists as much as party leaders, even sharing private vulnerabilities with newsmen to gauge reaction. The *Los Angeles Times's* Washington bureau chief, Jack Nelson, had such an encounter before the 1988 campaign season, when a prospective presidential candidate "literally asked me how long I thought the statute of limitations was" for marital infidelity. "I told him I didn't know, but I didn't think [the limit] had been reached in his case!" For whatever reasons, the individual chose not to run.

As the reader will see later in this volume, able members of the news corps offer impressive defenses for all the practices mentioned thus far, not the least of which is that the press has become more aggressive to combat the legions of image makers, political consultants, spin doctors, and handlers who surround modern candidates like a nearly impenetrable shield. Yet upon reflection, most news veterans recognize that press excesses are not an acceptable antidote for consultant or candidate evils. In fact, not one of the interviewed journalists even attempted to justify an increasingly frequent occurrence in news organizations: the publication of gossip and rumor *without convincing proof*. Gossip has always been the drug of choice for journalists as well as the rest of the political community, but as the threshold for publication of information about private lives has been lowered, journalists sometimes cover politics as "Entertainment Tonight" reporters cover Hollywood. A bitter Gary Hart* observed: "Rumor and gossip have become the coins of the political realm," and the *New York Times*'s Michael Oreskes seemed to agree: "1988 was a pretty sorry year when the *National Enquirer* was the most important publication in American journalism." With all the stories and innuendo about personal vice, campaigns appear to be little more than a stream of talegates (or in the case of sexual misadventures, tailgates).

The sorry standard set on the campaign trail is spilling over into coverage of governmental battles. Ever since Watergate,† government scandals have paraded across the television set in a roll call so lengthy and numbing that they are inseparable in the public consciousness, all joined at the Achilles' heel. Some recent lynchings such as John Tower's failure to be confirmed as secretary of defense,‡ rival any spectacle produced by colonial Salem. At the same time more vital and revealing information is ignored or crowded off the agenda. *Real* scandals, such as the savings-and-loan heist or the influence peddling at the Department of Housing and Urban Development in the 1980s, go undetected for years. The sad conclusion is inescapable: The press has become obsessed with gossip rather than governance; it prefers to employ titillation rather than scrutiny; as a result, its political coverage produces trivialization rather than enlightenment. And the dynamic mechanism propelling and demonstrating this decline in news standards is the "feeding frenzy." . . .

The term *frenzy* suggests some kind of disorderly, compulsive, or agitated activity that is muscular and instinctive, not cerebral and thoughtful. In the animal world, no activity is more classically frenzied than the feeding of sharks, piranhas, or bluefish when they encounter a wounded prey. These attack-fish with extraordinarily acute senses first search out weak, ill, or injured targets. On locating them, each hunter moves in quickly to gain a share of the kill, feeding not just off the victim but also off its fellow hunters' agitation. The excitement and drama of the violent encounter builds to a crescendo, sometimes overwhelming the creatures' usual inhi-

---

*Former Senator (D-Col.) Gary Hart's 1988 presidential candidacy ended after media revelations about his extramarital relations with Donna Rice.—EDS.

†Watergate began with the 1972 break-in at the Democratic National headquarters by several men associated with President Nixon's re-election committee. Watergate ended two years later with the resignation of President Nixon. Nixon and his closest aides were implicated in the coverup of the Watergate burglary. Tapes made by President Nixon of his Oval Office conversations revealed lying and obstruction of justice at the highest levels of government.—EDS.

‡In 1989, the Senate rejected President Bush's nominee for secretary of defense, former Texas Senator John Tower. Senate hearings produced allegations that Tower was an excessive drinker and a womanizer.—EDS.

bitions. The frenzy can spread, with the delirious attackers wildly striking any object that moves in the water, even each other. Veteran reporters will recognize more press behavior in this passage than they might wish to acknowledge. This reverse anthropomorphism can be carried too far, but the similarity of piranha in the water and press on the campaign trail can be summed up in a shared goal: If it bleeds, try to kill it.

The kingdom of politics and not of nature is the subject of this volume, so for our purposes, a feeding frenzy is defined as the press coverage attending any political event or circumstance where a critical mass of journalists leap to cover the same embarrassing or scandalous subject and pursue it intensely, often excessively, and sometimes uncontrollably. No precise number of journalists can be attached to the term *critical mass*, but in the video age, we truly know it when we see it; the forest of cameras, lights, microphones, and adrenaline-choked reporters surrounding a Gary Hart, Dan Quayle, or Geraldine Ferraro is unmistakable. [The following table] contains a list of thirty-six events that surely qualify as frenzies. They are occasions of sin for the press as well as the politicians, and thus ideal research sites that will serve as case studies for this book. A majority (twenty-one) are drawn from presidential politics, while seven examples come from the state and local levels, with the remaining eight focused on government scandals or personal peccadilloes of nationally recognized political figures. . . .

Conditions are always ripe for the spawning of a frenzy in the brave new world of omnipresent journalism. Advances in media technology have revolutionized campaign coverage. Handheld miniature cameras (minicams) and satellite broadcasting have enabled television to go live anywhere, anytime with ease. Instantaneous transmission (by broadcast and fax) to all corners of the country has dramatically increased the velocity of campaign developments today, accelerating events to their conclusion at breakneck speed. Gary Hart, for example, went from front-runner to ex-candidate in less than a week in May 1987. Continuous public-affairs programming, such as C-SPAN and CNN, helps put more of a politician's utterances on the record, as Senator Joseph Biden discovered to his chagrin when C-SPAN unobtrusively taped Biden's exaggeration of his résumé at a New Hampshire kaffeeklatsch in 1987. (This became a contributing piece of the frenzy that brought Biden down.) C-SPAN, CNN, and satellite broadcasting capability also contribute to the phenomenon called "the news cycle without end," which creates a voracious news appetite demanding to be fed constantly, increasing the pressure to include marginal bits of information and gossip and producing novel if distorting "angles" on the same news to differentiate one report from an-

FEEDING FRENZIES: CASE STUDIES USED FOR THIS BOOK

From Presidential Politics

1952	Richard Nixon's "secret fund"
1968	George Romney's "brainwashing" about Vietnam
1968	Spiro Agnew's "fat Jap" flap
1969	Ted Kennedy's Chappaquiddick
1972	Edmund Muskie's New Hampshire cry
1972	Thomas Eagleton's mental health
1976	Jimmy Carter's "lust in the heart" *Playboy* interview
1976	Gerald Ford's "free Poland" gaffe
1979	Jimmy Carter's "killer rabbit"
1980	Billygate (Billy Carter and Libya)
1983	Debategate (Reagan's use of Carter's debate briefing books)
1984	Gary Hart's age, name, and signature changes
1984	Jesse Jackson's "Hymietown" remark
1984	Geraldine Ferraro's family finances
1985/86	Jack Kemp's purported homosexuality
1987	Gary Hart and Donna Rice
1987	Joseph Biden's plagiarism and Michael Dukakis's "attack video"
1987	Pat Robertson's exaggerated résumé and shotgun marriage
1988	Dukakis's mental health
1988	Dan Quayle (National Guard service, Paula Parkinson, academic record, rumors such as plagiarism and drugs)
1988	George Bush's alleged mistress

From the State and Local Levels

1987/88	Governor Evan Mecham on the impeachment trail (Arizona)
1987/88	Chuck Robb and the cocaine parties (Virginia)
1983/90	Mayor Marion Barry's escapades (District of Columbia)
1987	Governor Dick Celeste's womanizing (Ohio)
1988	Mayor Henry Cisneros's extramarital affair (San Antonio, Texas)
1989/90	Governor Gaston Caperton's "soap opera" divorce (West Virginia)
1990	Texas governor's election: drugs, rape, and "honey hunts"

Noncampaign Examples

1973/74	The Watergate scandals
1974	Congressman Wilbur Mills and stripper Fanne Foxe
1986/87	The Iran-Contra affair
1987	Supreme Court nominee Douglas Ginsburg's marijuana use (and campaign repercussions)
1989	John Tower's losing fight to become secretary of defense
1989	Speaker Jim Wright's fall from power
1989	Tom Foley's rocky rise to the Speakership
1989/90	Barney Frank and the male prostitute

other. The extraordinary number of local stations covering national politics today—up to several hundred at major political events—creates an echo chamber producing seemingly endless repetitions of essentially the same news stories. This local contingent also swells the corps traveling the campaign trail. In 1988 an estimated two thousand journalists of all stripes flooded the Iowa caucuses, for instance. Reporters not infrequently outnumber participants at meetings and whistlestops. . . .

Whether on the rise or not, the unfortunate effects of pack journalism are apparent to both news reporters and news consumers: conformity, homogeneity, and formulaic reporting. Innovation is discouraged, and the checks and balances supposedly provided by competition evaporate. Press energies are devoted to finding mere variations on a theme (new angles and wiggle disclosures), while a mob psychology catches hold that allows little mercy for the frenzy victim. CNN's Frank Sesno captures the pack mood perfectly:

I've been in that group psychology; I know what it's like. You think you're on to something, you've got somebody on the run. How dare they not come clean? How dare they not tell the full story? What are they trying to hide? Why are they hiding it? And you become a crusader for the truth. Goddammit, you're going to get the truth! . . .

Sesno's crusader spirit can be traced directly to the lingering effects of the Watergate scandal, which had the most profound impact of any modern event on the manner and substance of the press's conduct. In many respects Watergate began the press's open season on politicians in a chain reaction that today allows for scrutiny of even the most private sanctums of public officials' lives. Moreover, coupled with Vietnam and the civil rights movement, Watergate shifted the orientation of journalism away from mere description—providing an accurate account of happenings— and toward prescription—helping to set the campaign's (and society's) agendas by focusing attention on the candidates' shortcomings as well as certain social problems.

A new breed and a new generation of reporters were attracted to journalism, and particularly its investigative arm. As a group they were idealistic, though aggressively mistrustful of all authority, and they shared a contempt for "politics as usual." Critics called them do-gooders and purists who wanted the world to stand at moral attention for them. Twenty years later the Vietnam and Watergate generation dominates journalism: They and their younger cohorts hold sway over most newsrooms, with two-thirds of all reporters now under the age of thirty-six and an ever-increasing share of editors and executives drawn from the Watergate-era class. Of course, many of those who found journalism newly attractive in the wake of Watergate were not completely altruistic. The ambitious saw the happy fate of the *Washington Post*'s young Watergate sleuths Bob Woodward and Carl Bernstein, who gained fame and fortune, not to mention big-screen portrayals by Robert Redford and Dustin Hoffman in the movie *All the President's Men*. As *U.S. News & World Report*'s Steven Roberts sees it:

A lot of reporters run around this town dreaming of the day that Dustin Hoffman and Robert Redford are going to play them in the movies. That movie had more effect on the self-image of young journalists than anything else. Christ! Robert Redford playing a journalist? It lends an air of glamour and excitement that acts as a magnet drawing young reporters to investigative reporting.

The young were attracted not just to journalism but to a particular *kind* of journalism. The role models were not respected, established reporters but two unknowns who refused to play by the rules their seniors had accepted. "Youngsters learned that deductive techniques, all guesswork, and lots of unattributed information [were] the royal road to fame, even if it wasn't being terribly responsible," says Robert Novak. After all, adds columnist Mark Shields, "Robert Redford didn't play Walter Lippmann and Dustin Hoffman didn't play Joseph Kraft." (Kraft, like Lippmann, had a long and distinguished career in journalism.) . . .

A clear consequence of Watergate and other recent historical events was the increasing emphasis placed by the press on the character of candidates. As journalists reviewed the three tragic but exceptionally capable figures who had held the presidency since 1960, they saw that the failures of Kennedy, Johnson, and Nixon were not those of intellect but of ethos. Chappaquiddick, Spiro Agnew, and the Eagleton affair reinforced that view. The party affiliations and ideology of these disappointing leaders varied, but in common they possessed defects of personality, constitution, and disposition. In the world of journalism (or academe), as few as two data points can constitute a trend; these six together constituted an irrefutable mother lode of proof. "We in the press learned from experience that character flaws could have very large costs," says David Broder, "and we couldn't afford to ignore them if we were going to meet our responsibility." . . .

[A] troubling consequence of modern media coverage for the political system has to do with the recruitment of candidates and public servants. Simply put, the price of power has been raised dramatically, far too high for many outstanding potential officeholders. An individual contemplating a run for office must now accept the possibility of almost unlimited intrusion into his or her financial and personal life. Every investment made, every affair conducted, every private sin committed from college years to the present may one day wind up in a headline or on television. For a reasonably sane and moderately sensitive person, this is a daunting realization, with potentially hurtful results not just for the candidate but for his or her immediate family and friends. To have achieved a nongovernmental position of respect and honor in one's community is a source of pride and security, and the risk that it could all be destroyed by an unremitting and distorted assault on one's faults and foibles cannot be taken lightly. American society today is losing the services of many exceptionally talented individuals who could make outstanding contributions to the commonweal, but who understandably will not subject themselves and their loved ones to abusive, intrusive press coverage. Of course, this problem stems as much from the attitudes of the public as from those of the press; the strain of moral absolutism in portions of the American people merely finds expression in the relentless press frenzies and ethicsgate hunts. . . . *New York Times* columnist Anthony Lewis is surely correct when he suggests, "If we tell people there's to be absolutely nothing private left to them, then we will tend to attract to public office only those most brazen, least sensitive personalities. Is that what we want to do?"

78

MORLEY WINOGRAD
MICHAEL HAIS

From *Millennial Makeover*

Former Governor Howard Dean's 2004 presidential bid did not succeed in vaulting the doctor into the White House, but it did break new ground in campaign tactics. Morley Winograd and Michael Hais trace the rise of the "Netroots" political activists, citizens who meet and participate in campaigns using Internet sites. The authors tell the story of two young Millennials who ran for the state legislature in New Hampshire using some then-obscure social networking strategies. The campaign became an "event," with the outcome successful for both. Winograd and Hais detail how the Internet has expanded the potential for candidates to reach voters—primarily young voters but older voters too—particularly through the use of YouTube. As those of you who followed the 2008 presidential election recall, YouTube campaign ads caused many flurries of excitement, with the most controversial commercials often reserved for the Net rather than for broadcast or cable TV. It is the sharing of online messages that make them so influential, Winograd and Hais remind us. They predict that "the resulting cataclysm will wash away the current politics of polarization and ideological deadlock, putting in place a new landscape of collective purpose and national consensus that involves individuals and communities in solving the nation's problems."

POLITICAL CAMPAIGNS ARE THE EQUALS of any media company when it comes to wanting to run things from the top and control every aspect of the product they are selling. As Joe Trippi, Howard Dean's campaign manager in 2004, wrote, "Most campaigns do everything in their power to control every element of the candidate's image and message, from the clothes he wears to each word out of his mouth." As a consultant to Silicon Valley start-ups, Trippi could see that the notion of running a campaign from the bottom up would require an "open source" approach, with control located, if at all, in the swarm of contributors to the campaign's efforts rather than at its headquarters. But, as he pointed out to Dean, attempting such a feat would be like "jumping from a fifteen-story building" and trusting the front line troops would be there to catch you. In a DeanNation blog posted in May 2003, Trippi wrote, "Every political

campaign I have ever been in was built on the top-down military structure. . . . This kind of structure will suffocate the storm [groundswell of
support], not fuel it. . . . The important thing is to provide the tools and
some of the direction . . . and get the hell out of the way when a big wave
is building on its own." The idea, as the Dean campaign itself proved, is
easier to articulate than to execute. But those candidates who master the
art of putting the voters in charge of the campaign will be rewarded with
victory. . . .

Those who cut their teeth in 2004 on this new way to involve the
voters soon found themselves in demand by all of the 2008 presidential
campaigns. Mark Warner, who left the governor's mansion in Virginia in
2005 to explore a presidential run (which he ultimately decided against),
recruited one of the more prominent members of the Dean campaign,
Jerome Armstrong, who had coined the term word "Netroots" in 2002 to
describe the growing community of people who became politically active
through online interaction. Armstrong was hired for what turned out to
be a one-year test of the ability of online campaigning to build support
for a relatively unknown presidential candidate. Warner, who had co-
founded Nextel and invested in other Internet start-ups before he became
governor, fully appreciated the potential of this new approach to campaigning. Joining Armstrong at the center of the candidate's Netroots activities was Trei Brundrett, whose knowledge of peer-to-peer technologies may have even surpassed Armstrong's. With Warner's full support, the
two Net organizers set out to build upon what the Dean campaign had
done and, in particular, to take advantage of social networking sites that
weren't widely used in 2004.

In 2006, the pair created a web initiative to complement Warner's
"Forward Together" political action committee, designed to attract interest and build a network of future volunteers and supporters. Their idea
was a contest among Democratic congressional candidates in Republican
districts called "Map Changers," a name given to Warner by a Missouri
Democrat in reference to Warner's impact in helping to change red districts to blue. The contest rules were simple: an individual visiting the web
site would "vote" for a Democratic challenger as a sign of support, at the
same time submitting his or her name, email address, and zip code to the
Warner PAC web site. That data, of course, was invaluable to the nascent
Warner effort, while the winning congressional candidates would receive
Warner's time and help in raising money. After an initial round of voting,
the ten candidates with the most online votes won a contribution from
Forward Together. Then, in the final round of the contest, those ten com-
peted to see who would get Warner to come to the candidate's district

and headline a fund-raiser for the campaign. In effect, Brundrett and Armstrong had created an incentive for the Democratic candidates to self-organize and create networks of political activists that might in turn help Warner in his own possible presidential run. The idea proved so successful that it was repeated for legislative candidates in the two key early presidential contest states, Iowa and New Hampshire.

In New Hampshire, two nineteen-year-old Millennials running for the state legislature, Andrew Edwards and Jeffrey Fontas, were among the top five online vote getters, each receiving a $1,000 check from Warner's PAC. Edwards attends Worcester Polytechnic Institute when he is not engaged in politics. Fontas majors in political science at Northeastern University, which allows him to count his time in the state legislature as his "co-op" semester of work. The account of their winning the Map Changer contest can still be read on their October 2006 blog postings. Having won the money, they asked their friends and supporters for ideas on how best to spend it in their campaigns. In the end, each opted to use the winnings from his online campaigning to buy the fundamentals of offline grassroots campaigns—lawn signs, literature, and local advertising.

But their skill in social networking was the key to winning Warner's contest. Edwards and Fontas each created a group on Facebook's social networking site specifically for his campaign and encouraged friends from around the world to join. Facebook's platform, or operating system, allows users to join or create any group that might be of interest—from a particular band or musical genre to a candidate or a political party or anything in between. Fontas and Edwards sought to streamline the process of mobilizing people they knew only through the Internet by making clear their groups' purposes: "Fontas for State House" and "Edwards for State Representative."

When the Forward Together contest was announced, they decided to use the site's NewsFeed feature to round up support. NewsFeed is designed to tell each user what is going on in a community that a member has joined, either by signing up for a group or by "friending" another user. News about the community shows up on the profile page of all members of the community for other friends to see whenever they check their profile. Normally what passes for community news is information about who is "friending" whom, what parties people went to the night before, or who has just posted pictures that others should view. But Edwards and Fontas grasped the potential for this feature to be used in their political campaigns long before most campaign gurus had even heard of the concept.

They both began by posting a "note" about the Map Changer contest on their personal profile, which meant that each of their friends or members of their group received notice of the contest as one "story" in that community's NewsFeed. But the two social networking gurus went one step further, using the "tagging" function within the Facebook platform as well. Technically, a "tag" is metadata, or "information about information," created when a user labels a particular piece of data, such as a photo, with information that will help categorize the item so it will be easier to find again. By mentioning each of their friends in the note, thereby "tagging" them, the note automatically appeared in all their friends' News-Feeds as well, so that people with whom neither of them were friends but who were "friends of their friends" also heard about the contest. By using the platform, or operating system, of Facebook's site, the news about the contest "spread like wildfire."

This frenzy of social networking was enabled by the Warner web site, which provided "widgets," or small Web-based applications, that each contestant was able to import to his own web site and include in the "post" or "note" about the contest. The widgets told visitors who clicked on them how to vote in the Map Changer contest and why they should vote, and also provided a sample ballot that could be copied to any other web site for further sharing. Based on his Dean campaign experience, Armstrong designed the Map Changer contest to provide contestants with the tools they might want to use to assist their individual organizing efforts, but he left it up to each participant to decide how best to spread the word and gain support.

Edwards's and Fontas's creative use of Facebook's NewsFeed application didn't end there. For instance, Edwards placed a notice on his campaign profile site of the contest but treated it as an "event." Under News-Feed's rules, this meant that each person invited to the event was sent an "invitation" to attend, or, in this case, to vote. The friends then either had to RSVP, in effect voting for Edwards in the contest, or take some other affirmative action to remove the invitation from the member's personal profile. He used this particular feature to avoid constantly emailing people to ask for their votes, which would have been viewed as a violation of Net etiquette. After the contest, he underlined the importance of these social networking features for his contest victory. "The NewsFeed, coupled with features like Notes and Media sharing, is such a perfectly integrated system to disseminate information. It's already *the* tool, in fact."

Edwards had more than 150 friends in his campaign Facebook group at the time of the contest, and Fontas had more than 250. Starting from that core, the two candidates then reached out to other Facebook users and traditional sources of online Democratic support, such as DailyKos .com, to get people to vote for them in the Map Changer campaign. Not satisfied with those efforts, the two candidates posted a plea for votes on the "Something Awful" forum, a comedy web site filled with messaging pranks, digitally edited pictures, and humorous movie reviews. The idea to use this particular site came from Fontas, who constantly checked the site's forum for news updates and commentary and posted his own thoughts about the news on the site for his fellow news addicts to read. However, in order not to have that history of his postings or comments interfere with their Map Changer contest, Edwards was chosen to be the one who actually asked for votes on the site. As he noted, "The politics of personal destruction have been amplified so much now by the Net that you need to go to extraordinary lengths to protect your privacy."

The two campaigners received many replies to their pleas for votes from people on "Something Awful" who wanted to know about the ethics of the contest, how much the two were being paid to send out the Warner-related message, and other questions that reveal the paranoia many "Netizens" feel toward people seeking power. But, in the end, the request generated more than one hundred votes, which helped put them into the winner's circle.

Each district in the lower house of the New Hampshire legislature elects multiple representatives depending on its size. In District 26, for instance, Edwards received 3,558 votes, or 5 percent, finishing seventh out of twenty candidates. The ten candidates winning the greatest number of votes were entitled to a seat, so Edwards was sworn in as one of the youngest members of the state legislature. Meanwhile, in District 24, Fontas received 1,134 votes, or 22 percent. There were only five candidates running for the three seats in that district, so his total was enough to give him a seat. Even though he admits that he is a terrible blogger, Fontas still was proud enough of his victory that, in classic Millennial style, he posted the "obligatory mom and pop shot" on his blog the day he was sworn in. Within months of their victories, the two friends were speaking on the floor of the legislature, resisting entreaties from lobbyists, and capturing all the action for their friends on Facebook....

The enormous advantage in the economics of campaigning via the Net compared to television means that it is only a matter of time until candidates who devote most of their energies, if not most of their money, to these new campaign tactics will gain the upper hand. Not only does the technology provide an economical way to reach voters, it does so with messages that are actually watched and heard and, if created properly, believed.

Nearly 80 percent of Americans are now online. About half of them are in the fast-growing group of broadband users. Over a third of Americans report that they spend more time online than they do watching television or listening to the radio. These numbers are even higher for the Millennial Generation, the first to be able to multitask by using all these media simultaneously and effectively. Broadcast technologies, requiring advertisers to interrupt the viewers' entertainment to sell them something they may not want, are simply not able to compete for the attention of a generation that expects communications to be authentic and relevant. History suggests that those who find ways to integrate the new technology with existing tactics to produce multi-faceted campaigns that reach all voters will be especially successful in future elections. . . .

The second trend arguing for the importance of online campaigning in the future is the increasing numbers of Millennials in the electorate. This emerging generation has a penchant for getting its information from the Net, especially on social networking sites.

Younger voters are twice as likely as others to use the Net, rather than newspapers, to get information about political campaigns. Thirty-five percent of younger broadband Internet users acquired most of their news about the 2006 elections online, compared to 57 percent who still obtained the bulk of their information from television. This is the lowest use of TV for information among all age groups, and its use continues to decline in importance among Millennials. If, as expected, these trends continue, the Net will become their primary source of information within the next several election cycles. . . .

Understanding what the future of online political campaigning will look like, therefore, begins with understanding Millennials' penchant for social expression on the Net. . . .

Since moving pictures are always more interesting than stills, it should have come as no surprise when three older Millennials struck gold in 2005 by combining the fundamentals of social networking technology with an easy to use flash video player application. Chad Hurley, Steve Chen, and Jawed Karim, three engineers at PayPal, a service that enables users to pay for products or make charitable contributions securely online, had found it hard to share videos they had created. Their solution was YouTube, and suddenly all one had to do was simply click on an onscreen image of the video from a web browser, thus shortening download times and significantly reducing the cost of creating and sharing video images. Originally launched in February 2005 as a way to enable online video auctions, the site soon became an overnight sensation. A year and a half later, the site was attracting 34 million unique visitors a month. Many of those users were heavily engaged in politics, which became the second most popular general type of channel, or topic cluster, on the site. (In 2006, the sixth most popular site on YouTube was one satirizing George Bush.) Just as television swamped radio in popularity by adding pictures to sound, YouTube achieved incredible growth by allowing people to share online not just text, photos, and audio, but full-motion video, regardless of quality.

By July 2006, 649 million videos had been streamed, or downloaded, from the site by over 30 million unique visitors. That placed the new site in third place among all U.S. video streaming sites, behind Yahoo! and MySpace. Six months later, YouTube visitors initiated almost one billion video streams, making the parent company, Google, the top web site for all video streaming activity on the Net. The 120 million worldwide visitors to YouTube in 2006 represented a 1,922 percent increase over the number of viewers the site had attracted in 2005. Not only does YouTube attract more viewers than any other online video site, but the site's average viewer spends more time browsing through the content than do visitors to the other, more text-oriented social networking sites.

YouTube's growth in popularity created an almost insatiable demand for new content from amateur video bloggers. By significantly lowering the cost of creation and providing an inexpensive way for the aspiring artists to share their work, YouTube tapped into a rich vein of previously frustrated videographers. By September 2006, 6.1 million videos had been uploaded into YouTube's database, one million more than the previous month.

By the fall of 2006, there were about 500,000 user profiles on the site, a number that began to grow exponentially as the site hit critical mass at the end of 2006, according to Jordan Hoffner, a YouTube executive. Even though no one was required to have a personal profile on the site to view individual videos, the desire to become a part of this fast-growing community was hard to resist. Seventy percent of YouTube's profiles came from Americans, about half of whom were under twenty years of age. By one calculation, between the time of YouTube's conception and the end of August 2006, users spent the equivalent of 9,305 years on the site sharing videos of all kinds with one another. . . .

Because of Millennials' desire to share their ideas and experiences with others online, contacting them through the Internet is now an imperative for any politician who wants to reach them. Sixty-four percent of Millennials believe everyone in their group is equal, so they tend to make decisions together, with the leader managing a search for consensus rather than trying to dictate what their response should be. As a result, there are no Millennial "political bosses" who can deliver the entire generation. Each group of friends needs to be collectively convinced to support a particular cause or candidate. About two-thirds of all Millennials consider their friends the most important source of information on what's cool. Web sites on the Net come in second (with magazines, cable TV, and parents rounding out the top five). The key to reaching Millennials is clearly through their friends on the Net.

When Millennials join the Netroots online, they are disproportionately more influential than the average citizen, precisely because they are so active in sharing their ideas and opinions with others. A 2004 study conducted by the Institute for Democracy, Politics, and the Internet at George Washington University found that fully 69 percent of those involved in politics online also met the Roper organization's definition of "'Influentials' or opinion leaders and trendsetters with their friends and neighbors." This stands in stark contrast to the general population, only 10 percent of which qualify as Influentials based on their tendency to share their ideas with others. Even among more prosperous and better educated Internet users, the percentage of Influentials doesn't exceed 13 percent. "If word of mouth is like a radio signal broadcast over the country, 'Influentials' are the strategically placed transmitters that amplify the signal, multiplying the number of people who hear it." . . .

Whether it's education or health care, energy policy or the environment, the way democracy functions or how we approach the world, no part of government will be untouched by the changes Millennial beliefs will bring to our public policy debate. The tectonic plates undergirding America's current political landscape are beginning to shift. The resulting cataclysm will wash away the current politics of polarization and ideological deadlock, putting in place a new landscape of collective purpose and national consensus that involves individuals and communities in solving the nation's problems. While such an outcome is hard to imagine before the shift actually occurs, especially for the inherently divided, pessimistic, and cynical generations now in positions of power, the evidence of the desire for such a change among much of the American public, especially Millennials, is clear. The battle lines between those locked in the dogmas of the past and those ready to present something new to the American public are already forming. Because of the sheer size of the Millennial Generation and its greater facility with new information and communication technologies, their attitudes and beliefs will overwhelm defenders of the status quo and reshape American politics for decades to come.

79

CASS SUNSTEIN

From *Republic.com 2.0*

Law professor Cass Sunstein challenges conventional wisdom about the Internet as a tool to enhance open debate and the exchange of ideas in a democratic society. Yes, individuals have great freedom to gather information, he writes, but often that freedom is exercised in very narrow, particularistic ways that end up limiting an individual's exposure to a few favorite topics and a few favorite points of view. Each individual finds her or his cyber-niche and settles into it. Sunstein points to the danger of this personalized world of information. The author also underscores the importance of "shared experiences" in a diverse society; they'll become less and less common as people carve out their own narrow spheres of interest. Sunstein then discusses the blogosphere, in which limitless numbers of Internet opinion leaders share views with their web readers. A chance for a more open democracy? Yes, in a sense, Sunstein thinks, but also a chance for error and for extreme, polarized views to flourish. The "echo chamber" is hardly Sunstein's ideal vision for the new communications technologies. The author's critique of the new media is especially interesting because early in President Barack Obama's administration, Professor Sunstein was selected as the head of the Office of Information and Regulatory Affairs within the president's Office of Management and Budget.

———

IN A DEMOCRACY, people do not live in echo chambers or information cocoons. They see and hear a wide range of topics and ideas. They do so even if they did not, and would not, choose to see and to hear those topics and those ideas in advance. These claims raise serious questions about certain uses of new technologies, above all the Internet, and about the astonishing growth in the power to choose—to screen in and to screen out.

Louis Brandeis, one of America's greatest Supreme Court justices, insisted that the greatest threat to freedom is "an inert people." To avoid inertness, a democratic public must certainly be free from censorship. But the system of free expression must do far more than avoid censorship; it must ensure that people are exposed to competing perspectives. The idea of free speech has an affirmative side. It imposes constraints on what government may do, but it requires a certain kind of culture as well. (George

Orwell's *Nineteen Eighty-Four*, with its omnipresent, choice-denying Big Brother, is the most familiar vision of democracy's defeat; a more subtle vision is Aldous Huxley's *Brave New World*, with its pacified, choice-happy, formally free citizenry.) Members of a democratic public will not do well if they are unable to appreciate the views of their fellow citizens, or if they see one another as enemies or adversaries in some kind of war. . . .

In many respects, our communications market is rapidly moving in the direction of this [personalized news]. As of this writing, many newspapers, including the *Wall Street Journal*, allow readers to create "personalized" electronic editions, containing exactly what they want, and excluding what they do not want.

If you are interested in getting help with the design of an entirely individual paper, you can consult an ever-growing number of sites, including individual.com (helpfully named!) and crayon.com (a less helpful name, but evocative in its own way). Reddit.com "learns what you like as you vote on existing links or submit your own!" Findory.com will help you to personalize not only news, but also blogs, videos, and podcasts. In its own enthusiastic words, "The more articles you click on, the more personalized Findory will look. Our Personalization Technology adapts the website to show you interesting and relevant information based on your reading habits."

If you put the words "personalized news" in any search engine, you will find vivid evidence of what is happening. Google News provides a case in point, with the appealing suggestion, "No one can read all the news that's published every day, so why not set up your page to show you the stories that best represent your interests?" And that is only the tip of the iceberg. Consider TiVo, the television recording system, which is designed to give "you the ultimate control over your TV viewing." TiVo will help you create "your personal TV line-up." It will also learn your tastes, so that it can "suggest other shows that you may want to record and watch based on your preferences." In reality, we are not so very far from complete personalization of the system of communications.

In 1995, MIT technology specialist Nicholas Negroponte prophesied the emergence of "the Daily Me"—a communications package that is personally designed, with each component fully chosen in advance. Negroponte's prophecy was not nearly ambitious enough. As it turns out, you don't need to create a Daily Me. Others can create it for you. If people know a little bit about you, they can discover, and tell you, what "people like you" tend to like—and they can create a Daily Me, just for you, in a matter of seconds.

Many of us are applauding these developments, which obviously increase fun, convenience, and entertainment. But in the midst of the applause, we should insist on asking some questions. How will the increasing power of private control affect democracy? How will the Internet and the explosion of communications options alter the capacity of citizens to govern themselves? What are the social preconditions for a well-functioning system of democratic deliberation, or for individual freedom itself?

My purpose . . . is to cast some light on these questions. I do so by emphasizing the most striking power provided by emerging technologies, *the growing power of consumers to "filter" what they see*. In the process of discussing this power, I will attempt to provide a better understanding of the meaning of freedom of speech in a democratic society.

A large part of my aim is to explore what makes for a well-functioning system of free expression. Above all, I urge that in a diverse society, such a system requires far more than restraints on government censorship and respect for individual choices. For the last decades, this has been the preoccupation of American law and politics, and in fact the law and politics of many other nations as well, including, for example, Germany, France, England, Italy, Russia, and Israel. Censorship is indeed the largest threat to democracy and freedom. But an exclusive focus on government censorship produces serious blind spots. In particular, a well-functioning system of free expression must meet two distinctive requirements.

First, people should be exposed to materials that they would not have chosen in advance. Unplanned, unanticipated encounters are central to democracy itself. Such encounters often involve topics and points of view that people have not sought out and perhaps find quite irritating. They are important partly to ensure against fragmentation and extremism, which are predictable outcomes of any situation in which like-minded people speak only with themselves. I do not suggest that government should force people to see things that they wish to avoid. But I do contend that in a democracy deserving the name, lives should be structured so that people often come across views and topics that they have not specifically selected.

Second, many or most citizens should have a range of common experiences. Without shared experiences, a heterogeneous society will have a much more difficult time in addressing social problems. People may even find it hard to understand one another. Common experiences, emphatically including the common experiences made possible by the media, provide a form of social glue. A system of communications that radically diminishes the number of such experiences will create a number of problems, not least because of the increase in social fragmentation.

As preconditions for a well-functioning democracy, these requirements hold in any large country. They are especially important in a heterogeneous nation, one that faces an occasional risk of fragmentation.
They have all the more importance as each nation becomes increasingly
global and each citizen becomes, to a greater or lesser degree, a "citizen of
the world." Consider, for example, the risks of terrorism, climate change,
and avian flu. A sensible perspective on these risks, and others like them, is
impossible to obtain if people sort themselves into echo chambers of their
own design. . . .

One of the more striking developments of the early twenty-first century has been the rise of weblogs, which can serve to elicit and aggregate
the information held by countless contributors. Weblogs, or "blogs," have
been growing at a truly astounding rate—so much so that any current
account will rapidly grow out of date. As of the present writing, there are
over 55 million blogs, and over 40,000 new ones are created each day,
with a new one every 2.2 seconds. (Question: How many blogs are created in the time it takes to read a short book?) In recent years, the most
highly rated political blogs—including Atrios, Instapundit, and the Daily
Kos—have received over tens of thousands of visitors *each day*.

You can easily find blogs on countless subjects. Often, of course, the
real topic is the life of the author, in an unintended reimagining of the
idea of the Daily Me; one survey finds that "the typical blog is written by
a teenage girl who uses it twice a month to update her friends and class-
mates on happenings in her life." Political blogs are a small percentage of
the total, but they are plentiful, and they seem to be having a real influence on people's beliefs and judgments. In my own field of law, there are
numerous blogs, and some of them are often quite good. For example, the
Volokh Conspiracy and Balkinization offer clear and illuminating analyses
of legal questions, often with amazing speed.

For most of those who write and read them, blogs can be a lot of fun.
And if countless people are maintaining their own blogs, they should be
able to act as fact-checkers and as supplemental information sources, not
only for one another but also for prominent members of the mass media.
If hundreds of thousands of people are reading the most prominent blogs,
then errors should be corrected quickly. No one doubts that the blogosphere enables interested readers to find an astounding range of opinions
and facts.

If the blogosphere is working well, we might understand it in two different ways. First, we might believe that the blogosphere serves as a huge
market, in a way that supports the claims of those who claim that free
markets can help society to obtain the widely dispersed information that

individuals have. Second, we might think that the blogosphere operates as a kind of gigantic town meeting, in a way that fits well with the claims of those who speak of the operation of the well-functioning public sphere. On this second view, the world of blogs is helping to improve the operation of deliberative democracy, because it involves a great deal of citizen involvement and because arguments are often supported by facts and reasons. These two understandings of the blogosphere lie behind many of the contemporary celebrations. Are the celebrations warranted? . . .

True enough, many blogs aggregate a lot of information; instapundit .com, for example, assembles material from many sources. We might even consider the most elite bloggers, who gather material from elsewhere in the blogosphere, as an aggregating mechanism of sorts. Daniel Drezner and Henry Farrell have shown that because of the networked structure of the blogosphere, "only a few blogs are likely to become focal points," but those few blogs "offer both a means of filtering interesting blog posts from less interesting ones, and a focal point at which bloggers with interesting posts and potential readers of these posts can coordinate." But . . . some of the elite or "focal point" bloggers have their own biases. Many of them are primarily interested in cherry-picking items of opinion or information that reinforce their preexisting views. In other words, we lack a blog that succeeds in correcting errors and assembling truths. Those who consult blogs will learn a great deal, but they will have a tough time separating falsehoods from facts.

There is another point. Participants in the blogospere often lack an economic incentive. If they spread falsehoods, or simply offer their opinion, they usually sacrifice little or nothing. Maybe their reputation will suffer, but maybe not; maybe the most dramatic falsehoods will draw attention and hence readers. True, some bloggers attract advertising, and they have a stake in preserving their credibility. But most bloggers do not, and it is hardly clear that the best way to attract advertising revenues is to tell the truth. Many advertisers on political blogs are themselves trying to sell products designed to appeal to those with strong partisan beliefs. They are unlikely to object to exaggerations and semifalsehoods that appeal to the prejudices of their target audiences.

By their very nature, blogs offer rival and contentious positions on facts as well as values. In many ways, this is a virtue. People who are curious can find a wide range of views, including those that oppose their own. But if truth is to emerge, it is because of the competition of the marketplace of ideas, and this particular marketplace is far from perfect. One of the undeniable effects of blogs is to spread misunderstandings and mistakes. This point leads to another possible understanding of blogs, closely connected to my central concerns here—an understanding that is rooted in the idea of deliberative democracy. . . .

. . . Certainly it can be said that as compared to many alternatives, the blogosphere is both "public and inclusive," and grants communication rights to countless participants. Perhaps the blogosphere can be said to operate, at least to some degree, in this idealized fashion, in a way that will promote the emergence of "the better argument."

In view of what we know about group polarization, however, it should be clear that this happy view of the blogosphere faces a big problem. Drezner and Farrell emphasize its networked structure, in which ideas from less popular blogs can "bubble up" to much larger audiences. But a serious question is whether people are mostly reading blogs that conform to their own preexisting beliefs. If so, the truth is not likely to emerge, and polarization is nearly inevitable. Liberals, reading liberal blogs, will end up being more liberal; conservatives will become more conservative if they restrict themselves to conservative blogs. . . .

It is entirely reasonable to think that something of this kind finds itself replicated in the blogosphere every day. Indeed some bloggers, and many readers of blogs, try to create echo chambers. Because of self-sorting, people are often reading like-minded points of view, in a way that can breed greater confidence, more uniformity within groups, and more extremism. Note in this regard that shared identities are often salient on the blogosphere, in a way that makes polarization both more likely and more likely to be large. On any day of any year, it is easy to find unjustified rage, baseless attacks on people's motivations, and ludicrous false statements of fact in the blogosphere. From the democratic point of the view, this is nothing to celebrate.

Of course the quality of bloggers is immensely variable, and some of them are very good, in part because they take account of reasonable counterarguments. . . . Information aggregation is likely to work best when many minds are involved, but it is also important that reasons and information are being exchanged in a way that can lead to corrections and real creativity. To some extent, this is happening already. I have not denied that we are better off with blogs than without them. But it is a big stretch to celebrate blogs as an incarnation of deliberative ideals. . . .

One study explores the degree to which conservative and liberal bloggers are interacting with each other. Focusing on 1,400 blogs, the study finds that 91 percent of the links are to like-minded sites. Hence the two sides sort themselves into identifiable communities. For example, power lineblog.com, a conservative blog, has links from only twenty-five liberal blogs—but from 195 conservative blogs. Dailykos.com, a liberal blog, has links from 46 conservative blogs—but from 292 liberal blogs. In the aggregate, the behavior of conservative bloggers is more noteworthy in this regard; they link to one another far more often and in a denser pattern. The study's authors also examined about 40 "A-List" blogs, and here too they found a great deal of segregation. Sources were cited almost exclusively by one side or the other. Those sites with identifiable political commitments, such as Salon.com and NationalReview.com, were almost always cited by blogs on the same side of the political spectrum. . . .

The general conclusion is that in the blogosphere, there is a significant divide between politically identifiable communities. Liberals link mostly to liberals and conservatives link mostly to conservatives. Much of the time, they do not even discuss the same topics. Of course, it is true that many people are using the blogosphere not to strengthen their antecedent convictions, and not to waste their time, but to learn about different views and new topics. The blogosphere increases the range of available information and perspectives, and this is a great virtue, above all for curious and open-minded people. There are networks here with multiple connections, not entirely segregated communities. But if linking behavior on blogs can be taken as a proxy for how people are using the blogosphere, it is reasonable to think that many readers are obtaining one-sided views of political issues. For many people, blunders, confusion, and extremism are highly likely, not in spite of the blogosphere but because of it.

80

DIANA MUTZ

How the Mass Media Divide Us

How the mass media divide us is by entertaining us with TV shows that are built on bitter debate, sharp disagreement, and angry confrontation. This makes for exciting shows but has negative consequences for American politics. When people watch these uncivil exchanges, Professor Diana Mutz believes, they become more extreme in their political views. Mutz, an expert in communications and political psychology, has conducted some interesting studies to substantiate her thesis. Perhaps you don't remember when former Senator Zell Miller told commentator Chris Matthews that he'd like to meet him in a duel: Hardball was definitely memorable that night! Perhaps C-SPAN's talking heads, who discuss issues calmly and drone on too long, are not very entertaining, but they would be more beneficial to political dialogue. There are many factors behind the polarization that has characterized American politics in the past decades, and Mutz has identified an important one.

——

"SHOUT-SHOW" TELEVISION has been the target of a tremendous amount of criticism from many quarters, academic and otherwise. The world of political disagreement as witnessed through the lens of political talk shows is quite polarized. Increased competition for audiences has led many programs on political topics to liven themselves up in order to increase audience size. Thus, political talk shows such as *The McLaughlin Group, The O'Reilly Factor, Meet the Press, Capital Gang, Hardball,* and many others tend to involve particularly intense and heated exchanges.

The issue of contentiousness and incivility in political discourse was brought to a head in October 2004, when *Daily Show* host Jon Stewart appeared on *Crossfire* and openly criticized this program (and others like it) for its "partisan hackery," which Stewart said was "hurting America." Is there any truth to Stewart's claim? Aside from the obvious distastefulness some find in watching politicians scream, yell, and interrupt one another for thirty minutes or more, how is this kind of in-your-face politics implicated as a potential cause of mass polarization?

The tendency on television is to highlight more emotionally extreme and less polite expressions of opinion, and research suggests that these expressions of incivility may have important consequences for attitudes toward the opposition. These consequences flow from the fact that politeness and civility are more than mere social norms; they are means of demonstrating mutual respect. In other words, uncivil discourse increases polarization by helping partisans think even less of their opponents than they already did.

And yet market forces seem to favor the kind of television that encourages polarization. Polarized political discourse and an angry opposition makes for compelling television. Viewers may claim that they find it disgusting, but they cannot help watching—just as passing motorists cannot help "rubbernecking" when there is an accident alongside the highway. It is not that people actually *enjoy* what they are seeing, but there is something about information of this kind—information about life and death, about conflict and warring tribes in a dispute—that makes it difficult to ignore. Evolutionary psychologists have pointed to the adaptive advantage of having brains that automatically pay attention to conflict as a means of staying alive in an earlier era. At a cognitive level, of course, no one really expects to be caught in the "crossfire" of a televised partisan shout-fest. But even when it is "only television," and thus poses no real threat of bodily harm, people cannot help but watch and react to incivility.

My own research suggests that psychologists are correct about the demands of incivility on human attentional processes. To examine the difference that incivility makes independent of political content, I produced a mock political talk show—on a professional television set using professional actors as congressional candidates. The candidates espoused the same issue positions and made exactly the same arguments for and against various issue positions in two different versions of the program. In one discussion, however, they raised their voices, rolled their eyes, and engaged in an impolite, uncivil exchange. In the civil version of the program, they spoke calmly, refrained from interrupting one another, and showed mutual respect simply by obeying the social norms for polite discourse.

The differences in viewer reactions to the two programs were startling. The group randomly assigned to the uncivil version of the political discussion came away with roughly the same feelings toward their preferred candidate as those in the civil group. But attitudes toward the "other side" became much more intensely negative when the two exchanged views in an uncivil manner. The more dramatic, uncivil exchanges encouraged a more black-and-white view of the world: their candidate was not just the best; the alternative was downright evil.

This effect was evident for partisans on both sides of the political spectrum and regardless of which candidate they liked best. Interestingly, watching the uncivil version led to greater polarization in perceptions of "us" versus "them," relative to a control group, but watching the civil version of the exchange led to *decreased* levels of polarization. This pattern of findings suggests that political television has the potential to *improve* as well as to exacerbate the divide among partisans of opposing views; it simply depends upon how those differences of opinion are aired. When differences of opinion are conveyed in a manner that suggests mutual respect, viewers are able to understand and process the rationales on the other side and are less likely to see the opposition in starkly negative terms. Differences of opinion are perceived as having some legitimate and reasonable basis. But when those same views and rationales are expressed in an uncivil manner, people respond with an emotional, gut-level reaction, rejecting the opposition as unfairly and viciously attacking one's cherished views.

Using indicators of physiological response, my studies also demonstrate that televised incivility causes viewers' levels of emotional arousal to increase, just as they do when people encounter face-to-face incivility. In the face of real-world conflict, this reaction supposedly serves a functional purpose—participants are given the rush of adrenaline they may need to flee the situation. But with televised incivility, this kind of reaction serves no purpose; it is simply a remnant of brains that have not adapted to twentieth-century representational technology.

Even though viewers are just third-party observers of other people's conflicts on television, they show heightened levels of emotional arousal, just as people do when encountering face-to-face disagreement. This is not so surprising if one considers how it feels to be a third-party observer of a couple's argument at a dinner party. The same discomfort, awkwardness, and tension exist, even for those not directly involved in the conflict. Likewise, when political commentator Robert Novak stormed off the set of a live broadcast of CNN's *Inside Politics* in August 2004, viewers were uncomfortable—and they paid attention. The tension was palpable to viewers, even though few may be able to remember what the substance of the conflict was.

The heightened arousal produced by incivility can make it difficult to process the substance of the exchange. Some arousal helps to call attention to what otherwise might be considered bland and uninteresting. But at extremely high levels of arousal, people will remember only the emotional content of the program (who screamed at whom, who stomped off in a pique) and recall little of the substance of the disagreement. As anyone who has ever had an argument knows, there is a point at which the emotional content of the exchange overwhelms any potential for rational discourse. As a result, viewers gain little understanding of the other side. They perceive their own side of the debate as unfairly attacked, and thus the incivility their own candidate displays is simply an appropriate level of righteous indignation in reaction to an unprovoked attack. The incivility demonstrated by the opponent demonstrates that he is a raving lunatic, wholly unfit for office.

In addition to this disdain for the opposing side, incivility produces a second important reaction—heightened attention. As Bill O'Reilly, host of *The O'Reilly Factor*, suggests, "If a radio producer can find someone who eggs on conservative listeners to spout off and prods liberals into shouting back, he's got a hit show. The best host is the guy or gal who can get the most listeners extremely annoyed—over and over and over again." Evidently, these sorts of shows have hooked Senator Hillary Rodham Clinton (D-N.Y.), who indicated that she and her husband Bill now have TiVo, a technology that allows a viewer to record and replay television programs. And for what purpose do the senator and the former president use TiVo? According to Senator Clinton, they use it to record the most outrageous statements made by their political opponents so they can play them over and over and yell back at the television. An optimist might regard this vignette as an example of how viewers are *not* necessarily selectively exposing themselves to politically compatible media. But the pessimist would undoubtedly point out that yet another media mechanism of polarization has kicked in to take its place. Uncivil political discourse that produces such strong emotional reactions is unlikely to further the cause of political moderation.

Controlled laboratory studies suggest, for better or worse, that O'Reilly is correct: incivility is extremely entertaining and people like to watch it, even if it is just to scream back. Despite the fact that many viewers claim to be repulsed by it, the respondents who viewed the identical but uncivil version of the same program always rated it as more entertaining, found it more exciting to watch, and indicated a greater desire to see the uncivil program again than the civil version. Polite conversation is boring, and the deliberative ideal for political discourse makes for dull television. "I acknowledge there are some good points on my opponent's side" will probably never make good television, whereas "These evil people must be stopped!" always will.

With these findings in mind, it is important to consider the extent to which the rise of televised political incivility can help explain mass polarization. Is political discourse truly any more uncivil now than in the past? Some have suggested that the United States is in the midst of a "civility crisis" in its public life. As then University of Pennsylvania president Judith Rodin argued in 1996, "Across America and increasingly around the world, from campuses to the halls of Congress, to talk radio and network TV, social and political life seem dominated today by incivility. . . . No one seems to question the premise that political debate has become too extreme, too confrontational, too coarse." Similar calls for greater civility in political discourse have come from a wide array of scholars, as well as from philanthropic organizations. . . .

Clearly, there is a widespread perception that political discourse is much more uncivil now than in the past, but there is little historical evidence to confirm such a trend. As then senator Zell Miller (D-Ga.) implied when he wistfully said he would like to challenge *Hardball* host Chris Matthews to a duel, violence among political opponents was once far more common than it is now. Senator Miller's statement was made during an uncivil exchange between himself and a journalist during the 2004 Republican National Convention. It made headlines, precisely because the idea of using weapons to resolve political differences seemed absurd. We have not had a duel to the death among politicians for many years, and thus one could easily characterize today's political talk shows as mild by comparison.

So is it fair to say that incivility is on the rise in political discourse? There is no definitive answer to this question, but the increased *visibility* of uncivil conflicts on television seems indisputable. Although politicians of past eras may frequently have exchanged harsh words, without television cameras there to record these events and to replay them for a mass audience their impact on public perceptions was probably substantially lower. The dominance of television as a source of exposure to politics suggests that public exposure to uncivil political discourse has increased. Moreover, it is one thing to read about political pundits' or candidates' contrary views in the press, and quite another to witness them directly engaged in vituperative argument. The sensory realism of television conveys a sense of intimacy with political actors that people were unlikely to encounter in the past, even among the few lucky enough to have face-to-face meetings.

Television provides a uniquely intimate perspective on conflict. In the literature on human proxemics, the distance deemed appropriate for face-to-face interactions with public figures in American culture is more than twelve feet. Yet exposure to politicians on television gives the appearance of being much closer. When people are arguing, the tendency is to back off and put greater space between those who disagree. Instead, when political conflicts flare up on television, cameras tend to go in for tighter and tighter close-ups. This creates an intense experience for the viewers, one in which they view conflict from an unusually intimate perspective. Political scientist Jane J. Mansbridge has noted that when open political conflict occurs in real life, bringing people together in one another's presence can intensify their anger and aggression. To the extent that a television presence has similar effects, incivility is likely to encourage polarization. . . .

The underlying question that still needs to be confronted—by scholars as well as those in the media business—is how to make a topic that is not inherently interesting to many Americans nonetheless exciting to watch. And if the answer is not behind-the-scenes coverage of election strategy, or mudslinging on political talk shows, or partisan extremists rallying the troops, then what will keep those politically marginal citizens from watching movies on cable instead?

81

RUSSELL PETERSON

From *Strange Bedfellows*

The "strange bedfellows" here are political news and late-evening comedy programs on TV. Do you, young readers, get most of your news from the witty satire that captivates viewers who stay up late for information and fun, rolled into one? "What are we laughing at, and why?" asks Russell Peterson. Using examples from the 2004 election, Peterson assesses the standards of the comedy that viewers enjoy. The funniest material is really a knock against politics and politicians. The jokes make fun of the quirks of people who are in politics and of the entire democratic system that's hopelessly inept. Peterson then turns to Saturday Night Live, *a show that has been an integral part of political campaigns—maybe unwittingly—for decades. You yourself can bring this excerpt up to date, adding the examples of* Saturday Night Live's *Tina Fey imitating 2008 vice presidential candidate Sarah Palin, or David Letterman's 2009 feud with Gov. Palin over a tasteless joke about her daughter.*

———

POLITICS, SAYS THE OLD CLICHÉ, makes strange bedfellows. So too with comedy and news; yet in the bleary late-night haze the twenty-four-hour urgency of CNN, Fox, and MSNBC blurs into the bubbling frivolity of Jay and Dave and *The Daily Show* in a strangely intimate way. It would be too glib simply to say that you can no longer tell where the news leaves off and the comedy begins, though in fact there are plenty of people saying just that. A survey conducted by the Pew Center for the People and the Press in 2004 found that 61 percent of people under the age of thirty got some of their political "news" from late-night comedy shows. This survey (which the Pew people have conducted in each presidential cycle since 1996) has provided the premise for a number of news stories raising concerns about the younger generation's information diet: by getting information directly from topical comics, the metaphorical argument goes, they are skipping their spinach and going straight for the pumpkin pie.

At the same time, the nutritional value of the news itself has come into some doubt. News programming is, according to the consensus, becoming almost indistinguishable from entertainment programming. With its snappy theme songs, soap-operatic continuities (Laci Peterson, runaway brides, the life and death of Anna Nicole Smith*), and a cast of characters ranging from photogenic newsreaders to egomaniacal pundits, contemporary television journalism rivals, in its shallowness and sensationalism, the finest works of the late Aaron Spelling. From the parapets of the Pew Center and other such watchtowers of serious discourse, the prospects for maintaining an informed electorate look bleak indeed. On the one hand, it's terrible how people choose entertainment over the news; on the other hand, *what* news?

The individual viewer, however, might see the blurring of the info/tainment boundary from a different perspective and ask: what difference does it make? The news says the system is broken, our leaders are crooks, and there's not a damn thing I can do about it. Comedians tell me the same thing, but at least they do it in a funny way. A vicious cycle of trivialization and cynicism is set in motion: people are focusing on the wrong things (Tom Cruise's sex life, high-speed car chases, *American Idol*), but the things they should be paying attention to (global warming, the trade deficit, the terrorist threat) are so beset by special-interest influence, partisan gridlock, and leaders who put their political survival ahead of the public good—that knowing about them wouldn't help anyway. Hell, we might as well laugh—gimme that remote.

Yet late-night comedy does more than simply induce apathy and dumb down our discourse. It adds its own dimensions to the interpretation of current events, even as it shuts out others. . . .

Topical comedy, in short, is not simply an inadequate substitute for the news; for good and for ill, it adds something of its own to our understanding of current events. Moreover, the problem is less that we pay it too much attention than that we don't pay it enough; after all, a joke—as Aristotle, Sigmund Freud, Henri Bergson, and the myriad other "serious" thinkers who have turned their minds to such matters would tell you—is rarely just a joke. On the one hand, not all late-night political humor deserves to be called "trivial." On the other hand, not all of it deserves to be called "political." (Some of it doesn't even deserve to be called "humor.") We ought to consider the subject in all its complexity. Above all, we ought to understand it for what it is, not just for what it isn't. Rather than simply

---

*Laci Peterson was a young woman whose husband was convicted of murdering her in a sensational 2005 trial in California. Also, in 2005, a Georgia woman ran away days before her wedding, garnering immense media attention by falsely claiming that she had been kidnapped. Anna Nicole Smith, Playboy model and celebrity personality, died in 2007, allegedly from a mixture of several prescription drugs.

dismissing this phenomenally popular genre as a symptom of civic decay or a cause of electoral apathy, we ought to be asking: what are we laughing at, and why? ...

While genuine satire arises from a sense of outrage, the topical jokes heard in mainstream late-night monologues are rooted in mere cynicism. Unlike satire, which scolds and shames, this kind of comedy merely shrugs. ...

The difference is easier to discern if we go back to a presidential election year. So pick up that remote, hit rewind, and keep going, all the way back to 2004:

> Political pundits are saying President George W. Bush has made gains in two key states: dazed and confused. (Letterman)

> You see the pictures in the paper today of John Kerry windsurfing? ... Even his hobby depends on which way the wind blows. (Leno)

> Earlier today, President Bush said Kerry will be a tough and hard-charging opponent. That explains why Bush's nickname for Kerry is "Math." (O'Brien)

> Kerry was here in Los Angeles. He was courting the Spanish vote by speaking Spanish. And he showed people he could be boring in two languages. (Leno)

A larger sampling would prove, as this selection suggests, that the political jokes told by network late-night hosts aim, cumulatively, for a bipartisan symmetry. Although election season "joke counts" maintained by the Center for Media and Public Affairs do not show a perfect one-to-one balance of jokes aimed at Democratic and Republican nominees, as the election got closer, a rough equity emerged, suggesting that George W. Bush was no more or less dumb than John Kerry was boring. So it is in every presidential election year. Even in between, care is taken to target the abuse at "both sides," even if, during the Bush years, it has often meant resorting to time-worn Monica Lewinsky jokes. Maintaining this equilibrium is understood as one of the ground rules of the genre—a tenet so well established that an industry-specific cliché has arisen to describe those who embrace it: "equal-opportunity offenders."

The phrase, or the ideal it expresses, is typically brandished by late-night comics as a shield against charges of bias. But it is a paradigm embraced even more fervently by journalists who write about comedy. Bill Maher, Robin Williams, and Carlos Mencia—even an Israeli/Lebanese comedy team who bill their show as "The Arab-Israeli Comedy Hour"— have been celebrated in press accounts as equal-opportunity offenders. Being branded an EOO by the journalistic establishment is something like getting the Good Housekeeping Seal of Approval, though the honor is bestowed with some subjectivity. . . .

Journalists' peculiar devotion to the equal-opportunity offender ideal results from a tendency to project their own profession's standards of objectivity onto comedians. Expecting Jay Leno to play by the same rules as Anderson Cooper is a bit like squeezing apples to get orange juice, but conventional wisdom seems to take this conflation of journalistic and comedic ethics for granted—the Pew poll, after all, asks its respondents to consider *The Tonight Show* and CNN side by side. Comedians' own reasons for maintaining balance, however, have little to do with abstract notions of fairness; it's more a matter of pragmatism than idealism. As Jay Leno put it, once a comedian takes a political side, "you've lost half the crowd already." These guys are in show *business,* after all, and it doesn't pay to alienate 50 percent of your potential viewers. Such bottom-line considerations, incidentally, help explain why *The Colbert Report* and *The Daily Show* can afford to be more politically "risky" than Leno's: a little over a million viewers—a narrowly interested but loyal core—amounts to a pretty respectable audience for a cable show like the *Report,* but for *The Tonight Show,* which averages six million viewers nightly, it would be a disaster.

The bigger difference between the network and cable shows' humor has to do with what the jokes say, not how many of them are aimed at Democrats versus Republicans. On closer examination, the only political thing about the mainstream jokes quoted above is that they happen to be about politicians. They are personality jokes, not that different from the ones those same comedians tell about Paris Hilton or Ozzy Osbourne—just replace "dumb" and "boring" with "slutty" and "drug-addled." And unlike [Stephen] Colbert's jokes about Bush's inflexibility or his tendency to think with his "gut," the jokes told on the network shows rarely transcend the level of pure ad hominem mockery to consider how such personal traits might manifest themselves in terms of policy.

The bottom line of all the jokes about Bush's dumbness, Kerry's dullness, Al Gore's stiffness, Bob Dole's "hey-you-kids-get-outta-my-yard" crankiness, and so on is that all politicians are created equal—equally unworthy, that is—and that no matter who wins the election, the American people lose. Thus, despite their efforts to play it safe by offending equally (and superficially), the mainstream late-night comics actually present an extremely bleak and cynical view of American democracy.

What, then, is the secret of their appeal? Why do millions of us tune in, night after night, to be told—not overtly, but insinuatingly and consistently—that our cherished system of self-government is a joke? Perhaps because this confirms what we have always suspected: democracy is a nice idea but not, ultimately, a practical one. And if Americans doubt democracy, we hate politics. Politics is treated like an infection, or a tumor. It is to be avoided if possible, and when found lurking—in a sitcom writers' room, in an Oscar acceptance speech, in the funnies (*Doonesbury* has been exiled to the editorial pages of many of the papers that carry it)—it must be excised before it can infect the nation's body non-politic. Politics is *icky*.

Even our politicians disdain politics. A candidate can't go wrong by running against Washington, D.C., and all that it supposedly stands for. George W. "I'm from Texas" Bush successfully campaigned as an anti-establishment "outsider"—and his dad was the president! Ronald Reagan got applause when he proclaimed that government was not the solution, but the problem—though he himself had just campaigned for, and achieved, the government's top job.

Most Americans see nothing strange in this; for as much as we like to wave the flag, and pledge our allegiance to the republic for which it stands, as a people we regard our government, its institutions, and its representatives (save those who take care to inoculate themselves with anti-political rhetoric) with contempt. This feeling is reflected not only in our appallingly low voter turnout rates but also in our culture—particularly in our humor.

Which is why most of this country's "political" humor—from Artemus Ward to Will Rogers, from Johnny Carson to Jay Leno, from Andy Borowitz to JibJab.com—has in fact been *anti*-political. "All politics is applesauce," Rogers once said, by which he did not mean that it was a tasty side dish with pork chops. He meant that progress was the opposite of Congress, that the Democrats were worse than any other party except for the Republicans and vice versa, that six of one was half a dozen of the other. Will Rogers was an equal-opportunity offender.

Rogers's observation that "both parties have their good and bad times . . . they are each good when they are out, and . . . bad when they are in" reappears almost seventy years later as Jay Leno's characterization of the 2000 election as a choice between "the lesser of two weasels." It appears again, in an "edgier" guise, when the *South Park* kids are given the opportunity to learn about democracy by nominating and voting for a new school mascot: "We're supposed to vote between a giant douche and a turd sandwich," Stan tells his parents, "I just don't see the point." His parents react with shocked sanctimony: "Stanley," scolds his mother, "do you know how many people died so you could have the right to vote?" Mom just doesn't get it.

Whether the metaphor describes electoral choice as a contest between a pair of rodents or between a feminine hygiene product and a piece of excrement, it's the same old joke. Anti-political humor is everywhere; clean or dirty, hip or square, as told by professionals over the airwaves and amateurs over the cubicle divider. In fact, what I think of as the quintessential anti-political joke is one I heard not from any television show but from my dad—and although this version dates from 1980, all that is necessary to make it work in any other presidential election year is to change the names:

Q: If Jimmy Carter, Ronald Reagan, and John Anderson [that year's third-party threat] were all in a rowboat in the middle of the ocean, and the boat flipped over, who would be saved?

A: The United States. . . .

The implications of the rowboat riddle are fairly grim: no choice would be better than the choices we have, and anyone who would presume to be worthy of the people's vote deserves to drown like a rat. Yet this nihilistic punch line is no more than a crystallization of the message repeated night after night, joke after joke, by Jay, Dave, and Conan. Late-night's anti-political jokes are implicitly anti-democratic. They don't criticize policies for their substance, or leaders for their official actions (as opposed to their personal quirks, which have little to do with politics per se); taken as a whole, they declare the entire system—from voting to legislating to governing—an irredeemable sham. . . .

In spite of its anti-democratic implications, anti-politics (and anti-political humor) is itself a bedrock American tradition: a contrarian habit as old as the republic itself. Atop this foundation of anti-political disdain, we have in recent decades been building a towering Fortress of Irony, reaching, by the turn of the twenty-first century, a point where it seems as if every communication is enclosed in air quotes. In contemporary America, sincerity is suspect, commitment is lame, and believing in stuff is for suckers.

Late-night comics did not invent the air-quote culture, anymore than they invented our anti-political sentiments, but they have played a leading role in proselytizing this cynical message. Election after election, night after night, joke after joke, they have reinforced the notion that political participation is pointless, parties and candidates are interchangeable, and democracy is futile.

This is not to suggest that comedy that takes politics as its subject matter is inherently destructive. Mocking our elected representatives and our institutions is an American birthright, and exercising that right is worthwhile, if only to maintain it. The problem is not the presence, or even the proliferation, of political comedy per se. The problem is that too little of it is actually "political" in any meaningful way. Genuine political satire, like good investigative journalism, can function as democracy's feedback loop. It can illuminate injustices, point out hypocrisy, and tell us when our government is not living up to its ideals, thereby raising the awareness that is the first step toward alleviating any of these problems. Real satire—such as Colbert's excoriation of the press and the president—sounds the alarm: something is wrong, people must be held to account, things must be made right. Anti-political humor—the far more common kind, practiced by Leno, Letterman, and O'Brien, among others—merely says, resignedly, "Eh, what are you gonna do?" . . .

"Satire," George S. Kaufman once quipped, "is what closes Saturday night." As the co-author of several of the American stage's most successful comedies, Kaufman presumably knew what he was talking about. The folks who buy the tickets just want to laugh, not think.

But if satire closes Saturday night, how do we explain *Saturday Night Live*'s thirty-two-year run? And what about the rest of the week's late-night lineup? Don't Jay, Dave, Conan, Kimmel, and what's-his-face with the Scottish accent joke about current events? Don't they regularly make fun of Republicans, Democrats, Congress, the president? Isn't *that* satire?

Not necessarily. The critical distinction between genuine satire and pseudo-satire has less to do with content than with *intent*. To put it another way, while the genuine satirist and the pseudo-satirist are both joking, only one of them is kidding. Real satire means it. The problem with this definition is that there is no way to objectively measure sincerity—the Mean-It-o-Meter has yet to be invented. And simply asking is no good: a professional comedian, whether he is a satirist or not, will deny having a "message" as a matter of course—it's part of the code. . . .

"If men were angels," James Madison famously observed, "no government would be necessary." And if politicians were angels, no satire would be necessary. That they are not is only to be expected—the people they represent aren't angels, either. But our representatives' foibles and our system's flaws—like our own human imperfection—are no cause for despair, or for cynicism. They are, and ever will be, cause for humility, for vigilance, and—whether as a corrective or merely a balm—for laughter.

82

BRADLEY PATTERSON

From *The White House Staff*:
The Advance Office

Never on screen, not even allowed to snack from the "reporters' buffet," the White House advance team is charged with planning every presidential visit down to the last detail. After reading this account of the painstaking attention to detail required to make a trip successful and memorable, the two minutes of footage of a presidential visit on the nightly news will never seem the same again. In this excerpt, Bradley Patterson describes the many elements that go into presidential travel, from security to transportation to celebration: "three thousand balloons are recommended," notes the author. And don't forget the president's plane. Some people, Patterson discovers, will show up at the airport only to see Air Force One. The advance team must make sure everything goes exactly as planned, including "The Moment" that sticks forever in the minds of the crowd and, the team hopes, that appears on page one of every newspaper.

———

PRESIDENTS NEVER stay home. From Shawnee Mission High School to the emperor's palace, from the Kentucky State Fair to the Kremlin, the president of the United States is visitor in chief, representing now his government, now his party, now all the people of the nation. As chief of state, he has words of encouragement for the National Association of Student Councils; as chief partisan, he addresses a Senate candidate's closing rally; as national spokesman, he stands on the cliff above Normandy Beach; and as chief diplomat, he spends weary hours at the Wye Retreat Center, extracting tenuous Middle East peace agreements from skeptical antagonists. The lines between his roles are of course never quite that distinct: in each place he travels, the president is all these "chiefs" at once.

His national and political roles are public and he wants them to be so: cameras and the press are invited to witness every handshake, film each ceremony, record all the ringing words. A presidential trip is often substantive, but it is also always theater: each city an act, every stop a scene. As the Secret Service recognizes, however, in any balcony can lurk a John Wilkes Booth, at any window a Lee Harvey Oswald; a Sara Jane Moore or a John Hinckley may emerge from any crowd.* One other presidential role is quintessential but usually more concealed: as commander in chief, the American president must always—no matter where he is in the world—be able to reach his national security command centers.

A presidential trip, therefore, is not a casual sojourn: it is a massive expedition, its every mile planned ahead, its every minute preprogrammed. The surge of cheering thousands must stop just short of a moving cocoon of security; curtained behind each VIP receiving line is the military aide with the "doomsday briefcase." Except for the military aide with the "satchel," all of the first lady's travel presents similar requirements for minute care and advance attention.

These massive expeditions are the responsibility of the White House Advance Office. How large a job is this? In seven years in office, President Clinton made some 2,500 appearances in over 800 foreign or domestic cities or destinations, plus some 450 appearances at public events in the Washington area. The pace of the work in the Advance Office was nothing short of breathtaking.

While each chief executive's travel style is different, trip preparations are similar; the art of "advancing" is common to presidency after presidency, although new technological gadgetry has made the whole trip-preparation process swifter and more efficient.

Within any White House staff, trip planning calls for intricate choreography among more than a dozen separate offices: cabinet affairs, communications, domestic policy, intergovernmental, legislative, medical, military, national security (if the trip is overseas), scheduling, political, public liaison, press, Secret Service, social, speechwriting, transportation, the vice president's office, and the first lady's staff. The Advance Office is the orchestrator of this cluster and the manager of all the forthcoming on-scene arrangements.

How does the Advance Office organize a presidential trip? . . .

A domestic presidential visit can get its start from any one of the hundreds of invitations that pour into the White House, but more likely it originates from within, as a homegrown idea. What policy themes is the president emphasizing? To which areas of American life does he wish to draw attention? Educational excellence, industrial competitiveness, athletic prowess, racial harmony, minority achievement, environmental improvement . . . ? At campaign time, of course, electoral issues are foremost: What voters are targeted, which senators need help?

*Booth assassinated President Abraham Lincoln. Oswald, at least according to official findings, was the assassin of President John Kennedy. Moore and Hinckley made assassination attempts on Presidents Gerald Ford and Ronald Reagan, respectively.—Eds.

Like the daily schedule . . . , a trip is not a casual event but a calculated piece of a larger theme—and, as such, is designed to convey a message. A presidential trip, in other words, is an instrument of persuasion.

Forward planning for domestic presidential trips may be done from four to eight weeks in advance but is more likely compressed into an even shorter lead time. As soon as the desired message is framed and agreed to, through discussions within the White House, the Advance Office reviews the choices for domestic travel: Where in the country can the presidential theme best be dramatized? Which groups, which sponsors, which cities or towns? What already-scheduled local event could the president join, transforming it into an illustration of his own policy initiative? Local and state calendars are scanned, the *Farmer's Almanac* is studied. Invitations are searched, private suggestions reviewed. Long lists are discussed with the Scheduling Office and vetted into short lists; tentative alternatives are identified. If the president is campaigning, all the processes mentioned here are melded together: the president may do twelve to eighteen events in a week.

For domestic trips, in previous years, "site surveys" would be undertaken perhaps six weeks ahead of time, and "pre-advance" teams would be sent out weeks beforehand. Money then became tighter and staffs smaller. The Bush Advance Office staff totaled eighteen; the Clinton White House had only twelve, four of whom were interns. Communications have speeded up as well. "Reactivity time"—that is, the period needed to respond to changes in circumstances—has dwindled, with the consequence that lead time for decisions may be greatly shortened, alterations more easily tolerated, last-minute revisions accepted. All arrangements can be more flexible; some can be consummated with only hours to spare. The final "go" decision, therefore, has sometimes been made as little as two weeks before the event—or less, as Clinton Advance Office director Paige Reffe described:

I was walking into an afternoon meeting in the deputy chief of staff's office that I thought was supposed to be about the first family's vacation . . . and the deputy turns to me and says, "By the way, we are thinking of the president going to New York at nine o'clock to meet with the TWA Flight 800 families." I said, "Nine o'clock when?" And she said, "Nine o'clock tomorrow morning," about eighteen hours from now. I said, "I didn't bring my top hat, I didn't bring my cane, and I don't have any rabbits to pull out today. . . . Let's stop *thinking* about this; there is a 5:30 P.M. flight to Kennedy; I can get people on that flight. I can actually get something set up if the decision is made in the next hour." In the end, sometimes those things are easier than normal events, because there isn't time for people to start picking them apart and making changes.

Floods, disasters, hurricane damage, funerals: a presidential presence is often required. But then the advance office looks less like a long-range-planning unit and more like a firehouse.

The White House counsel makes a key determination: Is any part of the trip for a clearly political purpose? Is the president going to be partisan in speech and act, or will he be entirely "presidential"? In scrupulous detail, all the proposed meetings, site events, rallies, and addresses are divided into rigid categories so that mathematically precise formulas can be used to allocate expenses between the political sponsors and the government: "21.7 percent of the trip is political, 78.3 percent is official," explains one illustrative memorandum. The counsel and the political affairs director sign off on the allocation. If the White House asks any federal political appointees to serve as volunteers on the advance team (which it often does), they must take annual leave if they work on any part of the trip that is political—and any expenses they incur must be paid for by the host political group or by party national headquarters.

Funding is a sensitive issue. There is a four-way division: (1) Assuming the trip is nonpolitical, the White House budget itself supports only the travel expenses of the advance teams and the presidential party (and its VIP guests), including the staff of the White House Press Office. (2) For any trip, political or not, the government covers those costs that relate to the president's security. In this category are the costs incurred by the White House Military Office (financed by the Department of Defense); this office covers the expenses of its medical personnel, military aides, and the White House Communications Agency (WHCA), which supplies lights and amplification equipment as well as its own ample communications gear. Also in this category are the costs incurred by the Secret Service (actually part of the Treasury Department), which has its own budget for travel and equipment (including the presidential limousine and other special cars). The Military Office's *Air Force One* will be supplied, but its costs must be reimbursed if the trip is political. (3) Members of the White House press corps pay for their own travel expenses (via reimbursement to the White House Travel Office). (4) All local "event" expenses must be borne by host groups: for example, the costs of renting a hall, constructing risers for the press, furnishing the stage backdrops, providing banners and hand-held signs, printing and sending out flyers, printing tickets, arranging for advertising, and providing motorcade vehicles for nonfederal dignitaries. A letter spelling out these financial obligations is sent to the host, who must send back a signed formal agreement.

The government's actual total cost for a domestic presidential trip is almost impossible to pin down, but it is high. No host group, political or otherwise, could afford all the charges, including those relating to security. Therefore, no matter what reimbursement is obtained, there is a significant publicly financed subsidy for any presidential expedition. It is simply the cost of having a president who travels.

Within the White House, an Advance Office "staff lead" is named who will head up all the advance work. In addition, a trip coordinator is designated—a stay-on-home-base "ringmaster" to whom the advance team's queries are directed and on whose desk all plans and all logistical details are centralized. "She is the lifeline for the advance people," explained Bush advance director John Keller. "Whenever the advance people call back to the office, that's the one they talk to."

Once the two lead people are designated, internal assignments are specified. It is a broad "ring": the Intergovernmental Affairs and Political Affairs Offices will recommend governors, mayors, or local officials to be asked to sit on the dais; the legislative affairs staff will identify the senators and representatives who would be affronted if they were not invited to accompany the president. If the trip is political, the political affairs director will compose a detailed list of themes that will gain a warm local reception, and of issues to avoid. The event will usually be designated as "open press"—but if not, the Press Office will organize a pool of the White House press corps, and the media relations unit will prepare credentials for the local press.

Speechwriters are at work, the medical staff makes its preparations, the Secret Service will ask its local field agents to supplement its regular presidential protective detail. WHCA will box up a mobile satellite sending and receiving station along with the president's armored "Blue Goose" podium. The Air Force will make sure that the local airport can handle the "footprint" of the huge 747 *Air Force One* and will stash two presidential limousines, the necessary Secret Service vehicles, and WHCA's "Roadrunner" communications van into a C-141 transport. If it is called for, the Marine Corps will add in HMX-1, one of the presidential helicopters.

The White House advance team itself is assembled. Headed by the staff lead, the team includes representatives from many of the offices just mentioned. Unless the occasion is unusually complicated, current practice is for the advance team for a domestic trip to leave the White House only six days before the president is scheduled to arrive (seven for a RON—"remain overnight"—visit). In what is likely to be a rather frantic final five days, the advance team must complete an unbelievably complicated checklist: one such list was twenty-six pages long and included 485 items.

The team visits the airport, draws (and faxes to Washington) rough site diagrams—showing where planes, helicopters, and cars will park—and reviews the planned arrival ceremonies. Who will the greeters be? (Each hand-shaker must be approved in Washington.) Are the toe strips in place to show the greeters where to stand? Where is the rope line? The team is admonished: "Inconvenience as few commercial airline passengers as possible." Not even a wheeled set of stairs needs to be commandeered; *Air Force One* has its own mobile stairs.

The motorcade is organized with minute precision. The advance team is reminded that "all the substantive success in the world can be overshadowed if those involved cannot get where they need to be." The motorcade may be the standard minimum of twenty-four vehicles or it may be a hundred cars long. Each car is labeled and spotted on the diagram; every driver must be approved by the Secret Service. The last two cars, which are called "stragglers," will pick up staff members who may have missed the departure; the stragglers can also be used as alternates in case of breakdowns. Motorcades used to be important for generating crowds of sidewalk spectators—but no longer. Primarily for security reasons, the line of cars speeds by: the onlookers not only don't see the president, they can't even figure out which limo he is in.

Each event site must be examined in detail: What will be the backdrop, the "storyboard"—that is, the picture that television will capture? "Distill the message into a brief and catchy phrase," advises the detail-conscious Advance Manual, but "you *do not* want shiny white letters on shiny yellow vinyl." This is not some "pizza-parlor's grand opening." Walking routes are plotted: for the president, the guests, the press, the staff, and the public (more diagrams). There must be a presidential "holding room" where he meets sponsors and guests. What will be the program? What kind of audience is expected—students? senior citizens? friendly? skeptical? How long will it take for them to go through the magnetometers? If hotel overnights are planned, floor plans are needed.

No team is without its conflicts. The press advance staffers want to have an airport arrival at high noon, big crowds, remarks, greetings, bands, balloons ascending, people pressing against the ropes. The Secret Service looks through different eyes. "If they had their way," commented one advance veteran, "they would have the president arrive after dark, in an out-of-the-way corner of the airport, put him into a Sherman tank, lead him to a bank, and have him spend the night in a vault." He added: "They would say, 'You cannot choose that route,' and we would counter, 'No, he *will* drive that avenue, you go ahead and protect him.'" Since the assassination attempt on Reagan, the Secret Service wins more of these battles.

There are conflicts with the local hosts as well: Who will sit on the dais? Will spaces be saved for the local as well as the national press? One sponsoring group for a fund-raiser had sold every seat on the floor of a gymnasium: the advance team had to insist that the tables and seats be squeezed together to make room for the camera platforms. There must be two sets of such risers: one facing the speaker and one at an angle in the rear, for over-the-shoulder "cutaway" shots of the president together with the audience he is addressing. With luck, the risers can be borrowed; the advance team is instructed: "Don't go cutting down virgin forest to build press risers for one-time-only use."

The White House advance person, the instructions make clear, is a diplomat-in-temporary-residence, "the mover and the shaker, the stroker and the cajoler, the smoother of ruffled feathers and the soother of hard feelings. The staff lead is the captain of a great team." But the captain is forewarned: shun all media interviews. "*Never* be a spokesman or go on the record with the press. . . . You are invisible to the camera. Your work is done just outside the four corners of the picture frame. You do not eat up an inch of the screen that is the canvas that you and your colleagues have designed to be a 'picture of the day.' You and your advance team colleagues are not the story, the *president's visit* is. . . . And don't snack on the buffet food which the working press has paid for. . . . But get the job done."

A former advance chief slyly recalls:

To be a successful advance person . . . you have to have that minor crooked side to you, and you have to be willing to do whatever you have to do. That doesn't nec-essarily mean breaking the law, but it means that you can't be shy and you have to be assertive. If I tell you to go find a podium, I know you're going to come back and you're going to find a podium. You may have just happened to have gotten it from that event three doors down, and they're wondering where their podium is right now, but the fallout had there not been a podium would be a hell of a lot bigger than somebody asking where the podium came from!

The advance team may include nongovernmental companions: tech-nical experts from the news networks, news photographers, and represen-tatives from the White House Correspondents Association. Satellite time must be reserved, transmitting "dishes" placed, camera angles planned. What will be the dramatic scenes? Where will the sun be?

The advance team's instructions leave no doubt as to the purpose of a presidential trip: "The President has a point to make and that's the mes-sage. The message of a trip . . . is the *mission* of a trip . . . The public events of a trip are the expression of the message. It is central to advance work and deserves a lot of time and energy. Every event or site must capture or reinforce the reason the President is there. . . . The trip's message has already been through a wringer of careful deliberation at the White House."

The government team and the news planning team represent institutions that are different and often at odds. In this mini-universe, however, they have a common purpose: to get the fullest stories and the best pictures to the most people the fastest. "All of them know that, visually and technically, there are right and wrong ways to do things," explained one former participant, "and this is true whoever is president; it's a professional business." Such symbiosis disturbed newsman Martin Schram, however. He quoted a colleague: "In a funny way, the . . . advance men and I have the same thing at heart—we want the piece to look as good as it possibly can. . . . That's their job and that's my job. . . . I'm looking for the best pictures, but I can't help it if the audiences that show up, or that are grouped together by the . . . [White House] look so good. . . . I can't help it if it looks like a commercial." Schram then adds, "That is what White House video experts . . . are counting on. Offering television's professionals pictures they could not refuse was at the core of the . . . officials' efforts to shape and even control the content of the network newscasts."

A Clinton advance officer described this duality from another angle:

The most frustrating part of my job: . . . the advance team will make sure that [the press] are supplied with very nice visuals, with a great venue for the speech, and then you will see the most unbelievable choice of pictures that the producer or editor or newspaper . . . will actually decide to run. . . . We put all that blood, sweat, and tears into creating this beautiful visual backdrop and instead they will wind up with pictures of the president talking with some aide backstage. . . . The picture that we actually got out of all this hard work was completely disconnected from the story we were trying to achieve. So I think that coziness may not be as prevalent as it used to be . . . not with the people who are deciding what goes on the evening news or the front page. . . . It is also a function of volume: President Clinton travels exponentially more than President Reagan; editors probably tire of running the pictures that we "give" them.

There are still other items on the final checklist: "Effect of the motorcade on normal commuting patterns," "Lighting: 320 foot-candles on the speaker and 200 foot-candles on the crowd," "Overtime cost estimate," "Other appropriate music—can the band play it?" "Empty seats filled or draped," "List of gifts accepted for the President," "Bad weather alternative."

The advance team has a daily "countdown" meeting, where the team members make sure that they are all on the same page. "Never miss it!" warns the manual. There is also a daily conference call to home base, with the trip coordinator and all the affected White House offices. "Date-time stamp and file every piece of paper," the team is instructed, and "Keep Everybody Informed."

If the trip is political and a big rally is scheduled, the advance team will include another specialist, a "crowd-builder," who comes with the attitude that this "is a historic occasion, a great party, the biggest thing to ever happen to this town. If Joe Public misses it, Joe Public will regret it for the rest of his/her life. So, Joe Public better pack up the kids and bring Grandma and Grandpa or they will have missed one of the biggest days in their town's history!"

The local hosts must do the actual work, mobilizing hundreds of enthusiastic volunteers. A vast menu of techniques is systematically used, but all are on the advance team's checklist: not a single step is left to chance. For illustration:

—Event sites should be "expandable" or "collapsible," so that new seats can be added or empty chairs removed.

—Ten times as many handbills should be printed as there are places to be filled: enough for every shopping-center grocery bag, for door handles in parking lots, to tape to mirrors in public rest rooms, even to lay (right side up) on busy sidewalks. One last idea is suggested: "Stand on top of the highest building in town and throw the handbills into the wind." Leaflets must list the event as beginning at least one half hour before it will actually start: a president on the platform with a crowd still at the gates is chaos.

—*Air Force One* should be mentioned in leaflets for an airport rally; some folks will come just to see the plane. News stories about the history of presidential aircraft should be used to spark the interest of the crowd (but mention of their cost should be avoided).

—Bands, cheerleaders, pom-pom girls, and drill teams are to be mobilized (but the Secret Service has to check every make-believe rifle).

—Banner-painting parties are suggested, with supplies of butcher paper and tempera paint; a "hand-held sign committee" should be organized.

—Three thousand balloons are recommended, with balloon rises preferred over balloon drops. The truly experienced may try to do both simultaneously in the same auditorium: helium in the ones to go up, air in the ones to come down. The hall manager must be consulted first, however: the risen balloons will cling to the ceiling for two days afterwards.

No matter how rah-rah some aspects of a trip may be, White House advance staffers are forever conscious that it is the president of the United States who is there. They strive for a "colorful and mediagenic setting"— but never at the expense of the dignity of the person or the office. Their instructions state:"The President must never be allowed into a potentially awkward or embarrassing situation, and the advance person is sometimes the only one who can keep that from happening.... For example, an oversized cowboy hat, a live farm animal, an Indian headdress, or a Shriner's 'Fez' could produce a decidedly un-presidential photograph. Common sense must be used to make sure that the dignity of the office of the President is never compromised by the well-intentioned generosity of local partisans."

And no thank you to sound trucks, bands on flatbed trailers, elephants, clowns, and parachutists.

Like crowd-raising, press-advancing is a special skill of the advance team. At a major event site, a press area must be set apart. Camera platforms and radio tables must be of the required size and height, and press-only magnetometers must be installed. Each event site must be equipped with a half-dozen long-distance telephones, and each desk needs an electric outlet for plugging in a laptop. Four nearby rooms are reserved (at their cost) for the three television networks to edit their tapes. A filing center is set up with tables and chairs for a hundred people; the press secretary and his staff need a large adjoining office area with six tables to hold their equipment. "We duplicate the White House Press Office on the scene of a presidential visit," one expert explained. "The White House press staff can do their work just as if they were at 1600 Pennsylvania Avenue."

The advance team stays on site, completing its prodigious checklist, until the very moment the president is to arrive.

Back at the White House, the formal press announcement is made, with the local sponsors tipped off ahead of time and the necessary representatives, senators, governors, and mayors likewise alerted just before the White House release. The speechwriters have prepared their drafts, idea notes, or complete remarks ahead of time for arrivals, departures, and each stop in between (but word processors and copiers are aboard *Air Force One* if last-minute changes are ordered). The earlier sketches of airports, motorcade arrival and departure points, corridors, rooms, and walkways are transformed into minute diagrams, with arrows drawn in showing each presidential footstep.

When its own thousand details are done, the White House Press Office compiles a "Press Schedule Bible," which is given out to the national press representatives.

On the morning before the day of departure, the Advance Office holds a final trip briefing for the chief of staff; it will be the chief of staff who gives the final imprimatur for the *Air Force One* manifest. The advance team staff lead composes the president's and first lady's personal schedule sheets. Even when airborne, *Air Force One's* communications desk buzzes with last-minute advice from the advance team waiting at the arrival site.

As the presidential party approaches the runway, what goes through an advance person's mind? One veteran remembers: "There are a hundred bad variables when you look at a situation and go down your list. What you try to do is to reduce those down to zero. You never get them to zero, but if you get them down to six or five or four when the event occurs, then the odds are with you, and if they do go wrong they are at least in the manageable range."

The Advance Manual emphasizes: Pictures of the president standing behind the podium are dull stuff, and could just as well be snapped in the Rose Garden. Plan to have the cameras catch the president doing something unique and special, of exciting human-interest quality:

The high point . . . is "The Moment," the one snippet of action that visually tells the story of why the trip was undertaken in the first place. Media organizations need this moment to encapsulate the event. It will be rare that a newspaper will carry the complete transcript and equally rare that a local affiliate will broadcast the event "live" on television. . . . So we strive to create a moment: that ten-second slice of uplifting video . . . or that full-color, top-of-the-fold newspaper photo. . . . As the cliche goes, a picture is worth a thousand words. . . . "The Moment" is what you make of it. Don't let a visit go by without creating one.

PART FIFTEEN

Political Economy and Public Welfare

83

MICHAEL HARRINGTON

From *The Other America*

Poverty in the United States is not new, but it took social critic Michael Harrington's acclaimed book, published in 1962, to bring the reality of "the other America" in the midst of the "affluent society" to the nation's attention. Harrington's study of the middle class's withdrawal from the problems of poor city-dwellers marked the philosophical start of the "war on poverty," which was to begin later in the 1960s. Harrington explored the situation of people who were poor within a society of plenty. His characterization of the poor as "socially invisible" and "politically invisible" led to wide public recognition of the problem of poverty in America. President Lyndon B. Johnson's "war on poverty" legislation has faded, but the "invisible" poor do, from time to time, reappear, never more poignantly than in the film footage of New Orleans's residents, many of them poor, calling out for help from the Superdome, from the Convention Center, and from city rooftops day after day while waiting in vain for a response from the Federal Emergency Management Agency (FEMA) following the disastrous 2005 Hurricane Katrina.

THERE IS a familiar America. It is celebrated in speeches and advertised on television and in the magazines. It has the highest mass standard of living the world has ever known.

In the 1950s this America worried about itself, yet even its anxieties were products of abundance. The title of a brilliant book was widely misinterpreted, and the familiar America began to call itself "the affluent society." There was introspection about Madison Avenue and tail fins*; there was discussion of the emotional suffering taking place in the suburbs. In all this, there was an implicit assumption that the basic grinding economic problems had been solved in the United States. In this theory the nation's problems were no longer a matter of basic human needs, of food, shelter, and clothing. Now they were seen as qualitative, a question of learning to live decently amid luxury.

While this discussion was carried on, there existed another America.

---

*Madison Avenue, in New York City, is the traditional home of the advertising industry. It is there that plans have been hatched for selling Americans products that they may not yet really know they want—like, in the 1950s, cars with tail fins.—EDS.

In it dwelt somewhere between 40,000,000 and 50,000,000 citizens of this land. They were poor. They still are.

To be sure, the other America is not impoverished in the same sense as those poor nations where millions cling to hunger as a defense against starvation. This country has escaped such extremes. That does not change the fact that tens of millions of Americans are, at this very moment, maimed in body and spirit, existing at levels beneath those necessary for human decency. If these people are not starving, they are hungry, and sometimes fat with hunger, for that is what cheap foods do. They are without adequate housing and education and medical care.

The Government has documented what this means to the bodies of the poor, and the figures will be cited throughout this book. But even more basic, this poverty twists and deforms the spirit. The American poor are pessimistic and defeated, and they are victimized by mental suffering to a degree unknown in Suburbia.

This book is a description of the world in which these people live; it is about the other America. Here are the unskilled workers, the migrant farm workers, the aged, the minorities, and all the others who live in the economic underworld of American life. . . .

The millions who are poor in the United States tend to become increasingly invisible. Here is a great mass of people, yet it takes an effort of the intellect and will even to see them. . . .

. . . The other America, the America of poverty, is hidden today in a way that it never was before. Its millions are socially invisible to the rest of us. No wonder that so many misinterpreted [economist John Kenneth] Galbraith's title and assumed that "the affluent society" meant that everyone had a decent standard of life. The misinterpretation was true as far as the actual day-to-day lives of two-thirds of the nation were concerned. Thus, one must begin a description of the other America by understanding why we do not see it.

There are perennial reasons that make the other America an invisible land.

Poverty is often off the beaten track. It always has been. . . .

. . . The American city has been transformed. The poor still inhabit the miserable housing in the central area, but they are increasingly isolated from contact with, or sight of, anybody else. Middle-class women coming in from Suburbia on a rare trip may catch the merest glimpse of the other America on the way to an evening at the theater, but their children are segregated in suburban schools. The business or professional man may drive along the fringes of slums in a car or bus, but it is not an important experience to him. The failures, the unskilled, the disabled, the aged, and the minorities are right there, across the tracks, where they have always been. But hardly anyone else is.

In short, the very development of the American city has removed poverty from the living, emotional experience of millions upon millions of middle-class Americans. Living out in the suburbs, it is easy to assume that ours is, indeed, an affluent society.

This new segregation of poverty is compounded by a well-meaning ignorance. A good many concerned and sympathetic Americans are aware that there is much discussion of urban renewal. Suddenly, driving through the city, they notice that a familiar slum has been torn down and that there are towering, modern buildings where once there had been tenements or hovels. There is a warm feeling of satisfaction, of pride in the way things are working out: the poor, it is obvious, are being taken care of. . . .

And finally, the poor are politically invisible. It is one of the cruelest ironies of social life in advanced countries that the dispossessed at the bottom of society are unable to speak for themselves. The people of the other America do not, by far and large, belong to unions, to fraternal organizations, or to political parties. They are without lobbies of their own; they put forward no legislative program. As a group, they are atomized. They have no face; they have no voice.

Thus, there is not even a cynical political motive for caring about the poor, as in the old days. Because the slums are no longer centers of powerful political organizations, the politicians need not really care about their inhabitants. The slums are no longer visible to the middle class, so much of the idealistic urge to fight for those who need help is gone. Only the social agencies have a really direct involvement with the other America, and they are without any great political power. . . .

Indeed, the paradox that the welfare state benefits those least who need help most is but a single instance of a persistent irony in the other America. Even when the money finally trickles down, even when a school is built in a poor neighborhood, for instance, the poor are still deprived. Their entire environment, their life, their values, do not prepare them to take advantage of the new opportunity. The parents are anxious for the children to go to work; the pupils are pent up, waiting for the moment when their education has complied with the law.

Today's poor, in short, missed the political and social gains of the thirties. They are, as Galbraith rightly points out, the first minority poor in history, the first poor not to be seen, the first poor whom the politicians could leave alone. . . .

What shall we tell the American poor, once we have seen them? Shall we say to them that they are better off than the Indian poor, the Italian poor, the Russian poor? That is one answer, but it is heartless. I should put it another way. I want to tell every well-fed and optimistic American that it is intolerable that so many millions should be maimed in body and in spirit when it is not necessary that they should be. My standard of comparison is not how much worse things used to be. It is how much better they could be if only we were stirred....

First and foremost, any attempt to abolish poverty in the United States must seek to destroy the pessimism and fatalism that flourish in the other America. In part, this can be done by offering real opportunities to these people, by changing the social reality that gives rise to their sense of hopelessness. But beyond that (these fears of the poor have a life of their own and are not simply rooted in analyses of employment chances), there should be a spirit, an élan, that communicates itself to the entire society.

If the nation comes into the other America grudgingly, with the mentality of an administrator, and says, "All right, we'll help you people," then there will be gains, but they will be kept to the minimum; a dollar spent will return a dollar. But if there is an attitude that society is gaining by eradicating poverty, if there is a positive attempt to bring these millions of the poor to the point where they can make their contribution to the United States, that will make a huge difference. The spirit of a campaign against poverty does not cost a single cent. It is a matter of vision, of sensitivity....

Second, this book is based upon the proposition that poverty forms a culture, an interdependent system. In case after case, it has been documented that one cannot deal with the various components of poverty in isolation, changing this or that condition but leaving the basic structure intact. Consequently, a campaign against the misery of the poor should be comprehensive. It should think, not in terms of this or that aspect of poverty, but along the lines of establishing new communities, of substituting a human environment for the inhuman one that now exists....

There is only one institution in the society capable of acting to abolish poverty. That is the Federal Government. In saying this, I do not rejoice, for centralization can lead to an impersonal and bureaucratic program, one that will be lacking in the very human quality so essential in an approach to the poor. In saying this, I am only recording the facts of political and social life in the United States....

[However] it is not necessary to advocate complete central control of such a campaign. Far from it. Washington is essential in a double sense: as a source of the considerable funds needed to mount a campaign against the other America, and as a place for coordination, for planning, and the establishment of national standards. The actual implementation of a program to abolish poverty can be carried out through myriad institutions, and the closer they are to the specific local area, the better the results. There are, as has been pointed out already, housing administrators, welfare workers, and city planners with dedication and vision. They are working on the local level, and their main frustration is the lack of funds. They could be trusted actually to carry through on a national program. What they lack now is money and the support of the American people. . . .

There is no point in attempting to blueprint or detail the mechanisms and institutions of a war on poverty in the United States. There is information enough for action. All that is lacking is political will. . . .

These, then, are the strangest poor in the history of mankind.

They exist within the most powerful and rich society the world has ever known. Their misery has continued while the majority of the nation talked of itself as being "affluent" and worried about neuroses in the suburbs. In this way tens of millions of human beings became invisible. They dropped out of sight and out of mind; they were without their own political voice.

Yet this need not be. The means are at hand to fulfill the age-old dream: poverty can now be abolished. How long shall we ignore this underdeveloped nation in our midst? How long shall we look the other way while our fellow human beings suffer? How long?

84

MILTON FRIEDMAN

From *Free to Choose*

Conservative economists are numerous today. But none can compete for style and consistency of viewpoint with Nobel Prize-winning Economics Professor Milton Friedman. Friedman has been the voice of conservative economics over the past half-century, during times when his ideas received little public acceptance. Free to Choose, written with his wife Rose Friedman, became the basis for an informative, entertaining—and controversial—TV series. Friedman's central theme is "freedom," both in economics and in politics. He advocates that the maximum amount of economic power be left to individual citizens, to make their own choices, with the least possible control placed in the central government's province. Big government is Friedman's target. In the excerpt, Friedman mentions his heroes, classical economists Adam Smith and Friedrich Hayek. The name of Milton Friedman will join that list for future generations of conservatives.

———

THE STORY of the United States is the story of an economic miracle and a political miracle that was made possible by the translation into practice of two sets of ideas—both, by a curious coincidence, formulated in documents published in the same year, 1776.

One set of ideas was embodied in *The Wealth of Nations*, the masterpiece that established the Scotsman Adam Smith as the father of modern economics. It analyzed the way in which a market system could combine the freedom of individuals to pursue their own objectives with the extensive cooperation and collaboration needed in the economic field to produce our food, our clothing, our housing. Adam Smith's key insight was that both parties to an exchange can benefit and that, *so long as cooperation is strictly voluntary*, no exchange will take place unless both parties do benefit. No external force, no coercion, no violation of freedom is necessary to produce cooperation among individuals all of whom can benefit. That is why, as Adam Smith put it, an individual who "intends only his own gain" is "led by an invisible hand to promote an end which was no part of his intention. Nor is it always the worse for the society that it was no part of it. By pursuing his own interest he frequently promotes that of the society more effectually than when he really intends to promote it. I have never known much good done by those who affected to trade for the public good."

The second set of ideas was embodied in the Declaration of Independence, drafted by Thomas Jefferson to express the general sense of his fellow countrymen. It proclaimed a new nation, the first in history established on the principle that every person is entitled to pursue his own values: "We hold these truths to be self-evident, that all men are created equal, that they are endowed by their Creator with certain unalienable Rights; that among these are Life, Liberty, and the pursuit of Happiness." . . .

Economic freedom is an essential requisite for political freedom. By enabling people to cooperate with one another without coercion or central direction, it reduces the area over which political power is exercised. In addition, by dispersing power, the free market provides an offset to whatever concentration of political power may arise. The combination of economic and political *power* in the same hands is a sure recipe for tyranny. . . .

Ironically, the very success of economic and political freedom reduced its appeal to later thinkers. The narrowly limited government of the late nineteenth century possessed little concentrated power that endangered the ordinary man. The other side of that coin was that it possessed little power that would enable good people to do good. And in an imperfect world there were still many evils. Indeed, the very progress of society made the residual evils seem all the more objectionable. As always, people took the favorable developments for granted. They forgot the danger to freedom from a strong government. Instead, they were attracted by the good that a stronger government could achieve—if only government power were in the "right" hands. . . .

These views have dominated developments in the United States during the past half-century. They have led to a growth in government at all levels, as well as to a transfer of power from local government and local control to central government and central control. The government has increasingly undertaken the task of taking from some to give to others in the name of security and equality. . . .

These developments have been produced by good intentions with a major assist from self-interest. [Yet] even the strongest supporters of the welfare and paternal state agree that the results have been disappointing. . . .

The experience of recent years—slowing growth and declining productivity—raises a doubt whether private ingenuity can continue to overcome the deadening effects of government control if we continue to grant ever more power to government, to authorize a "new class" of civil servants to spend ever larger fractions of our income supposedly on our behalf. Sooner or later—and perhaps sooner than many of us expect—an ever bigger government would destroy both the prosperity that we owe to the free market and the human freedom proclaimed so eloquently in the Declaration of Independence.

We have not yet reached the point of no return. We are still free as a people to choose whether we shall continue speeding down the "road to serfdom," as Friedrich Hayek entitled his profound and influential book, or whether we shall set tighter limits on government and rely more heavily on voluntary cooperation among free individuals to achieve our several objectives. Will our golden age come to an end in a relapse into the tyranny and misery that has always been, and remains today, the state of most of mankind? Or shall we have the wisdom, the foresight, and the courage to change our course, to learn from experience, and to benefit from a "rebirth of freedom"? . . . If the cresting of the tide . . . is to be followed by a move toward a freer society and a more limited government rather than toward a totalitarian society, the public must not only recognize the defects of the present situation but also how it has come about and what we can do about it. Why are the results of policies so often the opposite of their ostensible objectives? Why do special interests prevail over the general interest? What devices can we use to stop and reverse the process? . . .

. . . Whenever we visit Washington, D.C., we are impressed all over again with how much power is concentrated in that city. Walk the halls of Congress, and the 435 members of the House plus the 100 senators are hard to find among their 18,000 employees—about 65 for each senator and 27 for each member of the House. In addition, the more than 15,000 registered lobbyists—often accompanied by secretaries, typists, researchers, or representatives of the special interest they represent—walk the same halls seeking to exercise influence.

And this is but the tip of the iceberg. The federal government employs close to 3 million civilians (excluding the uniformed military forces). Over 350,000 are in Washington and the surrounding metropolitan area. Countless others are indirectly employed through government contracts with nominally private organizations, or are employed by labor or business organizations or other special interest groups that maintain their headquarters, or at least an office, in Washington because it is the seat of government. . . .

. . . Both the fragmentation of power and the conflicting government policies are rooted in the political realities of a democratic system that operates by enacting detailed and specific legislation. Such a system tends to give undue political power to small groups that have highly concentrated interests, to give greater weight to obvious, direct, and immediate effects of government action than to possibly more important but concealed, indirect, and delayed effects, to set in motion a process that sacrifices the general interest to serve special interests, rather than the other way around. There is, as it were, an invisible hand in politics that operates in precisely the opposite direction to Adam Smith's invisible hand. Individuals who intend only to promote the *general interest* are led by the invisible political hand to promote a *special interest* that they had no intention to promote. . . .

The benefit an individual gets from any one program that he has a special interest in may be more than canceled by the costs to him of many programs that affect him lightly. Yet it pays him to favor the one program, and not oppose the others. He can readily recognize that he and the small group with the same special interest can afford to spend enough money and time to make a difference in respect of the one program. Not promoting that program will not prevent the others, which do him harm, from being adopted. To achieve that, he would have to be willing and able to devote as much effort to opposing each of them as he does to favoring his own. That is clearly a losing proposition. . . .

Currently in the United States, anything like effective detailed control of government by the public is limited to villages, towns, smaller cities, and suburban areas—and even there only to those matters not mandated by the state or federal government. In large cities, states, Washington, we have government of the people not by the people but by a largely faceless group of bureaucrats.

No federal legislator could conceivably even read, let alone analyze and study, all the laws on which he must vote. He must depend on his numerous aides and assistants, or outside lobbyists, or fellow legislators, or some other source for most of his decisions on how to vote. The unelected congressional bureaucracy almost surely has far more influence today in shaping the detailed laws that are passed than do our elected representatives.

The situation is even more extreme in the administration of government programs. The vast federal bureaucracy spread through the many government departments and independent agencies is literally out of control of the elected representatives of the public. Elected Presidents and senators and representatives come and go but the civil service remains. Higher-level bureaucrats are past masters at the art of using red tape to delay and defeat proposals they do not favor; of issuing rules and regulations as "interpretations" of laws that in fact subtly, or sometimes crudely, alter their thrust; of dragging their feet in administering those parts of laws of which they disapprove, while pressing on with those they favor. . . .

Bureaucrats have not usurped power They have not deliberately engaged in any kind of conspiracy to subvert the democratic process. Power has been thrust on them. . . .

The growth of the bureaucracy in size and power affects every detail of the relation between a citizen and his government. . . . Needless to say, those of us who want to halt and reverse the recent trend should oppose additional specific measures to expand further the power and scope of government, urge repeal and reform of existing measures, and try to elect legislators and executives who share that view. But that is not an effective way to reverse the growth of government. It is doomed to failure. Each of us would defend our own special privileges and try to limit government at someone else's expense. We would be fighting a many-headed hydra that would grow new heads faster than we could cut old ones off.*

Our founding fathers have shown us a more promising way to proceed: by package deals, as it were. We should adopt self-denying ordinances that limit the objectives we try to pursue through political channels. We should not consider each case on its merits, but lay down broad rules limiting what government may do. . . .

We need, in our opinion, the equivalent of the First Amendment to limit government power in the economic and social area—an economic Bill of Rights to complement and reinforce the original Bill of Rights. . . .

The proposed amendments would alter the conditions under which legislators—state or federal, as the case may be—operate by limiting the total amount they are authorized to appropriate. The amendments would give the government a limited budget, specified in advance, the way each of us has a limited budget. Much special interest legislation is undesirable, but it is never clearly and unmistakably bad. On the contrary, every measure will be represented as serving a good cause. The problem is that there are an infinite number of good causes. Currently, a legislator is in a weak position to oppose a "good" cause. If he objects that it will raise taxes, he will be labeled a reactionary who is willing to sacrifice human need for base mercenary reasons—after all, this good cause will only require raising taxes by a few cents or dollars per person. The legislator is in a far better

---

*The Hydra was a mythical Greek monster that grew two heads for each one that was chopped off. It was killed by the hero Hercules.—Eds.

position if he can say, "Yes, yours is a good cause, but we have a fixed budget. More money for your cause means less for others. Which of these others should be cut?" The effect would be to require the special interests to compete with one another for a bigger share of a fixed pie, instead of their being able to collude with one another to make the pie bigger at the expense of the taxpayer. . . .

. . . The two ideas of human freedom and economic freedom working together came to their greatest fruition in the United States. Those ideas are still very much with us. We are all of us imbued with them. They are part of the very fabric of our being. But we have been straying from them. We have been forgetting the basic truth that the greatest threat to human freedom is the concentration of power, whether in the hands of government or anyone else. We have persuaded ourselves that it is safe to grant power, provided it is for good purposes.

Fortunately, we are waking up. . . .

Fortunately, also, we are as a people still free to choose which way we should go—whether to continue along the road we have been following to ever bigger government, or to call a halt and change direction.

85

SHARON HAYS

From *Flat Broke with Children*

When the welfare program in the United States was drastically changed in 1996, the impact was multifaceted. States gained much more power to tailor their welfare plans to fit their needs. The emphasis shifted from giving needy people money for an indefinite period of time to offering job training and childcare for a short time, with a job and independence as the ultimate goals. Sharon Hays assesses the decade-old welfare reform from several points of view. She talks to caseworkers in several cities about how well they think the new approach is working. She follows several welfare recipients through the system; their experiences suggest a mixed result. Yes, the bureaucratic rules remain and the hope of getting a decent job quickly is sometimes unrealistic. However, Hays finds that the changes to the welfare program have benefited many recipients. Beyond just a job, a sense of accomplishment and a future with real possibilities have opened up for some of those she studied.

———

A NATION'S LAWS REFLECT a nation's values. The 1996 federal law reforming welfare offered not just a statement of values to the thousands of local welfare offices across the nation, it also backed this up with something much more tangible. Welfare reform came with money. Lots of it. Every client and caseworker in the welfare office experienced this. New social workers and employment counselors were hired. New signs were posted. New workshops were set up. In Arbordale and Sunbelt City, the two welfare offices I studied to write this book, every caseworker found a new computer on her desk.* In small-town Arbordale, the whole office got a facelift: new carpets, new paint, a new conference room, new office chairs, and plush new office dividers. The reception area, completely remodeled with plants and posters and a children's play area, came to resemble the waiting room of an elite pediatrician's office more than the entrance to a state bureaucracy. Sunbelt City acquired new carpets, a new paint job, and new furniture as well. And all the public areas in that welfare office were newly decorated with images of nature's magnificence—glistening raindrops, majestic mountains, crashing waves, setting

———

*Arbordale and Sunbelt City are pseudonyms for the two towns where I studied the effects of welfare reform. I gave them these ficticious names to protect all the clients and caseworkers who shared with me their experiences of reform.

sun—captioned with inspirational phrases like "perseverance," "seizing opportunities," "determination," "succcss."

As I walked the halls of the Sunbelt City welfare office back in 1998, situated in one of the poorest and most dangerous neighborhoods of a western boom town, those scenes of nature's magnificence struck me as clearly out of place. But the inspirational messages they carried nonetheless seemed an apt symbolic representation of the new legislative strategy to train poor families in "mainstream" American values. Welfare reform, Congress had decreed, would "end the dependence of needy parents on government benefits by promoting job preparation, work, and marriage." Welfare mothers, those Sunbelt signs implied, simply needed a *push*—to get them out to work, to keep them from having children they couldn't afford to raise, to get them married and safely embedded in family life. Seizing opportunities.

States were awash in federal funds. And the economy was booming in those early years of reform. Everyone was feeling it. There was change in the air. A sense of possibilities—with just a tinge of foreboding.

The Personal Responsibility and Work Opportunity Reconciliation Act of 1996, the law that ended 61 years of poor families' entitlement to federal welfare benefits—the law that asserted and enforced a newly reformulated vision of the appropriate values of work and family life—provided all that additional funding as a way of demonstrating the depth of the nation's commitment to change in the welfare system. It provided state welfare programs with federal grants in amounts matching the peak years of national welfare caseloads (1992 to 1995)—even though those caseloads had everywhere since declined. This meant an average budget increase of 10 percent, before counting the tremendous amount of additional federal funding coming in for new childcare and welfare-to-work programs. Even though there was lots more money, most states did not pass it on to poor mothers in the form of larger welfare checks. In fact, only two states raised their benefit amounts, while two others lowered theirs at the inception of reform.

Most of the welfare caseworkers I met were optimistic about the new law, at least in the first year of its enactment. "Welfare reform is the best thing that ever happened," was a phrase I heard frequently. A number of caseworkers, echoing popular sentiment, told me that "welfare had become a trap" and the clients had become "dependent." Some focused on the tax money that would be saved. Others pointed out that lots of caseworkers are mothers too, and economic necessity forces them to come to work every day and leave their children in day care, so it seemed only fair that welfare mothers should be required to do the same. Still others em-

phasized that welfare reform provided caseworkers the opportunity to do
what they were meant to do all along—it allowed them to "help people."
Eligibility workers in particular, who had long had the job of simply processing applications and pushing papers, told me that they had grown
tired of just "passing out the checks." Welfare reform, one such worker
enthusiastically noted, offered the training and services necessary "to make
our clients' lives better, to make them better mothers, to make them more
productive." At the same time, some welfare workers, especially the social
workers and employment counselors, worried about the long-term consequences of reform and wondered about how some of their clients would
survive. But almost all caseworkers agreed that the old system was a problem and that the "self-sufficiency" and familial responsibility required by
welfare reform were (at minimum) good ideas. . . .

The Personal Responsibility Act offered wide discretion to states in
the enactment of welfare reform and in the use of welfare money. There
are, therefore, notable differences in the policies of Arbordale and Sunbelt
City. Arbordale's home state, for instance, has a "family cap" provision
that disallows welfare benefits to children born when their mothers are
already receiving aid; Sunbelt City's state does not. Sunbelt's state has a
provision to identify (and potentially protect) welfare mothers who are
the victims of domestic violence; Arbordale's state does not. Like most
states, both of these permit mothers with infants to be temporarily exempt from the work requirements: Arbordale allows mothers to stay at
home when their children are younger than 18 months old (a very generous provision relative to most states); Sunbelt City offers new mothers a
lifetime maximum of 12 months of work exemption. Also mimicking
wide variations among states, Arbordale and Sunbelt differ in the extent
to which they are willing to use the federal "hardship exemption" that
allows them to spare 20 percent of their cases from welfare time limits:
Sunbelt City maximizes its use of these exemptions; Arbordale exempts
almost no one.

Both Arbordale's and Sunbelt's home states have, as noted, instituted
two-year time limits on welfare, placing them among the 22 states that
have similarly chosen shortened time limits. Although some states are allowing welfare clients the federal maximum of one year of training toward work and some states are relatively flexible in the speed with which
they require their clients to get jobs, both Arbordale and Sunbelt City
have instituted "work first" policies that emphasize the expedient place-
ment of recipients in whatever jobs are available. Relative to other states
in the nation, neither Arbordale nor Sunbelt is particularly generous or
particularly miserly in its welfare benefit amounts or in the number of
programs they have instituted to aid welfare families. . . .

The first thing you see on entering the Arbordale welfare office is a large red banner, 12 feet long, 2 feet high, reading, "HOW MANY MONTHS DO YOU HAVE LEFT?" Underneath that banner is a listing of jobs available in the area—receptionist, night clerk, fast-food server, cashier, waitress, data entry personnel, beautician, forklift operator. In most cases, the hours, benefits, and pay rates are not listed. The message is unmistakable: you must find a job, find it soon (before your months run out), and accept whatever wages or hours you can get. . . .

Welfare recipients, of course, are not merely being encouraged to work. In Arbordale and Sunbelt City, they were reminded repeatedly that work requirements are backed up by strictly enforced time limits—two years at the state level, five years overall—and they were continuously admonished to "save their months." Welfare caseworkers and supervisors, for their part, were painfully aware of the time limits, and they were also aware that the work requirements are enforced through federal "participation rates" requiring states to place increasing percentages of their welfare clientele in jobs. Should a state fail in this task, its federal financial allotment will be decreased. If a caseworker failed in her piece of this task, she could lose her job. For welfare mothers, this translated into constant and intense pressure to find work. The symbolic device of the "ticking clock" measuring one's time on welfare was used incessantly by Arbordale and Sunbelt caseworkers and quickly found its way into the vocabulary of the welfare mothers I met.

Just as most of the public and the popular media have assumed all along, welfare reform's Work Plan thus takes center stage in the welfare office. According to the logic of this plan, if the welfare office can train mothers to value work and self-sufficiency, the need for welfare receipt will be eliminated, and former recipients will become respectable, "mainstream" American workers. In this model, the ideal of independence—long associated with values of citizenship, self-governance, and full social membership in Western culture—is thereby transformed into a simple demand for paid work.

There are a number of problems with that logic, as this chapter will demonstrate. A foundational problem is the false assumption that most welfare recipients were previously lacking the motivation to work. Another problem, apparent to anyone who has ever tried to survive on a minimum wage job, is that the low-wage work typically available to welfare recipients offers neither financial independence nor the independence associated with the higher ideals of American citizenship. These difficulties, I soon discovered, are made worse by the procedural enactment of reform. Immersed in a bureaucratic machine, the rigid rules and demanding regulations of reform not only diminish the dignity of the people being served, they also degrade the values that the Personal Responsibility Act purports to champion. . . .

As a start, consider Carolyn. A once-married, black Sunbelt City welfare mother with a high school diploma, her story contained a number of the patterns I saw in the lives of welfare recipients. She had worked for most of her adult life, and she had also spent nearly all her life hovering somewhere close to the poverty line. She had been employed as a waitress, a clerk at the District Attorney's office, a telephone operator, a nurse's aide, a receptionist at the power company, a childcare worker, and a discount-store cashier. She initially went on welfare when she had her first and only child with a man she planned to marry. Carolyn cried when she told me the story of how that man began to physically abuse her and ultimately raped her during her pregnancy: "When I first met him, he was a really good man," she said. "But then he started taking drugs. It was terrible. I was afraid all the time." Shortly after the rape, she escaped that situation and moved in with her sister, but lost her job. By the time she gave birth, she was suffering from a nervous breakdown. ("He had drove me insane: that's what they said, in the letter from the psychiatrist.") It was following her hospitalization for that breakdown, ten years before I met her, that she first went on welfare with her then two-month-old baby girl.

By the time her daughter was two years old, Carolyn went back to work. Three years after that she took on the full-time care of her three nieces (aged 3, 9, and 12) when their mother was imprisoned for selling drugs and Carolyn learned that those children were otherwise bound for the foster care system. At that point, she took a second job to care for those four kids, and tried hard to avoid returning to welfare. But after a few years her carefully organized (though always precarious and stressful) work/family balance was thrown into disarray. Her brother and sister-in-law who had been helping with childcare and transportation moved out of town. This left Carolyn trying to manage with the public bus system, paid caregivers, and after-school programs for her daily round of transportation to two jobs, the childcare provider, the older kids' schools, and back home again—along with all the added expenses that went with this new strategy.

Then came the final straw. Carolyn was laid off one of her jobs. By this time, she was deeply in debt and ill: the stress of her situation had contributed to serious heart problems, and her doctor was urging her to "take it easy." All these difficulties—transportation, relationships, low wages, precarious jobs, ill health, and the care of children—came together and landed her in the welfare office where I met her. It was clear to me that, at that point in her life, Carolyn was hoping for a little rest and recuperation. But the terms of the newly reformed welfare office, as you'll soon see, required just the opposite.

Although the poor mothers I met in Arbordale and Sunbelt City all came from different circumstances, many of them shared at least some of the troubles from which Carolyn had suffered. The primary point is that, in the vast majority of cases, when women end up on welfare it is not because they have lost (or never found) the work ethic. It is only because a moral commitment to work is, by itself, not always sufficient for the practical achievement of financial and familial stability. . . .

Overall, the rules designed to enforce work emerge as a relatively confusing mix of commands, backed up by some welcome gifts, and many, many, less welcome requirements. In pondering this system of rules, rewards, and punishments, the observer might consider to what extent it adds up to a model of the values of "mainstream" America.

The welfare clients I met heard two pieces of this message loud and clear: they knew they were expected to find jobs, and they knew they were expected to obey the rules. Many of them also heard, more faintly perhaps, the enthusiasm that was often conveyed by the caseworkers who enforced those rules, an enthusiasm for genuinely improving the lives of welfare families. Yet, just as the behaviorist model of welfare mixes rewards with punishments, that enthusiasm was also mirrored by another implicit message, one that emerged from the constant pressure, echoed persistently in the background, and was assimilated by most of the welfare mothers I encountered: "You are not wanted here. Americans are tired of helping you out, and we will not let you rest, not even for an instant, until you find a way to get off welfare."

The message of the importance of paid work is a very powerful message indeed. . . .

The welfare office is, first and foremost, a bureaucracy. It is a world of rigid rules and formal procedures. It is a world where every new welfare client can be represented as a series of numbers: a case number, a number of children, a number of fathers of those children, a number of dollars in cash income, a number of months on welfare, a number of required forms, oaths, and verifications. It is also a world where every welfare client has come to symbolize a potential case of fraud and a potential "error" in the calculation of appropriate benefits. It is no surprise, therefore, that the congressional Work Plan was simply translated into a complex system of bureaucratic rules and regulations. . . .

For all the hardships and discontent, for all those clients whose experiences with reform were unequivocally negative, most welfare mothers, most of the time, remained positive, chin up, eyes to the future. As much as almost no one was happy with *all* the rules and regulations, and although almost everyone recognized some problems, the largest proportion of the poor mothers I talked to were genuinely hopeful about reform and tried hard to make the best of it. They knew what the welfare office and the nation were asking of them, and they did whatever they could to get training, seek out work, find good childcare, manage their budgets, and get off the welfare rolls.

For those who clearly benefited from the programs instituted by reform their positive attitude was easy to understand. If they found both suitable childcare and decent jobs with regular hours that paid above the minimum wage, it made sense that they were grateful for the increased benefits offered as "transitional" (time-limited) assistance with childcare, transportation, medical insurance, and clothing. They were even more appreciative of the welfare checks they continued to receive if their wages were low in relation to their family size. Those benefits meant that this group of clients was, temporarily at least, clearly better off than they would have been prior to welfare reform. And, for some, this was just the boost they needed to achieve familial financial stability.

More surprising was the sense of hope that I regularly encountered among those who were having a harder time. This included mothers who ran through one training program after another, hoping that the next one would prove the "right" one—the one that would help them to get a good job, the kind that offered some flexibility and paid wages sufficient to support their family. It included all those women who took jobs paying minimum wage, jobs with irregular schedules, and jobs that were less than full time. It even included many of those who were forced to take unpaid workfare placements and who interpreted these placements as a chance to get much needed work experience.

Overall, for every client who complained to me of ill treatment and of the inappropriate logic of reform, there were at least two others who responded to my questions about their experiences by recounting positive encounters and emphasizing the helpful services. Shannon, a Sunbelt mother with two kids, was particularly enthusiastic. She'd been out of work for over a year before reform and, when I met her, she'd just started a three-month temporary job as a bill collector:

> I think welfare reform is great! It helps with the transportation and the day care, so it helps out a lot. And my caseworker is so nice—she takes care of me, and she tells me stuff. The classes teach you how to prepare yourself to go out for a job and have the right attitude. They taught me how to do my resume and things like that. And you learn how to feel good about yourself too. And, you know, things get tough sometimes, so the welfare office has helped me. I thank God for that.

Julia, pregnant with her second child, was equally positive. Even though she had not yet found work, she was still feeling hopeful, and grateful for the help that came with reform:

> They've been very good to me; I've never really had a problem with anything. I mean, the only thing that holds you back is you. My caseworker got me into classes for computer skills. I was looking at the lists and it's like $1,000 for a course like that! So welfare is really forking out the bucks. You know, people are saying, "This is our tax dollars!" and I think they're being put to good use.

Despite the rigmarole, the bureaucratic maze, the intrusions, the sanctions, and the massive number of strict requirements, many of the women I encountered expressed similar sentiments. Although I had read the statistics reporting that welfare recipients are nearly as likely as other Americans to support reform, in the context of the welfare office, I was more surprised by this fact than any other.

This ability to retain hope surely speaks to a resilience of the human spirit. And part of that hope, as I've suggested, clearly arose from practical calculations—no matter what one's circumstances, the supportive services and income disregards could make it feel like Christmastime, with gifts and pennies falling from heaven. Similarly, although the content of the training programs in computers, food service, and general office skills often bore little relation to what is actually required to achieve financial stability, and as often as I heard clients complain about bad teachers or demanding schedules, I also witnessed, firsthand, the way some of those programs offered some participants a sense of collective purpose and a feeling that they might actually have a better shot at the brass ring. Along the same lines, the new discretion and maternalism that entered the welfare office with reform meant that a number of clients established warm ties with their caseworkers and came to understand them as important life mentors. Those welfare mothers who made their way to the protection of Sunbelt's social workers often felt especially grateful for the help they received. In all this, there was no question that this welfare office was indeed different from the one where eligibility workers used to just "pass out the checks."

Practical considerations and warm ties, however, were not the only source of welfare mothers' positive assessment of reform. As you can begin to hear in the words of Shannon and Julia, the supportive programs offered by reform were also important because, for some welfare mothers, they seemed to indicate that not just the welfare office but also the nation as a whole wanted to help low-income families to achieve a *better* future. When Julia commented on those $1,000 training courses, even though she knew that Americans were primarily interested in getting her off the welfare rolls, she was also feeling that those Americans were standing with her, rather than against her.

Nonetheless, to maintain this positive attitude, this "ideal" vision of reform, often required welfare mothers to sustain a protective mental and emotional barrier between their hopes and their circumstances. The $6.00-an-hour jobs, the troubles in caring for one's children, the bureaucratic regulations, after all, didn't offer a perfect image of financial stability, happy family life, and a nation dedicated to the common good. But maybe, just maybe, many welfare mothers seemed to say, such a world was possible. . . .

The number of families that have been genuinely helped by reform is neither insignificant nor superfluous. At a practical as well as moral level, the services and income supports offered by the Personal Responsibility Act have clearly been positive. Yet in the long run and in the aggregate, poor mothers and children are worse off now than they were prior to reform. Among those who are working and still poor, among those without work or welfare, and among those who are still facing constant and intense pressure to find work and figure out some way to care for their children, we can only guess what impact this law will have on their ability to retain hope over the long term. Even the U.S. Census Bureau (not anyone's idea of a bleeding heart organization) has found itself answering the question, "Is work better than welfare?" in the negative, at least for those without substantial prior education and work experience. With a slower economy and increasing numbers of poor families due to hit their time limits in coming years, there are reasons to expect that conditions will become increasingly difficult.

Empathy for the downtrodden is one reason to worry about these results. As the following sections will emphasize, enlightened self-interest, a concern with financial costs, and a commitment to our collective future are also very good reasons to be troubled by the consequences of welfare reform. . . .

The extent to which the facts about the declining welfare rolls are read as a success ultimately depends on one's primary goals. If the goal of reform was solely to trim the rolls, then it has surely succeeded. If the goal was to place more single mothers in jobs regardless of wages, that goal has been met. If we sought to ensure that more welfare mothers would face a double shift of paid work and childcare, placing them on an "equal" footing with their middle-class counterparts, then some celebrations are in order. If the aim was to ensure that poor men are prosecuted for failure to pay child support, then welfare reform has been relatively effective. If the goal was to make low-income single mothers more likely to seek out the help of men, no matter what the costs, there is some (inconclusive) evidence that this strategy may be working. If the goal was to decrease poverty overall, there is no indication that anything but the cycle of the economy has had an impact. Beyond this, the answers are more complicated.

Thinking about losers, one can start with the families who have left welfare. One-half are sometimes without enough money to buy food. One-third have to cut the size of meals. Almost half find themselves unable to pay their rent or utility bills. Many more families are turning to locally funded services, food banks, churches, and other charities for aid. Many of those charities are already overburdened. In some locales, homeless shelters and housing assistance programs are closing their doors to new customers, food banks are running out of food, and other charities are being forced to tighten their eligibility requirements. . . .

Although the results of welfare reform may creep up on us slowly and almost imperceptibly, to proclaim this experiment in family values and the work ethic a "success" would be, at minimum, short-sighted. If we care only about our pocketbooks, the results of this reform will ultimately be more costly than the system that preceded it. If we care only about the nation's productivity, then the principles of enlightened self-interest would suggest that malnourished future laborers and caregivers stressed to the breaking point are not going to further that goal. If we care about the family, then tortured gender relations, double-shifts, family unfriendly employers, latch key kids, inadequately funded childcare centers, and high rates of domestic violence are nothing to celebrate. And if we care about the principles of independent citizenship and commitment to others, then it must be recognized that welfare reform represents little more than a weak-kneed retreat and a cowardly response to massive social change.

To confront the social problems that welfare reform was purported to solve requires public support for the work of care and directly addressing unjust social inequalities that leave so many Americans excluded from full citizenship. This is no small order. But this examination of welfare reform, I hope, can serve as a reminder that the effort required is important not only for those at the bottom of the social hierarchy, but for all of us.

86

MICHELE WUCKER

From *Lockout*

American history is the history of immigrants, but in the early twenty-first century, the debate over immigration is far from settled. Michele Wucker first offers some survey research data on the jobs that immigrants fill in the American economy. She finds that immigrants take both menial and highly technical positions; they could be uneducated laborers or they could be doctors. She finds that Americans' views toward recent immigrants reflect contradictory attitudes. Immigrants make important contributions but are simultaneously looked down on. Wucker then brings us to a New York town that's the scene of a confrontation between the Minutemen Civil Defense Corps, a group that has tried to guard the Mexican border, and pro-immigration demonstrators. A place for day laborer immigrants to gather was the immediate cause of the fray. Flags, digital cameras, banners, and chants all contributed to the tense confrontation, with news reporters finding themselves in the middle of the action. The author profiles one of the Minutemen whom she finds to be willing to exchange ideas in a friendly way. In fact, Wucker and her interviewee agree on a villain: employers who use immigrants' illegal status to cover up labor violations. Today, the issue of immigration remains a divisive one in American society, intertwined as it is with issues of the economy, of race, and of the nation's heritage.

⬤

DURING HIS TENURE AS FEDERAL RESERVE Board chairman, Alan Greenspan made the case often that the U.S. economy needs immigration of both skilled and unskilled workers. "As we are creating an ever more complex, sophisticated, accelerating economy, the necessity to have the ability to bring in resources and people from abroad to keep it functioning in the most effective manner increasingly strikes me as relevant policy," he testified to the U.S. Senate in 2000. During the 1990s, he frequently praised immigration for keeping inflation in check and thus enabling the Fed to keep interest rates low and in turn create the longest stretch of peacetime prosperity in memory. The low wages that kept inflation tame were, of course, a bane as well as a boon, since immigration of low-skilled workers was thought to hurt the job prospects of America's least educated and lowest-paid workers, and resentment soon grew over society's poorest members having to pay a heavy price for everyone else's prosperity.

There should be no doubt that immigration is a pillar of the U.S. economy as a whole. A 1995 survey polled a group of economists that included Nobel Prize winners, former members of the President's Council of Economic Advisers, and past presidents of the American Economic Association. When asked, "On balance, what effect has twentieth-century immigration had on the nation's economic growth?" an overwhelming 81 percent of respondents answered "favorable," with the remaining 19 percent replying "slightly favorable." Not a single one believed that immigration hurt America's economy.

Many Americans think of immigrants as doing "the jobs that Americans won't do"—the jobs that occupy most of the long-running U.S. argument over whether immigration is too high, too low, or at just about the right level. Certainly, these jobs—farming, construction, services—are so important to the day-to-day functioning of our economy that even Americans who believe that immigration is too high recognize that we depend on low-skilled immigrant workers. Immigrants make up a large percentage of employees in agriculture (37 percent), services (23 percent), and home maintenance work, such as landscaping and housecleaning (42 percent). Overall, however, this work is not representative of the jobs immigrants do.

Few Americans realize how much we depend on the immigrants at the other end of the socioeconomic spectrum: the engineers, scientists, entrepreneurs, and scholars who drive the knowledge economy. Immigrants make up only 20 percent of low-wage workers but represent 50 percent of research and development workers and 25 percent of doctors and nurses. About a quarter of foreign-born workers are managers and professionals; one-fifth are in technical, sales, and administrative support, and another fifth are in service occupations; 18 percent work as operators, fabricators, and laborers. Only 4 percent work in stereotypical fields like farming, forestry, and fishing.

Despite the stereotype of the immigrant as a low-skilled and poorly educated worker, the vast majority of foreign-born workers have completed high school, and 45 percent of foreign workers have attended or completed college—a rate higher than among American workers. To be sure, 30 percent of foreign-born workers here have not completed high school, compared with just 7 percent of those born in this country.

Although they are spread across occupations, immigrants nevertheless are overrepresented among low-skilled workers, underrepresented among those with high school and some college education, and overrepresented among the highest-skilled population. They represent only a small number relative to the total foreign-born population, yet the lowest-skilled immigrants are at the center of a growing controversy over how warm a welcome America should give immigrants. Although Americans are likely to agree that low-skilled immigrants, legal and illegal, make essential contributions to our economy, these immigrants are also the ones who attract the most profound resentment. They represent the other half of America's immigration mythology: the tired, the poor, the huddled masses yearning to breathe free. America's attitudes toward unskilled immigrants have come to define the national immigration debate and shape policies toward all the noncitizens on whom the U.S. economy depends—and thus the fate of the huddled masses will profoundly affect our future ability to attract the best and the brightest as well. . . .

On a clear late-summer day in the town of Babylon, a crowd gathered in front of American Legion Post 94 on an otherwise quiet Long Island street an hour's train ride from New York City. With pale yellow wood siding and white trim, the building could have come straight out of *Leave It to Beaver* had it not been for the graffiti freshly painted on it the night before. Several grim-faced men stood on the front steps, monitoring everyone who approached and letting in select groups, two or three at a time, of people whose main distinguishing feature was that they were so nondescript: the kind of typical white Americans you might see at the supermarket or the hardware store. They were members of the Minutemen Civil Defense Corps, the group that organized a month-long volunteer patrol of the U.S.-Mexico border in April 2005, and they had called this September meeting on Long Island to organize a similar vigil along the U.S.-Canada border in October 2005. The Minutemen had attracted attention not only for their border patrol efforts, but also for the white-supremacist groups that had embraced their work. The Minutemen tried to portray themselves as law-abiding concerned citizens, but it was hard to live down America's sad history of crimes committed when individuals have taken the law into their own hands. Nor did widely circulated photographs of Nazi flags being waved at a Minutemen rally help their cause. President George W. Bush and Secretary of State Condoleezza Rice had called the Minutemen vigilantes, a term that still rankled members of the group.

Long Island was far from the Canadian and Mexican borders, but it was nonetheless a major battleground in an intensifying war over illegal immigration. A few weeks earlier, Suffolk County Executive Steve Levy had ordered the expulsion of immigrants living in an overcrowded house, responding to residents' understandable complaints over building code violations but leaving the residents with no place at all to live. The new controversy stirred up emotions that were still raw from a fight that took

place after a brutal attack in 2000 on Mexican day laborers in Farmingville, a once bucolic town of 15,000. The attack, portrayed movingly in
the documentary film *Farmingville,* polarized residents, some of whom saw
illegal immigration as the main problem and deportation as the only solution, and others who felt that the blame fell on unscrupulous employers
and landlords. Residents fought tooth and nail over a proposal to provide
a central place where day laborers could seek work instead of congregat-
ing on streets and curbs. National pro- and anti-immigration groups had
adopted Farmingville as a cause, drawing the town into a high-stakes
struggle that was a proxy for national issues.

Eventually the Minutemen joined the fray. Not surprisingly, many of
the Long Islanders who had opposed the day laborer center were among
the forty or so people who showed up that September afternoon. The
Minutemen stationed on the American Legion hall steps warily eyed a
growing delegation of protesters on the sidewalk. Both sides were armed
with digital cameras and video recorders, photographing each other. As
the protesters marched back and forth on the sidewalk, a man who sympathized with the Minutemen stood in their midst, audio-recording the
whole thing.

The protesters were a hodgepodge: families of liberal Jewish New
Yorkers; serious-faced Mexican and Central American men and women;
greasy-haired teenagers dressed in black with pierced noses and eyebrows;
and white middle-class Long Islanders. Holding a saucepan and a wooden
spoon, a frightened-looking boy who was about six years old walked beside his mother, caught between the shouting protesters and Minutemen.
A poster reading "Stop the Hate," clearly a veteran of many marches, waved
above the protesters' heads next to an anarchist flag and several prints of a
Native American chief declaring "Deport Illegal Immigrants"—clearly
suggesting that the immigrants whose presence the Minutemen were
protesting had as much right to be here as the white Minutemen who
held their own "Deport Illegal Immigrants" signs. "No Human Being Is
Illegal!" read another placard.

"Are you Native American?" one of the protesters screamed. "If you're
not, then you're an immigrant too. We're all immigrants." A wiry Minuteman with sun-leathered skin and a nervous, angry energy screamed back
at them, "Illegal means illegal! Do you know what the word illegal means?"
The protesters tried out various chants against Nazis, fascists, racists, and
homophobes. "Racists Go Home!" they yelled. A heavyset middle-aged
woman sitting on the steps hollered back, "I *am* home!" Both sides mirrored the increasingly polarized tone of a national debate. To the protesters, the Minutemen were Nazis, vigilantes, fascists, racists. Too many of the

Minutemen, for their part, had taken the stance that anyone who wasn't with them was against them: if you didn't agree with their methods, then you were against protecting America.

At the foot of the steps of the American Legion hall, an argument broke out as several newspaper reporters—many of them from Hispanic media—protested loudly that they were not being allowed in to what had been billed as a public meeting. Reporters from two local television stations were allowed in, but no one else from the media (except for a Long Island newspaper reporter who pretended not to be one). Later, when a television reporter from Univision tried to get in, she was refused. "It's too bad my wife isn't here," said the gatekeeper. "She's from Venezuela and she's very upset by illegal immigration." The reporter stiffened at his condescension. "Sir, I was born in Puerto Rico and you should know that I am an American citizen," she said. The gatekeeper told her he'd send someone out to be interviewed, but after the reporter descended the steps, he made no move to do so. If the Minutemen hoped to control damage to their image by barring reporters from their meeting, they had succeeded in doing exactly the opposite through their unsubtle choices of which media representatives to let in and through the question they left in everyone's mind: If they were indeed the law-abiding citizens they claimed to be, what did they have to hide?

During the course of the afternoon, it became clear that there was no such thing as a typical Minuteman. There was, of course, Chris Simcox, the group's thin, tense-lipped founder, wound up with nervous energy, who had moved to Arizona from California and bought a local newspaper, which he used as a mouthpiece for his campaign. There were the angry men dressed in varying combinations of red, white, and blue. There were the Farmingville residents who complained about overcrowded homes, public urination, the illegal status of day laborers, and the government's failure to do anything about illegal immigration.

A Minuteman in a cowboy hat and boots was a Pennsylvania native who had made Arizona his home for more than a decade and become fed up with rising petty crime and the complaints of ranchers whose land the migrants were crossing indiscriminately. As I asked questions to try to understand where he was coming from—and he asked questions of his own to try to get a sense of how I might portray him—I was pleasantly surprised that he seemed open to information that contradicted his assumptions. When I told him about a recent study suggesting that there were many times more people who wanted to learn English in New York than there were classroom spaces for, he said he was glad to hear that. We disagreed, of course, on how to address the problem of illegal immigration. He was confident that it was possible to secure the Mexican border—after all, the Minutemen had succeeded in closing down part of it in April, he said. But, I pointed out, that was only twenty miles. To secure more than 2,000 miles would require more than 50,000 people, not just for one month but for a very long time. And that wouldn't solve the problem of making sure that the American economy had the workers it needed.

We agreed to disagree on the border issue, but he agreed wholeheartedly when I said I thought a big problem was the unscrupulous employers who used immigrants' illegal status to abuse them—some employers even call immigration authorities on themselves to clear out workers who complained about violations of labor and safety laws. It was that type of employer that dragged down wages and made American workers far less attractive than illegal immigrants to employers. Why hire someone at higher wages who was not afraid of being deported if he stood up for his rights? By making it impossible for honest businesses to find legal immigrant workers, and by not imposing any meaningful financial or other kinds of penalties on abusive employers, our lawmakers had been making the problem worse.

The Minuteman in the cowboy hat nodded. "I feel for them. I really do," he said. "The illegal immigrants are caught in the middle, and so are the American people." Our conversation was interrupted as the group on the sidewalk degenerated into a series of catch-all slogans. As they inveighed against President Bush and the war in Iraq, the Minuteman shook his head. "You know, I actually agree with those protesters on a lot of things." . . .

We Americans view ourselves as the most tolerant nation in the world, able to create *e pluribus unum,* one out of many. "The nature of this country is one that is good-hearted and our people are compassionate," President Bush declared in 2004 after he relaunched a plan to give guest worker status to undocumented immigrants who have been working hard in American jobs. Most of us would agree. We cannot separate our identity and our future from the question of whom to welcome to America and how to welcome them. The fear is that losing control of who is American means losing control of America. But our demographics are only part of our destiny. What has made America great has been our ability to shape that destiny as one nation made of many peoples.

When I told a friend who heads research at a respected New York think tank that I was writing about the growing pressures to close the doors to immigrants, he raised an eyebrow. But America is one of the most open countries in the world, he said, noting the president's guest worker proposal, the size of the foreign-born population, and our open society.

He is right. After all, roughly a million immigrants come here each year, more by far than to any other country in the world; America hosts one out of five immigrants worldwide. One in eight people in this country were born elsewhere, the highest level in a century. About half a million newcomers take the Oath of Citizenship each year to become naturalized Americans. The stars of the 2004 Democratic and Republican national conventions both came with stories of the immigrant's American Dream: Arnold Schwarzenegger, the Austrian immigrant turned movie star and California governor, and Barack Obama, the son of an American mother and a Kenyan father who had emigrated to America. We like to be inspired by our apparent openness to immigrants. We are even talking about amending the Constitution to allow a foreign-born president—inspired, of course, by the ultimate American Dream success story of an Austrian bodybuilder who became a movie superstar, married into American political royalty, and won a landslide election to become governor of California.

"In my book, anyone who comes here and gives an honest day's work for an honest day's pay is not only putting himself closer to the American Dream, he's helping the rest of us get there too," the Australian-born media mogul, Rupert Murdoch, wrote in the *Wall Street Journal*. "Frankly it doesn't bother me in the least that millions of people are attracted to our shores. What we should worry about is the day they no longer find these shores attractive. In an era when too many of our pundits declare that the American Dream is a fraud, it is America's immigrants who remind us— by dint of their success—that the Dream is alive, and well within reach of anyone willing to work for it." . . .

America is at a tipping point in our attitudes not only toward immigration but toward our country's role in the world. Today's mix of global interdependence with the threat of global terrorism and economic and demographic change has created a maelstrom of fears. Encompassing concerns about our borders, our cultural and national identity, and our ability to maintain unity, immigrants represent all of the touch-points of our collective insecurity. Any change that comes too rapidly creates anxiety in even the most tolerant of societies. The contradictory and uniquely American tendency to both demonize and romanticize the immigrant has only confused matters. Politicians and interest groups cynically invoke both emotions, sending the country swinging wildly from one pole to the other and making it all the harder to see through the fog of rhetoric.

The terrorist attacks of September 11, carried out by foreigners who

had come here under various immigrant and nonimmigrant visa categories (some of which had lapsed, making their continued presence illegal),
merely catalyzed an immigration debate that had already been building
for many years. With roughly a million immigrants arriving in the United
States each year through the 1980s and 1990s, the foreign-born population was approaching 12 percent of the U.S. population, the highest
proportion in a century. The sheer mass of people had long since overwhelmed our immigration bureaucracy, and as a result more and more
immigrants—about one in three, by some estimates—have been coming
here illegally. Many of the new immigrants, legal and illegal, come from
Latin America and Asia and are not white, which adds a racial element to
the massive demographic change taking place.

The ending in the 1950s and 1960s of race-based immigration bars,
combined with growing diversity and racial acceptance, opened many
doors for immigrants who did not happen to be born white. This change
speaks worlds of Americans' ability to find common ground in differences,
yet it also exposes the lingering prejudices that we have not yet overcome.
Recessions and the loss of manufacturing jobs in recent decades have
made Americans feel that their economic future is insecure even as they
noticed that immigrants who looked different no longer occupy mainly
the stereotypical jobs at the bottom of the ladder, the work that "Americans didn't want to do," but instead are solidly embedded in the American
middle class. The racial and ethnic differences represented by recent immigration catalyze the volatility of the country's reaction to them.

87

STEVEN COHEN

From *Understanding Environmental Policy*

The subject of the environment does not belong to any one set of experts, author Steven Cohen explains. That's part of the problem. Political scientists, economists, scientists, and business owners each have a unique but incomplete perspective. Cohen offers a simple but not simplistic way to approach environmental issues. While citizens often view the environment in very large and extremely complex terms—cap-and-trade legislation, multination anti-pollution pledges, global warming and melting ice caps—Cohen observes that environmental issues also exist in much smaller, more local, less dramatic yet still highly complicated ways, such as New York City's solid waste disposal: that is, garbage. The author gives us the basics on the city's waste disposal history, strategies, and upcoming crises. Many elements in this case study are applicable to other environmental problems in other places. NIMBY (Not In My Backyard) is a controversy that surfaces in almost every environmental debate in each city and town in America. Cohen provides a detailed analysis of the New York City garbage problem, with special emphasis on the role of new technologies—both good and bad—in the decision-making process. Cohen concludes by noting that New York City is not the only city with solid waste disposal problems. Some solutions may come from other U.S. cities that have tried innovative ideas.

ENVIRONMENTAL POLICY IS A COMPLEX and multidimensional issue. As Harold Seidman observed in *Politics, Position, and Power: The Dynamics of Federal Organization*, "Where you stand depends on where you sit." Put another way, one's position in an organization influences one's stance and perspective on the issues encountered. Similarly, one's take on an environmental issue or the overall issue of environmental protection varies according to one's place in society and the nature of one's professional training.

For example, to a business manager, the environmental issue is a set of rules one needs to understand in order to stay out of trouble. For the most part, environmental policy is a nuisance or at least an impediment to profit. Perhaps someday business managers will see it as a set of conditions that facilitate rather than impede the accumulation of wealth. For now, most business practitioners see a conflict between environmental protection and economic development, although this view of a trade-off is false. To an engineer, the environmental problem is essentially physical and subject to solution through the application of technology. Engineers tend to focus on pollution control, pollution prevention (through changes in manufacturing processes or end-of-pipeline controls), and other technological fixes. Lawyers view the environment as an issue of property rights and contracts, and the regulations needed to protect them. Economists perceive the environment as a set of market failures resulting from problems of consumption or production. They search for market-driven alternatives to regulation. Political scientists view environmental policy as a political concern. To them, it is a problem generated by conflicting interests. Finally, for philosophers, the environment is an issue of values and differing worldviews.

The environment is subject to explanation and understanding through all these disciplines and approaches. It is, in fact, a composite of the elements identified by the various disciplines and societal positions, and likely has dimensions where the disciplines and social perspectives intersect. The difficulty is that each view tends to oversimplify environmental problems, contending with only one facet of the situation. . . .

For purposes of this analysis, an environmental problem is conceptualized as follows:

• *An issue of values.* What type of ecosphere do we wish to live in, and how does our lifestyle impact that ecosphere? To what extent do environmental problems and the policy approaches we take reflect the way that we value ecosystems and the worth we place on material consumption?

• *A political issue.* Which political processes can best maintain environmental quality, and what are the political dimensions of this environmental problem? How has the political system defined this problem and set the boundaries for its potential solution?

• *A technology and science issue.* Can science and technology solve environmental problems as quickly as they create them? Do we have the science in place to truly understand the causes and effects of this environmental problem? Does the technology exist to solve the environmental problem or mitigate its impacts?

• *A policy design and economic issue.* What public policies are needed to reduce environmentally damaging behaviors? How can corporate and private behavior be influenced? What mix of incentives and disincentives seem most effective? What economic factors have caused pollution and stimulated particular forms of environmental policy? Economic forces are a major influence on the development of environmental problems and the shape of environmental policy. In this framework we view these economic forces as part of the more general issue of policy design. While most of the causes and effects of policy are economic, some relate to other factors such as security and political power.

• *A management issue.* Which administrative and organizational arrangements have proven most effective at protecting the environment? Do we have the organizational capacity in place to solve the environmental problem?

This multifaceted framework is delineated as an explicit corrective to analysts who narrowly focus on only one or two dimensions of an environmental problem. . . .

. . . We now turn to an application of that framework for understanding the problem of disposing New York City's garbage. Examining each dimension of the city's solid waste problem will provide a comprehensive explanation of the problem and its potential solution. The city's garbage problem will be examined as an issue of values, as a political issue, and as a problem for science and technology. Finally, we will address the policy design and management dimensions of the issue.

As noted, solid waste is not only an issue for New York City but is also a national problem. In 1960 Americans generated approximately 88.1 million tons of waste per year, which is equivalent to 2.7 pounds per person every day. By 1990 that number grew to 205.2 million tons per year and 4.5 pounds per person per day. During the next decade per capita waste remained stable at 4.5 pounds per day, but total waste rose to 232 tons in 2000. From 1960 to 2000 the total amount of waste generated grew from 88 to 232 tons per year. . . .

New York City's eight million residents and millions of businesses, construction projects, and nonresident employees generate as much as 36,200 tons of municipal solid waste per day. The city's Department of Sanitation (DOS) handles nearly 13,000 tons per day of waste generated by residents, public agencies, and nonprofit corporations; private carting companies handle the remainder. During the twentieth century the DOS relied on a number of landfills for garbage disposal. Then, in December 2001, the city's last garbage dump, Fresh Kills Landfill in Staten Island, closed. In response, the City Council adopted a twenty-year plan for exporting DOS-managed waste. Export became the exclusive waste disposal option for New York City.

Throughout New York City's history it has had problems with solid waste management. In 1894, four years before the incorporation of the City of Greater New York, the city stopped its practice of dumping garbage into the ocean. Instead, it began a new program that included recycling and composting. Soon, however, a new administration took office, and ocean dumping resumed. A federal lawsuit filed by a group of New Jersey coastal cities forced New York City to end ocean dumping in 1935. With plans for new incinerators slowed, first by the Great Depression and then by World War II, the city found it more and more difficult to meet its waste disposal needs. In 1947 the Fresh Kills Landfill opened. Initially the Staten Island dump was going to be a "clean fill," and the city's new mayor promised that "raw" garbage would only be landfilled at Fresh Kills for three years, the time it would take to design, site, and build a large incinerator in every borough. By the 1960s, however, one-third of the city's trash was burned in more than seventeen thousand apartment building incinerators and twenty-two municipal incinerators. The remaining residential refuse was still sent to Fresh Kills as well as to the city's other landfills.

As we noted in an Earth Institute report: "As environmental awareness grew, public pressure began to mount against incineration and landfilling. Old landfills and incinerators were gradually shut down, with the last municipal incinerator closed in 1992." By the late 1990s only Fresh Kills remained as a waste disposal option for the residential and public waste managed by the DOS.

In May 1996 Mayor Rudolph Giuliani and Governor George Pataki announced that Fresh Kills would receive its last ton of garbage no later than January 1, 2002. With the exception of the remains of the World Trade Center, that landfill has been closed since the last day of 2001. In an effort to determine how the city should go about disposing nearly 13,000 tons of daily waste previously sent to the site, a Fresh Kills Closure Task Force was established by the city government. The principal goal of the task force was to develop a short-term plan for diverting the waste from Fresh Kills up to its full closure in 2001. The next step was to develop a longer-term solution. . . .

In the summer of 2002 the city began to take some steps to develop elements of a true long-term plan for managing waste. While the overall waste export strategy was still being pursued, Mayor Michael Bloomberg announced a plan to develop garbage transfer stations that would compact refuse and ship it by barge for disposal. These stations would be placed in waterfront locations in each of the five New York City boroughs and would replace a system of land-based waste transfer that currently uses thousands of diesel-fueled trucks daily to haul garbage through city streets to disposal sites in other states. In late 2003 the projected expense of building these transfer stations grew, putting the plan on hold.

The current system of waste export in 2005 still leaves the city vulnerable over the long run, as both restrictions on waste disposal and its costs are likely to escalate. . . .

Our discussion of New York City's solid waste problem begins with an analysis of the values intrinsic to the issue, beginning with those that shape the consumption patterns responsible for creating 13,000 tons of residential garbage each day. The use of large amounts of packaging material, and the relatively minimal level of recycling, reflect the community's collective values. The preference for exporting waste is based on a desire to avoid the potential environmental insult of treating garbage and on the values underlying the "not in my backyard" (NIMBY) syndrome. The consumption behaviors described show little sign of fundamental change from decade to decade. Although the growth in per capita waste disposal in New York City has begun to slow, mirroring national trends, New Yorkers clearly value the benefits of a throwaway society. The value system supporting this mode of consumption dominates and has kept waste reduction off the political agenda. The issue does not pertain only to New York City; although the size and density of that city's population intensify its solid waste problem. At the root of the problem are consumption patterns that currently prevail in all modern, developed economies. New Yorkers probably place a higher value on convenience and service than may be typical, but the difference is one of degree rather than kind.

A subtle choice of values is also reflected in the way the public and the governing elite try to avoid the waste issue. Perhaps that is partly because garbage is physically unpleasant and also because it is a reminder of the great wealth some of us enjoy in the face of poverty. We discard food and clothing that could provide sustenance to the world's poor. And then, too, garbage is ugly and foul-smelling; we prefer not to think about it or where it ends up. Coupled with this attitude is the historic tendency to process garbage as far away as possible from the middle and upper classes. This helps to propagate the fantasy that all those green plastic mounds of garbage bags on the street are placed in a garbage truck and magically transported to some mythical solid waste heaven.

This pairing of convenience-driven consumption with waste avoidance is the value underpinning the city's solid waste management crisis. In contrast, throughout the twentieth century, New York invested many billions of dollars in a water supply system that is arguably the best in the world. As this demonstrates, the city does have the capacity and resources to develop long-term plans for infrastructure investment to address environmental problems—just not for garbage. . . .

The value issues described . . . have created a climate of opinion for the politics of waste that makes it difficult for local decision makers to address the city's solid waste issues. At the core of this issue is the local politics around choosing the sites for waste disposal, transfer, and treatment facilities. Garbage is inherently undesirable, and obviously there is no positive spin that can be placed on being the host site for a community's waste. The political antipathy to waste in New York was demonstrated for more than two decades by the local politics of waste in Staten Island. The highest priority for most of Staten Island's elected officials during the 1990s was to close the Fresh Kills Landfill. In the late 1980s and early 1990s the borough engaged in an effort to secede from New York City, partly to end the use of Staten Island as the city's dump. As a sparsely populated and predominantly Republican borough in a Democratic city, Staten Island had little leverage until Republican Rudolph Giuliani was elected mayor in 1993.

Local politicians, with few exceptions, have caved in to the longstanding antipathy toward locating waste facilities in New York City. In the 1980s, highly conflicted but with enormous political courage, the then mayor Ed Koch obtained an agreement to site a waste incinerator in each borough. Mayor Koch's incinerator agreement collapsed during the Dinkins and Giuliani administrations, as each subsequent mayor decided that community opposition to the siting was too intense to override. Even environmentalists, while arguing against landfilling and long-distance waste transportation, are even more opposed to siting a garbage incinerator or a waste-to-energy plant within New York City's five boroughs. The politics of waste, particularly the community politics of siting, has been the principal constraint on policy options for managing the city's waste. . . .

New York City's extreme population density has necessitated a number of technological innovations including an extensive mass transit network, electricity and water systems, modern sewage treatment and removal, product packaging, food refrigeration, preservatives, and, of course, solid waste removal. The technology of waste incineration has advanced dramatically since the 1960s, when much of the city's waste was burned in apartment building and municipal incinerators. Today probably the most environmentally sound methods for disposing the daily waste generated by the city's eight million residents and four million workers or visitors are regional or local waste-to-energy plants or other new and advanced waste treatment technologies. The remaining smaller volume of waste would be exported via marine waste transfer stations or rail transfer through a train tunnel from New Jersey to Brooklyn. Marine or rail transfer of waste and modern incineration or waste treatment can significantly reduce the number of collection truck miles and also maximize the ability to collect and recycle toxic materials and heavy metals. The potential for waste leakage from landfills would also be reduced. But despite the existence of appropriate and effective waste disposal technology that is actually more affordable than the current waste system, the politics of siting continues to dominate the issue.

Experts in waste disposal are not trusted and the government lacks credibility, and so even though there is a scientific solution to the problem, politics disallows the use of the new technology. If science could reduce waste plant emissions to zero, and if experts credible to the public and interest groups could confirm the improved technology, scientific fact *might* influence the political dialogue. A non-incinerator-based technology in which garbage is treated by a closed-system chemical process and transformed into a more useful, non-waste product or lower-volume material might achieve greater public acceptance. But as demonstrated by the debate over the global climate change, the more complex the issue, the more likely that scientific uncertainty remains. Thus the NIMBY syndrome and the political self-interest of some local community-based organizations continue to take precedence over scientific progress. . . .

Another aspect of the solid waste dilemma as a policy issue is its regulatory dimension. Local, state, and federal governments in the United States regulate waste disposal. Individuals and apartment building staff must package and sort garbage in specified ways. If it is packaged or sorted incorrectly, fines or noncollection may result. The visibility of the issue and the immediacy of enforcement make the regulatory dimensions of this issue relatively straightforward.

One partial solution is a policy that encourages waste reduction. The tax system or command-and-control regulation can be used to reduce packaging or to encourage the development and use of biodegradable packaging. For several reasons, however, these kinds of policies would be difficult for a city government to implement. . . .

More than five thousand communities nationwide have implemented a Pay-As-You-Throw system, making it available to 20 percent of the population. This number includes many smaller municipalities but also urban centers such as San Francisco, Seattle, Fort Worth, Austin, Buffalo, New Orleans, and the second largest U.S. city, Los Angeles, with a population of 3.8 million. As noted above, these cities have a distinct advantage in implementing this type of program as they consist largely of single-family or small-unit apartments in contrast to the high-rise residential buildings of New York City.

Arguably, Chicago and San Francisco offer the greatest comparisons to New York because of their population density and prevalence of older, multi-family structures. Chicago, with a population of 2.85 million, offers residential solid waste pickup only to structures that have fewer than five housing units. Residential buildings with more than four units must contract with a private solid waste removal or recycling company. The City of Chicago, Department of Streets and Sanitation collects 1.1 million tons of residential garbage and 300,000 tons of recycling annually. All this was collected from approximately 750,000 residential structures. Thus the waste from more than 300,000 larger residential units and all commercial properties were managed by private firms.

San Francisco has a residential population of nearly 800,000. Its entire municipal waste system is contracted out to the private firm Norcal Waste Systems. Sixty percent of housing in the city is comprised of structures of five units or fewer. These smaller units participate in a Pay-As-You-Throw program through a privately contracted firm. The remaining 40 percent of the city's housing is six-units or more. The city has been in a state of flux for several years trying to implement appropriate volume/frequency rates that still provide an appropriate level of incentive for individual residents to reduce waste. To its credit, San Francisco has one of the most aggressive recycling campaigns in the United States. Recycling, which is also conducted by Norcal, is available to nearly 90 percent of the city's apartment houses. The city reports a diversion rate upward of 63 percent. San Francisco has set an ambitious goal to divert 75 percent of the garbage generated by city businesses, residents, and visitors from landfills by 2010. Clearly, other cities in the United States are more successful than New York in managing solid waste. Perhaps New York can learn from these other cities and will some day be able to take out its own garbage.

88

KEVIN PHILLIPS

From *Bad Money*

The severe recession that hit the American economy in 2008 presented policymakers with daily challenges: saving banks, bailing out automobile companies, aiding foreclosed homeowners. The news was punctuated with talk of unemployment, stimulus, deflation, fear of inflation, executive compensation, and debt, debt, debt. Noted commentator Kevin Phillips, who has taken on some of the big issues of the twentieth century, turns our focus here to the causes of the economic crisis that transformed the American economy. If we understand how it happened, maybe it won't happen again. "The great credit bubble" had been building up for quite a while, Phillips notes. He traces how one problem led to the next and the next. He indicts the nation's reliance on the financial industry as a replacement for the old manufacturing economy.

FOR CENTURIES, THE IMPORTANCE of harvesttime in the affairs of men made August and September months notorious for declarations of war, crop failures, and, eventually, bank crises. . . .

By the twenty-first century, of course, farm calendars no longer guided major events in North America or Europe, save for well-attended fairs and festivals or the pleasure of buying raspberries, peaches, sweet corn, and cider at roadside stands. However, in the United States, a new economic seasonality—the high point in late spring and summer of new and existing home sales—helped set the time frame for the financial markets' 2007 mortgage and credit spasms. Falling prices fanned concern that housing's giddy five-year buoyancy had created a bubble, indeed one already starting to pop; concern crystallized into panic, at least in the mass media and the financial markets, when June and July data dashed any lingering hopes for a sales and price rebound.

Nearly a year earlier, very different public concerns—a quagmire in Iraq, and Republican sexual scandals and attendant moral hypocrisies—had taken over the 2006 midterm elections, returning control of Congress to the Democrats after twelve Republican years. Worry about soon-to-be-inadequate world oil supplies and the mountainous U.S. buildup of public and private debt, particularly home mortgages, were merely clouds on the horizon—perils, but not ones determining how people voted . . . yet.

That changed in mid-2007. Surging gasoline demand as springtime put motorists back on the road had focused May attentions on oil prices. Now roiling financial markets took global center stage, spooked by home foreclosure data, several hedge fund problems, and ominous projections of further foreclosures and price declines to come. As the days passed, fear spread—from subprime mortgages to the collateralized debt obligations (CDOs) into which asset loans had been opaquely repackaged. In August, apprehensions also stalled leveraged buyouts for want of funds, made banks unwilling to loan to one another, and froze the normal activity in commercial paper and other suddenly hard-to-value situations and product innovations. The impact was worldwide. From London to Tokyo, credit market after credit market froze toward illiquidity. Buyers sat on their hands, kept inactive by too little information about the new products' enigmatic content and wary of undisclosed risk. The once-sought-after CDOs could no longer be valued or "marked to market," or even marked to model, the next resort, but only, as skeptics remarked, marked to make-believe, a poisonous perception. Investors heard talk of the possible deleveraging of the global credit bubble—the privately feared "great unwind." Recession and deflation might be just over the hill. Other financial shivers—trembling municipal bonds, money market funds, and plain vanilla stocks—added to the worst August market chills since the mobilizations of 1914 had shut down bourses on both sides of the Atlantic. (The New York Stock Exchange, closed on July 31, 1914, did not resume full trading for four months.)

The 2007 crisis quickly revealed watershed characteristics. The great credit bubble, over two decades in its shaping, had since the 1980s been kept aloft and generally expanding by uplifts of monetary expansion from the U.S. Federal Reserve and other central banks. Having taken so long to form, cycle watchers thought, it would take years, not months, to unwind and deleverage. Proximate and wobbly currency and petroleum situations might add their own domino effects. Nor was the process assured of a happy ending through the wave of a central bank magic wand. Not unless, as the old adage says, God once again took particular care of fools, drunks, and the United States of America.

. . . [F]ar-reaching economic and political events and consequences began to unfold in midsummer's melee—developments that at least in part followed the direction that many specialists had foreseen—regarding U.S. housing prices, credit-bubble risk, the instability of so many financial innovations never crisis-tested, the ever-more-apparent inadequacy of global oil production, the related vulnerability of the dollar, and, behind it all, the false assurance of American "imperial" hubris. The administration of George W. Bush, rarely known for strategic grasp, miscued again in the early days of the crisis. Statements by the president, the secretary of the treasury, and the chairman of the Federal Reserve Board that the low-quality-mortgage meltdown would be short-lived and safely contained were disproved almost overnight. The principal catalysts of marketplace panic were some $500 billion of collateralized debt obligations seen to be tainted by subprime mortgages: "Ninja" loans, so called because unqualified borrowers had "no income, no job or assets." The CDOs quickly spread wider destruction than had been rumored for the vaunted weapons never found in Iraq (investor Warren Buffett, in 2003, had prophetically nominated derivatives as the "weapons of mass destruction" especially to be feared).

History does seem to repeat itself, if only in outline or rhyme. Unfortunately, vague memories of past financial bubbles almost never suffice to inoculate a people or nation against repeating an earlier generation's mistakes. Despite highly cautioning precedents, the U.S. financial services circa 2007, swollen to an unprecedented and unstable 21 percent of gross domestic product, had laid down a national and international playing field no more controllable than the earlier venues of the Gilded Age and the Roaring Twenties. Technology, quantitative mathematics, and leverage allowed more to go wrong more quickly, and with much greater global reach. Twenty-first-century risk turned out to be spread and distributed in a negative rather than positive way.

Aggravating matters, America's sprawling financial debtscape of 2007—some $11 trillion in federal, state, and local obligations, plus a towering private issuance of $37 trillion (mostly financial, corporate, and mortgage)—had attained most of that size and clutter over the two previous frenetic decades. When Alan Greenspan had taken up the eagle feathers of Federal Reserve Board chieftainship in 1987, public and private debt in the United States had totaled $10.5 trillion. By 2006, following his departure, total credit market debt had quadrupled to $43 trillion. The best-publicized part of the surge, in various forms of mortgage borrowing, came when the Fed, anxious to stimulate the weakened post-9/11 economy, dropped the key overnight interest rate, already low, several times more to an ultrastimulative 1 percent in July 2003. In the abstract, this mortgage bet was plausible; in its multiyear government and private implementation, though, the mistakes and abuses are still surfacing.

Huge sums were involved. Debt in record quantities had been piled on top of the trillions still extant from the binges of the eighties and nineties, so that by 2007 the nation's overseers watched a U.S. economy in which public and private indebtedness was three times bigger than that year's gross domestic product. This ratio topped the prior record, set during the years after the stock market crash of 1929. However, in contrast to the 1920s and 1930s, when manufacturing retained its overwhelming primacy despite the economy's temporary froth of stockmarket and financial ballyhoo, the eighties and nineties brought a much deeper transformation. Goods production lost the two-to-one edge in GDP it had enjoyed in the seventies. In 2005, on the cusp of Greenspan's retirement, financial services—the new übercategory spanning finance, insurance, and real estate—far exceeded other sectors, totaling over one-fifth of GDP against manufacturing's gaunt, shrunken 12 percent. During the two previous decades (and only marginally stalled by the early 1990s debt bailouts), the baton of economic leadership had been passed.

In the new century, a burgeoning debt and credit complex—vendors of credit cards, issuers of mortgages and bonds, architects of asset-backed securities and structured investment vehicles—occupied the leading edge. The behemoth financial conglomerates, Citigroup, JPMorgan Chase, et al., were liberated in 1999 for the first time since the 1930s to marshal banking, insurance, securities, and real estate under a single, vaulting institutional roof. Hedge funds, the bold boutiques, had multiplied from just a couple of hundred in the early 1990s to roughly ten thousand in mid-2007, deploying over $1.8 trillion in assets. Like digital buccaneers, and hardly more restrained than their seventeenth-century predecessors, they arbitraged the nooks and crannies of global finance, capturing even more return on capital than casino operators made from one-armed bandits and favorable gaming-table odds.

As the mortgage markets seized up in mid-2007, shrewd players understood the virginity of the terrain. Jack Malvey, the chief global fixed-income strategist for Lehman Brothers, explained: "This is what we would characterize as the first correction of the neo-credit market. We've never had a correction with these types of institutions and these types of instruments." Others distilled the doubts about hedge funds themselves— the exotic quantitative mathematics, the obscure language of fixed-leg features and two-step binomial trees, and the humongous bank loans needed for the fifteen- or twenty-to-one leverage that alchemized mere decimal points into financial Olympic gold medals.

New products often turned out to have Achilles' heels, like the misbehaving index arbitrage of so-called program insurance, the derivative innovation widely blamed for the 1987 crash, and the junk bonds derogated after their inventor went to jail. In 2007, the failures were multiple: besides the CDO and exotic mortage embarrassments, hedge funds' mathematical vulnerabilities included too many copycats doing the same thing, as well as an inability to deal with anarchic, almost random, volatility.... Some future congressional investigating committee would have a field day. Mathematically, what was theoretically impossible often manages to occur anyway. But the hedgies were big players, first-tier customers of first-tier lenders, and their bets sometimes accounted for as much as half the daily trading volume on the New York exchanges.

The average American, with other things to worry about, had little inkling of the financial sector's gargantuan size and clout or its resemblance to a laboratory of digital wagering....

Many insiders, of course, had sensed for months, even years, what was coming. The valuation of U.S. homebuilders' stocks hit a zenith in 2005, pulled down thereafter by sagging new-home demand and slowing price appreciation. New mortgage borrowing by households peaked in the third quarter of 2005, and had declined by 45 percent a year later. Building permit applications topped out in late 2005. The index of real estate investment trusts crested in 2006. California was already a patchwork quilt of cut-rate sales and unraveling prices. Housing foreclosures were setting national records during the last quarter of 2006 and the first quarter of 2007, even though the April–May–June peak-season disaster got the page 1 headlines.

By September 2007, the Mortgage Lender Implode-O-Meter—real enough, and easily found on the Internet—listed 150 U.S. mortgage lenders as having gone out of business or stopped making certain loans since December 2006, including American Home Mortgage and Ameriquest, once the nation's largest subprime lender. Even in late winter and spring, several dozen had already closed their doors. In May and June, endangered hedge funds also came to light. By late July and August, the bond and credit markets should not have been surprised. On the other hand, neither should markets have been surprised nine decades earlier when war came in August 1914. But they were. British bonds (consols) did not plunge until July 27, 1914, just days before. If markets are not always rational, the same is true of their willingness to anticipate bad news....

Huge stakes also drove the intense politics. In the United States, the UK, Canada, and Australia, your-home-is-your-castle nations where ownership reaches the 70 percent level, housing-centered crises are usually the ones that cut deepest into middle-class well-being. The explanation is simple. By some hypotheses, an informal, broadly defined "housing sector" of the U.S. economy—mortgage finance, construction, furnishings, lumber, and related industries—might represent a 25 percent share of the national gross domestic product, enough to include several million vulnerable jobs on top of the frightening blow to the national psyche's sense of well-being and stability.

And on top of that, between 2001 and 2006, an unprecedented number of Americans used their homes as ATMs, turning huge chunks of residential equity into borrowed, but spendable, cash. Harvard economist Martin Feldstein, a former Republican chairman of the White House Council of Economic Advisers, calculated in 2007 that over "the past five years, the value of U.S. home mortgage debt has increased by nearly $3 trillion. In 2004 alone, it increased by almost $1 trillion." He went on: "Net mortgage borrowing that year *not* used [my italics] for the purchase of new homes amounted to nearly $600 billion, or almost 7 percent of disposable personal income." In short, borrowing against homes enabled stressed consumers to keep consuming. . . .

. . . I've given this book the title *Bad Money,* and part of the explanation is caught up in what I think of as the malfeasance of "money," including lax oversight of the financial sector by Washington past and present. These failures laid the foundation for both of this volume's main concerns: first, the deadly interplay of financial sector growth and debt hubris with a hot-wired American housing crash; and second, the intertwined vulnerability of U.S. oil supremacy and the embattled, targeted dollar. Should both perils impact the U.S. financial markets simultaneously, as August 2007 hinted, the word "crisis" might prove to be an inadequate description.

In recent decades, many book titles and names for television programs have placed hot, flavorful adjectives—"old," "new," "easy," "dirty," "mad," "smart," and "dumb"—in front of greed's best-loved noun, "money." The pairing for this volume, *Bad Money,* is not intended to evoke nineteenth-century robber barons, twentieth-century salad oil swindlers, or twenty-first-century Enron architects. For now, that is too parochial. The reason for applying a negative characterization is historical and institutional, with a deep bow to the inherent vulnerability of human nature exposed to pecuniary temptation, witnessed today on an unprecedented scale. Money is "bad," in the historical sense, when a leading world economic power passing its zenith—before the United States, think Hapsburg Spain, the maritime Dutch Republic (when New York was New Amsterdam), and imperial Britain just before World War I—lets itself luxuriate in finance at the expense of harvesting, manufacturing, or transporting things. Doing so has marked each nation's global decline. *To institutionalize the dominance of minimally regulated finance at this stage of U.S. history is a bad idea.*

"Bad" in the systemic sense further applies to letting a financial elite elevate, expand, and entrench itself as a country's GNP- and profits-dominating sector, as has been done in the United States over the last quarter century. Doing this so hurriedly has wound up institutionalizing runaway public and private debt, gross speculative biases, tenfold and twentyfold leveraged gambling, unchecked and barely regulated "product" innovation, and a tendency toward periodic panics and instability. In such a short time frame, though, finance could probably not have consolidated and entrenched in a meeker or more civic-minded fashion. Former Federal Reserve chairman Alan Greenspan has openly stipulated, now that he is again a private citizen free to speak, what most people know well: that manic boom and bubble periods bring the weakness of human nature to the fore. As for the financial sector's behavior in such circumstances, surely there must be some applicable variation of Lord Acton's famous thesis about the greater the power, the greater the abuse and corruption.

It's also "bad" to promote an overbearing financialization of America's economy and culture, lesser versions of which in both U.S. and world history have led to extremes of income and wealth polarization, a culture of money worship, and overt philosophic embrace of speculation and wide-open markets. Minimally bridled finance, extraordinarily rewarding to the top 1 or 2 percent of the population possessing capital, skills, and education, indulges all of these tendencies. Bridling that sector was possible in 1933, when Franklin D. Roosevelt orated about throwing the money changers out of the temple. To a degree, at least, he did. Tossing political and governmental nets around the giant, cyberspatial King Kong who prowls early-twenty-first-century Manhattan (or, for that matter, the City of London financial district) represents an entirely different magnitude of challenge. . . .

The crisis is no longer in the future, but upon us. The debacle started in August [2007], when collateralized debt obligations, built in part around bad debt and distributed globally by Wall Street, began making a slow train wreck relating to weak sections of the U.S. mortgage market into a crisis of top American banks and of the global credit markets. The crux, beyond unsafe mortgage lending, was the recklessness of the speculative mind-set that lay at the heart of Anglo-American finance in an era when the rest of the world was beginning to look for capitalism more rooted and conscious of its responsibilities. . . .

There is no better distillation of the harm inflicted—and probably yet to be inflicted—than that of hedge fund manager Richard Bookstaber in his 2007 volume, *A Demon of Our Own Design: Markets, Hedge Funds, and the Perils of Financial Innovation.* His underlying point is that even though financial strategists can keep dreaming up new instruments, it's not a good idea to do so, because each innovation adds layers of increasing complexity, tight coupling, and risk. By way of comparison, "consider the progress of other products and services over the past century. From the structural design of buildings and bridges, to the operation of oil refineries or power plants, to the safety of automobiles and airplanes, we learned our lessons. In contrast, financial markets have seen a tremendous amount of engineering in the past 30 years, but the result has been more frequent and severe breakdowns. . . . The integration of the financial markets into a global whole, ubiquitous and timely market information, the array of options and other derivative instruments—have exaggerated the pace of activity and the complexity of financial instruments that makes crises inevitable."

Countertrends toward realism and greater regulation may well become excessive and overreach, much like the market excesses and Anglo-American hubris they now challenge. But it is well to understand the provocation offered by the blind-to-human-nature, history-ends-with-us millennial capitalism. . . . My summation is that American financial capitalism, at a pivotal period in the nation's history, cavalierly ventured a multiple gamble: first, financializing a hitherto more diversified U.S. economy; second, using massive quantities of debt and leverage to do so; third, following up a stock market bubble with an even larger housing and mortgage credit bubble; fourth, roughly quadrupling U.S. credit-market debt between 1987 and 2007, a scale of excess that historically unwinds; and fifth, consummating these events with a mixed performance of dishonesty, incompetence, and quantitative negligence.

How fully the complicit politicians will investigate the culpable regulators and financial architects remains to be seen. But there will be many further market events, energy and climate problems, books, essays, congressional hearings, and political campaigns to guide us.

PART SIXTEEN

America in a Changing World

89

SAMUEL HUNTINGTON

From *The Clash of Civilizations*

Renowned scholar Samuel Huntington's 1996 book has received much attention since the terrorist attacks against the United States in 2001. Writing several years earlier, Huntington anticipates the vastly changed landscape of world conflict after the collapse of Soviet communism and after the end of the U.S.-Soviet Cold War. "Power is shifting from the long predominant West to non-western civilizations," Huntington writes. He explores the reasons why he believes this is happening, emphasizing the renewal of religion as central to the changes in power. Religious conflicts, especially between Islam and Christianity, are inevitable, the author believes. Not all Americans will agree with Huntington's grim thesis, but his ideas are important reading for people who have been brought up in the United States. Modernism, reason, progress, and prosperity are key American values, but not necessarily those of much of the rest of the world.

IN THE POST-COLD WAR WORLD,* for the first time in history, global politics has become multipolar *and* multicivilizational. During most of human existence, contacts between civilizations were intermittent or nonexistent. Then, with the beginning of the modern era, about A.D. 1500, global politics assumed two dimensions. For over four hundred years, the nation states of the West—Britain, France, Spain, Austria, Prussia, Germany, the United States, and others—constituted a multipolar international system within Western civilization and interacted, competed, and fought wars with each other. At the same time, Western nations also expanded, conquered, colonized, or decisively influenced every other civilization. During the Cold War global politics became bipolar and the world was divided into three parts. A group of mostly wealthy and democratic societies, led by the United States, was engaged in a pervasive ideological, political, economic, and, at times, military competition with a group of

---

*The Cold War refers to the hostility that existed between the United States and the Soviet Union from the end of World War II until recent times. The Cold War involved many forms of hostility: democracy versus communism; America's NATO allies versus the Soviet Union's Warsaw Pact military partners; the threat of nuclear war; economic competition; the dividing of Third World nations into pro-U.S. and pro-Soviet camps. With the demise of communism in Eastern Europe and the disintegration of the Soviet Union, the Cold War era has ended.—EDS.

somewhat poorer communist societies associated with and led by the So-viet Union. Much of this conflict occurred in the Third World outside these two camps, composed of countries which often were poor, lacked political stability, were recently independent, and claimed to be non-aligned.

In the late 1980s the communist world collapsed, and the Cold War international system became history. In the post-Cold War world, the most important distinctions among peoples are not ideological, political, or economic. They are cultural. Peoples and nations are attempting to answer the most basic question humans can face: Who are we? And they are answering that question in the traditional way human beings have answered it, by reference to the things that mean most to them. People define themselves in terms of ancestry, religion, language, history, values, customs, and institutions. They identify with cultural groups: tribes, ethnic groups, religious communities, nations, and, at the broadest level, civiliza-tions. People use politics not just to advance their interests but also to define their identity. We know who we are only when we know who we are not and often only when we know whom we are against.

Nation states remain the principal actors in world affairs. Their be-havior is shaped as in the past by the pursuit of power and wealth, but it is also shaped by cultural preferences, commonalities, and differences. The most important groupings of states are no longer the three blocs of the Cold War but rather the world's seven or eight major civilizations. Non-Western societies, particularly in East Asia, are developing their economic wealth and creating the basis for enhanced military power and political influence. As their power and self-confidence increase, non-Western soci-eties increasingly assert their own cultural values and reject those "im-posed" on them by the West. The "international system of the twenty-first century," Henry Kissinger has noted, " . . . will contain at least six major powers—the United States, Europe, China, Japan, Russia, and probably India—as well as a multiplicity of medium-sized and smaller countries." Kissinger's six major powers belong to five very different civilizations, and in addition there are important Islamic states whose strategic locations, large populations, and/or oil resources make them influential in world affairs. In this new world, local politics is the politics of ethnicity; global politics is the politics of civilizations. The rivalry of the superpowers is replaced by the clash of civilizations. . . .

The philosophical assumptions, underlying values, social relations, customs, and overall outlooks on life differ significantly among civiliza-tions. The revitalization of religion throughout much of the world is rein-forcing these cultural differences. Cultures can change, and the nature of their impact on politics and economics can vary from one period to another. Yet the major differences in political and economic development among civilizations are clearly rooted in their different cultures. East Asian economic success has its source in East Asian culture, as do the difficulties East Asian societies have had in achieving stable democratic political systems. Islamic culture explains in large part the failure of democracy to emerge in much of the Muslim world. Developments in the postcommunist societies of Eastern Europe and the former Soviet Union are shaped by their civilizational identities. Those with Western Christian heritages are making progress toward economic development and democratic politics; the prospects for economic and political development in the Orthodox countries are uncertain; the prospects in the Muslim republics are bleak.

The West is and will remain for years to come the most powerful civilization. Yet its power relative to that of other civilizations is declining. As the West attempts to assert its values and to protect its interests, non-Western societies confront a choice. Some attempt to emulate the West and to join or to "bandwagon" with the West. Other Confucian and Islamic societies attempt to expand their own economic and military power to resist and to "balance" against the West. A central axis of post-Cold War world politics is thus the interaction of Western power and culture with the power and culture of non-Western civilizations.

In sum, the post-Cold War world is a world of seven or eight major civilizations. Cultural commonalities and differences shape the interests, antagonisms, and associations of states. The most important countries in the world come overwhelmingly from different civilizations. The local conflicts most likely to escalate into broader wars are those between groups and states from different civilizations. The predominant patterns of political and economic development differ from civilization to civilization. The key issues on the international agenda involve differences among civilizations. Power is shifting from the long predominant West to non-Western civilizations. Global politics has become multipolar and multi-civilizational. . . .

The distribution of cultures in the world reflects the distribution of power. Trade may or may not follow the flag, but culture almost always follows power. Throughout history the expansion of the power of a civilization has usually occurred simultaneously with the flowering of its culture and has almost always involved its using that power to extend its values, practices, and institutions to other societies. A universal civilization requires universal power. Roman power created a near-universal civilization within the limited confines of the Classical world. Western power in the form of European colonialism in the nineteenth century and American hegemony in the twentieth century extended Western culture throughout much of the contemporary world. European colonialism is over; American hegemony is receding. The erosion of Western culture follows, as indigenous, historically rooted mores, languages, beliefs, and institutions reassert themselves. The growing power of non-Western societies produced by modernization is generating the revival of non-Western cultures throughout the world.

A distinction exists, Joseph Nye has argued, between "hard power," which is the power to command resting on economic and military strength, and "soft power," which is the ability of a state to get "other countries to *want* what it wants" through the appeal of its culture and ideology. As Nye recognizes, a broad diffusion of hard power is occurring in the world and the major nations "are less able to use their traditional power resources to achieve their purposes than in the past." Nye goes on to say that if a state's "culture and ideology are attractive, others will be more willing to follow" its leadership, and hence soft power is "just as important as hard command power." What, however, makes culture and ideology attractive? They become attractive when they are seen as rooted in material success and influence. Soft power is power only when it rests on a foundation of hard power. Increases in hard economic and military power produce enhanced self-confidence, arrogance, and belief in the superiority of one's own culture or soft power compared to those of other peoples and greatly increase its attractiveness to other peoples. Decreases in economic and military power lead to self-doubt, crises of identity, and efforts to find in other cultures the keys to economic, military, and political success. As non-Western societies enhance their economic, military, and political capacity, they increasingly trumpet the virtues of their own values, institutions, and culture.

Communist ideology appealed to people throughout the world in the 1950s and 1960s when it was associated with the economic success and military force of the Soviet Union. That appeal evaporated when the Soviet economy stagnated and was unable to maintain Soviet military strength. Western values and institutions have appealed to people from other cultures because they were seen as the source of Western power and wealth. This process has been going on for centuries. Between 1000 and 1300, as William McNeill points out, Christianity, Roman law, and other elements of Western culture were adopted by Hungarians, Poles, and Lithuanians, and this "acceptance of Western civilization was stimulated by mingled fear and admiration of the military prowess of Western princes." As Western power declines, the ability of the West to impose

Western concepts of human rights, liberalism, and democracy on other civilizations also declines and so does the attractiveness of those values to other civilizations.

It already has. For several centuries non-Western peoples envied the economic prosperity, technological sophistication, military power, and political cohesion of Western societies. They sought the secret of this success in Western values and institutions, and when they identified what they thought might be the key they attempted to apply it in their own societies. To become rich and powerful, they would have to become like the West. Now, however, these Kemalist attitudes have disappeared in East Asia. East Asians attribute their dramatic economic development not to their import of Western culture but rather to their adherence to their own culture. They are succeeding, they argue, because they are different from the West. Similarly, when non-Western societies felt weak in relation to the West, they invoked Western values of self-determination, liberalism, democracy, and independence to justify their opposition to Western domination. Now that they are no longer weak but increasingly powerful, they do not hesitate to attack those same values which they previously used to promote their interests. The revolt against the West was originally legitimated by asserting the universality of Western values; it is now legitimated by asserting the superiority of non-Western values.

The rise of these attitudes is a manifestation of what Ronald Dore has termed the "second-generation indigenization phenomenon." In both former Western colonies and independent countries like China and Japan, "The first 'modernizer' or 'post-independence' generation has often received its training in foreign (Western) universities in a Western cosmopolitan language. Partly because they first go abroad as impressionable teenagers, their absorption of Western values and life-styles may well be profound." Most of the much larger second generation, in contrast, gets its education at home in universities created by the first generation, and the local rather than the colonial language is increasingly used for instruction. These universities "provide a much more diluted contact with metropolitan world culture" and "knowledge is indigenized by means of translations—usually of limited range and of poor quality." The graduates of these universities resent the dominance of the earlier Western-trained generation and hence often "succumb to the appeals of nativist opposition movements." As Western influence recedes, young aspiring leaders cannot look to the West to provide them with power and wealth. They have to find the means of success within their own society, and hence they have to accommodate to the values and culture of that society. . . .

In the first half of the twentieth century intellectual elites generally assumed that economic and social modernization was leading to the withering away of religion as a significant element in human existence. This assumption was shared by both those who welcomed and those who deplored this trend. Modernizing secularists hailed the extent to which science, rationalism, and pragmatism were eliminating the superstitions, myths, irrationalities, and rituals that formed the core of existing religions. The emerging society would be tolerant, rational, pragmatic, progressive, humanistic, and secular. Worried conservatives, on the other hand, warned of the dire consequences of the disappearance of religious beliefs, religious institutions, and the moral guidance religion provided for individual and collective human behavior. The end result would be anarchy, depravity, the undermining of civilized life. "If you will not have God (and He is a jealous God)," T. S. Eliot said, "you should pay your respects to Hitler or Stalin."

The second half of the twentieth century proved these hopes and fears unfounded. Economic and social modernization became global in scope, and at the same time a global revival of religion occurred. This revival, *la revanche de Dieu*, Gilles Kepel termed it, has pervaded every continent, every civilization, and virtually every country. In the mid-1970s, as Kepel observes, the trend to secularization and toward the accommodation of religion with secularism "went into reverse. A new religious approach took shape, aimed no longer at adapting to secular values but at recovering a sacred foundation for the organization of society—by changing society if necessary. Expressed in a multitude of ways, this approach advocated moving on from a modernism that had failed, attributing its setbacks and dead ends to separation from God. The theme was no longer *aggiornamento* but a 'second evangelization of Europe,' the aim was no longer to modernize Islam but to 'Islamize modernity.' "

This religious revival has in part involved expansion by some religions, which gained new recruits in societies where they had previously not had them. To a much larger extent, however, the religious resurgence involved people returning to, reinvigorating, and giving new meaning to the traditional religions of their communities. Christianity, Islam, Judaism, Hinduism, Buddhism, Orthodoxy, all experienced new surges in commitment, relevance, and practice by erstwhile casual believers. In all of them fundamentalist movements arose committed to the militant purification of religious doctrines and institutions and the reshaping of personal, social, and public behavior in accordance with religious tenets. The fundamentalist movements are dramatic and can have significant political impact. They are, however, only the surface waves of the much broader and more fundamental religious tide that is giving a different cast to human life at the end of the twentieth century. The renewal of religion through-out the world far transcends the activities of fundamentalist extremists. In society after society it manifests itself in the daily lives and work of people and the concerns and projects of governments. The cultural resurgence in the secular Confucian culture takes the form of the affirmation of Asian values but in the rest of the world manifests itself in the affirmation of religious values. The "unsecularization of the world," as George Weigel remarked "is one of the dominant social facts in the late twentieth cen-tury." . . .

How can this global religious resurgence be explained? Particular causes obviously operated in individual countries and civilizations. Yet it is too much to expect that a large number of different causes would have produced simultaneous and similar developments in most parts of the world. A global phenomenon demands a global explanation. However much events in particular countries may have been influenced by unique factors, some general causes must have been at work. What were they?

The most obvious, most salient, and most powerful cause of the glob-al religious resurgence is precisely what was supposed to cause the death of religion: the processes of social, economic, and cultural modernization that swept across the world in the second half of the twentieth century. Long-standing sources of identity and systems of authority are disrupted. People move from the countryside into the city, become separated from their roots, and take new jobs or no job. They interact with large numbers of strangers and are exposed to new sets of relationships. They need new sources of identity, new forms of stable community, and new sets of moral precepts to provide them with a sense of meaning and purpose. Religion, both mainstream and fundamentalist, meets these needs. As Lee Kuan Yew explained for East Asia:

We are agricultural societies that have industrialized within one or two genera-tions. What happened in the West over 200 years or more is happening here in about 50 years or less. It is all crammed and crushed into a very tight time frame, so there are bound to be dislocations and malfunctions. If you look at the fast-growing countries—Korea, Thailand, Hong Kong, and Singapore—there's been one remarkable phenomenon: the rise of religion. . . . The old customs and reli-gions—ancestor worship, shamanism—no longer completely satisfy. There is a quest for some higher explanations about man's purpose, about why we are here. This is associated with periods of great stress in society.

People do not live by reason alone. They cannot calculate and act ra-tionally in pursuit of their self-interest until they define their self. Interest politics presupposes identity. In times of rapid social change established identities dissolve, the self must be redefined, and new identities created.

For people facing the need to determine Who am I? Where do I belong? religion provides compelling answers, and religious groups provide small social communities to replace those lost through urbanization. All religions, as Hassan al-Turabi said, furnish "people with a sense of identity and a direction in life." In this process, people rediscover or create new historical identities. Whatever universalist goals they may have, religions give people identity by positing a basic distinction between believers and nonbelievers, between a superior in-group and a different and inferior out-group.

In the Muslim world, Bernard Lewis argues, there has been "a recurring tendency, in times of emergency, for Muslims to find their basic identity and loyalty in the religious community—that is to say, in an entity defined by Islam rather than by ethnic or territorial criteria." Gilles Kepel similarly highlights the centrality of the search for identity: "Re-Islamization 'from below' is first and foremost a way of rebuilding an identity in a world that has lost its meaning and become amorphous and alienating." In India, "a new Hindu identity is under construction" as a response to tensions and alienation generated by modernization. In Russia, the religious revival is the result "of a passionate desire for identity which only the Orthodox church, the sole unbroken link with the Russians' 1000-year past, can provide," while in the Islamic republics the revival similarly stems "from the Central Asians' most powerful aspiration: to assert the identities that Moscow suppressed for decades." Fundamentalist movements, in particular, are "a way of coping with the experience of chaos, the loss of identity, meaning and secure social structures created by the rapid introduction of modern social and political patterns, secularism, scientific culture and economic development." The fundamentalist "movements that matter," agrees William H. McNeill, " . . . are those that recruit from society at large and spread because they answer, or seem to answer, newly felt human needs. . . . It is no accident that these movements are all based in countries where population pressure on the land is making continuation of old village ways impossible for a majority of the population, and where urban-based mass communications, by penetrating the villages, have begun to erode an age-old framework of peasant life."

More broadly, the religious resurgence throughout the world is a reaction against secularism, moral relativism, and self-indulgence, and a reaffirmation of the values of order, discipline, work, mutual help, and human solidarity. Religious groups meet social needs left untended by state bureaucracies. These include the provision of medical and hospital services, kindergartens and schools, care for the elderly, prompt relief after natural and other catastrophes, and welfare and social support during periods of economic deprivation. The breakdown of order and of civil society creates vacuums which are filled by religious, often fundamentalist, groups. . . .

. . . "More than anything else," William McNeill observes, "reaffirmation of Islam, whatever its specific sectarian form, means the repudiation of European and American influence upon local society, politics, and morals." In this sense, the revival of non-Western religions is the most powerful manifestation of anti-Westernism in non-Western societies. That revival is not a rejection of modernity; it is a rejection of the West and of the secular, relativistic, degenerate culture associated with the West. It is a rejection of what has been termed the "Westoxification" of non-Western societies. It is a declaration of cultural independence from the West, a proud statement that: "We will be modern but we won't be you." . . .

Some Westerners, including [former] President Bill Clinton, have argued that the West does not have problems with Islam but only with violent Islamist extremists. Fourteen hundred years of history demonstrate otherwise. The relations between Islam and Christianity, both Orthodox and Western, have often been stormy. Each has been the other's Other. The twentieth-century conflict between liberal democracy and Marxist-Leninism is only a fleeting and superficial historical phenomenon compared to the continuing and deeply conflictual relation between Islam and Christianity. At times, peaceful coexistence has prevailed; more often the relation has been one of intense rivalry and of varying degrees of hot war. Their "historical dynamics," John Esposito comments, " . . . often found the two communities in competition, and locked at times in deadly combat, for power, land, and souls." Across the centuries the fortunes of the two religions have risen and fallen in a sequence of momentous surges, pauses, and countersurges. . . .

A . . . mix of factors has increased the conflict between Islam and the West in the late twentieth century. First, Muslim population growth has generated large numbers of unemployed and disaffected young people who become recruits to Islamist causes, exert pressure on neighboring societies, and migrate to the West. Second, the Islamic Resurgence has given Muslims renewed confidence in the distinctive character and worth of their civilization and values compared to those of the West. Third, the West's simultaneous efforts to universalize its values and institutions, to maintain its military and economic superiority, and to intervene in conflicts in the Muslim world generate intense resentment among Muslims. Fourth, the collapse of communism removed a common enemy of the West and Islam and left each the perceived major threat to the other. Fifth, the increasing contact between and intermingling of Muslims and Westerners stimulate in each a new sense of their own identity and how it differs from that of the other. Interaction and intermingling also exacerbate differences over the rights of the members of one civilization in a country dominated by members of the other civilization. Within both Muslim and Christian societies, tolerance for the other declined sharply in the 1980s and 1990s.

The causes of the renewed conflict between Islam and the West thus lie in fundamental questions of power and culture. *Kto? Kovo?* Who is to rule? Who is to be ruled? The central issue of politics defined by Lenin is the root of the contest between Islam and the West. There is, however, the additional conflict, which Lenin would have considered meaningless, between two different versions of what is right and what is wrong and, as a consequence, who is right and who is wrong. So long as Islam remains Islam (which it will) and the West remains the West (which is more dubious), this fundamental conflict between two great civilizations and ways of life will continue to define their relations in the future even as it has defined them for the past fourteen centuries. . . .

The underlying problem for the West is not Islamic fundamentalism. It is Islam, a different civilization whose people are convinced of the superiority of their culture and are obsessed with the inferiority of their power. The problem for Islam is not the CIA or the U.S. Department of Defense. It is the West, a different civilization whose people are convinced of the universality of their culture and believe that their superior, if declining, power imposes on them the obligation to extend that culture throughout the world. These are the basic ingredients that fuel conflict between Islam and the West.

In the 1950s Lester Pearson warned that humans were moving into "an age when different civilizations will have to learn to live side by side in peaceful interchange, learning from each other, studying each other's history and ideals and art and culture, mutually enriching each others' lives. The alternative, in this overcrowded little world, is misunderstanding, tension, clash, and catastrophe." The futures of both peace and Civilization depend upon understanding and cooperation among the political, spiritual, and intellectual leaders of the world's major civilizations. In the clash of civilizations, Europe and America will hang together or hang separately. In the greater clash, the global "*real* clash," between Civilization and barbarism, the world's great civilizations, with their rich accomplishments in religion, art, literature, philosophy, science, technology, morality, and compassion, will also hang together or hang separately. In the emerging era, clashes of civilizations are the greatest threat to world peace, and an international order based on civilizations is the surest safeguard against world war.

90

FAREED ZAKARIA

From *The Post-American World*

Dr. Fareed Zakaria is a scholar, writer, and TV host whose views on American foreign policy and international affairs are highly regarded by people of varying political ideologies. In this book, Zakaria addresses the changing nature of international politics and the United States' place within it. As the rest of the world—especially Asia—grows dramatically, the United States is no longer in the position of uncontested dominance that it had enjoyed over the past century. Zakaria is careful to distinguish between an "anti-American world" and a "post-American world." The latter, not the former, is the reality. The author sketches out a role for the United States in the world order that is developing: "global broker." More like a "chair of the board" than the single superpower, this role is not a familiar one for America, but one that promises great influence and power in the global community. Zakaria concludes his vision for the future with a plea for less fear about the rest of the world and more of the American generosity of spirit that he experienced first hand decades ago, as a young visiting college student.

THIS IS A BOOK not about the decline of America but rather about the rise of everyone else. It is about the great transformation taking place around the world, a transformation that, though often discussed, remains poorly understood. This is natural. Changes, even sea changes, take place gradually. Though we talk about a new era, the world seems to be one with which we are familiar. But in fact, it is very different.

There have been three tectonic power shifts over the last five hundred years, fundamental changes in the distribution of power that have reshaped international life—its politics, economics, and culture. The first was the rise of the Western world, a process that began in the fifteenth century and accelerated dramatically in the late eighteenth century. It produced modernity as we know it: science and technology, commerce and capitalism, the agricultural and industrial revolutions. It also produced the prolonged political dominance of the nations of the West.

The second shift, which took place in the closing years of the nineteenth century, was the rise of the United States. Soon after it industrialized, the United States became the most powerful nation since imperial Rome, and the only one that was stronger than any likely combination of

other nations. For most of the last century, the United States has dominated global economics, politics, science, and culture. For the last twenty
years, that dominance has been unrivaled, a phenomenon unprecedented
in modern history.

We are now living through the third great power shift of the modern
era. It could be called "the rise of the rest." Over the past few decades,
countries all over the world have been experiencing rates of economic
growth that were once unthinkable. While they have had booms and busts,
the overall trend has been unambiguously upward. This growth has been
most visible in Asia but is no longer confined to it. That is why to call this
shift "the rise of Asia" does not describe it accurately. In 2006 and 2007,
124 countries grew at a rate of 4 percent or more. That includes more
than 30 countries in Africa, two-thirds of the continent. Antoine van
Agtmael, the fund manager who coined the term "emerging markets," has
identified the 25 companies most likely to be the world's next great mul-
tinationals. His list includes four companies each from Brazil, Mexico,
South Korea, and Taiwan; three from India; two from China; and one each
from Argentina, Chile, Malaysia, and South Africa. . . .

. . . For the first time ever, we are witnessing genuinely global growth.
This is creating an international system in which countries in all parts of
the world are no longer objects or observers but players in their own
right. It is the birth of a truly global order.

A related aspect of this new era is the diffusion of power from states to
other actors. The "rest" that is rising includes many nonstate actors. Groups
and individuals have been empowered, and hierarchy, centralization, and
control are being undermined. Functions that were once controlled by
governments are now shared with international bodies like the World
Trade Organization and the European Union. Nongovernmental groups
are mushrooming every day on every issue in every country. Corporations and capital are moving from place to place, finding the best location
in which to do business, rewarding some governments while punishing
others. Terrorists like Al Qaeda, drug cartels, insurgents, and militias of all
kinds are finding space to operate within the nooks and crannies of the
international system. Power is shifting away from nation-states, up, down,
and sideways. In such an atmosphere, the traditional applications of national power, both economic and military, have become less effective.

The emerging international system is likely to be quite different from
those that have preceded it. One hundred years ago, there was a multipolar order run by a collection of European governments, with constantly
shifting alliances, rivalries, miscalculations, and wars. Then came the bipo-

lar duopoly of the Cold War,* more stable in many ways, but with the superpowers reacting and overreacting to each other's every move. Since 1991, we have lived under an American imperium, a unique, unipolar world in which the open global economy has expanded and accelerated dramatically. This expansion is now driving the next change in the nature of the international order.

At the politico-military level, we remain in a single-superpower world. But in every other dimension—industrial, financial, educational, social, cultural—the distribution of power is shifting, moving away from American dominance. That does not mean we are entering an anti-American world. But we are moving into a *post-American world,* one defined and directed from many places and by many people.

What kinds of opportunities and challenges do these changes present? What do they portend for the United States and its dominant position? What will this new era look like in terms of war and peace, economics and business, ideas and culture?

In short, what will it mean to live in a post-American world? . . .

Imagine that it is January 2000, and you ask a fortune-teller to predict the course of the global economy over the next several years. Let's say that you give him some clues, to help him gaze into his crystal ball. The United States will be hit by the worst terrorist attack in history, you explain, and will respond by launching two wars, one of which will go badly awry and keep Iraq—the country with the world's third-largest oil reserves—in chaos for years. Iran will gain strength in the Middle East and move to acquire a nuclear capability. North Korea will go further, becoming the world's eighth declared nuclear power. Russia will turn hostile and imperious in its dealings with its neighbors and the West. In Latin America, Hugo Chávez of Venezuela will launch the most spirited anti-Western campaign in a generation, winning many allies and fans. Israel and Hezbollah will fight a war in southern Lebanon, destabilizing Beirut's fragile government, drawing in Iran and Syria, and rattling the Israelis. Gaza will become a failed state ruled by Hamas, and peace talks between Israel and the Palestinians will go nowhere. "Given these events," you say to the sage, "how will the global economy fare over the next six years?"

*The Cold War refers to the hostility that existed between the United States and the Soviet Union from the end of World War II until the late 1980s. The Cold War involved many forms of hostility: Democracy versus communism; America's NATO allies versus the Soviet Union's Warsaw Pact military partners; the threat of nuclear war; economic competition; the dividing of Third World nations into pro-U.S. and pro-Soviet camps. With the demise of communism in Eastern Europe and the disintegration of the Soviet Union, the Cold War era has ended.—Eds.

This is not really a hypothetical. We have the forecasts of experts from those years. They were all wrong. The correct prediction would have been that, between 2000 and 2007, the world economy would grow at its fastest pace in nearly four decades. Income per person across the globe would rise at a faster rate (3.2 percent) than in any other period in history.

In the two decades since the end of the Cold War, we have lived through a paradox, one we experience every morning when reading the newspapers. The world's politics seems deeply troubled, with daily reports of bombings, terror plots, rogue states, and civil strife. And yet the global economy forges ahead, not without significant interruptions and crises, but still vigorously upward on the whole. Markets do panic but over economic not political news. The front page of the newspaper seems unconnected to the business section. . . .

What explains this mismatch between a politics that spirals downward and an economy that stays robust? First, it's worth looking more carefully at the cascade of bad news. It seems that we are living in crazily violent times. But don't believe everything you see on television. Our anecdotal impression turns out to be wrong. War and organized violence have declined dramatically over the last two decades. Ted Robert Gurr and a team of scholars at the University of Maryland's Center for International Development and Conflict Management tracked the data carefully and came to the following conclusion: "the general magnitude of global warfare has decreased by over sixty percent [since the mid-1980s], falling by the end of 2004 to its lowest level since the late 1950s." Violence increased steadily throughout the Cold War—increasing sixfold between the 1950s and early 1990s—but the trend peaked just before the collapse of the Soviet Union in 1991 and "the extent of warfare among and within states lessened by nearly half in the first decade after the Cold War." Harvard's polymath professor Steven Pinker argues "that today we are probably living in the most peaceful time in our species' existence."

One reason for the mismatch between reality and our sense of it might be that, over these same decades, we have experienced a revolution in information technology that now brings us news from around the world instantly, vividly, and continuously. The immediacy of the images and the intensity of the twenty-four-hour news cycle combine to produce constant hyperbole. Every weather disturbance is "the storm of the century." Every bomb that explodes is BREAKING NEWS. It is difficult to put this all in context because the information revolution is so new. We didn't get daily footage on the roughly two million who died in the killing fields of Cambodia in the 1970s or the million who perished in the sands of the Iran-Iraq war in the 1980s. We have not even seen much footage from the war in Congo in the 1990s, where millions died. But now, we see almost daily, live broadcasts of the effects of IEDs or car bombs or rockets—tragic events, to be sure, but often with death tolls under ten. The randomness of terrorist violence, the targeting of civilians, and the ease with which modern societies can be penetrated add to our disquiet. "That could have been me," people say after a terrorist attack.

It *feels* like a very dangerous world. But it isn't. Your chances of dying as a consequence of organized violence of any kind are low and getting lower. The data reveal a broad trend away from wars among major countries, the kind of conflict that produces massive casualties.

I don't believe that war has become obsolete or any such foolishness. Human nature remains what it is and international politics what it is. History has witnessed periods of calm that have been followed by extraordinary bloodshed. And numbers are not the only measure of evil. The nature of the killings in the former Yugoslavia in the early 1990s—premeditated, religiously motivated, systematic—makes that war, which had 200,000 casualties, a moral obscenity that should register very high on any scale. Al Qaeda's barbarism—cold-blooded beheadings, the deliberate targeting of innocents—is gruesome despite its relatively low number of casualties.

Still, if we are to understand the times we are living in, we must first accurately describe them. And they are, for now, in historical context, unusually calm. . . .

Islamic terror, which makes the headlines daily, is a large and persistent problem, but one involving small numbers of fanatics. It feeds on the dysfunctions of the Muslim world, the sense (real and imagined) of humiliation at the hands of the West, and easy access to technologies of violence. And yet, does it rank as a threat on the order of Germany's drive for world domination in the first half of the twentieth century? Or Soviet expansionism in the second half? Or Mao's efforts to foment war and revolution across the Third World in the 1950s and 1960s? These were all challenges backed by the power and purpose of major countries, often with serious allies, and by an ideology that was seen as a plausible alternative to liberal democracy. By comparison, consider the jihadist threat. Before 9/11, when groups like Al Qaeda operated under the radar, governments treated them as minor annoyances, and they roamed freely, built some strength, and hit symbolic, often military targets, killing Americans and other foreigners. Even so, the damage was fairly limited. Since 2001, governments everywhere have been aggressive in busting terrorists' networks, following their money, and tracking their recruits—with almost immediate results. In Indonesia, the largest Muslim nation in the world, the government captured both the chief and the military leader of Jemaah Islamiah, the country's deadliest jihadist group and the one that carried out the Bali bombings in 2002. With American help, the Filipino army battered the Qaeda-style terrorist outfit Abu Sayyaf. The group's leader was killed by Filipino troops in January 2007, and its membership has declined from as many as two thousand guerrillas six years ago to a few hundred today. In Egypt and Saudi Arabia—Al Qaeda's original bases and targets of attack—terrorist cells have been rounded up, and those still at large have been unable to launch any new attacks in three years. Finance ministries—especially the U.S. Department of the Treasury—have made life far more difficult for terrorists. Global organizations cannot thrive without being able to move money around, and so the more terrorists' funds are tracked and targeted, the more they have to resort to small-scale and hastily improvised operations. This struggle, between governments and terrorists, will persist, but it is the former who have the upper hand. . . .

Here is the bottom line. In the six years since 9/11, Al Qaeda Central—the group led by Osama bin Laden and Ayman Zawahiri—has been unable to launch a major attack anywhere. It was a terrorist organization; it has become a communications company, producing the occasional videotape rather than actual terrorism. Jihad continues, but the jihadists have had to scatter, make do with smaller targets, and operate on a local level—usually through groups with almost no connection to Al Qaeda Central. And this improvised strategy has a crippling weakness: it kills locals, thus alienating ordinary Muslims—a process that is well underway in countries as diverse as Indonesia, Iraq, and Saudi Arabia. Over the last six years, support for bin Laden and his goals has fallen steadily throughout the Muslim world. Between 2002 and 2007, approval of suicide bombing as a tactic—a figure that was always low—has dropped by over 50 percent in most Muslim countries that have been tracked. There have been more denunciations of violence and fatwas against bin Laden than ever before, including from prominent clerics in Saudi Arabia. Much more must happen to modernize the Muslim world, but the modernizers are no longer so scared. They have finally realized that, for all the rhetoric of the madrassas and mosques, few people want to live under the writ of Al Qaeda. Those who have, whether in Afghanistan or Iraq, have become its most dedicated opponents. In contrast to Soviet socialism or even fascism in the 1930s, no society looks with admiration and envy on the fundamentalist Islamic model. On an ideological level, it presents no competition to the Western-originated model of modernity that countries across the world are embracing.

A cottage industry of scaremongering has flourished in the West—especially in the United States—since 9/11. Experts extrapolate every trend they don't like, forgoing any serious study of the data. Many conservative commentators have written about the impending Islamization of Europe (Eurabia, they call it, to make you even more uncomfortable). Except that the best estimates, from U.S. intelligence agencies, indicate that Muslims constitute around 3 percent of Europe's population now and will rise to between 5 and 8 percent by 2025, after which they will probably plateau. The watchdogs note the musings of every crackpot Imam, search the archives for each reference to the end of days, and record and distribute the late-night TV musings of every nutcase who glorifies martyrdom. They erupt in fury when a Somali taxi driver somewhere refuses to load a case of liquor into his car, seeing it as the beginning of sharia in the West. But these episodes do not reflect the basic direction of the Muslim world. That world is also modernizing, though more slowly than the rest, and there are those who try to become leaders in rebellion against it. The reactionaries in the world of Islam are more numerous and extreme than those in other cultures—that world does have its dysfunctions. But they remain a tiny minority of the world's billion-plus Muslims. And neglecting the complicated context in which some of these pseudoreligious statements are made—such as an internal Iranian power struggle among clerics and nonclerics—leads to hair-raising but absurd predictions, like Bernard Lewis's confident claim that Iran's President Mahmoud Ahmadinejad planned to mark an auspicious date on the Islamic calendar (August 22, 2006) *by ending the world.* (Yes, he actually wrote that.)

The ideological watchdogs have spent so much time with the documents of jihad that they have lost sight of actual Muslim societies. Were they to step back, they would see a frustration with the fundamentalists, a desire for modernity (with some dignity and cultural pride for sure), and a search for practical solutions—not a mass quest for immortality through death. When Muslims travel, they flock by the millions to see the razzle-dazzle of Dubai, not the seminaries of Iran. The minority that wants jihad is real, but it operates within societies where such activities are increasingly unpopular and irrelevant. . . .

In some unspoken way, people have recognized that the best counterterrorism policy is resilience. Terrorism is unusual in that it is a military tactic defined by the response of the onlooker. If we are not terrorized, then it doesn't work. And, from New York and London to Mumbai and Jakarta, people are learning this fact through experience and getting on with life even amid the uncertainty. The most likely scenario—a series of backpack or truck bombings in the United States—would be a shock, but in a couple of weeks its effects would fade and the long-term consequences would likely be minimal. In vast, vigorous, and complex societies—the American economy is now $13 trillion—problems in a few places do not easily spill over. Modern civilization may be stronger than we suspect. . . .

The rise of the rest, while real, is a long, slow process. And it is one that ensures America a vital, though different, role. As China, India, Brazil, Russia, South Africa, and a host of smaller countries all do well in the years ahead, new points of tension will emerge among them. Many of these rising countries have historical animosities, border disputes, and contemporary quarrels with one another; in most cases, nationalism will grow along with economic and geopolitical stature. Being a distant power, America is often a convenient partner for many regional nations worried about the rise of a hegemon in their midst. In fact, as the scholar William Wohlforth notes, American influence is strengthened by the growth of a dominant regional power. These factors are often noted in discussions of Asia, but it is true of many other spots on the globe as well. The process will not be mechanical. As one of these countries rises (China), it will not produce a clockwork-like balancing dynamic where its neighbor (India) will seek a formal alliance with the United States. Today's world is more complicated than that. But these rivalries do give the United States an opportunity to play a large and constructive role at the center of the global order. It has the potential to be what Bismarck helped Germany become (briefly) in the late nineteenth-century—Europe's "honest broker," forging close relationships with each of the major countries, ties that were closer than the ones those countries had with one another. It was the hub of the European system. Being the global broker today would be a job involving not just the American government but its society, with all the strengths and perspectives that it will bring to the challenge. It is a role that the United States—with its global interests and presence, complete portfolio of power, and diverse immigrant communities—could learn to play with great skill.

This new role is quite different from the traditional superpower role. It involves consultation, cooperation, and even compromise. It derives its power by setting the agenda, defining the issues, and mobilizing coalitions. It is not a top-down hierarchy in which the United States makes its decisions and then informs a grateful (or silent) world. But it is a crucial role because, in a world with many players, setting the agenda and organizing coalitions become primary forms of power. The chair of the board who can gently guide a group of independent directors is still a very powerful person. . . .

Before it can implement any of these specific strategies, however, the United States must make a much broader adjustment. It needs to stop cowering in fear. It is fear that has created a climate of paranoia and panic in the United States and fear that has enabled our strategic missteps. Having spooked ourselves into believing that we have no option but to act fast and alone, preemptively and unilaterally, we have managed to destroy decades of international goodwill, alienate allies, and embolden enemies, while solving few of the major international problems we face. To recover its place in the world, America first has to recover its confidence.

By almost all objective measures, the United States is in a blessed position today. It faces problems, crises, and resistance, but compared with any of the massive threats of the past—Nazi Germany, Stalin's aggression, nuclear war—the circumstances are favorable, and the world is moving our way. In 1933, Franklin Delano Roosevelt diagnosed the real danger for the United States. "The only thing we have to fear is fear itself," he said. "Nameless, unreasoning, unjustified terror." And he was arguing against fear when America's economic and political system was near collapse, when a quarter of the workforce was unemployed, and when fascism was on the march around the world. Somehow we have managed to spook ourselves in a time of worldwide peace and prosperity. Keeping that front and center in our minds is crucial to ensure that we do not miscalculate, misjudge, and misunderstand.

America has become a nation consumed by anxiety, worried about terrorists and rogue nations, Muslims and Mexicans, foreign companies and free trade, immigrants and international organizations. The strongest nation in the history of the world now sees itself as besieged by forces beyond its control. While the Bush administration has contributed mightily to this state of affairs, it is a phenomenon that goes beyond one president. Too many Americans have been taken in by a rhetoric of fear. . . .

We will never be able to prevent a small group of misfits from planning some terrible act of terror. No matter how far-seeing and competent our intelligence and law-enforcement officials, people will always be able to slip through the cracks in a large, open, and diverse country. The real test of American leadership is not whether we can make 100 percent sure we prevent the attack, but rather how we respond to it. Stephen Flynn, a homeland-security expert at the Council on Foreign Relations, argues that our goal must be resilience—how quickly can we bounce back from a disruption? In the material sciences, resilience is the ability of a material to recover its original shape after a deformation. If one day bombs do go off, we must ensure that they cause as little disruption—economic, social, political—as possible. This would prevent the terrorist from achieving his main objective. If we are not terrorized, then in a crucial sense we have defeated terrorism. . . .

At the end of the day, openness is America's greatest strength. Many smart policy wonks have clever ideas that they believe will better American productivity, savings, and health care. More power to them all. But historically, America has succeeded not because of the ingenuity of its government programs but because of the vigor of its society. It has thrived because it has kept itself open to the world—to goods and services, to ideas and inventions, and, above all, to people and cultures. This openness has allowed us to respond quickly and flexibly to new economic times, to manage change and diversity with remarkable ease, and to push forward the boundaries of individual freedom and autonomy. It has allowed America to create the first universal nation, a place where people from all over the world can work, mingle, mix, and share in a common dream and a common destiny.

In the fall of 1982, I arrived here as an eighteen-year-old student from India, eight thousand miles away. . . .

. . . Everywhere I went, the atmosphere was warm and welcoming. It was a feeling I had never had before, a country wide open to the world, to the future, and to anyone who loved it. To a young visitor, it seemed to offer unlimited generosity and promise.

For America to thrive in this new and challenging era, for it to succeed amid the rise of the rest, it need fulfill only one test. It should be a place that is as inviting and exciting to the young student who enters the country today as it was for this awkward eighteen-year-old a generation ago.

91

CHALMERS JOHNSON

From *Blowback*

A scholar on American foreign affairs, Chalmers Johnson applies the CIA term "blowback" to the dilemma of this nation's military and diplomatic actions: many problems we grapple with currently are "unintended consequences of policies that were kept secret from the American people." Johnson discusses drug trafficking, terrorist acts, and economic retaliation as examples of other nations reacting to American policies, no matter how unintentional the negative results of those policies were. The country's actions may well produce more future blowback without citizens realizing what's ahead. Johnson's warning about American foreign policy is harsh: " . . . a nation reaps what it sows, even if it does not fully know or understand what it has sown."

———

NORTHERN ITALIAN COMMUNITIES HAD, for years, complained about low-flying American military aircraft. In February 1998, the inevitable happened. A Marine Corps EA-6B Prowler with a crew of four, one of scores of advanced American jet fighters and bombers stationed at places like Aviano, Cervia, Brindisi, and Sigonella, sliced through a ski-lift cable near the resort town of Cavalese and plunged twenty people riding in a single gondola to their deaths on the snowy slopes several hundred feet below. Although marine pilots are required to maintain an altitude of at least one thousand feet (two thousand, according to the Italian government), the plane had cut the cable at a height of 360 feet. It was traveling at 621 miles per hour when 517 miles per hour was considered the upper limit. The pilot had been performing low-level acrobatics while his co-pilot took pictures on videotape (which he later destroyed).

In response to outrage in Italy and calls for vigorous prosecution of those responsible, the marine pilots argued that their charts were inaccurate, that their altimeter had not worked, and that they had not consulted U.S. Air Force units permanently based in the area about local hazards. A court-martial held not in Italy but in Camp Lejeune, North Carolina, exonerated everyone involved, calling it a "training accident." Soon after, President Bill Clinton apologized and promised financial compensation to the victims, but on May 14, 1999, Congress dropped the provision for aid to the families because of opposition in the House of Representatives and from the Pentagon....

I believe it is past time for such a discussion to begin, for Americans to consider why we have created an empire—a word from which we shy away—and what the consequences of our imperial stance may be for the rest of the world and for ourselves. Not so long ago, the way we garrisoned the world could be discussed far more openly and comfortably because the explanation seemed to lie at hand—in the very existence of the Soviet Union and of communism. Had the Italian disaster occurred two decades earlier, it would have seemed no less a tragedy, but many Americans would have argued that, given the Cold War, such incidents were an unavoidable cost of protecting democracies like Italy against the menace of Soviet totalitarianism. With the disappearance of any military threat faintly comparable to that posed by the former Soviet Union, such "costs" have become easily avoidable. American military forces could have been withdrawn from Italy, as well as from other foreign bases, long ago. That they were not and that Washington instead is doing everything in its considerable powers to perpetuate Cold War structures, even without the Cold War's justification, places such overseas deployments in a new light. They have become striking evidence, for those who care to look, of an imperial project that the Cold War obscured. The by-products of this project are likely to build up reservoirs of resentment against all Americans—tourists, students, and businessmen, as well as members of the armed forces—that can have lethal results.

For any empire, including an unacknowledged one, there is a kind of balance sheet that builds up over time. Military crimes, accidents, and atrocities make up only one category on the debit side of the balance sheet that the United States has been accumulating, especially since the Cold War ended. To take an example of quite a different kind of debit, consider South Korea, a longtime ally. On Christmas Eve 1997, it declared itself financially bankrupt and put its economy under the guidance of the International Monetary Fund, which is basically an institutional surrogate of the United States government. Most Americans were surprised by the economic disasters that overtook Thailand, South Korea, Malaysia, and Indonesia in 1997 and that then spread around the world, crippling the Russian and Brazilian economies. They could hardly imagine that the U.S. government might have had a hand in causing them, even though various American pundits and economists expressed open delight in these disasters, which threw millions of people, who had previously had hopes of achieving economic prosperity and security, into the most abysmal poverty. At worst, Americans took the economic meltdown of places like

Indonesia and Brazil to mean that beneficial American-supported policies of "globalization" were working—that we were effectively helping restructure various economies around the world so that they would look and work more like ours. . . .

If Washington is the headquarters of a global military-economic dominion, the answers will be very different than if we think of the United States as simply one among many sovereign nations. There is a logic to empire that differs from the logic of a nation, and acts committed in service to an empire but never acknowledged as such have a tendency to haunt the future.

The term "blowback," which officials of the Central Intelligence Agency first invented for their own internal use, is starting to circulate among students of international relations. It refers to the unintended consequences of policies that were kept secret from the American people. What the daily press reports as the malign acts of "terrorists" or "drug lords" or "rogue states" or "illegal arms merchants" often turn out to be blowback from earlier American operations.

It is now widely recognized, for example, that the 1988 bombing of Pan Am flight 103 over Lockerbie, Scotland, which resulted in the deaths of 259 passengers and 11 people on the ground, was retaliation for a 1986 Reagan administration aerial raid on Libya that killed President Muammar Khadaffi's stepdaughter. Some in the United States have suspected that other events can also be explained as blowback from imperial acts. For example, the epidemic of cocaine and heroin use that has afflicted American cities during the past two decades was probably fueled in part by Central and South American military officers or corrupt politicians whom the CIA or the Pentagon once trained or supported and then installed in key government positions. For example, in Nicaragua in the 1980s, the U.S. government organized a massive campaign against the socialist- oriented Sandinista government. American agents then looked the other way when the Contras, the military insurgents they had trained, made deals to sell cocaine in American cities in order to buy arms and supplies.

If drug blowback is hard to trace to its source, bomb attacks, whether on U.S. embassies in Africa, the World Trade Center in New York City, or an apartment complex in Saudi Arabia that housed U.S. servicemen, are another matter. One man's terrorist is, of course, another man's freedom fighter, and what U.S. officials denounce as unprovoked terrorist attacks on its innocent citizens are often meant as retaliation for previous American imperial actions. Terrorists attack innocent and undefended American targets precisely because American soldiers and sailors firing cruise missiles from ships at sea or sitting in B-52 bombers at extremely high altitudes or supporting brutal and repressive regimes from Washington seem invulnerable. As members of the Defense Science Board wrote in a 1997 report to the undersecretary of defense for acquisition and technology, "Historical data show a strong correlation between U.S. involvement in international situations and an increase in terrorist attacks against the United States. In addition, the military asymmetry that denies nation states the ability to engage in overt attacks against the United States drives the use of transnational actors [that is, terrorists from one country attacking in another]." . . .

Blowback itself can lead to more blowback, in a spiral of destructive behavior. A good illustration of this lies in the government's reaction to the August 7, 1998, bombings of American embassy buildings in Nairobi and Dar es Salaam, with the loss of 12 American and 212 Kenyan and Tanzanian lives and some 4,500 injured. The U.S. government promptly placed the blame on Osama bin Laden, a Saudi who had long denounced his country's rulers and their American allies. On August 20, the United States retaliated by firing nearly eighty cruise missiles (at a cost of $750,000 each) into a pharmaceutical plant in Khartoum, Sudan, and an old mujahideen camp site in Afghanistan. (One missile went four hundred miles off course and landed in Pakistan.) Both missile targets had been identified by American intelligence as enterprises or training areas associated with bin Laden or his followers. It was soon revealed, however, that the intelligence on both places had been faulty and that neither target could be connected with those who were suspected of attacking the embassies. On September 2, 1998, the U.S. secretary of defense said that he had been unaware that the plant in Khartoum made medicines, not nerve gas, when he recommended that it be attacked. He also admitted that the plant's connection to bin Laden was, at best, "indirect." Nonetheless, President Clinton continued to insist that he had repelled an "imminent threat to our national security," and Secretary of State Madeleine Albright called Sudan a "viper's nest of terrorists."

Government spokesmen continue to justify these attacks as "deterring" terrorism, even if the targets proved to be irrelevant to any damage done to facilities of the United States. In this way, future blowback possibilities are seeded into the world. The same spokesmen ignore the fact that the alleged mastermind of the embassy bombings, bin Laden, is a former protégé of the United States. When America was organizing Afghan rebels against the USSR in the 1980s, he played an important role in driving the Soviet Union from Afghanistan and only turned against the United States in 1991 because he regarded the stationing of American troops in his native Saudi Arabia during and after the Persian Gulf War as a violation of his religious beliefs. Thus, the attacks on our embassies in Africa, if they were indeed his work, are an instance of blowback rather than unprovoked terrorism. Instead of bombing sites in Sudan and Afghanistan in response, the United States might better have considered reducing or removing our large-scale and provocative military presence in Saudi Arabia. . . .

In a sense, blowback is simply another way of saying that a nation reaps what it sows. Although people usually know what they have sown, our national experience of blowback is seldom imagined in such terms because so much of what the managers of the American empire have sown has been kept secret. As a concept, blowback is obviously most easy to grasp in its most straightforward manifestation. The unintended consequences of American policies and acts in country X are a bomb at an American embassy in country Y or a dead American in country Z. Certainly any number of Americans have been killed in that fashion, from Catholic nuns in El Salvador to tourists in Uganda who just happened to wander into hidden imperial scenarios about which they knew nothing. But blowback, as demonstrated in this book, is hardly restricted to such reasonably straightforward examples. . . .

I do not believe that America's "vast array of strategical commitments" were made in past decades largely as the result of attempts to exploit other nations for economic gain or simply to dominate them politically and militarily. Although the United States has in the past engaged in imperialist exploitation of other nations, particularly in Latin America, it has also tried in various ways to liquidate many such commitments. The roots of American "imperial overstretch" today are not the same as those of past empires. Instead they more closely resemble those that brought down the Soviet Union.

Many Americans do not care to see their country's acts, policies, or situations compared with the Soviet Union's; some condemn such a comparison because it commits the alleged fallacy of "moral equivalence." They insist that America's values and institutions are vastly more humane than those of Stalin's Russia. I agree. Throughout the years of the Cold War, the United States remained a functioning democracy, with rights for its citizens unimaginable in the Soviet context (even if its more recent maintenance of the world's largest prison population suggests that it should be cautious in criticizing other nations' systems of criminal justice). Comparisons between the United States and the former Soviet Union are useful, however, because those two hegemons developed in tandem, challenging each other militarily, economically, and ideologically.

In the long run, it may turn out that, like two scorpions in a bottle, they succeeded in stinging each other to death. The roots of both modern empires lay in World War II and in their subsequent contest to control the forces that the war unleashed. A stress on the costs of the Cold War to the United States also draws attention to the legacies of that struggle. America's role as the planet's "lone superpower"—as leader of the peace-loving nations and patron of such institutions as the United Nations, the World Bank, and the World Trade Organization—is made much more difficult by the nature of the harvest we continue to reap for imprudent, often secret operations undertaken in the past. . . .

Terrorism by definition strikes at the innocent in order to draw attention to the sins of the invulnerable. The innocent of the twenty-first century are going to harvest unexpected blowback disasters from the imperialist escapades of recent decades. Although most Americans may be largely ignorant of what was, and still is, being done in their names, all are likely to pay a steep price—individually and collectively—for their nation's continued efforts to dominate the global scene. Before the damage of heedless triumphalist acts and the triumphalist rhetoric and propaganda that goes with them becomes irreversible, it is important to open a new discussion of our global role during and after the Cold War. . . .

The American military at the end of the century is becoming an autonomous system. We no longer have a draft army based on the obligation of citizens to serve their nation. When the Vietnam War exposed the inequities of the draft—for example, the ease with which college students could gain deferments—Congress decided to abolish conscription rather than enforce it in an equitable manner. Today, the military is an entirely mercenary force, made up of volunteers paid salaries by the Pentagon. Although the military still tries to invoke the public's support for a force made up of fellow citizens, this force is increasingly separated from civilian interests and devoted to military ones.

Equipped with the most advanced precision-guided munitions, high-performance aircraft, and intercontinental-range missiles, the American armed forces can unquestionably deliver death and destruction to any target on earth and expect little in the way of retaliation. Even so, these forces voraciously demand more and newer equipment, while the Pentagon now more or less sets its own agenda. Accustomed to life in a half-century-old, well-established empire, the corporate interests of the armed forces have begun to take precedence over the older idea that the military is only one of several means that a democratic government might employ to implement its policies. As their size and prominence grow over time, the armed forces of an empire tend to displace other instruments of foreign policy implementation. What also grows is militarism, "a vast array of customs, interests, prestige, actions, and thought associated with armies and wars and yet transcending true military purpose"—and certainly a reasonable description of the American military ethos today.

"Blowback" is shorthand for saying that a nation reaps what it sows, even if it does not fully know or understand what it has sown. Given its wealth and power, the United States will be a prime recipient in the foreseeable future of all of the more expectable forms of blowback, particularly terrorist attacks against Americans in and out of the armed forces anywhere on earth, including within the United States. But it is blowback in its larger aspect—the tangible costs of empire—that truly threatens it. Empires are costly operations, and they become more costly by the year. The hollowing out of American industry, for instance, is a form of blowback—an unintended negative consequence of American policy—even though it is seldom recognized as such. The growth of militarism in a once democratic society is another example of blowback. Empire is the problem. Even though the United States has a strong sense of invulnerability and substantial military and economic tools to make such a feeling credible, the fact of its imperial pretensions means that a crisis is inevitable. More imperialist projects simply generate more blowback. If we do not begin to solve problems in more prudent and modest ways, blowback will only become more intense.

92

JOSEPH NYE

From *Soft Power*

When the United States flexes its military or economic muscle, it is using "hard power," a long used and much relied upon strategy for a superpower. Foreign policy specialist Joseph Nye introduces us here to "soft power," a littler known but no less important source of international influence. "Soft power," Nye explains, "rests on the ability to shape the preferences of others." Culture, values, and the legitimacy of foreign policy all contribute to a nation's soft power. In this selection, Nye gives a brief introduction to some of the competing views of foreign policy, including the Realists, the Wilsonians, the Neoconservatives, and the New Unilateralists. Nye believes that the ultimate success of the United States in protecting its interests in today's world lies in learning how to better utilize soft power along with the hard power we so quickly embrace. Whether you fully agree or not, Nye raises interesting points about the importance of soft power, the power that brought the United States into such prominence after World War II and won the Cold War.

MORE THAN FOUR CENTURIES AGO, Niccolo Machiavelli advised princes in Italy that it was more important to be feared than to be loved. But in today's world, it is best to be both. Winning hearts and minds has always been important, but it is even more so in a global information age. Information is power, and modern information technology is spreading information more widely than ever before in history. Yet political leaders have spent little time thinking about how the nature of power has changed and, more specifically, about how to incorporate the soft dimensions into their strategies for wielding power....

Everyone is familiar with hard power. We know that military and economic might often get others to change their position. Hard power can rest on inducements ("carrots") or threats ("sticks"). But sometimes you can get the outcomes you want without tangible threats or payoffs. The indirect way to get what you want has sometimes been called "the second face of power." A country may obtain the outcomes it wants in world politics because other countries—admiring its values, emulating its example, aspiring to its level of prosperity and openness—want to follow it. In this sense, it is also important to set the agenda and attract others in world politics, and not only to force them to change by threatening military force or economic sanctions. This soft power—getting others to want the outcomes that you want—co-opts people rather than coerces them.

Soft power rests on the ability to shape the preferences of others. At the personal level, we are all familiar with the power of attraction and seduction. In a relationship or a marriage, power does not necessarily reside with the larger partner, but in the mysterious chemistry of attraction. And in the business world, smart executives know that leadership is not just a matter of issuing commands, but also involves leading by example and attracting others to do what you want. It is difficult to run a large organization by commands alone. You also need to get others to buy in to your values. Similarly, contemporary practices of community-based policing rely on making the police sufficiently friendly and attractive that a community wants to help them achieve shared objectives.

Political leaders have long understood the power that comes from attraction. If I can get you to want to do what I want, then I do not have to use carrots or sticks to make you do it. Whereas leaders in authoritarian countries can use coercion and issue commands, politicians in democracies have to rely more on a combination of inducement and attraction. Soft power is a staple of daily democratic politics. The ability to establish preferences tends to be associated with intangible assets such as an attractive personality, culture, political values and institutions, and policies that are seen as legitimate or having moral authority. If a leader represents values that others want to follow, it will cost less to lead. . . .

The soft power of a country rests primarily on three resources: its culture (in places where it is attractive to others), its political values (when it lives up to them at home and abroad), and its foreign policies (when they are seen as legitimate and having moral authority.)

Let's start with culture. Culture is the set of values and practices that create meaning for a society. It has many manifestations. It is common to distinguish between high culture such as literature, art, and education, which appeals to elites, and popular culture, which focuses on mass entertainment.

When a country's culture includes universal values and its policies promote values and interests that others share, it increases the probability of obtaining its desired outcomes because of the relationships of attraction and duty that it creates. Narrow values and parochial cultures are less likely to produce soft power. The United States benefits from a universalistic culture. The German editor Josef Joffe once argued that America's soft power was even larger than its economic and military assets. "U.S. culture, low-brow or high, radiates outward with an intensity last seen in the days of the Roman Empire—but with a novel twist. Rome's and Soviet Russia's cultural sway stopped exactly at their military borders. America's soft power, though, rules over an empire on which the sun never sets."

Some analysts treat soft power simply as popular cultural power. They make the mistake of equating soft power behavior with the cultural resources that sometimes help produce it. They confuse the cultural resources with the behavior of attraction. For example, the historian Niall Ferguson describes soft power as "nontraditional forces such as cultural and commercial goods" and then dismisses it on the grounds "that it's, well, soft." Of course, Coke and Big Macs do not necessarily attract people in the Islamic world to love the United States. The North Korean dictator Kim Jong-il is alleged to like pizza and American videos, but that does not affect his nuclear programs. Excellent wines and cheeses do not guarantee attraction to France, nor does the popularity of Pokémon games assure that Japan will get the policy outcomes it wishes. . . .

The values a government champions in its behavior at home (for example, democracy), in international institutions (working with others), and in foreign policy (promoting peace and human rights) strongly affect the preferences of others. Governments can attract or repel others by the influence of their example. But soft power does not belong to the government in the same degree that hard power does. Some hard-power assets such as armed forces are strictly governmental; others are inherently national, such as oil and mineral reserves, and many can be transferred to collective control, such as the civilian air fleet that can be mobilized in an emergency. In contrast, many soft-power resources are separate from the American government and are only partly responsive to its purposes. In the Vietnam era, for example, American popular culture often worked at cross-purposes to official government policy. Today, Hollywood movies that show scantily clad women with libertine attitudes or fundamentalist Christian groups that castigate Islam as an evil religion are both (properly) outside the control of government in a liberal society, but they undercut government efforts to improve relations with Islamic nations. . . .

Hard and soft power sometimes reinforce and sometimes interfere with each other. A country that courts popularity may be loath to exercise its hard power when it should, but a country that throws its weight around without regard to the effects on its soft power may find others placing obstacles in the way of its hard power. No country likes to feel manipulated, even by soft power. . . .

. . . Moreover, as we saw earlier, hard power can sometimes have an attractive or soft side. As Osama bin Laden put it in one of his videos,

"When people see a strong horse and a weak horse, by nature, they will like the strong horse." And to deliberately mix the metaphor, people are more likely to be sympathetic to underdogs than to bet on them.

The 2003 Iraq War provides an interesting example of the interplay of the two forms of power. Some of the motives for war were based on the deterrent effect of hard power. Donald Rumsfeld is reported to have entered office believing that the United States "was seen around the world as a paper tiger, a weak giant that couldn't take a punch" and determined to reverse that reputation. America's military victory in the first Gulf War had helped to produce the Oslo process on Middle East peace, and its 2003 victory in Iraq might eventually have a similar effect. Moreover, states like Syria and Iran might be deterred in their future support of terrorists. These were all hard power reasons to go to war. But another set of motives related to soft power. The neoconservatives believed that American power could be used to export democracy to Iraq and transform the politics of the Middle East. If successful, the war would become self-legitimizing. As William Kristol and Lawrence Kaplan put it, "What is wrong with dominance in the service of sound principles and high ideals?" . . .

Foreign policies also produce soft power when they promote broadly shared values such as democracy and human rights. Americans have wrestled with how to integrate our values with other interests since the early days of the republic, and the main views cut across party lines. Realists like John Quincy Adams warned that the United States "goes not abroad in search of monsters to destroy," and we should not involve ourselves "beyond the power of extrication in all the wars of interest and intrigue." Others follow the tradition of Woodrow Wilson and emphasize democracy and human rights as foreign policy objectives. As we shall see . . . , today's neoconservatives are, in effect, right-wing Wilsonians, and they are interested in the soft power that can be generated by the promotion of democracy.

During the 2000 election campaign, when George W. Bush frequently expressed traditional realist warnings that the United States should not become overextended, leading neoconservatives urged him to make human rights, religious freedom, and democracy priorities for American foreign policy and "not to adopt a narrow view of U.S. national interests." After 9/11, Bush's policy changed and he spoke of the need to use American power to bring democracy to the Middle East. As Lawrence Kaplan and William Kristol put it, "When it comes to dealing with tyrannical regimes like Iraq, Iran and, yes, North Korea, the U.S. should seek transformation, not coexistence, as a primary aim of U.S. foreign policy. As such, it commits the U.S. to the task of maintaining and enforcing a decent world order."

The neoconservatives are correct that such a world order could be a global public good, but they are mistaken to assume that their vision will be shared by all those affected by it. Whether the neoconservative approach creates rather than consumes American soft power depends not only on the results but also on who is consulted and who decides. The neoconservatives pay less heed than traditional Wilsonians to consultation through international institutions. But because the currency of soft power is attraction, it is often easier to generate and wield in a multilateral context.

In recent years, other countries have increasingly complained about the unilateralism of American foreign policy. Of course such differences are a matter of degree, and there are few countries that are pure unilateralists or multilateralists. International concerns about unilateralism began well before George W. Bush became president, and involved Congress as well as the executive branch. The president has disclaimed the label but most observers describe his administration as divided between traditional pragmatists and a more ideological school that the columnist Charles Krauthammer celebrated as "the new unilateralism."

The "new unilateralists" advocate an assertive approach to promoting American values. They worry about a flagging of internal will and a reluctance to turn a unipolar moment into a unipolar era. American intentions are good, American hegemony is benevolent, and that should end the discussion. To them, multilateralism means "submerging American will in a mush of collective decision-making—you have sentenced yourself to reacting to events or passing the buck to multilingual committees with fancy acronyms." They deny that American "arrogance" is a problem. Rather, the problem is "the inescapable reality of American power in its many forms." Policy is legitimized by its origins in a democracy and by the outcome—whether it results in an advance of freedom and democracy. That post hoc legitimization will more than compensate for any loss of legitimacy through unilateralism.

Unfortunately, the approach of the new unilateralists is not very convincing to other countries whose citizens observe that Americans are not immune from hubris and self-interest. Americans do not always have all the answers. As one realist put it, "If we were truly acting in the interests of others as well as our own, we would presumably accord to others a substantive role and, by doing so, end up embracing some form of multilateralism. Others, after all, must be supposed to know their interests better than we can know them." Since the currency of soft power is attraction based on shared values and the justness and duty of others to contribute to policies consistent with those shared values, multilateral consultations are more likely to generate soft power than mere unilateral assertion of the values. . . .

Anti-Americanism has increased in the past few years. Thomas Pickering, a seasoned diplomat, considered 2003 "as high a zenith of anti-Americanism as we've seen for a long time." Polls show that our soft-power losses can be traced largely to our foreign policy. "A widespread and fashionable view is that the United States is a classically imperialist power. . . . That mood has been expressed in different ways by different people, from the hockey fans in Montreal who boo the American national anthem to the high school students in Switzerland who do not want to go to the United States as exchange students." An Australian observer concluded that "the lesson of Iraq is that the US's soft power is in decline. Bush went to war having failed to win a broader military coalition or UN authorization. This had two direct consequences: a rise in anti-American sentiment, lifting terrorist recruitment; and a higher cost to the US for the war and reconstruction effort." Pluralities in 15 out of 24 countries responding to a Gallup International poll said that American foreign policies had a negative effect on their attitudes toward the United States. . . .

Skeptics about soft power say not to worry. Popularity is ephemeral and should not be a guide for foreign policy in any case. The United States can act without the world's applause. We are so strong we can do as we wish. We are the world's only superpower, and that fact is bound to engender envy and resentment. Fouad Ajami has stated recently, "The United States need not worry about hearts and minds in foreign lands." Columnist Cal Thomas refers to "the fiction that our enemies can be made less threatening by what America says and does." Moreover, the United States has been unpopular in the past yet managed to recover. We do not need permanent allies and institutions. We can always pick up a coalition of the willing when we need to. Donald Rumsfeld is wont to say that the issues should determine the coalitions, not vice versa.

But it would be a mistake to dismiss the recent decline in our attractiveness so lightly. It is true that the United States has recovered from unpopular policies in the past, but that was against the backdrop of the Cold War, in which other countries still feared the Soviet Union as the greater evil. Moreover, . . . while the United States' size and association with disruptive modernity is real and unavoidable, smart policies can soften the sharp edges of that reality and reduce the resentments they engender. That is what the U.S. did after World War II. We used our soft-power resources and co-opted others into a set of alliances and institutions that lasted for 60 years. We won the Cold War against the Soviet Union with a strategy of containment that used our soft power as well as our hard power.

It is true that the new threat of transnational terrorism increased American vulnerability, and some of our unilateralism after September 11 was driven by fear. But the United States cannot meet the new threat identified in the national security strategy without the cooperation of other countries. They will cooperate up to a point out of mere self-interest, but their degree of cooperation is also affected by the attractiveness of the United States. Take Pakistan for example. President Pervez Musharraf faces a complex game of cooperating with the United States in the war on terrorism while managing a large anti-American constituency at home. He winds up balancing concessions and retractions. If the United States were more attractive to the Pakistani populace, we would see more concessions in the mix.

It is not smart to discount soft power as just a question of image, public relations, and ephemeral popularity. As we argued earlier, it is a form of power—a means of obtaining desired outcomes. When we discount the importance of our attractiveness to other countries, we pay a price. Most important, if the United States is so unpopular in a country that being pro-American is a kiss of death in that country's domestic politics, political leaders are unlikely to make concessions to help us. Turkey, Mexico, and Chile were prime examples in the run-up to the Iraq War in March 2003. When American policies lose their legitimacy and credibility in the eyes of others, attitudes of distrust tend to fester and further reduce our leverage. For example, after 9/11 there was an outpouring of sympathy from Germans for the United States, and Germany joined a military campaign against the Al Qaeda network. But as the United States geared up for the unpopular Iraq War, Germans expressed widespread disbelief about the reasons the U.S. gave for going to war such as the alleged connection of Iraq to 9/11 and the imminence of the threat of weapons of mass destruction. German suspicions were reinforced by what they saw as biased American media coverage during the war, and by the failure to find weapons of mass destruction or prove the connection to 9/11 in the aftermath of the war. The combination fostered a climate in which conspiracy theories flourished. By July 2003, according to a Reuters poll, one-third of Germans under the age of 30 said that they thought the American government might even have staged the original September 11 attacks.

Absurd views feed upon each other, and paranoia can be contagious.

American attitudes toward foreigners harden, and we begin to believe that the rest of the world really does hate us. Some Americans begin to hold grudges, to mistrust all Muslims, to boycott French wines and rename French fries, to spread and believe false rumors. In turn, foreigners see Americans as uninformed and insensitive to anyone's interests but their own. They see our media wrapped in the American flag. Some Americans in turn succumb to residual strands of isolationism, and say that if others choose to see us that way, "To hell with 'em." If foreigners are going to be like that, who cares whether we are popular or not. But to the extent that Americans allow ourselves to become isolated, we embolden our enemies such as Al Qaeda. Such reactions undercut our soft power and are self-defeating in terms of the outcomes we want.

Some hard-line skeptics might say that whatever the merits of soft power, it has little role to play in the current war on terrorism. Osama bin Laden and his followers are repelled, not attracted, by American culture, values, and policies. Military power was essential in defeating the Taliban government in Afghanistan, and soft power will never convert fanatics. Charles Krauthammer, for example, argued soon after our swift military victory in Afghanistan that it proved that "the new unilateralism" worked. That is true up to a point, but the skeptics mistake half the answer for the whole solution.

Look again at Afghanistan. Precision bombing and Special Forces defeated the Taliban government, but U.S. forces in Afghanistan wrapped up less than a quarter of Al Qaeda, a transnational network with cells in 60 countries. The United States cannot bomb Al Qaeda cells in Hamburg, Kuala Lumpur, or Detroit. Success against them depends on close civilian cooperation, whether sharing intelligence, coordinating police work across borders, or tracing global financial flows. America's partners work with us partly out of self-interest, but the inherent attractiveness of U.S. policies can and does influence their degree of cooperation.

Equally important, the current struggle against Islamist terrorism is not a clash of civilizations but a contest whose outcome is closely tied to a civil war between moderates and extremists within Islamic civilization. The United States and other advanced democracies will win only if moderate Muslims win, and the ability to attract the moderates is critical to victory. We need to adopt policies that appeal to moderates, and to use public diplomacy more effectively to explain our common interests. We need a better strategy for wielding our soft power. We will have to learn better to combine hard and soft power if we wish to meet the new challenges. . . .

Americans are still working their way through the aftermath of September 11. We are groping for a path through the strange new landscape created by technology and globalization whose dark aspects were vividly illuminated on that traumatic occasion. The Bush administration has correctly identified the nature of the new challenges that the nation faces and has reoriented American strategy accordingly. But the administration, like the Congress and the public, has been torn between different approaches to the implementation of the new strategy. The result has been a mixture of successes and failures. We have been more successful in the domain of hard power, where we have invested more, trained more, and have a clearer idea of what we are doing. We have been less successful in the areas of soft power, where our public diplomacy has been woefully inadequate and our neglect of allies and institutions has created a sense of illegitimacy that has squandered our attractiveness.

Yet this is ironic, because the United States is the country that is at the forefront of the information revolution as well as the country that built some of the longest-lasting alliances and institutions that the modern world has seen. We should know how to adapt and work with such institutions since they have been central to our power for more than half a century. And the United States is a country with a vibrant social and cultural life that provides an almost infinite number of points of contact with other societies. What's more, during the Cold War, we demonstrated that we know how to use the soft-power resources that our society produces. . . .

. . . In short, America's success will depend upon our developing a deeper understanding of the role of soft power and developing a better balance of hard and soft power in our foreign policy. That will be smart power. We have done it before; we can do it again.

PERMISSIONS
ACKNOWLEDGMENTS

1. From *Democracy in America* by Alexis de Tocqueville, translated by Henry Reeve, published by Schoeken Books, 1961. Originally published in 1835.
2. From *The American Commonwealth* by James Bryce. Published by Macmillan, 1888.
3. From "Dinner with Democracy" by Cynthia Farrar in *Democratic Vistas: Reflections on the Life of American Democracy*, edited by Jedediah Purdy. Copyright © 2004 by Yale University. Reprinted by permission of the publisher, Yale University Press.
4. From "The Enduring Culture War" by James Davison Hunter in *Is There a Culture War?* by James Davison Hunter and Alan Wolfe. Copyright © 2006 by the Brookings Institution and Pew Research Center. Reprinted by permission of the Brookings Institution Press.
5. From *Race Matters*, by Cornel West. Copyright © 1993, 2001 by Cornel West. Reprinted by permission of Beacon Press, Boston.
6. From *People of Paradox* by Michael Kammen. Copyright © 1972 by Michael Kammen. Reprinted by permission of Alfred A. Knopf, a Division of Random House, Inc.
7. From *Habits of the Heart: Individualism and Commitment in American Life* by Robert Bellah, et al. Copyright © 1985, 1996 The Regents of the University of California. Reprinted by permission of The University of California Press in the format Textbook *via* Copyright Clearance Center.
8. From *The American Political Tradition* by Richard Hofstadter. Copyright © 1948 by Alfred A. Knopf, Inc. and renewed 1976 by Beatrice Hofstadter. Reprinted by permission of Alfred A. Knopf, a Division of Random House, Inc.
9. From *Democracy in America* by Alexis de Tocqueville, translated by Henry Reeve, published by Schoeken Books, 1961. Originally published in 1835.
10. *The Federalist 10*, by James Madison, 1787.
11. From *A Machine That Would Go of Itself* by Michael Kammen (Knopf, 1986). Copyright © 1986 by Michael Kammen. Reprinted by permission of the author.
12. From *The Power Elite, New Edition* by C. Wright Mills. Copyright © 1956, 2000 by Oxford University Press, Inc. Used by permission of Oxford University Press, Inc.
13. From Richard Zweigenhaft and G. William Domhoff, *Diversity in the Power Elite.* Copyright © 1998, 2006 by Rowman and Littlefield. Reprinted by

David O'Brien, by permission of W. W. Norton & Company, Inc. Copyright © 1996, 1993, 1990, 1986 by David O'Brien. Used by permission of W. W. Norton & Company, Inc.

46. From *Pursuit of Justices: Presidential Politics and the Selection of Supreme Court Nominees* by David Alistair Yalof. Copyright © 1999 by The University of Chicago. Used by permission of the University of Chicago Press.

47. From Richard H. Fallon, Jr. *The Dynamic Constitution*. Copyright © 2004 by Richard H. Fallon, Jr. Reprinted by permission Cambridge University Press.

48. From *Gideon's Trumpet* by Anthony Lewis. Copyright © 1964 and renewed 1992 by Anthony Lewis. Used by permission of Random House, Inc.

49. Excerpts from *Miranda v. Arizona*, 384 U.S. 436, 86 S.Ct. 1602 (1966).

50. From *System Under Stress: Homeland Security and American Politics*, by Donald F. Kettl. Copyright © 2004 by CQ Press, a division of Congressional Quarterly, Inc. Reprinted by permission of Congressional Quarterly, Inc.

51. From *Simple Justice* by Richard Kluger. Copyright © 1975 and renewed 2003 by Richard Kluger. Reprinted by permission of Alfred A. Knopf, a division of Random House Inc.

52. From *All Deliberate Speed: Reflections on the First Half Century of* Brown v. Board of Education, by Charles J. Ogletree, Jr. Copyright © 2004 by Charles J. Ogletree, Jr. Used by permission of W. W. Norton & Company, Inc.

53. From Craig A. Rimmerman *The Lesbian and Gay Movements: Assimilation or Liberation?* Copyright © 2008 by Craig A. Rimmerman. Reprinted by permission of Westview Press, a member of the Perseus Books Group, in the format Textbook *via* Copyright Clearance Center.

54. Eight pages from *In Our Defense* by Ellen Alderman and Caroline Kennedy. Copyright © 1991 by Ellen Alderman and Caroline Kennedy. Published by William Morrow & Company, Inc. Reprinted by permission of HarperCollins Publishers.

55. Reprinted with the permission of The Free Press, a Division of Simon & Schuster, Inc., from *Rights Talk: The Impoverishment of Political Discourse* by Mary Ann Glendon. Copyright © 1991 by Mary Ann Glendon. All rights reserved.

56. From David E. Bernstein *You Can't Say That! The Growing Threat to Civil Liberties from Antidiscrimination Laws*. Copyright © 2003 by the Cato Institute. Reprinted by permission of the Cato Institute.

57. From *Public Opinion and American Democracy* by V. O. Key, published by Alfred Knopf, 1961. Permission granted by the executors of the Key Estate.

58. From *Direct Democracy: The Politics of Initiative, Reform, and Recall*, by Thomas Cronin, pp. 1–3, 5, 6, 10–12, 196–199, 222, Cambridge, Mass.: Harvard University Press, Copyright © 1989 by the Twentieth Century Fund, Inc. Reprinted by permission of Harvard University Press.

59. From *Politicians Don't Pander: Political Manipulation and the Loss of Democratic Responsiveness* by Lawrence R. Jacobs and Robert Y. Shapiro. Copyright © 2000 by The University of Chicago. Used by permission of the University of Chicago Press.

60. From *The Opinion Makers: An Insider Exposes the Truth Behind the Polls* by David W. Moore. Copyright © 2008 by David W. Moore. Reprinted by permission of Beacon Press, Boston.

61. From *Democracy in America* by Alexis de Tocqueville, translated by Henry Reeve, published by Schoeken Books, 1961. Originally published 1835.

right © 2007 by Ronald Brownstein. Used by permission of The Penguin Press, a division of Penguin Group (USA), Inc.

76. Selections from *Boiling Mad: Inside Tea Party America* by Kate Zernike. Copyright © 2010 by Kate Zernike. Reprinted by permission of Henry Holt and Company, LLC.

77. From *Feeding Frenzy* by Larry Sabato. Copyright © 2000 by Larry J. Sabato. Reprinted by permission of LANAHAN PUBLISHERS, INC., Baltimore.

78. From Morley Winograd and Michael D. Hais *Millennial Makeover: MySpace, YouTube, and the Future of American Politics.* Copyright © 2008 by Morley Winograd and Michael D. Hais. Reprinted by permission of Rutgers University Press.

79. From Cass R. Sunstein *Republic.com 2.0.* Copyright © 2007 by Princeton University Press. Reprinted by permission of Princeton University Press.

80. From "How the Mass Media Divide Us" by Diana C. Mutz in *Red and Blue Nation?* edited by Pietro S. Nivola & David W. Brady. Copyright © 2006 by the Brookings Institution and Hoover Institution on War, Revolution and Peace. Reprinted by permission of the Brookings Institution Press.

81. From *Strange Bedfellows: How Late-Night Comedy Turns Democracy into a Joke* by Russell L. Peterson. Copyright © 2008 by Russell L. Peterson. Reprinted by permission of Rutgers University Press.

82. From *The White House Staff: Inside the West Wing and Beyond* by Bradley H. Patterson, Jr. Copyright © 2000 The Brookings Institution. Reprinted by permission of The Brookings Institution.

83. Reprinted with the permission of Scribner, a division of Simon & Schuster, Inc. from *The Other America: Poverty in the United States* by Michael Harrington. Copyright © 1962, 1969, 1981 by Michael Harrington; copyright renewed © 1990 by Stephanie Harrington. All rights reserved.

84. Excerpts from *Free to Choose: A Personal Statement*, copyright © 1980 by Milton Friedman and Rose D. Friedman, reprinted by permission of Houghton Mifflin Harcourt Publishing Company.

85. From *Flat Broke with Children: Women in the Age of Welfare Reform*, by Sharon Hays. Copyright © 2003 by Sharon Hays. Used by permission of Oxford University Press.

86. From Michele Wucker *Lockout: Why America Keeps Getting Immigration Wrong When Our Prosperity Depends on Getting It Right.* Copyright © 2006 by Michele Wucker. Reprinted by permission of Public Affairs, a member of the Perseus Books Group, in the format Textbook *via* Copyright Clearance Center.

87. From *Understanding Environmental Policy* by Steven Cohen. Copyright © 2006 by Columbia University Press. Reprinted with the permission of the Publisher.

88. From *Bad Money: The Global Crisis of American Capitalism* by Kevin Phillips, copyright © 2008 by Kevin Phillips. Used by permission of Viking Penguin, a division of Penguin Group (USA), Inc.

89. Reprinted by permission of Simon & Schuster, Inc. from *The Clash of Civilizations and the Remaking of World Order* by Samuel P. Huntington. Copyright © 1996 by Samuel P. Huntington. All rights reserved.

90. From *The Post-American World* by Fareed Zakaria. Copyright © 2008 by Fareed Zakaria. Used by permission of W. W. Norton & Company, Inc.